Paradox for Windows Power Programming

Vince Kellen
Gail Meisner
David Randolph
William Yock
William Todd

Dedication: The authors would like to thank Liz, Sheila, Heather, Dan Ehrmann, Borland staff, Que, and supportive family members who helped make this book possible.

Paradox for Windows Power Programming

© 1993 by Que® Corporation

All rights reserved. Printed in the United States of America. No part of this book may be used or reproduced in any form or by any means, or stored in a database or retrieval system, without prior written permission of the publisher except in the case of brief quotations embodied in critical articles and reviews. Making copies of any part of this book for any purpose other than your own personal use is a violation of United States copyright laws. For information, address Que Corporation, 11711 N. College Ave., Carmel, IN 46032.

Library of Congress Catalog No.: 93-84801

ISBN: 1-56529-091-7

This book is sold *as is*, without warranty of any kind, either express or implied, respecting the contents of this book, including but not limited to implied warranties for the book's quality, performance, merchantability, or fitness for any particular purpose. Neither Que Corporation nor its dealers or distributors shall be liable to the purchaser or any other person or entity with respect to any liability, loss, or damage caused or alleged to be caused directly or indirectly by this book.

96 95 94 93   8 7 6 5 4 3 2 1

Interpretation of the printing code: the rightmost double-digit number is the year of the book's printing; the rightmost single-digit number, the number of the book's printing. For example, a printing code of 93-1 shows that the first printing of the book occurred in 1993.

Trademarks

All terms mentioned in this book that are known to be trademarks or service marks have been appropriately capitalized. Que cannot attest to the accuracy of this information. Use of a term in this book should not be regarded as affecting the validity of any trademark or service mark.

Publisher: *David P. Ewing*

Associate Publisher: *Rick Ranucci*

Acquisitions Editor: *Sarah Browning*

Managing Editor: *Corinne Walls*

Credits

Title Manager
Walter R. Bruce, III

Product Director
Timothy S. Stanley

Production Editor
Don Eamon

Copy Editors
William A. Barton
Fran Blauw
Lori Cates
Philip Kitchel
Ginny Noble

Technical Editors
Tina Grubbe
Ed Jones
Randy Spitz

Proofreading/Indexing Coordinator
Joelynn Gifford

Production Analyst
Mary Beth Wakefield

Book Designer
Amy Peppler-Adams

Graphic Image Specialists
Dennis Sheehan
Susan VandeWalle
Jeff Shrum

Production Team
Claudia Bell
Laurie Casey
Brook Farling
Michelle Greenwalt
Bob LaRoche
Caroline Roop
Linda Seifert

Indexers
Michael Hughes
Joy Dean Lee
Craig Small

Composed in *ITC Century Light* and *MCPdigital* by Prentice Hall Computer Publishing

About the Authors

Vince Kellen
Vince Kellen is a senior consultant at Kallista. Specializing in systems analysis/design and business management, he developed Paradox applications for a variety of Fortune 500 corporate clients and was winner of the Best Case Study at the 1991 Borland Paradox Conference. Vince was a speaker at the Borland Paradox Conference for the last three years and has published several articles on Paradox in industry journals. Vince is an IEEE and ACM member. He can be reached on CompuServe at 70511,3511 or at Kallista, Inc., 312-663-3900.

Gail Meisner
Gail Meisner is an independent consultant, specializing in Paradox development and training. She spent four years working for Borland, supporting Paradox and other business applications. She is a member of Team Borland, which provides technical support for Paradox on CompuServe and is a co-founder of the Rhode Island Paradox Users Group. Gail can be reached on CompuServe at 70523,3542.

David Randolph
David Randolph is Director of Technical Resources for Shared Logic, a San Diego-based consulting firm that specializes in Paradox and Windows application development, training, and consulting. Mr. Randolph has presented Paradox for Windows topics for the Borland Database Conference and has written articles that appeared in *Data Based Advisor* and *Instant Scripts* (the newsletter for the Southern California Paradox Users Group). Dave can be reached on CompuServe at 76340,1012.

Bill Yock
Bill Yock, a consultant at Kallista, has been developing Paradox applications and providing Paradox training for more than six years. Previously, Bill was a database consultant for the University of Iowa, where he cofounded the Iowa Paradox Users Group. Bill was a speaker at the 1993 Borland Database Conference. He can be reached on CompuServe at 71024,213.

Bill Todd
Bill Todd, Vice-President of Kallista, is a former Director of the Chicago Computer Society and co-founder of the CCS Paradox Users Group. Bill is a nationally published author on Paradox. He has worked and trained in Paradox since the program was first released and has been a speaker at all the Borland Conferences. Bill can be reached on CompuServe at 75046,1354.

Overview

Introduction 1

I Developing Applications in Paradox for Windows 5

1. Objects and Properties: The Object-Based Paradigm 7
2. Relational Database Design 21
3. User Interface Design in Windows 47

II Getting Started: The Paradox for Windows Environment 59

4. The Desktop 61
5. The ObjectPAL Editor 75
6. Using the ObjectPAL Debugger 93
7. Inspecting Object Properties 103

III Interactive Use: Tables, Forms, Reports, and Queries 115

8. Building Tables 117
9. Data Models and Referential Integrity 137
10. Designing and Using Forms 151
11. Designing and Using Reports 185
12. Using Query By Example 199

IV Programming in ObjectPAL 219

13. ObjectPAL Basics 221
14. Events: Controlling User Interactions 265
15. UIObjects: Controlling the User Interface 295
16. TCursors 329
17. Building and Using Menus 341
18. Using Dialog Boxes 365
19. Understanding Error-Handling Strategies 385
20. Debugging Techniques 401
21. Delivering the Application: Putting the Pieces Together 413

V Interoperability 457

22. Using DLLs To Extend ObjectPAL 459
23. Using DDE 469
24. Using OLE 487
25. Sharing Data with Other Applications 503
26. IDAPI: What Is It? 517
27. Sound and Video 521
28. The Multiple Document Interface (MDI) 531

VI	**Special Topics**	**543**
	29 Multiuser Strategies	545
	30 Using Indexes	567
	31 Performance Tuning	577
	32 Neat Tricks and Bad Traps	585

Appendixes **597**

    A Paradox for Windows Installation and Configuration   599
    B An Overview of ObjectPal for the PAL Programmer   613
    C An Overview of ObjectPal for Non-PAL Programmers   621
    D A Brief Discussion of Containership and the Object-Oriented Paradigm   627
    E Issues in Developing Large Applications   633
    F Object Type Reference   649
    G Methods by Type   661
    H Constants and Properties   691
    I Glossary   727

    Index   733

Table of Contents

Introduction — 1
- What Makes Paradox for Windows Unique? — 1
- Who Should Read This Book — 2
- What Makes This Book Different — 2
- How This Book Is Divided — 2

I Developing Applications in Paradox for Windows — 5

1 Objects and Properties: The Object-Based Paradigm — 7
- Object-oriented — 8
  - Objects — 8
  - Encapsulation — 9
  - Polymorphism — 10
  - Inheritance — 10
- Object-based — 11
  - Paradox Objects — 12
  - Objects and Forms — 13
  - Object Properties — 14
  - Objects for Programmers — 15
  - Objects and Actions — 17
- Summary — 18
- Bibliography — 19

2 Relational Database Design — 21
- Some Basic Terms — 21
  - Database — 22
  - Entities — 22
  - Relationships — 22
  - Properties — 22
  - Tables, Tuples, Attributes—What Are They? — 22
  - Table Properties — 24
  - Maintaining Relational Integrity — 26
  - Integrity Rules — 29
  - Views — 33
  - Relational Operators — 33
  - Extensions to the Relational Model — 33
- Data Normalization — 34
  - First Normal Form — 34
  - Second Normal Form — 37
  - Third Normal Form — 38
  - Fourth and Fifth Normal Forms — 41
  - Avoiding Normalization Problems — 43
- Summary — 44
- Bibliography — 45

3 User Interface Design in Windows — 47
- Parts of the Windows Interface — 47
- Data Input Elements — 50

	Application Design Philosophy	51
	Some Windows Terms Defined	56
	Miscellaneous Windows Conventions	56
	Summary	57

II Getting Started: The Paradox for Windows Environment — 59

4 The Desktop — 61

Paradox as an MDI Application	61
Dialog Boxes	62
Running Multiple Instances of Paradox	63
Desktop Components	63
The SpeedBar	64
The Status Bar	65
Desktop Properties	66
Title	66
Background Bitmap	66
SpeedBar	67
ObjectPAL Level	67
Desktop Menus	68
Summary	73

5 The ObjectPAL Editor — 75

Accessing the Editor	75
Review SpeedBar Tools	78
Run	79
Check Syntax	79
Save	79
Breakpoints	80
The Object Tree	80
Menu Items	82
File	82
Edit	82
Language Menu	83
Property Menu	85
Window Menu	86
Using Help in the Editor	87
Setting Bookmarks	87
Using Another Help File	89
More on the Methods Dialog Box	89
Built-in Methods	90
Custom Methods	90
Uses Window	90
Type Window	90
Const Window	91
Var Window	91
Proc	91
Multiple Editor Windows	91
Summary	92

6 Using the ObjectPAL Debugger — 93

- The Debugger Menu — 94
  - Inspect — 94
  - Stack Backtrace — 95
  - Set Breakpoints, List Breakpoints — 95
  - Trace Execution, Trace BuiltIns — 96
  - Enable Debug, Enable Ctrl+Break — 97
  - View Source, Origin — 98
  - Step Over, Step Into — 98
  - Quit This Method — 98
  - Run — 98
- The Debugger SpeedBar — 99
- Debugger Keys — 99
- Summary — 100

7 Inspecting Object Properties — 103

- Object Properties — 103
- Table Properties — 105
  - Heading Properties — 105
  - Grid Properties — 108
  - Data Properties — 109
  - Direct Manipulation — 112
  - Saving Table Properties — 112
- Form Properties — 113
- Summary — 113

III Interactive Use: Tables, Forms, Reports, and Queries — 115

8 Building Tables — 117

- How To Build a Table — 117
- Field Types — 118
- Reordering Fields — 119
- Table Properties — 119
- Validity Checks — 120
- Validity Checks Applied to Existing Data — 123
- Table Lookups — 124
- Secondary Indexes — 125
- Password Security — 126
- Table Language — 127
  - Borrowing a Table's Structure — 128
  - Restructuring a Table — 128
  - Table Resources — 128
  - Field Sizes — 129
  - Record Sizes — 130
  - Block Sizes — 131
- The Struct Table — 132
- Files Associated with Paradox Tables — 134
  - Forms and Reports — 134
  - Index Files — 135
  - Other Paradox Files — 135
- Summary — 136

9	**Data Models and Referential Integrity**	**137**
	Data Model Dialog Box	138
	Define Link Dialog Box	141
	Building Queries Based on Data Models	142
	Changing Data Models	144
	Referential Integrity	145
	Defining Referential Integrity on Tables with Data	146
	Deleting and Inserting Records with Referential Integrity Defined	146
	Strict Referential Integrity	148
	Self Referential Integrity	149
	Summary	150
10	**Designing and Using Forms**	**151**
	Form Design Basics	151
	Quick Forms	151
	Page Layout	152
	Design Layout	153
	UIObjects in Forms	156
	Noise Names	157
	Containership	158
	Selecting Multiple Objects	159
	Grouping Objects	159
	Bring to Front and Send to Back	159
	Aligning Objects	160
	Pinning Objects	160
	Duplicating Objects	160
	Using Unbound Fields	161
	Special Fields	161
	Calculated Fields	162
	Summary Fields	163
	Field Properties	164
	Word Wrap	165
	Display Type	165
	Format	167
	Special Issues for Memo and Formatted Memo Fields	170
	Other UIObjects	171
	Text Objects	171
	Graphic Objects	172
	Pushbutton (Button) Objects	172
	MROs	173
	Table Frames	175
	Graphs	176
	Crosstabs	178
	OLE Objects	179
	Form Designer Properties	180
	Form Properties	182
	Delivered Forms	183
	Summary	183

11 Designing and Using Reports — 185

- Page Layout — 185
- Report Bands — 186
- Resizing Bands — 187
  - Report Band Properties — 188
  - MROs and Tableframes in Reports — 188
  - Detach Header — 189
  - Show All Records — 189
  - DeleteWhenEmpty — 189
  - Breakable — 190
  - Shrinkable — 190
- Grouping Reports — 190
- Group Band Properties — 191
- Adding Calculated and Summary Values — 192
  - Aligning Columns of Totals — 193
  - Page Breaks — 193
- Using a Query as the Basis of a Report — 194
  - Change Table — 194
- Mailing Labels — 195
- Mail Merge — 195
- Quick Reporting on a Table — 195
- Report Restart Options — 196
- Reporting to a File — 196
- Using Variables in Reports — 197
- Summary — 197

12 Using Query By Example — 199

- Creating Queries Using Data Models — 199
  - Answer Table Properties — 201
  - Sorting the Answer Table — 202
- Example Elements — 203
  - Using Example Elements in Search Conditions — 203
  - Using Example Elements in Calculations — 205
  - Using Example Elements in Insert Queries — 206
  - Example Elements in ChangeTo Queries — 207
- Delete Queries — 208
- The Inclusion Operator — 210
- Set Queries — 214
- Summary — 218

IV Programming in ObjectPAL — 219

13 ObjectPAL Basics — 221

- Method Notation — 222
- Control Structures — 223
  - for — 224
  - foreach — 224
  - if — 225
  - switch — 225
  - while — 226

try-onFail	226
Condition Evaluation	226
Data Types	227
Numeric Data Types	229
Date and Time Data Types	230
String Type	231
Array Data Types	232
Record Data Type	234
Object Types	236
Converting Data Types	237
Constants	238
Explicit versus Implicit Variable Declaration	238
Formatting and Commenting Code	238
Methods and Procedures	239
Parameter Passing and Returning Values	240
Parameter Passing	240
Returning Values	241
Parameter Passing and Performance	243
The Containership Model	243
Scope of a Variable	247
Scope of Methods and Procedures	249
Binding and Program Compilation	250
Libraries	251
Libraries and Encapsulation	253
Library Scope	253
The Event Model	254
What Is an Event?	254
Action Events	258
Creating Your Own Events	260
Bubbling	261
Summary	263

14   Events: Controlling User Interactions   265

Internal, External Events, and Bubbling	266
Events and eventInfo	269
Handling Form-Level Events	270
Events Keywords	271
Denying Events	275
Built-In Methods and Status Messages	277
Events—Where To Place Code	278
Events and Placing the Code in a Library	280
Manipulating Bubbling	281
Top Events: The Big Eight	282
open( )	282
action( )	283
menuAction( )	284
error( )	284
keyPhysical( )	284
canDepart( )	288

canArrive( )	289
arrive( )	289
Top Events: The Little Six	289
changeValue( )	290
newValue( )	290
pushButton( )	291
setFocus( )	291
removeFocus( )	291
timer( )	292
Creating Events Out of Thin Air	293
Summary	294

15 UIObjects: Controlling the User Interface — 295

Table Frames	295
Multi-Record Objects	302
Record Objects	303
Programming Field Objects	304
Programming a List Object	306
Fields and the Editing Property	309
ObjectPAL and Calculated Fields	309
Assigning a Value to Fields Not in the Form	310
Graph Object Properties	311
Object Variables	314
UIObject and ObjectPAL Trivia	316
Form as UIObject	316
Key UIObject Methods and Procedures	317
attach( )	317
copyFromArray( ), copyToArray( )	318
deleteRecord( )	318
empty( )	319
edit( ), endEdit( )	319
enum..( ) Methods/Procedures	319
insert..( ) Methods	321
locate..( )	321
method..( )	324
moveTo..( )	324
nextRecord( ), priorRecord( ), skip( )	325
postRecord( ), unlockRecord( )	325
recordStatus( )	325
setFilter( ), switchIndex( )	326
Summary	327

16 TCursors — 329

Defining TCursor	329
Declaring a TCursor	329
Opening a Table	330
Creating a Table	331
Closing a TCursor	332
Moving Around	333
Moving to a Specific Record	334

	Working with Records	334
	Accessing Fields	336
	Column Calculations	336
	Table Operations	337
	Generating a Unique Key	338
	Summary	339
17	**Building and Using Menus**	**341**
	Menu Basics	341
	Pop-up Menus	343
	The & Character, Separators, Bars, and Breaks	344
	SwitchMenu	346
	Using addArray( )	347
	Other PopUpMenu Methods	347
	Creative Pop-Up Menu Uses	348
	Using Menu Attributes	348
	Pull-Down Menus	350
	Adding and Using Menu Items	351
	Adding Accelerators	353
	Changing Pull-Down Menu Attributes	355
	Turning Off the SpeedBar	356
	Using Paradox's Menu Ids	356
	Building a Window Menu Item	358
	Using the menuAction( ) Built-In Method	358
	Problems with Changing Menu Attributes	360
	Pull-Down Menu Design Issues	360
	Menus and Multiple Forms	361
	Intercepting a Paradox SpeedBar Event	362
	Creating Your Own Speedbar	362
	Summary	363
18	**Using Dialog Boxes**	**365**
	Using Messages	365
	Using the View( ) Method	367
	Using Paradox's Built-In Dialog Boxes	369
	Using Windows Built-In Dialog Boxes	371
	Creating Your Own Dialog Boxes	372
	Assigning Form Properties	373
	Using Modal and Non-Modal Dialog Boxes	376
	Using Wait( ) and FormReturn( )	378
	Transferring Information between Forms	379
	Using Nested Waits( )	382
	Summary	383
19	**Understanding Error-Handling Strategies**	**385**
	Using an Error-Handling Manifesto	385
	Understanding How Paradox Handles Errors	386
	Looking at Programmers' Error-Trapping Mechanisms	388
	Examining Problems with action( ), keyPhysical( )	390
	Using Error-Handling Methods and Procedures	395

	Saving and Manipulating the Error Stack	396
	Designing an Error-Handling Mechanism	397
	Summary	399
20	**Debugging Techniques**	**401**
	Using the Tracer Window	401
	tracerOn( )	402
	tracerOff( )	402
	tracerClear( )	403
	tracerHide( )	403
	tracerShow( )	403
	tracerSave( )	403
	tracerWrite( )	403
	tracerToTop( )	403
	Taking a Closer Look at the Tracer Window	404
	Debugging menuAction Events	409
	Examining Other Debugger Limitations	410
	Summary	411
21	**Delivering the Application: Putting the Pieces Together**	**413**
	Creating and Launching the Main Form	414
	Opening and Using Libraries Properly	416
	Table-level Password Protection	417
	Integrating Reports into the Application	420
	Displaying Reports: Using the open( ) Method	420
	Report Restart Options	421
	Using the print( ) Method	422
	Selecting a Printer	424
	Changing Report Properties	425
	Integrating Queries into the Application	426
	Using QBE Files	427
	Using Query Types	429
	Using Query Strings	432
	Interacting with the Operating System	447
	Using the fileBrowser( ) Procedure	447
	FileSystem Type	451
	Reading ASCII Text Files	452
	Delivering Forms and Reports	455
	Summary	456
V	**Interoperability**	**457**
22	**Using DLLs To Extend ObjectPAL**	**459**
	Declaring DLL Functions with the Uses( ) Method	460
	Specifying the Library Name	460
	Specifying the Routine Name	460
	Specifying the Routine Parameters	461
	Specifying the Return Data Type	462
	Calling a DLL Function	462
	Calling a Third-Party DLL	463
	Summary	467

23 Using DDE — 469

- Overview of DDE — 469
  - DDE Server Capabilities — 470
  - DDE Server Limitations — 471
  - Interactive DDE Client Capabilities — 471
  - ObjectPAL DDE Client Capabilities — 473
- DDE Tutorial — 475
  - Controlling the Program Manager by Using DDE — 475
  - Integrating with a Word Processor — 476
  - Integrating with a Spreadsheet — 479
- Summary — 485

24 Using OLE — 487

- OLE Servers and Clients — 487
- Linking and Embedding an OLE Object — 487
- Verbs — 488
- Packages — 488
- The Benefits of OLE in Paradox — 489
- Using an OLE Field — 489
- Using the OLE UIObject — 491
- Using the OLE Type in ObjectPAL — 492
  - Declaring an OLE Variable — 492
  - OLE Methods — 492
- Tutorial — 494
  - Embedding a Bitmap into an OLE Field — 494
  - Playing a Sound Clip Using the OLE Type Variable — 497
  - Playing a Video Clip Using the action() Method — 497
  - Embedding a Windows Write Document Using the Object Packager — 498
  - Embedding a CorelDRAW! Drawing into an OLE UIObject — 500
- Summary — 501

25 Sharing Data with Other Applications — 503

- Interactive Export/Import Tools — 503
- Third-Party Export/Import Tools — 507
- Solutions to Problems with Sharing Data — 508
  - Using a TextStream Object — 508
  - Using Third-Party Batch Tools — 512
  - Other Options — 512
- Working with Graphics — 513
- Using Quattro Pro and Paradox — 514
- Summary — 516

26 IDAPI: What Is It? — 517

- Record-Oriented versus Set-Oriented Applications — 517
- Under the Hood — 518
- Summary — 519

27 Sound and Video — 521
- Video — 521
  - Application Ideas for Video — 521
  - Still Video Issues — 522
  - Still-Image Cameras — 523
  - Understanding Graphic File Formats — 523
  - Full-Motion Video Issues — 525
- Sound — 526
- An Example: Using Still Video Images — 527
- Summary — 529

28 The Multiple Document Interface (MDI) — 531
- The Application Window — 531
- The Document Window — 533
  - Minimized Document Window — 533
  - Maximized Document Window — 533
  - The Window Menu — 535
  - Keyboard Shortcuts — 537
- Controlling the Application Window — 538
  - Changing the Title — 538
  - Changing the Menu — 539
  - Removing the SpeedBar — 541
  - Changing the Status Bar — 541
- Summary — 542

VI Special Topics — 543

29 Multiuser Strategies — 545
- Configuration Issues — 545
  - How Paradox Locks Tables — 546
  - Single and Multiple File Server Issues — 549
- Multiuser Table Issues — 549
  - Table Locks — 550
  - Paradox for Windows and Paradox for DOS Table Locks — 551
  - Record Locks — 553
  - Query Restart Options — 554
  - Retry Period — 554
  - Refresh Rate — 556
- ObjectPAL Issues — 556
  - Locking Tables in ObjectPAL — 557
  - Detecting Locks You Placed with lockStatus( ) — 560
  - Locking and Unlocking Records — 560
  - Other ObjectPAL Issues — 562
- Summary — 565

30 Using Indexes — 567
- Primary versus Secondary Indexes — 567
  - Creating a Secondary Index — 568
  - Multi-Field Secondary Indexes — 569

xvii

	Indexes with ObjectPAL	570
	How Paradox Uses Indexes	570
	Sorting/Viewing	570
	Querying	573
	Zoom/Locating	573
	Linking	573
	How Paradox Stores Indexes	574
	Index Names	576
	Summary	576
31	**Performance Tuning**	**577**
	PC Configuration	577
	Network Performance	579
	Table Access Performance	580
	Using Secondary Indexes Wisely	580
	Using Queries and TCursors Properly	580
	TCursor versus Query Performance Test	580
	Using Multi-Step Queries	582
	ObjectPAL Performance	582
	Summary	584
32	**Neat Tricks and Bad Traps**	**585**
	Summary	596
VII	**Appendixes**	**597**
A	**Paradox for Windows Installation and Configuration**	**599**
B	**An Overview of ObjectPAL for the PAL Programmer**	**613**
C	**An Overview of ObjectPAL for Non-PAL Programmers**	**621**
D	**A Brief Discussion of Containership and the Object-Oriented Paradigm**	**627**
E	**Issues in Developing Large Applications**	**633**
F	**Object Type Reference**	**649**
G	**Methods by Type**	**661**
H	**Constants and Properties**	**691**
I	**Glossary**	**727**
	Index	**733**

Introduction

In many ways, Paradox for Windows represents a radical departure from the old ways of creating database applications. Gone is the monolithic source code file and the usual way of building applications through the slow accretion of lines of source code. In comes a visually-based, sophisticated way to program not just database applications, but highly complex Windows applications. To handle this new era of programming, Borland built Paradox for Windows from the ground up as a no-holds-barred, no compromises Windows database, fully equipped with an event-driven, object-based, visual programming development environment.

This environment creates a brave new world for application developers. The interactive environment builds on the interactive strengths found in previous versions of Paradox. The programming language, ObjectPAL, is a full-grown, complete, robust, and detailed programming language which gives us unprecedented power not found in previous versions of Paradox or in many other application development environments. The relationally complete Query-By-Example (QBE) interface that Paradox made famous has been adapted to the Windows environment faithfully, sacrificing nothing.

These advances, coupled with the new object-based paradigm, make for wonderful application development possibilities, but represent a major shift in orientation for most developers. Rather than organizing applications along logical lines within source code files, applications are organized along visual lines, from a forms-based, user-oriented point of view. Paradox for Windows carves up the programmable world into small, discrete, physical, modifiable objects with which users interact. This new order requires changes in the way programmers design, build, and maintain applications. The new order is not for the timid. Rather, it is for those who want both ease-of-use and tremendous power together in one application.

This book is designed to help make this transition for programmers and developers easier.

What Makes Paradox for Windows Unique?

Paradox for Windows is not just a database package for end users; the package is a complete, sophisticated programming language and application development environment. ObjectPAL, the Paradox for Windows programming language, comes with over 1,000 methods and procedures that programmers can use to create applications. These methods and procedures run the gamut from very high-level database manipulation methods to lower-level text file and directory accessing methods. In addition, developers will find in Paradox for Windows approximately 170 discrete events that they can intercept and provide their own code to handle.

With all this power comes the capability of doing exciting stuff. We not only explain the theory and the metaphor behind Paradox for Windows, we also give real-world examples and offer a frank assessment of Paradox's strengths and show you how to work around any weaknesses in the product. As serious developers, we know that you want the straight scoop. We will give you insight into what works, what doesn't, what other developers are doing, and we will give it to you unfiltered.

Who Should Read This Book

Anyone who wants to learn how to write applications in Paradox for Windows will find this book useful. Experienced programmers in previous versions of Paradox and other programming languages such as C, C++, Basic, Pascal, and other languages are the primary audience. New programmers are the secondary audience. Paradox for Windows is a large and complex piece of software, and we cannot write a book for everyone. However, ambitious newcomers to the programming world who read this book, along with other references and programming books, also learn something.

What Makes This Book Different

This book is geared for developers.

Rather than focusing on the minutia of ObjectPAL or of all possible interactive uses of the product, this book focuses on the concepts and issues that you are most likely to encounter—and not what you will likely find answers to in the standard documentation. Had we taken the former—rather than the latter—approach, you would not have this book in your hands today. Paradox for Windows is much too rich, powerful, and complex to cover exhaustively in one book.

With our expertise in Paradox and Borland products, and experience based on years of developing real-world applications for all kinds of clients and teaching other developers how to use Paradox, we felt that a discussion of the critical issues (some of these issues are philosophical) that will make or break an application, is more beneficial and gives you information difficult to find elsewhere. At many points throughout the book, we attempt to convey the depth of this real-world experience building systems in Paradox for clients who expect results. As application developers yourselves, you deserve no less.

How This Book Is Divided

This book is divided into seven parts.

Part I, "Developing Applications in Paradox for Windows," introduces you to the object-based, relational-database, Windows user-interface world of Paradox for Windows. Paradox for Windows demands that developers know more about object-oriented design and construction techniques, the relational model, and how to create Windows user interfaces. These chapters provide some grounding in those areas. Experienced object-oriented programmers, relational database programmers, and Windows programmers will find the appropriate chapters in this section an easy read.

Part II, "Getting Started: The Paradox for Windows Environment," introduces you to the Paradox development environment. This part introduces the new environment, focusing on the ObjectPAL editor, debugger, and property inspector.

Part III, "Interactive Use: Tables, Forms, Reports, and Queries," shows you how to create tables, forms, and reports, and how to use the QBE feature in Paradox for Windows. These two sections are a must if you want to understand how to program in Paradox for Windows. Because all application code is placed in a form with which users will interact, all developers need to become experts in forms. In addition, if you learn the interactive portions of the product well, you will find learning ObjectPAL much easier.

Part IV, "Programming in ObjectPAL," discusses the nitty-gritty details about programming in ObjectPAL. Rather than discussing every ObjectPAL method—there are hundreds—we focus extensively on the areas that are crucial for application development or areas that are much more complex and need special treatment. This section is perhaps the most ambitious part of the book. Programmers need to turn here to find out the best way to program in Paradox for Windows.

Part V, "Interoperability," discusses Paradox for Windows interoperability, an exciting new area in PC-based database development. Topics covered include extending ObjectPAL by writing DLL's in other languages, using DDE and OLE, sharing tables and files with other applications, and using sound and video in Paradox for Windows. For many Windows developers, this area certainly is important and cannot be overlooked.

Part VI, "Special Topics," covers areas also critical for application development. These topics include a good discussion of Paradox for Windows' multi-user locking commands and locking strategies; Paradox for Windows installation and configuration; understanding and effectively using primary and secondary indexes; and performance tuning. The section ends with an interesting chapter that lists dozens of small yet significant tricks and traps.

Finally, Part VII, "Appendixes," includes information that you may want to read first, or at any time. An overview of ObjectPAL for experienced PAL programmers is designed to help explain ObjectPAL for those programmers. The overview of ObjectPAL for programmers new to Paradox is designed to help explain ObjectPAL to programmers new to Paradox, but not new to writing programs in other languages or environments.

One appendix compares ObjectPAL and the Paradox for Windows containership model with object-oriented theory. This appendix goes into greater depth on if, how, and why Paradox for Windows fits into the object-oriented paradigm. Another appendix discusses issues and strategies that may help you in building larger applications. The last few appendixes provide some basic description of the ObjectPAL classes, methods, and properties.

We hope that you take advantage of other resources that have taught us many things about Paradox. One resource is the Borland forum on CompuServe, which is one of the best places to get fast real-world answers to tough questions. The authors of this book and many other top Paradox experts and users frequent the Borland forum. If you are a member of CompuServe, just type GO PDOXWIN at the CIS prompt to enter the Paradox for Windows forum. If you aren't a member of CompuServe, you may want to look into joining. Other industry journals also provide valuable insight into Paradox. Three journals stand out: the *Paradox Informant*, the *Paradox Users Journal*, and the *Paradox Developers Journal*. These journals publish some of the best Paradox tips and traps.

As you read this book, you may find that the concepts come fast and furious, partly because Paradox for Windows is like a race car—anyone can drive it, but only the skilled can make it scream. Paradox for Windows only appears to have a steep learning curve. After you understand some of the basic concepts and begin to apply what is discussed in this book to a real-world application, learning becomes easy.

Put on your racing helmet and gloves and hold on tight, because from here on, the ride gets exciting.

I

Developing Applications in Paradox for Windows

1
Objects and Properties: The Object-Based Paradigm

"Objects, objects everywhere..."

In order to develop applications in Paradox for Windows, you have to think in terms of objects. Everything with which you work in Paradox for Windows is an object. If you create a *table* (Paradox's term for a file), the table is an object. If you create a menu, the menu is an object. If you create a data entry form, the data entry form is an object. When you work with Paradox interactively, notice that the desktop has a SpeedBar. This too is an object.

Of all the things you need to learn to work with Paradox for Windows, this is the most important: *all things are objects and objects have properties and behavior.*

If you are an experienced C++ or other object-oriented language developer, you undoubtedly will have an easier time applying this concept in Paradox for Windows. If you are new to object-oriented or object-based concepts or if you are used to developing traditional procedural applications in languages like COBOL, C, or Pascal, making the transition to object-based thinking takes a little practice.

Object-oriented and object-based programming paradigms are based on the way the human mind tends to categorize things that we experience. We naturally and intuitively group similar or like objects. Dogs and cats are four-legged mammals. So are horses, cows, and goats. Dogs and cats are house-broken four-legged animals. Horses, cows, and goats usually are not. Chairs and desks are not mammals, although both animals may have four legs. Dogs and horses are race animals; cats, cows, and goats are not. Horses and cows are large animals; dogs, cats, and goats usually are not nearly as large.

As you can see from this simple example, you can build several categories for the objects, based on their properties.

All items we experience are clustered around a kind of taxonomy of objects. Some things fit into certain parts of this hierarchy. Other things fit into other parts of the hierarchy. Object-oriented and object-based approaches to software development try to capitalize on this natural human tendency to allow programmers and system designers to better understand the world they are trying to model.

Paradox for Windows, being object-based, captures this idea. You will encounter a hierarchical ordering of objects in Paradox's form-based application development environment. Rather than thinking about how to build the main menu and where to hook in your own programs to build an application, you will begin to see programming in terms of identifying the salient objects and how these objects need to interact.

As you begin this shift, please note that computers, unlike the mind, are rigid, deterministic machines. Object-oriented and object-based paradigms implement categories that have hard edges and clear boundaries, and the human mind does not. As you begin to organize an application around key objects, you will need to make sure that the objects you create are clearly and carefully defined.

Before delving further into particulars, however, we will define some terms by tackling the term *object-oriented* first.

Object-oriented

The computer industry has been deluged with marketing hype about object-oriented software. It seems that everything is object-oriented, as long as it has at least one object, even if the only object is a shrink wrap.

The term object-oriented has a very specific and formal definition in computer science. The term is applied to a way of analyzing systems, designing systems, and constructing systems. You can apply the object-oriented paradigm in all three areas, but for now, just confine your study to the construction, or the programming, aspect.

A programming language or application development environment is object-oriented if the environment supports these basic concepts: some notion of an object or object identity, encapsulation, polymorphism, and inheritance. Although the terms may sound imposing, the concepts behind the terms are rather simple.

Objects

An object is a combination of programs and the data the programs operate on. If you were to write a payroll program, for example, one important object might be the paycheck. The paycheck is the data, and the operations on the data may include writing, posting, and depositing. By placing the data, (in this case, paycheck information such as gross wages, taxes deducted, and so on), and the operations on the data (calculating, writing, posting, and depositing), into one entity, you begin to see one of the advantages of object-oriented programming: increased abstraction. The world is carved into clearly defined, discrete objects that are easier to comprehend, extend, and manipulate.

Objects are categorized into classes. Classes and objects are different; classes are abstract categories, and objects are real. In a class, several objects can exist. My dog, Rover, for example, is a member of the class of dogs, German Shepherd; but he is just one of many German Shepherds. German Shepherd is an abstraction, a class. Rover is the living, breathing instance of a German Shepherd.

To create a paycheck, you create an *instance* of the paycheck class and give the instance a name, such as "MyPayCheck." Then, you apply some of the programs, such as Calculate( ) (to determine the salary and taxes) to supply the data. In Paradox for Windows and in some object-oriented development environments, you perform this work by writing some code that looks like this:

```
MyPayCheck.Calculate()
```

The name of the object is on the left side of the period, and the name of the *program* (the method) is on the right side of the period. When you work with objects in Paradox for Windows, you often will work with multiple instantiations of a class: multiple objects. You may want to create and then calculate several paycheck objects like this:

```
YourPayCheck.Calculate()
HerPayCheck.Calculate()
BobsPayCheck.Calculate()
```

Each object has a unique repertoire of methods that you can invoke to perform certain tasks. From the perspective of the programmer, the data and the programs that operate on the data are inseparable. Throughout the book, these two parts of an object—the programs and the data—are commonly referred to as methods and data.

Encapsulation

Encapsulation means data-hiding. In object-oriented programing languages such as C++ and other object-oriented environments, *encapsulation* means that portions of the object are hidden from view and manipulation, which allows system designers and programmers to create objects and hide data and methods that perform critical work. These data and programs are internal to the object and should be out of view of the rest of the application. Encapsulation ensures that certain parts of the application are hidden, which means that changes in other parts of the application won't affect the encapsulated parts.

Although Paradox for Windows does not support encapsulation directly in the language syntax, you can exploit properties of various programming objects to enforce data and program hiding. This exploitation is discussed in greater detail in Chapter 13.

Polymorphism

Polymorphism means that a particular class hierarchy can have objects whose behavior may take on different forms. A paycheck may not always be the same kind of paycheck. One kind of paycheck, for example, may have a special type of deduction that all other paychecks don't have. So, the Calculate( ) method has to deal with one extra piece of data to calculate a net pay amount for some checks and one less for others, or one type of paycheck may require an entirely different kind of data for a different kind of employee than another type of paycheck. Polymorphism makes possible having the Calculate( ) method behave differently, depending on the type of paycheck object on which the method is operating, without having to create a separate method name for each calculation type.

To be more precise, the concept of polymorphism is the use of a single name to refer to a superclass (the top level, or great-grandparent class, if you will) that represents the common behavior of multiple sub-classes, which allows multiple objects to respond in slightly different ways to the same message or method. An example of polymorphism in ObjectPAL is the important UIObject (*user interface object*) class. You can create and work with different objects, such as a box or a button, using the same methods (such as MyUI.Create( ), MyUI.Visible = TRUE), which means that you, as a programmer, don't have to learn the syntax for a different method for similar objects.

Polymorphism is a useful concept because system developers can use it to create powerful methods that can take many different types of data as parameters, or operate on different types of objects, and perform the appropriate task. By identifying the number and types of parameters, the method (or the compiler) can decide on the course of action to take.

In addition, polymorphism is the means by which the concept of inheritance comes to life.

Inheritance

Inheritance means that the application development environment allows developers to create a hierarchy of classes in which descendants can "inherit" methods (behavior) and data from their ancestors (see fig. 1.1).

In this example, the top checks class serves as the basic object type; the grandparent, so to speak. In object oriented parlance, this is the *base class*, where class refers to the type of object with which you are dealing, which in this case is checks.

The Checks class has three descendent classes: a Payroll, a Payables, and a Petty Cash class. The Payroll class also has two descendent classes: a Salaried and Hourly employee check class. Creating this kind of taxonomy can be useful because all checks need at least one method that is identical in all classes: PrintCheckAmount( ).

Inheritance allows programmers to create objects and pass on the methods to child objects without extensive code revisions.

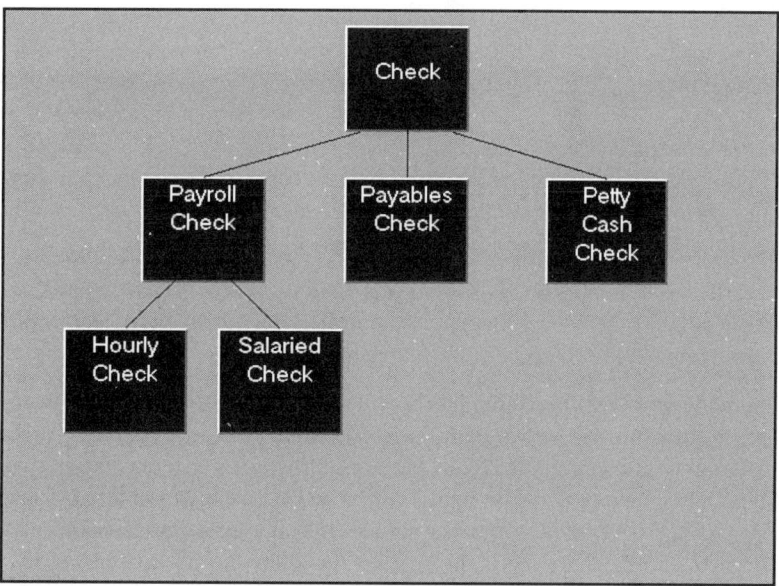

Figure 1.1. Inheritance.

Object-based

Paradox for Windows is an object-based—not an object-oriented—development environment. As an object-based environment, Paradox makes extensive use of objects, allowing developers to create objects with methods attached. Paradox does not allow developers to create truly polymorphic objects or to endow objects with robust inheritance capabilities.

The programming language in Paradox for Windows, ObjectPAL, also is not an object-oriented language. ObjectPAL differs from C++ and other object-oriented languages which fully support encapsulation, polymorphism, and inheritance.

Don't be alarmed that Paradox for Windows is object-based, not object-oriented. This difference doesn't mean that Paradox for Windows is not a powerful development environment—it is. All this means is that polymorphism, encapsulation, and inheritance are not required to create powerful, sophisticated applications. In Paradox for Windows, the concept of objects provides so much capability that, frankly, you can create great applications and never feel the need for true object-orientation. In addition, mastering the object-based environment can ease the transition to an object-oriented one.

As you work with Paradox for Windows, you will see that Borland took the power of object-oriented programming and made it useful in this object-based approach. Paradox for Windows is written in C++, an object-oriented language, which you will see when we discuss ObjectPAL methods. Several ObjectPAL methods are overloaded: that is, they take several types and numbers of arguments. The open( ) method, for example, which is used to open form objects, has three possible syntaxes—each syntax has different parameters. This overloading gives the developer flexibility in using the open( ) method without having to remember three method names. Many ObjectPAL methods are also polymorphous and can operate on many different types of objects.

You will see Paradox for Window's object-oriented construction when you examine this application's methods, which are organized by class. Beneath the surface, you will see the object-oriented structure which takes advantage of all the object-oriented terms just discussed.

In addition, the concept of containership lets you, the developer, create an arbitrary hierarchy of objects. Objects in the hierarchy can easily be moved around, deleted, or copied to new hierarchies. Objects in the hierarchy can automatically use methods already present or can bring along their own methods. Although this kind of programming model is not a customary object-oriented one, it has significant advantages, with flexibility and ease of use chief among them. This object based-model is a visual one and lets objects share methods and data as defined by a visual hierarchy. The rules of programming are determined visually. The concepts and relationships embodied in the application, therefore, are more concrete because they are anchored in a strong visual metaphor.

Paradox Objects

Because Paradox for Windows is object-based, take a closer look at some of its basic objects:

Object	*Definition*
Tables	The most basic and important object in Paradox for Windows: tables have records that store data in fields.
Forms	Objects that let users and developers create data entry screens so that users can put data into tables. Forms also are used to display data in different ways with graphs and cross tabs. Forms are binary objects that require no programming to create.
Reports	Binary objects that let users and developers define how data in the tables is printed or displayed.
Queries	The heart and soul of interactive Paradox. Queries let users and developers apply relational database operators to view, search, add, change, and delete data in tables.
Scripts	Files that can hold ObjectPAL statements. In many ways, Paradox for Windows scripts are similar to scripts in the DOS versions of Paradox or to source code files in other languages.

Object	Definition
Libraries	Hold ObjectPAL methods and code that you as a developer may want to create. Libraries are not the only object that can contain ObjectPAL statements. Forms, for example, allow developers to attach ObjectPAL statements to other objects within the form.
Design objects	Special objects, such as boxes, circles, graphs, buttons, graphic images, and other items that can be placed on forms.

Some of these Objects have objects embedded within them. A table object, for example, holds records and fields. Records and fields also are objects.

Objects and Forms

Obviously, objects are a crucial concept. In Paradox for Windows, however, the objects that you, as a developer work with must exist *on* something. Objects can't be placed on thin air. Objects are placed on forms. Not restriction only makes Paradox for Windows object-based; but also, for the most part, makes it *form-based*. Nearly everything of importance you do in Paradox for Windows is done on a form. Table objects, field objects, library objects, graph objects all will be placed on a form. Even the code you write to create applications is placed on a form!

For programmers used to more traditional development environments, this form-based approach will seem strange. Rather than writing code in a script or a source code file, where the source code file is an object separate and distinct from the data the code handles, you write code that becomes attached to an object which, in turn, is embedded on a form.

This coupling of program code attached to data on forms is an example of an object. This approach gives you a new, intuitive way to work with objects. We can inspect any object and attach a "snippet" of code to it, which modifies the object's behavior in some way. If you do this to many objects on a form, sooner or later, you have an entire application built into a form. When the user opens the form, everything springs to life.

If the source code contains errors, simply open the form in a design mode, look for the object that is having a problem, and modify the snippet of code, rather than examining hundreds or thousands of lines of source code in a source code file.

This object-based and form-based approach to system development gives a built-in way to divide an application into dozens or even hundreds of small components or objects. By itself, each component is small and manageable. Therefore, the source code modules, which are called methods, are more likely to be small and manageable. The object-based paradigm gives us a powerful way to automatically decompose an application into more manageable chunks.

Object Properties

Perhaps the most important thing about objects is that they have changeable properties. A display window, for example, has a certain height and width. If you can create this kind of object in Paradox for Windows and can't change the height and width, what good is the object? Fortunately, Paradox gives us great control over object properties.

The Desktop, for example, is the part of Paradox for Windows that includes the display background and the tools SpeedBar. This object has properties, as figure 1.2 shows.

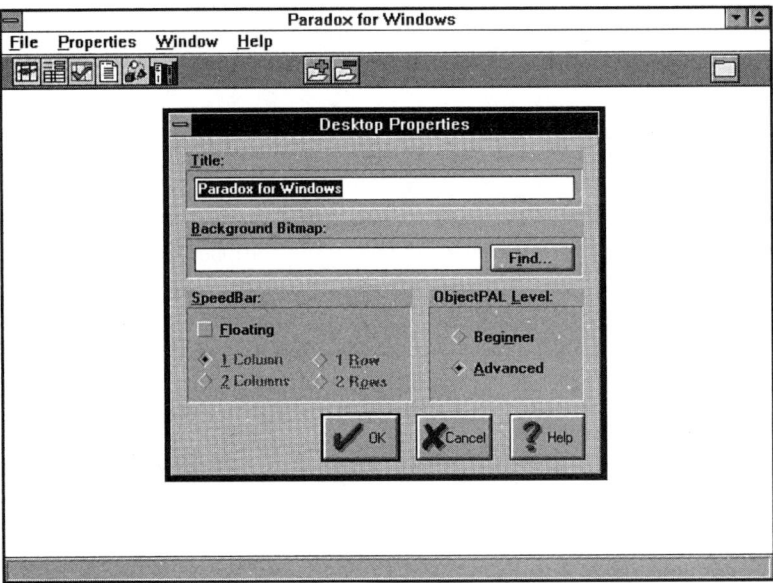

Figure 1.2. Desktop properties.

You can change the properties of the desktop by selecting the Properties ¦ Desktop menu items. You can change the desktop title, attach a bit mapped image to the desktop, or change the look and location of the tools SpeedBar.

All Paradox for Windows objects have changeable properties. In tables, the field headers that display the field names for the appropriate columns in the table have changeable properties. The field display areas also have properties you can set. For example, you can change the field colors, make the field colors change depending on the value of the data, select a different font, have the field left or right justified, and so on (see fig. 1.3).

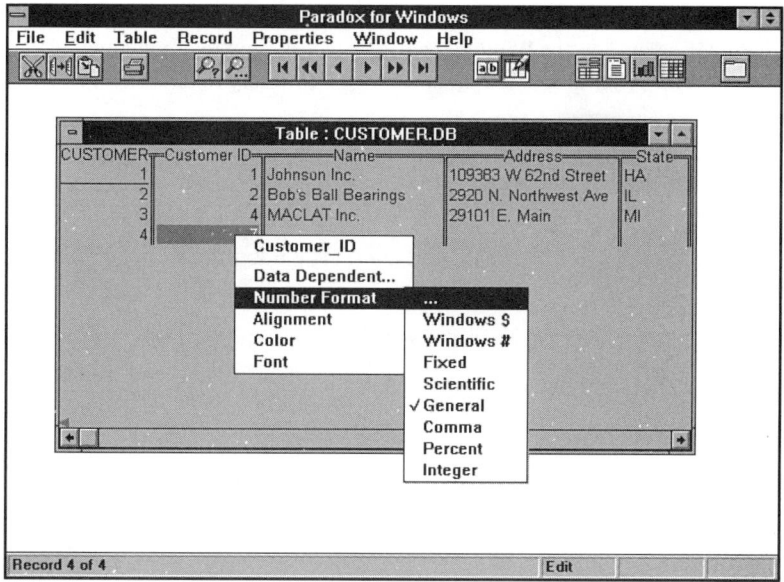

Figure 1.3. Field properties.

As you may have noticed, Paradox for Windows gives you quite a bit of control over object properties. The use of properties as a means to control the appearance of an object is used heavily in ObjectPAL, and will be one of the primary means you will have to achieve the programmatic effects you want. In fact, many important properties you may want to set as a programmer can't be set interactively; these properties must be set under ObjectPAL control.

Again, remember that everything is an object and that all objects have properties.

Under ObjectPAL control, for example, you can specify the properties for the font style of a given object. You can select bold, italic, normal, strikeout, or underline. In this case, the object property is changeable. In some cases, the object property is read-only and can't be altered.

Objects for Programmers

It should be fairly clear by now how one can manipulate object properties. What isn't always clear, however, is determining all the object types, especially because some objects make sense only in a programming environment, which can be deceiving, because if you only deal with Paradox for Windows interactively and don't look under the hood, you miss a host of valuable objects.

So far, I've been discussing objects in an accurate, but rather informal way. It is fairly obvious that forms, reports, and tables are objects. A class of objects exist, however, that have a more precise meaning to ObjectPAL programmers—objects that a programmer can create by using ObjectPAL source code. This code is where the real action is.

Just like a skilled auto mechanic can find ways to make cars run faster and farther, a skilled ObjectPAL programmer can make Paradox for Windows perform nearly any task imaginable. The ObjectPAL language is this rich. It's "programmer's" objects give us the ability to exert tremendous control over the user interface.

Some of these objects explained in the following list:

Building a user interface

- Menu objects that allow you to create and control menus, which appear on the top of the screen.
- Popup menu objects allow you to create vertical menus.
- Graphic objects that store bit-mapped images.

Controlling access and display of tables

- Table view objects, which display a table in it's own window.
- Table objects, which allow you to perform operations on tables, such as deleting, locking, and password protection.
- UIObjects (user interface objects), which are any objects placed in a form, including fields, records, lists, and others.
- Form objects allow you to open and close forms, change the form position, size, and other options.
- TCursor objects, which allow you to manipulate a table without the overhead of displaying it. A TCursor object is similar to a UIObject, except that the TCursor object never is displayed.
- Query objects, which allow you to execute Paradox QBE queries under program control.
- Database objects, which control access to a directory of related tables. In Paradox for Windows, a directory of related tables is called a Database.

Accessing DOS and system-level objects

- File system objects allow you to copy DOS files, determine a file's attributes, make and delete directories, and perform other tasks.
- System objects enable you to display messages in standard dialog boxes; invoke Paradox for Windows standard dialog boxes which perform various tasks, such as prompting the user to empty a table and displaying a list of locks; and read and write DOS environment variables.
- Text stream objects enable you to read and write a DOS text file.
- Binary objects let you read and write binary files.

Objects and Actions

So far I've told you only two-thirds of the story. Yes, all things are objects, and objects have properties. The last important piece, however, is that objects act or are acted upon. These acts are known as *events*, which completes the three basic rules for Paradox for Windows programming:

1. All things are objects.
2. All objects have properties.
3. Interaction with objects creates events.

Moving to event-driven, object-based programming can be a significant shift in orientation. In typical procedural languages such as C or COBOL, the lines of code you write create the actions. Nothing occurs unless you create the code to make it happen.

Paradox for Windows is different. Paradox supplies you, the developer, with all kinds of built-in capabilities. All you have to do is create the proper objects and sit back and *watch for events of interest*. The italics in the preceding sentence is important: in event-driven, object-based programming, you will find yourself on the back of your heels, trying to respond to events properly rather than aggressively leaning forward and controlling all aspects of user interaction.

The latter, control-oriented approach is easier to understand, because you, as the programmer, create the whole programming universe for the user. The former, event-driven approach is more difficult at first, because you must create objects that fit in an already existing universe with objects that behave according to predefined laws. These predefined laws are the default behaviors Paradox for Windows provides. If you study these behaviors well, you may find that you are writing short, compact pieces of code that by themselves do little but collectively perform tasks that would take longer to write using the "control-everything" approach. Programming in Paradox's event-driven interface is kind of like surfing. "Riding the wave" is much easier than trying to fight it.

Figure 1.4 shows a Paradox for Windows dialog box which enables you to select an event to which you will attach code.

As you can see, several events are available. These events are grouped into types. Some of these events are crucial to understand because they will be the events you likely will be most interested in. I will discuss these events in detail in this book. Some of the more important events that you as a developer absolutely need to understand include:

- *Error events* convey information about any errors that occur.
- *Key events* convey information about the keystroke the user pressed.
- *Menu events* convey information about the menu interaction that occurred.
- *Mouse events* convey information about the type of mouse interaction which occurred.

Information about events is stored in a packet, which you can evaluate to take action. Events are covered in greater detail in chapter 14.

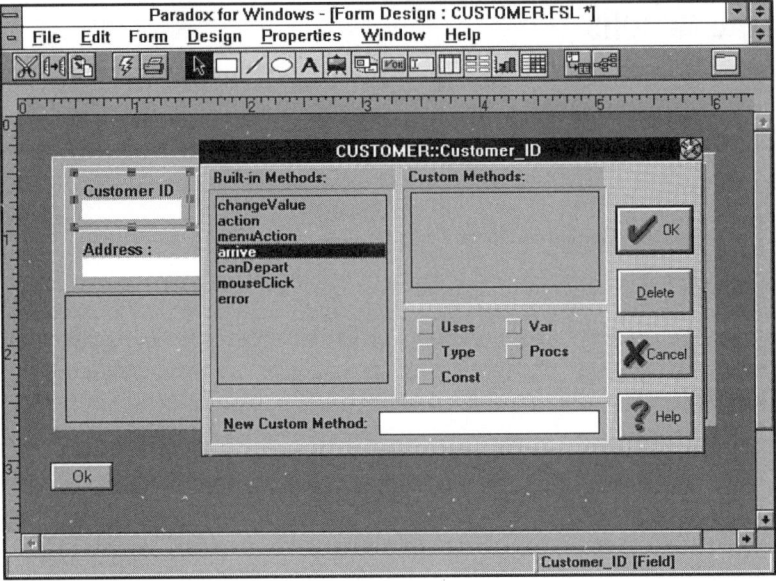

Figure 1.4. Paradox For Windows Events.

Events allow you to bring life to applications in Paradox for Windows. Without events, you couldn't trap for user-interactions, such as pressing the F1 key for help or selecting a menu item. You will build applications by taking the following steps:

1. Properly placing objects on a form.
2. Using the interactive environment or ObjectPAL to set these objects properties.
3. Attaching code to the objects to trap for events.

Summary

Paradox for Windows is object-based, not object-oriented. This approach retains the powerful concept of objects, *without* adding the complexities of object-oriented programming. You can build an application by aggregating many objects. You can modify the object properties by using Paradox interactively and by using ObjectPAL. Finally, you can use ObjectPAL to trap for interactions between objects, which allows you to extend or redefine Paradox's default way of handling the event.

By modifying objects' properties and trapping for interactions between objects, you can easily change the behavior of any objects in the application. In an object-based world, modifying an object's properties and behavior is the essence of programming.

Because of this object-based approach, many programmers may feel like a stranger in a strange land, groping a familiar hand hold. Don't worry. Throughout this book we'll have examples showing you how to navigate in this new world.

Bibliography

G. Booch, "Object-Oriented Development," IEEE Transactions on Software Engineering, February, 1986.

G. Booch, *Object Oriented Design with Applications*, Benjamin-Cummings Publishing Co., 1991.

P. Coad, E. Yourdon, *Object-Oriented Analysis*, Yourdon Press, 1990.

R. Ege, *Programming in an Object-Oriented Environment*, Academic Press, 1992.

A. Snyder, "The Essence of Objects: Concepts and Terms," IEEE Software, January 1993.

2
Relational Database Design

Because Paradox for Windows is a relational database, it is crucial for developers to understand the basics of relational design. Experienced SQL (Structured Query Languages) programmers or programmers who worked with other relational database packages such as IBM's DB2, DEC's RDB, Sybase SQL Server, or Oracle have a leg up here because they most likely were exposed to the basic relational theory and relational terms.

For programmers who are new to relational theory, don't fret. Building relational databases is both easy and fun. In fact, the more you know about relational theory, the easier Paradox will seem to you, especially when you read about the Paradox Query By Example (QBE) facility in Chapter 12.

Relational theory is a body of knowledge that has undergone much research over the past two decades. By tapping into some of this research, you can enhance your ability to create database applications in Paradox for Windows. We strongly encourage developers new to relational theory to not only read this chapter, but to seek out other, more complete texts on relational theory.

Paradox for Windows implements many aspects of the relational theory. Some of these aspects have not yet been seen on other database products and are very powerful. Paradox's QBE is an excellent implementation of the relational calculus, which is a systematic approach to querying data based on predicate logic. Understanding these and other relational concepts is crucial to understanding Paradox for Windows.

Some Basic Terms

Every industry has special terms and acronyms. Knowing a term's meaning differentiates the *insiders* from the *outsiders*. The following sections help you get inside relational theory by defining some basic terms.

Database

In relational theory, a database is just a collection of data that needs to be stored in some more or less permanent, or persistent fashion. Typical business applications have databases which store employee, customer, and vendor information. This data is stored on the computer's disk drives and is available at any time for viewing, editing, and other manipulation. The term database does not distinguish between different levels of organizations of data.

Entities

You may have heard the term entity thrown about in discussions on relational databases. In certain areas of relational theory, the term entity has a specific and rigorous meaning. The most common meaning, however, and the one applicable here, says that an *entity* is an object that needs to be represented in the database.

A customer, for example, is an entity that needs to be represented somewhere in the database. So is a vendor. The same is true of invoices, employees, products, and so on. The entity refers to the real-world concept that must be reduced, in some way, to bits and bytes in a computer file.

Relationships

Entities have relationships between them. In some businesses, employees produce many products. Customers purchase many products. Each vendor supplies many parts.

In a relational database system, you can consider the relations between entities as entities themselves, in that the relationship needs to be recorded somewhere in the database. The interesting side of relational databases is that, unlike other database systems, the relationships among data do not necessarily have to be recorded in the database, which is the beauty of relational databases! You can, at any time, create new relationships between entities, or change existing ones, without having to reconstruct the data.

Properties

Entities represented in databases have *properties*, that is, they have distinguishing characteristics. For example, employees have names, customers have addresses, and vendors have credit terms. Each property that describes entities also can be stored in the database.

Tables, Tuples, Attributes—What Are They?

As you can see, objects as described in Chapter 1 have a great deal in common with entities. In fact, the relational theory places entities in the same place as object-based approaches place objects.

And both approaches use the term property in a similar fashion. In this way, an entity is an object, and all the properties that describe the object are stored in fields in the database.

This brings us to the next concept: translating entities from abstract concepts to real, tangible computer files. Relational theory has additional nomenclature here as well, and they are covered in the following sections so that you all have the same understanding of their meaning.

Table

Basically, a *table* is a file or a collection of files that appear to the user as a single representation of an entity. You may represent the customer entity, for example, in one table in Paradox for Windows. You can ignore, for now, that Paradox may use more than one DOS file name to store all the data about customers. In fact, most users are totally unaware that when they access a memo field in a Paradox table, they are accessing data stored in a DOS file, separate from the file that holds the customer table.

Tables also are called *relations*. In functional dependency theory, which relational theory draws from, the term relation has a strict mathematical definition. In relational database theory, relation often refers to a table. Although the two terms mean different things, the term table is similar enough to the mathematical term relation that table is used an informal equivalent of relation. The authors use the term table throughout this book.

Tuple

A *tuple* is another word for a record in a table. There may be many customers in a table and each occurrence of a customer is one tuple, or record. If a table has 20,000 records, and each record contains a different customer, then the table also has 20,000 tuples. In some relational texts, you often hear about the cardinality of a table. Cardinality refers to the number of records in the table.

Tuples are instantiations of an entity. In much the same way, objects are instantiations of a class, where a class is described as a particular kind of an object. Tuples, however, are rigid instantiations of the same entity. All customers have the same number and kind of attributes or properties represented in the database.

Attributes

Each record, or tuple, in a table can have many fields. A customer record may have the following fields: address, city, state, zip, phone, contact, and name. In this way, a field is the same as an attribute. If you want to be a bit more formal, you can say the properties of an entity are stored as attributes in a table.

A common alternative to the term field or attribute is column. People frequently refer to records and fields in a relational table as rows and columns. This terminology reminds us of spreadsheets, where information is stored in rows and columns and presented the same way.

Because many terms in relational theory are used to refer to the same or similar things, from now on, the term table will refer to the representation of an entity, record will refer to a tuple, and *field* will refer to a column or attribute.

In some relational texts, you may often read about the degree of a table. The degree just refers to the number of fields in a table. A table with five fields, for example, has a degree of five.

Table Properties

Now, apply some object-based terms here. A table, being an object in the relational database theory, has properties that make it a member of the relational class. These properties distinguish relational database systems from non-relational ones and include the following specifics:

- Every record in a table has the same number of fields.
- Each record must be unique; there can be no duplicates.
- Every field must be atomic; it can't be broken down into other fields.
- Records are considered an unordered list.
- Fields are considered an unordered list.

Now, look at each of these properties:

1. ***Every record in the table has the same number of fields.***

    Tables are like spreadsheets because they are tabular. Paradox for Windows, like other relational databases, does not allow tables with a variable number of fields. A great number of applications in use today handle data in a non-tabular format. Generally, relational databases do not allow a variable number of fields, and Paradox for Windows, a relational database, does not either (setting aside memo fields and BLOB fields for now).

2. ***Every record must be unique.***

    There can't be duplicates in a table, which makes sense. Two identical customer records in the customer table would be confusing. Which record should be updated with a new balance? Paradox for Windows helps you enforce this rule by specifying one or more key fields in the table. These key fields make sure that a user can't enter two customer records with the same customer number. This property doesn't prevent the user from entering the same customer twice, one with one number and another time with a different number, but at least you can determine the difference between the two customers.

    Frequently, programmers create tables that ignore this rule, which commonly done when using temporary tables for reporting purposes. When building applications in Paradox for Windows, however, every table that holds important information should absolutely meet this rule.

3. ***Every field must be atomic.***

    A classic example of a field that is not atomic is a name field. If the name field includes both the last and first name, querying the table and getting a list of first names becomes difficult. Instead, break the name field into at least two other fields: a first name field and a last name field. Every field in a table should be atomic. Another example is commonly called a *repeating group*, which occurs when one field holds a list of information, such as a list of contact names and phone numbers. To be a table in the relational sense, this list of values should be broken out into separate fields, if not into separate tables.

It is common for programmers and developers to occasionally break this rule. For example, occasionally, developers create a customer identification field by taking the first five characters of the customers last name and adding an incrementing number, such as **01** to the end of the name. Using this scheme, several customers named Smith are represented as *Smith01*, *Smith02*, *Smith03*, and so on.

You could split this information into two field: a field to hold the first five characters and a field to hold the number. On the other hand, you can think of the field as one unique identifier to the customer record, just as a social security number identifies a person, even though the social security number is divided visually into three parts.

In fact, as a developer, you can—if you need to—decide to violate this rule of atomicity. What counts is that, from the perspective of the users of the data, the field is not made up of two or more significant pieces of data. If a table meets this and all other five properties, then the table is considered to be in first normal form. First normal form and database normalization are discussed later in this chapter.

4. ***Records are considered an unordered list.***

    The physical placement of the record in the file should not matter—don't rely on the physical placement of a record in a file as a means to find the file. Just because a record, for example, happens to be placed last in the file should not matter in terms of searching for the record. Of course, the records always can be sorted into another table, which will physically order the records. Sorting the records, however, doesn't make them an ordered list.

    You should be able to find the record based on some field value or combination of field values. As long as this holds true, the records are considered an unordered list. If you need to preserve some order to the list, then a field should be used to do so. For example, invoice numbers can be a simple incrementing number. This scheme lets you place the record in order. Because the invoice number is represented as a field in the record, however, this particular record still can be found. Therefore, the records still are considered an unordered list.

    Other database environments commonly use a record number, which refers to the record's physical placement in the table to locate a record. Only in very restricted circumstances should you ever use the record number to locate a record in a table. Always use a field value, or some combination of field values to find a record in a table.

5. ***Fields are considered an unordered list.***

    This rule is similar to the preceding one. Although developers often place fields in a certain order in a table, usually for display purposes, or so that they can group similar fields together, the physical placement ultimately should not matter.

Maintaining Relational Integrity

Paradox gives you the ability of ensuring your data's integrity. Relational theory describes several aspects involved in maintaining integrity, which include domains, primary keys, alternate keys, and foreign keys.

Domains

The term domain refers to the universe of possible values for a given field. Phone numbers, for example, have almost unlimited combinations of numbers available, with at least one restriction—they can't begin with 0. Otherwise, how would you call the operator? If you had a field in an invoice table which served as a flag to tell you whether the invoice has shipped or not, the range of possible values for the flag may be rather limited, perhaps only to Y and N. A domain is a set of possible values that a field can have.

Paradox for Windows provides significant support for maintaining domain integrity. When you create or restructure a table, you can place restrictions on the kind of information that can be placed in a field by assigning table lookups, or validity checks. Table lookup assignments allow you to restrict the entries in the current field to only the list of primary keys from another table (see fig. 2.1).

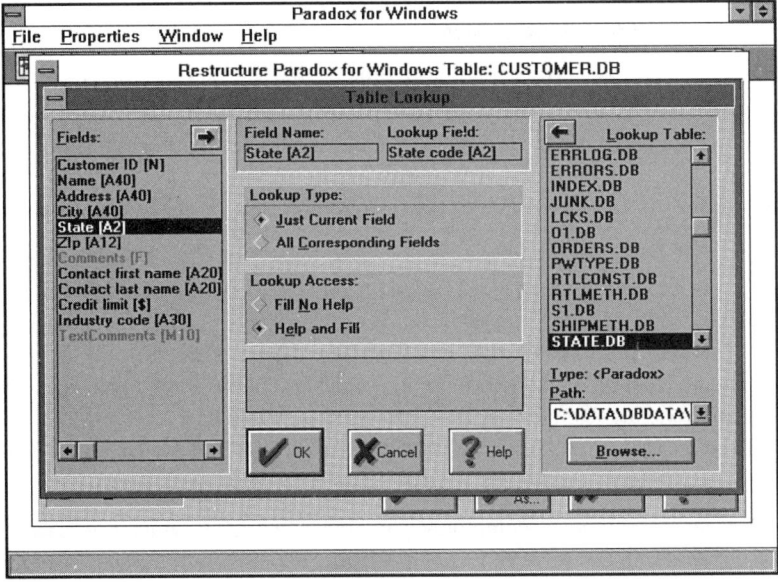

Figure 2.1. Setting table lookups.

With validity checks, you can specify minimum and maximum values for entries in a field, flag the field as a required field and prevent the user from leaving until the field is filled in, provide a default value for the field, and create pictures to restrict entry in the field.

Pictures are a powerful means of restricting user input to a combination of characters. Paradox for Windows comes with some predefined pictures that properly format and restrict user entry into phone number fields, zip code fields, fields which need to be restricted to colors, and so on. You can exploit the power of pictures to restrict data entry to many other formats and you can save these formats for later use. Figure 2.2 shows how validity checks are set.

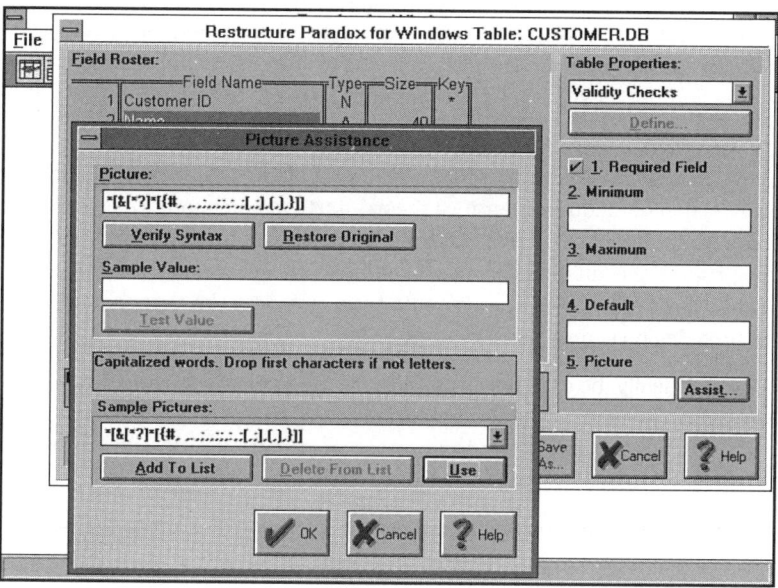

Figure 2.2. Setting validity checks.

Table lookups and validity checks are discussed more fully in Chapter 8. The important thing to note here is that Paradox provides support for enforcing domain integrity during data entry sessions. The domain support also is provided during the batch adding of data using queries or the Add utility, which allows you to add records from one table into another. If any record does not meet any of the validity checks, the record is not added to the table.

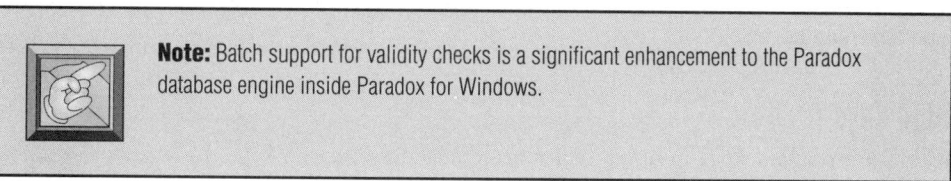

Note: Batch support for validity checks is a significant enhancement to the Paradox database engine inside Paradox for Windows.

Primary Keys

Relational theory also has rules about how to keep the records in tables. The most important rule, and perhaps the most basic, is that all tables should have primary keys.

To preserve rule 4 (records are considered an unordered list), you must have a means of identifying a record. Primary keys do just that. The primary key must be unique. Paradox for Windows won't let you place two records with the same primary key into a keyed table. (A *keyed table* is a table created with primary keys defined.) However, Paradox does allow you to place duplicate records in an unkeyed table.

Primary keys are best when you keep them short. A single field is always best, for example, as in using a part number to uniquely identify a part or using a check number to uniquely identify a payroll check. Often, one field won't do the job, as in the case of trying to store part numbers from multiple vendors in one table. Here, you need two fields in the primary key, a vendor identification field and a part number field.

Fields can be concatenated in this way to construct a primary key. A word of caution: if you find the number of fields needed to uniquely identify a record starts to reach four, five, or six fields, you may need to evaluate your database design. Usually an arbitrarily created number or sequence of characters can provide the uniqueness you need without consuming several fields. Arbitrarily determined primary keys are known as *surrogate keys*. Surrogate keys are common when the real-world situation provides no simple primary keys.

Primary keys should, ideally, be as short as possible. Using a company name field with a width of 60 as a primary key is not a good idea. Numbers, short character fields, and the combination of date and time all make for possible primary keys. In any case, a primary key should contain the minimum number of fields needed to ensure that the record can be identified uniquely.

Paradox enables you to create tables with primary keys by placing these fields first in the table structure and marking these fields as key fields. If multiple fields exist in the primary key, these fields must be listed in order, after the first field in the primary key (see fig. 2.3).

Key fields should be considered carefully. After you create your tables and start developing a system in Paradox for Windows, changing the key fields will prove costly.

Always carefully analyze and design each table's primary key!

Alternate Keys

Some records can contain more than one unique identifier. These are known as *alternate keys*. In these cases, you actually may have a choice in picking a primary key. The field or fields not chosen become alternate keys.

Foreign Keys

Field that are primary keys in other tables are considered foreign keys. In an invoice table, for example, which has an invoice number serving as the primary key, you may want to store the customer number as well, which allows you to know which customer has to pay this invoice. The customer number field, then, is a foreign key, because it points to a record in the customer table.

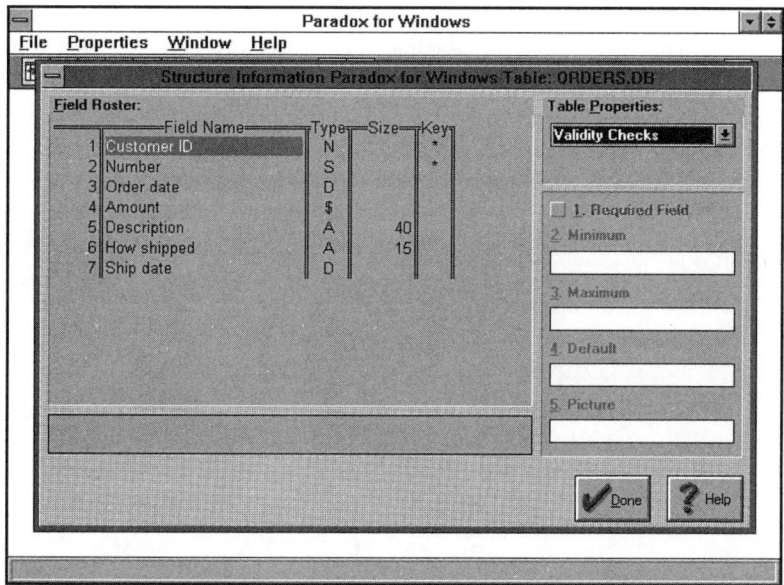

Figure 2.3. A table with multiple primary keys.

Always remember: foreign keys point to primary keys.

Paradox for Windows provides good facilities for handling foreign keys. Among the most popular forms of support is being able to look up the customer record from the invoice table and see the customer record rather than just looking at the customer number. You also may want to select a customer record if you don't know the customer number. Paradox allows you to do this, as shown in figure 2.4, through the table lookup facility.

Integrity Rules

Relational theory has a few rules that help maintain data integrity. The first rule we will discuss often is overlooked.

Entity Integrity Rule

Called the *entity integrity rule*, it says that the primary key should not contain null values.

In relational theory, null values are considered to have no identifiable value. In fact, null values never can be tested as equal to themselves because, by definition, null values are the absence of all value. Because this is the case, never allowing null values in any part of the primary key makes sense. After all, the primary key is designed to uniquely identify the record and by placing a null value, all or part of the primary key would be illogical. Essentially, you would be saying that you want to identify this record by not identifying it!

Paradox for Windows does provide some support for this rule. On the one hand, null values are treated as special values in numeric fields so that when you calculate counts, averages or perform math on these fields, you can choose whether to treat null values as zero or as null. On the other hand, Paradox, by default, does not prevent you from placing null values in primary key fields. By making entries in the primary key fields required, however, Paradox for Windows allows no records with null or blank primary key values. You can make any field, not just primary key fields, required entry fields.

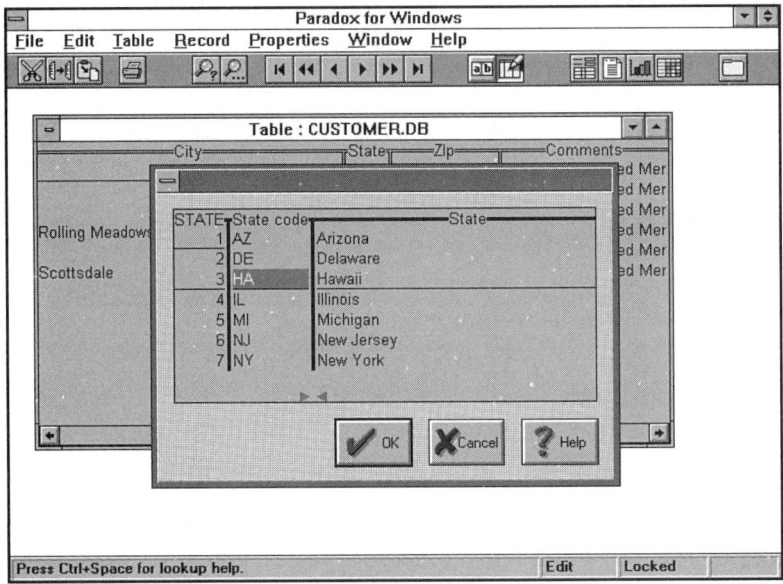

Figure 2.4. Using table lookup.

In practice, full support for the entity integrity rule usually is not needed. Because the design of primary keys in developed applications is considered carefully, and because the filling of values for the primary key is mostly under the control of the programmer, the programmer usually needs to provide more than just support for the entity integrity rule.

Referential Integrity Rule

The next rule, called the referential integrity rule, is much more important to developers and users alike. Remember the discussion earlier on foreign keys? Foreign keys are fields in a table which contain the primary key from another table: the customer number field in the invoice record allows you to know which customer ordered the items on the invoice.

The *referential integrity rule* says that the database must have no unmatched foreign keys. If a nonsense value is placed in the customer number field in the invoice table, then you would not be able to match the invoice to a customer, or, if you wanted to delete the customer record, but you had records in the invoice table that were matched to the customer record, what do you do? You probably can take one of the following actions:

- Deny the delete.
- Delete all the invoice records first and then delete the customer record.
- Delete the customer record and place a null value in the customer number field for all invoice records that once belonged to the deleted customer record.

These three options are, respectively, the *restricted*, *cascading*, or *nullify* options on referential integrity. Fortunately, Paradox for Windows provides good support for referential integrity rules. When you create tables, you can make referential integrity assignments to any foreign keys. Foreign keys can include one or more fields, but these fields must match the primary key in the parent table. Paradox allows two options: cascade and prohibit (see fig. 2.5).

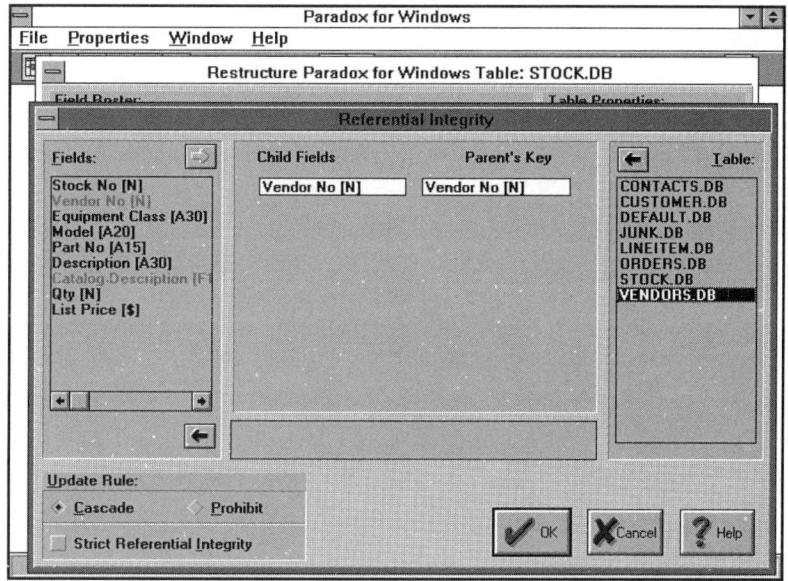

Figure 2.5. Creating referential integrity rules.

The *cascade* option cascades the updates and changes the foreign key values in the dependent table. For example, if you changed the customer number and you had referential integrity in Paradox for Windows set to cascade, then Paradox will change the customer number value in all records in the invoice table that matched the old customer number.

The *prohibit* option in setting referential integrity rules is the same as the restricted case in relational theory. In this case, Paradox does not allow you to change the customer number field in the customer table if the customer had any invoices. In relational theory terms, Paradox restricts the update to the case where the customer has no dependent invoices.

In addition, if you deleted a customer record that had dependent invoices, Paradox for Windows prohibits the delete. Relational theory describes the same three cases—restricted, cascades, and nullifies—for both the delete operation and the update operation. Paradox for Windows provides support only for the restricted case for deletes.

This restriction is somewhat of a bother, because in many circumstances, you may want Paradox to automatically delete a large number of dependent records. Paradox for Windows simply won't allow this deletion to occur, and for good reason. Because Paradox for Windows is an interactive product and users can create their own referential integrity rules (provided they have the proper table security), users could easily create a cascading delete rule (if one existed), which could be catastrophic, especially if you or the user accidentally deleted a record that had thousands of dependent records!

In any case, providing support for the cascading deletes of dependent foreign key records by using ObjectPAL is simple.

Paradox enables you to specify several referential integrity rules for a table and name these rules separately. This is an example of the relationship between tables being stored in the database. Paradox for Windows also lets you see if the current table has any dependent tables.

You may have a payments table that tracks all the payments that customers make to their account. In the payment table you may want to record the customer number so that you can match the payment to the customer. In this case, you can set a referential integrity rule in the payments table that says the customer number field is a foreign key that depends on the customer table. You then could view the customer table and determine which tables depended on customer tables for foreign key values. In the example we have created so far, that would be two tables: the invoices table and the payments table.

In fact, Paradox for Windows enables you to define a foreign key in a table that depends on its own primary key. A common example of this dependency is an employee table that contains the following fields:

Employee number*

Employee name

Manager employee number

Here the employee number is the primary key, denoted by the asterisk.

In this case, the managers also are stored in the employee table, and each employee has a manager. Here, the manager employee number field is a foreign key that points to the employee number primary key. Paradox for Windows handles this special "self referential integrity" case.

Remember, Paradox for Windows allows you to identify foreign key rules on the child table, not the parent table.

Views

The relational model also discusses views. Views are not tables, but to the user, views look, feel, smell, and act like tables. Views allow developers to combine tables, select certain records from tables, and present the transformed tables as one table. The user may have no idea that such gymnastics may be occurring behind the scenes, which is one of the powerful aspects of views. *Views* provide an additional level of indirection between the actual tables and the application or users that work with the tables. Therefore, any changes in the table structure, access requirements and so on, are confined to the definition of the view.

Paradox for Windows does not provide full support for views. Although Paradox has an excellent QBE, the QBE does not allow for the results of the QBE to be treated entirely as a subset or a *window* to the original tables. The result of the QBE is a separate and distinct table. Paradox does allow users to open forms and reports based on a query, but the query isn't a table.

Views certainly would help developers in building applications. However, some problems exist with views. Although you are supposed to treat views as tables, complete with the capability to update records in the view, some types of views are inherently not updatable. Moreover, there is, as of this writing, no way to algorithmically determine which views are not updatable.

Most developers simulate views by controlling Paradox's QBE and carefully controlling user access to data. After all, with ObjectPAL, you can achieve just about all the effects of views.

Relational Operators

Relational theory holds that relational database systems should provide support for certain relational operators. These operators allow you to manipulate a table in a variety of ways. This area is where Paradox for Windows shines because it supports nearly all relational operators in QBE. These operators enable you to select, insert, delete and change records, join tables, and perform set operations on tables.

Paradox's QBE are discussed in greater detail in Chapter 12.

Extensions to the Relational Model

Paradox for Windows supports some useful extensions to the relational model: *memo* fields, *OLE* fields, and *BLOB* fields. Memo fields allow users to type a large amount of text to store notes, comments, or even a book in one field. Clearly, this kind of usage is a violation of atomicity rule. This extension to the relational model, however, is so useful that developers and users can't do without it. The extension to the relational model solves some basic problems that the relational model was not originally designed to solve.

The Binary Large Object field (or BLOB for short) allows users and developers to store graphic images and other binary forms of data into a field. The OLE (Object Linking and Embedding) capabilities are based on Microsoft's Windows OLE facilities, which allow you to embed a document from another application (the *server*) into the *client* document. When you click on the OLE field in the client document, the embedded document is opened with the server's application program running. These extensions are discussed in a following part of the book.

Data Normalization

Data normalization can appear like a daunting, abstract, and painful exercise. When you read books and articles on relational theory, the passages that cover data normalization often sound fuzzy and ethereal. In reality, data normalization is a practical exercise that all good developers do, whether or not they understand relational theory because it actually is an intuitive process designed to eliminate redundancy in databases. All developers, at one time or another, have had to deal with redundancy issues. If the same data exists in more than one place, each copy of the data must be properly maintained.

In building relational databases, redundancy is the chief enemy, which is why data normalization is so important. When data is stored in a database, you don't want to have to spend extra effort chasing after duplicate copies of data. Relational theory provides a set of rules that help eliminate redundancy.

The first concept that you need to understand to develop normalized tables is *functional dependency*. When primary keys were discussed, you learned that a primary key describes, uniquely, the record in question. If you look at the relationship the other way around—from the perspective of the fields in the record in question—you can say that the fields are dependent on the primary key. This seems all too obvious because you wouldn't put vendor information in a customer table. The vendor fields are certainly not dependent on the customer number. Rather, vendor fields are dependent on the vendor number.

The concept of functional dependency is a powerful concept that can help you normalize databases without needing to memorize the rules of normalization. If every field in the table describes the primary key, the whole primary key and nothing but the primary key, then you probably have a table that was normalized well.

Remember: make sure that every field in a table is completely dependent on the entire primary key, or that not one field can exist as an entity independent of the primary key.

There are many subtle variations on this gross error, however, which you will soon see. To see and avoid these errors, start by diving in and tackling more definitions.

First Normal Form

"Egads! Not first normal form! No!" The words sound imposing: First Normal Form. Say the words aloud a few times. You will know what we mean. Despite the tone of the words, all developers usually create tables in first normal form at the first crack, which is why normalization is much easier to understand than you think.

The definition of first normal form is simple: a table is in *first normal form* if all the field values are atomic. Name fields have been split up into their components—last name and first name. Address fields will need to be split up into street address fields, city, state, and zip fields and so on. If all this work is done, the table is in first normal form.

The following table in figure 2.6 is not in first normal form.

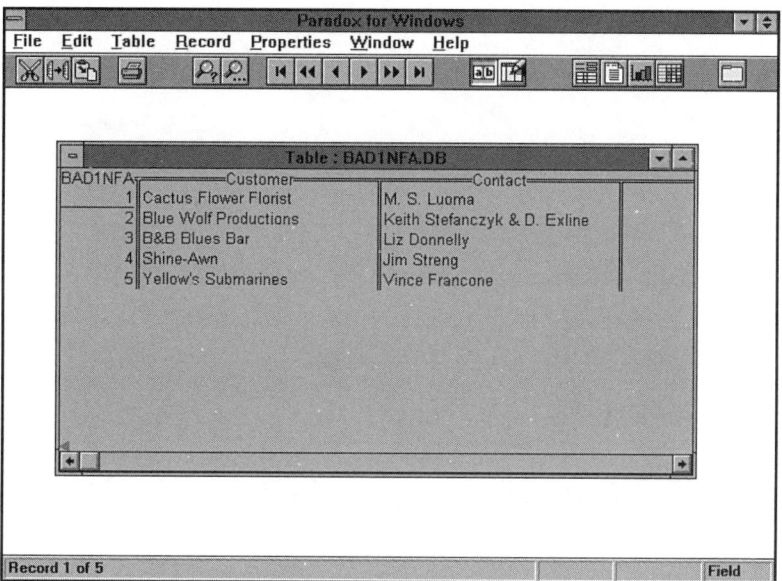

Figure 2.6. Table not in first normal form.

The table in figure 2.7 is in first normal form.

Wasn't that easy?

In fact, the term first normal form is so basic, it is common to illustrate the rule by phrasing it in another way. This rule also could tell us to eliminate repeating groups. Users and developers unfamiliar with relational database theory often create tables that seem to be in first normal form, but have repeating groups. You may have seen a customer table, for example, that has fields containing the all the contacts at the customer site. These fields often are names like Contact 1, Contact 2, Contact 3, and so on, as shown in figure 2.8:

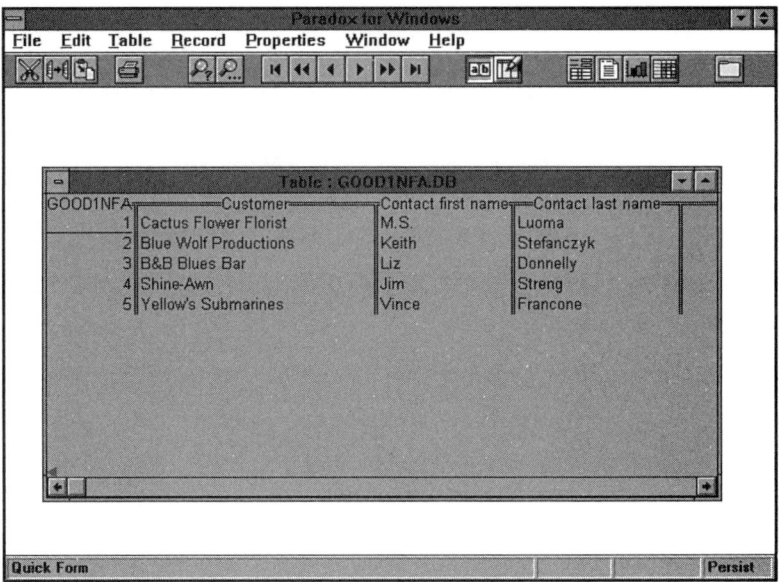

Figure 2.7. Table in first normal form.

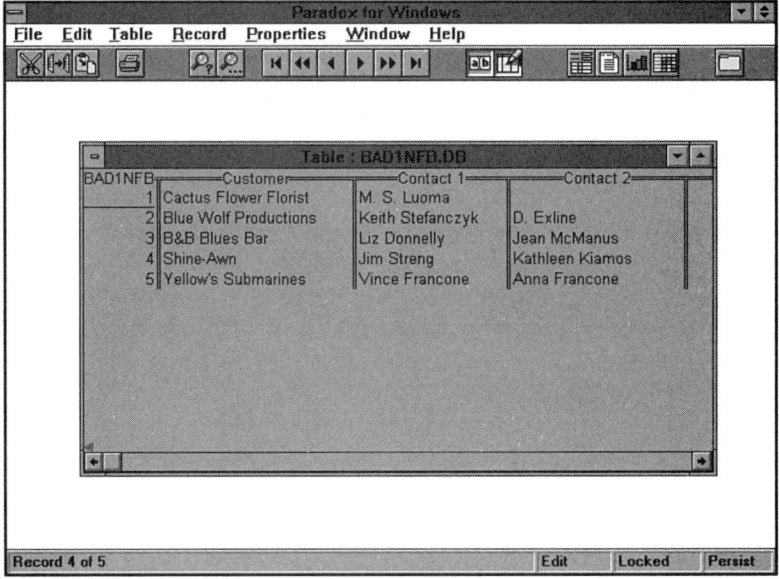

Figure 2.8. An example of repeating groups.

If you see repeating groups like this, you can remove and place these fields in a new table where you can provide an unlimited number of contacts (see fig. 2.9).

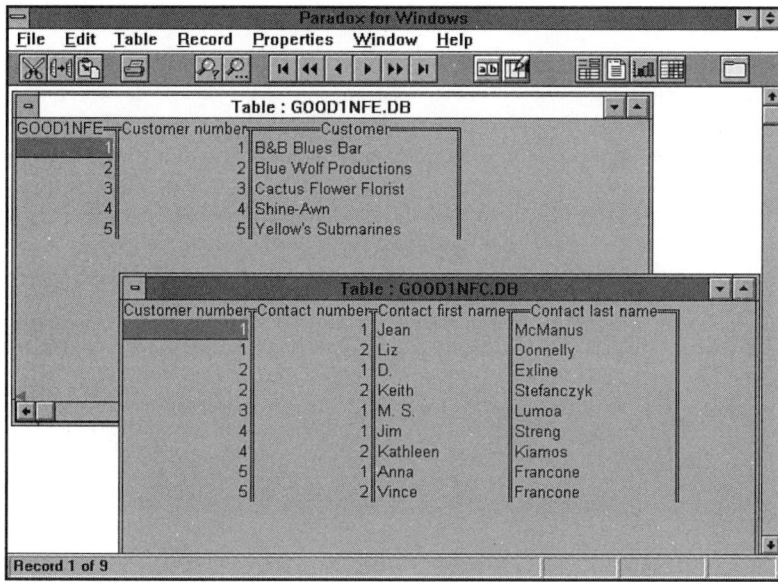

Figure 2.9. Eliminating repeating groups.

By moving information into a second table, you eliminate some problems, which relational theorists call *anomalies*. If, for example, you had repeating groups and you needed to find all customers who had contacts with the first name "John," you would have to look in each of the contact first name fields.

In addition, repeating groups can be viewed as a field that is not atomic. The repeating groups actually are one field with many occurrences of data, as is common in mainframe databases that maintain lists of values in repeating groups.

Second Normal Form

A table is in second normal form if it is first normal form already, and all the fields are completely dependent on the primary key, which sounds simple and intuitive enough. In fact, the previous example of putting vendor information in a customer table is a pathological example of violating the second normal form.

Occasionally, however, developers put fields in a table that don't belong there. The following example in figure 2.10 is a table in first normal form, has no repeating groups, but is not in second normal form.

In this example, two new fields—product type and product cost—are introduced. These fields imply that the customer buys a certain product at a set cost. Moreover, suppose that the company sells a set of product types that every customer can and does buy. If you delete all customers who buy a certain product, you lose the information on the product's cost. If you wanted to update the product cost information, you need to look for all occurrences in the customer table and change the product type's cost.

Obviously, information is redundantly stored. The product cost field is not fully dependent on the primary key, which includes the customer number and the product type. Product cost, as an entity, exist independent of customers. Products' costs can exist without customers or customers without product to sell. Because the product cost field is dependent only on part of the primary key, namely the product type field, you can solve the update and delete anomalies by splitting the product information into a new table called the products table (see fig. 2.11).

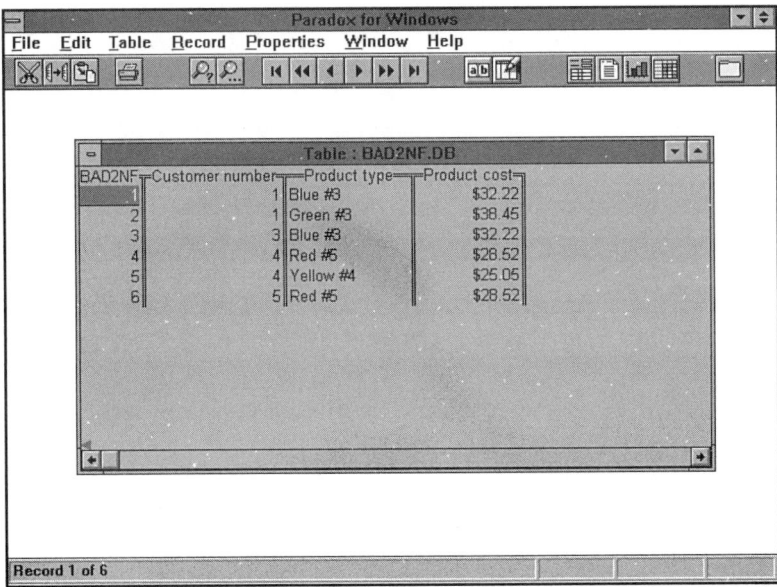

Figure 2.10. A table not in second normal form.

Although this last example was a bit more work, you still can easily see where the rules of data normalization came in handy.

Third Normal Form

A table is in third normal form if it is already in first and second normal forms and if every field other than the primary key fields are not dependent—in a transitive fashion—on the primary key. To understand this rule, it's best to look at a violation of the rule.

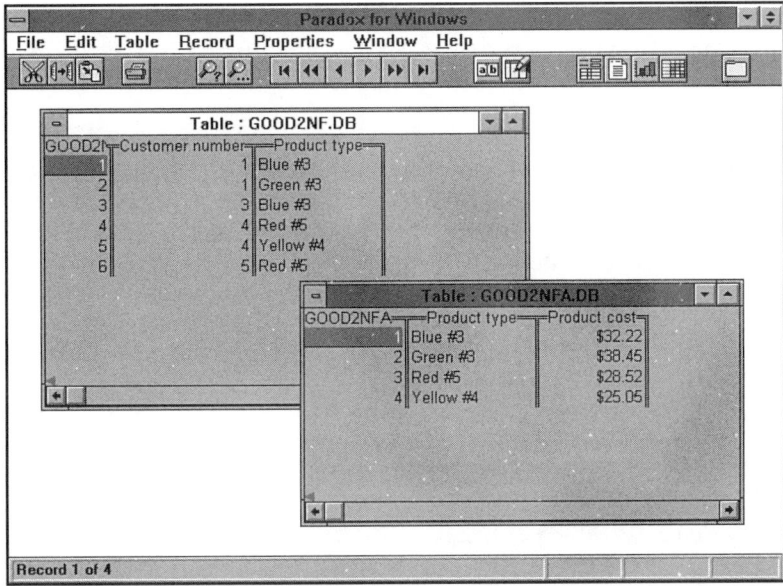

Figure 2.11. Tables in second normal form.

The following table shows another variation of previous example. Here, the product type and cost were moved to a separate table. However, a new field—a region code field, which determines the region of the country the customer is in (see fig. 2.12)—was added to the customer table.

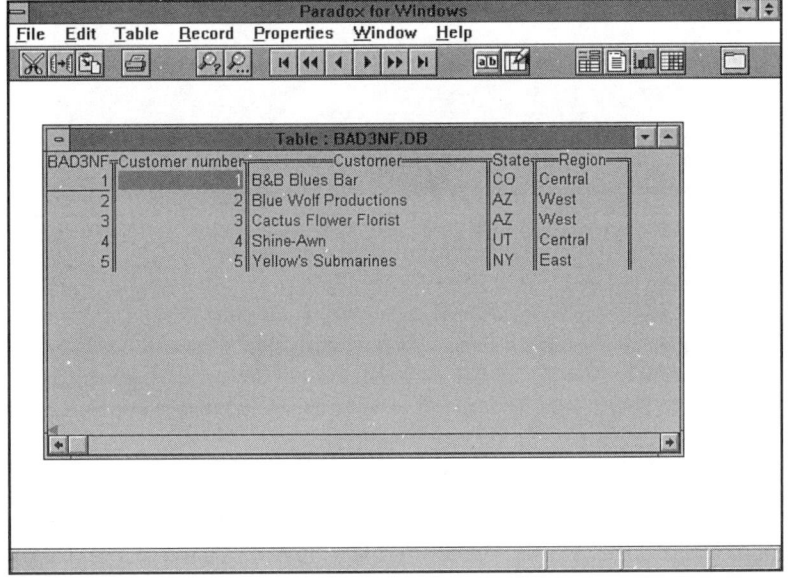

Figure 2.12. A table not in third normal form.

Examine this example closely and notice that the region code field is dependent on the state field, and that the state field is dependent on the customer number. After all, it is the customer that exists somewhere in the state. This example shows a transitive dependency, where one field is indirectly dependent on the primary key.

This example creates some update and delete anomalies. If all customers in region 2 are deleted, all information about region 2 is lost, including the most important information: that region 2 actually exists. Further, if other pieces of information about region 2 are, like the regions name, stored in the customer table, then redundant information exists. What happens when the company decides to call the west region the southwest region? The region name has to be changed in more than one place.

This problem can be solved by moving the region code field into a new table that just contains two fields: a state code and a region number (see fig. 2.13). This change solves the update and delete anomalies by eliminating redundancy.

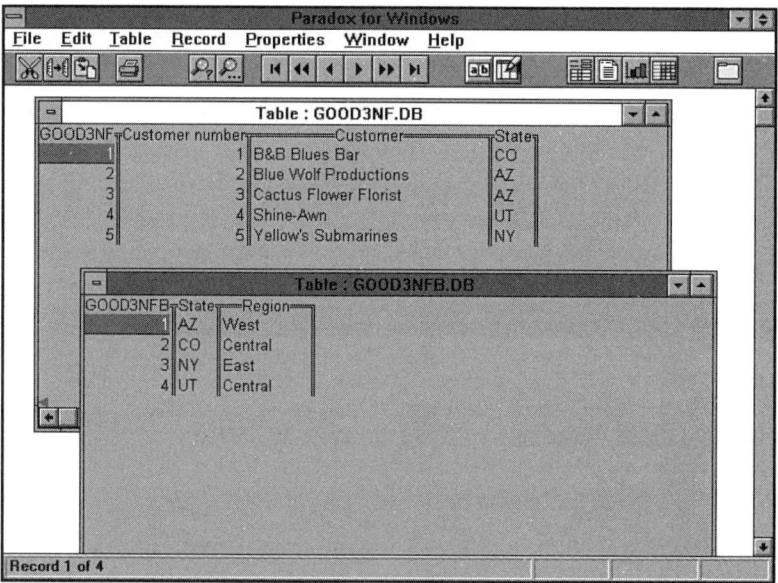

Figure 2.13. Tables in third normal form.

Another level of normalization closely related to the third normal form is the *Boyce-Codd normal form* (BCNF). Tables are in BCNF if all fields are dependent on the primary key or on the alternate keys only. The BCNF solves problems with tables in third normal form that have a primary key and at least one other alternate key.

However, because the majority of tables that you create in Paradox for Windows won't have alternate keys, you don't run into tables in third normal form that aren't in BCNF. We recommend that you be careful in determining primary keys and treat alternate keys with suspicion. Careful selection of your primary keys will prevent trouble from occurring.

Fourth and Fifth Normal Forms

Fourth and fifth normal forms are less frequently encountered, but deserve a brief mention.

Tables in BCNF but not in fourth normal form have key fields that don't belong together. A classic example is the class, teacher, books example in which the class name, the teacher's name, and the book name make up the primary key of a table. In this example, the table holds a list of all the classes, the teachers for the class, and the books that the teacher uses. All three fields are part of the primary key and no other fields are in the table. Figure 2.14 illustrates this point.

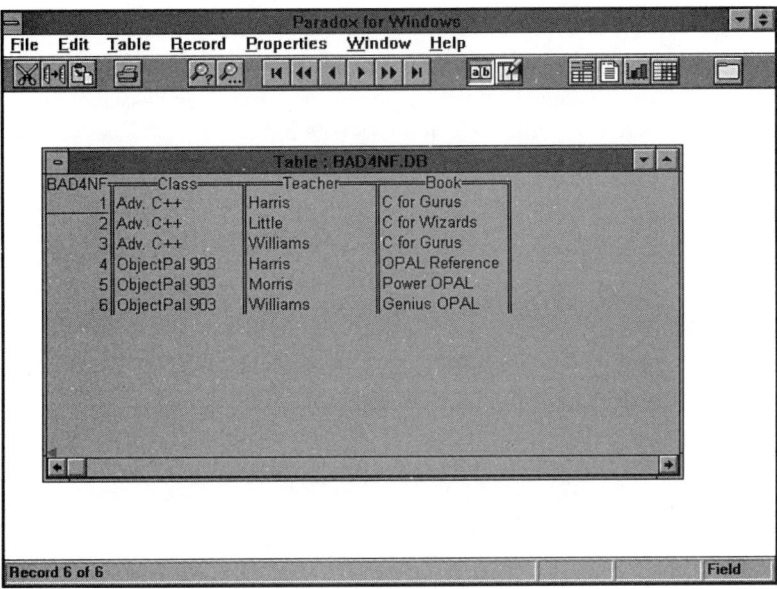

Figure 2.14. Table not in fourth normal form.

This table clearly is in BCNF, but something is odd about it. The books for the class should exist independent of the teacher. In addition, there should be a table somewhere to hold the teachers for each class independent of the books for the class. Otherwise, to change a teacher's name, you have to change it in several places. If you happen to delete all of one teacher's classes, we lose all references to this teacher. In this case, the value for the teacher is dependent on the class and the value for the book is dependent on the class. In addition, each class can have multiple books and multiple teachers.

We can clearly identify the dependencies:

1. Classes determine teachers.
2. Classes determine books.

Notice that classes can have multiple teachers and multiple books. If only one teacher and one book were allowed, you have a single value dependency. In other words, the relationship would be phrased, "The field classes determines one value of teacher," or alternately, "one teacher is assigned to each occurrence of a class." If this were the case, we need not key the teachers and books fields because both fields can have only one value for each class.

This situation is called a *multi-valued dependency*, where there are multiple teachers and books. We can use functional dependency notation to describe this situation:

1. classes ⇉ teachers
2. classes ⇉ books

One way to solve this problem is to place the teachers, classes, and books into separate tables and create two new tables: one class/teacher table to indicate which teacher has which class and one class/book table to indicate which class uses which books (see fig. 2.15).

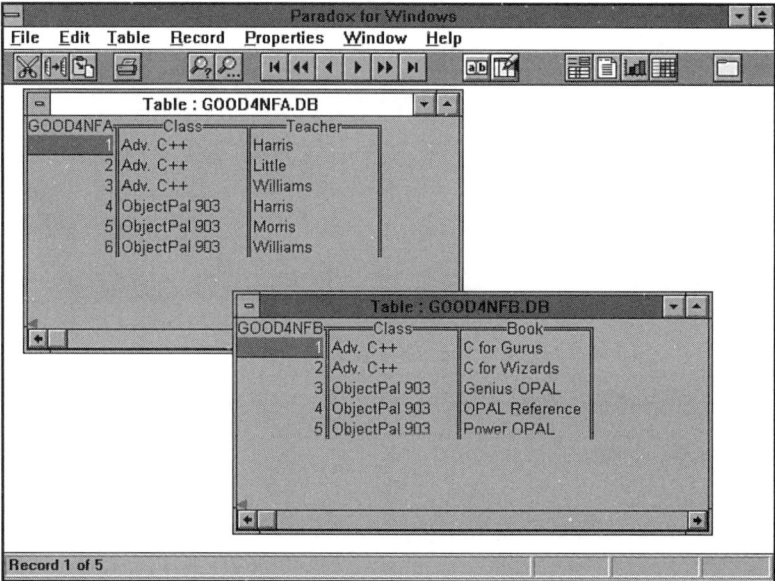

Figure 2.15. Table in fourth normal form.

The fifth normal form is a generalization of the fourth normal form, where a table can be decomposed into 3 or more tables, rather than just two tables as shown in the previous example. In a fifth normal form, a cyclic dependency exists between three or more fields, where Field 1 determines Field 2, which determines Field 3, which determines Field 1. In fifth normal form, the table is decomposed into three or more tables. You will rarely encounter a table in fourth normal form but not in fifth normal form. For this reason, the discussion of fifth normal form is brief.

Fourth normal form often is a goal for normalization, but often third normal form or BCNF is good enough for developing robust applications.

Avoiding Normalization Problems

Most developers automatically create tables in third normal form, if not fourth normal forms. The reason for this lies in the developers' ability to clearly identify the entities before actually creating the tables and programming. If you look at normalization as a process of seeking out any life form (a field) that can exist on its own and creating a separate table for it, you hardly ever run into problems.

In fact, each step of normalization involves identifying fields that not only can be more effectively stored in a separate table, but also don't need to be stored in the original, poorly designed table. If you look closely at each normalization example, you see that in each case, a new table was created.

In addition, during the analysis of a system, we recommend that you take a hard look at the entities you have identified to make sure these entities cannot be decomposed even further and that the entities represent succinct and distinct items in the real world. After you have completely decomposed all your entities, you usually can faithfully convert these entities to tables in a fully normalized way. When all your entities are clear, distinguishable real-world items, chances are you won't have to redesign your databases as frequently.

Identify clearly the relationships that exist between entities. Do you see a single valued or a multi-valued relationship between them? These relationships often are denoted as one-to-one and one-to-many relationships. *One-to-one relationships*, rather easy to understand, allow for exactly one occurrence of a record between two tables that have the same primary key value. *One-to-many relationships* allow for one table, often known as the *parent table*, to have multiple child records. In this case, the child record must have at least one more primary key field than the parent table. Many-to-many relationships are more difficult to handle and occasionally involve creating a table that is placed between the two tables, effectively creating two one-to-many relationships, as shown in figure 2.16.

Identifying the type of relationship between tables helps you determine primary keys for your tables.

We cannot emphasize enough that good clear design in advance of writing code is good. Trying to change all your key fields well into the development of a system is more costly than just adding an additional field to the table. In Paradox for Windows, reports, queries, and your ObjectPAL code will make extensive use of your tables' primary keys. Because the primary keys uniquely identify records in the table, and because access by the primary key is very fast, primary keys are extremely important.

The following rules summarize three points about avoiding normalization problems:

1. To make normalization simple, look for fields than can exist independent of the original table's primary key, and move these fields to separate tables.

2. Identify relationships between tables, and transform many-to-many relationships into two one-to-many relationships.

3. Avoid redefining key fields late in application's development.

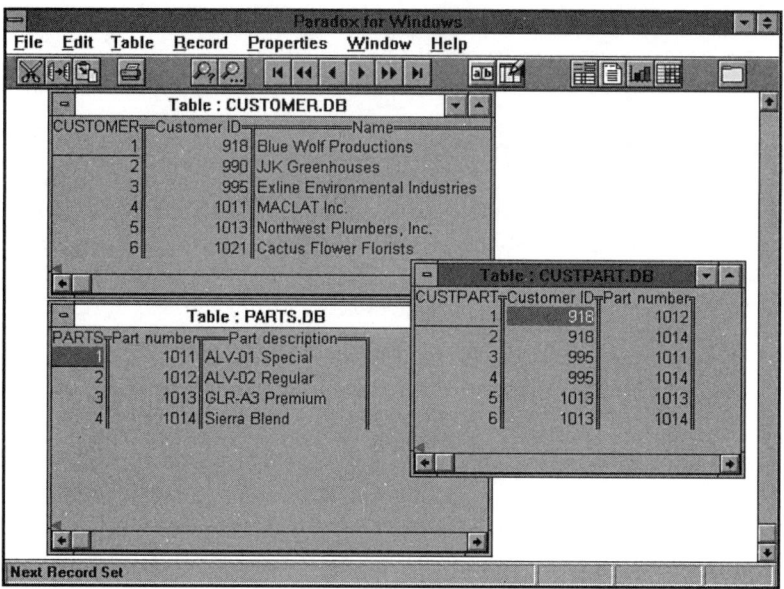

Figure 2.16. Converting M:M relationships to M:1:M.

Summary

Paradox for Windows supports and extends the relational model in many extremely important and useful ways. To develop solid applications in Paradox for Windows, you eventually will have to become comfortable with the ins and outs of relational databases.

Because Paradox's QBE and several portions of the user interface remain fairly truthful to the relational model, a better understanding of the relational model will help you create better applications.

Finally, data normalization is important, but don't get caught up in trying to memorize the rules of data normalization. Instead, keep a clear focus on identifying the entities in the real world you want to transform into tables; clearly identify each table's primary key and make sure that the key is succinct and accurate; and look for any fields in those tables that can exist independent of the tables' primary key.

Mastering relational databases makes application development in Paradox for Windows flow easily.

Bibliography

E. F. Codd, *The Relational Model for Database Management*, Version 2, Addison-Wesley Publishing, 1990

C.J. Date, *An Introduction to Database Systems*, Addison-Wesley Publishing, 1990

C. Fleming and B. von Halle, *Handbook of Relational Database Design*, Addison-Wesley Publishing, 1989

I. T. Hawryszkiewycz, *Relational Database Design*, Prentice Hall, 1990

3
User Interface Design in Windows

Paradox for Windows is indebted to three mainstreams of computing: object-based and object-oriented technology, relational databases, and graphical user interfaces. To take full advantage of Paradox, developers need skills in all three areas. This chapter introduces you to the basics of the Windows world of graphical user interfaces. For developers who come from a non-Windows background, Windows introduces some new terminology and application design philosophies that you need to know.

Parts of the Windows Interface

To develop Paradox applications in Windows, you need to know something about what's included in a Windows application. Windows is a *graphical user interface* that gives users pictures rather than words to manipulate. Figure 3.1 shows a Paradox for Windows screen, with the various parts of the Windows interface pointed out.

Figure 3.1 shows a form displayed with Paradox for Windows. Paradox and the form are both contained within windows. Each window has a title bar, a control menu box and sizing controls. Some windows have scroll bars with scroll bar controls. An active window, which is the window with which the user is interacting, has a different color title bar than an inactive windows. Paradox is a Windows application and it can have windows (called document windows) opened inside of it. In figure 3.1 the form is the document window.

As you may already know, windows can be *cascaded* (placed one on top of the other, each slightly offset to reveal the title of the window beneath) or *tiled* (where each window is placed adjacent to the next window).

Part I ■ Developing Applications with Paradox for Windows

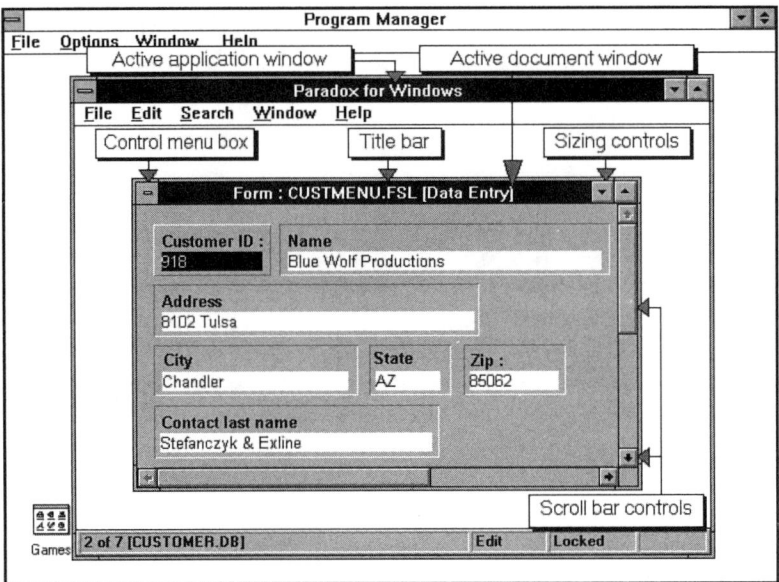

Figure 3.1. The Paradox for Windows window elements.

Each window has sizing controls to maximize, minimize, or restore the window. The sizing controls are shown in the following list:

 Restore. This control returns a minimized window back to the state it was in before it was minimized.

 Minimize, maximize. The control on the left minimizes the window. Minimize turns the window into an icon at the bottom of the application window. Maximize control enlarges the window to take up all of the application's window. If you maximized the form in figure 3.1 the customer form would fill Paradox's window space. The Paradox application window, however, would not change in size.

Each window's control box enables the user to bring up a control menu. Each window's control menu allows the user to minimize, maximize, size, move or close the window. There are two types of control menus, shown in the following example:

 The menu box on top is the application's control box, and is activated by a mouse click or by pressing Alt+space bar. The menu box below is the document window's control menu, and is activated with a mouse click or by pressing Alt+hyphen (-).

Not only can the user move and resize a window by using the control menu, the user also can move and resize a window by grabbing and moving a window's frame with the mouse (see fig. 3.2).

48

Chapter 3 ■ User Interface Design in Windows

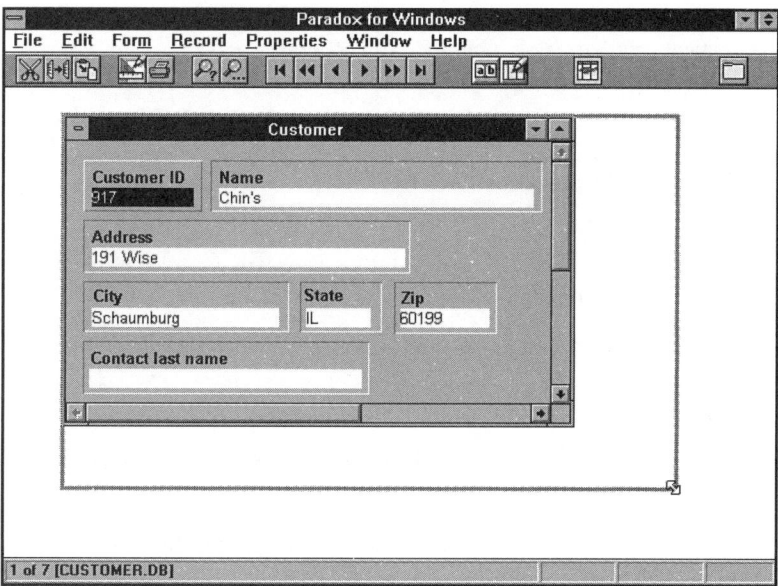

Figure 3.2. Resizing a Paradox form window.

As you see, Windows gives the user a fair amount of control over the user interface. Windows can be moved, iconized, closed, resized, restored, maximized, minimized, cascaded, and tiled. Users can move these windows around to get the desktop organized *the way they want it organized*.

Windows has several pointer types so you can see what the mouse is doing (see table 3.1).

Table 3.1. Mouse Pointer Types.

Pointer Type	*Description*
Arrow	The normal Windows mouse pointer.
I-Beam	Looks like the letter I, used to indicate the text entry insertion point.
Hourglass	The mouse changes to an hourglass whenever an application is doing something that takes time, like saving a file.
Vertical and horizontal pointers	When the user resizes something vertically, horizontally, and diagonally, these mouse pointers appear (refer to fig. 3.2).
Cross-hair	Used in design mode to line up boxes, circles, text, and other elements in a window.

Windows also supports some other mouse pointer types, such as a magnifying glass, pointers for horizontal and vertical split bars, help pointers, and others.

Data Input Elements

Window's applications use dialog boxes to get user input. Paradox uses forms, which are document windows to get input from the user and store it in tables. However, Paradox also enables you to create dialog boxes, but these dialog boxes are just a special type of a form.

Table 3.2 lists some typical dialog box elements that most Windows applications use.

Table 3.2. Data Input Elements.

Element	Description
Buttons	Otherwise known as pushbuttons, these perform some action, such as closing the dialog box, opening a new one or performing some task.
Text boxes	Users type values into text boxes. Paradox calls these text fields.
List boxes	Users can select an item from a list.
Combo boxes	This is a combination of the list box and the text box. Users can either select an item from a list or type in a value.
Spin boxes	Users can increment and decrement a value
Check box	A check or X will appear in this box if the user selects it.
Radio buttons	Otherwise known as option buttons, this control lets users select from a list of values by "pushing" the button. Users can select only one button from the list.
Sliders	These let the user select a value from a range of values. Sliders are not the same as scroll bars. Scroll bars are a kind of slider that lets the user scroll through a window, list, text box or some other element.

Each of these data input elements—except for the slider—is depicted and identified by the respective box labels in figure 3.3.

List boxes come in two styles: standard and drop-down. The list box in figure 3.3 is a standard list box. In a standard list box, the list is always open and visible. In a drop-down list box, the list is not visible until the user pushes the button with the down arrow. Drop-down lists are used to save space. The list isn't visible until the user wants it visible. Paradox provides support for standard list boxes only.

Combo boxes also come in two styles: standard and drop-down. The one in figure 3.3 is a drop-down combo box. The drop-down list is visible only when the user presses the down-arrow button. In a standard combo box, the list is always visible with the text box above it. Paradox supports the drop-down combo box, but not the standard combo box.

Chapter 3 ■ User Interface Design in Windows

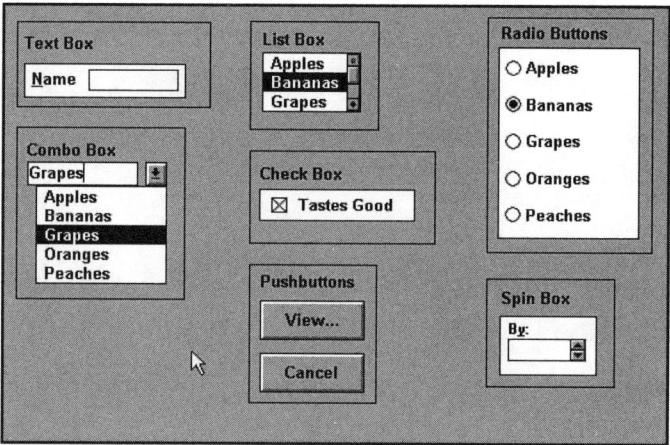

Figure 3.3. Data input elements.

In addition, Paradox provides no support for spin boxes. In Paradox for Windows, however, you can construct spin boxes, closed list boxes, and standard combo boxes by combining data input elements and adding some ObjectPAL code to these objects. In Paradox, scroll bars always come with the objects that need them. Paradox doesn't have the ability to create a slider.

Paradox for Windows has implemented a meaningful subset of the data input element usually found in Windows applications and given them a slightly different look and feel. In addition, Paradox dialog boxes have a distinctive style compared with Windows dialog boxes. Figure 3.4 shows several of the data input elements, but this time Paradox style. Figure 3.5 shows a standard Windows dialog box and figure 3.6 shows a standard Paradox for Windows dialog box. Notice the differences.

Application Design Philosophy

When you design applications in Paradox for Windows, you have to ask questions, such as the following:

- Do you want the application to behave like a Windows application or like a DOS application?
- How close to the Windows interface model do you want the new application to get?
- How close to the Paradox for Windows interface model do you want the new application to get?
- Should users be able to maximize, restore, and resize windows?
- Should users be able to move and minimize windows?
- Should all the data input elements have hot key equivalents?

Part I ■ Developing Applications with Paradox for Windows

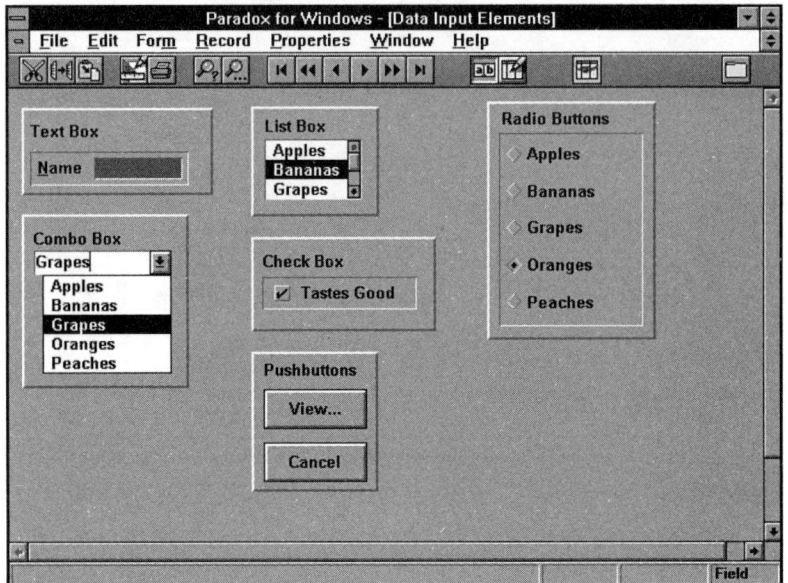

Figure 3.4. Data input elements: Borland style.

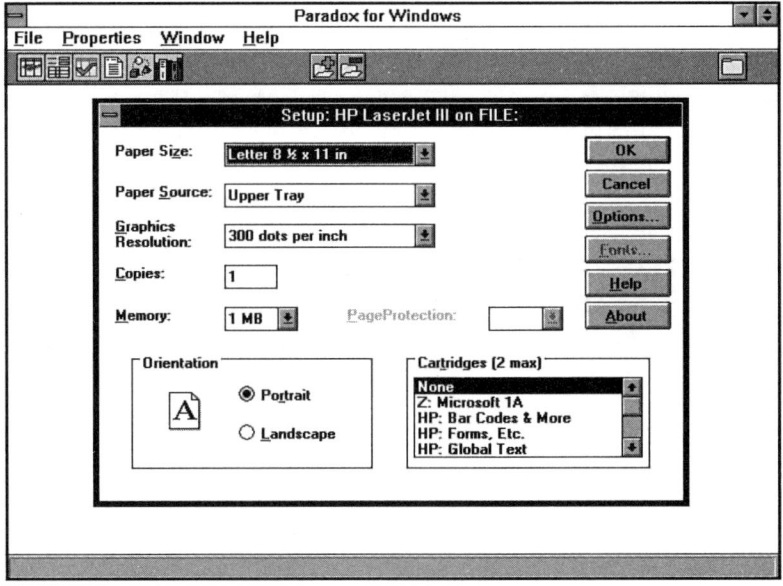

Figure 3.5. A Windows-style dialog box.

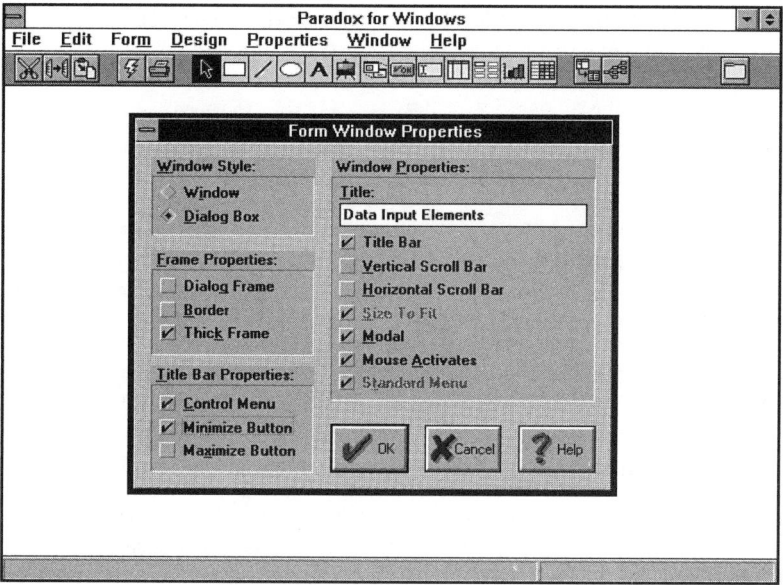

Figure 3.6. A Borland-style dialog box.

You have more or less work cut out for yourself, depending on how you answer these questions, so take them in order.

Do you want the application to behave like a Windows or a DOS application?

Many developers who start developing Paradox application in Windows complain that Windows requires too much knowledge of the user. The developer usually tries to *limit* or *restrict* what Windows can do. For example, these developers often try to prevent the user from ever seeing the Program Manager or prevent them from switching between Paradox and other tasks. Some developers will remove any Windows games, utilities, or miscellaneous applications in an attempt to shield the user from the Windows environment.

Using Paradox for Windows to create these kinds of applications begs a fundamental question: *Why are you using Windows in the first place?* If the application needs to be this restrictive with the operating system, then perhaps you shouldn't use Windows and Paradox for Windows.

Windows and Paradox for Windows are *enabling* environments that enable the user to do *more* with the computer and let them *tie together* various applications. They give the user *control* over the computing environment. If you are unhappy with the freedom that Windows provides, you may have to find another operating environment or spend some time altering the Windows installation and setup.

Many DOS developers, because DOS does not provide these enabling tools, could create a restrictive and simple operating environment for their applications with just a little work and were able to give the illusion that the computer is designed to run the custom application *and nothing else.* This style of programming is frequently done in the name of training efficiency, reduced support costs and troubles, and to accommodate many users of varying computer skill levels.

For rank novices and users who haven't yet developed the skills necessary to master a Windows interface, these kinds of restrictive applications provided some benefit. For more skilled users, an enabling environment often is better than a restrictive one. Most of the time, skilled users demand an enabling environment.

We don't to discourage application development in Paradox simply because some users haven't mastered the Windows operating environment. We just want to alert you to the fact that Windows assumes users have made some investment in training and self-practice to master the requisite hand-mouse skills and the Windows navigation skills.

Restricting a Windows application's environment takes more work and effort than restricting a DOS application's environment. With this warning said, let's move on to the next question.

How close to the Windows interface model do you want the new application to get?

How close to the Paradox for Windows interface model do you want the new application to get?

As you see in figure 3.5 and 3.6, there are some differences between Windows and Paradox for Windows. Borland has opted to develop a more visually interesting interface than standard Windows applications. Borland's dialog boxes have a 3-D *chiseled steel* look. When you decide to build your Paradox application, you have the option to do it the Microsoft way or the Borland way and either way is equally easy. Which way do you think is more appropriate for your application and your users?

Should users be able to maximize, restore, and resize windows?

Should users be able to move and minimize windows?

If you have decided that you want the new application to take advantage of Windows' enabling environment, you may be leaning towards a yes answer to these two questions. In fact, if you wanted to stick faithfully to a Windows-style application, you should allow your users to maximize, restore, resize, move, and minimize document windows in your application.

For many DOS developers, this option is confusing. These developers are used to writing applications where *the user can do one thing, and one thing only, at a time.* This design usually is referred to as *modal applications.* To many DOS developers, giving the users the ability to open many windows at the same time looks too difficult and challenging to program. Nothing could be further from the truth.

Managing multiple document windows in Paradox is easy. In fact, we've had discussions with several developers who said that they weren't intentionally creating modal applications in Paradox. They were just forgetting that in Windows, you can do many things at the same time and that Paradox easily accommodates this kind of programming.

This means that, if you wanted, you could let your users open the customer form, which edits the customer table, five times and then let them tile or cascade the five windows! DOS applications almost never attempt this trick, yet in Windows it's no trick but a fact of life. These applications often are known as *amodal applications*.

You may have to make some real-life considerations and *cripple* parts of your Paradox application somewhat to prevent users from opening too many windows, or from moving, resizing, or minimizing them. Again, you must decide the appropriate options for your application and your users. Paradox enables you to create windows that can't be resized, minimized, or moved, so you have some latitude.

Should all the data input elements have hot key equivalents?

This question indicates that you want to design an interface that isn't so biased towards mouse use. Many Windows applications provide shortcut keys to bring the user directly to a data input element when a certain key combination, such as Ctrl+J, is pressed. With a small amount of ObjectPAL code, you can provide this keystroke-driven user interface design in your applications.

However, keep in mind that Windows has established some common shortcut keys and access for several menu commands. Try to keep your data input element shortcut keys different than those listed in table 3.3.

Table 3.3. Common Windows Shortcut and Access Keys.

Menu or Command Name	*Keystroke*
Copy (as in Edit ¦ Copy to clipboard)	Ctrl+Ins or Ctrl+C
Cut	Shift+Del or Ctrl+X
Paste	Shift+Ins or Ctrl+V
Undo	Alt+Backspace or Ctrl+Z
File menu choice	Alt+F
Edit menu choice	Alt+E
Help menu choice	Alt+H
Window menu choice	Alt+W

Some Windows Terms Defined

Because the age of the graphical user interface is upon us, it is important to define the new terms that people use. Table 3.4. lists these terms.

Table 3.4. Windows Terms.

Action Type	Term	Meaning
Mouse	Click	Press and release a mouse button quickly without moving the mouse.
Mouse	Double-click	Clicking the mouse button twice in succession rapidly.
Mouse	Drag	Hold the mouse button down while moving the mouse.
Mouse	Drop	Release the mouse button after dragging.
Mouse	Point	Move the mouse pointer to the desired location.
Window	Close	Close the window.
Window	Hide	Make the window temporarily invisible.
Window	Move	Drag the window to a new location.
Window	Resize or Size	Change the windows size.
Window	Switch	Activate the next open window.
Input content	Clear	Discard the current data input selection without placing it on the Clipboard.
Input content	Copy	Copy the current selection to the Clipboard.
Input content	Cut	Remove the current selection and copy it to the Clipboard.
Input content	Delete	Similar to Clear, except if an object is selected, delete the object as well.
Input content	Paste	Copy the Clipboard contents to the current insertion point.

Miscellaneous Windows Conventions

Windows applications have somewhat standardized several other conventions. For example, pushbuttons sometimes have ellipsis after the button's label text, as in Approve... or the pushbutton has chevrons after the label text as in Approve>>.

The ellipsis indicates that another dialog box is displayed if the button is pressed. The current dialog box can be closed before the other dialog box is displayed, or the current dialog box is suspended, but still visible, when the new dialog box opens. When the new dialog box closes, the original dialog box regains control. These two types of new dialog boxes are known as *goto* and *gosub* dialog boxes. The goto dialog box does not return control to the calling dialog box, and a gosub dialog box does.

Menu access keys (as in Alt+F for the File menu or Alt+W for Window menu) and command button access keys should try to use the first letter of the menu or button name, a distinctive consonant or any other unique letter in the menu or button name.

Many applications include toolbars, otherwise called speedbars, to enhance the user interface. Although Paradox doesn't have a toolbar utility, you can create a toolbar by using the form designer and pushbuttons. Speedbars usually provide graphic equivalents to menu names and menu commands. Some of the graphics on these buttons are standard, such as a pair of scissors for Edit ¦ Cut, a picture of a clipboard for Edit ¦ Paste and a picture of a printer for File ¦ Print.

Summary

To develop applications in Paradox for Windows, you need to be versed in Windows user interface design and Windows terminology. Although Windows provides a standard interface, you have considerable options. You can design an application that meets the Microsoft Windows interface model or the Borland Windows interface model. You can make applications behave just like DOS applications, or you can take advantage of the benefits of the amodal, enabling environment Windows offers.

No matter which approach you take, keep in mind the following rule: the further you gravitate away from the Windows style of application development, the more work you will have to do in Paradox.

II

Getting Started: The Paradox for Windows Environment

4
The Desktop

The Desktop is your interface with Paradox for Windows. It's the first thing you see when you start Paradox. All your tables, forms, and reports open onto the Desktop. The Desktop's status area keeps you apprised of everything that's happening as you work through your application.

Much of what you do with the Desktop is intuitive; you can just rely on it as the backdrop. This chapter introduces you to the concepts that are important when working with the Desktop—including what's contained within it and how to customize it. We begin with a discussion of how the Desktop operates within the Window's MDI specification.

Paradox as an MDI Application

MDI, which stands for *multiple document interface*, is the Microsoft Windows standard interface for dealing with multiple documents within an application. For example, Paradox allows you to view more than one table, form, report, or query—all at the same time—each in its own window. The MDI specification is a component of CUA (Common User Access).

The Windows documentation refers to two kinds of windows: application windows and document windows. The Desktop is an example of an *application window*; tables open in windows, forms, reports, and queries are examples of *document windows*. The PAL documentation briefly mentions MDI frame and child windows—these windows correspond to application and document windows, respectively. The MDI frame is the backdrop window for an application. The Paradox for Windows Desktop is an MDI frame window.

The rules for the MDI dictate much of the behavior of windows within Paradox. Child windows are physically confined to their frame window (the Desktop). A maximized child window is never larger than the size of the related frame window. Child windows share the menu contained in the frame window—they do not contain their own menus.

Figure 4.1 shows the Desktop (frame window) that contains three different child windows:

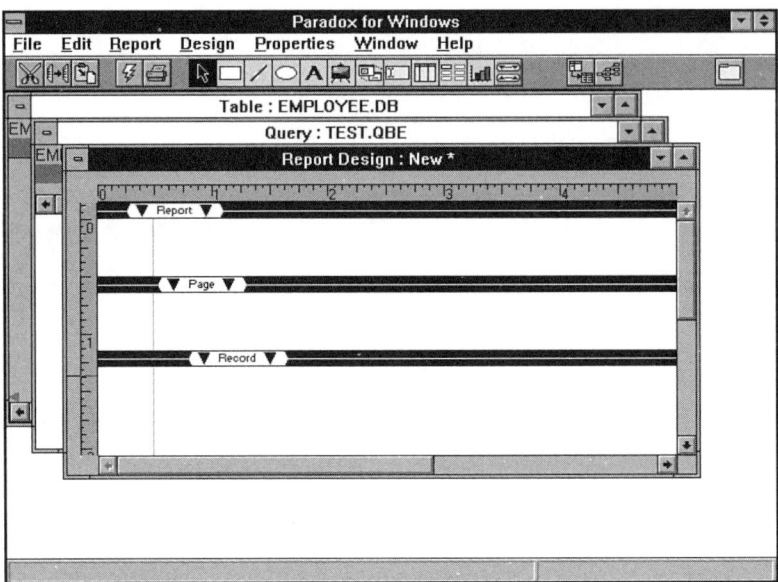

Figure 4.1. Multiple child windows.

Notice that the MDI defaults to cascading child windows as they are opened. Notice, also, that the menu always appears in the frame window, although the window changes to reflect the options available for the currently selected child window.

Dialog Boxes

Dialog boxes present a special case—they fall outside the realm of the MDI. Dialog boxes are *not* MDI children, and as such, are free from many of the limitations imposed on MDI child windows. Notice how the dialog box in figure 4.2 has been moved outside the boundary of the Desktop.

When a dialog box is active, the application menus and SpeedBar are *not* accessible.

Paradox's own dialog boxes are modal, which means that the user is required to interact with them before moving on to other windows within the application. To make your own forms act as true dialog boxes, you need to both open them as dialog boxes (making them non-MDI children) and set their modal property to true. Specific techniques for doing this are presented in Chapter 18.

Running Multiple Instances of Paradox

Because Paradox allows you to launch multiple instances, it is important to remember that each instance has its own frame window to control its child windows. Each *instance*, or frame, can run only one application at a time. This application can be native Paradox for Windows or your custom ObjectPAL application.

Within each Paradox instance, you may open multiple sessions. A *session* is a channel to the database engine. Each session utilizes a user count.

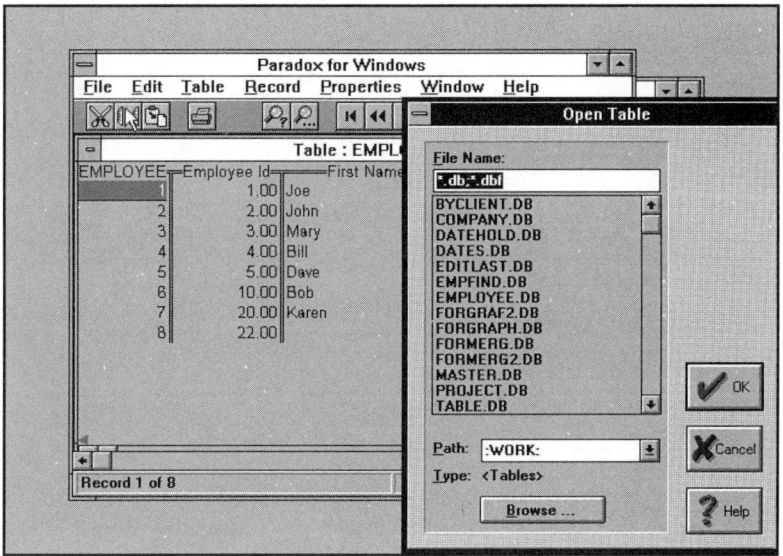

Figure 4.2. A Paradox for Windows dialog box.

Desktop Components

Now look at the Desktop once again, this time in greater detail in figure 4.3.

Figure 4.3 shows the Paradox for Windows Desktop, with no open windows.

At the very top are the usual windows boxes—the control menu box at the upper left and the minimize and maximize buttons in the upper right corner. In the middle is the application's title.

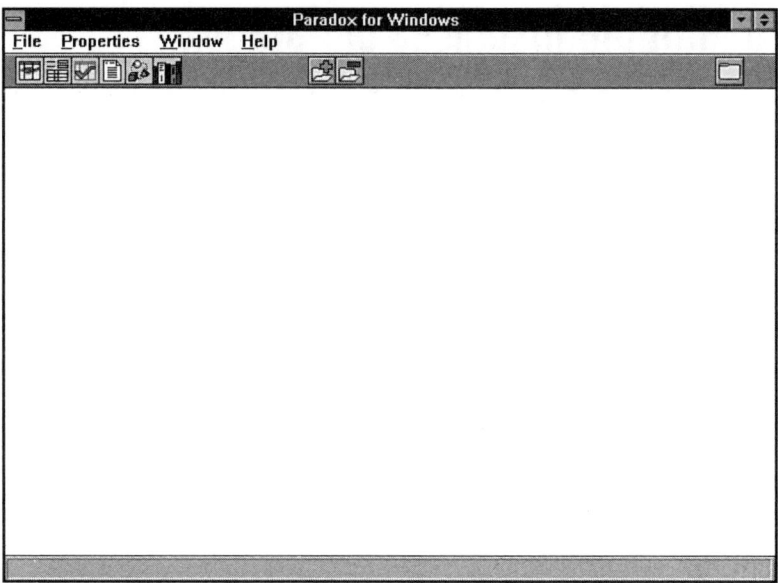

Figure 4.3. The default Paradox Desktop, with no windows open.

The SpeedBar

Using Paradox's default configuration, the SpeedBar appears immediately below the title bar. (We'll show you how to change the SpeedBar's position in the following section.) SpeedBars are common to Windows applications; they serve as shortcuts to commonly used menu actions. Like menus, SpeedBars are context-sensitive. SpeedBars in form windows contain a different set of icons than SpeedBars for table windows and query windows. As menu shortcuts, SpeedBars share some important menu features:

- SpeedBars appear only on MDI parent windows.

- SpeedBars show options relevant to the current operation. If you move through different child windows, the SpeedBar is updated to reflect the options available to the active window.

- SpeedBars generate the corresponding menu event. If you use the SpeedBar in your application, you can treat SpeedBar selections like menu selections. You can test the MenuEvent that results from a SpeedBar interaction. (Chapter 17 discusses this testing in detail.)

Three ObjectPAL procedures work specifically with the SpeedBar; their functions should be evident from their names:

1. HideSpeedBar( )
2. ShowSpeedBar( )
3. IsSpeedBarShowing( )

The Status Bar

The status bar is the area at the bottom of the screen. It, too, is common to many windows applications. Its contents also are dependent on the current activity.

ObjectPAL messages are displayed within the status bar. StatusEvent methods are used to control the display here. The four regions within the status bar are accessed with the ObjectPAL constants StatusWindow, ModeWindow1, ModeWindow2, and ModeWindow3, respectively. Figure 4.4 shows these four status areas.

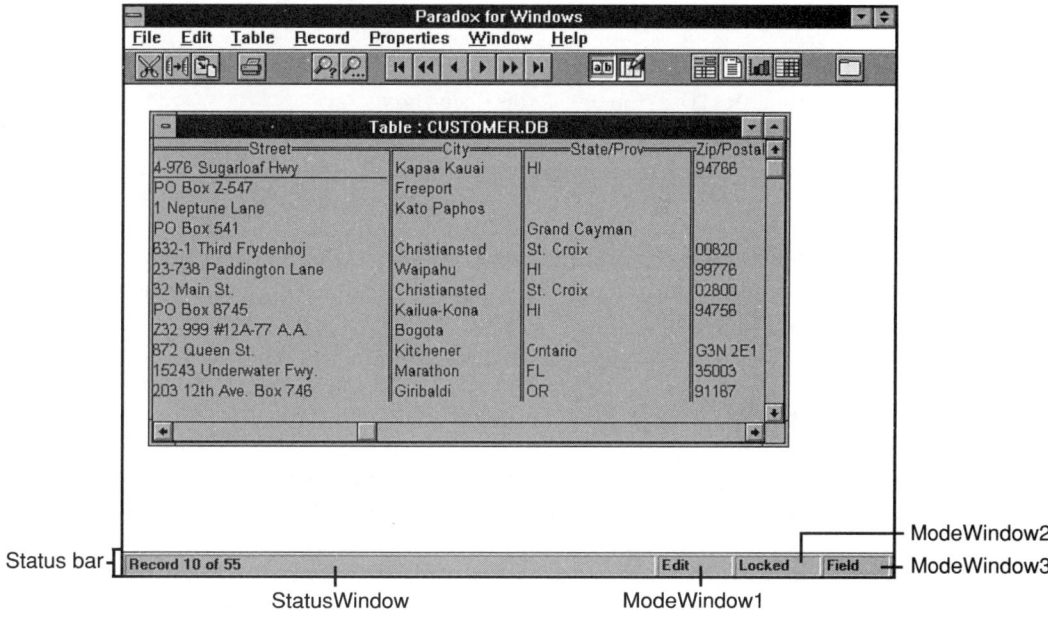

Figure 4.4. Status areas.

Desktop Properties

A variety of properties exist that describe the working Desktop. The Desktop Properties dialog box is shown in figure 4.5.

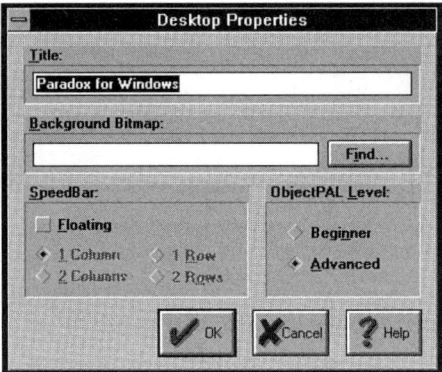

Figure 4.5. The Desktop Properties dialog box.

The menu selection Properties | Desktop opens this dialog box.

Title

The Title text box is where you specify the title for the current desktop. If you run multiple instances of Paradox, it is helpful to give them different titles so that you can easily identify which instance is active by glancing at the title bar.

Background Bitmap

This region of the Desktop Properties dialog box allows you to tell Paradox to display a custom graphic as the background for your application. This graphic can be in any of the graphic formats supported by Paradox: .BMP, .PCX, .GIF, .TIF, or .EPS. (The name of the property is *Background Bitmap*: Paradox converts the other graphic formats into .BMP format for display.) You can either type the name of the file that contains the graphic into the text box, or select BROWSE to find the file using the browser. Figure 4.6 shows the Desktop with the Windows file, CARS.BMP as the background bitmap.

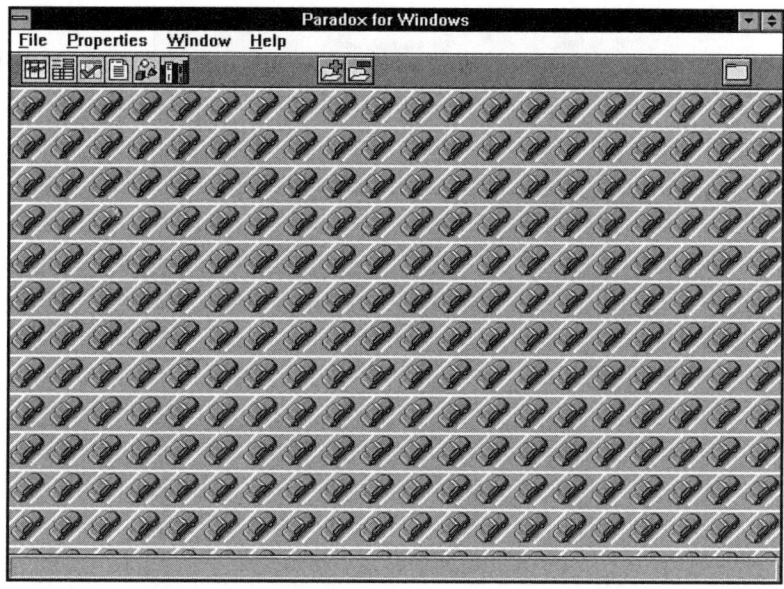

Figure 4.6. The Desktop, with custom bitmapped background.

To clear the Desktop, simply empty this text region.

SpeedBar

The SpeedBar region of the Desktop Properties dialog box allows you to define the following settings:

1. Whether or not the SpeedBar floats. A floating SpeedBar is always visible in its own window, on top of other windows and can be moved anywhere on the screen—even outside the Desktop.

2. The number of rows or columns used to display the icons in the SpeedBar. A nonfloating SpeedBar can be displayed only as a single row.

ObjectPAL Level

This section has two options: Beginner and Advanced. The ObjectPAL level tells Paradox how exhaustive the list of methods should be. It was included in an effort to not baffle new ObjectPAL programmers with *all* the available methods for each object. With Beginner selected, only the more commonly used methods are listed in the Methods dialog box. Figures 4.7 and 4.8 show the difference in the options available in the Beginner and Advanced level Methods dialog boxes.

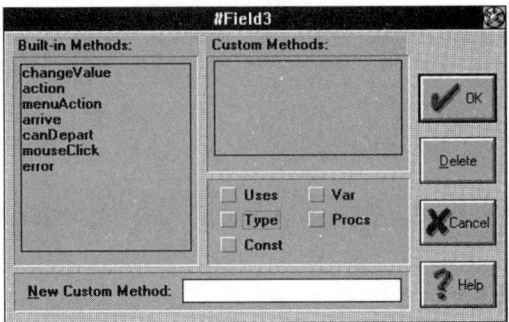

Figure 4.7. Beginner Methods options.

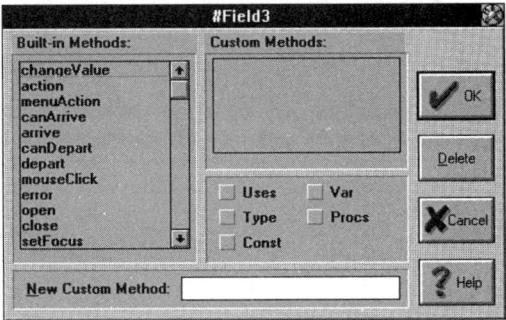

Figure 4.8. Advanced Methods options.

Whereas only 7 methods are listed with the ObjectPAL level set to Beginner, 27 methods are actually available, and all are listed when the ObjectPAL level is set to Advanced.

Note that this setting in no way limits the methods that are available—only methods that are displayed to the user. You are free to select Properties | Desktop to change this setting at any time during development.

Desktop Menus

Although the menu selections in Paradox for Windows are dynamic, representing options that are relevant to the current context, the Desktop menu options are available throughout the product.

The File menu is the workhorse of menus—if you don't know where to look for a function, the File menu is a good bet. The File menu is where you open existing and new Paradox objects, copy, rename or delete files, set your working and private directories, and more.

The New menu option allows you to open a new form, report, table, query, library, or script. Open enables you to open an already existent instance of these same objects. You also can open the Folder from this menu. Notice that all these menu options also are available as shortcuts from the SpeedBar.

Save, Save As, and Print are grayed when you look at a blank Desktop. These options are used for saving a query, form, library, or report design. People have been known to become confused by the absence of these options when working in table view. Because Paradox handles all changes to tables on a record by record basis, the table is essentially *saved* as soon as a record is posted. Therefore, it is meaningless to "Save" a table. Print is enabled as soon as an object is opened on the Desktop and prints the current document—the form or report. Reports print each record in the associated table(s), whereas forms print the data for the current record. It you are looking at the table in table view, Print will print the default or preferred report associated with the table.

The Printer Setup is available to customize the selected printer. This menu item takes you to the same dialog box that you see when using the Printer Setup option from the Windows Control Panel.

The Utilities submenu leads to a host of Paradox table operations. Figure 4.9 shows the options available from the Utilities menu.

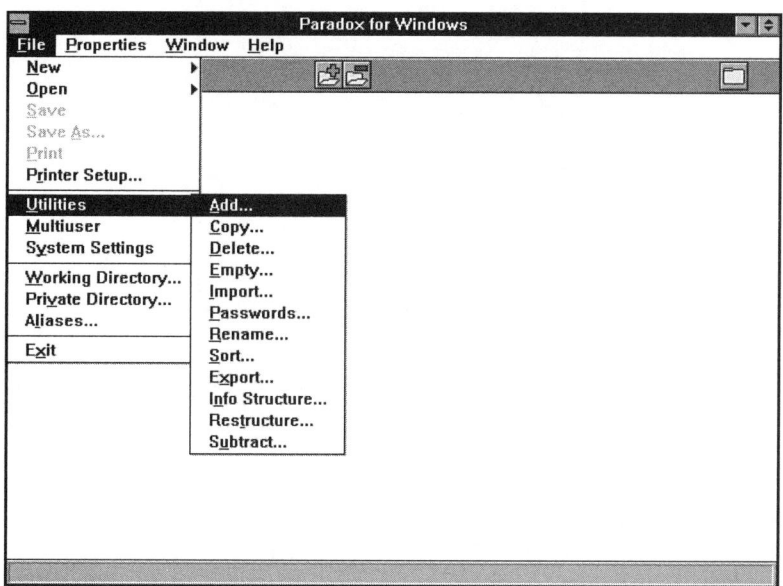

Figure 4.9. The Utilities menu options.

Use Add to add tables to one another. Don't forget that you can mix and match Paradox and dBASE tables and many of the operations under the Utilities menu. Choosing Append only appends new records to the table. Update only modifies key values in the existing table with records with identical key values in the new table. Append and Update do both—they add new records if the values do not exist and update existing records with the corresponding values in the source table.

69

Copy duplicates an existing object as a new object. You can transfer Paradox to dBASE files this way, by just changing the file extension for the new table. Copy works for forms, reports, libraries, and queries as well as tables. When you use Copy to copy tables, all the associated files are transferred with the table.

Delete erases an existing object from disk. If you use Delete to delete a table, all its associated files also are deleted.

Empty simply deletes all the records from a table.

The Import options allow you to bring data into Paradox from other formats. Figure 4.10 shows the import formats supported by Paradox for Windows.

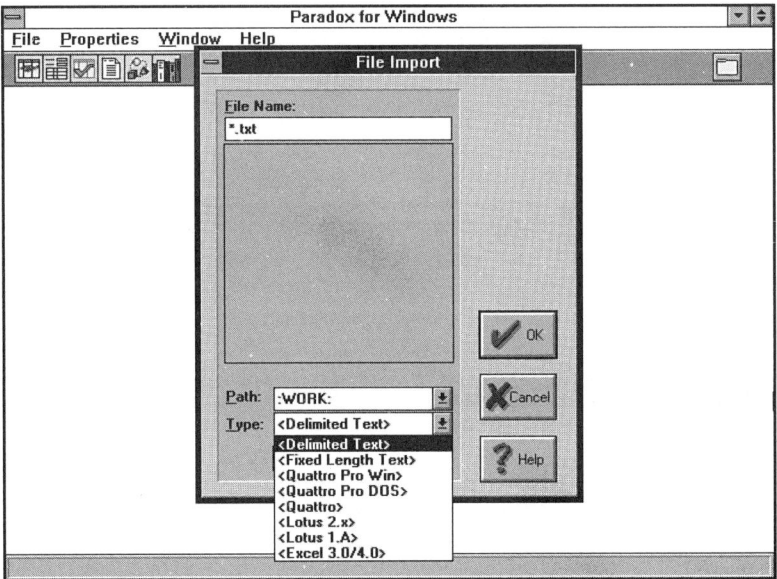

Figure 4.10. The Import Format options.

The Password menu selection allows you to add or remove passwords from the system. It does *not* allow you to assign passwords, which is done at the time you create or restructure your table.

Rename is where you change the name of a Paradox object. If you rename a table, all its associated objects are renamed as well.

Sort allows you to sort a table. Keyed tables must be sorted to a new table. Given Paradox for Windows' capability of displaying table *views* sorted by secondary index, you should think hard about using secondary indexes rather than sorting your tables.

Paradox for Windows allows you to Export to the same file formats that are allowed for Import. A serious limitation is that neither of these operations can be accessed directly under ObjectPAL control.

Info Structure brings up a dialog box that shows the structure of a table. The details of the resultant STRUCT table are discussed in Chapter 8.

The Restructure dialog box allows you to modify the structure of a table. This selection's features also are covered in depth in Chapter 8.

Subtract is used to remove records from a table as a batch operation, based on the contents of another table.

As the name implies, the options in the MultiUser menu deal with network and multiple-instance issues. We only touch briefly on these menu options here, because we devoted all of Chapter 29 to multiuser issues.

Display Locks shows all the locks on the selected table. Set Locks enables you to place a lock on the specified table. UserName shows you the UserName used by your network; this feature is for display only—the UserName cannot be set through this menu. Who displays a list of user names of the current users. Set Retry allows you to set the number of seconds that Paradox will retry a network operation.

The System settings contains a combination of four system setting options. Two options are read only and two options can be set from this menu. ODAPI shows the current settings in the ODAPI Configuration utility. Driver displays a dialog box of the currently installed driver list, again from the ODAPI Configuration Utility. Auto Refresh allows you to view or set the number of seconds Paradox waits between screen refreshes. See Chapter 29 for a complete discussion of the Refresh options. The Blank as Zero menu item is used to tell Paradox how to handle blank values in calculations. With Blank=Zero check marked, Paradox will see and treat blank values in numeric fields as zero. With it unchecked, Paradox ignores blank values in numeric fields when performing calculations on these fields. Suppose that you have a calculated field in a form or report that displays the result of the multiplication of two other fields. With Blanks=0 checked, any time either of the fields contained a zero, the calculated field would display 0; with Blanks=0 unchecked, the calculated field would display blank if either of the regular fields were blank.

Because the concept of Aliases is new, the next three options are presented out of order. Not only is it important for the discussion of setting your working and private directories, it is an important concept throughout the product.

An alias is an alternate name for a directory. You might, for example, give the directory C:\PUBLIC\ACCTS\ACME the alias :AC_ACT:. Aliases serve the following two purposes:

1. It is easier to refer a directory with a single name than to use an entire directory path.

2. Your applications are much more portable if you use aliases for directory references, rather than hard-coding complete directory paths.

Aliases are available in all the Paradox dialog boxes that allow you to choose a file. The Path drop-down list, for example, will show you any available aliases. This can be significantly faster than using the browser to navigate through levels of directories to find the file you need. For anything bigger than a basic application, creating aliases for such things as forms, libraries, and lookups is helpful.

To assign a new alias, select File ¦ Aliases to bring up the Alias Manager, shown in figure 4.11.

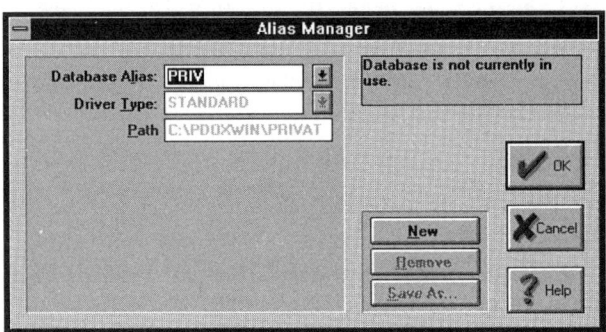

Figure 4.11. The Alias Manager.

If you click the New button, the Define Alias text region is blanked and ready for you to enter a name. Although Paradox allows you to enter a name as long as 31 characters, it's advisable to make aliases only as long as necessary to identify the directory contents. After giving the alias a name, type the drive and directory path into the Path text region. Notice that you can create multiple aliases that point to the same directory. In Chapter 9, we show you examples of how this procedure can be used to get around some data modelling restrictions.

There are two ways to save the alias, after the alias is defined, that seem to especially confuse new users. In fact, these two functions are quite straightforward. The Keep New button saves the alias *for the duration of the Paradox session*. Save As saves the alias to the ODAPI.CFG file, making the alias permanently available.

Two aliases have reserved names—:PRIV: and :WORK:. It shouldn't be surprising that these represent the currently defined private and working directories, respectively.

This brings us to the discussion of the last two File menu items—Working Directory and Private Directory, shown in figures 4.12 and 4.13, respectively. These items can be used both as information dialog boxes and to set the appropriate directories.

Notice the Alias drop-down list, which allows you to choose from any predefined alias. If no alias is assigned to the directory you need, you need to Browse to find the directory. The Alias list is unavailable in the Set Private Directory dialog box, but it always is available from the top of the Browser:

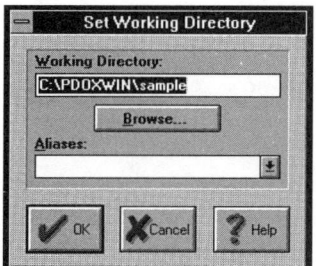

Figure 4.12. The Working Directory dialog box.

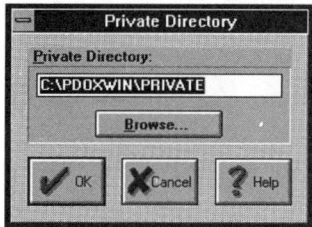

Figure 4.13. The Private Directory dialog box.

Summary

Although the Desktop's primary function is just to sit behind your application, it is important to understand its MDI interaction with other windows. For example, it is critical that you understand the distinction between an MDI child, or document window and a dialog box. This distinction is important both as you work with the interactive product and when you design your own applications.

This chapter introduced you to those menu options available from the Desktop. When you work with the Desktop directly, you can access a subset of the menu options that are available when you work with application windows in Paradox.

You also learned about some of the ways to customize your Desktop. Paradox gives a choice of where and how the SpeedBar should display. You can limit the number of ObjectPAL methods to display. By defining a custom background bitmap, you can change the background that you look at while working within.

5

The ObjectPAL Editor

Past versions of Paradox have been criticized for their rather lackluster programming editors. Paradox for Windows has a substantially improved editor with the following capabilities:

- Multiple window editing
- Syntax checking
- A tracer window with good tracing options
- Breakpoints
- A Variable inspector
- On-line assistance with method names, properties, and constants

Because editors are extremely important to developers (many a vociferous argument between developers has been over editors), it's imperative that you understand not only the basics of accessing and using the editor, but also the alternate ways to do things.

Accessing the Editor

In keeping with the Windows convention of giving multiple ways to perform the same procedure, Paradox for Windows has at least four ways to access the editor. To access the editor, you must be in form designer with the object to which you want to add code selected, and then take one of the following actions:

1. Use the right mouse button to bring up the current objects property menu. Select Methods, the last property on the list.

2. Use the Property | Current Object menu choices to bring up the property pop-up menu and select Methods.

3. Press F6 to bring up the properties pop-up menu for the current object and select Methods.

4. If you want to cut to the chase, just press Ctrl+space bar, and the methods dialog box pops up for the currently selected item on the form (see fig. 5.1).

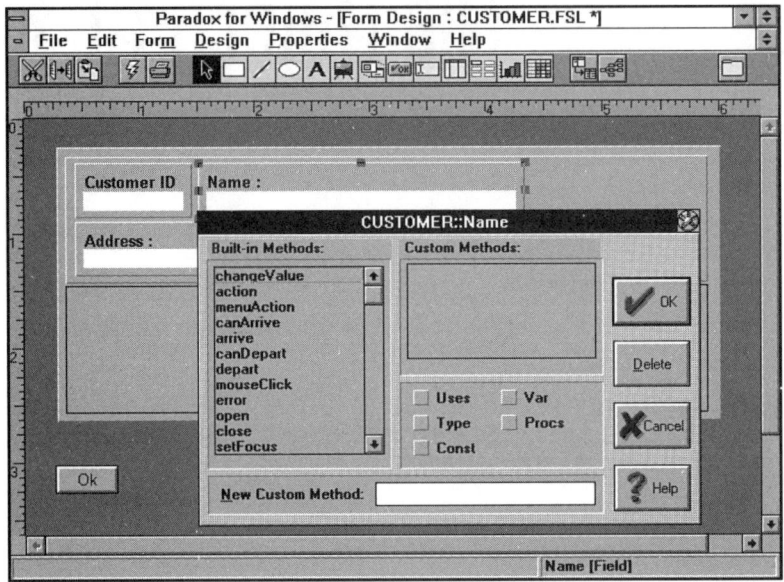

Figure 5.1. The Methods dialog box.

The basic idea is to select the item to which you want to attach code and then invoke the methods dialog box. Although this procedure is useful for objects on the form, what about the form itself? The form, after all, is an object that contains other objects. The form is actually the highest level container that exists in Paradox for Windows, which means the form is a significant object to which you most likely will attach code.

To bring up the property pop-up menu for the form, deselect all items on the form—including the page—by pressing Esc. Notice that the vertical and horizontal rulers will be colored to show you the selected item (if you have the rulers displayed). When no items are selected (when the form is selected), the vertical and horizontal rulers will not be colored. Then press F6 to bring up the Property pop-up menu. From this menu, select Methods to bring up the Methods dialog box. You also can use the Property | Form | Methods menu choices to bring up the methods dialog box for the form.

After the method dialog box is displayed, you then can select the event to which you want to attach code. We won't go into events and the Paradox for Windows event model here; this material is discussed in following chapters. The idea here is that you want to detect certain events and perform actions that Paradox for Windows, by default, doesn't perform. In this case, select the mouseEnter event because mouseEnter is a simple yet useful event. This event is triggered when the mouse pointer passes over the selected object. Trapping for this event lets you endow your application with the same capabilities that Paradox for Windows provides when the mouse pointer passes over a SpeedBar item. The details of the methods dialog box are discussed in following sections of this chapter.

To select the event, you can double-click the mouse or use the cursor keys to select the event. After the event is selected, an editor window opens (see fig. 5.2). You can select multiple events by using the Shift+Click and Ctrl+Click combinations. Shift+Click selects a contiguous region, and Ctrl+click selects multiple discontinuous regions. If you select multiple events, when you press the OK button several editor windows open, which you then can tile or cascade.

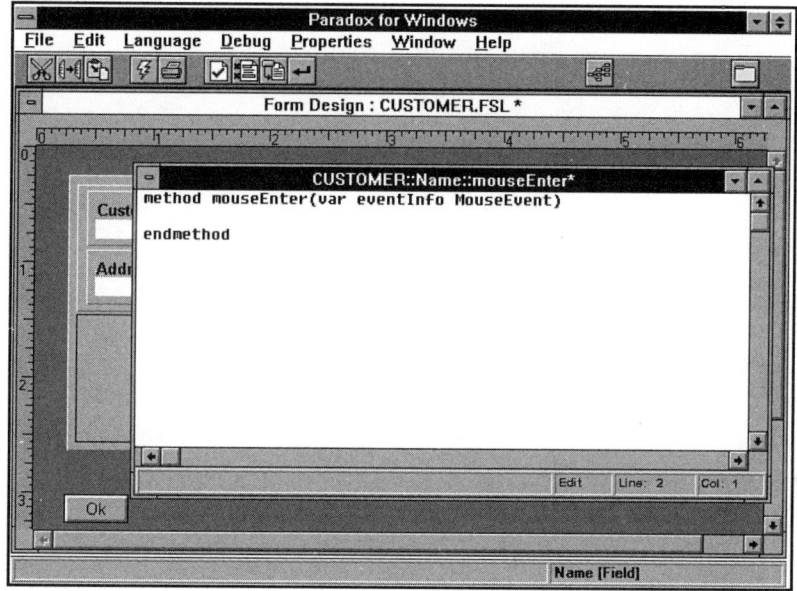

Figure 5.2. The Editor Window.

The editor follows typical Windows conventions for marking, deleting, and moving text around. Pressing the shift key and the cursor movement key highlights text. Pressing Ctrl+Shift+Left, for example, highlights the previous word.

Table 5.1 lists the more common editing action keys.

Table 5.1. Editing Keys

Keys	Result
F1	Help
Shift+F2	Close the editor window, keeping any changes
F5	Go to a line number
F6	Bring up the language menu
Ctrl+M	Bring up the language menu
F8	Run the form
Ctrl+F8	Save the form and run
F9	Check the syntax
Ctrl+Y	Check the syntax
Ctrl+space bar	Bring up the methods dialog box
Ctrl+Ins	Copy to the clipboard
Shift+Del	Delete to the clipboard
Shift+Ins	Paste from the clipboard
Esc	Undo the last change
Alt+Backspace	Undo the last change
Ctrl+Z	Search
Ctrl+A	Search again
Ctrl+Shift+Z	Search and replace

Inside the editor window, some new tools are available. Perhaps the most useful tool is the SpeedBar.

Review SpeedBar Tools

Like most Windows software, Paradox for Windows has a SpeedBar that makes it easier to select menu items. The editor SpeedBar is shown in figure 5.3.

From left to right, the SpeedBar items are:

1. Cut to the clipboard
2. Copy to the clipboard
3. Paste from the clipboard
4. Run this form
5. Print

6. Check syntax
7. Set breakpoints
8. Display the methods dialog box
9. Save the source code and exit
10. Display the object tree
11. Open a folder

All these items aren't discussed here, but we will discuss the important ones.

Figure 5.3. The Editor SpeedBar.

Run

The lightening bolt SpeedBar item always means *run the form*. When you press this SpeedBar item, Paradox for Windows checks the syntax in the active editor windows and, if no errors are found, runs the form. As in the Save SpeedBar item, pressing the Run SpeedBar item will not actually save your source code to the form and to your computer's hard drive. To do this procedure, from the form designer, just save the form.

Check Syntax

This SpeedBar item checks the syntax for the currently active editor window. If Paradox detects errors, the error messages are displayed in the message bar at the bottom of the current editor window, not the button of the editor session window.

A problem with this option is that the message is displayed at the bottom of the editor window, not the bottom of the Paradox for Windows Desktop window, which at first can be confusing. In addition, on some video displays, the message at the bottom of the editor window can be a little hard to read or may be obscured from view if the editor window is clipped.

Save

This SpeedBar item does not check your syntax, but it does save your source code and close the editor session window. Although the editor window closes, your source code is not written to the form and your computer's hard disk until you actually save the form.

Breakpoints

Used for debugging, this SpeedBar item enables you to designate a breakpoint without having to traverse the menus. When you press this SpeedBar item, Paradox displays the breakpoint dialog box (see fig. 5.4).

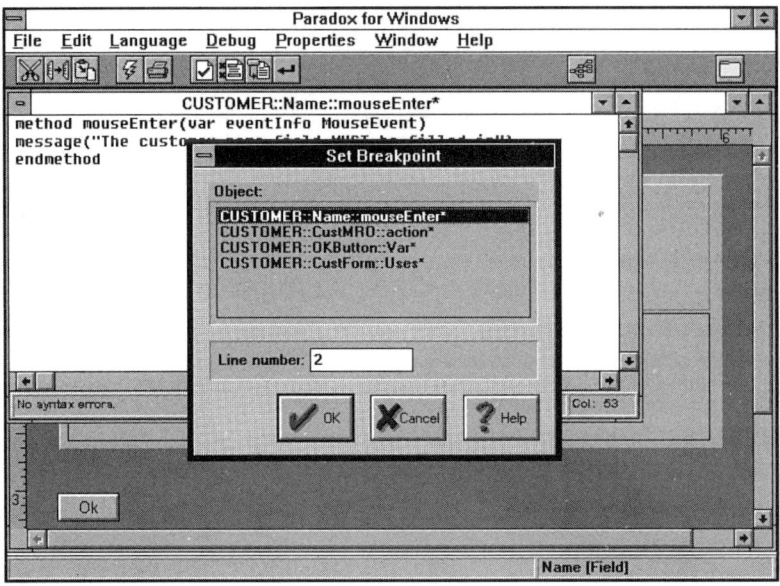

Figure 5.4. The Breakpoint dialog box.

This dialog box shows you all the objects you currently have attached code to and enables you to select a line number. When the form runs, as soon as this method for the object selected is encountered, you are placed in the Paradox for Windows debugger. The debugger is covered more extensively in Chapters 6, "Using the ObjectPAL Debugger," and 20, "Debugging Techniques."

The Object Tree

Pressing the object tree SpeedBar displays the form's containership hierarchy in a tree-like fashion. If you click the object tree SpeedBar item, the object tree appears in its own window.

The object tree is an innocuous-looking SpeedBar item that you shouldn't overlook. Besides the language menu items, the object tree probably is the most valuable object that you will use because the object tree shows the containership hierarchy for your current form. The object tree is a useful mechanism for searching the form for existing code and determining the exact relationship between all the items in the form. We feel so strongly about the object tree that we will go out on a limb to say that no serious developer can do without it. A bit of an overstatement, perhaps, but we hope that you get the idea.

To understand the object tree, you must understand the tree structures that programmers use. Tree structures usually display the trunk on top with all the branches below, which really is an upside-down tree in the physical world of nature. For programmers, the upside-down tree structure is a useful artifact because it tends to mimic an entire range of data structures.

The object tree is one of these data structures because it always displays higher level objects to the left and lower level objects to the right, which means that higher, or more fundamental objects, like the form and the page, are displayed to the left, and more particular objects, such as field objects and button text objects, are displayed to the right. So, the direction left— or up in the tree— corresponds to items that are visually behind or beneath other objects, and right— or down in the tree— corresponds to items on top of or surrounded by other objects. An example of an object tree is shown in figure 5.5.

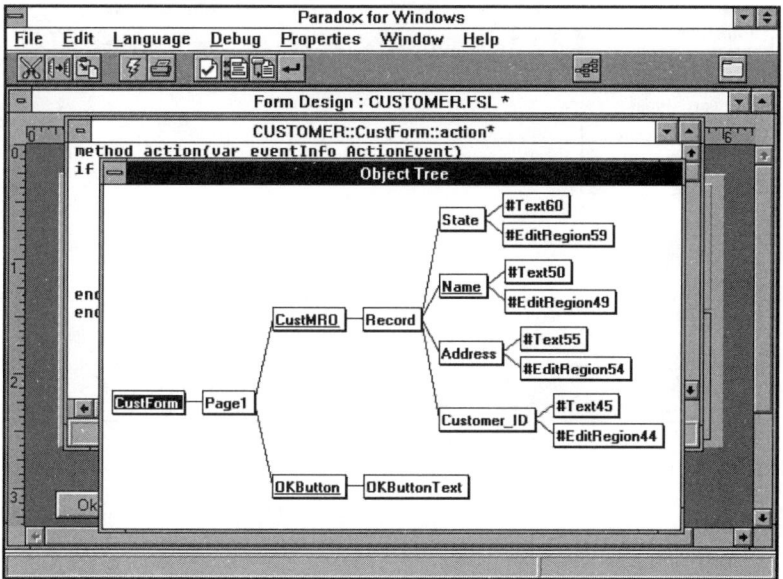

Figure 5.5. The Object Tree.

When you first enter a form in design mode, the screen looks like you have no object selected. You do; the form itself is selected. If you press the object tree SpeedBar item, you will see the form furthest left in the object tree. As you select an item in the form (including what, at first glance, may seem like the form but actually is the page object) and then press the object tree SpeedBar item, you see the object tree for the currently selected item downward. On complex forms this visual is helpful because you can restrict the display of the object tree to just a portion of the tree.

Menu Items

Now that you reviewed the SpeedBar and the various ways to access the editor from the form designer, review the menu items. Many of the menu items may be familiar to if you who worked with Windows software before, so we'll be brief.

File

While in the editor, the file menu is the same in Paradox for Windows as in other modes (see fig. 5.6).

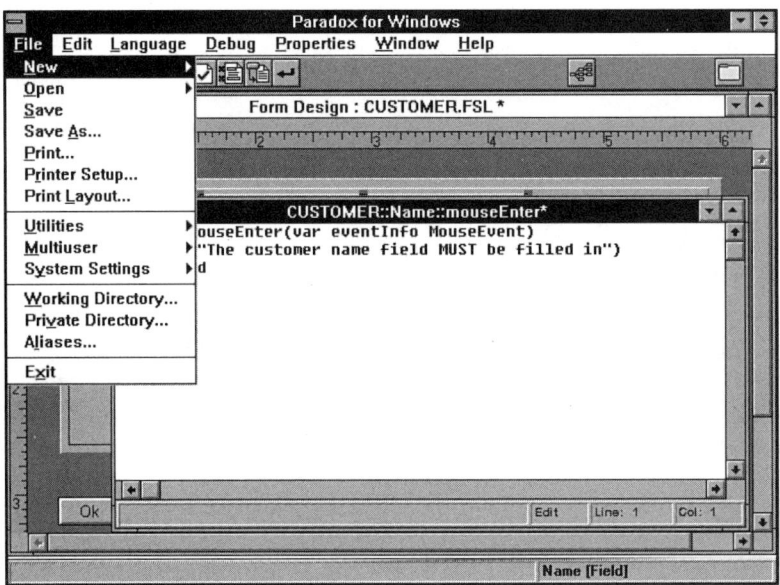

Figure 5.6. The File menu in the editor.

While you are in the editor, you can create tables, edit tables, look at other forms, and basically do anything you want. Paradox for DOS developers have long been used to being unable to do these sorts of things from within the editor. If you're a die-hard Paradox for DOS programmer, you probably will forget that you can be editing a table, designing a form, and editing methods at the same time.

Edit

The edit menu has the equivalents to the SpeedBar cut and paste tools, plus a few more items. Perhaps the most important thing to remember here is that when you copy or cut an item from the form to the clipboard, all the object's methods go with the item. This feature is useful because it makes it very easy to create an object with a generic behavior and copy the object into the forms that need this behavior.

The Select all menu item selects all objects within the currently selected object, which is useful to change the color or some other property for all the objects selected.

Language Menu

This menu item has the equivalent for the Check syntax, Object tree, and Methods SpeedBar items (see fig. 5.7). The language menu also has several useful items (see table 5.2).

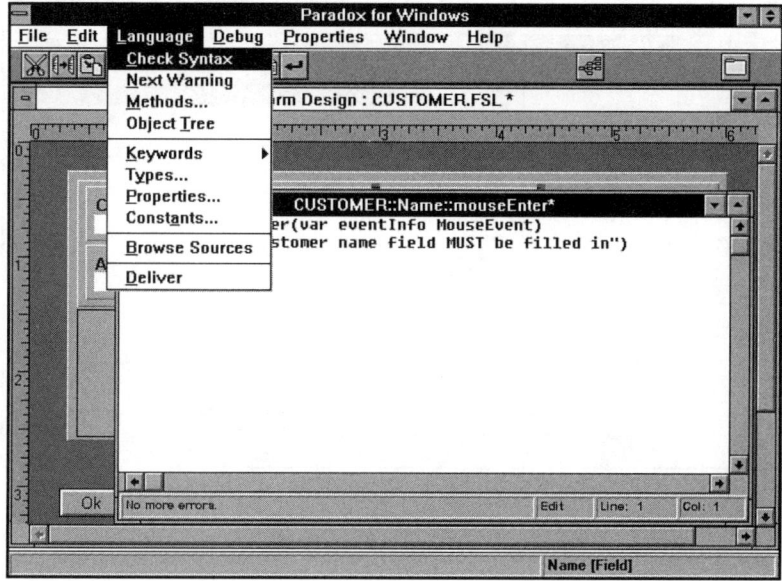

Figure 5.7. The Language menu.

Table 5.2. Language Menu Options.

Option	Definition
Next Warning	Move to the next compiler warning.
Keywords	Display the list of basic language elements and optionally insert one.
Types	Browse a list of methods and procedures.
Properties	Browse a list of object properties.
Constants	Browse the list of ObjectPAL constants.
Browse Sources	View all source code for the current form.
Deliver	Remove source code from the form so it can't be changed.

The four most useful menu items are Keywords, Types, Properties, and Constants.

Keywords

The ObjectPAL language has basic language elements: conditional constructs, looping constructs, and error constructs. This menu item lists each of the basic language elements for quick reference. These language elements are discussed in more detail in Chapter 13.

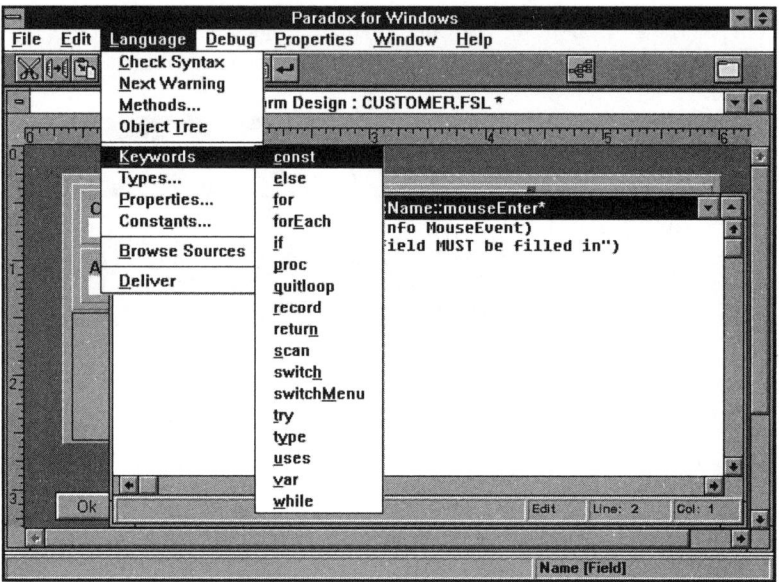

Figure 5.8. The Keywords menu.

The Types Dialog Box

Almost everything you manipulate in ObjectPAL is an object. Different types of objects exist. For example, one object may be a string, which is different from a form object. Each object type has dozens of methods and procedures you use to manipulate and control the object.

If you add up all the methods for all the object types, Paradox for Windows has over 1,000 methods and procedures, hundreds of constants, and hundreds of properties. Most of us can't remember everything, much less even a small fraction. This menu item enables you to scroll through lists of all the available methods and procedures for each object type (see fig. 5.9). Because of this advantage, developers may use this menu item most.

This dialog box displays the arguments that the method requires as well as what variable type the method returns. For this reason, the Type menu is most often used as a quick reference utility. From this dialog box, you can insert the currently selected method or procedure, or you can enter the selected type into the current cursor position in the active editor window, which saves you editing keystrokes and prevents typing errors.

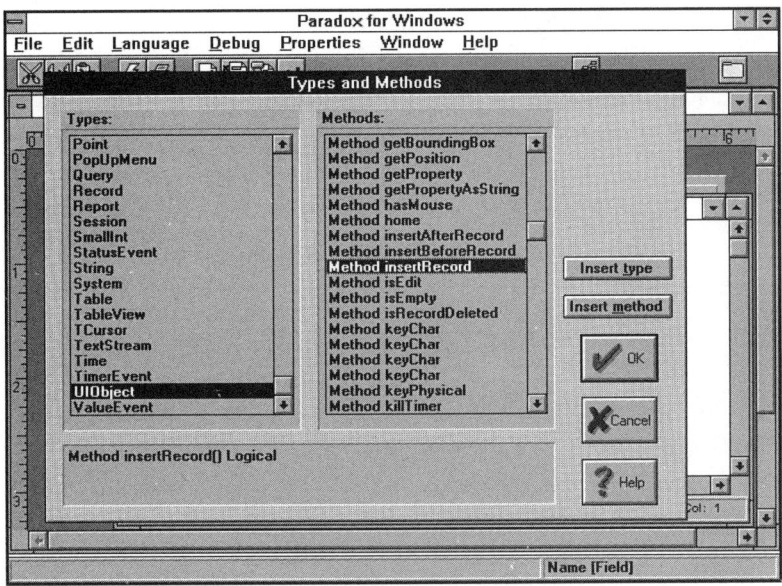

Figure 5.9. The Types dialog box.

Properties Dialog Box

Every object you work with has properties. A text field label, for example, has a font style and color, an ellipse has a certain color, a multi-record object has a certain frame style. Some properties can be set, and some properties are there for read-only purposes (Paradox needs these properties to do internal processing). Rather than memorize all these properties, the property menu will display a dialog box listing each object type and the properties associated with it (see fig. 5.10). From this dialog box, you can insert an object. In addition, you can insert the object's property.

Constants Dialog Box

Paradox for Windows has hundreds of predefined constants that refer to such diverse things as system colors, data entry actions, and system menus. The reason Paradox for Windows uses so many constants is so that developers don't have to memorize or use strange and cryptic numbers to refer to these items. This menu item enables you to browse the list of constants (see fig. 5.11).

Property Menu

The property menu enables you to set several desktop properties or editor defaults. With the Property | Desktop menu items, for example, you can make the following four changes:

Part II ■ Getting Started: The Paradox for Windows Environment

1. Change the Paradox for Windows desktop window title.
2. Change the ObjectPAL level to beginning or advanced. Marking advanced displays all built-in methods in the methods dialog box. Marking beginner limits the display of built-in methods to a handful or so of methods.
3. Change the background bitmap.
4. Make the SpeedBar floating or fixed.

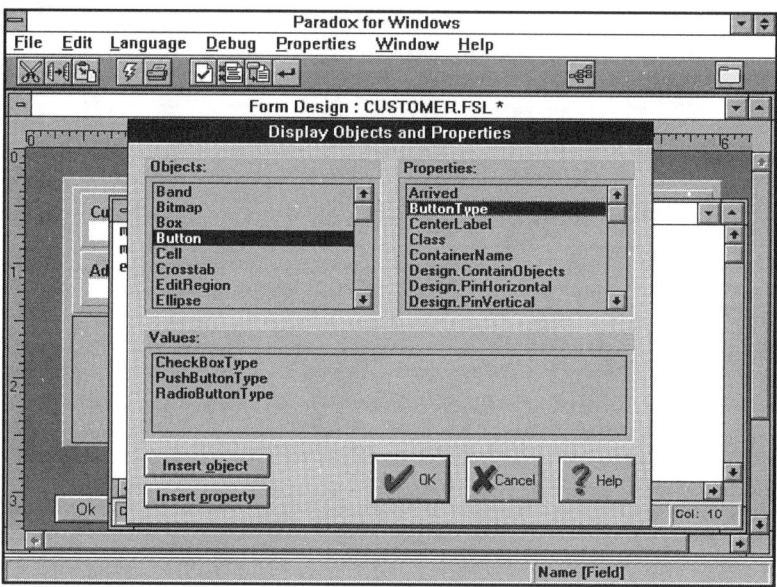

Figure 5.10. The Properties dialog box.

With the Property ¦ Alternate Editor menu selections, you can tell Paradox for Windows to use another editor instead of the built-in editor. The last item, Show Compiler Warnings, lets you disable or enable compiler warnings. Warnings include messages about undeclared variables and other things that may cause a problem during runtime.

Window Menu

With the Window menu, you tile, cascade, and close your windows. You also can select which window you want to become active. If you have multiple editor windows active, you can use the Window menu to select a specific editor window.

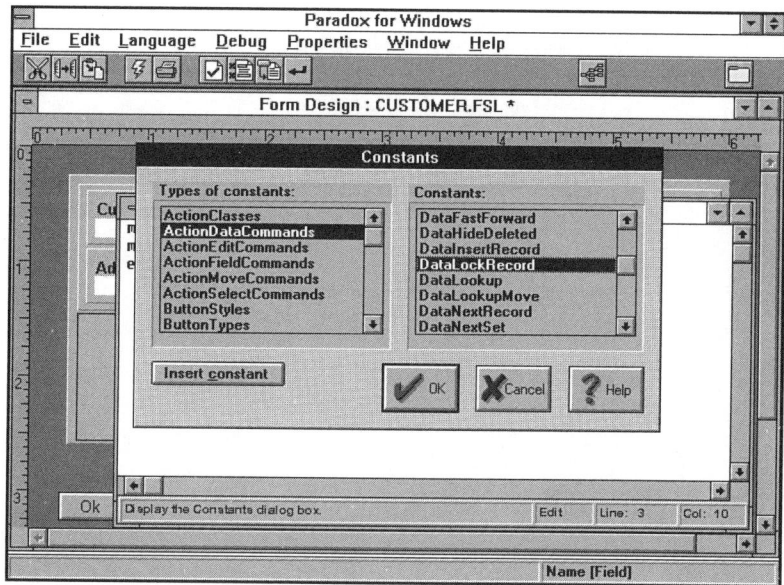

Figure 5.11. The Constants dialog box.

Using Help in the Editor

One of the most useful menu choices in the editor is the Help menu item. Paradox for Windows has an extensive context-sensitive help system, which is implemented through the Windows help facility. You can access help by using the menus, or by pressing F1 at any time.

The help system is always displayed in a window that belongs to the Windows session, not the current session of Paradox. If you run multiple tasks in Windows and you invoke Paradox for Windows help, the help window appears as a separate task in the task list.

Setting Bookmarks

A little-known feature of the Windows Help system lets you define a bookmark. A bookmark is a tag that appears on the Bookmark menu item that will bring you to a specific menu item quickly. Often, you can get lost or are unable to remember where you found a particular help screen.

A useful help screen is the alphabetical list of ObjectPAL methods. Once you select a method and the particular class for the method, the help system displays the method's argument list, return type, a description, and some examples. Figure 5.12 shows the help system with the list of ObjectPAL methods and the bookmark menu. Figure 5.13 shows a sample ObjectPAL method help screen.

Part II ■ Getting Started: The Paradox for Windows Environment

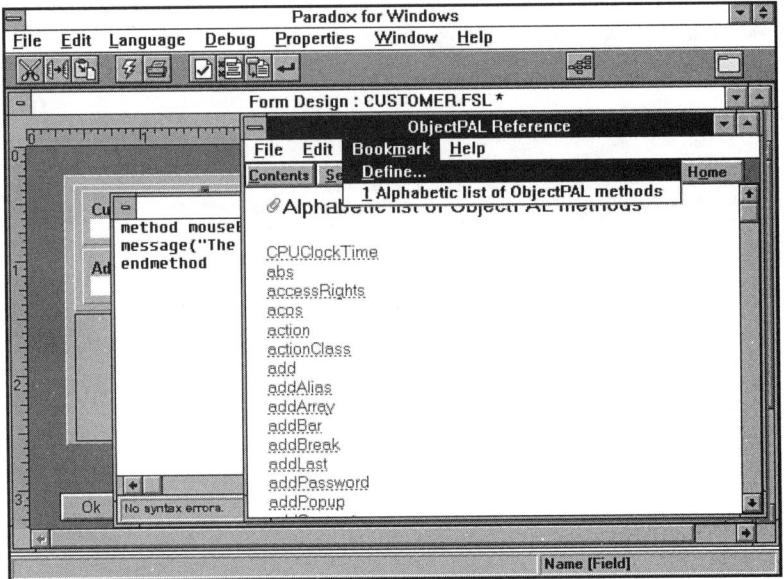

Figure 5.12. The Help system list of ObjectPAL methods.

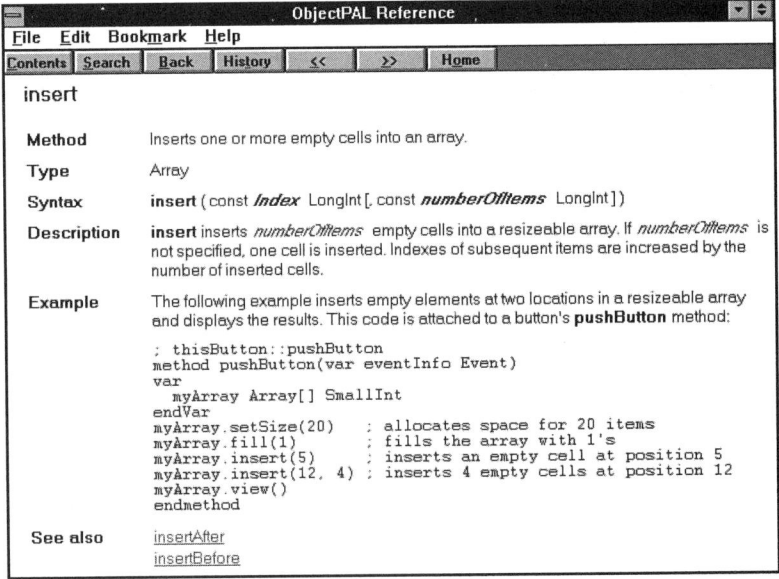

Figure 5.13. The Help system Method help screen.

Using Another Help File

You can select different help files from the help system File menu. In fact, the help screens for Paradox for Windows are distributed across several help files, which means that you can select any file that meets the Windows Help file format specification and can be opened as a help file.

To open another help file, press F1 to display the Paradox Help window. Choose File ¦ Open from the Help window menu and select another help file.

Figure 5.14 shows the File ¦ Open dialog box. Because you can select another help file, you can create and add your own help files to your application. To create a help file, however, you need a help compiler. Borland includes a help compiler with the Borland C++ package.

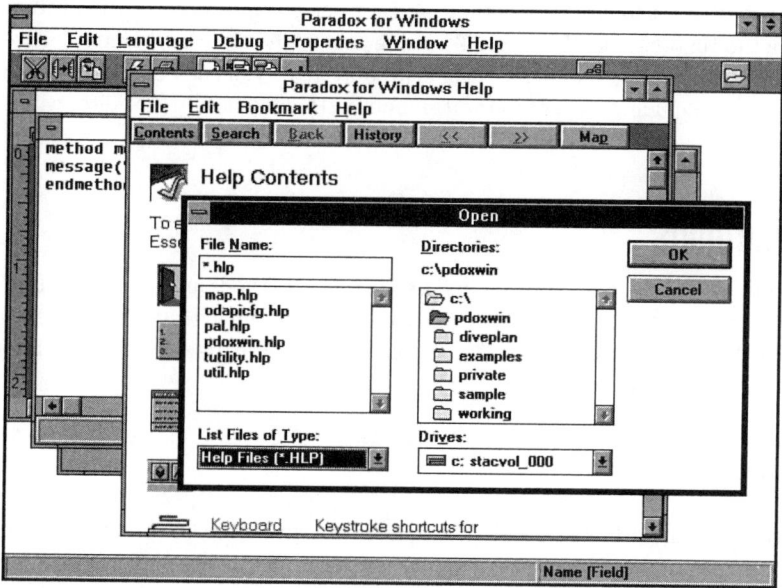

Figure 5.14. Opening another help file.

More on the Methods Dialog Box

We've already discussed how to access the methods dialog box. Because this dialog box is going to be your only means of adding ObjectPal code, you should review some of the other items inside this dialog box.

Built-in Methods

The methods dialog box always displays a list of built-in methods available for the current object. Built-in methods are programming stubs, or empty methods, to which you can add code. The methods are named after the event they respond to. You don't need to worry about understanding everything about built-in methods here, because they are discussed more fully in Chapters 13 and 14. What is important to know is that the list is rather long and that, as soon as you attach code to one of the built-in methods, the built-in method appears at the top of the list. This lets you quickly find objects that have code added.

In addition, all built-in methods to which you added code are underlined and are followed by an asterisk, giving you another indication that the method has code attached.

To bring up the editor for the built-in method, you can select the built-in method you want, double-click on the method or press the OK button. To delete your code for the built-in method, you can select the built-in method you want and press the Delete button, or you can edit the built-in method and delete everything—including the method and endmethod keywords—in the editor window, and save the editor window.

Custom Methods

Custom methods are methods you create. Invariably, these methods are called from the form's built-in methods. You add custom methods by typing the method name in the name field at the bottom of the methods dialog box and pressing the OK button. Custom methods always appear in the list on the right hand side of the methods dialog box.

Uses Window

If you mark the Uses check box in the Methods dialog box and press OK, you then can edit the Uses window. With this window, you can declare the methods that are external to this form. Methods external to the form reside either in a library or in a DLL. These ideas are discussed in more detail in Chapter 13.

Type Window

Marking the Type box and then pressing OK opens a type window. In the type window, you can declare user-defined types and record structures. This feature comes in handy if you need to pass arrays as arguments to other methods or procedures or if you need to create records similar to the C struct construct. Chapter 13 discusses types in greater detail.

Const Window

You have already seen the Constant dialog box from the Language menu. If you mark the Const check box in the Methods dialog box, you can define your own constants. Constants are somewhat like variables, except that their values can never change. The compiler makes sure that these values cannot and do not change.

Constants are useful tools that can provide meaning where a number may create confusion. Constants also are more efficient than variables. Because constants never change, the compiler can pass the constant by reference without making a copy of the variable. This process is discussed in more detail in Chapter 13.

Var Window

The Var check box opens a Var window where you can declare variables. You will use the Var window quite a bit in your ObjectPAL applications, because every time you want a variable visible to anything other than the object to which it is attached, you need to create a variable in an object's Var window. This topic and variable visibility are discussed in detail in Chapter 13.

Proc

The Proc check box enables you to open a Proc window. In a Proc window, you can add as many procs as you want. Procs are different than methods. These differences are discussed in Chapter 13.

Multiple Editor Windows

What happens when you mark all the boxes in the methods dialog box and select several events? Figure 5.15 shows the result: many editor windows!

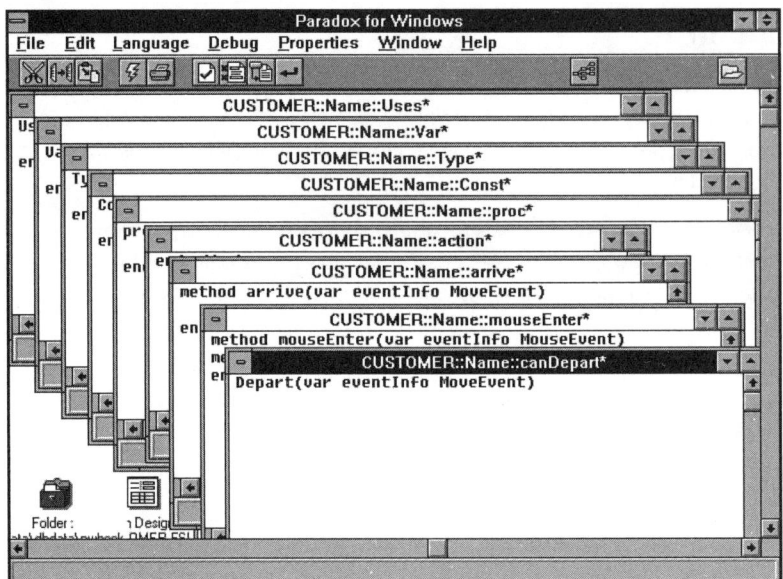

Figure 5.15. Several Editor windows open at the same time.

Summary

Compared with previous versions of Paradox, Paradox for Windows has a much improved, easy to use programming editor. While not having all the features of a full-blown, high-end programmer's editor, Paradox for Windows does include some very important features, which are recapped in the following list:

- An object browser, so that you can see where your source code is located.
- An on-line list of available methods, procedures, constants, properties, and keywords.
- An on-line help system.
- The capability of cutting and pasting not only sections of code, but entire objects with code.

6

Using the ObjectPAL Debugger

Debugging tools for traditional third generation languages are well established. Companies have been writing debugging tools for these environments for years, refining the tools and enhancing them along the way. Most programmers know how to debug traditional programs.

In object-oriented and object-based environments, however, debugging has a few new wrinkles.

Traditional programming environments have a main module and a traceable calling hierarchy. Nearly all programmers start at the top module and work their way down to discover the source or the cause of the problem. In Paradox for Windows' object-based environment, no main method exists that calls all the other methods. Most forms don't actively do anything; they just sit and wait for events to occur and dispatch the event to the appropriate method. Viewing all the lines of code that are executed usually tells you little about what the application is doing right or doing wrong. You have to see the application in action and catch it *in the act*.

In addition, in Paradox for Windows, your source code often is scattered among many objects on the form. Quickly finding the offending object is important. The concept of source code line number, while still present in Paradox for Windows, has less meaning because each method you write tends to be rather small. There also is no concept of a *universal* line count for all methods in a form. After all, the methods you write are not kept in a single text file, but are stored with their parent object *within* the form.

Other problems arise. Method names are not unique. Each form can have many duplicate method names, both built-in (provided by Paradox) and custom (provided by you). Although method names are unique to an object, each form can have many objects. In fact, this aspect of the Paradox for Windows model is the most crucial because it enables you to perform some object-oriented techniques, such as polymorphism, within the structure of the containership hierarchy. The problem occurs when you think a problem exists with an open( ) method somewhere in the form. The questions arise: which open( ) method—the form's? The table frame's? The record object's? The field's?

Debugging in this new environment requires slightly different thinking. Fortunately, Paradox for Windows has just enough tools to get the debugging job done. Perhaps the most important tool is the object tree. The object tree gives you an unambiguous map of all the objects in the form (the object tree is discussed in greater detail in Chapters 10 and 13). With the object tree, you can inspect the form visually and quickly determine which objects have code attached to them and which don't. The objects that have code attached are underlined. Objects that have no code aren't underlined. Using the object tree, you can quickly spot the objects you have attached code to.

This chapter reviews debugging basics. Chapter 20, "Debugging Techniques," reviews some debugging issues related to the Paradox for Windows event model. These issues are discussed in Part IV, after Paradox for Window's event model has been explained in more detail.

The Debugger Menu

The debugger menu is accessed several ways:

1. From within the editor while you have one or more edit windows open.

2. By pressing Ctrl+Break when running the form. This feature must be enabled with the debugger menu option Enable Ctrl+Break to Debugger.

3. Invoking the debugger menu by placing the debug( ) proc in your code and then running your form. The form is suspended and the debugger menu is activated when the debug( ) proc is encountered. This feature must be enabled with the debugger menu option Enable DEBUG statement.

Figure 6.1 shows the debugger menu during a debug session. All debugger menu options are available during a debugger session. When you are editing your source code, some options don't make sense, like stepping through your source code or inspecting a variable. You can only do these when running the form.

Inspect

The inspect menu item let's you view variables you have declared. When you inspect a variable, the debugger will automatically place the current line of code in the editor window into the inspect dialog box. If you want the variable inspector to come up with the name of your variable, move your cursor to the line that has that variable name in it before you inspect the variable.

The inspect facility, however, has some limitations you need to be aware of:

1. You cannot view an array element. You can, however, view an entire array and the dialog box will let you scroll through array elements.

2. You cannot view a record element. You can, however, view an entire record structure and scroll through the record's fields.

3. You cannot inspect an object's property. This limitation is more critical, because if you need to evaluate an object's property during a debugging session, you first need to assign the property to a variable.

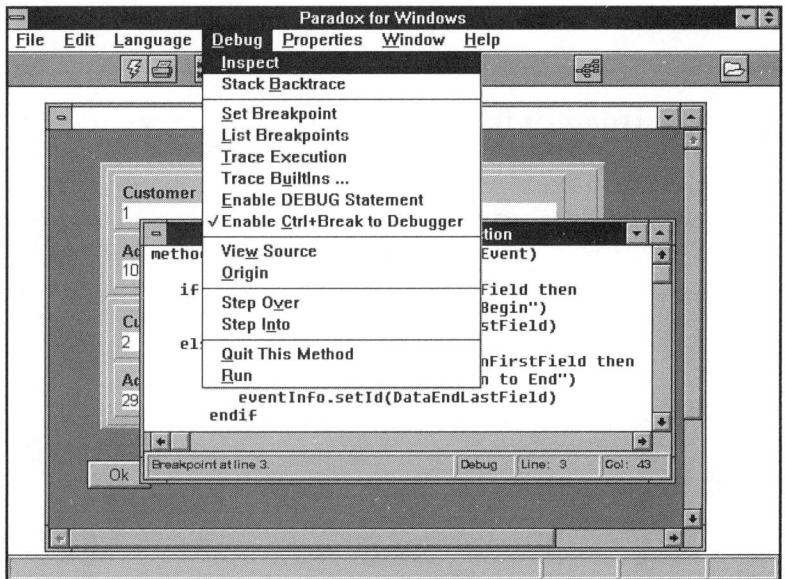

Figure 6.1. The Debug menu.

Stack Backtrace

Stack backtrace will show you the hierarchy of methods and procedures which got you to the current method. For simple event trapping, such as adding code to an open event or an action event, the stack backtrace usually shows you one line—the name of the method with the debug statement.

The method or procedure you are in will be listed first, and all prior methods and procedures are listed in order.

Set Breakpoints, List Breakpoints

Breakpoints automatically suspends the form and invokes the debugger when the method and line number indicated are encountered. If you select this menu item, a breakpoint dialog box will pop up for the current method. You then can enter the line number you want to set as the breakpoint. When the dialog box pops up, it uses the current line number as the default line number.

Breakpoints cannot be set for a procedure, which can be a significant limitation if your application uses procedures liberally. To get around this limitation, set a breakpoint in the method that calls the procedure. You then can step through each line of code until you get into a procedure.

The List Breakpoints menu item brings up a dialog box that lists all breakpoints set. From this dialog box, you also can delete any or all breakpoints.

Trace Execution, Trace BuiltIns

When the Trace Execution menu item is checked, the debugger opens a tracer window and writes to the tracer window the lines of code along with an object name for which the code is executing. Unless you select the Trace BuiltIns menu item, only code that you have attached to any objects will be traced.

The Trace BuiltIns menu item brings up a dialog box (see fig. 6.2) that enables you to trap any or all of Paradox for Windows built-in methods, whether or not the built-in method contains code.

Figure 6.2. Trace BuiltIns dialog box.

You can trace built-in methods only if you have Trace Execution enabled or you use the tracerOn( ) procedure in the System type to specifically turn on the tracer. In fact, using tracerOn( ) and tracerOff( ) procedures from within your code is a useful technique because so many events get generated that determining what events are occurring where is sometimes difficult.

If you want to see the Paradox for Windows blizzard of events, check all the built-in methods, turn on trace execution, and watch the tracer window. Figure 6.3 shows what happens.

Chapter 6 ■ Using the ObjectPAL Debugger

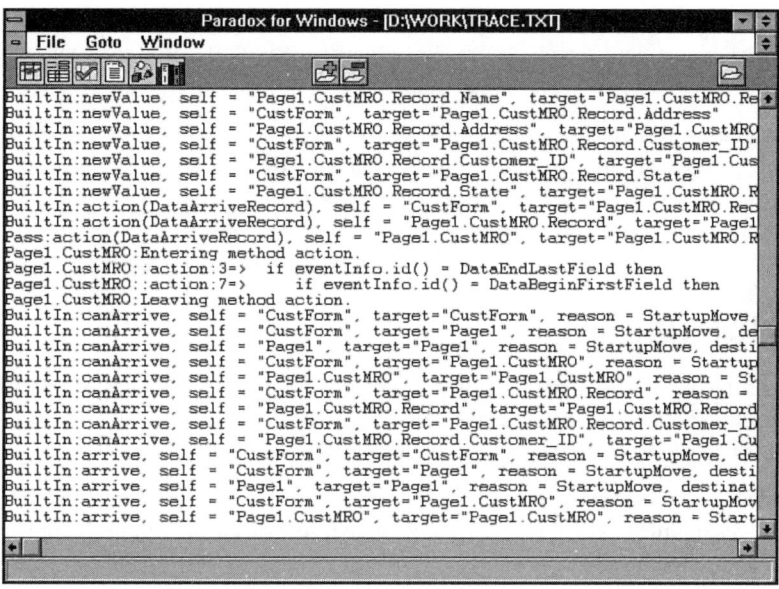

Figure 6.3. The Tracer window with all built-ins traced.

Obviously, if you want to trace all events, you will want to save your tracer window to a file, which you can do by either clicking on the tracer window to make it active or selecting the tracer window from the Window menu item. The file menu allows you to save the tracer window to a file of your choice. This file, however, is not continually updated. You must select the tracer window specifically and save it to your file. The file created is a text file except that the ASCII 10 character is used to separate lines, not the normal CR/LF sequence (ASCII 13 and ASCII 10). To bring this file into a text editor, you first need to replace the ASCII 10 character with a CR/LF sequence.

If you don't want to see the tracer window output while your form is running, the tracer window can be minimized.

By the way, the tracer execution status is saved with the form, which can be confusing if you forget to set tracer execution to off before you save the form. If you don't set tracer execution off and then save the form, the next time you run the form, the tracer window appears.

Enable Debug, Enable Ctrl+Break

The Enable Debug menu item allows you to enable any debug( ) procs in your code, which is useful because you may want to place one or more debug statements in your code so that you can invoke the debugger at problem areas. These debug( ) procs do not invoke the editor if Enable Debug isn't checked. If you want to keep the debug statements in your code but run the form with all debug( ) procs disabled, just make sure that the Enable Debug menu option is not checked.

97

If the Enable Ctrl+Break menu option is checked (turned on), pressing the Ctrl+Break key activates the debugger when the next event occurs. Pressing Ctrl+Break doesn't automatically invoke the debugger; some event after the Ctrl+Break must occur.

Usually, you don't want Enable Debug and Enable Ctrl+Break turned on when an application is complete. This setting will cause your form to run slightly slower because Paradox for Windows has to perform extra work to trap for debug( ) statements and Ctrl+Break keystrokes. During testing and debugging, however, you will find yourself using these two options frequently.

View Source, Origin

These two options make working with multiple editor windows active an easier process. The View Source option enables you to select and view another method from any object on the form. You won't be able to edit this source code, but you can view it.

The Origin menu item returns you to the editor window with the method and line number that triggered the breakpoint. This item is useful if you have several editor windows open and you want to return to the original breakpoint.

Step Over, Step Into

These two items allow you to step through your source code, one line at a time. Suppose that you insert a debug( ) proc right before a custom method. If you use Step Over, the debugger will not show you all the lines of code for this custom method. Instead, the debugger executes the custom method, but it will not show you any of the source code within the custom method.

If you want to see all the lines of code for the method, use Step Into. Frequently, Step Over is used when you don't care to see all the lines of code for a particular proc or method because you know that the proc and method is debugged and is not the source of the error.

Quit This Method

This menu item will quit the method you are debugging and close any of the debug windows. If your debugging session usually ends with the form running, you may trigger a breakpoint by interacting with the form again. Quit This Method does not automatically close the form.

Run

This menu item will run the form. If you are in the debugger, Run continues execution from the current breakpoint. If you are in the editor, Run saves any source code—but will not save the form—and then runs the form.

The Debugger SpeedBar

When the debugger is active, a different SpeedBar is displayed (see fig. 6.4).

Figure 6.4. The Debugger SpeedBar.

From left to right, the SpeedBar items represent the following actions:

- Run the form
- Print
- Set breakpoints
- Display the methods dialog box
- Step over
- Step into
- Inspect variables
- Display the object tree
- Open a folder

Each SpeedBar item is a shortcut for the equivalent menu command. Just like the menu command, the object tree SpeedBar item does not display the full object tree, only the object tree for the currently selected object— only the object tree for the object that contains the debug( ) proc or has a breakpoint set will be displayed.

Debugger Keys

Several keys, shown in Table 6.1, are active in the debugger.

Table 6.1. Debugger Keys.

Key	*Definition*
F1	Help
F3	Inspect variables
Ctrl+I	Inspect variables

continues

Table 6.1. Continued.

Key	Definition
Shift+F3	Stack backtrace
Ctrl+K	Stack backtrace
Ctrl+F3	Set breakpoints
Ctrl+B	Set breakpoints
F5	Go to a line
F6	Bring up the debugger menu
F7	Step over
Shift+F7	Step into
F8	Run
Ctrl+space bar	Display the methods dialog box
Ctrl+Z	Search
Ctrl+A	Search again

For some reason, Shift+Ctrl+Z—the replace menu item—is allowed in the debugger. This command will actually change your source code, which you cannot do either from the Edit menu or by editing the debugged source code. Any editor windows open during a debugging session cannot be edited. However, although the source code is changed in the debugger window, the changes are not saved and the next time the method is debugged, the changes are lost.

Summary

The Paradox for Windows debugger contains the basics that a debugger in an object-based environment needs to be effective. Missing, however, are two helpful features: the capability of inspecting object properties and the capability to automatically go to a method and line when a runtime error occurs. We have already discussed the inability to inspect object properties, so there's no need to review it again. For now, look at the second issue.

Although ObjectPAL is compiled, which prevents many errors from occurring, some errors do occur at run time, especially if you use an AnyType variable and forget the variable's type and assume it is a number when the variable is actually a string. Trying to add a number and a string is impossible.

When Paradox for Windows encounters these run errors, it displays a dialog box listing the error message, the name of the object and the method, a line number (although the line number is not identified as a line number), and the option to go into design mode. When you press the design push button, you are placed in design mode, but the method that caused the error is not automatically opened. Although these features are nice to have, the ObjectPAL debugger has enough capabilities to effectively debug an application.

Debugging an application involves other issues. We have not discussed how the Paradox for Windows event model can cause minor problems during debugging nor have we discussed the various tracer procedures which give you the ability to control the tracer window. These and other debugging issues are discussed more fully in Chapter 20.

7

Inspecting Object Properties

Recall from Chapter 3 that the term *object* is very broad, which can include design UIObjects, as well as events, data types, menus, display managers, queries, and Tcursors. One of the most difficult concepts to grasp is the breadth and variety of object types. Remember also that objects consist of data and code; in Paradox for Windows parlance, data and code are referred to as properties and methods. Nearly everything you work with in Paradox for Windows—including forms, reports, tables, fields, and design objects—has properties. This chapter covers issues dealing with setting properties interactively. It focuses primarily on table properties, leaving the specific form and report properties to the chapters that deal with design documents.

Object Properties

An object is described by its properties, including appearance and content. Most of the properties that you can set interactively describe the object's appearance. Interactively, you can assign properties only to UIObjects; to set other object properties, you need to use ObjectPAL. This section shows you how to assign properties interactively.

Each object type has its own set of properties. For example, font style and size properties are available for text objects. These same properties make no sense with regard to ellipses, boxes, table frames, or multi-record objects (MROs). Compound objects like MROs, table frames, crosstabs, and graphs have properties that apply to the entire object; each component object has additional appropriate properties, which means that although font style and size are not relevant to a table frame, the component text objects (such as headers and field text) do support those same properties. (UIObject properties are discussed in detail in Chapter 10.)

You can assign properties interactively in one of four ways:

- Right-clicking the object
- Right-clicking the object in the object tree
- Choosing Properties | Current Object from the menu
- Selecting the object and pressing F6

Note: All these methods require that the correct item is selected. Only the properties pertinent to the selected object will display.

The first method, right-clicking the object, is known as *object inspection*; the menu that pops up is the *object inspector*. For example, the following menus appear when you inspect the objects in the following list:

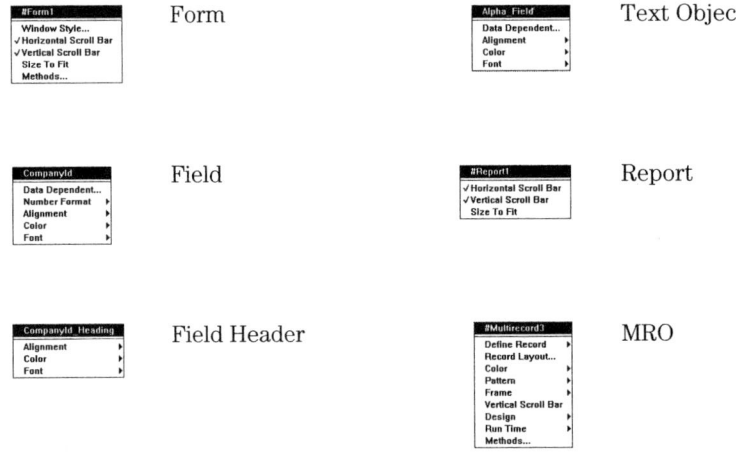

Now, examine the properties associated with a text object in detail to see some of the features available from the object inspector. As shown in the previous related illustration of the Text Object, the text object's property menu has three kinds of options that you find in standard Windows menus:

- Options followed by ellipses
- Options followed by right arrows
- Options that can be toggled on and off

When you choose a menu option followed by an ellipsis, a dialog box opens. Choosing Search Text, for example, opens the Search and Replace dialog box as shown in figure 7.1.

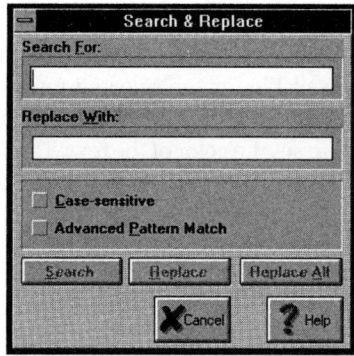

Figure 7.1. The Search and Replace dialog box.

When you choose a menu option followed by a right arrow, a submenu opens.

A menu option that isn't followed by anything acts as a toggle. This kind of option is toggled on or off each time you choose it.

Table Properties

Three components of a table can be customized in table view:

- Heading Properties
- Grid Properties
- Data Properties

Heading Properties

Table headings are text objects, which means that they share the same properties as all text objects: font, alignment, and color. Font and color are ubiquitous text properties, meriting their own discussions in the following sections.

Each field heading, as well as the table heading listed in the leftmost column, can be customized. Therefore, you have complete control over the table display; you can customize the table headings to look alike, and you can give each column a different heading style.

Font

Font properties includes typeface, size, style, and color. Choosing Typeface brings up a list of installed fonts. Size shows you the sizes available for the selected font. You use the Style submenu to tell Paradox whether to display the selected font in a special style: italicize, underscore, or bold. You use the Color option in the Font menu to set the color of the text. This option should not be confused with the Color option on the Header menu, which is used to set the background color.

If you look at the Font and Color submenus—figures 7.2 and 7.3, respectively—notice that both submenus have the same icon at the top:

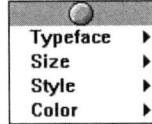

Figure 7.2. The Font menu.

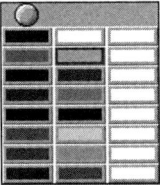

Figure 7.3. The Color menu.

This icon represents a thumbtack, which allows you to *pin* the menu onto the screen by clicking on the tack. When the menu is pinned, it becomes nonmodal; it stays on-screen so that you can reuse it when needed. When you pin the Font menu, Paradox displays the dialog box shown in figure 7.4.

With this dialog box on-screen, you can move among the elements of the underlying table; the descriptive text at the bottom of the dialog box updates to reflect the currently selected object. If you select new font settings, they are applied to the current object.

To *unpin* this dialog box, move the cursor over the thumbtack until it changes shape, then click. (This new shape is supposed to represent the bottom of a snap—like the kind found on your Levi's.)

Color

Choosing a color on the palette changes the color of the currently selected item. You just saw that the Color menu can be snapped in place, making the color palette a nonmodal dialog box, like the following example:

Chapter 7 ■ Inspecting Object Properties

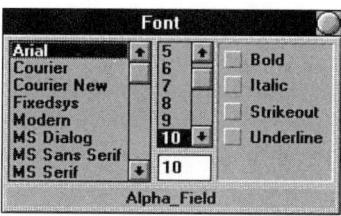

Figure 7.4. The *Pinned* Font Selection dialog box.

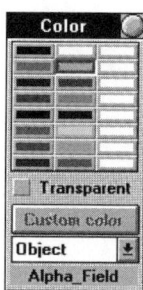

Figure 7.5. The *Pinned* Color Palette.

As you move through objects in the table, the descriptive text at the bottom of the dialog box is updated to reflect the current object. A drop-down list in this dialog box enables you to choose between the object and the related font. With Object selected, color is applied to the object background. With Font selected, the text color is affected.

Notice the bank of white boxes along the right side of the color palette. You use these boxes for setting custom colors. As soon as you select one of these color options, the Custom Color button is enabled. Click on it to see the Custom Color dialog box, shown in figure 7.6.

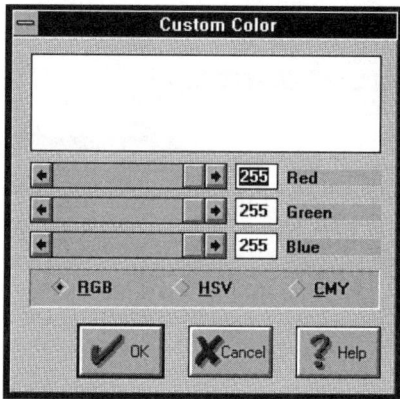

Figure 7.6. The Custom Color dialog box.

107

You use this dialog box to mix your own colors and save them with the palette for future use. Three color schemes are available:

- Red/Green/Blue
- Hue/Saturation/Value
- Cyan/Magenta/Yellow

These three schemes provide different ways of representing the same color. You choose a color scheme based on the ultimate output device. When you are designing for a color monitor, RGB is the color scheme of choice.

Grid Properties

The *grid* is the backdrop for the table frame; grid lines separate the rows and columns of the table frame. Specifically, the horizontal grid separates rows, and the vertical grid separates columns. When you first install Paradox, the vertical grid displays as a double line; the horizontal grid is not displayed.

Because the grid lines may or may not be displayed at any time, consider using the Grid menu to work with grid properties, which include the following:

    Color

    Grid Lines

    Current Record Marker

With the Color option, you set the grid color. The entire grid is affected by this setting.

You use the Grid Lines option to work with just the grid line colors. With Grid Lines, you can specify which grid lines to show and which style to use to display the lines. The Heading Lines, Column Lines, and Row Lines options beneath the Grid Lines submenu enable you to toggle the display of these lines. Line Style offers the options shown in figure 7.7.

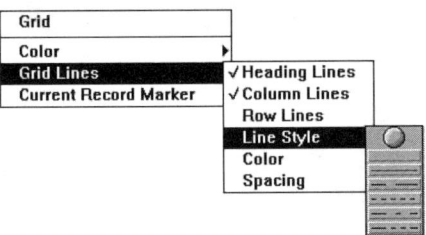

Figure 7.7. The Grid Line ¦ Line Style submenu, showing the available line styles.

The Color option from this menu directly affects the color of the grid lines.

Spacing is a little misleading because it is used to indicate *how many* lines are displayed per grid line.

Figure 7.8 shows a table with the grid spacing property set to 1, 2, and 3:

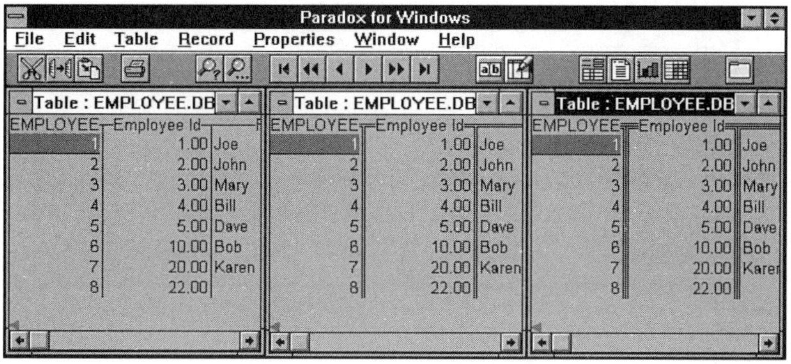

Figure 7.8. The EMPLOYEE Table, with Grid Spacing set to 1,2,3, displayed in three different windows.

Data Properties

A table's data has the same properties as all text objects: alignment, color, and font. Besides these properties, table data may have *data-dependent properties*. As the name implies, data-dependent properties vary, depending on the value of the data. For example, numbers within a certain range can be displayed in a different color; specific alpha values can appear in a special font.

Data-dependent properties are applied on a field-by-field basis. Such properties can be set on data in table view only. Setting conditional properties in form view requires ObjectPAL. ObjectPAL also gives you more control of data-dependent properties and allows you to do such things as mentioned in the following list:

- Control associated text objects based on the value in a field
- Cause a field to display or not display based on data values
- Use conditional properties based on the value in another table or tables—even a table not on the workspace

When you select the Data Dependent from a field's object inspector, Paradox presents the Data Dependent Properties dialog box, as seen in figure 7.9.

The Ranges section shows any existing data-dependent properties. You use the New Range button to define a new data-dependent setting. As soon as either a new or an existing range value is selected, the Data Dependent dialog box changes. The Set Properties and Apply Changes buttons are activated, and a new button, Sample, is added to the dialog box.

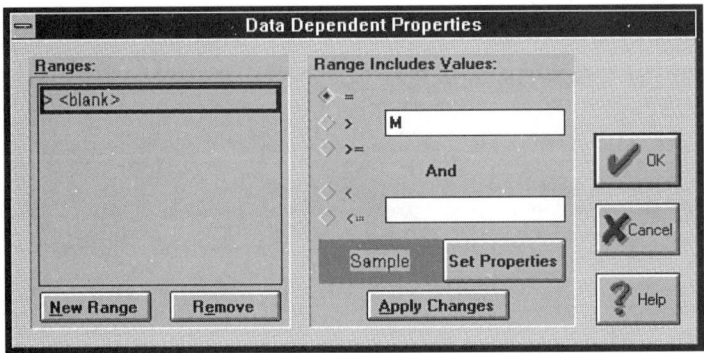

Figure 7.9. The Data Dependent Properties dialog box.

The Range Includes Values section is where you define the parameters for the range. To set special properties for values equal to "Smith," click on the = radio button and type the value, Smith, in the box. Figure 7.10 shows the Data Dependent Properties dialog box with the value "Smith" filled in.

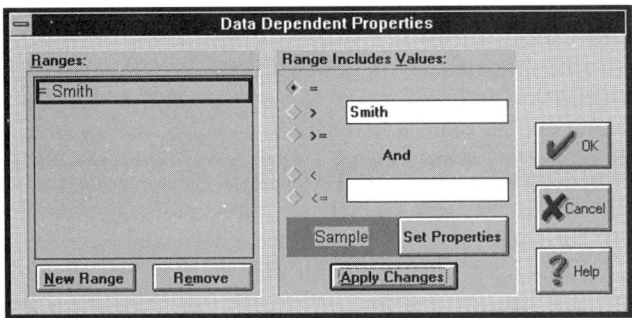

Figure 7.10. The Data Dependent Properties dialog box, with "Smith" as the value.

To specify a range of values, use both the upper and lower sections of the Range Includes Values section. Use either > or >= to specify the low end of the range. Then in the And portion, use < or <= and indicate the maximum values to include in the data-dependent range.

After the range is defined, you need to use the Set Properties button to tell Paradox how you want the selected values to be displayed. You have the same font and color properties that you have with field objects. It is important to keep in mind that data-dependent properties take precedence over any other field properties.

Apply Changes accepts your changes and enables you to continue working with this dialog box.

Data-dependent properties can get extremely intricate. For example, you can easily set up multiple levels of data dependency, performing the interactive equivalent of a lengthy switch-case statement.

Suppose that you had a field that contained a Marital Status field. You could set up four levels of data-dependent properties to cause the field values to display in seven corresponding colors, depending on whether the value is S (Single), M (Married), D (Divorced), or W (Widowed). The completed Data Dependent dialog box would look like figure 7.11.

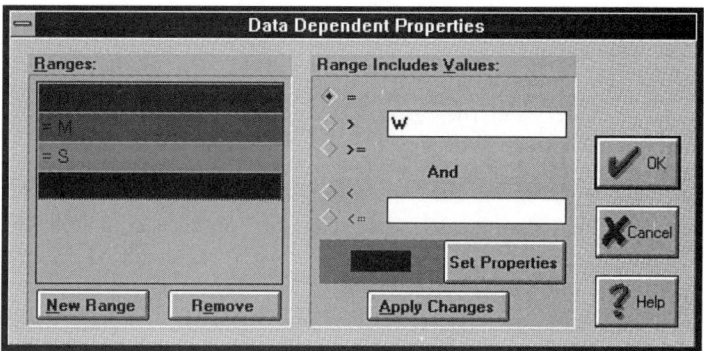

Figure 7.11. A filled-in multi-level Data Dependent Properties dialog box.

The resulting table view is shown in figure 7.12.

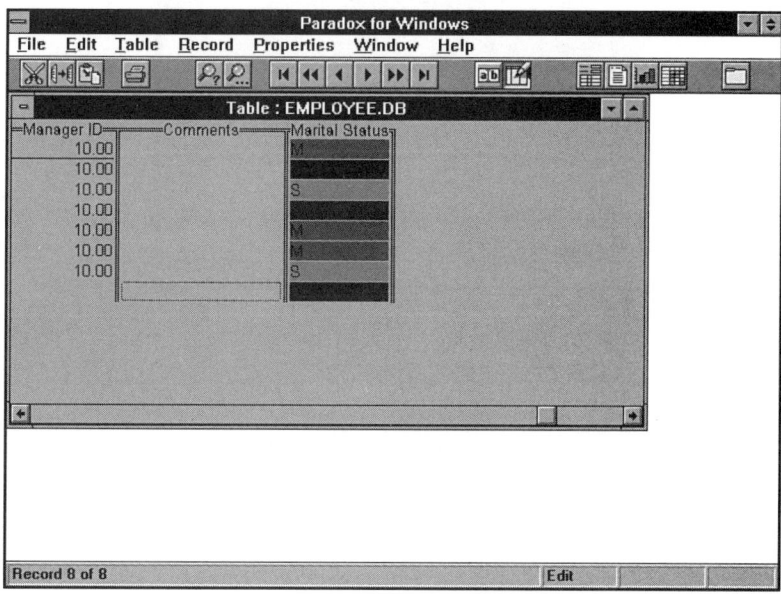

Figure 7.12. Table with Multiple Data Dependent properties set.

Direct Manipulation

One method of setting properties, *direct manipulation*, is most often used in table view, although some of the same techniques can be applied to table frames placed on forms. Direct manipulation involves using the mouse to interactively change the shape and size of an object. In table view, for instance, you can use direct manipulation to change the display width and height of fields. To change the width, simply move the cursor over the vertical grid until the cursor becomes a double arrow, and then widen or narrow the field width as you like. To change the height, you need to be in the leftmost column, under the table header. When the cursor becomes a double vertical arrow, drag the grid line up or down to make the row smaller or larger.

You also can use direct manipulation to click and drag columns to new positions. Move the cursor over the field header until the cursor changes to a field icon; then drag the column to the new location.

Saving Table Properties

Changes to the table view display are saved in the TV file. (TV stands for *T*able *V*iew.) Paradox lets you know if you made changes that affect the table's properties and gives you the option to save them by presenting you with the dialog box shown in figure 7.13.

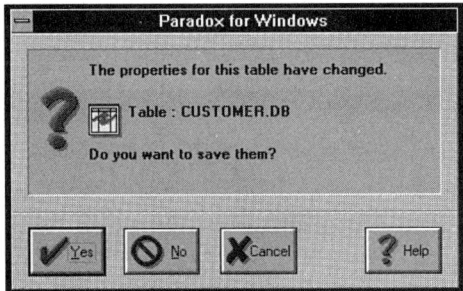

Figure 7.13. The Save Table Properties prompt.

If you want to set up default table-view properties, create a file called DEFAULT.DB in your private directory, and set the properties there. Paradox looks to this file for default values for all new tables the program creates. To use the properties from one table for an already existing table, you can copy the TV file. For example, if you want to apply the properties from DEFAULT.DB to your table, CUSTOMER.DB, type the following line at the DOS prompt:

    copy DEFAULT.TV CUSTOMER.TV

 **Caution:** Remember that multiple users may be viewing the same table, and a single user may view the same table a number of times. The last copy of the file saved overwrites any existing properties. Consider a network scenario in which you open the table first and start to make changes to the table properties. Joe then opens a copy of the table while you are still working on it. You save your changes. If Joe then decides to save his changes, his copy will overwrite all your work.

Form Properties

Forms are somewhat special objects because they fall within both the UIObject type and the display manager type. In application development, forms serve as the backdrop for nearly everything. Forms are the ultimate container for all UIObjects within an application.

Besides the three ways of inspecting an object discussed in this chapter, a fourth method is available, but only for forms: you can set form properties by right-clicking the form's title bar. This method is available regardless of whether the form is the selected object.

Specific form properties and properties of specific UIObjects are discussed in Chapters 10 and 11.

Summary

Nearly everything you work with in Paradox for Windows is an object—forms, reports, UIObjects, fields, and even things as specific as table grid lines and heading fonts. Since all objects have properties, you can change the way these various objects display by changing their properties. This chapter introduced you to some of the more common and important properties.

III

Interactive Use: Tables, Forms, Reports, and Queries

8

Building Tables

Tables are the backbone of database applications. For this reason, it is important for you as a developer to understand the intricacies of Paradox tables—what to include, what to leave out, and where the various components are stored.

Paradox for Windows stores much more information with the actual table than with previous versions. All validity checks, secondary indexes, and referential integrity rules are defined at the time you create or restructure your table. Paradox for Windows allows you to define relatively sophisticated validity checks, referential integrity rules and secondary indexes—all interactively. After you learn what's available interactively, you can use these features to create and restructure tables programmatically.

No single Paradox for Windows *native* table structure exists; Paradox for Windows transparently reads, writes and creates Paradox 3.5, Paradox for Windows, dBASE III+, and dBASE IV tables. Paradox 4.0 and Paradox for Windows share the same table format. With a few minor exceptions discussed in this chapter, both programs can read files created in the other.

How To Build a Table

You can create a new table in one of the two following ways:

1. Right click on the Desktop table icon, and select New.
2. Select File ¦ New ¦ Table from the menu.

Both options lead you to the Table Type dialog box (see fig. 8.1), which has a drop-down list that contains the supported table types.

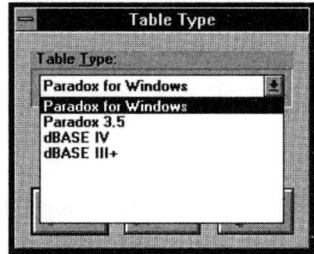

Fig. 8.1. The Table Type dialog box.

Field Types

The table you create allows a different set of features, depending on the table type you choose. dBASE III+ tables, for example, support the following field types:

- Character
- Number
- Date
- Logical
- Memo

The dBASE IV tables support a Float field type, in addition to the field types in the previous list.

Paradox 3.5 tables may contain the following field types:

- Alphanumeric
- Number
- Currency
- Date
- Short Number

Besides the field types available in Paradox 3.5, Paradox for Windows supports the following field types:

- Memo
- Formatted Memo
- Binary

- Graphic
- OLE

Memo and Binary field types are available in Paradox 4.0 for DOS.

Paradox tables and dBASE tables differ in that Paradox tables require a field size for numeric field types. The DEC field in the Create dialog box is used to specify the number of decimal places used by the field and is available only for dBASE files.

Reordering Fields

As you create or restructure a table, you may decide that you want to rearrange the order of the fields. To do so, you can take advantage of a wonderful GUI feature: at the left edge, click on the field and drag to the new location in the table structure. To delete a field, select the field and press Ctrl+Delete.

Table Properties

The different table types allow for different settings in the Table Properties section of the Create dialog box. The only option for dBASE tables is Indexes. All indexes for dBASE tables are created with this option. The following list shows index possibilities for dBASE III+ tables:

- Expression index
- Unique indexes
- Descending indexes

In addition, dBASE IV tables support Subset condition expressions.

The Create dialog box for dBASE IV tables also has a check box that enables you to toggle the Record Lock option on or off. When this box is marked, you can tell Paradox what kind of information to display about locked records. A hidden field is added to the table that contains information on the user with the record lock, the date locked, and whether the other user has modified the record. This field is displayed when you attempt to access a record that was locked by another user.

Paradox 3.5 tables support the following table properties:

- Validity Checks
- Table Lookup
- Single field, case-sensitive secondary indexes
- Password security
- Table Language

Paradox for Windows tables support the same table properties as Paradox 3.5, with the following additions:

- Referential Integrity
- Multi-field secondary indexes
- Case-insensitive secondary indexes

All of the various indexing possibilities are discussed in detail in Chapter 31. The rest of this section focuses on the remaining Paradox for Windows table properties.

Validity Checks

You use validity checks to confine your data in a variety of ways. For example, validity checks are used to set minimum or maximum allowable values for a field and can be used to set a field's default value, to make a field required, or to define a picture or template for the characters entered in a field.

Minimum and maximum values can be set on Number, Short, Date, and Alphanumeric field types. To impose the restriction, for example, that a date field's values fall within the year 1994, enter **1/1/94** as a minimum field value and **12/31/94** as the maximum value.

Notice that for alphanumeric fields, Paradox enforces minimum and maximum values based on ASCII order, which means that, if you enter a maximum value of Z, Paradox doesn't allow you to enter a value in the field that begins with a lowercase letter, because lowercase letters follow uppercase letters. Remembering that a single character value is smaller than a longer entry that begins with the same letter also is important. For example, you don't want to set the maximum field for an alphanumeric last name field to Z, because this setting disqualifies entries such as Zimmer and Zeff.

Required fields are applied at the record level, which means that whether or not the cursor ever touches the required field, it must be entered. If you try to leave the record—by moving to another record, toggling out of edit mode, or closing the table, Paradox presents you with the following error message:

```
Field value required: Field: fieldname
```

Default validity checks are values entered in a field if the user does not enter a value. Default values also are applied at the record level. Paradox places the default value into the field as soon as a new record is opened.

Picture values enable you to specify the format of the characters in the fields. You also can use pictures to add literal values to a field or to specify optional literal characters. The following list shows characters that are available for picture strings:

Character	Definition
#	Represents a *number*.
?	Represents any *letter* (upper- or lowercase).
&	Accepts any *letter* and converts it to uppercase.
@	Accepts any *character*.
!	Any *character* and converts letters to uppercase.
;	Takes the following *character* literally.
*	Repeats the following character the specified number of times.
[ ]	Characters (either literal or picture mask) are optional components of the field value.
{ }	Choice of characters (either literal or picture mask) contains within the curly braces.

Paradox for Windows also offers assistance with defining pictures through the Picture Assistance dialog box, shown in figure 8.2.

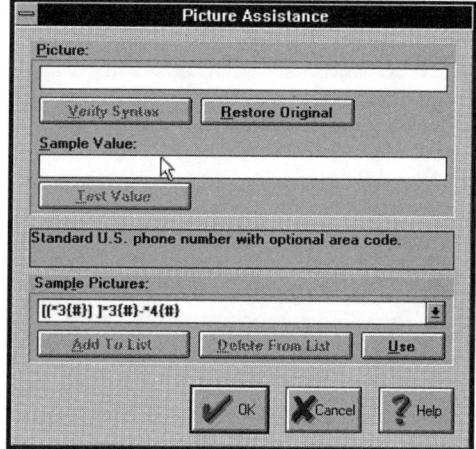

Figure 8.2. The Picture Assistance dialog box.

To open this dialog box, click the Assist button that appears next to the Picture specification in the Create or Restructure dialog box.

The Sample Pictures list gives some examples on-line that you can use directly as your picture or that you can use as a starting point for creating a custom picture format A description of the picture is displayed in the box above the sample list. To use one of the sample pictures, highlight it in the list, then click the Use button.

121

You can change any sample picture and change the new setting. You can use the Restore Original button in case you modify a sample picture, and then decide to abandon the changes.

You can add a new picture, either by typing it directly into the Picture type-in box in the Create or Restructure dialog box, or you can use the Picture Assistance dialog box (see fig. 8.3). To use this second dialog box, type the new value in the Picture type-in region. For example, to define a picture mask for a Social Security field, you fill in the dialog box.

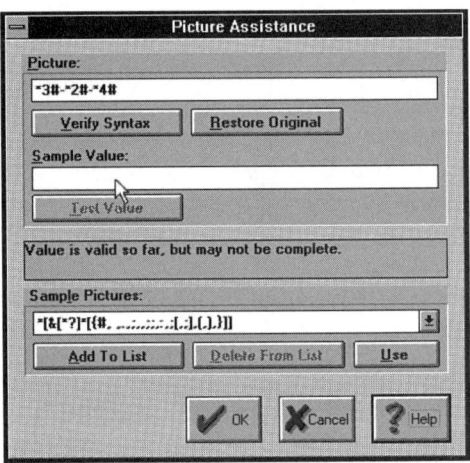

Figure 8.3. The Picture Assistance dialog box, filled in for a Social Security field.

The Verify Syntax button only tests that the picture that you entered is valid. A picture with invalid syntax, for example, may have mismatched braces or brackets.

Use the Sample Value box to try the field with a test value. When you click on the Test Value button, Paradox tells you whether or not the value conforms to the picture. If the sample value is valid, but Paradox tells you that the value doesn't match the picture, you need to adjust your picture. When you achieve an acceptable picture, click on the Use button to use the picture for the current field. To save the picture specification for use with other fields or other tables—or both—click on Add to List. In the Save Picture dialog box, you see the information shown in figure 8.4.

You can give the picture a custom description; in this case, the description is `Social Security Number`. The picture will appear in the sample list from this point forward. The description that you give the field in the Save Picture dialog box appears in the box above the sample picture list when the new picture is highlighted in the list. The new picture is stored in the file PDOXWIN.INI.

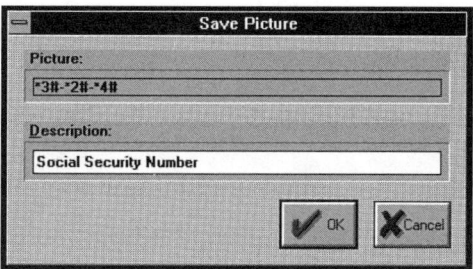

Figure 8.4. The Save Picture dialog box.

Validity Checks Applied to Existing Data

If you add or modify validity checks during a restructure operation, these changes may affect existing data. For example, values may already exist in your table that do not fall within newly defined minimum and maximum constraints. Blank entries may be present in a field that gets a new required validity check, or blank entries may be present in a field that gets a new default validity check. In all these cases, Paradox gives you the option of applying or not applying the new validity check to existing data in figure 8.5.

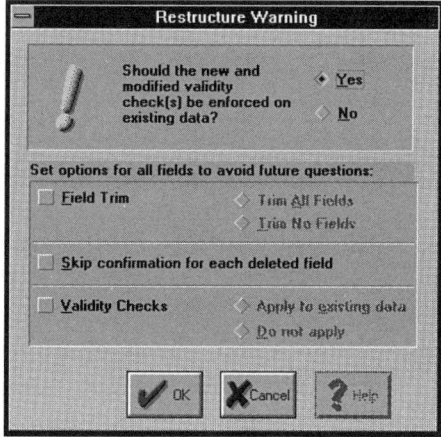

Figure 8.5. The Restructure Warning dialog box.

Enforcing new validity checks on existing data causes the new default values to be entered in blank fields in the table. Records with blank values in a newly defined required field are removed to a KEYVIOL table. Records with fields that do not conform to minimum and maximum validity checks also are removed to a KEYVIOL table.

You cannot apply any of the preceding validity checks to fields in tables involved in referential integrity relationships.

Nothing happens to existing records with pictures that do not conform to a new picture—they remain in the table in the same format. To change the display format of existing fields requires some ObjectPAL.

Table Lookups

Table lookups are used to limit the values in a field to the values contained in the first field of another table. The options available in the Table Lookup dialog box are shown in figure 8.6.

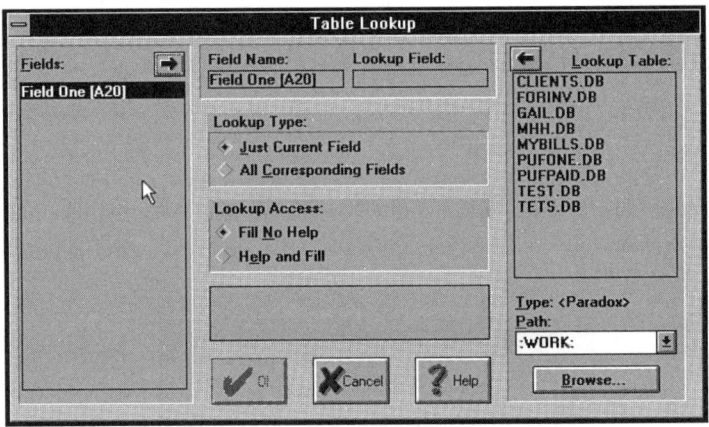

Figure 8.6. The Table Lookup dialog box options.

The Lookup field name doesn't need to be the same, but the field types must match, which means that a date field must lookup a date field. Alphanumeric fields must be the same length, and number, short, and currency field types can all be used interchangeably.

With the Lookup Type option, you specify whether you want to just use the first field in the table, or whether you want to fill in all fields in the current table that have corresponding fields in the lookup table. Corresponding fields must have the same field names and field types.

Lookup Access is where you tell Paradox whether or not to allow the user to display the lookup table. If not, all attempts to add a value that is not contained in the lookup table generates the error message, `Unable to find lookup value.`

If Fill No Help is selected, the person entering data is responsible for knowing the values in the lookup table.

If instead you choose Help and Fill as the Lookup Access option, the field value can be typed from the keyboard or entered through a visible lookup table. The key combination used to access the lookup table is Ctrl+space bar. The lookup table is displayed in a separate dialog box. You can maneuver through the table as you do through any Paradox table; Ctrl+Z is available to look up a value in any field. With the correct record selected, press OK to accept the dialog and copy the current record value into the underlying table.

A distinction needs to be made between the table properties Table Lookup and Referential Integrity. A referential integrity relationship is much stronger and more permanent than a lookup table relationship. For example, when a value is added to a table by using a lookup table, nothing prevents you from deleting or changing the original value in the lookup table. If you do, nothing happens to the value in the table that looked to it for the original value. A referential integrity relationship, by contrast, continues to monitor changes in the master table and update the dependent table accordingly. Referential Integrity is discussed in more detail in Chapter 2.

Secondary Indexes

Secondary indexes are used for speeding up searches on a field and sorting your table to a different view. Sorting to a view allows you to view the same table in a different sort order. The Define Secondary Index dialog box is shown in figure 8.7.

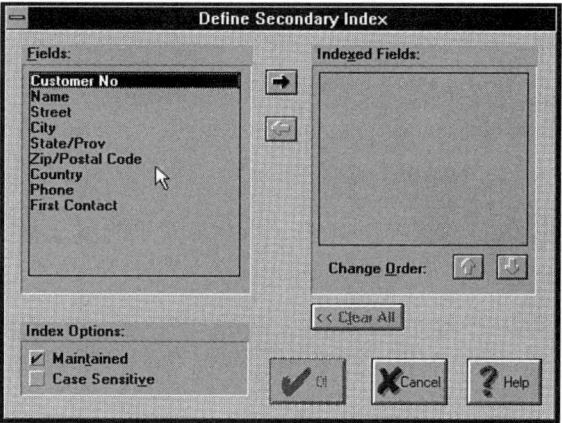

Figure 8.7. The Define Secondary Index dialog box.

Notice that all the fields in the current table are available for secondary indexes. Multiple fields can be used to define a secondary index. For example, if you created a secondary index on the Last Name and First Name fields, and then viewed the table in this secondary index order, all entries in the Last Name field would be sorted alphabetically. Duplicate last names would be sorted according to their first name values.

The Index options for a Paradox for Windows table are Maintained and Case Sensitive. By default, secondary indexes are both maintained and case sensitive. The exception to this rule is non-keyed tables. If a table does not have a primary index, Paradox cannot maintain a secondary index. (See Chapter 31 for a complete discussion.) Maintained indexes are always current—they are updated after each change to the table—and therefore always immediately available for viewing tables and using in queries.

Case-sensitive indexes sort in ASCII order, with capital letters sorting before lowercase letters. Case-insensitive indexes treat all characters as capital letters, and therefore, sort upper- and lowercase letters together.

 **Note:** A discussion of how Paradox stores and accesses secondary indexes is presented in Chapter 31. Refer to chapter 2 for a thorough discussion of referential integrity.

Password Security

Password Security is the first of the table properties you encountered so far that isn't necessarily associated with the currently selected field, but rather is related to the entire table. Table passwords are stored as part of the table structure in Paradox for Windows. The Password Security dialog box is shown in figure 8.8.

Figure 8.8. The Password Security dialog box.

You type the table level password once in the Master Password type-in box, then use the Verify Master Password area to ensure that your initial entry was correct. If you define only a master password, then your users will have *all or nothing* rights to the table.

After a password is defined for a table, this table remains visible for the duration of the current session because the password was entered into the system. After you either terminate the Paradox session or remove the password by using the File ¦ Utilities ¦ Password menu selection. The next time a user attempts to access the table, for the table password prompt appears.

For more control over specific rights for specific fields, click on the Auxiliary Password button. This button is available only after a master password is entered and verified. The Passwords section in the upper left corner displays passwords that were already defined for the table. Type a new, auxiliary password into the Current Password type-in box.

The Table Rights section of this dialog is where you tell Paradox which rights you want granted upon receipt of this password entry. These rights are defined in the following list:

All	Allows the user to do whatever they like with the table. They are free to do such things as empty it, restructure it, or even delete it. Users with All privileges to a table *cannot* use this password to change the master table.
Insert & Delete	Users with this password are limited to adding and deleting (and changing) records.
Data Entry	Allows the user to add records, and change—but not delete—existing records.
Update	Allows the user to change non-key values in the table. These users can neither add nor subtract records.
Read Only	No modifications are allowed to the table; the user can view the table only.

The Field Rights section of this dialog box allows you to fine tune user access on a field by field basis. The same options are available for each field as are available for the entire table.

You cannot give a user greater rights to a field than the user has to the entire table.

Click the Add button to add a newly defined auxiliary password to the system. Click the New button to add another auxiliary password. The Change button is used to change the rights associated with an existing password.

Table Language

This table property allows you to change the table's language driver. The default table language is set in Paradox's Configuration Utility. Table language is used to determine the default sort order and available character set for the table.

Borrowing a Table's Structure

By borrowing the structure of an existing table, you can save a great deal of time when you create a table. Use the Borrow button at the bottom of the Create dialog box. Paradox for Windows lets you borrow, independently or together, the following table properties:

- Primary key
- Validity Checks
- Lookup Tables
- Secondary Indexes
- Referential Integrity

Although, by default, Paradox borrows all the fields from a table, you can delete as many fields as you want before you save the table. To delete a field from the table structure, press Ctrl+Delete.

You can borrow from only one table, and you can only borrow into a new table structure. As you begin to enter fields in the table, the borrow button becomes dimmed.

Restructuring a Table

You can access the Restructure dialog box in the following two ways:

1. Select File ¦ Utilities ¦ Restructure from the menu.
2. With the table open, select Table ¦ Restructure.

If you are viewing a table, only option 2 works.

The Restructure dialog box is almost identical to the Create dialog box. Two features are available that are available only in the Create dialog box—Dependent Tables and Pack Table.

Dependent tables, listed under Table Properties, is for informational purposes only, and is here to show you any child tables that are linked to the current table in a referential integrity relationship.

Pack Table, a check box in the bottom left corner of the Restructure dialog box, is used to release the space occupied by records deleted from the table. Packing Paradox tables can significantly reduce the size the tables take on disk.

Table Resources

This section covers the internals of how Paradox stores data on disk, including the space required for various field types, how records are stored in blocks, and which information is stored in which files on disk. The more you know about the product's resource utilization, the more efficiently you can design your tables.

Field Sizes

The amount of disk space required for each field type in Paradox is predictable. In fact, in previous versions of Paradox, you could easily figure out the amount of disk space a table consumed. Starting with Paradox for DOS 4.0, the ability to predict total disk use was muddied with the introduction of Memo and Blob field types. Although these fields use a predictable amount of space in the .DB, they allow for variable amounts of information, some or all of which gets stored in a related file, called the .MB file. The .MB file is a file that Paradox automatically creates when you use a Memo, Blob, Graphic, or OLE field. It has the same name as the table, but is given the .MB file extension.

The number of bytes used by the various field types are shown in the following list:

Field Type	*Bytes Used*
Alpha	1 byte per character. For example, an A5 field uses 5 bytes and an A30 field uses 30 bytes.
Date	4 bytes.
Number	8 bytes.
Short	2 bytes.
Currency	8 bytes.
Memo	1 byte per character defined with the table structure, plus 10 additional bytes. For example, an M10 field consumes 20 bytes.
Formatted Memo	Same as Memo field.
Graphic	Same as Memo field.
Blob	Same as Memo field.
OLE	Same as Memo field.

Paradox requires a memo field to have a size of at least one. All the other extended field types (F, G, B, and O) have allowable sizes from 0 to 240. All the extended field values are duplicated in both the .DB and the .MB files. Memo fields, by contrast, are only duplicated in the .MB file if they don't fit within the size specified in the table structure. If you define a Memo field as M10 in the table structure, for example, the first ten characters of the field are stored in the .DB file. If the field contains ten characters or less, nothing is placed in the .MB file. As soon as the field size exceeds ten characters, however, the following changes happen:

1. The first ten characters remain in the .DB file.
2. The entire field is stored in the .MB file.

In this example, Paradox displays the first ten characters with the table in table view. You must enter memo view (Shift+F2) to see the rest of the field.

Carefully consider the size of the memo field when you are designing your tables. Be sure that you make the field large enough that the display is meaningful as you view the table in table view. Probably more important, however, you want to size the field to reduce data redundancy as much as possible. If your memos are all likely to be large, for example—such as greater than 240 characters—but usually begin with unique text, you don't want to define the memo field size at 200. If you do, the first 200 characters of the field are stored in the table in the .DB and again in the .MB file. In a file with many records, using this field size unnecessarily takes a significant amount of disk space.

If the first 15 characters give the user the gist of the memo, you can set up the field as an M15, thereby using significantly less disk space. Remember that the user (or the programmer) has the option to view the field in memo view if seeing the entire memo becomes necessary.

If your memo data usually falls within a predictable size, such as 50 characters, with an occasionally larger entry, then defining the memo field as M50 makes good sense. This way, you won't have the duplication that you have on disk if you chose a smaller field size. Making the memo large enough to accommodate the largest entry possible, in this case, unnecessarily wastes disk space. Because the field is a memo and not an alpha, Paradox has access to the .MB file for the occasional field that doesn't fit within the 50 characters.

There really is little reason to store any of the other extended field types (G, B, or O) with the table, for the following reasons:

1. It's unlikely that you will know the size of these field types.

2. Even if you know the field sizes, the entire field value is stored within the .MB file anyway.

3. When displaying the field in table view, the amount of the field displayed depends on the table properties and type, not on the size of the field.

The behavior of formatted memo fields falls somewhere between this and memo field behavior. The number of characters displayed with the table in table view is determined by the size of the field in the table structure. The memo text that displays when the field is not active, however, is *not* formatted. Any alignment, color, or font changes applied to the text only display when the field is fully rendered.

Record Sizes

Knowing the number of bytes taken by each field type is the first step in understanding how Paradox uses disk space. The next question becomes *How does Paradox use these field sizes to determine the record size?*

Paradox just adds together the fields sizes. Take, for example, the table structure shown in figure 8.9.

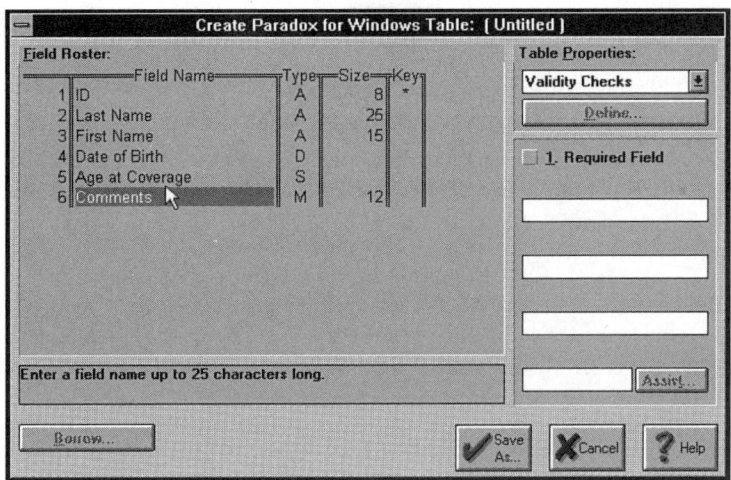

Figure 8.9. An example of how Paradox adds together field sizes when creating a table structure.

Based on the field size information in the preceding section, the field sizes for this record are shown in the following list:

Field Type	Field Size
ID	8 bytes
Last Name	25 bytes
First Name	15 bytes
Date of Birth	8 bytes
Age at Coverage	2 bytes
Comments	22 bytes
Total	80 bytes

This simple calculation shows that each record in this table needs 70 bytes of disk space. Paradox uses a fixed size record format; each record is the same size, which means that if you only enter one character in the ID field, or if you fill each field completely the record takes 80 bytes.

Block Sizes

With the information on field and record sizes, you may think that you are ready to calculate the amount of disk space needed for your table. But you are not there yet—a few other complicating factors remain. (Remember that the size of the .MB file is *completely* variable. If you use extended field types, you can predict the .DB file size, but not the total disk requirements!) The next item that you need to understand is the way that Paradox stores records in blocks.

Paradox can store data in 2K or 4K blocks—2K is the default size, which means that when Paradox needs more space to store record information, the chunks (blocks) are allocated either in 2048 or 4096 bytes. A total of six bytes per block are reserved for internal use, making the real space available for 2K and 4K block 2042 and 4090, respectively. A block needs to accommodate one record for an unkeyed table and three records from a keyed table.

These limitations on block storage explain Paradox's maximum record size. Given a maximum block size of 4K, and the requirement that one unkeyed record must fit within a block, the maximum record size for an unkeyed table is 4K. By the same reckoning, if three records need to fit within each block for a keyed table, it makes sense that keyed records are limited to 1350 bytes.

Table block size is adjusted using the ODAPI Full Tree Editor in the Advanced section of the ODAPI Configuration utility. Although this utility accepts any block value that is a multiple of 1024, Paradox tables have a lower limit of 2K and an upper limit of 4K blocks. If you define a block size smaller than 2K, Paradox uses a 2K block; if you define a block size larger than 4K, Paradox uses a 4K block.

The .MB files are *not* affected by the table size specified in the ODAPI configuration. Regardless of the block size set for tables, .MB files are always allocated in 4K blocks.

Our sample table has 80 bytes per record. Assuming a 2K block size (minus 6 bytes for overhead), 2042/80, or 25.525 records per block. Because Paradox allows no records to be split between blocks, each 2K block actually holds 25 records. Because 25*80=2000, each block contains 42 bytes of unused, or wasted, space. If the block were 4K, or 4090 bytes, each block could hold 4090/80 51.125, or 51 records. Because 51*80=4080 and 4090-4080=10, there would only be 10 wasted bytes per block. In this situation, a 4K block provides a significant improvement in disk use. As your tables grow larger, these differences become more significant.

The Struct Table

Previous versions of Paradox could view a table's structure into a table—STRUCT.DB. Paradox for Windows also allows you to see the STRUCT table interactively though the File ¦ Utility ¦ Info Structure menu selections. The Structure Information dialog box is similar to the Create and Restructure dialog box, except that this dialog box, shown in figure 8.10, is for informational purposes only:

You can look through the Table Properties of each field to see what kinds of secondary indexes, referential integrity, validity checks, and so on have been defined for the table. However, an easier way exists to see all this information.

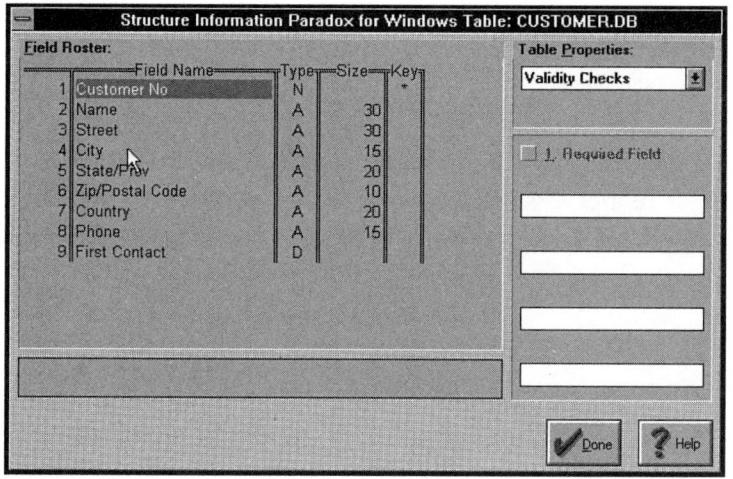

Figure 8.10. The Structure Information dialog box.

When you display a table's structure, Paradox creates a STRUCT table in your private directory. This table contains far more information about your table than was contained in previous versions of Paradox. Each record in the STRUCT table represents a field in the most recent table to view. The STRUCT table in Paradox for Windows contains the following fields:

Field Name
Type
Size
Key
Invariant Field ID
Required Value
Min Value
Max Value
Default Value
Picture Value
Table Lookup
Table Lookup Type

The field name contains the names of the field in the table.

Type displays A,D,N,S,$,M,F,G,B,or O to indicate the Paradox field type.

The Size field contains the size of all alphanumeric and memo fields, as well as the size of all of the other extended field types that have sizes specified with the table.

The Key field displays an asterisk (*) for fields that are included in the table's primary index. This field is blank for non-key fields.

The Invariant Field ID field indicates the field's ordinal position within the table structure. This field exists in case the STRUCT table is displayed in other than default order. If the STRUCT table were sorted somehow, for example, the Invariant Field ID still would reflect the field's position in the original table.

The Required Value field, displays an asterisk (*) if the field was designated as required in the table structure. Otherwise, the field is blank.

If a minimum validity check is assigned to the field, you see the check displayed in the Min Value field.

The Max Value field shows the maximum value validity check, if this setting is active.

The Default Value field contains the value entered in the Default validity check, if a value was selected.

The Picture Value shows any defined picture for the current field.

Table Lookup shows the name of the table used as a lookup to the current field.

Table Lookup Type has one of the following values:

Value	Definition
0	No lookup defined
1	Just Current Field / Fill No Help
2	All Corresponding Fields/ Fill No Help
3	Just Current Field / Help and Fill
4	All Corresponding Fields/ Help and Fill

Files Associated with Paradox Tables

Paradox for DOS uses the notion of *family objects*—a combination of files associated with the table that need to follow wherever the table goes. How Paradox deals with these objects is discussed in the following sections.

Forms and Reports

Paradox for Windows has limited support for the notion of families, and differs significantly in the way it handles forms and reports. In the DOS versions of Paradox, forms are given the same name as the table to which they belong and have either an .F, or .F1 through .F14 extension. Similarly, reports in the DOS version have the master table's name and an .R or .R1 through .R14 extension. A form or report must be copies, using the Paradox menus to avoid corruption. For a form or report to copy correctly, the structure of the source and destination tables must be the same.

Forms and reports differ significantly in Paradox for Windows. First, these items can exist *independent of any table*. You can design a form with only design objects—text, graphics, lines, and so on. Second, forms and reports are not limited to taking the name of their master table, but can have any eight character prefix. Forms are given either .FSL or .FDL extensions, depending on whether or not they have been delivered. Reports either have a .RSL or .RDL extension, again depending on whether or not they have been delivered. Forms and reports are actually Windows DLLs, which are discussed in Chapter 22.

Form and report files do not need to reside in the same directory as the tables with which they are associated. Another way to look at it is to realize that you can build a form by using tables from different directories.

Forms and reports can be associated with different tables by pressing a button—the Change Master button on the Open Document dialog box. If the structure of the new master differs from the original table, fields are deleted from the form. Adding field from the new master back to their place is simple. Not only can forms and reports be associated with different tables, they also can be associated with queries. These issues are discussed in detail in Chapters 10 and 11.

Index Files

When you create a table with a primary index, Paradox creates a file on disk with the same first name as the table but with a .PX extension. If you delete the .PX file, the table would no longer be keyed.

If you create a secondary index on a Paradox table, Paradox create two new files on disk, a file with an Xnn extension and a file with a Ynn extension. Because there can be multiple secondary indexes on the same table—even on the same field—you may find quite a few of these .Xnn and .Ynn files.

Index fields always appear in the directory with the .MB file.

Other Paradox Files

The .MB file and this file's purpose were discussed previously in this chapter. This file also must reside in the same directory as the .DB file.

Three other files also are closely associated with the table, and all the files except forms and reports and these files must be in the same directory as the table.

The .VAL file stores all defined validity checks. Minimum, maximum, required, default, and picture specifications are stored here, as are referential integrity rules. One interesting thing to note is that although referential integrity is defined on the child table, a .VAL file is created for the parent table as well. In fact, if you delete the .VAL file for one of the tables, Paradox does not allow you to open the other—and displays a `Corrupt or missing VAL file` message.

Whenever you change table properties in table view, Paradox asks you whether or not you want to save the new properties. If you select Yes, the new properties are saved to a file with the same name as the table with a .TV extension.

The last file you may see has the .FAM extension. This file is used during certain operations such as copying or renaming a table to point to the .TV file. Currently, this file contains only information on the .TV file; presumably, it will play a larger role in future versions of Paradox for Windows. If you delete the .FAM file, then rename or copy the table, the table properties cannot be transferred to the new table.

Summary

Knowing how Paradox stores table data on disk, and applying this information wisely can both save disk space and speed your applications. Carefully selecting the size of memo fields, for example, can avoid data duplication. If you know that Paradox Windows uses 2K and 4K blocks, you know that reducing one field's size incrementally can have a drastic effect on resource requirements. You also can know that, in many cases, you have nothing to lose by adding a few characters to an Alpha or Memo field.

This chapter also introduced the various files associated with a Paradox table. Some files are associated much more closely than others. The .PX, .Xnn, .Ynn, and .VAL files, for example, directly impact the table's structure. Forms and reports, by contrast, can be based on a master table or query, are easily linked to a different table, or can exist independently of any table at all.

Remember that the Borrow dialog box allows you to indicate whether you also want to borrow the table's primary key, secondary index, validity checks, or referential integrity. It should be clear where Paradox looks for that information, knowing the functions of the various files.

9

Data Models and Referential Integrity

Paradox for Windows has taken PC relational databases to new heights in its quick and graphical data modeling capabilities. With the click of a few mouse buttons you can join tables together creating data models on which forms, reports, and queries are based. Once created, data models also are easy to modify with quick access from the Data Model SpeedBar icon within the Document Designers and the Open Query dialog box.

To safeguard the data that is entered and modified, Paradox for Windows supports expanded referential integrity constraints. Referential integrity guarantees that related tables, tables linked together on common fields, are updated consistently. If you change a customers ID number in a customer table, for example, referential integrity makes sure that the customer ID is updated correspondingly in an orders table. Inserting and deleting records also must pass Referential Integrity rules. Referential Integrity is no longer defined and limited by using a form, as was the case in DOS versions of Paradox, but created and applied at the table level to make sure that all operations that potentially change data have the referential integrity rules enforced.

To take full advantage of these capabilities, it is important that your database tables are properly indexed. Paradox for Windows is intelligent enough to automatically suggest default links based on the tables primary key fields. In a well-normalized database design, table structures usually are defined appropriately for Paradox to make the right type of relational link. Refer to Chapter 2 for a detailed discussion of normalization techniques and definitions of the possible relationships between tables.

Data Model Dialog Box

When creating a new form or report, you first must define the data model in the Data Model dialog box (see fig. 9.1). This dialog box enables you to quickly select the tables to use and define the links between tables. You define a link by clicking the mouse on a table button and dragging a line to another table. When you click the mouse on the first table, the pointer turns to the data model icon while you drag a line to the linked table.

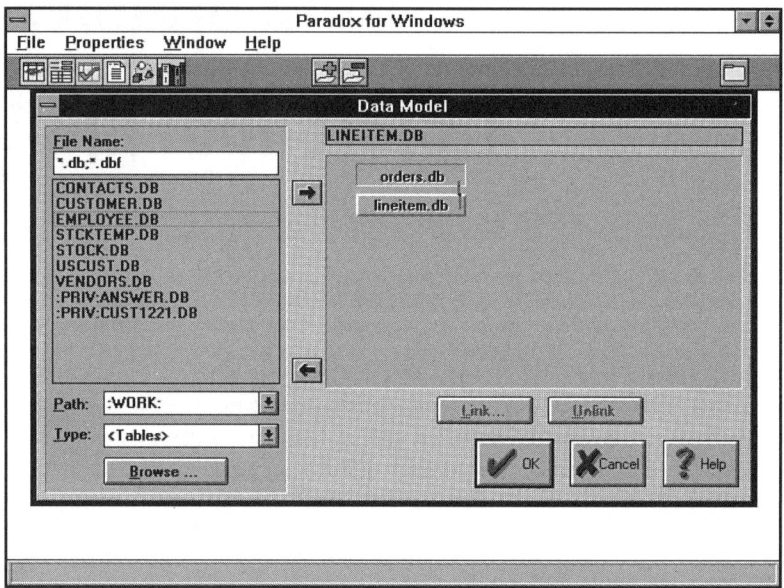

Figure 9.1. The Data Model dialog box.

After a link is defined, Paradox displays either a line with a single arrow or a line with a double arrow. The single arrow line represents a single-valued relationship between tables, and a double arrow represents a multi-valued relationship. A *single-valued relationship* is defined when the linked tables are either a 1:1 (one to one) or M:1 (many to one) relationship. A *multi-valued relationship* is for 1:M (one-to-many) table relationships. Single-valued relationships are always displayed downward in a vertical fashion, and multi-valued relationships are displayed to the right horizontally.

The number of tables and types of relationships can be simple or complex. You do not have to select any tables in the data model. Forms defined as dialog boxes, for example, may not be based on any tables. Figure 9.2 shows a rather complex relationship. Notice that the customer table has three 1:M relationships defined, and two of these relationships have their own relationships defined, which in turn have single-valued relationships defined.

Chapter 9 ■ Data Models and Referential Integrity

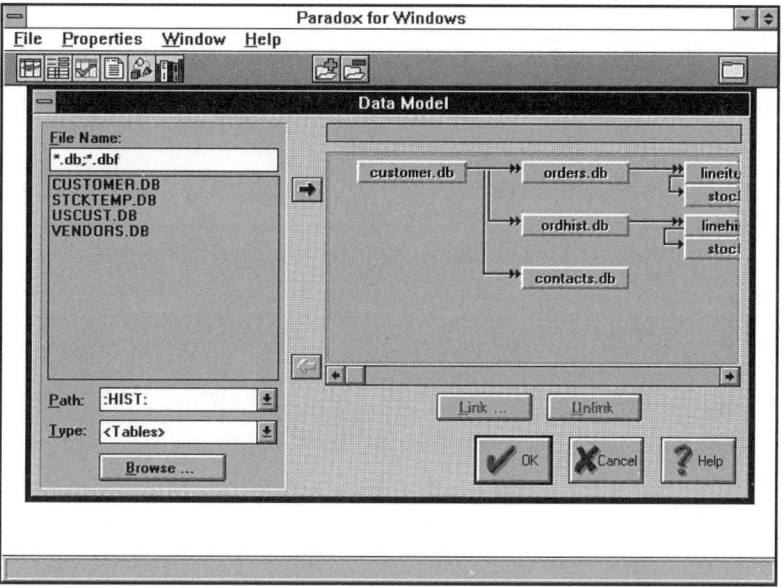

Figure 9.2. A complex data model.

You cannot select the same table twice in the same data model. Notice, however, that the stock table is used twice in this data model, which is done with the use of the Alias feature of Paradox for Windows (see fig. 9.3). You can define an Alias to the same directory as the working directory and access the same table by using this Alias from the Path pull down.

An even easier way exists to construct data models than the point, click, and drag method. Any queries that you may have defined can be translated automatically into the corresponding data model. To use a query as the basis of a data model, you select Queries from the Types pull-down box of the Define Data Model dialog box (see fig. 9.4).

When selected, a QBE query file appears just like a table button. It appears as a single button, even if the query joins together several tables. You can join tables to queries in a Data Model in the same way you can with regular tables, as demonstrated in figure 9.4, by linking the Lineitem table to the 91Orders query.

The order in which tables are linked is important in determining the type of relationship. Consider the relationship between the Customer and Orders tables. Starting with Customer and linking to the Orders table creates a multi-valued (1:M) relationship. Starting with the Orders table and linking to the Customer table defines a single-valued (M:1) relationship.

Part III ■ Interactive Use: Tables, Forms, Reports, and Queries

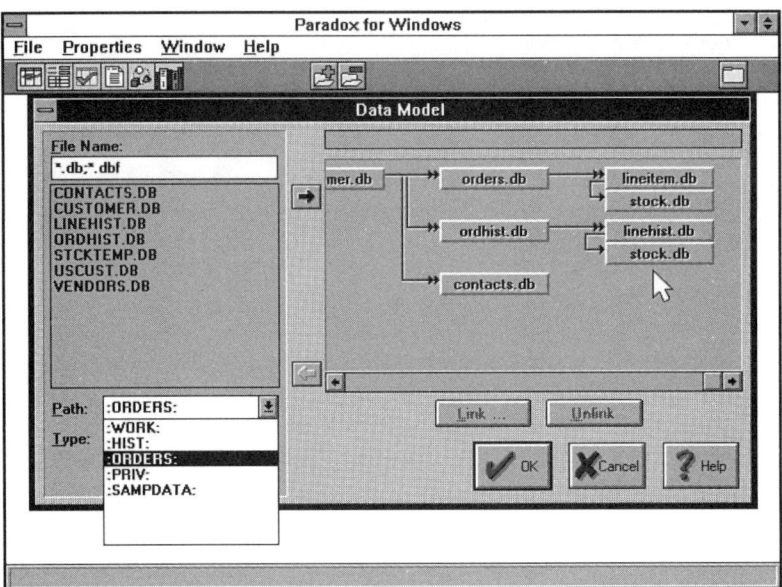

Figure 9.3. Using an Alias to reference the same table twice.

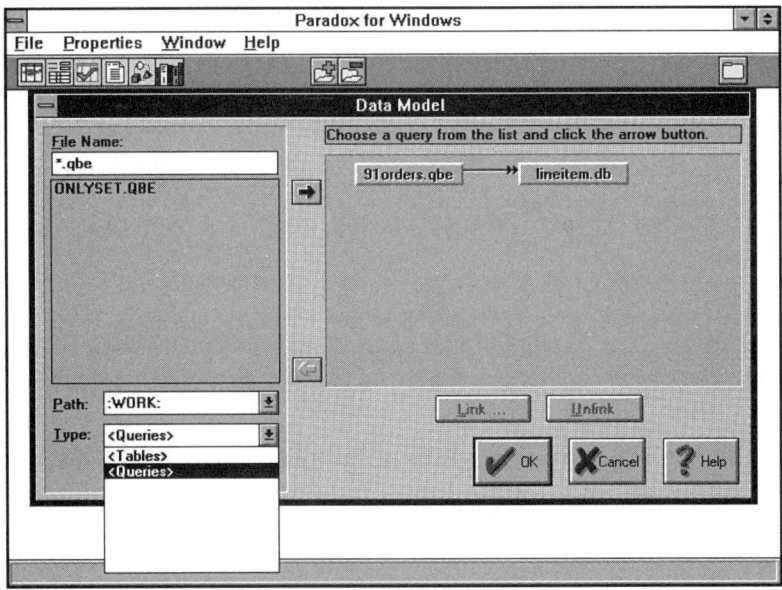

Figure 9.4. Defining Data Models by using Query files.

Define Link Dialog Box

Table relationships are based upon links established between fields of the tables. By default, Paradox defines a relationship between tables if common field names exist in the primary indexes of the tables. If a link cannot be safely assumed, Paradox presents the Define Link dialog box for the user to explicitly define the link. You always can change a link after it is established by selecting the child table and clicking the Link button—or right-clicking on the arrowed line—to bring up the Link dialog box.

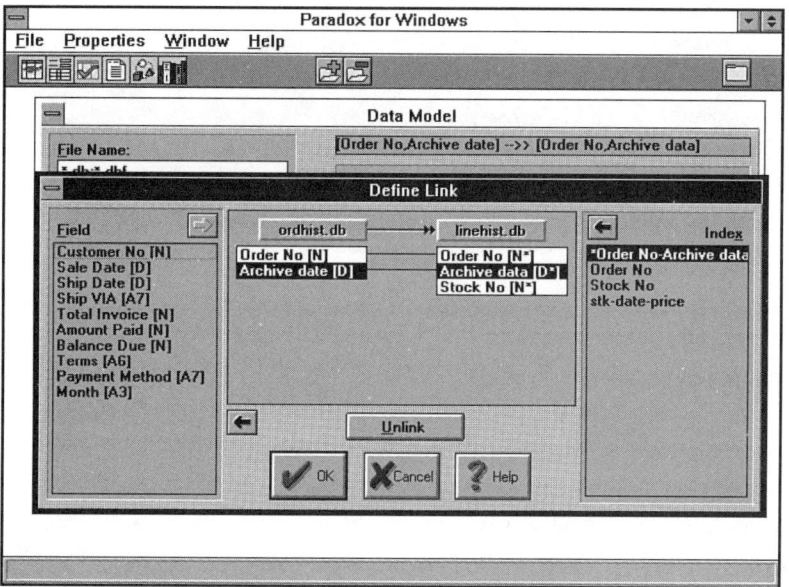

Figure 9.5. The Define Link dialog box.

This link is being defined from the Ordhist to the Linehist history tables. The Parent tables fields are displayed on the left side, and the Child tables indexes appear on the right side. You can select any field from the Parent table that has at least one field defined in a Child index with the same type and width. If you link more Child fields than Parent fields, you define a multi-valued relationship. If you have the same number of Child fields, you define a single-valued relationship. Obviously, you need to make sure that you define links between fields that contain similar data, otherwise your forms and reports will not display the data appropriately.

Paradox treats the table on the one side of a (M:1) single-valued relationship different than others. Many-to-one relationships are commonly known as a table lookup relationship, or a virtual tuple. For this reason, Paradox makes the lookup table, the one side of the relationship, a read-only table (see fig. 9.6). If you right-click on a table in the data model you can remove the read-only attribute.

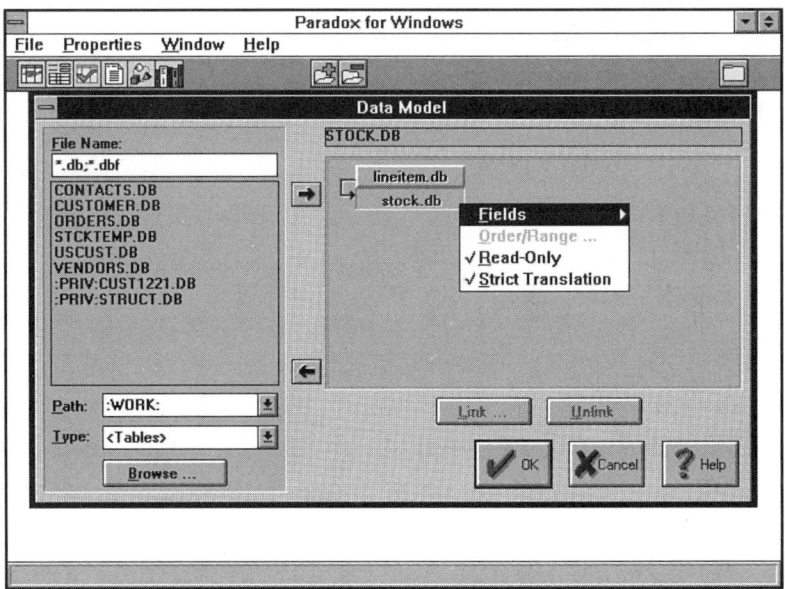

Figure 9.6. The Read Only table property.

This property pop-up menu is a shortcut to setting the same properties from the table menu when viewing a table. Only the master table of the data model can have the Order/Range attribute set. Strict translation refers to how Paradox handles different character sets. With Strict Translation checked, Paradox for Windows limits enterable characters to the ANSI character set, and does not translate the character to the corresponding DOS OEM code page character set, defined in the tables language driver. With Strict Translation unchecked, Paradox for Windows converts the characters into a common DOS OEM character in the supported set because Paradox for Windows tables can be accessed by DOS versions of Paradox. The Fields option just displays a list of the fields in the table.

Building Queries Based on Data Models

Queries can be constructed quickly by using a data model. When you define a new query, the dialog box contains the Data Model icon, to the right of the Browse button (see fig. 9.7).

Selecting this icon brings up the Define Data Model dialog box. Paradox uses the links defined in the data model to construct the corresponding links for a query using example elements. For example, figure 9.8 is the result of the data model displayed in figure 9.3.

Notice that Paradox inserts the Inclusion Operator in the Customer table. Paradox realizes that the Customer table has three 1:M Foreign key relationships. Because a Foreign Key relationship can have zero values in the child relationship (a customer may exist in the Customer table even if they have not placed an order), Paradox uses the inclusion operator to return customers even if they have no matches in the other tables. Only one field is checked when constructing a query from a data model to minimally make the query valid.

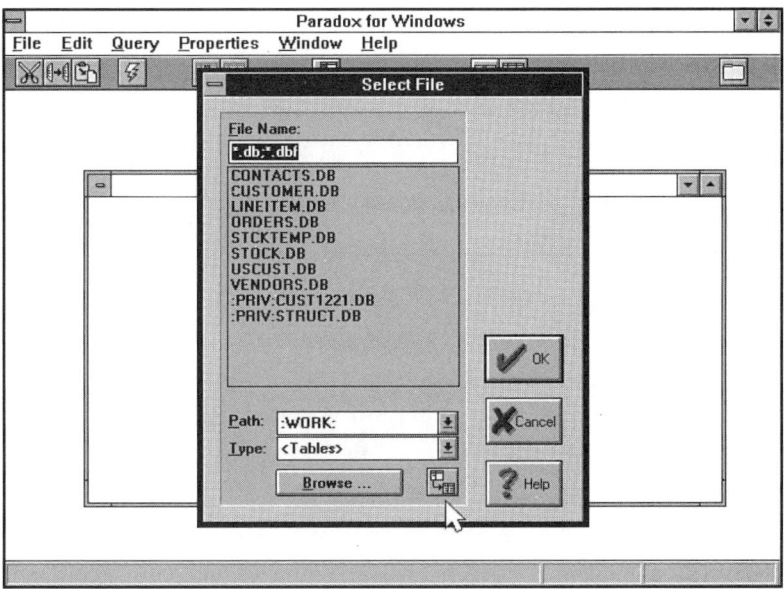

Figure 9.7. The Data Model icon in the Query Select File dialog box.

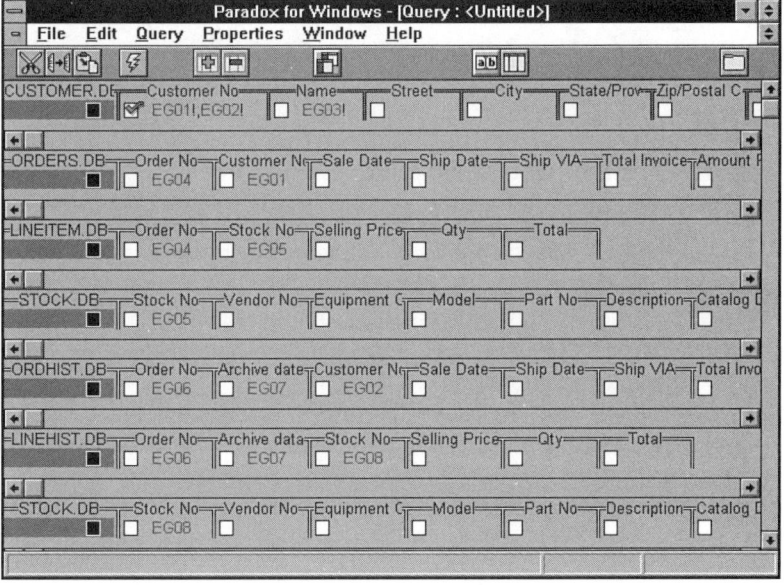

Figure 9.8. A query automatically created from a data model.

Queries also can be derived from a data model already defined for a form or a report. Rather than selecting the data model icon from the New Query dialog box, use the Types pulldown and select an existing form or report.

Changing Data Models

Data models can be changed easily even after you start designing your forms and reports (see fig. 9.9). Clicking the Data Model icon on the SpeedBar of the form or report designer brings up the same Data Model dialog box. You then can delete or add tables to the data model or redefine links between tables. If you delete tables that have defined objects placed on the form or report, you see a warning message.

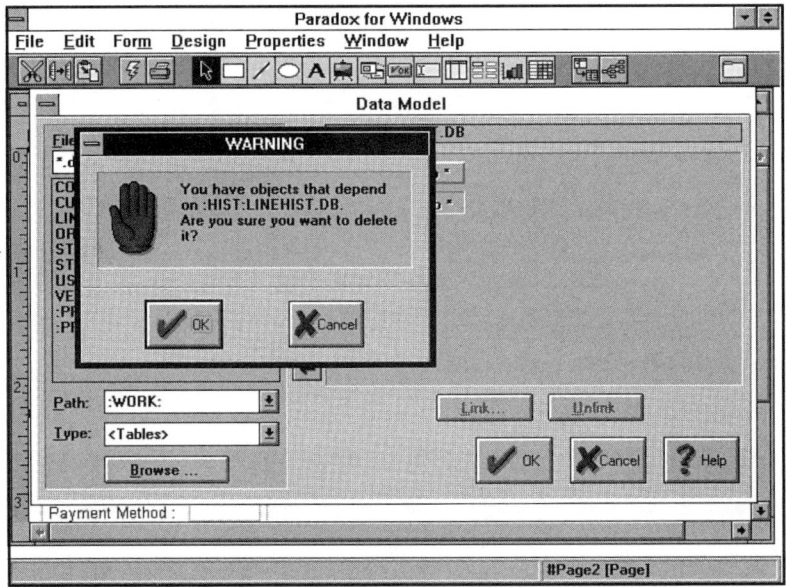

Figure 9.9. Changing data models from within the form or report designer.

If you delete a table that had fields placed on the form or report, they remain on the form in an unlabelled format. All table frames or multi-record regions also remain. You will need to select and delete these objects in the designer, or redefine them for other tables. If you add a new table when changing a data model, none of the fields is placed automatically in the designer, as happens when you first define the default design layout.

Referential Integrity

A major issue of any relational database is how it handles referential integrity. *Referential integrity* is the rule that constrains how related data is entered. It is important that data be entered consistently so that you can join tables properly. Paradox for Windows automatically checks referential integrity after you define the links between tables.

Referential integrity is established when you create a new or restructure an existing table. Selecting Referential Integrity from the Table Properties pulldown provides a dialog box much like the Define Link dialog box when creating data models (see fig. 9.10). However, one very big difference exists that is important to remember: *Referential Integrity rules are defined on Child tables.*

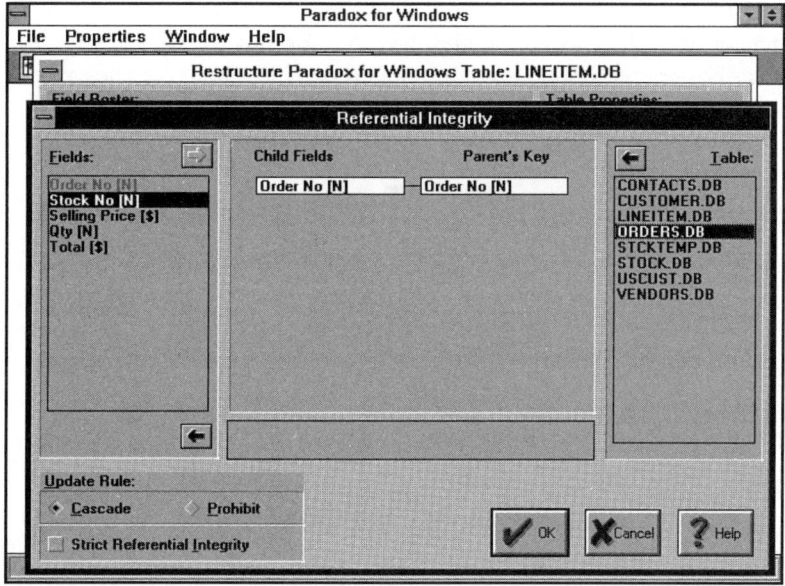

Figure 9.10. The Define Referential Integrity dialog box.

Here, the Child table fields are displayed on the left side and the Parent tables on the right. You can select any field of a Child table and then select the Parent table. The Parent table's key fields are used to link to the Child table fields you specify. In the example above the referential integrity link guarantees the following:

- No order number is entered in Lineitem that does not already exist in Orders.
- No Order record can be deleted if there is a corresponding order number in the Lineitem table.

Besides these rules, Paradox also allows you to define how to define a Cascading Updated rule. By selecting Cascade in the Update Rule, you tell Paradox to change the values in the linked Child table when the values in the Parent tables key field change.

 **Note:** Unlike the DOS versions of Paradox, the Cascading Update works even when you make changes without using a form.

If you select Prohibit in the Update Rule box, you prohibit all changes to be made to the key fields of the Parent table if Child records exist that depend on the Parent table. All of these referential integrity rules are automatically maintained by Paradox. If you try to edit a record that is Prohibited, deleting dependent records, or entering values not in the Parent table, Paradox issues a message that the action is not allowed.

Defining Referential Integrity on Tables with Data

When defining multiple referential integrity rules, for tables that contain data, the order in which you define the rules is important (see fig. 9.11). Suppose that you defined referential integrity between the Lineitem table to the Orders table, and you then want to define a rule between Order and Customer. When you try to define the rule between Order and Customer you get an error message.

To overcome the problem of improper order of rules, you need to delete the referential integrity rule defined on the Lineitem table, set the rule between Orders and Customer, and then redefine the rule between Lineitem and Orders.

If you define a referential integrity rule on a table that contains data, and the data fails the referential integrity rules, Paradox removes and places the records into a KeyViol table (see fig. 9.12).

Deleting and Inserting Records with Referential Integrity Defined

One referential integrity rule not supported by Paradox is Cascading Deletes. Cascading Deletes allows you to delete all dependent Child records when you delete a Parent record. To accomplish this deletion in Paradox, you can issue a series of delete queries to get rid of all the records. The order in which you delete these records is important (see fig. 9.13). If you try deleting records—by using a delete query—that have dependent Child records, Paradox doesn't delete the records and displays in a table—ErrorDel—the records that would have been deleted.

Chapter 9 ■ Data Models and Referential Integrity

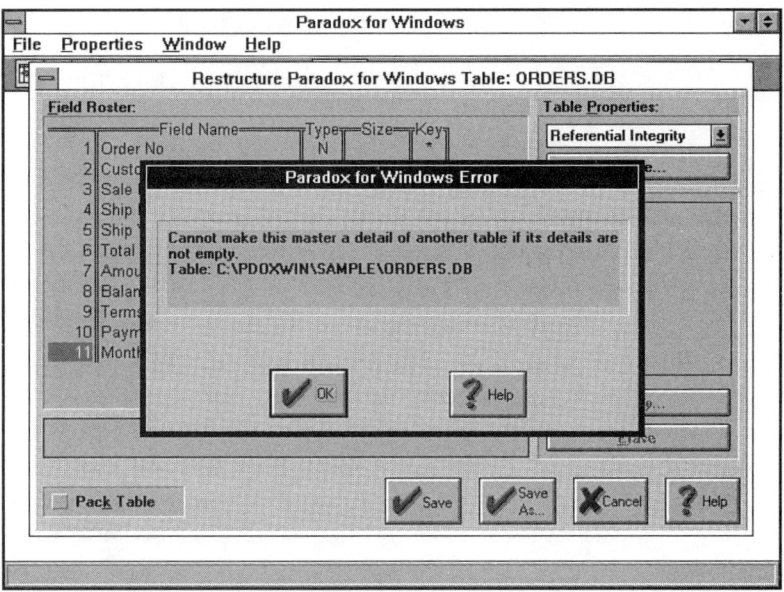

Figure 9.11. The order of defining referential integrity rules.

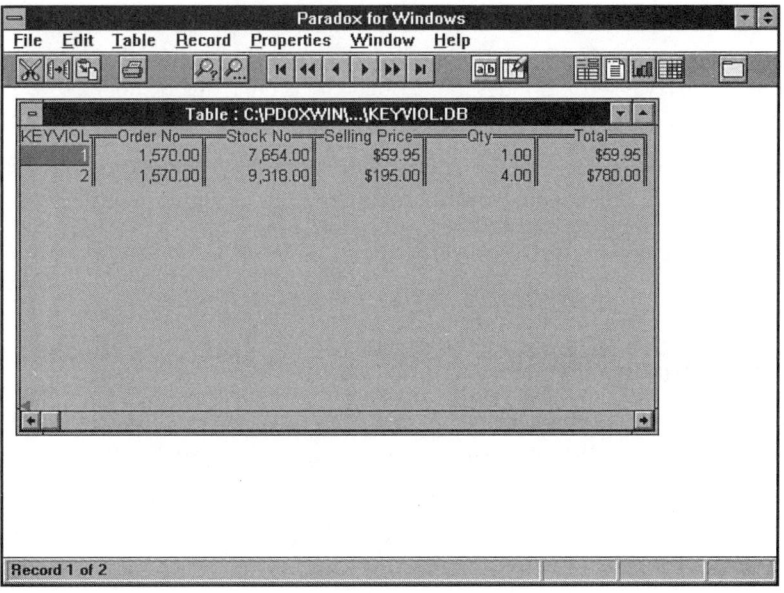

Figure 9.12. A KeyViol table, if table with existing data does not pass the referential integrity check.

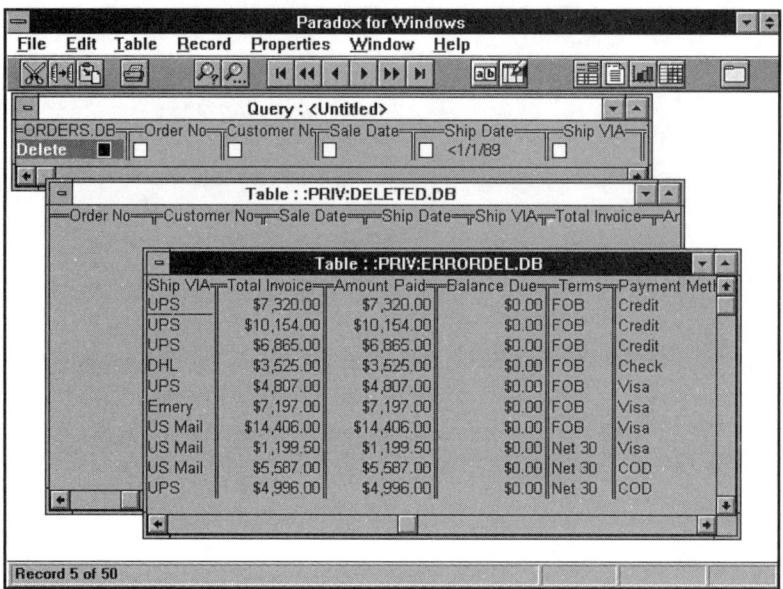

Figure 9.13. Inserting and Deleting records on tables with Referential Integrity defined.

Notice that the Deleted table is empty, which indicates that nothing was deleted. Insert queries work in a similar way, by creating a blank Inserted table and an ErrorIns table with the records that could not be inserted. If you try inserting values into a Child tables field, that do not have a corresponding value in the Parent tables key field, Paradox will create an ErrorIns table.

Besides Delete and Insert queries, Paradox applies referential integrity rules when Changeto queries are used. In addition, Import or Add operations from the File ¦ Utilities menu also will be verified against the referential integrity rule. Virtually all the ways that data can change in a table have referential integrity applied.

Strict Referential Integrity

The Referential Integrity dialog box has a check box, Strict Referential Integrity, in the lower left corner. If you check this box, Paradox displays a warning message (see fig. 9.14).

If more than one referential integrity rule is defined for the table, strict referential integrity is applied to all. What Strict Referential Integrity means is that Paradox for Windows does not allow a DOS version of Paradox to access the table. Paradox for DOS only enforces referential integrity when entering data from a form. Because you can access a table from Paradox for DOS that doesn't respect the referential integrity rules established with Paradox for Windows, you may have to restrict access to the table. If Paradox for DOS users try to access a table in Paradox for Windows that has the Strict Referential Integrity rule defined, they see a message that says the table is write-protected.

Chapter 9 ■ Data Models and Referential Integrity

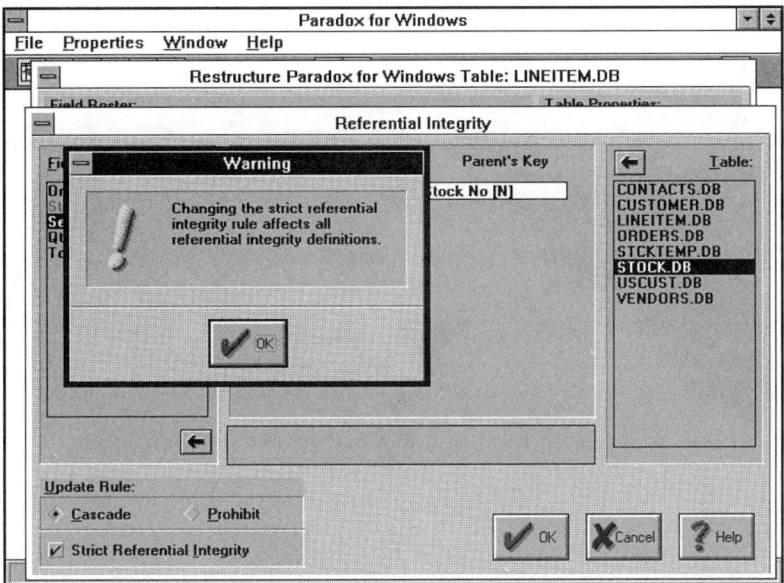

Figure 9.14. Strict Referential Integrity warning.

Self Referential Integrity

It is possible to have a field of a table linked to the primary key of that table to define a self referential integrity rule on the table (see fig. 9.15). If you have an employee table with a supervisor field, for example, you can link this field to the primary key of the employee table.

Notice that when you take this action, the only Update Rule possible is Prohibit, which means you cannot change any employee IDs that also are supervisor IDs, if these supervisor IDs are assigned to employees.

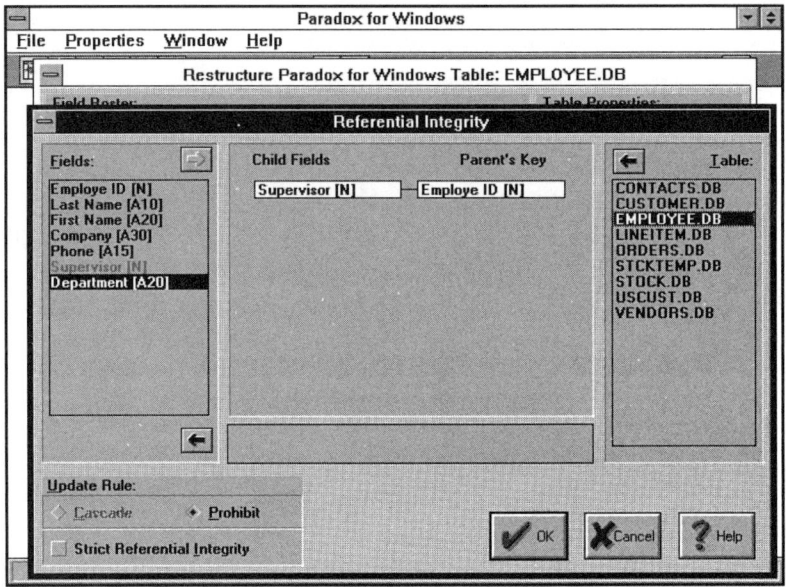

Figure 9.15. Defining Self Referential Integrity on the same table.

Summary

This chapter presented two of the most significant new features of Paradox for Windows, Data Modeling, and Referential Integrity. These features save the developer a tremendous amount of time by performing basic relational database functions. You can quickly define complex data relationships and help guarantee the integrity of the data in these relationships. By understanding the basics of how to use these features, you can take full advantage of their power and ease of use.

10
Designing and Using Forms

It is probably clear by now that, in many ways, forms serve a critical role in application development in Paradox for Windows, which often are the nonprogrammers' and your application's end users' only direct contact with the data. As such, they need both function and aesthetic appeal. Paradox for Windows forms provide limitless opportunity for customization, including the use of color, fonts, graphics, shapes, and graphs, to name just a few.

For the developer, forms also are the primary point of contact; with the exception of an occasional script, all ObjectPAL code gets attached to forms. As in the DOS-based versions of Paradox, it is important for the developer to understand the interactive features of the product. Form design is a perfect example. More than a few times, we have seen developers go through serious contortions to do something that can be done interactively quite easily.

Form Design Basics

This section introduces you to the elements that you encounter when you first design a form. As with nearly all aspects of this product, you almost always have more than one way to access these features.

Quick Forms

Quick Forms are the Paradox for Windows way of generating a quick-and-dirty form. These forms are extremely basic, at least initially. You generate Quick Forms by clicking the Quick Form icon in the SpeedBar, with the master table on the Desktop. Unless you specify a preferred form (discussed at the end of this chapter), Paradox creates a default form. Figure 10.1 shows a default Quick Form for the CUSTOMER table.

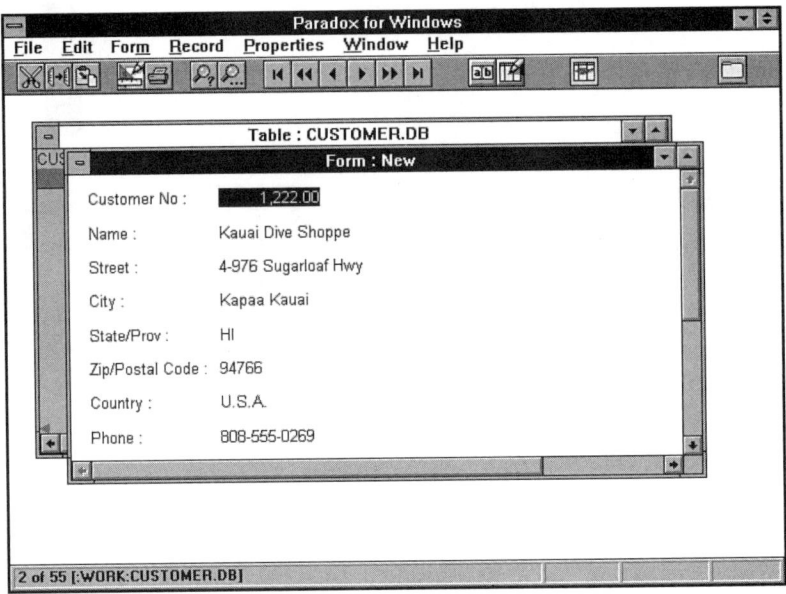

Figure 10.1. A Paradox for Windows default form.

This default form is extremely boring, but occasionally fits the bill; when it doesn't, the default form frequently can serve as a starting point for a customized form. Paradox simply places as many (labeled) fields as possible along the left side of the form. When the program runs out of room, it continues to lay out the fields in a top-down, left-right pattern.

Page Layout

You use the Page Layout dialog box to tell Paradox the dimensions of your form. Whether you are designing a form for the first time, or modifying an existing form, you have the option of using the Page Layout dialog box to customize a form. When you design a new blank form, Paradox always presents the Page Layout dialog box. When you design a new nonblank form (a form that includes tables or queries in the Data Model), the Page Layout dialog box is available through the Page Layout button on the Design Layout dialog box (see fig. 10.2). When you are in design mode for a new or existing form, you always have access to the Page Layout dialog box through the menus, Form ¦ Page ¦ Layout.

By default, forms are created for the screen. Reports, by contrast, are designed for the printer. Both of these defaults are overridden easily by changing the selection in the Design For section of this dialog box.

If you choose to design the form for the printer, Paradox uses only fonts supported by your printer. Paradox substitutes from the available screen fonts to approximate the printer fonts as well as it can. This substitution can cause a slight mismatch between screen and printer, giving you a not-quite-WYSIWYG form. Text objects on-screen may appear wrapped or clipped; however, these same fonts print just right.

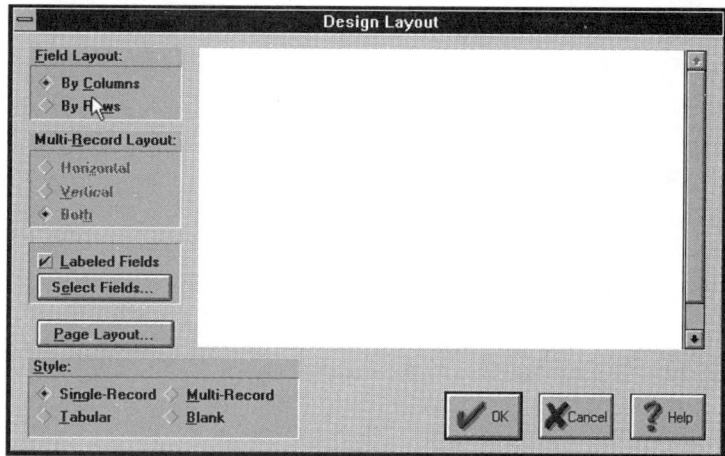

Figure 10.2. The Design Layout dialog box, showing the Page Layout button.

If you design for the screen, then the Screen Size area defaults to the current screen driver, in pixels, but can be changed to a custom size. You also can specify the custom size in either inches or centimeters. If you design a form for the printer, the Orientation option is enabled, allowing you to specify whether you want the form to print landscape or portrait. The predefined page sizes listed in the Paper Sizes area are the sizes supported by your printer. These sizes also can be customized, using either inches or centimeters as the unit of measure.

Design Layout

Paradox for Windows offers tremendous flexibility when placing the various fields and tables from your data model on the form. For a single-table form, the default design layout that is presented when you first see the Design Layout dialog box is the same layout that you see in the default Quick Form (refer to fig. 10.2). For multitable forms the layout is similar—single fields display in a top-down then left-right orientation. Tables that represent the *many* side of a relationship appear in a table frame. Like the default Quick Form, this default is extremely flexible. You can use the design layout as specified in this dialog box, you can modify the layout after you are in form design mode, or you can leave it blank and place the objects from scratch within the form designer.

The Design Layout dialog box has a few more options if you are designing with multiple tables (see fig. 10.3).

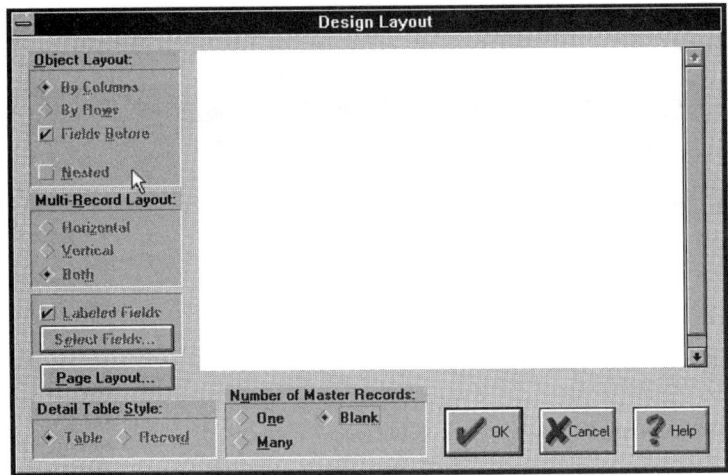

Figure 10.3. Layout options for a multitable form.

The Field Layout (single table only) section of this dialog box tells Paradox whether to place the fields in the data model top-down and then left-right (by columns), or left-right and then top-down (by rows). The default is by columns.

For multitable designs, the Field Layout area is referred to as Object Layout, because you then need to be concerned with placement of both fields and records. The Fields Before Records option places the single records before any tabular information.

The Nested option merits special discussion. The Nested option becomes available whenever you have multiple master records, which can happen in a 1:M data model if you choose to display multiple master records. It also happens with the middle table in a 1:M:M relationship. In a nested display, the master record and its potentially multiple details display together within the same MRO (multi-record object). Using the nested MRO approach, you can see multiple records of the master, along with its multiple details.

The Multi-Record Layout region is activated only when you select Multi-Record from the Style area. Similar in concept to the Field Layout region, this is where you tell Paradox whether you want to orient the records in a multi-record object horizontally (left-right) or vertically (top-down), or both.

Labeled Fields is a toggle. Click it once to mark the check box; this causes all your fields to display with their labels. Click the check box again to unmark it and have fields display without labels. The status of this check box determines the default setting for fields on your form; you are always free to modify certain field(s).

The Select Fields button brings up the dialog box shown in figure 10.4.

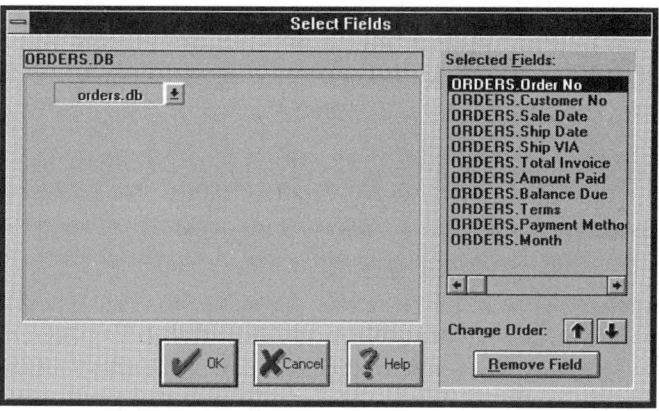

Figure 10.4. The Select Fields dialog box.

By default, Paradox includes all the fields in the master table of the data model. Any linking fields from the detail table(s) are not included, because they would only duplicate the information contained in the master. Paradox displays the included fields from the selected table in the Selected Fields section. You can choose between the different tables in the data model by clicking them; the field list updates to show fields from the selected table. The Remove Field button removes the currently selected field or fields. The Change Order up and down arrows change the display position of the currently selected field.

Use the Page Layout button to access the Page Layout dialog box, discussed in the previous section.

The Style area for single table forms has four options. Single-Record is the default style; it places the fields in a top-down, then left-right fashion. Multi-Record displays the table as an MRO. After you select Multi-Record, you can use the options under Multi-Record Layout to determine how you want them displayed. A tabular layout uses a table frame (see fig. 10.5).

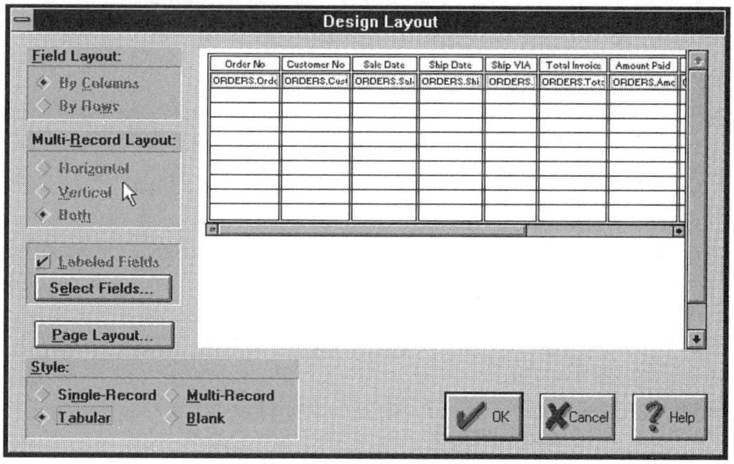

Figure 10.5. A tabular layout.

The tabular layout places as many fields as can fit within the specified page width. If you plan to use a tabular display, it is important to limit the displayed fields so that all fields are visible. Although to a certain extent Paradox allows you to resize the columns in a table frame, you cannot make these columns narrower than the field header.

It is usually better to opt for an MRO than a table frame because an MRO affords more design flexibility. One thing to remember when designing forms is that both MROs and table frames require that all their fields fit on a single page, which is another argument for making sure that your data is as normalized as possible and that you carefully select the fields that you include in a form.

Multitable forms, especially forms with tables linked 1:M or 1:M:M, add another layer of complexity to the design layout. You can use the Number of Master Records section to determine whether you want to display One or Many master records. In other words, you can display the master records either as individual fields or within an MRO. You can use Detail Table Style to tell Paradox whether to use an MRO or a table frame to display the details. If you display Many master records, then the Detail Table Style setting also affects the master record display.

As your data model grows in complexity, so does this dialog box. At some point, it no longer makes sense to try to let Paradox *help* you here. Often, you do better by selecting Blank and placing UIObjects yourself. The data model still enforces the appropriate table linking, but you can have more control over which fields and tables are placed, and where they are placed on the form. Working with UIObjects is the topic of the following section.

UIObjects in Forms

The UI in UIObject stands for *User Interface*. If the form requires some interaction with the user, you must have at least one UIObject on the form. A good place to see the UIObjects available on a form is on the SpeedBar in form design mode (see fig. 10.6).

Figure 10.6. UIObjects on the SpeedBar.

The UIObjects on this SpeedBar begin with the Ellipse tool and end with the Crosstab tool. (Remember that if you need a reminder about the function of any SpeedBar icon, pass over the icon with the mouse and look at the description on the status line.)

You can place all these UIObjects on the form by clicking the appropriate SpeedBar icon and then dragging to an area on the form. Notice that the icon changes to represent the UIObject type as you place it on the form and then changes back to the selection arrow after the object is placed. To place multiple objects of the same type, Shift+click the SpeedBar icon. The icon doesn't return to the selection arrow until you click on the selection arrow on the SpeedBar. This procedure allows you to continue placing objects of the selected type without continuously clicking on the SpeedBar to select the same type.

Noise Names

Understanding how Paradox assigns names to objects placed on a form is helpful. By default, all objects are given noise names. The Object Tree in figure 10.7 shows objects addressed by their noise names.

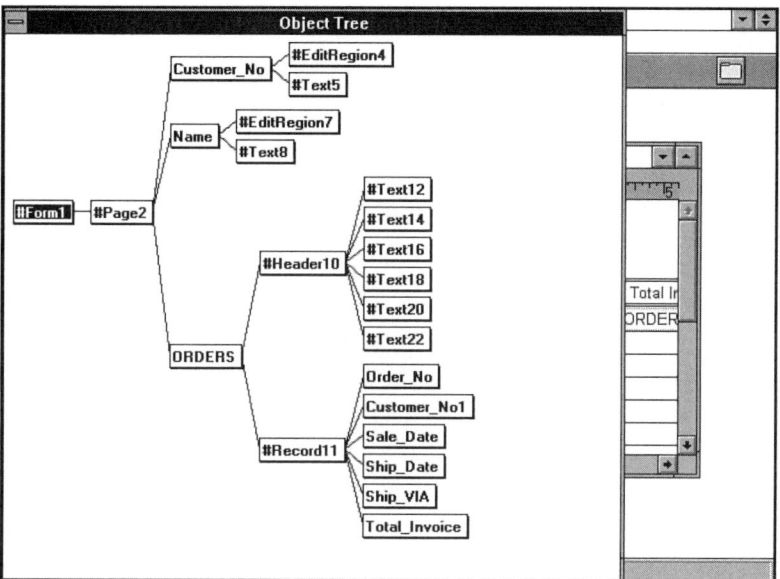

Figure 10.7. A Paradox for Windows Object Tree.

Notice that the form is displayed on the far left side of the form, with the name #Form1. The name comes from the obvious fact that it represents the form and from the perhaps not-quite-as-obvious fact that it was the first object opened on the form. Next comes the page, with the predictable name #Page2, because it was the next object opened on the page. Bound fields and table frames are given their field names or associated table names; Paradox assumes that these may be the names you would use. But notice that their corresponding numbers are not available in the numbering scheme—there is no object with a noise name #object3. In the figure 10.7, the Customer_No field is the third object. The numbering continues with the field's edit region.

A few other things should be pointed out in this Object Tree. First, spaces in field names are translated to underscores (_) because spaces are not allowed in object names. Second, take a close look at the different components of a compound object. Labeled fields, for example, are comprised of the label (text region) and the edit region. Table frames have even more component objects: the table frame itself, the headers for the various fields, a record object, and the frame's component field objects.

For the sake of readability, we usually advise you to assign your own names to objects that you work with in your forms. An object's name is a property and therefore can be set through property inspection. Inspect the object, click the name (which appears at the top to the popup menu), and type the new name in the Object Name dialog box. You also can set an object's name from within the Object Tree: right click, select the name at the top of the menu, and then type the new name.

Containership

The notion of containership is pervasive throughout Paradox for Windows and is discussed in detail in other chapters of this book. It is worth revisiting here briefly, however, to understand how containership works with respect to objects in forms. If you place an object on a form and then place another object *completely within its boundaries*, the first object *contains* the second object. When an object is contained by another object, this situation affects much of how it is treated in the form and report designers.

Something that is sometimes confusing to new users is the way Paradox handles the properties of contained objects. Assume that, for example, you had a text region that contained a button, which in turn contained a label. You might expect that changing the font—or color, or any other property—in the text region would automatically change the same property in the label, or other contained objects. It doesn't.

Having Paradox automatically change the property in the contained object, however, is easy. Paradox has a feature known as *penetrating properties* that allows you to set, in one step, the properties of both the selected object and all the objects contained by it. With the object selected, Ctrl+right click to bring up the Objects in Text, or penetrating properties menu.

Figure 10.8 shows what the menu looks like for the preceding example. If you change the font, color, or other property from this menu, it affects the selected objects and all the objects it contains. Another impact of containership is that contained objects get moved with their containers.

Figure 10.8. The Objects In Text menu.

By default, Paradox assumes that you want objects that are completely surrounded by another object to be contained by the larger object. You can break the containership by moving the inner, smaller object outside the container, even if only slightly. By default, Paradox checks a UIObject property called Contain Objects. If you want a smaller object to coexist in the space within a larger object without being contained by the larger object, you can turn off the Contain Objects property for the larger object.

Selecting Multiple Objects

You now know that Paradox moves objects within a container together and that you can use penetrating properties to set properties for all the objects within a container. Suppose that, however, you want to move objects, or set properties for objects, that do not fall within the same container, or that if, when they do fall within the same container, you don't want to include *all* the objects within the container? Paradox for Windows offers options for this type of selection.

There is a standard windows technique of pressing Shift while clicking to select multiple contiguous *things* in many Windows applications. Ctrl+click usually selects multiple noncontiguous items. You can see this technique at work when you open multiple files from a dialog box. In Paradox for Windows forms, you can use either technique for selecting multiple objects in a form. After the objects are selected, you can use the Ctrl+right click technique to set properties for all the objects at once.

The other technique for selecting multiple objects requires that they be contiguous on the form. Holding down the Shift key and dragging a box around objects causes all the objects within the boundary of the box to become selected. Again pressing Ctrl+right click allows you set properties for all the selected objects.

Grouping Objects

After you select multiple objects by using either of the preceding techniques, you can group them by selecting the Design ¦ Group menu. When you create a group, you create an artificial container object for all the selected objects. From this point on, you can move the objects together and set their properties together.

By default, Paradox visits the fields in a top-down, left-right pattern as you tab through a form. Grouping also is helpful in forcing a different tab order. Paradox tabs to all objects within a group before moving to other objects. You can nest groups within groups to force a very exact tab order.

Group objects have the property, *ungroup*; inspect the group and select Ungroup to dissociate the grouped objects.

Bring to Front and Send to Back

When objects overlap on a form, Paradox sees the object placed last on the form as *on top* of the other. You can see this overlap, for example, if you place one colored object on top of another colored object. The top object masks the underlying object. If you move an older object to the same position as a new one, the old object appears to slide underneath the new one.

Although objects on a form are placed from the bottom up, you can change this placement by using two commands from the Design menu: Bring to Front and Send to Back. Choosing Bring to Front for an object causes it to display on top of other UIObjects. Send to Back moves the objects to the bottom of the UIObject pile.

Aligning Objects

The Paradox form and report designers are highly visual tools. You are free to place objects essentially anywhere on the design document. With this freedom comes the associated risk of creating a form that looks haphazard—as if you had drawn the form freehand. Paradox provides tools to help ensure that the objects on a form display with the proper alignment.

Paradox uses *alignment* in two unrelated places—one pertains to aligning multiple objects relative to one another, and the other to describing the placement of an individual text object relative to its container. Regarding the alignment property of text objects, Paradox allows you to right-, left-, or center-align text, or to justify it. Justified text fills the space between the assigned margins, aligning on both the left and right.

Aligning multiple objects in a form can be very important to the appearance of a document. The Design ¦ Align menu allows you to align multiple objects horizontally or vertically. Vertically, Paradox allows you to align the top, bottom, or middle of the selected objects; horizontally, you can choose between left, right, or center alignment.

If the alignment causes objects to overlap, they display in the top-down order described in the previous paragraphs. By default, the object placed last appears on top, unless Bring to Front or Send to Back was applied to any of the aligned objects.

Pinning Objects

A complex form can spend a few hours in the form designer. You don't want to risk the possibility of accidentally moving one or more carefully placed objects. You can avoid this possibility by using the Pin property associated with all design objects. The object inspector for design objects always has a Design ¦ Pin Horizontal and Design ¦ Pin Vertical option. Choosing Pin Horizontal fixes the horizontal placement of the object; you can move it up and down, but not left to right, or right to left. Vertical Pin fixes the object in the vertical plane. Checking both objects causes the object to become absolutely fixed.

Duplicating Objects

Paradox allows you to copy one or many objects, both within a form and between forms. Choosing Design ¦ Duplicate from the menus duplicates the selected object(s) within the same form. All properties of the form are assigned to the duplicate object. If the object was using its noise name, such as #field1 or #box2, the new objects are named according to the standard noise-naming rules. When the objects have given names, the new object(s) are given a sequentially numbered extension. When you duplicate an object named NewField, for example, the duplicated object receives the name NewField1.

Besides using the Duplicate menu option, the Clipboard is available for moving or duplicating objects, which is especially useful for copying between different pages or even different forms. When you transfer an object by using the Clipboard, all the object's properties also are transferred, including any methods associated with the field, which is a great way to reuse segments of code from application to application.

An interesting ramification of copying objects between forms is that, if the object that you copy is bound to a table, this table is added to the new form's data model if it is not already there.

Using Unbound Fields

Usually, you think of fields as objects associated with tables. Paradox for Windows, however, lets you use fields *not* associated with tables—*unbound fields*—for a variety of purposes. For the interactive user, the primary purpose of an unbound field is to hold a special or calculated value. For the ObjectPAL programmer, an unbound field is handy for receiving a variable or holding the results of a calculation.

One thing to consider when you work with unbound fields is whether or not you want them to be able to be tabbed. Unmarking Runtime ¦ Tab Stop essentially makes the field display-only to the interactive user—the cursor cannot land on the field as you tab through the form. There is another property under the Runtime menu—Read Only— which when set, does not allow the user to modify the field. A field can be tab-able, but unchangeable by checking both the Tab Stop and the Read Only properties. Although these properties are available for other design objects, these properties often are an important consideration when dealing with unbound fields.

Special Fields

Special fields are used to display information about a table on your computer system. You can access the special field types in the following two ways:

1. From the object inspector, choose Define Field to see the menu shown in figure 10.9. The special fields Today, Now, Page Number, and Number of Pages are available for this menu.

2. Click the ellipsis (...) to bring up the Define Field Object dialog box. The lower right corner contains a drop-down list with the same special field types included in figure 10.10.

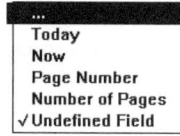

Figure 10.9. Field properties, showing special field options.

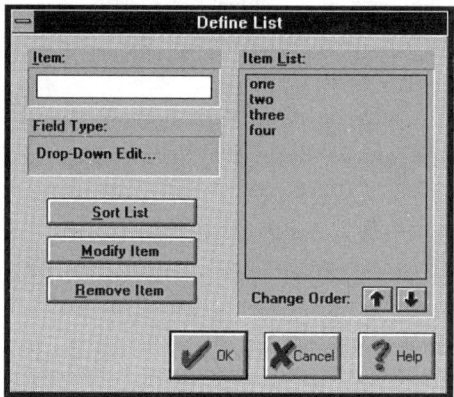

Figure 10.10. Special fields, available from Define Field Object dialog box.

Calculated Fields

You also can use the Define Field Object dialog box to place calculated and summary fields. As soon as you mark the Calculated check box, the Copy Field button becomes available, which allows you to copy the field from the data model region and place it into the Calculated box. If you want to use one of the fields from the data model in the calculation, you can click on the table icon in the data model region and select the appropriate field from the drop-down list associated with the table. Fields used in calculated fields do *not* need to be fields selected from the Design Layout dialog box; all fields in the tables included in the Data Model are available.

Besides selecting the fields from the data model region, you also can type the fields into the Calculated text box, using the following syntax:

    [Tablename.fieldname]

To add a flat 6-percent tax to a field, you use the following calculation:

    [Tablename.moneyfield]*1.06

No discussion of calculated fields is complete without a demonstration of how to concatenate alphanumeric fields, using the example of First and Last name:

    [Tablename.First_Name]+" "+[Tablename.Last__Name]

Essentially any combination of fields, arithmetic operators, and constants is acceptable for calculated fields. ObjectPAL methods also are allowable here:

```
UPPER([Tablename.NameField])
MOY([Tablename.Datefield])
```

A conditional if (IIF) statement here can solve many problems:

```
IIF([Tablename.Fieldname]="","N/A",[Tablename.Fieldname])
```

ObjectPAL functions that would result in a change in the value of another field are not allowed. For example, you might be tempted to use a calculation like:

```
IIF([Tablename.State]="HI",[TableName.State]="WA",[TableName.State]="MI")
```

This calculation does not change the value of the State field, but instead always evaluates to false. Paradox sees that [TableName.State] *does not* equal "WA" (because the calculation was already selected for "HI"), so the value of the true condition is the result of this evaluation, which is false. The state clearly also is MI, so the false condition also evaluates to false, causing the value "False" to display in the calculated field in either case. Paradox uses only the second and third parameters of the IIF statement as the value to display in the calculated field based on whether the initial parameter is true.

Summary Fields

The summary operators also are available from within the Define Field Object dialog box, and vary depending on the selected field type, but the total set of options includes the following:

- None
- Sum
- Count
- Min
- Max
- Avg
- Std
- Var

You can use any combination of copying fields, typing fields, selecting summary operators, and typing summary operators to enter your calculation:

```
sum([table.fieldname])
```

To perform summary calculations on multiple fields, use the following:

```
SUM([Table.Fieldname])/SUM([Table.Fieldname])
```

The range of summary fields is dependent on the placement of the field's (or fields') data model. For a single-table form, the calculation is based on the entire table. In a multitable form, summary calculations work differently depending on whether you are summarizing on a master or a detail table. Summaries on the master table always take into account the entire table; summaries on the detail table(s) respect the link to the master and operate only on the fields linked to the current master. In figure 10.11, the first calculated field counts records in the Customer table. The second calculated field counts records in the Orders detail table *that are associated with the current master record.*

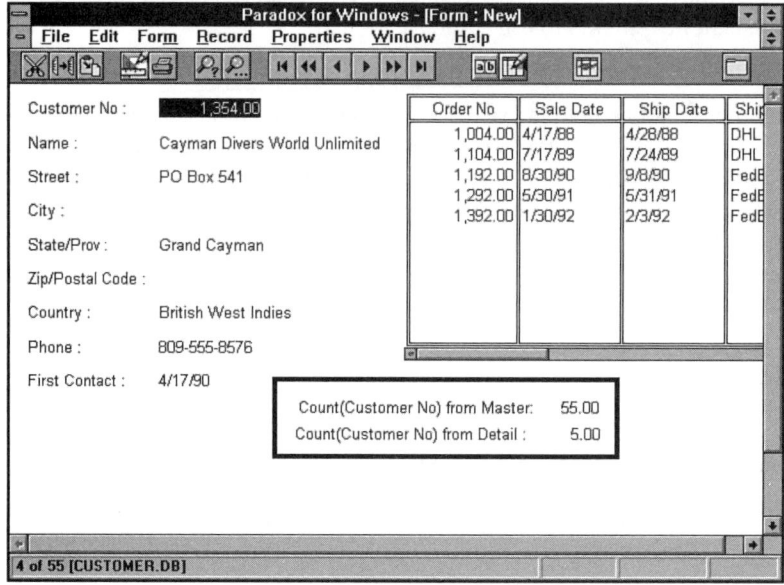

Figure 10.11. The first calculated field, showing records being counted in the Customer table.

Field Properties

Many field properties, such as color, size, line spacing, and font, are very intuitive and don't deserve special attention. As mentioned previously, the alignment property determines the justification of the text within its container. The pattern property is available for many of the UIObjects and determines the object's background display pattern. Similarly, field objects share the same frame property options as other UIObjects. Setting a field's display type and format also are important topics discussed in this section.

Word Wrap

If you need to enter a significant amount of text in a field, you probably want to turn on word wrap. With the field property word wrap turned off, text that doesn't fit on the current line scrolls to the left, out of the object's visible area. With the word-wrap property on, when text reaches the left border of the field, it wraps to the next line.

Display Type

Paradox gives you a variety of choices to displaying fields. These options are available under the field's Display Type property. You can display field objects as any of the following types:

- *Labeled.* The default field type, which consists of a text region for the label and an edit region representing the field value. For bound fields, the text defaults to the associated field name.

- *Unlabeled.* The same as labeled fields, but, as their name implies, these fields display without the text region.

- *Drop-Down Edit.* Initially displays a blank field with an arrow that indicates its drop-down list. You can open the list box and select one of the existing values, or type in a new value.

  Entering values into drop-down edit, radio button, and list field types (discussed in the following text) involves essentially the same steps. When you choose any of these field types from the field property inspector, you see the Define List dialog box (see fig. 10.12).

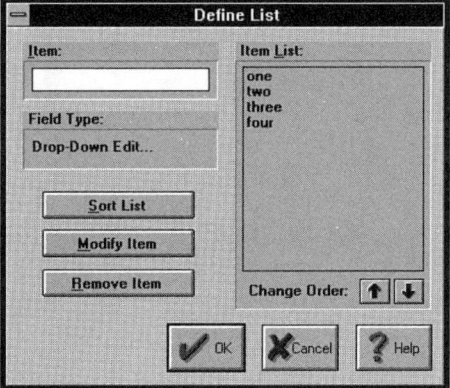

Figure 10.12. The Define List dialog box.

The possible values for the field are entered into the Item text box. Pressing Enter adds them to the Item List. The Sort Item button is used to perform a case-insensitive sort.

- *List* (or list boxes). Similar to drop-down edit field types, except that you can select only an item that exists in the list.
- *Radio Buttons.* Display a list of mutually exclusive options. As soon as you select one button, any other selected button is deselected. Paradox treats these radio buttons as one field, whose value is determined by the selected button. Notice that a radio button consists of three parts: a text region contained within a button region, which is contained within the field. The text region corresponds to the label in a labeled field, whereas the values you enter in Define List dialog box represent the values entered into the table. So, although the label text defaults to displaying the values from the field definition, you are free to customize it.

Notice also that these compound field types have all the field properties of other field types, besides having properties associated with their component objects. For example, you can change the frame style of the entire field object, the individual fields, or both.

Another issue that you need to be aware of is when defining optional field values using lists: Paradox makes no evaluation of the contents of this list, which means that you can add a 10-character choice for an A5 field, use an alphabetic value in numeric field, and violate any validity checks defined for the table. When you attempt one of these values at runtime, however, Paradox generates an error and does not accept the field.

- *Check Box.* Check boxes display as a single box, with an assigned *marked* or *checked* and *unmarked*, *unchecked*, or *blank* value. Although they often appear in groups, each check box represents a different field and can be marked or not, independent of the status of all the other boxes. Paradox uses the dialog box shown in figure 10.13 for assigning the marked and blank values to the field.

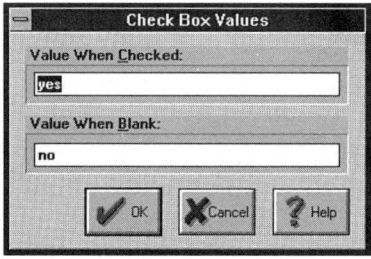

Figure 10.13. The Check Box Values dialog box.

It is easy to misunderstand check boxes and equate the Value When Blank value with the default value. They are not the same!

Using the values in the picture, you may think that not accessing this field during a data entry session sets the field value to *no*. In fact, the value is blank unless you move through the field without checking it. The Default validity check is the tool of choice for interactively setting the default field value. Using ObjectPAL, you can always initialize the field value.

Format

The format property is available for dates and all the numeric field types. Besides the built-in formats for these field types, Paradox allows custom formats. For date, numeric, and currency field types, as well as time, the International dialog box (accessed by choosing the International option from the Windows Control Panel) contains default formats (see fig. 10.14).

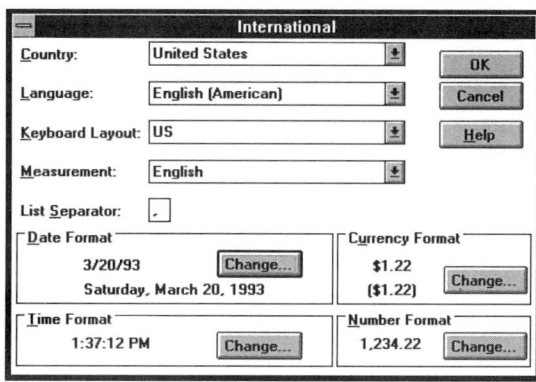

Figure 10.14. The Windows International dialog box.

Figure 10.15 shows a cascading menu from the Format ¦ Number Format menu.

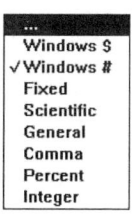

Figure 10.15. Default Number Format options.

The default options for the number formats are shown in table 10.1.

Table 10.1. Number Format Default Options.

Display Format	Decimal Places	Thousands Separator	Negative Numbers	Trailing Zeros	Example	Comments
Windows $					$1,234.00	The default currency format. Uses the currency format defined in the Windows Control Panel.
Windows #					1,234.00	Uses the default number format from the Windows Control Panel.
Fixed	2	None	minus	yes	1234.00	
Scientific	4		minus	no	1.2340e+3	Uses exponential notation.
General	<2	None	minus	yes	1234	
Comma	2	Comma	( )	yes	1,234.00	
Percent		None	minus		123400%	Numbers followed by %.
Integer	0	None	minus		1234	Rounds decimal values.

Besides these predefined number formats, Paradox allows you to create your own new custom number format. You create a new format by pressing the Add Format button from the Select Number Format dialog box (see fig. 10.16).

Click the Create button to create a new number format. After you set all the properties of the number format, give it a name in the Name text box. The Permanent option enables you to save the new format permanently; otherwise, the new format is available for the duration of the current Paradox session. If you choose to make the format permanent, it is saved to the file PDOXWIN.INI in the WINDOWS directory. The Add Format button adds the format to the list of existing formats and allows you to continue to work within the dialog box.

Chapter 10 ■ Designing and Using Forms

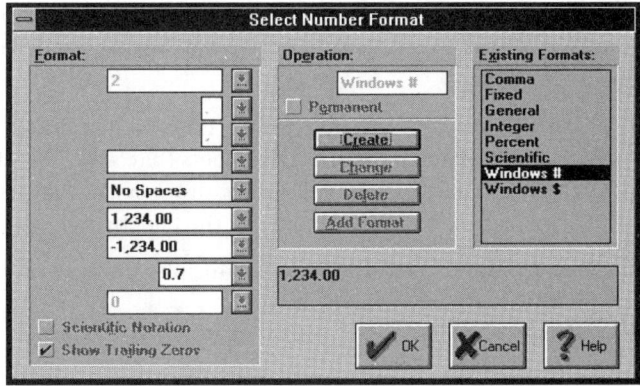

Figure 10.16. The Select Number Format dialog box.

After you create a custom number format, you have the option of changing or deleting it—to do either, highlight the format in the Existing Format list and click the appropriate button, either Change or Delete. Notice that the Change and Delete buttons are enabled only when a custom format is highlighted; you cannot change or delete a predefined format.

Selecting and modifying date formats is similar in concept to working with number fields. Only three predefined date formats are available:

Windows Short

Windows Long

mm/dd/yy

The first two date formats are read from the Windows control panel settings. The third format is self-explanatory.

To add a new date or customize an existing date specification, inspect the field, then select Format ¦ Date Format. Click the ellipsis to display the Select Date Format dialog box (see fig. 10.17).

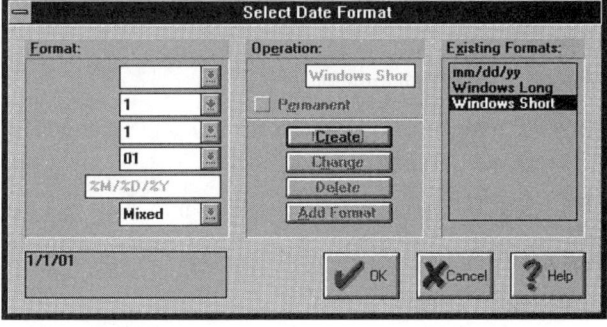

Figure 10.17. The Select Date Format dialog box.

169

The right two columns of this dialog operate in exactly the same way as they do with custom numbers. New date formats also are written to PDOXWIN.INI. Click on the Create button to create a new date/format.

The Order type-in area (which is available from the Create Date Format dialog box) works like a picture for the date format by telling Paradox which components (day, date, month, year) to display and the order of the display. The parentheses are replaced with actual date values. You also can use literal values to display text as part of the date or to modify the punctuation.

The Weekday option allows you to specify whether and how to display the day of the week. This option is disabled until you type **%W** in the Order type-in area.

Special Issues for Memo and Formatted Memo Fields

Extended fields are fields that have the potential of being stored in the external .MB file. They include Memo, Graphic, Formatted Memo, Blob, and OLE field types.

When you first land on a memo field in a form, the entire memo is highlighted or selected. As you begin typing, if you are in edit mode, the highlighted text is replaced. If you put the field into Field View, by either using the Field View SpeedBar icon, or by clicking within the field, the text becomes deselected. In Field View, you are free to type all the characters you like. If you try adding a tab or a carriage return, however, Paradox moves to the next record. An additional editing *mode* is available for memo fields—Memo View. You get there by pressing Shift+F2. In Memo View, you can press the Tab key and the Enter key and still remain within the memo field.

The Runtime ¦ Complete Display property tells Paradox whether to display the entire memo (or as much as fits within the field object) or only the part of the memo stored with the .DB file. Often, you can shorten the time it takes to scroll through records if you do not require that Paradox refresh the field with the contents of the .MB file, by turning off Complete Display.

Memo fields have a word-wrap property that behaves similarly to the word-wrap property of other fields and text objects (discussed later in this chapter). Interestingly, if you are in Memo View, with word wrap disabled, the Enter key has no effect; the Tab key, however, inserts a tab. By default, Paradox uses 1/2-inch tabs.

Formatted memo fields are similar to regular memos, except that you have the option to add color, fonts, line spacing, tab stops, and text alignment.

In the Properties menu, you can toggle the expanded ruler on and off. Figure 10.18 shows what the expanded ruler in the form (and report) designer looks like.

The set of icons on the left side of the expanded ruler are similar to those you see in a word processor. Select left, center, right, or justify to align your text. If you select alignment with text selected, Paradox aligns the selected text. If text is not selected, any subsequent text aligns according to the choice you make in the expanded ruler.

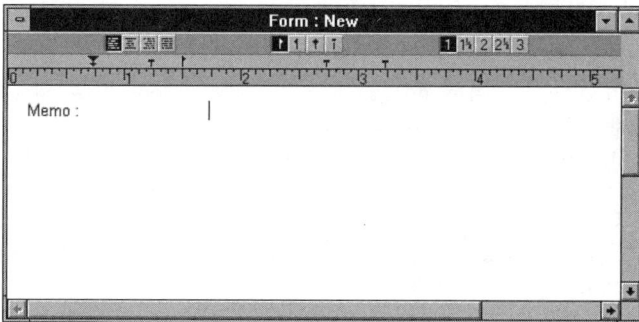

Figure 10.18. The expanded ruler.

To set tabs, the horizontal ruler must be visible. The gray area that displays below the tab, alignment, and line-spacing icons and just above the horizontal ruler is the *tab well*. To set left, right, center, or decimal tabs, click the appropriate icon, and then click the tab well at the spot you want the tab.

Left tabs are the standard tab stop that you are probably familiar with; text is pushed to the right so that the tab stop defines its left edge. Right tabs define the right edge of the text; text is pushed left to align on the right. Center tabs cause the text to center itself relative to the tab stop. And decimal tabs are used to force decimal places to line up at the position of the tab stop.

All the formatting features available for formatted memo fields also can be used by text objects (discussed in the following section).

Other UIObjects

The other UIObjects—text, graphic, pushbutton, MRO, table frames, graphs, crosstabs, and OLE objects—share many of the same properties as the objects already discussed. A discussion of their unique behavior and properties follows.

Text Objects

Text objects have many of the same properties as the text portion of field objects, such as enabling you to set fonts, sizes, word wrap, and the other formatting features mentioned in the preceding sections.

There are two ways to place text objects on forms:

- Click the Text tool icon and drag out the desired shape and size of the text object. Then fill in the text.

- Click the Text tool icon; then click on the form at the spot you want the text to appear. Type the text.

There is a property of text objects—Design Sizing—with three options: Fixed Size, Fit Text, and Grow Only. Fixed Size causes the text area to remain static; if you add more text or change the font, you risk the possibility of having some of the text object not on the visible form. Fit Text allows the text object to grow or shrink as necessary to accommodate the text it holds. Grow Only uses the design size as the minimum size, but allows the text box to grow when necessary to hold more or larger text. If the object grows to accommodate new text that is subsequently deleted, the object size doesn't shrink; you must manually resize the object.

An important distinction exists between these two methods of placement that impacts the default Design Sizing setting of the object. If you use the first option to place the text object, the object's Design Sizing property defaults to Fixed Size; if you use the second option, the property defaults to Fit Text. You can, of course, overwrite either of these settings.

Graphic Objects

After a graphic object is placed on a form, you can paste a value into it, either through the Clipboard or from an appropriate graphic file on disk. Allowable graphic formats are BMP, PCX, TIF, GIF, and EPS. If you inspect the graphic object and then choose Define Field, you have the Paste or Paste From options. Paste pastes a graphic contained in the active Clipboard. If a graphic isn't in the Clipboard, this option is unavailable.

Paradox allows you to increase the graphic display size by 200 or 400 percent, or decrease it to 25 or 50 percent of original size, by using the magnification property. Choosing Best Fit from the Magnification menu displays the graphic as large as possible within its container, keeping the vertical/horizontal proportions intact. The Size to Fit property causes the frame to adjust to the size of the graphic image, whereas Best Fit causes the image to adjust with respect to the frame.

If the graphic size is larger than its container, Paradox shows a hand icon as you move the cursor over the graphic. When the hand cursor is visible, you can click and drag the image within its container. The border is a fixed window under which you can slide the larger graphic.

Graphic fields support sophisticated *raster operations*. Raster operations tell Paradox how the source graphic (the image pasted from the Clipboard or file) interacts with already visible on-screen elements.

Pushbutton (Button) Objects

Two notable properties are associated with pushbuttons: type and tab stop. Buttons are really not functional without at least some ObjectPAL code associated with them. Without code, a pushbutton just pops in and back out.

The button type property allows you to display a pushbutton, radio button, or a check box. Pushing a pushbutton causes it to appear pushed in as long as the mouse button is down; when the mouse button is released, the button pops back up. Marking a check box causes the check mark to toggle on and off. Similarly, pushing a radio button toggles its selection on and off.

Check boxes and radio buttons have two optional display styles: Borland and Windows. The Borland styles are the defaults and display in the familiar *chiseled steel* look. Figure 10.19 shows the different types of styles for the three button types.

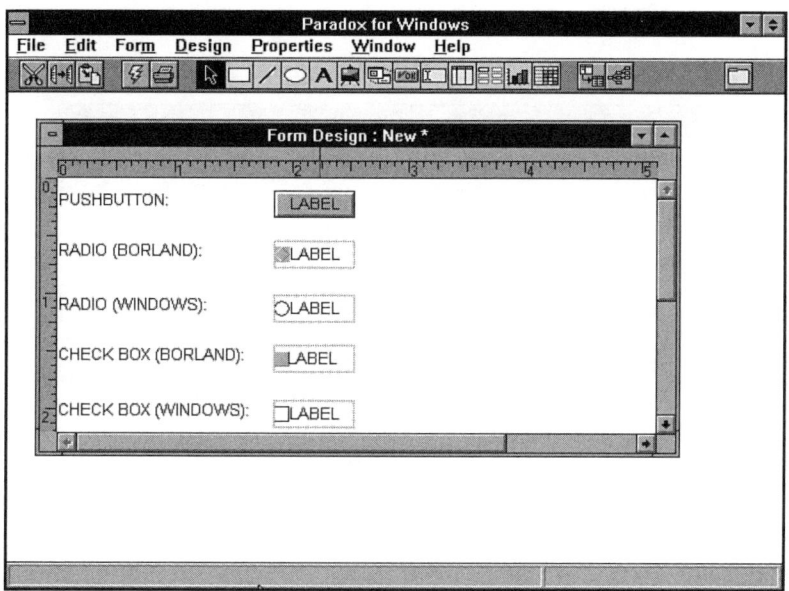

Figure 10.19. Form with various button display options.

A pushbutton's Tab Stop property is off by default, which means that it must be pressed with the mouse; using the cursor keys or the Tab key will not give the button focus. You need to check the Tab Stop property to allow the user to actuate the button with the keyboard. After the button has focus, pressing the Enter key *presses* the button and causes all attached code to execute.

MROs

The section, "Design Layout," near the beginning of this chapter discusses some issues to consider when choosing between MROs and table frames. This section shows you the properties important to MROs—defining a record and record layout.

When you choose Multi-Record from the Design Layout dialog box, Paradox sizes and places the MRO on the form. For more control, however, you can choose to place the MRO manually by using the Multi-Record tool on the SpeedBar.

When you choose Define Record from the MROs property inspector, Paradox displays a menu with the names of the tables in the dialog's data model. After you select a table, the MRO then contains all the fields in the table (regardless of whether you limited the field selection in the Design Layout dialog box). To create an MRO with select fields, select Define Record from the MRO's property inspector, and click the ellipsis at the top of the menu. Then, from within the Define Multi-Record Object dialog box, select the fields to include by clicking on them from the drop-down list associated with the table (see fig. 10.20).

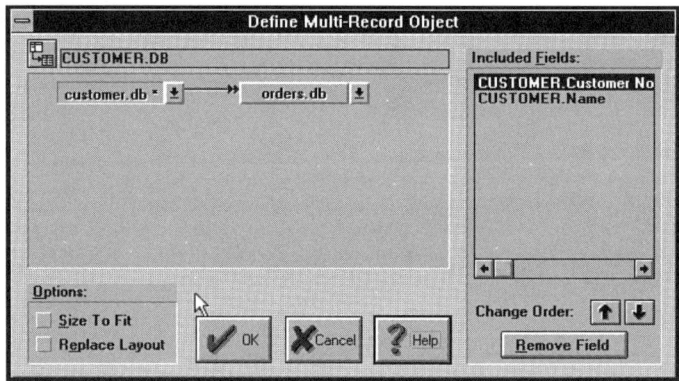

Figure 10.20. The Define Multi-Record Object dialog box.

In the lower left corner of the Create Multi-Record Object dialog box are two check boxes: Size To Fit and Replace Layout. Size To Fit is not relevant to MROs, but Replace Layout enables you to tell Paradox whether you want a newly defined field list and field order to replace an existing one.

If you are working with an 1:M data model, for example, Paradox doesn't allow you to select fields from more than one table when working in the Define Multi-Record Object dialog box. (If the data model is x:1m, there's no problem mixing and matching fields.) The way around this limitation is to first select the fields from the table on the one side, and then modify the MRO to add fields from the second table, *making sure that Replace Layout check box is unmarked*. If you add the fields from the many side of the relationship first and then try to add fields from the one side, the first fields become undefined.

If you check Replace Layout, the existing fields are deleted and the new fields are added. Even if the same fields are used, marking this box causes all ObjectPAL code and any custom properties associated with the existing fields to be unassigned.

The Record Layout dialog box is where you specify how the multiple records get displayed within the overall object (see fig. 10.21).

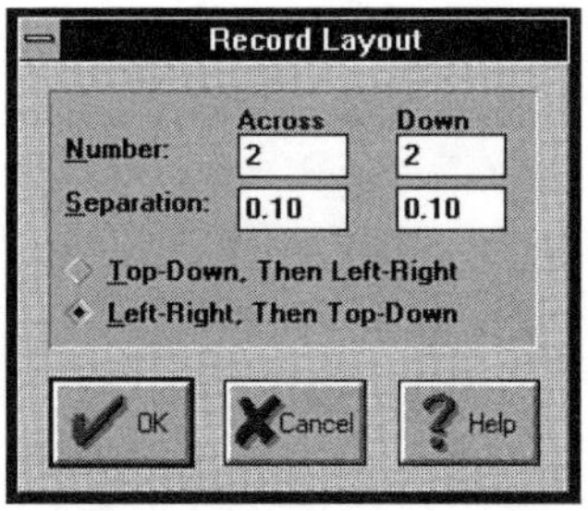

Figure 10.21. The Record Layout dialog box.

The setup in the figure indicates that the records should be displayed in a 2-by-2 grid, two records across and two records down. If more records exist than can be displayed in the indicated rows and columns (four in this case), you have to use the F11 and F12 keys or the VCR buttons to maneuver through them. If the MRO is associated with a detail table, you must first move to the detail and then use either of these techniques to move through the detail records.

The Separation setting indicates the distance between records, measured in inches. Using the settings shown in the figure, tell Paradox whether to place the second record below the first record or to the right of it. The Left-Right, Then Top-Down setting results in the following pattern:

    Record 1   Record 2

    Record 3   Record 4

Checking Top-Down, Then Left-Right, however, displays the records in the following pattern:

    Record 1   Record 3

    Record 2   Record 4

Table Frames

Because you cannot attach any ObjectPAL code to a Table View, table frames contained in forms are the method of choice for performing data entry operations on tabular data. Many issues discussed in the preceding section on MROs are applicable to table frames.

For example, you can select a table from the data model when the Define Table list appears, or you can click the ellipsis to use the Define Table Object dialog box (see fig. 10.22). Replace Layout works the same way with table frames as it works with MROs.

The Size To Fit check box appears in the dialog box for MROs, but has no effect. Here, however it does. If you add fields to the table frame, it grows to accommodate them, with the limitation that it must display on the page. If the table frame adds fields that cause it to exceed the page width, horizontal scroll bars are added. Conversely, the table frame shrinks when fields are deleted.

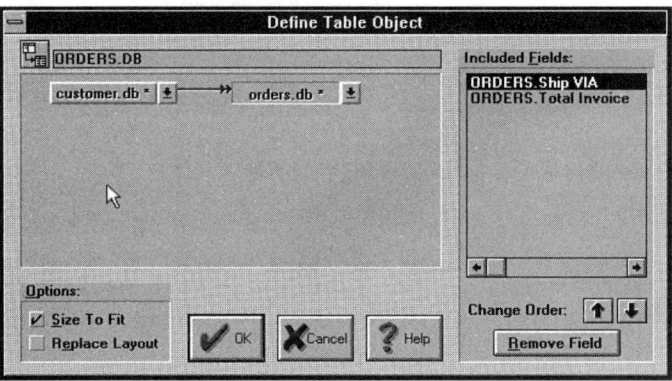

Figure 10.22. The Define Table Object dialog box.

Because the Replace Layout option causes Paradox to lose field properties and code attached to the replaced fields, working directly with the table frame, rather than with the Define Table Object dialog box, often is a better idea. You can resize a file easily by selecting its vertical grid and pulling or pushing it larger or smaller.

Another thing many developers don't realize is that you can use direct manipulation to rearrange fields in a table frame. All you need to do is move the cursor to the topmost grid of the table frame, until it changes to a field icon, and then drag the field to the new position.

Table frames are complex objects, consisting of a grid, multiple fields, and a header with multiple field objects. The header is detachable, which is another property of table frames. After the header is detached, you can either place the header elsewhere on the form or delete it completely.

Graphs

Graphs translate the data points in your table into a pictorial representation. Do not confuse Graphs with Graphic Objects, which are static graphics read from file or the Clipboard; graphs hold data. As with all aspects of form design, Paradox allows tremendous flexibility using graphs. You can create a form that contains nothing but a graph or graphs, or you can display a graphic representation of your data alongside the data. You also have control over nearly every graph component.

After you place a graph on the form, you can inspect it and set properties for the following areas: the x-axis, the y-axis, each individual series, the graph background, and the graph as a whole.

The first item from the Object Inspector that you need to define the graph, which tells Paradox the table to use as the basis for the graph. Here, you can either select one of the tables used in the data model or define your own fields. You can mix and match fields from linked tables, *as long as the fields are linked in an x:1 fashion*.

If you choose to let Paradox create a default graph on a single table, the first field in the table provides the x-axis values. The numeric fields—including Short and Currency—are used as series, with their values displaying along the y-axis. Of course, if you define a graph, you can modify the x- and y-axis fields, as long as you use numeric field types for the y-axis value(s).

Paradox provides three basic graph types, used to represent increasing amounts of information:

- *Tabular graph.* This is the basic graph type. The table is the direct source of its information. The tabular graph doesn't perform analysis or summary on the data.

- *1-D summary graph.* This graph type analyzes one field with respect to one or more other fields. When you choose the y-value button, the summary list becomes available, allowing you to pick the desired summary operation on the selected y-value. If the y-value field is not numeric, the only available summary operator is Count. Numeric field types support Count, Sum, Avg, Min, and Max operators.

- *2-D summary graph.* This graph type adds the capability of grouping your summary information according to the values in a third field. In addition to these general graph types, the following display options exist:

    XYGraph
    2-D Bar
    2-D Stacked Bar
    2-D Rotated Bar
    2-D Area
    2-D Lines
    2-D Columns
    2-D Pie
    3-D Bar
    3-D Stacked Bar
    3-D Rotated Bar
    3-D Area
    3-D Surface
    3-D Pie
    3-D Columns
    3-D Ribbon
    3-D Step

With the Min x values and Max x values property, you specify minimum and maximum values for the graph series. The graph doesn't display less than the minimum number of data points or more than the maximum. With the Options submenu, you toggle on and off the display of the title, the legend, the grid, the axes, and labels. If you want to inspect any of these graph components, they must be displayed in the design window.

The 3-D graphs (except 3-D pie and 3-D columns) have a rotation and elevation property, allowing you to look at the graph from any angle.

If you use a graph in a form or report next to data, the graph respects the data model (see fig. 10.23). Assume that you had a form with the CUSTOMER table and the INVOICE table, linked 1:M. If you had a graph of total sales per invoice, the graph would show only the invoices associated with the current customer.

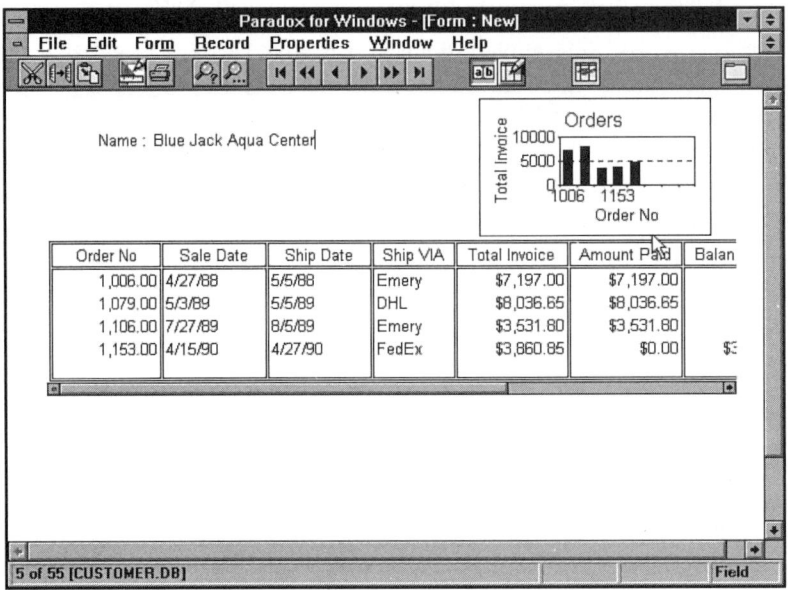

Figure 10.23. A form with an embedded graph, reflecting displayed data.

As you scroll through the table, the graph updates to reflect the data linked to the selected record.

Crosstabs

Crosstabs share many features with graphs. In fact, Paradox internally crosstabulates data before generating a graph. Like graphs, *crosstabs* are composite objects, with many sub-objects, each with their own set of properties. Again like graphs, crosstabs can appear alone on a form or in conjunction with other data. If associated with data, crosstabs take into account data relationships and display only the data points associated with the current record. Another similarity between graphs and crosstabs is the limitation that values can be crosstabbed only within the same table, or across x:1 links.

The Define Crosstab dialog also is similar to the Define Graph dialog (see fig. 10.24).

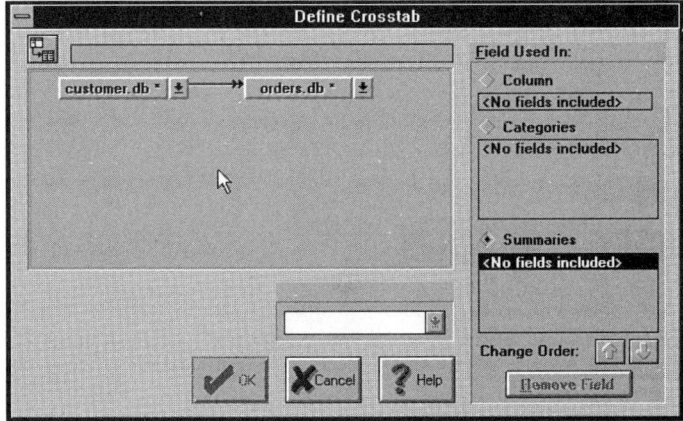

Figure 10.24. The Define Crosstab dialog box.

To generate a crosstab, you need a value in the Column area (to provide the column headers) and you need a summary value (displayed as the data points within the cells). The Define Crosstab dialog box also has an optional Categories area that you use to group the data. The groups, or categories, are displayed down the left side of the screen, and the cells are filled with per column per category information. In other words, a matrix of values is created with column field values shown across the top and category field values displayed down the leftmost column. The first type of crosstab is referred to as a *one-dimensional crosstab*; the crosstab broken into categories is a *two-dimensional crosstab*.

OLE Objects

Chapter 8 visits OLE briefly in its discussion of OLE fields. OLE objects differ from OLE fields in that OLE objects are static objects on the form. OLE objects can be manipulated during form design, but not when the form is running. OLE objects are placed from the Windows Clipboard. The Paradox form designer is an OLE client. This means the form designer can receive OLE objects from an OLE server, which is an application that can generate and work with the OLE object.

The classic example of the OLE server used to serve to the Paradox form designer as client is PaintBrush. If you copy a graphic from PaintBrush to the Clipboard, you can paste it into the OLE object by inspecting the object and selecting Paste.

179

After the object is placed, the name of the OLE server where the object originated is available by inspecting the object and selecting the Define OLE submenu. This menu choice points to a list of verbs or actions supported by the server (Play or Edit). PaintBrush supports only the Edit action, so Edit is what you see under this menu selection. If you choose Edit, PaintBrush is launched, ready for you to make modifications to the OLE object.

Chapter 24 discusses OLE Objects and OLE fields in greater detail.

Form Designer Properties

The previous section in this chapter, "Special Issues for Memo and Formatted Memo Fields," discusses the expanded ruler and the horizontal ruler. Paradox also has a vertical ruler that can be toggled on or off. Besides the horizontal ruler's function for setting tab stops, all the rulers can be used to assist you with the placement of objects on the form.

Perhaps even more helpful for precision placement of objects is the form's grid. You can toggle the grid on or off by using the Properties ¦ Show Grid menu choice. When turned on, Show Grid can be used to place and help align your objects. The Properties ¦ Grid Settings menu selection brings up the Grid Settings dialog box (see fig. 10.25).

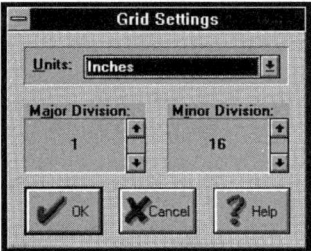

Figure 10.25. The Grid Settings dialog box.

Grid marks can be set by using either inches or centimeters as the unit of measure. The number that displays in the Major Division area indicates the distance, using the unit of measure specified in the units, between the major grids.

After you designate the layout of the grid, you can choose whether to show it by marking or unmarking the Show Grid selection in the Properties menu.

To keep these settings and make them defaults, choose Properties ¦ Form Options ¦ Save Defaults. These grid and ruler settings are saved in the file PDOXWIN.INI, which resides in your Windows directory.

Another set of properties closely related to the preceding form options is *designer properties*. This set impacts some general aspects of how objects behave or look. Choosing Properties ¦ Designer accesses these settings in the Designer Properties dialog box (see fig. 10.26).

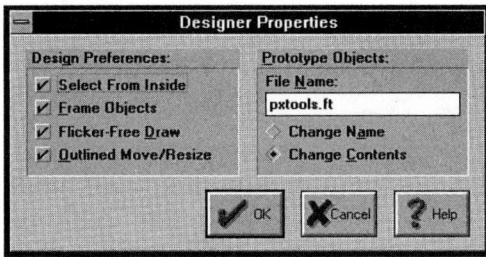

Figure 10.26. The Designer Properties dialog box with default settings displayed.

Check Select From Inside if you want to be able to select an object contained by another object by clicking on the object directly. Subsequent clicks cause objects within the containership hierarchy to be selected from the inside out. The disadvantage of this setting is that you may want to select the larger object to move or just select it. But to select it, you need to click enough times to get to the outermost container. If Select From Inside is not checked, the outermost container is selected first, then the next one in, and so on, so that the number of mouse clicks needed to select an object depends on how many container levels exist above it.

Frame Objects causes a light gray (ghost) frame to appear at the border of each object, regardless of the setting of its frame style. Seeing the frame makes it easier to find the object's boundary when you go to resize it. The best argument for *not* showing the frame is that without the frame the form in design mode more closely represents the form when it runs.

Flicker-Free Draw may or may not make a difference with your screen display. Turning off Flicker-Free Draw is often suggested when screen redraw appears to take too long. With this option turned off, the display is less smooth, but quicker.

Outlined Move/Resize tells Paradox whether to show the entire object as it gets resized or moved, or just its outline. Again, you trade better visuals for speed, because displaying the entire object takes longer than just displaying its outline. If you have a fast video card or fast CPU, the settings for both Outlined Move and Flicker-Free Draw may not make a difference.

All these settings also are saved to the file PDOXWIN.INI in the Windows directory.

The final option in the Designer Properties dialog box allows you to save changed SpeedBar properties to a file. You can change the properties of the SpeedBar in the following two ways:

- You can select an object of the appropriate type (a field, for example) and then select Design CopyToSpeedBar. Any subsequent objects (fields, in this instance) have the same properties as the field used as the prototype.

- You can click the SpeedBar icon with the right mouse button and set the properties there. This approach usually is considered safer because you are explicitly setting the properties you want to change. The other method leaves the possibility open of unintentionally copying more properties than you want to set.

These settings last for the duration of the current Paradox session. To save them permanently, you need to check the Change Contents button in the Designer Properties dialog box. You can create multiple files that contain different SpeedBar settings (all must have an .FT extension), but the file PXTOOLS.FT contains the default settings.

Form Properties

The preceding sections cover the important properties associated with the form designer and with specific design objects. More properties need to be addressed, however—additional properties that belong to the entire form. In contrast to the previous discussion of settings that apply to multiple forms, these properties are specific to the current form. To open the Form Properties dialog box, perform one of the following procedures:

- Choose Properties ¦ Current Object with the form selected.
- Right-click the form's title bar.

Properties ¦ Form allows you access to a subset of the form's properties, so this option is of limited use, given the alternatives.

The combinations of Windows styles are almost staggering, but are critical for large applications that require different combinations of modal and nonmodal dialog boxes and windows. Refer to Chapter 18 for a complete discussion of the form's Windows Properties.

The Horizontal and Vertical Scroll Bar properties are straightforward. When they are checked, the bars appear; the bars do not appear if the properties are not checked.

Not quite so straightforward is the form's Size To Fit property. If you check the form's Size To Fit property, the form always opens to the size of the page, as specified in the Page Layout dialog. Especially if you work with different monitor resolutions, it is possible to create a page larger than your monitor, which can cause problems. For example, when Paradox tries to shift focus to an object that doesn't appear on-screen, the form appears to shift up or to the right to move to an object that can receive focus.

When you set the form's Size To Fit property, you also need to close and reopen the form for this property to take effect; switching from design mode to run mode doesn't cause the window to resize.

Delivered Forms

When you are through designing your form—when all the objects are placed and all the attached code is debugged—you are ready to deliver your forms. To deliver a form, choose Form ¦ Deliver. This command creates a file on disk with the same name as your form, but with an .FDL extension.

Delivered forms are protected from further design changes, which means that the end user cannot modify the form in any way and that no one else can access the code attached to your form. If you are familiar with Paradox for Windows, delivered forms share the same protection as libraries in that product; if you have developed in C++, delivering forms is like doing a *no-debug* make in C++. The delivered form is stored in the form of a Windows DLL.

The delivered file maintains no connection to the original .FSL file. If you make changes to the nondelivered forms that you want to deliver, you need to deliver the form again.

Summary

In this chapter, you learned that nearly everything you do in ObjectPAL, you do through forms. With the exception of occasional stand-alone scripts and libraries, ObjectPAL code is placed on forms. Much of your application's behavior is dictated by your form design. Forms hold UIObjects, which, as the name implies, are those things with which the user interfaces. Understanding these various objects and their ultimate container, the form, is imperative to working with Paradox for Windows.

# 11

Designing and Using Reports

Report design shares many similarities with form design. Most of the UIObjects are identical, and most of the time they operate in the same way, with two notable exceptions:

- No support exists for crosstab objects in reports.
- You cannot attach ObjectPAL code to design objects contained in reports. In fact, if you open an existing form as a report, Paradox strips all ObjectPAL code from the form.

With these two exceptions, if you are comfortable designing forms, you will feel right at home working with reports—especially working with UIObjects in reports. This chapter focuses on the aspects of report design that differ from form design.

Page Layout

As discussed in Chapter 10, the default setting in the Page Layout dialog box for forms is Design For Screen; reports, as output tools, use Printer as the default in the Page Layout dialog box. Figure 11.1 shows the default report Page Layout dialog box. Besides using the printer as the default setting, the report page layout allows you to specify margins.

The predefined sizes are taken from the sizes supported by your selected printer. As with forms, you can choose from one of the predefined paper sizes or define your own custom size. For example, if you are working with mailing labels, or printing on custom forms, you may need to change the page height or width. An example of working with mailing labels occurs later in this chapter.

Your choice between Screen or Printer affects the fonts you can display or use for your document's text objects. Suppose you have a laser printer font, for example, that isn't installed as a screen font. If you design a new form for a printer, you can choose the printer font as a text object font. However, if you change your default printer to one that doesn't support the same font, Paradox may need to substitute fonts supplied by the currently selected printer. TrueType fonts, therefore, are the safest bet when selecting fonts for UIObjects.

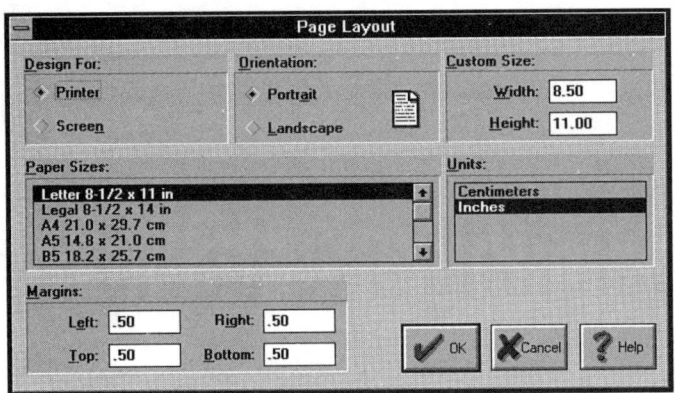

Figure 11.1. The report Page Layout dialog box with default settings.

You can access the Page Layout dialog box in two ways:

- From within the Design Layout dialog box. You see this dialog when you first create a form; you can also access it by selecting Design ¦ Design Layout. From this dialog, click on the Page Layout button.

- From within the report designer, select Report ¦ Page Layout from the menus.

If you modify your page layout so that it can no longer contain all its UIObjects, Paradox offers the option of deleting the offending objects or not modifying the layout.

Report Bands

Paradox uses bands to indicate where text, fields, and other UIObjects should appear in a report. By default, Paradox reports contain three types of bands—Report bands, Page bands, and All Records—each of which appear in pairs. These bands are described in the following list:

Report bands	Contain information that appears only once for the entire report. Objects placed in the report header print once at the beginning of the report; objects placed in the report footer print once at the end of the report.
Page bands	Objects in the Page bands print once per page. Anything in the top page band (page header) prints at the top of each page. Objects in the page footer print at the bottom of each page.
All Records	Almost always where the *meat* of the report resides, and contains the data from the table. In a single record report, everything within this band prints once per record.

The various report areas are shown in figure 11.2.

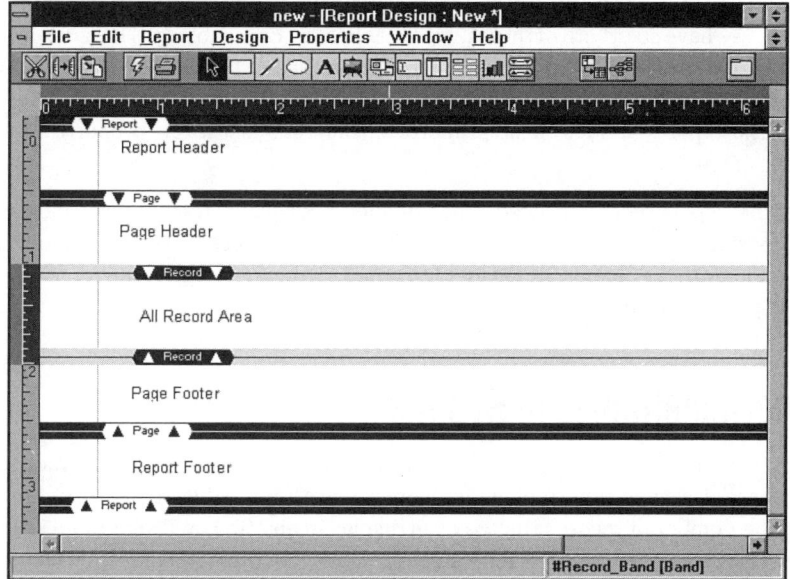

Figure 11.2. A Paradox screen, showing the various report areas.

Group bands are discussed in "Grouping Reports," a following section of this chapter.

There is a property under the report's Property menu called Show Bands. If this property is unchecked, the report bands take up no space on the report designer, which allows you to visualize the report as it appears when printed. It has the disadvantage, however, of making the selection and moving of report bands difficult. Usually, it is advisable to keep Show Bands checked.

Resizing Bands

To resize any of these bands, use the mouse to select and then drag the band either up or down. Each band is displayed with an arrow pointing either up or down (assuming that the Show Bands property is checked). This arrow points to the other report band, which the selected band uses as a reference point. For example, the top Report band points downward, indicating that it moves in relation to the top Page band. The top Page band points downward, telling you that it moves relative to the All Records band, which means that if you want to increase the distance between the Report band and the Page band, pull the Report band *up*. Although you may be tempted to try to pull the Page band down, this action doesn't achieve the desired effect. Because it moves relative to the All Records band, pulling the Page band down will move the Page band closer to the All Records band and does not change the distance between the Report band and the Page band. If other objects exist between the bands, they act as boundaries to the movement of either band.

Report Band Properties

All reports bands, with the exception of the Page Band have two properties in common—Breakable and Shrinkable. We have seen both of these properties before. Breakable tells Paradox whether or not to continue printing the contents of the selected band on the next page if they are too large to fit on the current page. Shrinkable is used to indicate whether or not the object can eat into the white space at the end of the report. Besides these properties, there are just a few properties unique to the different types of bands.

A property of the Report Header, Precede Page Header, is available; this property indicates whether to print the report header before the Page Header. The Page Header band has a property that enables you to tell Paradox whether or not the Header is printed on the first page of the report. This property is appropriately named Print on 1st Page.

MROs and Tableframes in Reports

A few aspects of working with TableFrames and MROs, that are true for forms, are more pertinent to reports. There are also a few important areas where reports behave differently than forms. In a form, for example, the number of records that you can display in an MRO or TableFrame is limited to the size of the currently selected page (or screen if you're designing for the screen), which makes sense because these objects cannot extend across pages. So, if you are working with an MRO that allocates exactly one inch per record and you're working with an 11-inch form, you cannot use a number larger than 11 in the Down box of the Record Layout dialog box (see fig. 11.3).

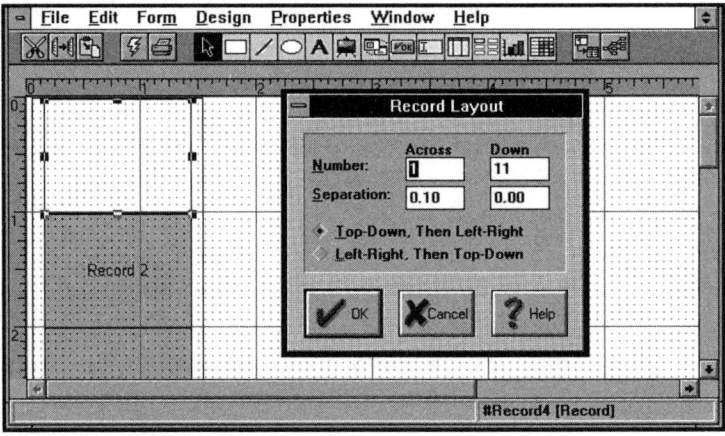

Figure 11.3. The Record Layout dialog box, with Down set to 11.

Reports, by contrast, do not use pages in the same way that forms do. A report grows to accommodate the number of records—you can actually see that the report footer gets pushed down and the "page" grows to fit the number of records. When you run the report, the object spans more than one page if necessary. (If you do uncheck the Breakable property, discussed later in this chapter, you get an error at runtime that tells you that the record band is too large to fit on the page.)

Two additional limitations arise on working with MRO's that, although true for forms, may be more limiting with reports:

- You cannot size individual records smaller than .25 inch.
- You cannot display more than 100 records total within an MRO.

Detach Header

Tableframes, by default, display with a table header. A TableFrame property called Detach Header exists that allows you to place the header anywhere on the report. Specifically, you may want to move the header within a group band (discussed in the following section, "Grouping Reports"), or you may want to delete the header altogether. If the header is detached, it doesn't retain a connection to the table; if you resize, rearrange, or delete fields in the TableFrame, you need to update the header manually to display it correctly.

Show All Records

Tableframes and MROs share a property—Show All Records. Selecting Runtime ¦ Show All Records in a TableFrame causes the TableFrame to expand to accommodate as many records as fit on a page; otherwise, the TableFrame only displays the number of records that the design UIObject allows. Additional records display in new TableFrames, and each contains the fixed number specified in design mode. If you have Show All Records checked and *don't* check the Breakable property, a TableFrame with more records than fit on a page will cause an error.

MROs respond in the same way to the Show All Records property, with one twist: if the layout is Left-Right Then Top-Down, the object expands vertically. If the layout is Top-Down Then Left-Right, the expansion happens horizontally. As you might imagine, this second option can lead to extremely wide pages.

DeleteWhenEmpty

DeleteWhenEmpty is another property of TableFrames that is available only for reports. This property determines whether to delete a record from the report when the fields are blank. DeleteWhenEmpty is available for TableFrames, as well as for the records within TableFrames. For TableFrames, DeleteWhenEmpty tells Paradox not to show the TableFrame if it doesn't contain any records. Although you may have reason to display a header without data, more often than not you do not want to display a lone header. For records, DeleteWhenEmpty tells Paradox not to display the record if the fields included in the TableFrame are all blank, which can happen, for example, if you place a key field value in a group band and display a subset of the records' fields in the TableFrame.

Breakable

Runtime ¦ Breakable is a property of many UIObjects, including TableFrames and MROs, that tells Paradox whether it can break the object over more than one page. With the breakable property checked, the object continues on the next page. With the property unchecked, when the entire object doesn't fit on the current page, it gets sent to the next page; if the object doesn't fit on that page (which means it won't fit on *any* page), Paradox generates an error message telling you that the object is too large and your report does not run.

Shrinkable

The Runtime ¦ Shrinkable property, if checked, overrides the breakable property. Shrinkable tells Paradox to use any white space in the design document if doing so enables the current object to fit on the page. In other words, with both properties set, an object does not break if there is enough white space that Paradox can use to display the object on the current page.

Grouping Reports

Grouping is an extremely important concept when dealing with reports. This feature allows you to group the output on a per salesperson, per state, or per invoice basis. Besides grouping fields with same values, Paradox allows you to group on a specified number of records or range of field values. Groups serve the additional purpose of sorting the report on the group field or fields.

Placing a group band is relatively easy: just click on the Add Band icon in the report designer, or choose Report ¦ Add Band from the menus. After performing either of these procedures, the Define Group dialog box opens (see fig. 11.4).

The two radio buttons, Group By Field Value and Group By Record, allow you to choose the basis for the group. Group By Field Value allows you to select any of the fields in the master table in a x:M linkage. If you want to group on a field from the many side of a 1:M relationship, you need to build the report with the M table as the master. A report linked in an x:1 fashion allows you to link on fields from either table.

After you choose Group By Field Value, the Range Group check box becomes available. This allows you to indicate the number of values of the current field to group together. For example, if you group a numeric field on a range value of 3, records with values of 1-3 in the selected field share a group, 4-6 appear in the next group, 7-9 in the next, and so on. If you select Range Group with a date field the following options display in the associated box: Day, Week, Month, Quarter, and Year. Alphanumeric fields also use a number to indicate the range values. A range group value of 1 tells Paradox to group by the first letter (such as grouping all A's together); a range group of 5 tells Paradox to place all records with the same first five characters in the selected field together. An example might be a telephone number field, with the format (###) ###-####. Specifying a range group of 5 causes records to display grouped by area code.

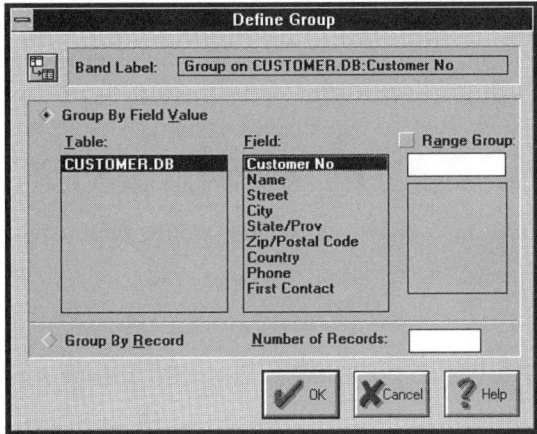

Figure 11.4. The Define Group dialog box.

If you select Group By Record, the Number of Records box is activated, allowing you to specify how many records you want to appear in each group. For example, if you place the number 10 in this box, each group prints with ten records, then inserts a group break.

If you group on a field value, Paradox inserts a space in the group header containing the field value. If you do not want your group to display with the group name, this field can be modified or removed. If you want to use a group for sorting, but don't want to see it in the final report, you just resize the header and footer to have no height.

To delete a group, select the group, then press the Delete key.

Group Band Properties

Group bands have some unique properties. The Define Group item allows you to redefine the field, range or records for the group. Headings enable you to choose whether you want the group header to display just at the top of each group or at the top of each group and at the top of the page. Having the group header display at the top of the page, gives you a phone book-like index, allowing you to see the starting group values for each page.

Finally, group values can be displayed in ascending or descending order.

Adding Calculated and Summary Values

Calculated fields are available for reports as they are available for forms. These fields are placed in the same way—place a field object, select define field, and click on the ellipses to bring up the Define Field dialog box. Summary calculations are sensitive to placement within groups. If you place a count field within a group, for example, the field defaults to counting the values within the group. If, however, you place the calculated field outside the group, it counts overall values. You can override these defaults by selecting a different value from the summary list in the Define Field dialog box. To display a running total within a group, for example, place the unbound field, bring up the Define Field dialog box, and instead of checking Normal under the Summary list, check Cumulative.

You also can include calculated fields with a TableFrame or MRO, to display a calculated field on a per record basis. For example, if you want to display the total for an order based on the quantity and unit price, just fill in the Define Field dialog box as shown in figure 11.5.

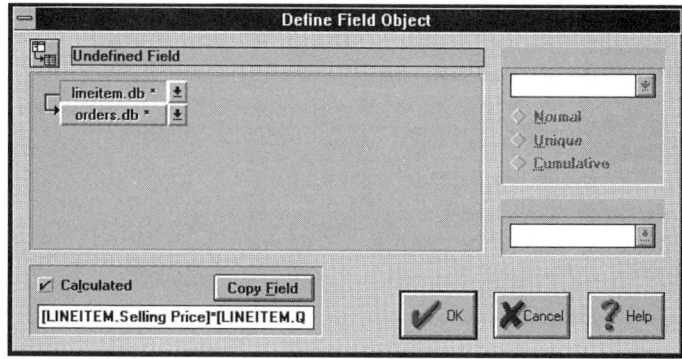

Figure 11.5. The Define Field dialog box, showing a calculated field.

```
(The full calculation is: [Lineitem.Selling Price]*[Lineitem.Quantity].)
```

To place a summary calculated field, place a field object in the appropriate group band. Define this field as calculated, with the following expression: Sum([tablename One])*Sum([table.field Two]). You either can type the expression directly into the Calculated Field area, or you can select the field, define the summary operation so that the correct expression appears in the field description at the top of the dialog box, then press Copy Field to place the expression into the calculated field area. If you need to perform a calculation like Sum([Field One]*[Field Two]), you must perform the calculation in a query, then build your report on the query, which is discussed in a following section, "Using a Query as the Basis of a Report."

Aligning Columns of Totals

A common requirement that frequently throws people is aligning column totals under their columns. To align column totals, place the summary field under the column, turn off the Fit Width property for both the field in the column and the summary field. Select the two field objects using Shift+click and select Design ¦ Align ¦ Right to right-justify both numbers. With Runtime ¦ Fit Width unchecked, the field resizes itself to accommodate the data the field contains. So, even though the field may be right justified within its boundaries, if the total field size shrinks to fit a smaller display, the field will not align correctly relative to other fields.

Page Breaks

If you are generating a form letter, you want only one letter to print on a page, even if the page can accommodate two records. To force a page break, just click the mouse on the well area (the Sidebar) to the left of the vertical ruler. The vertical ruler, of course, needs to be displayed for this to work. A page break marker appears, to indicate the placement of the page break, as shown in figure 11.6.

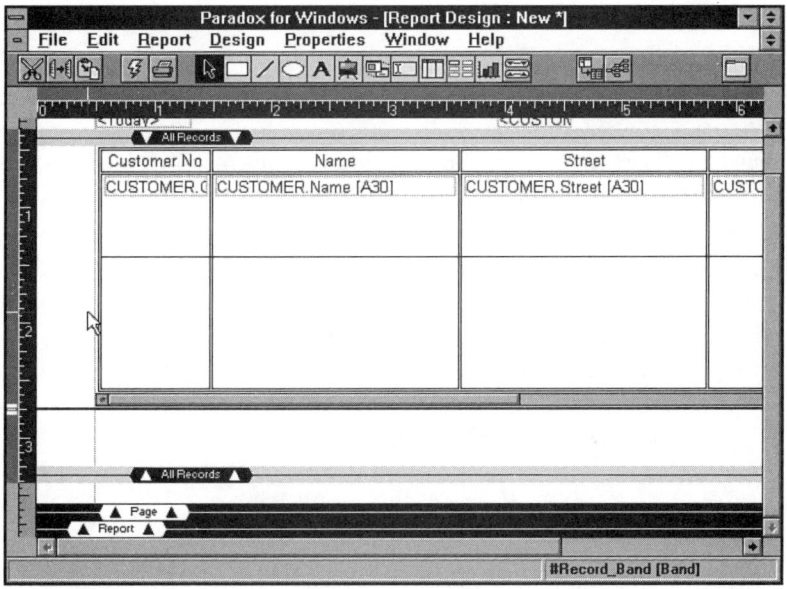

Figure 11.6. A page break marker, indicating the point of the page break.

You can move this marker up or down by clicking and dragging the marker to a new location. The marker, however, cannot be placed in an area occupied by an existing design object. To remove a page break, grab the marker with the mouse and pull it off screen. It helps to think of pulling the marker up or down and to the right of the screen.

Using a Query as the Basis of a Report

Paradox for Windows supports a great deal of sharing of objects: you can open a form as a report, use the data model of a form or report to define query link, and probably most useful, you can attach a report to a query, which is one way to generate a report on a subset of the records in your table—just fill in the query with the desired selection criteria. Reports built on queries also allow you to get around Paradox's inability to perform summary operations on calculated fields; if you do the calculation as part of the query, then the calculated field becomes part of the answer table and is treated as a regular field when you design your report.

When you are presented with the Data Model dialog box for a report, the Types box drops down to give you the option of using tables or queries for the report. You also can mix and match tables and queries in the Data Model. Because the detail table must be keyed, and because Answer tables are not by definition keyed, the query needs to be the master table in a multiple table report.

When you run the report, all selection criteria and field selections in the query are applied (although no actual Answer table is generated).

In addition, any Answer table properties defined in the query are applied. If you specify the sort order for the answer table, for example, the report (absent any overriding groupings) displays in the specified sort order.

This technique of specifying the sort order as a property of the Answer table is a great way to get around the limitation in the report designer of sorting on a calculated field. Perform the calculation in the query, build the report on the query. You can either use the Answer table properties to sort the records or place a group in the report based on the field that results from the calculation.

There are a few aspects of hanging a report on a query that differ from reports built on tables. If you restructure the underlying table used in a report, for example, the report will notice that the fields aren't there and—if you proceed—will open with any references to those fields as undefined. The rest of the report remains intact, including any fields that may have changed position. By contrast, if you delete a field that is used in a query, the query cannot open, and the report built on the query cannot open correctly. Although the report will open and give you the option of attaching it to a different table, all references to the original master table are lost.

Change Table

You can use the Change Table button, available from the Open Document dialog box, to attach the report (or form) to a different table or to a query. All matching field names are used; fields that don't match are deleted from the original document. One particularly handy use for this button is to reuse a report that you designed for a table, on a query. Suppose that you already customized a report for the entire table, and then decide after the fact that you want to use the report for a subset of the records. Just create and then save a query with the selection criteria, and use the new query as the new master for the report. From then on, you can modify the query at will and generate the report on the records the query retrieves.

Mailing Labels

As with most database applications on the market, mailing labels are easy to do, after you learn the idiosyncrasies of the particular product. The MRO serves for mailing labels. The size of the label is defined by the size of the record object. For one 1-by-4-inch mailing label, make your MRO an inch high and four inches wide. Remember, however, that the MRO includes both the field area and the inter-record spacing, so if the labels are actually 7/8 inch with 1/8 between labels, make the MRO 1 inch high, and the record area 7/8 inch high. You have the vertical and horizontal rulers to help you place these objects; you also have the Resizing indicator in the lower left status area. This indicator displays the precise dimensions of the object you resize and the exact coordinates as you move it.

If your labels are contained on a page with a margin, it is important that you set the margins correctly in the Page Layout dialog box. Make sure that you delete all white space outside the All Records band—including removing the default page and date fields in the page header.

Finally, if you have any lines in your label report that may not exist for each record (Address2 or Title, for example), you need to enclose all the fields in a text box, then turn on the text box's Line Squeeze property.

Mail Merge

Mail merge documents are easy to create by using Paradox reports. The only trick to making these documents work is to enclose the text *and fields* in a text box. Setting the Field Squeeze property to On causes the values from the fields to merge seamlessly with the text of the report.

Quick Reporting on a Table

The Quick Report SpeedBar prints a basic report for the currently displayed table. One useful application of the Quick Report is to generate a *quick and dirty* print out a table's structure. You can get the information on the fields and table properties of a table by selecting Info Structure from the Utilities menu. The result is a table named STRUCT.DB. With the STRUCT table open in table view, click the Quick Report icon to produce the report.

If you use the Properties ¦ Preferred menu selection to define a preferred report for the table, Paradox uses the Preferred Report to print the Quick Report. (The same holds true for the Preferred Form, Crosstab, and Graph.)

Report Restart Options

If you are working in a multi-user environment, data may be changed while you are generating a report. Paradox enables you to indicate how changes made by other users are reflected in your output. These options can be set from the Report ¦ Restart Options while you are designing a report.

- *Restart report if data changes*. This option tells Paradox to regenerate the report if any changes occur in the data. This selection ensures that your report is an exact representation of the data *at the time the report was produced* and allows other users editing the table complete access. The drawback is that, if a lot of editing activity is occurring on the table, the report may take an unacceptably long time to complete.

- *Lock tables to prevent changes*. This selection favors the person generating the report at the expense of other users. After the report begins, other users cannot modify the table until the report is complete. Conversely, Paradox needs to be able to place the lock, which it cannot do if another user has a Record lock, Write lock, or Exclusive lock on the table already.

- *Lock and copy tables, run from copies*. This option is the default. Behaves like the previous option, but locks the only table long enough to copy it to another temporary table. This selection then releases the lock immediately, so that it is available to other users more quickly.

- *Ignore data changes and continue*. Paradox doesn't care if data changes while the report is running, which leaves open the possibility of producing a report with less than accurate results. If you are looking only for ballpark information or if you are reporting on a set of records that doesn't intersect with the set of records currently being edited, this option is fastest.

Reporting to a File

Paradox for Windows does not have a built-in *report to file* feature. Besides the possibility of simply exporting the data to an ASCII file, there is a way to print to a file. Printing to file prints only the most basic components of your report, because the file will support only ASCII text.

First, go into the Control Panel and make sure that the Generic/Text Only printer driver is installed and connected to the device FILE. If you don't know how to perform this procedure, refer to the documentation supplied with your Windows software.

From Paradox, select the Generic/Text Only print driver in File|Print Setup. Print the report. The print driver eventually prompts you for a file name before writing the file. All graphics, including object frames are removed from the report.

Using Variables in Reports

Using a variable within a report is a common requirement. You may want, for example, to prompt the user for a value and then display the value in the report. Some simple ObjectPAL code is required to perform this process. The process involves putting the report in design mode just long enough to assign the value of the variable to a text object, as detailed in the following code (which you may want to attach to a pushbutton):

```
var
    rept    report
    varval    string
endvar
varval.view("Enter the new value")
rept.load("YOURREPT.RSL")
rept.textfield=varval
rept.save()
rept.run()
```

If you want to load the report without the user seeing the report going into design mode, use the following line of code:

```
rept.load("YOURREPT.RSL",WinStyleHidden)
```

The WinStyleHidden constant makes the report design window invisible.

Summary

The Paradox for Windows report writer provides you with a powerful tool for data output. In addition to standard report output, you can easily generate mailing labels, mail merge documents, and other highly customized types of output. By appropriately using the various report bands, you can carefully control where each object is printed on your report.

12

Using Query By Example

Query By Example (QBE) was always one of Paradox's most shining features. This feature truly represents the famous Paradox claim—ease of use yet powerful data management capabilities. Luckily, the same intuitive and graphical query definition system was brought over from the DOS version of Paradox to Paradox for Windows. Only minor modifications were made to make QBE look and feel more like a Windows application and to provide some new functionality.

This chapter uses many examples to present some of the more sophisticated capabilities of QBE. The authors assume that the reader has a basic understanding of constructing queries in Paradox using QBE. This chapter does not address using queries in ObjectPAL; please refer to Chapter 21 for a discussion of using QBE files in ObjectPAL. Examples are developed by using the sample tables that come with Paradox for Windows. You begin by examining some of the new query features found in Paradox for Windows.

Creating Queries Using Data Models

To access Paradox's QBE facility, right-click the Open Query icon on the Desktop SpeedBar and select New, or pull down the File menu, and then choose New ¦ Query. You see the Select File dialog box, filtered to show only Tables. However, you can base a new query on items other than tables. If you click on the Types drop-down list in the dialog box, you can select from Tables, Forms, Reports, or other Queries on which to base the new query.

If you already established a data model on a Form, Report, or Query, you can save time in constructing a query by letting Paradox use the tables and links established by the data model. The Select File dialog box also has the Data Model icon, next to the Browse button, to let you create a new data model. When you click this icon, you see the Data Model dialog, which was discussed in detail in Chapter 9. From this dialog box, you can quickly select and link the tables you want to use in your query (see fig. 12.1).

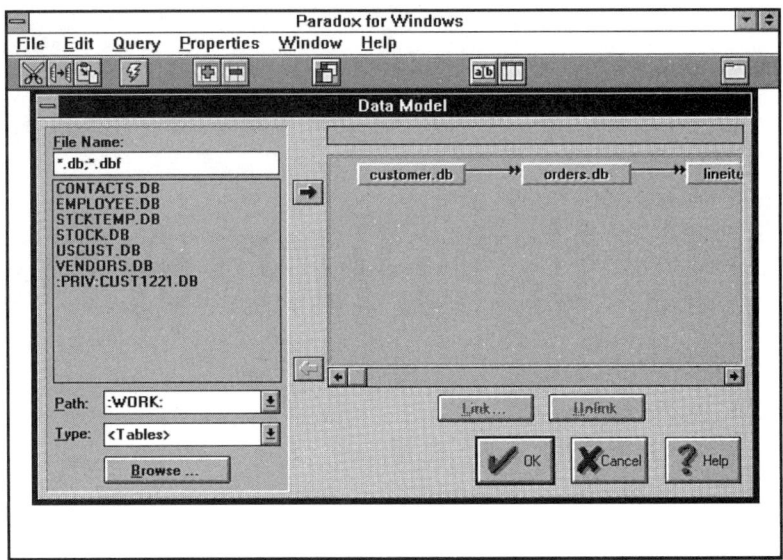

Figure 12.1. The Data Model dialog box.

This data model creates a 1:M:M (One to Many to Many) relationship between Customer, Orders, and the line item tables. Using this data model results in the query being automatically filled in (see fig. 12.2).

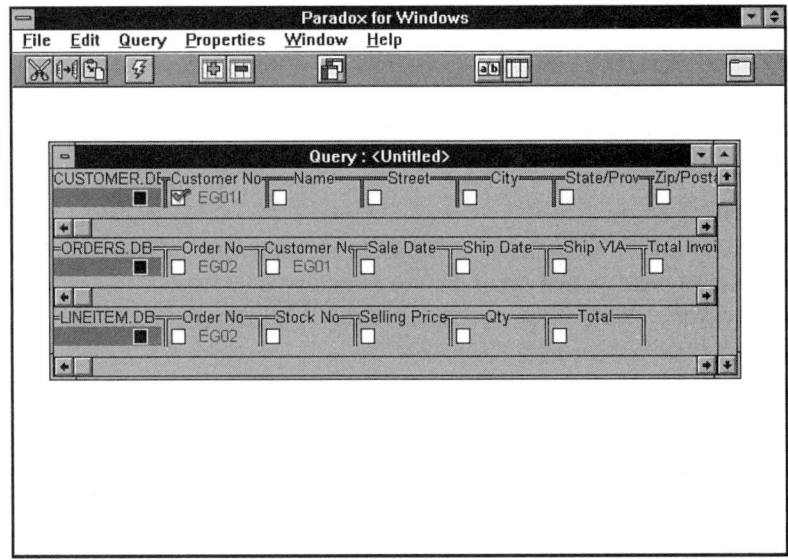

Figure 12.2. The default Query from a data model.

Paradox has placed only one check mark in the first field to make this a valid query if run. Notice that, within the Data Model, the query automatically placed linking example elements in the fields linked on. Another important change that Paradox automatically included is the *inclusion operator* (!) after the first example element in the Customer table. Paradox calculated from the Data Model that the Customer table has a 1:M (One to Many) Foreign Key relationship with the Orders table, which basically means that customers can exist in the Customer table that have not placed orders. Because by default Paradox doesn't include records in an Answer table that have no matching value in all linked tables, the inclusion operator was included to add Customer records in the Answer table, even if these customers have placed no orders. Inclusion operators is covered in detail in a following section of this chapter.

Answer Table Properties

Before executing a query, Paradox allows you to control certain properties of the Answer table. If you click on the Answer Table Properties icon, or select Properties ¦ Answer Table ¦ Options from the menu, the dialog box shown in figure 12.3 appears.

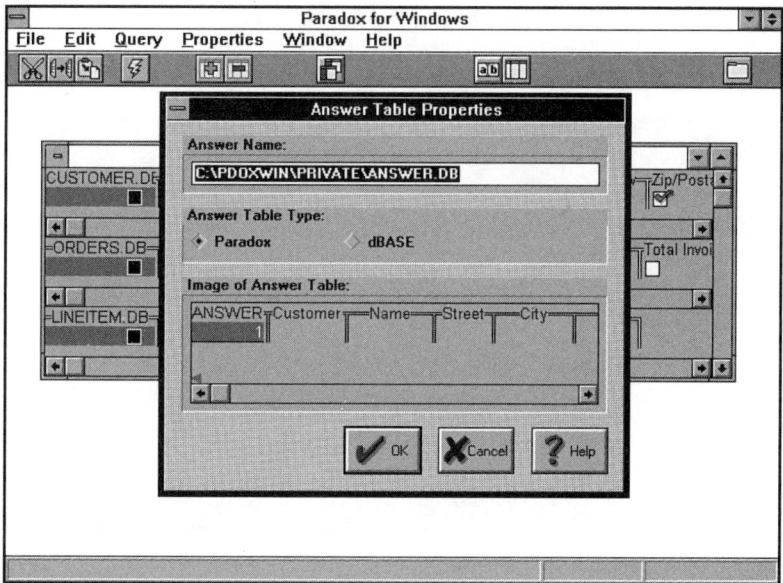

Figure 12.3. Answer Table Properties dialog box.

This dialog box allows you to save the Answer table under a different name. This enhancement may not, at first glance, seem major. However, what this means is that gone are the days of DOS Paradox running a query, copying a report from a report holding table to the Answer table, and then running the report. This change is an unfortunate necessity because Answer tables are only temporary tables that are overwritten the next time a query is performed. Answer tables also are deleted at the end of a Paradox session. You now can create a report based on the renamed Answer table and this report is not lost the next time you run the query.

This dialog box also enables you to create the table as a Paradox for Windows or a dBASE table. Using the Image of Answer Table section, you can define the properties of the table, like changing field fonts and colors, or rearranging the order of fields. You can set properties for the column headings, field values, and the table grid. Just as with any other table, these properties are saved in a Tablename.TV (Table View) file. This table displays only the fields that were check marked in the query.

Sorting the Answer Table

You can specify the order that records are displayed in an Answer table by using the Sort Answer Dialog box. Selecting the Properties ¦ Answer Table ¦ Sort option from the menu displays the Sort Answer dialog box (see fig. 12.4).

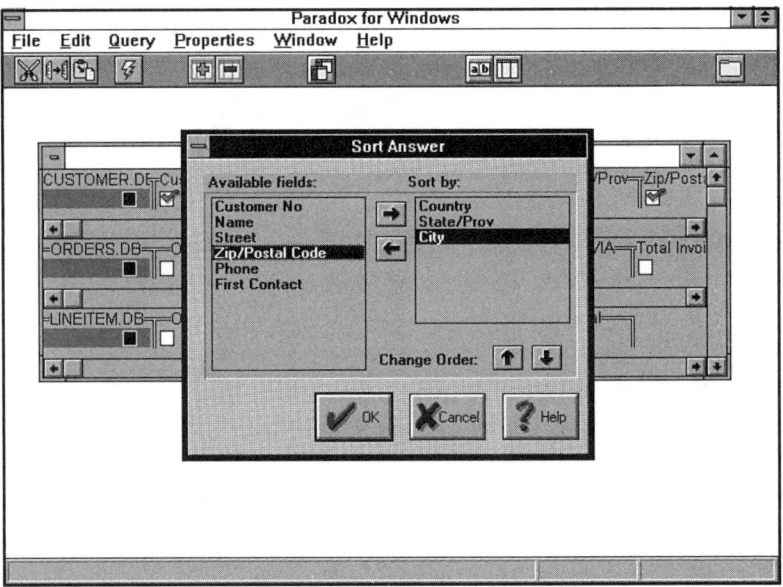

Figure 12.4. Sort Answer dialog box.

By default, queries that use Check marks sort the records of the Answer table according to the order of the fields of the Answer table. To specify a different sort order simply select the fields in the order you want them sorted in the Sort Answer dialog box. The above example sorts the records first by Country, and then within Country by State/Prov, and then within State/Prov by City. If you want to sort in a descending sequence, first place a CheckDescending mark in the field of the query and then specify that field in the Sort Answer dialog box.

Example Elements

Example elements serve several functions in Paradox queries. These elements enable you to join tables together on fields with common data, perform calculations on data, insert data from one table to another, and represent values so you can ask a variety of questions. You can place example elements in one of three different ways:

- Press the F5 key and type a value.
- Press the underline character and type a value.
- Click the Join table icon and then click in the field where you want to place the value.

Each of these methods displays the typed value in red highlight. If you choose the last method, Paradox enters a default numbered value that is sequenced each time you click the icon—in other words, EG01, EG02, EG03, and so on. This method is convenient for linking together tables because you can click on multiple fields of different tables and place the same example element. This is the same method of placing example elements for new queries based on a data model, as seen above in figure 12.2. However, many designers prefer entering their own example element values that can be mnemonic values that more readily identify the link, and possibly the data type of the field in which the element is placed.

Using Example Elements in Search Conditions

Example elements can be used to represent values in records that meet a search condition. You then can use these elements to display the results of the query. Suppose that you want to find all Vendors that manufacture stock items in the Equipment Class of Tools (see fig. 12.5).

Three Vendors manufacture stock items in the Equipment Class Tools. The first line of the query uses the search condition Tools in the Equipment Class field. The results of this search condition are represented by the example element placed in the Vendor No field. The next line of the query defines a new search condition by using the example element from the first line. The resulting Answer table also shows additional Equipment Class items made by the three vendors because the Equipment Class field also is checked.

You can use this same technique to define a range of values. Suppose that you want to find all Orders that have a Total Invoice greater than the order placed by Customer No 1221 on 4/3/88, which was for $7,320.00 (see fig. 12.6).

203

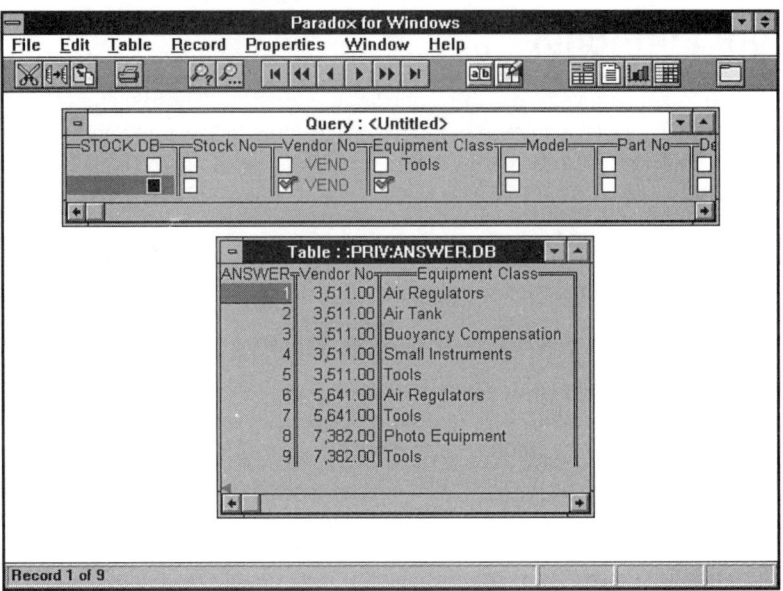

Figure 12.5. An example element in search condition.

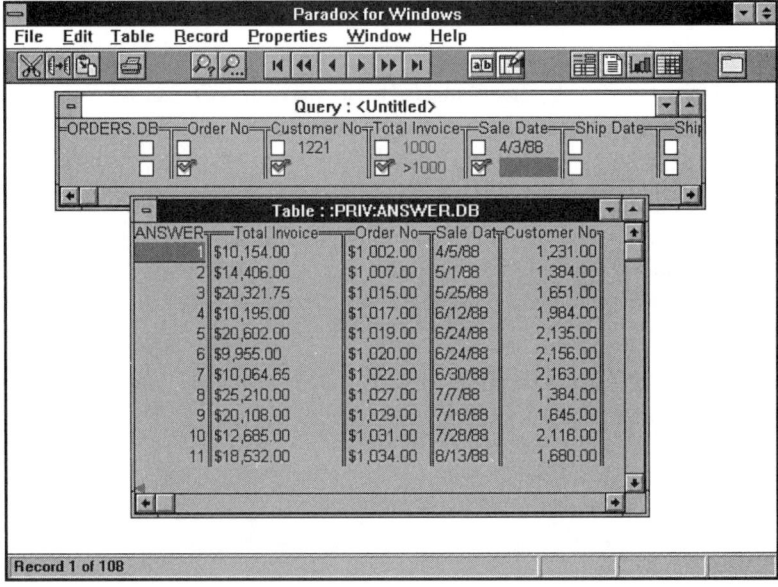

Figure 12.6. An example element in range search condition.

In this example, using a range operator in the second line works best if the search condition on the first line returns only one value. Note that the query will run if the first line returns more than one value, but the results may not be what you expect because the example element represents the last value found in the table that meets the search condition. In the preceding example, if the Sale Date criteria is omitted, the first line example element represents the last order placed by Customer No. 1221, which was $350.00.

Using Example Elements in Calculations

Example elements can be used in calculations using the *calc query operator*. A query that uses example elements in a calculation creates a new field in the Answer table that stores the results of the calculation. Suppose that you want to see the actual order prices as opposed to suggested list prices (see fig. 12.7).

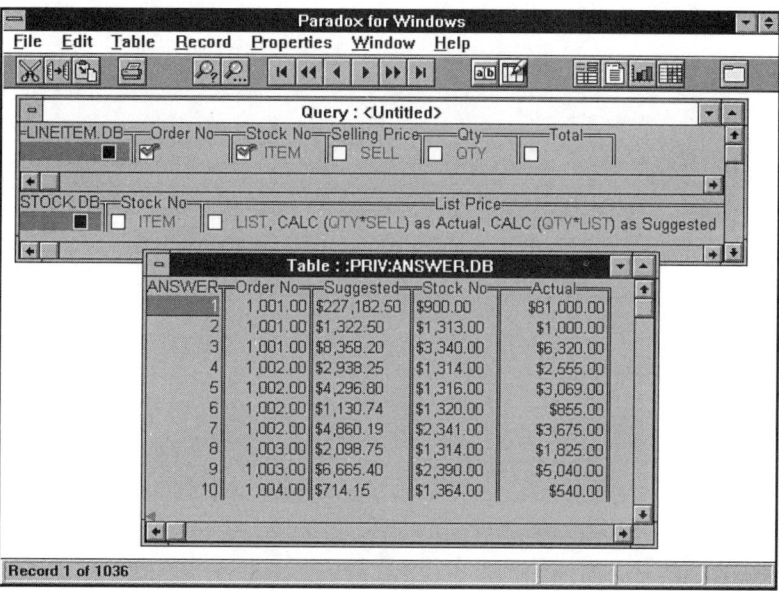

Figure 12.7. Using example elements in calculations.

This example uses several example elements. The ITEM example element in the Stock No field serves to link the two tables together. ITEM basically says, "Take the values in the Stock No table of the line item table and match them up to the same values in the Stock table." The other example elements are used in the two *calc* operations. Here, you are using the same QTY element in both calculations. Both calculations are entered into the same field, but they could have been entered in different fields. The query operator *as* allows you to give your own name to the field displayed in the Answer table.

Example elements also can be used to combine alphanumeric fields by using the (+) *concatenation operator*. You can combine the elements with literal strings at the same time. To combine the stock item's Model and Part No fields, for example, you could do something like the example in figure 12.8.

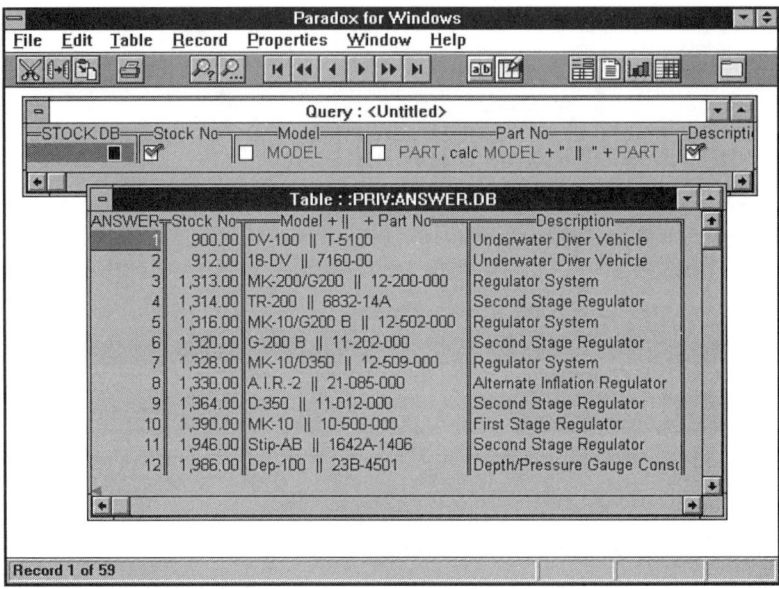

Figure 12.8. Concatenating fields with example elements.

This query allowed you to quickly create a new field that combines two fields together and separates them with the double bar mark, entered as a literal string between two quotes. Concatenating fields together using example elements is commonly used with Insert queries, as can be seen in the following example.

Using Example Elements in Insert Queries

Paradox enables you to copy data from one table to another by using an Insert query. To perform an insert query, you need to place example elements in the like fields of the two tables (see fig. 12.9). In the record number column, under the table name of the query form into which you want to have the values copied, click and hold the left mouse button. A drop-down menu appears with Insert as one of the choices. The next example queries for customers from the U.S.A. and copies certain fields meeting that criteria into a different table.

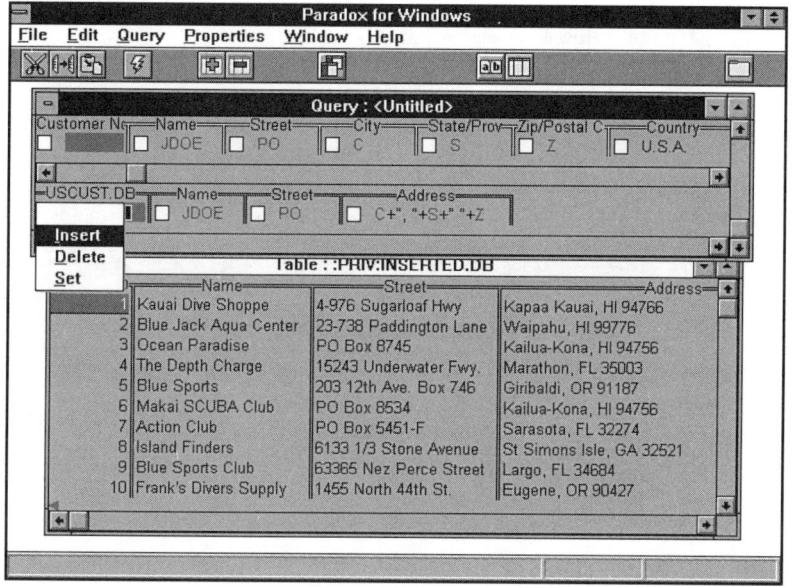

Figure 12.9. An Insert query.

Insert queries are useful for copying data between tables with incompatible structures. Unfortunately, you cannot use this technique to copy data from any of the Paradox extended field types of Memo, Formatted Memo, Blob, Graphic, or OLE. Notice that the table displayed as the result of the query is not an Answer table, but rather a table, named Inserted. This table holds all the records that were inserted into the table and is a safeguard table that allows you to undo the Insert query by performing a File ¦ Utilities ¦ Subtract from the Desktop menu.

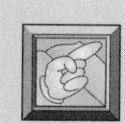 **Note:** Records not passing any Referential Integrity rules defined for the target table are put into the table, ErrorIns. Records not passing any Validity Checks, except Pictures, are put into the table, Problems.

Example Elements in ChangeTo Queries

Another flexible way of modifying data in tables is to use the ChangeTo query operator. When combined with example elements that represent field values, ChangeTo can make wholesale changes to selected records. Suppose that your Scuba Professionals vendor increased prices by 15 percent, and you need to update all of your stock items accordingly (see fig. 12.10).

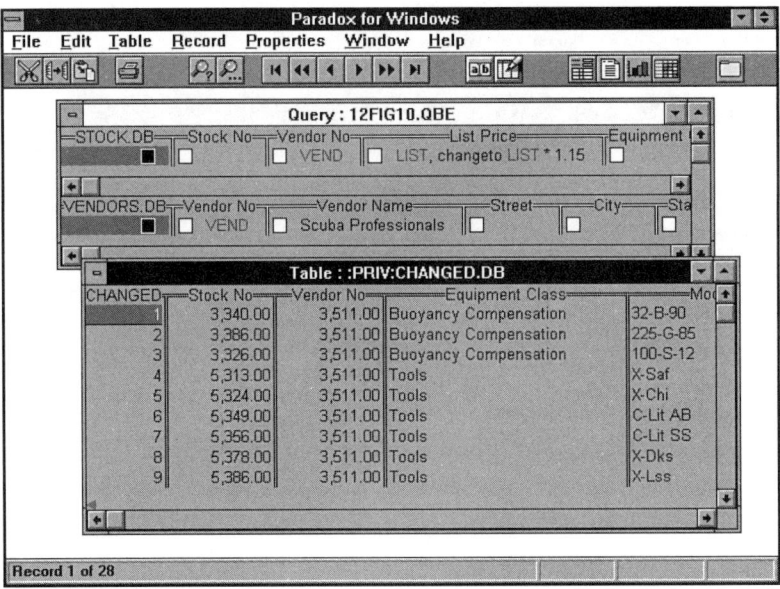

Figure 12.10. A ChangeTo query.

Similar to the Insert query, a ChangeTo query doesn't produce an Answer table. Rather, it creates the table, Changed, which again is a safeguard in case you need to undo the changes just made. The Changed table, like Inserted and Deleted tables, is a temporary table stored in the Private working directory and is automatically deleted when you exit Paradox.

Delete Queries

A new feature of Paradox for Windows is the Cascading Update capability, established when defining Referential Integrity on a table. This feature propagates changes to the key field values of a master table automatically to any detail tables. Unfortunately, no corresponding Cascading Delete feature exists. To perform Cascading Deletes you need to execute a series of Delete queries. If you try to delete records from a table declared as a Parent table in a Referential Integrity (a table that still has child records), Paradox creates the table, ErrorDel (see fig. 12.11).

The example in Figure 12.12 is trying to delete all the orders of customers from the British Virgin Islands. This query fails because a Referential Integrity constraint exists on the Orders table that does not allow deletes when line item detail records are associated with it. Before performing the previous query, you need to delete the line items.

Chapter 12 ■ Using Query By Example

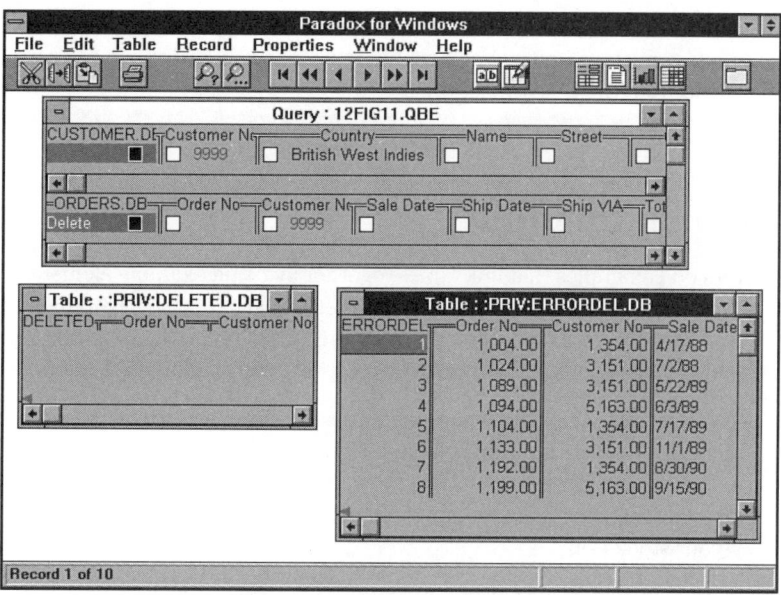

Figure 12.11. The ErrorDel table.

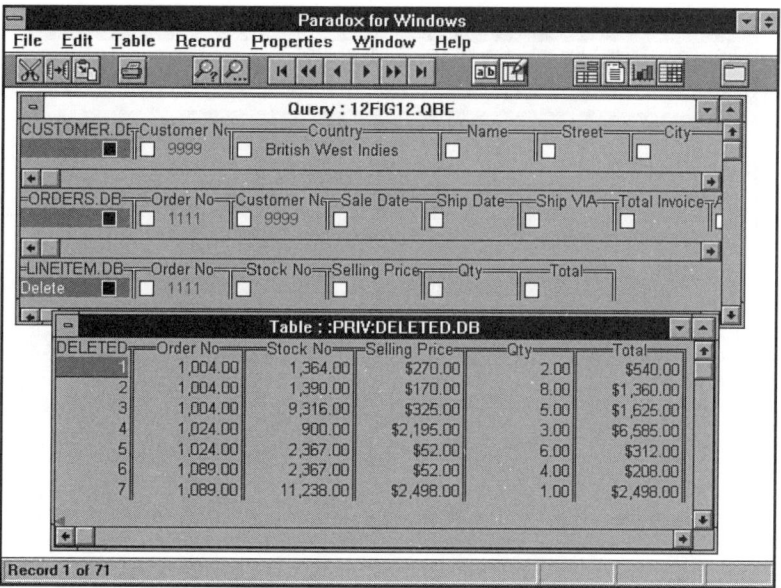

Figure 12.12. A Delete query.

Notice that just like Insert and ChangeTo queries Delete queries do not result in an Answer Table. If you made a mistake and deleted the wrong records, you can simply restore them doing Files ¦ Utilities ¦ Add from the Desktop menu.

The Inclusion Operator

You have seen several examples that link tables together by using example elements. Linking tables, also known as *joining*, is a fundamental function of relational databases. By default, Paradox treats tables linked together with example elements such as *Exclusive Links*, or *inner Join*. This kind of join only retrieves records if matching values existed between the linked fields of the table.

To include records even if there are no matching values, Paradox provides the Inclusion Operator (!). By including this operator with example elements in a query, Paradox creates *Inclusive Links*, or *outer joins*, which return all records in the table that contain an inclusion operator, even if no matching values exist. Suppose that you want a list of all vendors, even if they are not currently being used to supply your stock items.

This kind of query is known as an *Asymmetrical* outer join (see fig. 12.13). A *Symmetrical* outer join (see fig. 12.14) also can be created by including the Inclusion Operator with both of the example elements in a link.

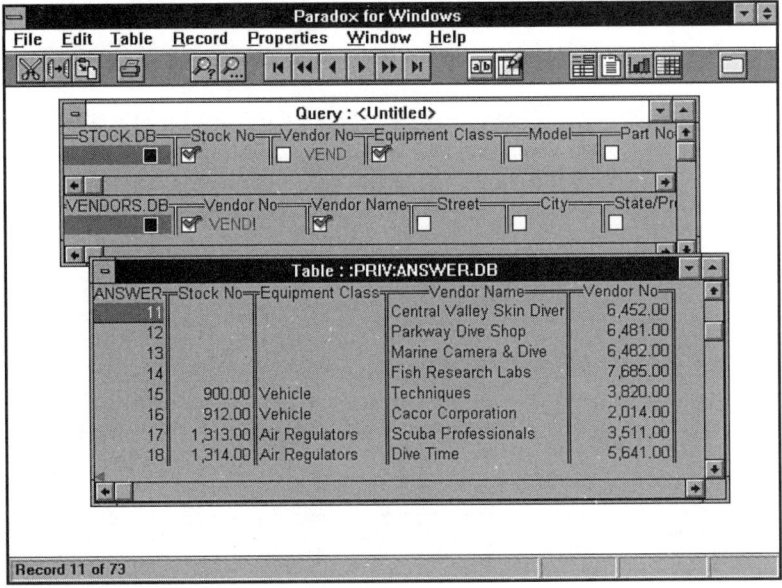

Figure 12.13. An Asymmetrical outer join.

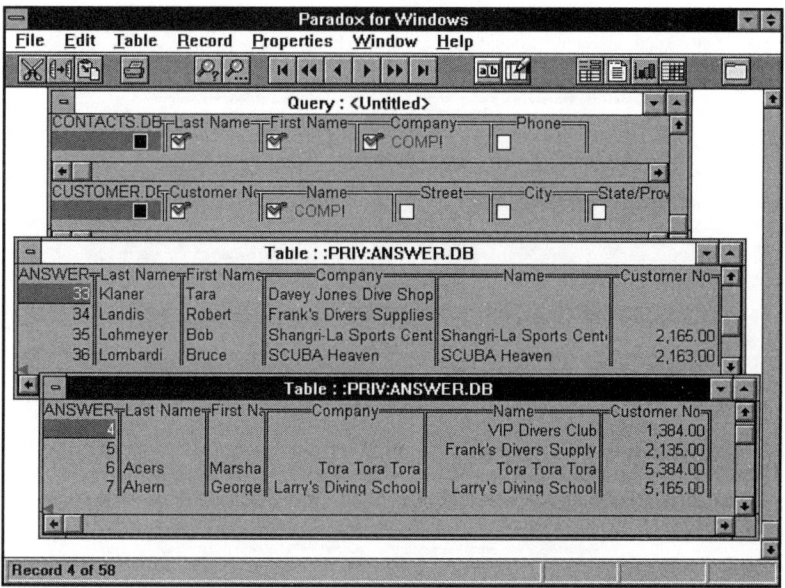

Figure 12.14. A Symmetrical outer join.

This query shows all customers that have no matching contacts, and all contacts that have no matching customers, plus all customers that do match. The same Answer table is displayed in two windows to help demonstrate. Inclusive linked queries are a good way of finding records that do not have matches in another table. Unfortunately, these queries have a side effect of also displaying the records that match. But, with the help of the Count group operator you can avoid this problem (see fig. 12.15).

The Inclusive link defines all the vendors, even vendors that do not have matching records in the stock table. The *count=0* group operator counts vendors that equal zero in the stock table, that is vendors that do not appear in stock.

Both Inclusive and Exclusive links can be combined in one query. Suppose that you want to show all customers with an outstanding balance due greater than zero, who ordered items in quantities larger than 20, and list all orders that have order items in quantities greater than 20 (see fig. 12.16).

This query first shows all orders that have a line item quantity greater than 20, and then those customers with balance dues greater than zero and a line item greater than 20. Now, suppose that besides the preceding search requirements, you want to include all customers that have an outstanding balance greater than zero, even if the items ordered have been for quantities less than zero.

The only difference between figure 12.17 and the query to the previous one is that the Inclusive link (!) also was placed on the query line of the Order table, which has the selection condition of a balance due greater than zero.

Figure 12.15. The Count = 0 query, or the Not-In query.

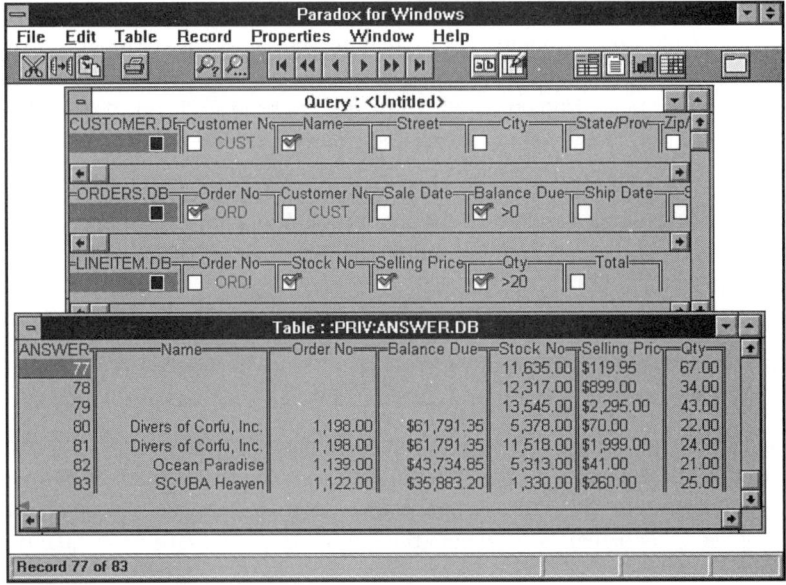

Figure 12.16. Inclusive and Exclusive links.

Chapter 12 ■ Using Query By Example

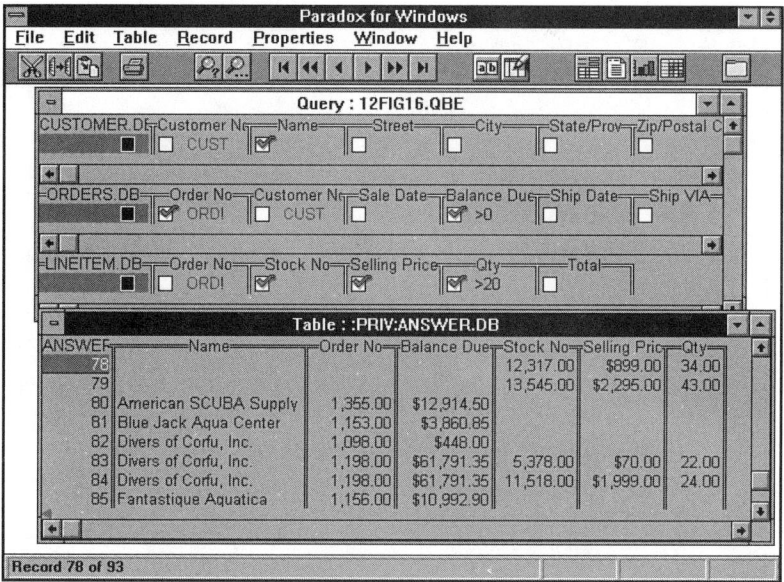

Figure 12.17. Double Inclusive link query.

You can use Inclusive and Exclusive links in the same query as long as you follow one rule: *For any two linked lines of a query you can use either an Inclusive link or an Exclusive link but you can't use both.*

You can use the inclusion operator (!) with any example element only once per line and twice per query, which means you can use only one type of link to join any two lines in a query. When developing Inclusive link queries with many tables, you probably will run up against this limitation of being able to use the Inclusive links with example elements only if there are no more than two of these example elements. The query in figure 12.18 shows one way of working around this limitation.

This example shows all customers that have balance dues greater than zero or have sale dates greater than 1/1/91, plus any customers that do no fall in that classification. Because this is an "or" type of query you need to link tables together using both lines of the Order table. Because an Inclusive link cannot be placed on example elements that occur more than twice you create different example elements for the multiline linking needs.

When processing queries that involve multiple types of links Paradox follows the same rules to guarantee consistency. If a query involves both Inclusive and Exclusive links Paradox processes in order of least to most inclusive, which means that Paradox first processes all Exclusive links, then Asymmetrical Inclusive, and finally Symmetrical links.

213

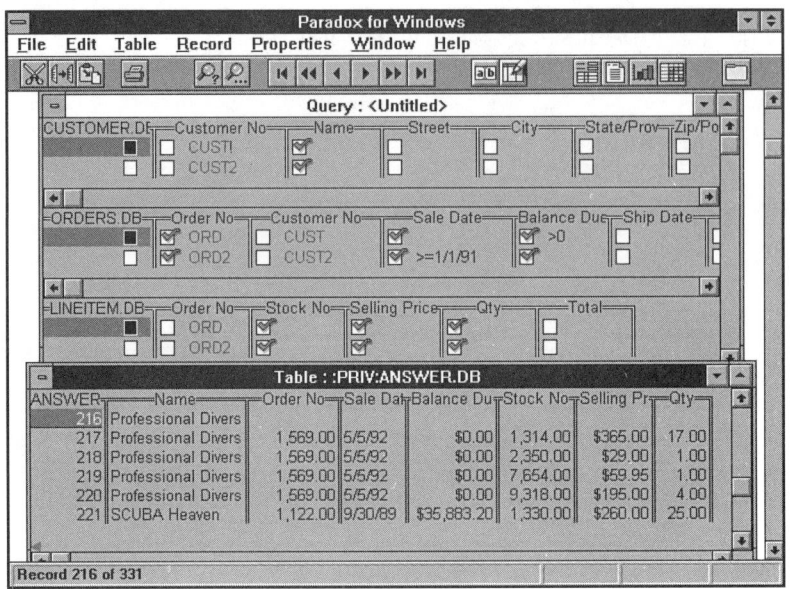

Figure 12.18. Multiline Inclusive Link query.

Set Queries

Set queries are a powerful analysis tool in Paradox that enables you to define one set of records and then compare the set to another set of records. You define a set of records by selecting Set from the drop-down list of choices you get when clicking on the first column of a query image, and then you define the search condition. The search condition identifies the set of records you want to use in the comparison. Defining the group of records to compare the set to is done by placing Check marks in fields, on a different query line than the Set definition.

Comparisons can be done in several ways. One method involves using group summary operators. The following example uses the *average* group operator to find all orders with Total invoices greater than the average Total invoice of Orders paid by using a Visa card, which is $12,793.22.

The first line of the query in figure 12.19 defines the set of orders paid by Visa. The second line uses Check marks to define the group to compare to, which is basically all orders. The example element in the Total Invoice field on the first line represents all the values defined by the set of records. The second line then uses this example element to assign the grouping records a greater than average Total Invoice representation.

Chapter 12 ■ Using Query By Example

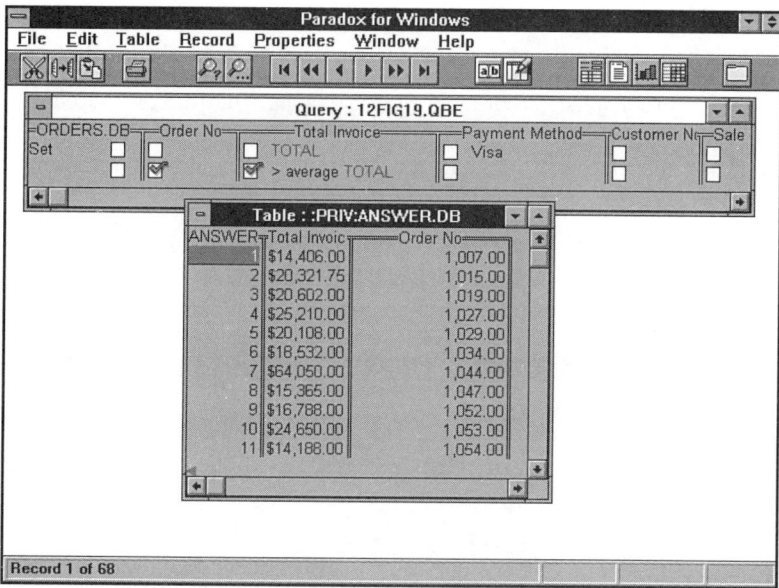

Figure 12.19. A set query with group summary operators.

Set queries often involve comparisons between multiple tables. When defining set queries between several tables, example elements are used in conjunction with special set operators to define the link and the type of comparison.

This query in figure 12.20 first defines the set of stock items that belong to the Tools Equipment Class, then defines the group of line item orders with a Check mark in the Order No field. By using the example element in the Stock No field, you now can compare the two sets of records on the values of that field. In this case you are using the set comparison operator *Only* to define a special comparison. The Only operator says find orders in which only line items for Tools have been purchased.

Three other set comparison operators can be used in the same way, No, Every, and Exactly. In the context of the preceding example, each of the set operators is interpreted as:

- *Only*. Find all orders that have line items that contain *only* stock items in the Tools category. The tools category is the set and line items is the subset. Each line item per order must exist in the tools category, but not all items in the tools category have to be in each order's line items.

215

- *No.* Find all orders that have line items that contain *no* stock items in the Tools category. Each order's line items must have nothing in common with the Tools category.

- *Every.* Find all orders placed that have *every* stock item of the Tools category, even if there are more line items with different categories. Line items are the set and the tools category is the subset. Every tools category item must exist in each order's set of line items.

- *Exactly.* Find all orders that have *every* stock item in the Tools category and *only* stock items in the Tools category. Exactly combines the *every* and *only* operators. In other words, the tools category set is exactly equal to the list of stock items per order. Each order's set of stock items must exactly match the tools category.

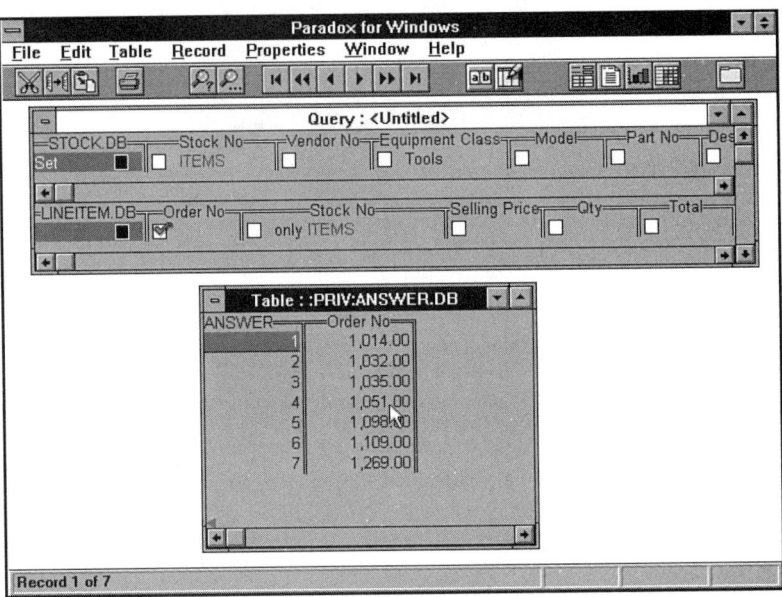

Figure 12.20. An Only set query.

The set diagram in figure 12.21 helps explain these set relationships.

Suppose that you want a list of all customer names that placed orders for every type of vehicle in stock. You would need to construct a query using the *every* set operator (see fig. 12.22).

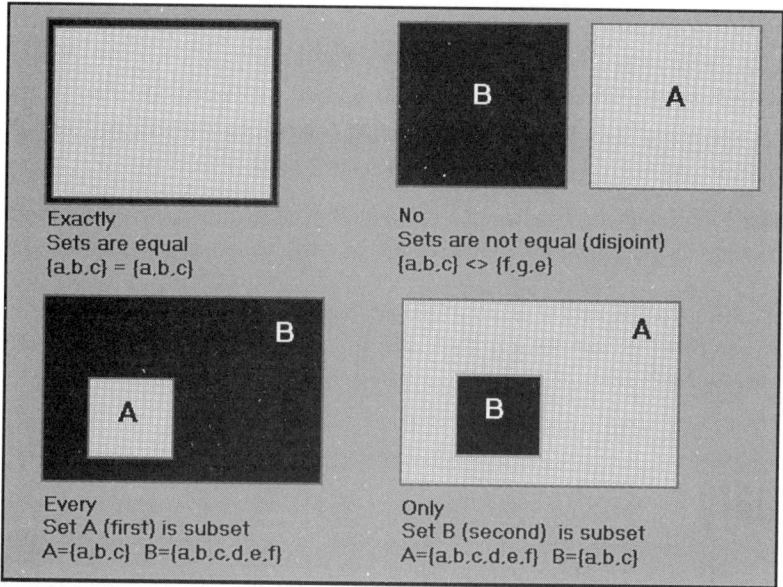

Figure 12.21. Set query meanings.

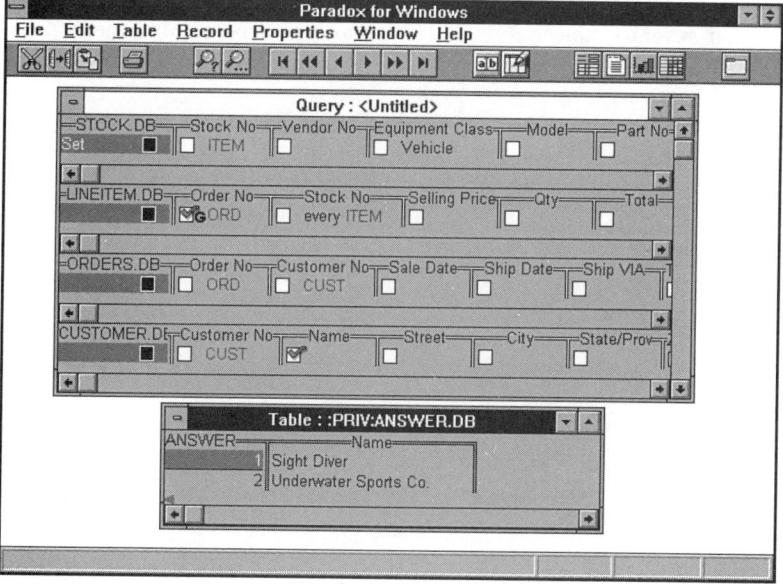

Figure 12.22. An Every set query and a Top X, Bottom Y query.

Notice the use of the GroupBy Check mark in the line items Order No field. If you need to define a group of records by using a field, but you do not want the field displayed in the Answer table, then you need to use the GroupBy Check mark.

A query can have more than one set of records defined. Figure 12.22 also shows how you can use a set query to find out the top three orders according to Total Invoice amounts.

This example is based on a query demonstrated by Dan Ehrmann in the February 1993 issue of *The Paradox Informant* magazine and demonstrates how to solve a class of questions known as the *Top X, Bottom Y* values. The logic of this query can be reversed easily to show the bottom three orders by using the *min* group operator and the opposite range operators. The examples, or number of set definitions, can be extended down to 64 levels, the maximum number of query lines allowed in a Paradox query form.

Summary

This chapter gave you a better understanding of how Paradox's Query By Example feature works. Although the QBE facility is fairly intuitive and easy to use, understanding some of the intricacies helps exploit the true power of Paradox.

As you become more comfortable with Paradox's QBE, you will begin writing complex queries, and you will have several ways to implement the same query. You may be tempted to use one complex query rather than several simpler queries. Don't be easily persuaded. Many times the same results can be arrived at in a series of queries, which may be even quicker than one sophisticated query.

IV

Programming in ObjectPAL

13
ObjectPAL Basics

ObjectPAL is a full-featured *programming language*.

We say these words with emphasis because Paradox for Windows has been designed from the ground up as an object-based, Windows relational database with a programming language. It is not an interactive database package with some programming commands added on, nor is it just a programming language with some interactive features thrown in. Paradox for Windows still remains a paradox: it comes with an easy-to-use interface that all interactive users, beginners and experts alike, can quickly learn, and it has a complete programming language for the serious developer. This product serves both groups.

Although many additions have been made to the programming language of the DOS version of Paradox over the years, it looks tame compared to ObjectPAL. ObjectPAL contains hundreds of methods that vary in scope from the simple to the complex. Along with the concepts of containership, objects, and events, this makes for a very powerful and sometimes difficult-to-understand environment.

Although Paradox is designed for all types of users, ObjectPAL is designed more *for the professional application developer than the casual interactive user*.

Again, we say these words with emphasis. We don't believe that most casual users, or interactive users without a little programming background or introductory training in programming, will use ObjectPAL. With Paradox for Windows, the stakes are raised. The programming language has more power and gives the programmer more control. You therefore are faced with greater responsibility to learn and master that language. Fortunately, after you start working with ObjectPAL and learn the concepts presented in this book, ObjectPAL becomes easy to use.

When Borland designed ObjectPAL, they made it an object-based language rather than an object-oriented language for a specific reason: they wanted it to be accessible to all programmers. Making the language object-oriented would have introduced an additional set of complexities. By not doing so and by introducing the concept of containership, Borland has made concrete the abstract qualities of object-based thinking. The programmer attaches code to a *physical* object on a visible, manipulable form. Although ObjectPAL is an industrial-strength language with an impressive arsenal of weapons, the effort required to make minor changes is very little. Programmers can learn by increments very easily. Perhaps even interactive users may venture forward and add a few lines of code here and there to modify an object's default behavior. Those who do will be rewarded. After you learn the ObjectPAL basics, it is very easy to add a few lines of code to a form and begin experimenting.

ObjectPAL has other, not so obvious benefits. Because all code is attached to some concrete object and because an application can be made up of hundreds of concrete objects, the programming code is automatically decomposed into hundreds of small "chunks." Each section of code is smaller, is less ambitious, and tends to be restricted to a small number of tasks. This makes ObjectPAL code more maintainable. Because the programmer has a visual frame of reference to locate the defective object, and because the code that does the work is broken into to small tasks, changes are usually simpler.

As a programming language, ObjectPAL is similar to C or Pascal and offers programmers some similar basic data types and almost the same level of control over data types as conventional programming languages. It may seem easy to infer that because of this, ObjectPAL development will be slower than development in DOS versions of Paradox or other database application environments.

We don't believe that this is the case.

Although the ObjectPAL language offers greater control and flexibility, it operates on objects created in an interactive environment. These objects can be very simple or they can be very complex, representing thousands of lines of C code. ObjectPAL also offers default behavior for all of these objects that you, as a developer, probably won't have to alter. Despite ObjectPAL's rather large number of rich and varied methods and procedures, application development that sticks closely to the Paradox for Windows way of doing things should proceed as fast or faster than development in previous versions of Paradox or in other database environments.

As you read further in this book and as you read the documentation that comes with Paradox for Windows, you will be surprised at the sheer number and variety of ObjectPAL methods that come with the product. This may look daunting, but don't fret. Many of the methods are easily learned. This book will not exhaustively cover ObjectPAL. That would take too much valuable time. What we will discuss are the features that are most critical for serious application development.

This chapter reviews ObjectPAL programming fundamentals. Begin the excursion into ObjectPAL by reading about some of the most basic and easy-to-grasp parts of the programming language.

Method Notation

In ObjectPAL, almost all programming is done by using ObjectPAL methods or using your own methods that you can create. As discussed in Chapter 1, methods operate on an object. In many cases, the object on which the method is operating is a basic variable, such as a number or a string. For example, all variables come equipped with a view( ) method that displays the contents of the variable in a dialog box. The following example shows how to declare a variable in ObjectPAL, assign it a value, and view it.

```
var
    greeting String
endvar
greeting = "Welcome to ObjectPAL"
greeting.view()
```

When this code executes, a dialog box with the greeting, Welcome to ObjectPAL, is displayed.

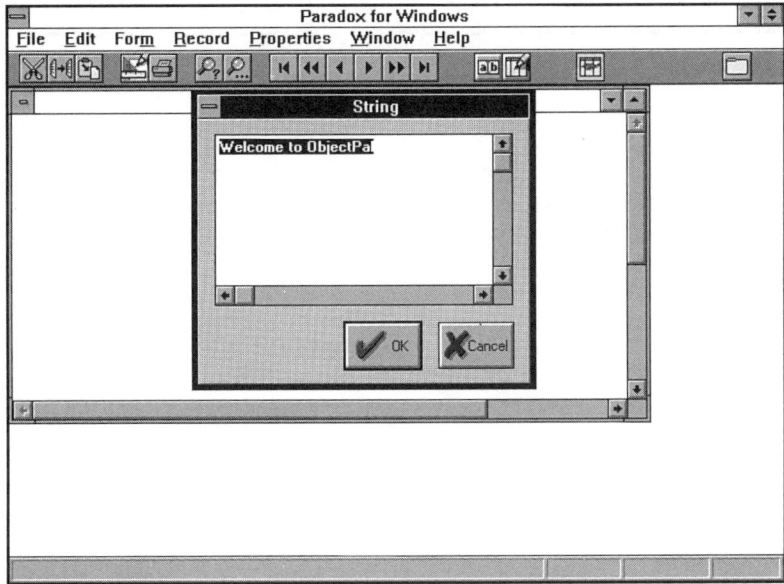

Figure 13.1. Viewing a variable.

Control Structures

Paradox for Windows supports the standard control structures that most programming languages support. Table 13.1 lists these control structures.

Table 13.1. Standard Paradox for Windows control structures.

Structure	Purpose
for	Repeats a series of commands a number of times
foreach	Repeats a series of commands for each element in a DynArray
if-else	Executes two series of commands depending on a logical value

continues

Table 13.1. Continued.

Structure	Purpose
switch	Executes one of several series of commands depending on a logical value
while	Repeats a series of commands as long as a condition is True
try-onFail	Executes a series of commands; upon failure, executes the on fail commands

for

The for command has some interesting twists. The from, to, and step clauses all are optional. This means a for loop executes forever if you leave off the to clause. The following example illustrates some typical for statement uses:

```
var
    x, y SmallInt
endvar
; this steps x from 1 to 10
for x from 1 to 10
    Y = X * 2
    Y.view()
endfor
; this steps x from 10 to 1 in steps of 2, e.g., 10, 8, 6...
for x from 10 to 1 step -2
    y = x * 2
    y.view()
endfor
; this steps x from 1 to 10 in steps of 1
x = 1
for x to 10
    y = x * 2
    y.view()
endfor
; this steps x from 1 until an overflow error occurs
x = 10
for x
    y = x * 2
    y.view("Press Ctrl+Break to stop this loop")
endfor
```

foreach

The foreach command repeats a series of statements for every element in a DynArray. DynArrays are discussed later in this chapter. However, here is a simple example of a foreach command:

```
var
   dynKey String
   myDyn DynArray[] String
endvar
myDyn["First name"] = "Santa"
myDyn["Last name"] = "Clause"
foreach dynKey in myDyn
   myDyn[dynKey].view()
endforeach
```

if

The if command executes one of two series of commands depending on the value of the if condition. The following examples illustrate the use of if:

```
var
   x SmallInt
endvar
x = 33
if x=100 then
   message("X is one hundred")
else
   if x = 32 then
      message("X is thirty two")
   else
      message("X is not one hundred")
   endif
endif
```

switch

The switch statement is an extended version of an if statement in that it enables you to test a large number of cases and execute a series of ObjectPAL statements for which the condition was true. The following examples show the point:

```
var
   x,y SmallInt
endvar
for x from 1 to 5
   switch
      case x = 1 : message("X is one")
      case x = 2 : message("X is two")
      case x = 3 : message("X is three")
      otherwise  : message("X is either four or five")
   endswitch
endfor
```

Only the first case statement that evaluates to True is executed. The other case statements and the otherwise clause are ignored. The statements after the otherwise clause are executed if no other conditions are true. If none of the conditions are true and the otherwise clause is left out, none of the statements in the switch command are executed. All switch statements can be nested.

while

The while statement repeats a series of statements as long as a certain condition is true. In the following example, the value of x is continually displayed until x is set to 100.

```
var
    x SmallInt
endvar
x = 1
while x <= 100
    x.view()
    x = x + 1
endwhile
```

try-onFail

The try-onFail construct enables the developer to build an error recovery mechanism into Paradox for Windows applications. This control structure is so powerful that Chapter 19 is dedicated to a discussion of it and other error recovery issues. The syntax, however, is covered here.

```
var
    x SmallInt
    y AnyType
endvar
x = 1
y = "Hello"
try
    x = x + y
onfail
    msgStop("Error","Y is not a numeric type")
    y = True
    fail()
endtry
```

You can nest try-onFail blocks.

Condition Evaluation

Some programming languages use what is often called *short-circuit evaluation* of conditions. For example, in the following example, there are two conditions in the if statement:

```
if x = 1 and y = 2 then
    message("X is oneand Y is two")
endif
```

For a message to be shown, both conditions must evaluate to True. Conversely, if one or the other condition is not true, the message is not shown. But notice that the test to determine if the message should not be shown can involve, at the least, testing only one of the conditions. If one of them is not true, it is not necessary to test the other condition. If you know that x is 4, why bother to check what y is?

Some compilers and environments do precisely that: they ignore the other conditions if the evaluation of the statement can be concluded without doing so, hence the term, *short-circuit evaluation*.

Paradox for Windows evaluates both sides of an AND or OR statement and does not perform short-circuit evaluation. Often, programmers exploit short-circuit evaluation for their own advantages. In ObjectPAL, you cannot use this technique.

Data Types

Paradox for Windows supports variables from two groups of data types:

- Data that can be represented in a table
- Data that you can manipulate in memory with ObjectPAL

Most developers manipulate data in tables, because that is usually where the application's data is stored. However, some developers find uses for the data types that can't be stored in a table, especially if the application requires extensive use of Arrays or other data structures.

The data that you can manipulate in ObjectPAL can be further divided into two groups:

- Basic data types
- Object types

The basic data types are the usual programmer's data types, numbers, strings, dates, and so on, in which variables are created and values are placed or manipulated. The second group, object types, is used to create variables that can manipulate the various Paradox for Windows objects.

Although we have just divided variables into two groups, basic data types and object types, all variables are really just instances of object types. Even basic data types can be viewed as objects in and of themselves. In fact, Paradox for Windows treats all variables as objects. Each variable type is a member of an object type with associated methods. A UIObject variable is an instance of the UIObject type. A string variable is an instance of the String type. A date variable is an instance of the Date type. We have divided the variables into the two groups because most programmers are familiar with basic data types. We discuss the basic data types first; then we discuss the object types.

Paradox for Windows has a variety of basic data types, as well as a rich set of methods to manipulate each data type. Table 13.2 lists the data types, and table 13.3 lists the data types that can be stored in a table.

Table 13.2. Data types.

Data Type	Allowable values
Numeric data types	
Currency	±1.1 * 104930, precise to six decimal places
LongInt	–2,147,483,648 to +2,147,483,647, 4 bytes
Number	±1.1 * 104930, up to 18 digits of precision
SmallInt	–32,768 to +32,767, 2 bytes
Date and Time data types	
Date	1/1/100 to 12/31/9999, valid dates only
DateTime	Date and time together
Time	Hour, minute, second, millisecond format
String data type	
String	Up to 32,767 characters
Array data types	
Array	All data types supported, including AnyType
DynArray	Array index can be any string ObjectPAL expression
Other data types	
AnyType	Any data type is allowed
Binary	Used to hold binary files
Logical	True or false values
Memo	Up to 512M, for formatted and unformatted text
OLE	Object linking and embedding data type
DDE	Dynamic data exchange data type
Point	Screen x, y value in twips (1/1440 inch, 1/20 point)
Record	User-defined, as in C struct or Pascal record

Table 13.3. Data types that can be stored in tables.

alphanumeric (equivalent to String)
number
currency
date
short number (equivalent to LongInt)

memo
formatted memo
binary
graphic
OLE

Numeric Data Types

The numeric data types are straightforward. However, number data types can be expressed using scientific notation:

```
x = 1.43E+5
```

Here, x is assigned the value of 143,000.

Numbers have a wide assortment of methods available. Some of these methods are listed in table 13.4.

Table 13.4. Some number methods.

Method	Result
pow( )	Raises the number to a given power, as in x.pow(3) = 27, where x = 3.
pow10( )	Raises 10 to the power given by x, as in x.pow10( ) = 100, where x = 2.
sin( )	Returns the sine of x.
tan( )	Returns the tangent of x.
floor( )	Returns the floor of x, as in x.floor( )=2, where x=2.76, which rounds the number down to the nearest whole number.
ceil( )	Returns the ceiling of x, as in x.ceil( )=3, where x=2.21, which rounds the number up to the nearest whole number.
sqrt( )	Returns the square root of x.
ln( )	Returns the natural logarithm of x.
log( )	Returns the logarithm of x.
abs( )	Returns the absolute value of x.

The currency data type is almost identical to the numeric data type. It inherits all the numeric methods. The difference is in the level of precision. Currency data types are precise up to six decimal places, whereas numbers are precise up to 18 digits in the *significand* (the first term in a scientific number), expressing the number in scientific notation.

LongInt and SmallInt variables inherit all the number methods and have a few additional methods for bitwise operations. Table 13.5 lists the bitwise methods available for SmallInt and LongInt.

Table 13.5. Integer bit-level methods.

Method	Result
bitAND( )	Performs a bitwise AND operation on two variables
bitOR( )	Performs a bitwise OR operation on two variables
bitXOR( )	Performs a bitwise XOR operation on two variables
bitIsSet( )	Determines if a bit is on (1) or off (0)

Date and Time Data Types

You can create three types of date and time variables: date variables, time variables, and date/time variables. DateTime variables store both the date and time in a single variable, whereas Date variables do not. More important, you cannot store a DateTime or a Time variable in the database because, as of this version, Paradox for Windows doesn't support a DateTime variable in the table format. You can convert the date and time variables to strings and store these strings in the database. In addition, with the DateTime and Time types, you can easily perform math on dates and time with ObjectPAL.

You can use the following code to create a Date variable, a DateTime variable, and a Time variable:

```
var
   dt   Date
   dtTm DateTime
   tm   Time
endvar
dt = Date("01/31/94")      ; convert in mm/dd/yy format
dtTm = DateTime("07:30:00 am 01/31/94")
tm = Time("07:30:00 am")
```

Math can be performed on Date, DateTime, and Time variables. The following operations are legal:

```
var
   dt Date
   tm Time
   dtTm DateTime
   result AnyType
endvar
dt = today()
tm = Time("10:00:00 am")
dtTm = DateTime("11:00:00 am 01/15/95")
result = dt + 100      ; add 100 days to dt
result.view()
result = tm + 10000    ; add 10 seconds to tm
result.view()
result = dtTm + 10000  ; add 10 seconds to dtTm
result.view()
result = dtTm + dt     ; add dtTm and dt
result.view()
result = dtTm + tm     ; add dtTm and tm
result.view()
```

Dates have a variety of methods. Table 13.6 lists some of them.

Table 13.6. Example date methods.

Method	Result
day( )	Returns a small integer between 1 and 31 for the day of the month
dow( )	Returns the day of the week as a string, as in `"Wednesday"`
doy( )	Returns a small integer between 1 and 366 for the day of the year
isLeapYear( )	Returns True or False
moy( )	Returns the month of the year as a string, as in `"March"`
today( )	Returns today's date
year( )	Returns the year as a small integer

String Type

A string data type can hold up to 32,767 characters. The following example shows how to create and display a string variable:

```
var
    myString String
endvar
myString = "Hello world"
myString.view()
```

Although a string can hold 32,767 characters, you can assign only 255 characters as a *literal*, or what is otherwise referred to as a *quoted string*. You can concatenate several of these strings (using the + operator), up 32,767 characters. If you want to hold more than 32,767 characters in a variable, you have to use the memo variable type.

The <, >, and = operators are allowed on strings and are used to determine equality, inequality, and rank. For example, `"A"` < `"B"` is true, whereas `"Z"` < `"A"` is not.

Certain characters cannot be represented directly in a string because they would create confusion for the compiler. The " character is an example. To represent the " character in a string, proceed it with a backslash (\), as in the following:

```
var
    myString String
endvar
myString = "\"Hello\\Goodbye\""
myString.view()       ; displays "Hello\Goodbye",
                      ; not Hello\Goodbye in a dialog box
```

Other backslash codes are listed in table 13.7.

Table 13.7. Backslash codes.

Code	Represents
\"	Double quotation mark (")
\\	Backslash (\)
\t	Tab (^T)
\r	Carriage return (^M)
\n	New line (^S)
\f	Formfeed (^L)
\v	Vertical tab
\b	Backspace
\a	Bell (^G)
\xxx	Three-digit ASCII code less than 128

Although the concept of a string is simple, the methods associated with the string type are numerous and significant. Table 13.8 lists the more significant and useful string methods.

Table 13.8. Important string methods.

Method	Result
advMatch( )	Performs advance pattern matching in text strings with Awk-like expressions
breakApart( )	Splits a string into an Array of substrings based on separator(s)
format( )	Formats a string into one of more than 100 formats
search( )	Searches for the position of one string in another
size( )	Returns the length of the string
substr( )	Returns a portion of a string
upper( )	Converts a string to uppercase
lower( )	Converts a string to lowercase

Array Data Types

Paradox for Windows has exceptional support for Array data types. Three flavors of Arrays are available: static Arrays, resizeable Arrays, and dynamic Arrays.

Static Arrays are the most familiar to traditional programmers. Programmers must declare exactly how many elements a static Array has. The following is an example of a static Array:

```
var
    myArray Array[10] SmallInt
    x SmallInt
endvar
for x from 1 to 10
    myArray[x] = x * x
    myArray[x].view()
endfor
```

Static Arrays can have elements of type AnyType. This enables you to store different types of data in one Array.

```
var
    myArray Array[5] AnyType
endvar
myArray[1] = "John Smith"
myArray[2] = "102 W. Main Street"
myArray[3] = "Bedford Falls"
myArray[4] = 39
myArray[5] = Date("08/22/54")
for x from 1 to myArray.size()
    myArray[x].view()
endfor
```

A resizeable Array looks much like a static Array, except that you don't specify how many elements it will have, and you have at your disposal several methods to add items to and delete items from the Array. The following example shows how to create resizeable Arrays:

```
var
    myArray Array[] String
    x SmallInt
endvar
for x from 1 to 5              ; add the word "Hello" 5 times
    myArray.addlast("Hello")
    myArray.view()
endfor
myArray.empty()                ; empty the array
myArray.grow(5)                ; add 5 empty slots in the array
for x from 1 to 5
    myArray[x] = "Hello"       ; put in the word "Hello"
endfor
myArray.view()
```

You will notice that in these two examples, you can add elements one at a time using the addLast( ) method or other methods, or you can allocate space in the Array by using the grow( ) method before you actually assign the Array element values. In addition, you can use the view( ) method to view an entire Array or just one item in the array.

A dynamic Array is similar to a resizeable Array, except that the index to the Array element is not an integer; it can be anything that evaluates to a string. In addition, when you assign a DynArray element, you automatically create storage space for it, so preallocation of space is not required. The following example shows how to declare and use a DynArray:

```
var
    myDyn DynArray[] String
endvar
```

```
myDyn["Breakfast"] = "French Toast"
myDyn["Lunch"] = "Italian Salami Sub"
myDyn["Dinner"] = "Grilled Salmon"
myDyn["Dessert"] = "Mud Pie"
myDyn.view()
```

The DynArray is composed of two parts: a *key* (often called an *index*) and a *value*. The key is the string placed between the brackets. The value is the item assigned to the particular DynArray key.

One type of array that is not directly supported in Paradox for Windows is a multidimensional Array. Languages such as C and Pascal have always supported this basic Array type, and many programmers find the multidimensional Arrays useful for matrix processing. By using a DynArray, it is possible to simulate an N-dimensional DynArray. You are limited only by the allowable length of the string in a DynArray key. The following example shows how to create and manipulate a multidimensional DynArray:

```
var
   myDyn DynArray[] SmallInt
   x, y SmallInt
endvar
for x from 1 to 5
   for y from 1 to 5
      myDyn[String(x)+":"+String(y)] = x - y
   endfor
endfor
for y from 5 to 1 step -1
   for x from 5 to 1 step -1
      message( String(x)+":"+String(y)+" = "+
               String(myDyn[String(x)+":"+String(y)]) )
      sleep(1000)
   endfor
endfor
myDyn.view()
```

Arrays can be copied to each other simply by assigning one Array to another.

```
var
   arrayA array[3] SmallInt
   arrayB array[3] SmallInt
endvar
arrayA[1] = 1
arrayA[2] = 9
arrayA[3] = 4
arrayB = arrayA
arrayB.view()
```

Figure 13.2. shows the multidimensional array.

Record Data Type

The record data type enables you to group several other data types together under one name, in much the same manner as you would use a struct in C. To implement a record, however, you must use the type keyword. This keyword enables you to create your own data types based on the ObjectPAL basic data types. The following is an example of how to use type:

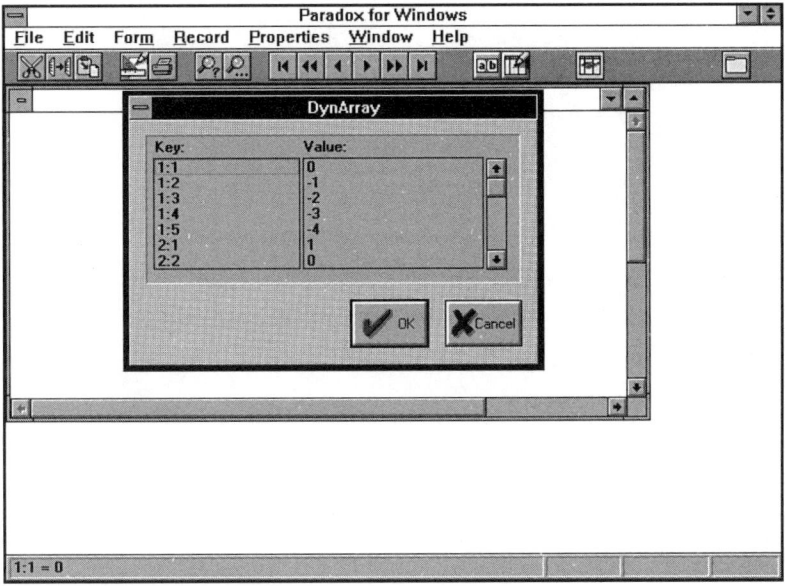

Figure 13.2. Multidimensional Array simulation.

```
type
   myType = SmallInt
endType
var
   myVar myType
endvar
myVar = 1
myVar.view()
```

In this example, a new type called myType was created. To create a record, you use a similar scheme, except you add the keyword record.

```
type
   myRecord = Record
      firstName String
      lastName String
      age SmallInt
      occupation String
   endRecord
endType
var
   myVar myRecord
endvar
myVar.firstName = "Jean-Luc"
myVar.lastName = "Picard"
myVar.age = 55
myVar.occupation = "Captain"
myVar.view()
```

Executing this code sample displays the dialog box in figure 13.3.

Part IV ■ Programming in ObjectPAL

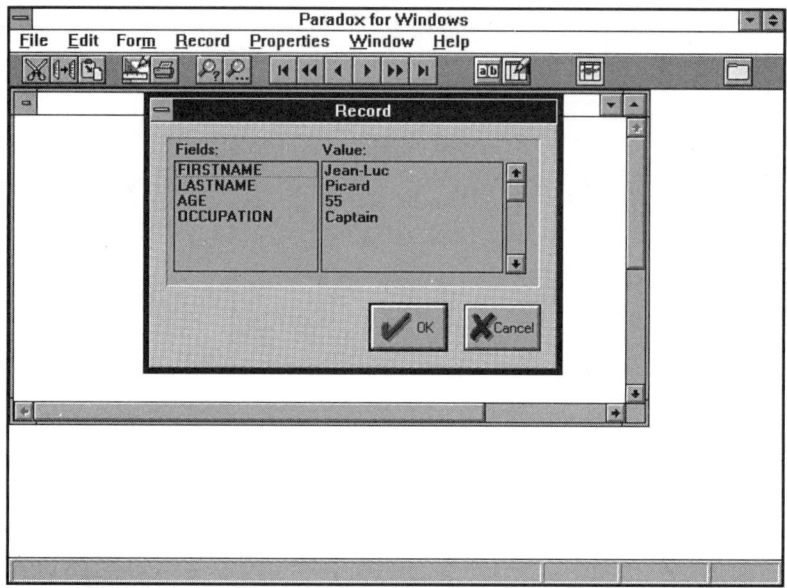

Figure 13.3. Record data type.

Object Types

Variables can also be instances of object types rather than just basic data types. For example, you can create a Form variable. This Form variable is an instance of the Form type. Each Form variable has a host of methods and procedures that enable you to control and manipulate the object. For example, the open( ) method opens a form. Another important type of variable is a TCursor variable. A TCursor variable enables you to manipulate a table as if it were visible on the desktop, when in fact it is not. The table is hidden from view. To use a TCursor, you declare a variable of the TCursor type, open the TCursor, then manipulate it. (TCursors are discussed at length in Chapter 16.)

The following example shows how to create an object variable and manipulate the object by using the variable. In this case, the object is a TCursor, which determines how many records are in the customer table.

```
var
    cust       TCursor
    recCount   LongInt
endvar
method test()
    cust.open("CUSTOMER")
    recCount = cust.nRecords()
    cust.close()
    recCount.view()
endmethod
```

Table 13.9 lists some more object data types.

Table 13.9. Object data types.

ActionEvent	Library	StatusEvent
Application	Menu	System
Database	MenuEvent	Table
ErrorEvent	MouseEvent	TableView
Event	MoveEvent	TCursor
FileSystem	MoveEventPopUpMenu	TextStream
Form	Query	TimerEvent
Graphic	Report	UIObject
KeyEvent	Session	ValueEvent

Chapter 39 details what each of these object types is for. In addition, we will discuss several of the object types at length throughout this book. At this time, it is not important to know everything about them. It is important to know, however, that many of these object types are extremely useful, and that each type comes with many methods. In fact, if you add up all the methods and procedures available for each type, you come up with more than 1,150 total methods and procedures.

Converting Data Types

Every data type comes equipped with a casting procedure, which enables you to assign one variable of one type to another variable of a different type. You saw examples of this in converting a number to a string, or converting a string literal to a date. The following code contains some examples of casting methods:

```
var
   dt Date
   n Number
   i SmallInt
   l LongInt
   s String
endvar
dt = Date("01/01/93"); assign a date variable
dt.view()
s = String(dt)    ; convert the date to a string and assign it to s
s.view()
n = 1.3           ; assign a number variable
n.view()
s = String(n)     ; convert the number to a string, assign it to s
s.view()
i = SmallInt(n)   ; convert the number to a small int, assign it to i
i.view()
```

Constants

ObjectPAL lets you declare constants. Constants are similar to variables, except you cannot change them. To declare a constant, you must use the const keyword:

```
const
   systemVersionNumber = Number(1)
   systemName = "Project Tracking System"
   systemDate = DateTime("03:00:00 pm 01/01/92")
endconst
```

Constants are more efficient than variables, because the compiler knows they cannot be changed or deleted. In addition, constants ensure that certain variables cannot be changed. In the absence of any casting, the compiler determines the type of the constant by examining the literal. We recommend that you be as explicit as possible by using casting procedures, as in the previous example, in which the systemVersionNumber constant is set to a number via the Number( ) procedure rather than an integer type, which makes clear your intent when you created the constant.

Explicit versus Implicit Variable Declaration

As you can see from these examples, ObjectPAL is a strongly typed language in which explicit type declaration of variables, arguments, and return values is encouraged and enforced by the compiler. Strongly typed languages, however, make it difficult to write procedures that can accept values of different types or return values of different types. ObjectPAL enables you to declare a variable of AnyType to get around this limitation. If you declare variables, arguments, and return values as AnyType, any basic ObjectPAL type will be allowed. If you assign a value to a variable that isn't explicitly declared in a var..endvar block, Paradox for Windows implicitly declares it for you as an AnyType variable. If it weren't for the AnyType variable, it would be difficult to write generic procedures that could act on variables of very different types. However, we recommend that you explicitly declare your variable types and use AnyType variables with caution for two reasons:

- The variable's type is unambiguous, resulting in better, maintainable code.

- Your program will run faster because Paradox can determine the type of the variable at compile time rather than runtime.

Formatting and Commenting Code

Paradox for Windows is case-insensitive. You can freely mix case in variable names, constant names, method names, and procedure names. for the most part, Paradox for Windows doesn't care how you format the code. The compiler can tell when a command begins and ends because every ObjectPAL command has an end block associated with it. You are free to choose the style of formatting and indenting that you prefer.

For example, the if statement can be formatted in a variety of ways:

```
if x=1
   then
      message("X is 1")
endif

if x=1 then message("X is 1") endif

if x=1 then
   message("X is 1")
endif
```

You can enter comments by preceding the comment with a semicolon (;). The comment can continue until the end of the line and can't wrap around to the next line. If you need to comment a large block of text that wraps to multiple lines, you can use the curly braces—{ and }—before and after your comment.

The following examples make this clear:

```
; This is a valid comment
x=1
; This is not
a valid comment
x=1
{ this is a valid
   comment }
x=1
{
This is also
a valid comment
}
x=1
```

Methods and Procedures

So far, we used the term *method* to describe an ObjectPAL module or routine. ObjectPAL actually has two types of programming modules: methods and procedures. In addition, methods and procedures have two flavors: those that are part of the product and those that you create on your own. The methods and procedures supplied in Paradox, of which there are hundreds, are the tools to build your application. The methods and procedures you create represent the customization you bring to the Paradox environment.

As you work with ObjectPAL, it is important to distinguish between methods and procedures. Methods manipulate an object or are associated with an object. You've seen several examples of this, such as the grow( ) method from the Array type, which enables you to expand the size of a resizeable Array.

Procedures are different. Procedures aren't associated with any particular object. You've seen examples of this in the type casting procedures, Date( ), SmallInt( ), Time( ), and others, which aren't associated with any object. The System type class has many procedures which perform tasks that also aren't associated with any object. Some examples are the message( ), msgInfo( ), and msgStop( ) procedures, which simply display a message either on the message line at the bottom of a window or in a dialog box.

Procedures can operate on a variety of objects without an object identifier. One example is the close( ) procedure in the Form type. This procedure closes the form it is attached to. It doesn't need a form identifier in front of it, as in myForm.close( ).

In Paradox for Windows, a custom procedure (one that you create) has properties that differ from the various procedures that Paradox supplies. We examine these differences in greater detail later in this chapter. For now, it is important to keep in mind the following points:

- Paradox comes with hundreds of methods and procedures
- Methods always refer to or operate on an object
- Procedures do not require an object identifier
- You can create either custom procedures or custom methods

Paradox for Windows has several *built-in* methods. You see these built-in methods whenever you access an object's methods dialog box. Built-in methods are simply method stubs that are automatically called when the corresponding event occurs. (Events are discussed later in this chapter and in more depth in Chapter 14.)

For example, the built-in arrive( ) method for a field object is called every time the user arrives on that field. You can enter your own code in these built-in methods.

Don't be confused by the term *built-in*. All it means is that for the given event, the corresponding, predefined method will be called. Built-in methods are empty methods waiting for you to insert code.

Parameter Passing and Returning Values

To do something useful in code, your custom methods and procedures need to receive and return data. ObjectPAL enables you to pass data to procedures and methods as arguments, and it enables you to return values from the called method or procedure to the calling method or procedure.

Parameter Passing

ObjectPAL allows you to call both ObjectPAL methods as well as your own methods with parameters, or arguments, supplied. The arguments must be declared and their type specified, otherwise the compiler gives you an error message. ObjectPAL supports three conventions for parameter passing. You can pass by reference, by value, or as a constant.

If you pass a variable by reference, the variable can be modified by the invoked method and any changes in the variable are reflected in the parent method. If you pass by value, the invoked method receives a copy of the variable and any changes in the variable are not reflected in the parent method's copy of the variable. If you pass a variable as a constant, the invoked method will not be able to modify the variable.

To call a method by reference, use the keyword, var. The following example shows how:

```
proc subtractWeek(var d Date)
   d = d - 7
endproc
method test()
   var
      dt Date
   endvar
   dt = today()
   subtractWeek(dt)
   dt.view()
endmethod
```

To pass as a constant, use the constant keyword, as in the following:

```
proc subtractDays(var d Date, const days SmallInt )
   d = d - days
endproc
method test()
   var
      dt Date
   endvar
   dt = today()
   subtractDays(dt, SmallInt(10))
   dt.view()
endmethod
```

If you don't use the const or var keywords, pass by value is assumed by Paradox.

Returning Values

To return a value from your procedure or method, use the return keyword along with an expression to leave the procedure or method and return a value. To do this, the procedure and method must be declared as returning a value of some kind. The following example shows how to do this:

```
proc subtractDays(const d Date, const days SmallInt ) Date
   return d - days
endproc
method test()
   var
      dt Date
   endvar
   dt = today()
   dt = subtractDays(dt, SmallInt(10))
   dt.view()
endmethod
```

The subtractDays( ) procedure is declared with the Date keyword following the argument declaration. This tells the compiler that this procedure returns a date type.

All of the basic data types can be returned except for Arrays and DynArrays. Arrays and DynArrays must be converted to a new type with the type construct before either returning the Array or DynArray as a value or passing it as an argument. The following code shows an example of creating a new type based on an Array type:

```
; declare an new array type
type
    myType = array[10] SmallInt
endtype
; array argument is passed as a constant
proc changeArray( const source myType ) myType
    ; declare a temporary array variable
    var
        tempArray array[10] SmallInt
    endvar
    ; copy the source array to the target array
    tempArray = source
    ; change one array element in the temporary array
    tempArray[2] = source[2] + source[3]

    ; return the temporary array
    return tempArray
endproc
method test()
    ; declare 2 variables of the new type
    var
        myArray, yourArray myType
        x SmallInt
    endvar
    ; initialize the first array
    for X from 1 to 10
        yourArray[X] = X
    endfor
    ; fill up myArray with new values based on yourArray
    myArray = changeArray( yourArray )
    myArray.view()
endmethod
```

What is interesting in this example is that you can treat your own types as Arrays and perform operations such as assignment on the new types based on Array variables. In other words, variables based on types that you create are treated the same as variables based on the equivalent data type. In changeArray( ), we are returning the variable tempArray of type Array[10] SmallInt, even though changeArray( ) expects us to return a variable of myType. As far as Paradox for Windows is concerned, the two variables are of identical types.

Parameter Passing and Performance

Whenever you pass by constant or by reference, Paradox for Windows passes a pointer to the argument rather than the whole argument. This can be important when your arguments are strings or other larger data types. Because a string can occupy hundreds or thousands of bytes of storage, it is more efficient to pass by constant or pass by reference. This improves the performance of your application because Paradox doesn't have to copy the entire argument onto the stack as your methods and procedures are called. Instead, Paradox copies the pointer to the argument on the stack.

For this reason, we recommend that you choose your argument-passing method wisely. Passing by constant always is preferred if the called method or procedure does not need to change the argument. Passing by reference is preferred if the called or child procedure or method needs to change the argument, and the argument change needs to be reflected in the calling or parent procedure or methods. Passing by value, the most expensive—in terms of performance—of the options, should be used when the child procedure or method needs to change a copy of the argument, not the real argument itself. Always choose pass by reference or constant, if possible, for larger data types such as strings.

The Containership Model

The containership model is what makes ObjectPAL and Paradox for Windows unique. It is the metaphor that runs through all aspects of Paradox for Windows: designing forms, interactive use, and programming. It is a highly visual and concrete rather than abstract metaphor that makes programming in Paradox for Windows easy yet powerful.

A container holds things. In Paradox for Windows, a form is a container. It holds many things, including buttons, table objects, multi-record objects, field objects, and other objects. Those objects are also containers. The multi-record object can hold a field object, which in turn can hold a text object. A button object contains a text object, which is the text on the button.

An object contains another object if it completely surrounds the other object and the object's Contain Objects property is set on. You can arbitrarily create your own container by using the Box tool to draw a box around any number of objects.

Because of the containership model, ObjectPAL program structure becomes an integrated part of the form. In other words, ObjectPAL code becomes coupled to the form. For this reason, it is critical that you understand the form creation process and interactive use before you begin writing ObjectPAL code.

The following is an example of a containership hierarchy. Figure 13.4 shows a simple form that can be used to edit a customer table, and figure 13.5 shows the containership hierarchy for that form.

Part IV ■ Programming in ObjectPAL

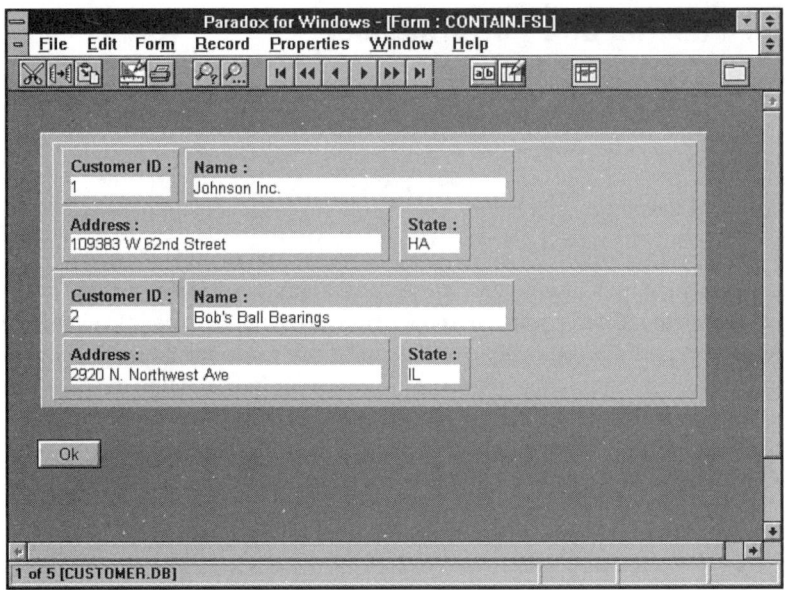

Figure 13.4. A simple customer table form.

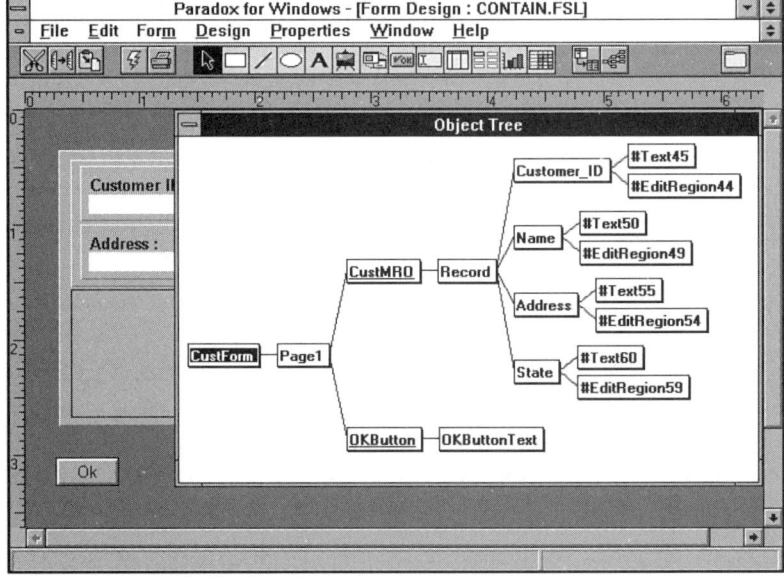

Figure 13.5. The containership hierarchy for CustForm.

As you can see, each object contains several other objects. You can attach ObjectPAL code to any or all objects. Your code, then, also is part of the containership hierarchy. If you attach ObjectPAL code to the Customer ID field object in figure 13.4, that ObjectPAL code is contained within the Record object, which is contained by the Page1 object, which is contained by the CustForm object.

The containership metaphor is so simple, yet it is deceiving. The idea of placing objects inside other objects is so intuitive—like stacking cups inside each other—yet it can create a wealth of complexity if you need it to. To understand this complexity, you need to compare ObjectPAL with conventional programming languages.

In languages such as C, Pascal, and PAL, program modules—whether we call them procedures, functions, or methods—also are stacked hierarchically. All programmers are well-versed in creating a main module which calls another module, which calls another module, and so on, as in figure 13.6.

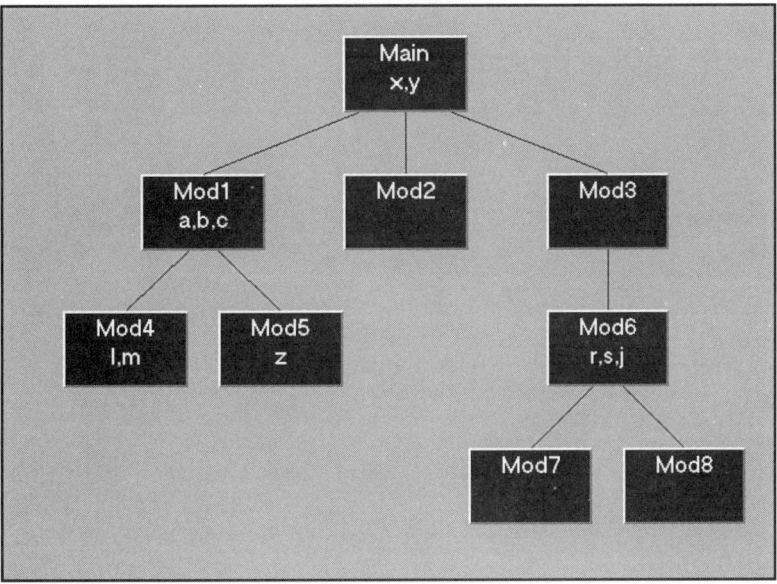

Figure 13.6. A traditional language module tree.

Each module has its own private variables that it can see. In dynamic scoping programming languages such as PAL, both Mod7 and Mod8 would be able to see variables r, s, and j, as well as variables x and y. In static scoping languages, Mod7 and Mod8 would not be able to see variables r, s, or j unless Mod6 passed them as parameters. Regardless of the scoping rules, the hierarchy of modules is fixed by how the programmer has the modules call each other.

Paradox for Windows still has a hierarchy, but it is achieved differently. The real action is in the containership hierarchy, which is one composed of objects rather than modules. Each object has various methods attached, and those attached methods may call other methods. In addition, method and variable visibility rules are determined by the hierarchy of objects rather than the hierarchy of program modules (see fig. 13.7). If you want to determine what method and what variable is accessible to what object, you will find yourself visually inspecting the object tree. In procedural languages, you find yourself stepping through the hierarchy of programming modules.

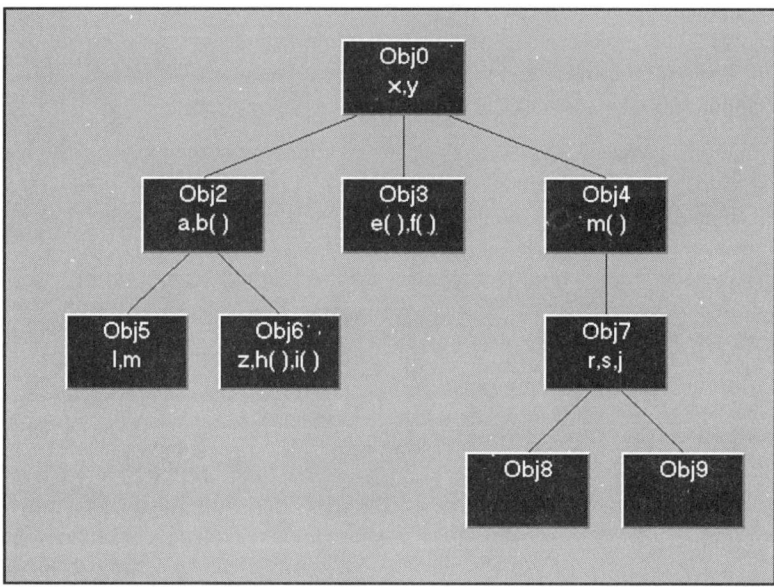

Figure 13.7. The object-based language object tree.

In the containership hierarchy in Paradox for Windows, method m( ) in Obj4 is automatically visible to Obj7, Obj8, and Obj9 because Obj4 contains the other three. Variables r, s, and j can be declared as visible to Obj8 and Obj9—not because any module has called another module, but because object Obj7 contains objects Obj8 and Obj9. Each object has methods and data attached to it. Each object can be easily added to or removed from the object tree, or any object can be repositioned within the object tree. The object tree, and hence the application's functionality, is visually modified.

The rules of visibility are determined by the visual organization of the objects, and therefore the application's logic will be intertwined with its visual construction. Using this scheme, the programmer's task is to create each object, empower it with attached methods that extend its behavior, and organize dependencies between the objects carefully by manipulating the containership hierarchy.

The downside to this approach is diminished maintainability. Because the relationship between objects is easily modified, if the code is not attached in the proper places, moving one object to another part of the containership hierarchy might disrupt the application logic. If you incorrectly place several important methods in Obj4, moving Obj4 to another part of the containership tree can cause the application to function improperly. Because methods can be made visible to descendent nodes in the containership tree, if any of Obj4's descendant objects explicitly referred to method m( ), moving Obj4 might cause problems.

There is another problem. It is possible to create an entire object, which in turn can be composed of many contained objects, and then use that object as a prototype to create copies. Each copy might be placed on many different forms. If the code for this prototype changes, you are faced with an arduous maintenance task: change all the code in all the copies. Obviously, you want to avoid this problem as well. The containership model gives you the freedom in placing custom methods in one of several locations. This gives you the flexibility and control needed to solve code maintenance and application logic problems.

Now that we have discussed some of the fundamental properties of the containership hierarchy, we can discuss the specifics of how Paradox for Windows finds variables, methods, and procedures when you access them from any object.

Scope of a Variable

Most programming languages have some concept of variable scope, or variable visibility. ObjectPAL supports several ways to control the scope of a variable. Unlike in other programming languages, however, the scoping rules are not always determined by looking at the source code. Instead, the accessibility of a variable can be determined by its object's location in the form's containership hierarchy.

There are three basic approaches to setting the scope of a variable:

- Declare the variable within a method
- Declare the variable just above a method
- Declare the variable in the object's Var window

The first approach restricts the variable's scope the most. Any variables declared within a method or procedure are private to that method or procedure. No other method or procedure has access to that variable, unless the variable is returned from that method or procedure to another method or procedure. In addition, any time that method or procedure is called, the variables are reinitialized. In this chapter, you have seen numerous examples of this, so we don't need to review it here.

The second approach is simple to implement. All you have to do is place a var statement immediately above the method or procedure name. Variables declared this way behave exactly like variables declared in the first approach, except they are not initialized each time the method or procedure is called. This approach is useful if you want to declare a variable that can be seen only by that method, yet is not reinitialized each time the method is called. The following example shows how to do this:

```
var
    oStatus Logical
endvar
```

```
method SwitchStatus()
   if oStatus.isAssigned() = False then
      msgStop("Stop","oStatus is not assigned")
   oStatus = True
   endif
   oStatus = not oStatus
endmethod
```

This example will constantly change oStatus from True to False to True and so on every time SwitchStatus is called. The variable oStatus will not be reinitialized each time it is called. Its value persists between calls.

The third method is perhaps the most useful approach because here is where the containership hierarchy meets ObjectPAL code. To declare variables in the object's Var window, check the Var check box in the methods dialog box (see fig. 13.8).

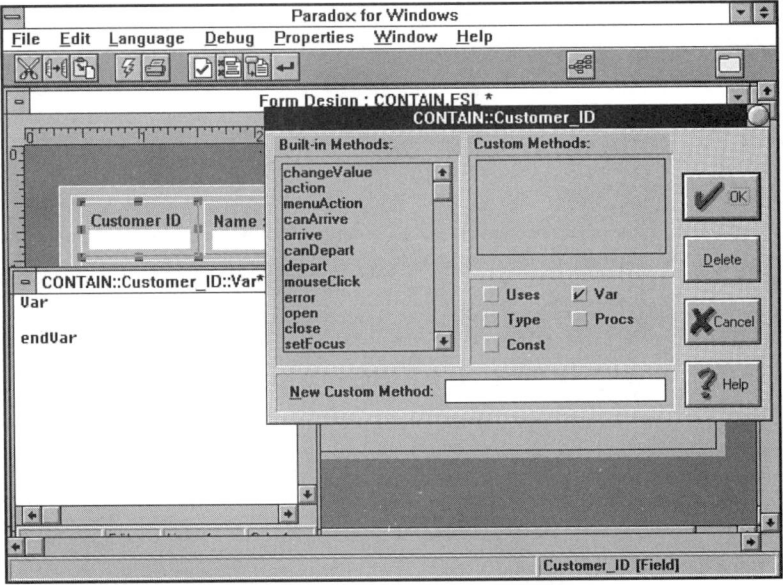

Figure 13.8. The methods dialog box.

Variables declared in the object's Var window are visible to all methods and procedures attached to that object and any other objects that object contains. If you look at figure 13.8, you can see that the Var check box is checked. If you clicked the OK button, you would be able to enter the variables declared for the selected object, in this case the Customer_ID field. Also examine figure 13.5, which is the forms containership hierarchy. Any variables attached to the Customer_ID field object are accessible to any other methods attached to the Customer_ID field object, as well as any methods attached to the Customer_ID edit region object and Customer _ID text object. If you want to make a variable visible to all objects within the form, declare the variable in the form's Var window.

This way of declaring variables attached to an object and automatically visible to objects in the containership hierarchy is very different than the way most traditional programming languages handle scoping. The approach taken by Paradox for Windows creates a tremendous amount of flexibility. With that flexibility, however, comes responsibility. It is your job to find the best place to declare variables.

If you think about this containership concept, you will see that there are no such things as global variables in Paradox for Windows. All variables fit in somewhere in the containership hierarchy. And because the form is the highest container in the containership model, the most *global* a variable can get is to be declared in the form's Var window.

If you have become accustomed to programming using large numbers of global variables, this idea might sound disturbing to you. Don't worry. If you need global variables that are accessible to multiple forms, you can do so by employing libraries, which is discussed in a following section.

Scope of Methods and Procedures

Methods are accessed much like variables. If you attach your own custom method to the CustMRO object in figure 13.5, all the objects within CustMRO have access to that custom method. If from within the Name object in figure 13.5, for example, you call a method declared in the CustMRO object, Paradox for Windows searches upward from the Name object in the containership tree to find the custom method you called.

This automatic searching mechanism is not the only way you can invoke a method or access a variable. You can directly access a method by using dot notation to call a method. For example, if you have a custom method called ApproveCustomer( ) attached to the OKButton object, you can invoke the ApproveCustomer( ) method directly with any of the following lines of code attached to the Name object:

```
CustForm.Page1.OkButton.ApproveCustomer()
```
```
Page1.OKButton.ApproveCustomer()
```
```
OKButton.ApproveCustomer()
```

Because the button and the Name object are both on the CustForm and the Page1 objects, these identifiers are optional. Because the OKButton is not part of the same subtree as the Name object, some qualification about where the ApproveCustomer( ) method is attached is needed. Paradox for Windows begins searching at the OKButton object for ApproveCustomer( ). If it can't find it there, it searches OKButton's container. Paradox keeps searching each object's container until it finds the ApproveCustomer( ) method or reaches the form level of the containership tree. What this means is that you could attach the following line of code to the Name object:

```
OKButtonText.ApproveCustomer()
```

Paradox for Windows still finds the ApproveCustomer( ) method because it starts the search for the method at the OKButtonText object; it won't find it there. Then Paradox will search the OKButton object, where it will find the method. In addition, Paradox for Windows allows you to place another custom method called ApproveCustomer( ) to another object anywhere on the form, which means that you can have two custom methods with the same name attached to different objects on the same form. Which method gets invoked depends on how you have identified the containing object with dot notation, and on where the actual methods are attached.

This method of automatically resolving conflicts between method names is a powerful mechanism, yet it is potentially dangerous. It gives you nearly unlimited flexibility in designing your objects and attaching custom methods. If also can be a maintenance problem if you haphazardly copy ill-designed objects. It is possible that your forms could suffer from *method clutter*, in which your form has unnecessary or conflicting methods attached to objects. Debugging and maintaining these objects can be easy if you carefully design your objects and decide what behavior you want to give them before you create them.

Custom procedures are different than methods. You can invoke methods attached to other parts of the containership tree that are not part of the current object's subtree. Custom procedures are available to the objects they are attached to, and any of its containers' custom procedures or methods. You cannot call a custom procedure, however, from outside the current object's containership hierarchy.

Procedures and variables share one important property that distinguishes them from methods: they cannot be accessed outside the current object's containership hierarchy. Although you can invoke a method attached to another object *outside* the current object's containership tree, you can't invoke a procedure or access a variable *attached to an object outside* the current object's containership tree.

Binding and Program Compilation

ObjectPAL is a compiled programming language. The ObjectPAL compiler searches the containership hierarchy for variable declarations. If it can't find an explicit variable declaration anywhere in the containership tree, the variable is treated as an AnyType variable, with the exact type and properties to be determined at runtime. In fact, the properties of all AnyType variables, even if they are explicitly declared (using a Var..EndVar block), must be determined at runtime rather than compile time.

Your code will run more efficiently if you explicitly declare your variables as any type other than AnyType. If the compiler knows the type of the variable, it doesn't have to determine the type of variable that the AnyType variable happens to be. This saves extra computing steps. This is not to say that AnyType variables are useless; they're not. In fact, they can be very useful. It is just not wise to make all variables AnyType variables.

All references to procedures and methods are bound at compile time, which makes accessing any of your custom methods and procedures very fast.

Libraries

Creating many forms and attaching code to several forms is useful, but it doesn't go far enough. What if you have a bunch of generic methods that you want to have available to many forms? Libraries make this possible. Libraries are simply special forms that serve as repositories for custom methods, procedures, variables, and constants.

To create a library, you simply click on the library speedbar item or use the File|New|Library menu selection to create a new library. The library form is blank and doesn't have any of the design tools that are available in forms. However, if you right-click the mouse on the form, the methods dialog box is displayed for the library. Notice that a library has only three built-in methods: open( ), close( ), and error( ). The open( ) method is useful if you need to initialize variables or create tables or other objects when the library is open. The close( ) method is useful if you need to remove any tables, files, or other objects that were created when the library was opened or during its use.

Figure 13.9 shows an example of a library with two methods attached to it.

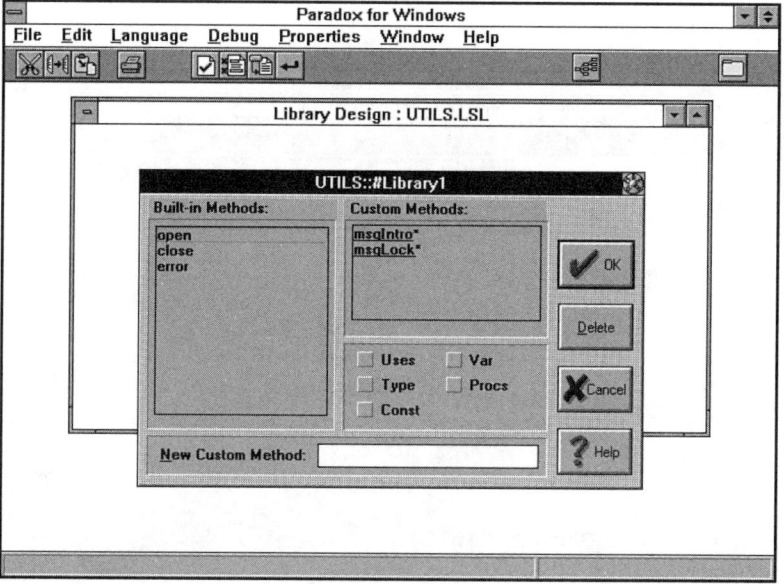

Figure 13.9. The Library1 form.

Libraries are extremely important items. They provide the mechanism to endow forms with a bunch of generic methods. To add a method, all you have to do is type the method name in the Custom Methods field and click the OK button. Libraries can have multiple procedures in them, as well. By opening a Procs window, you can add as many procedures as you need.

To call a method attached to a library, you must create a library variable so that the library can be opened. Perhaps the most common place to do this is at the form level in the containership tree in the form's Var window.

```
var
   myUtils Library
endvar
```

The library can then be opened by adding an open( ) method in the form's *arrive* built-in method:

```
myUtils.open("Utils.lsl")
```

To access the methods in the library, you have to tell the form what these methods are. Because the methods are not in the current form at all, Paradox for Windows considers them external to the form. To get around this problem, all you have to do is check the Uses box in the form's method dialog box and add a few lines to the Uses statement.

The Uses window enables you to declare external methods. You can make the two methods in figure 13.9 available to the current form by placing the proper lines in the Uses window (see fig. 13.10). By the way, the same Uses window is used to declare external C and Pascal functions that reside in a dynamic link library (DLL).

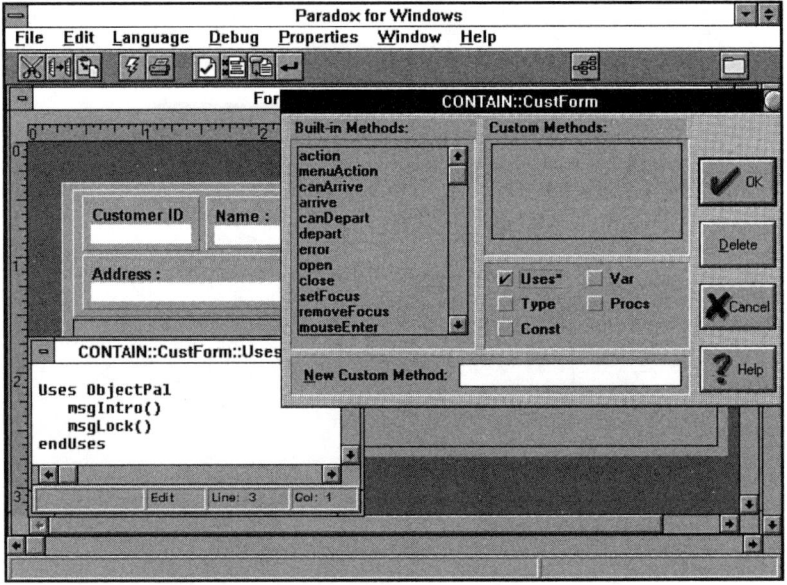

Figure 13.10. Declaring library methods in a Uses window.

Libraries and Encapsulation

You can add methods, procedures, constants, variables, and user-defined types to a library, but only methods will be visible to any form that has the library open. You can exploit this fact and provide some level of encapsulation in your generic routines by recognizing the following issues:

- Because procedures in a library can't be called by a form, they are internal to the library.
- Because methods can be called by the form, the methods can serve as interface modules to the procedures that perform all the work.
- Because the application's forms cannot access variables in the library, you must write custom methods to get and set the variable values.

Libraries are not only useful holders of methods and procedures, they also provide a level of insulation between your generic routines and the form that uses them. Access to all the data in the library is strictly controlled through your custom get and set methods, all procedures are hidden, and methods become the interface modules to the generic code.

Library Scope

Each form on the desktop needs to declare a library variable, open a library, and list the methods to access in the Uses window. If you have 10 forms in your application, each form must open a library properly. When you open the library from a given form, you can tell Paradox that this instance of the library is either private to the current form or global to all forms.

Two constant arguments can be passed to the library's open method: GlobalToDesktop or PrivateToForm. If no second argument is supplied, GlobalToDesktop is assumed. The PrivateToForm constant opens the library with all methods available to only the current form. If each form opens the same library as PrivateToForm, each form has a private copy of the library. Each form has its own private copy of any variables that are stored and set in the library.

If the library is opened as GlobalToDesktop, all forms that open the library as GlobalToDesktop share the same instance of the variables in the library. This action is important because it provides a mechanism for creating and manipulating global variables.

Keep in mind that if two forms open a library as GlobalToDesktop and a third form opens the same library as PrivateToForm, two instances of the library are created: one instance is shared by the two forms which opened the library as GlobalToDesktop, and the other instance is available to the third form.

Note: If you want true global variables accessible to all parts of your application, place the variables in the library, write the necessary methods to set and get the variable values, and make sure every form opens the library as GlobalToDesktop.

The Event Model

Events are object interactions. At one level, events are things the user does, such as moving the mouse or pressing a key. At another level, Paradox for Windows creates an event, such as posting a record or moving to the next field in a data entry form when the user presses the Tab key. Of course, it is valuable to be able to trap for all the keystrokes and mouse interactions the user can create; however, the real value of events is being able to take action on all the internal events Paradox for Windows creates as part of its routine work.

Buried somewhere in the Paradox for Windows DLLs are the routines that handle the mundane tasks such as posting a record, opening a form, and leaving a field. By letting developers attach their own code that will run whenever the Paradox for Windows routines for the various internal events occur, Borland has created an extremely powerful and sophisticated event model.

Some people claim that the event model in Paradox for Windows is too complex. We disagree. It can seem bewildering at first, especially to developers who aren't used to event-driven applications or developers who haven't had to tackle some complex issues in a PC database package. But when you understand the basic concepts, the event model is easy to understand. More importantly, it has the necessary flexibility to enable you to tackle just about every data-entry challenge.

What Is an Event?

So far, we discussed how the object-based model differs from the traditional models in which the programmer controls every aspect of the environment by controlling the exact sequence of events and the range of possibilities at each moment in time. We also said that in Paradox for Windows, you will be creating objects that respond to all kinds of events without having a *master* module handle all the dispatching.

Although that may be true, there is a master module or modules that dispatch all events in Paradox for Windows. That module does handle many events in distinct linear fashion. That module is internal to Paradox for Windows and is only partially revealed to the programmer. As programmers, we can't determine the exact sequence of all events, although we have great flexibility to respond to them. In the following case, a user, Casey, is editing a record and wants to leave the current record she is on and move to another record. For this event to occur, many internal events *must* proceed in an *exact* sequence, otherwise there would be mass confusion in the database.

The following is a hypothetical sequence of events that should transpire for this data entry example:

1. Casey presses the down-arrow key to go to the next record in the database.

2. The system must check to make sure that the record Casey was on is properly filled.

3. The system must post the record changes to the table so that they are committed to disk.

4. The system must leave the current record and position Casey at the next record in the database.

5. When Casey is positioned at the next record in the database, the system must position Casey at the proper field in the new record.

Each of these steps is a discrete event. Although Casey was responsible for only one event (pressing the down-arrow key), several events were actually created. These *internal* events are initiated by the database system so that it can keep its house in order and its data intact. For this reason, each user interaction creates a series of internal events, in which you might be equally interested.

Paradox for Windows has the same linear, discrete nature in its event model. The sheer number and variety of events that lay open for modification gives you some bewildering choices. Paradox for Windows has really exposed just about all the events you might want to handle. Throughout this book, we will show you which events are considered the work-horse events, the ones you will most likely use, and which events are less critical.

Paradox for Windows has 28 built-in methods which respond to events. These built-in methods are where you will write a large percentage of your code. Table 13.10 lists these built-in methods.

Table 13.10. Built-in methods for events.

Event	*When it occurs*
Internal events	
open	When a form is opened; occurs for each object
close	When a form is closed; occurs for each object
canArrive	Can the user enter an object?
arrive	After the user has entered an object
canDepart	Can the user depart an object?
depart	After the user has left an object
changeValue	Post changes in a field
newValue	After a field has received a new value
setFocus	When an object is ready for keyboard interaction
removeFocus	When an object is no longer ready for keyboard input
mouseEnter	When the mouse pointer moves on top of an object
mouseExit	When the mouse pointer leaves an object
pushButton	When a button is pushed
timer	Whenever a set interval of time elapses
External events	
mouseClick	Mouse left-click on an object
mouseMove	On a mouse movement
mouseDown	Left mouse button press

continues

Table 13.10. Continued.

Event	When it occurs
External events	
mouseUp	Left mouse button release
mouseDouble	Left mouse button double-click
mouseRightDown	Right mouse button press
mouseRightUp	Right mouse button release
mouseRightDouble	Right mouse button double-click
keyPhysical	Whenever a key is pressed
keyChar	After keyPhysical, when the key maps to an action
error	Error condition
action	When a keypress creates an internal action
menuAction	Choosing a menu item or speedbar equivalent
status	Whenever a message is displayed on the status bar

Not all of these events can be trapped for every type of object on a form. For example, the pushButton event makes sense only on a pushbutton, and the newValue and changeValue events are appropriate only for field objects.

As you scan the list of events in table 13.10, you may wonder why a particular event was classified as an internal or an external event. For example, an error condition may be the result of a user's mouse movement or keyboard interaction, but clearly it is Paradox's internal response to an external event. Don't get hung up on the distinction between internal and external events. The real difference between internal an external events lies in the way Paradox for Windows dispatches the event. We discuss this in the Bubbling section, later in this chapter.

Every event, internal or external, creates an object. This object is a packet of information called eventInfo. This packet of information looks different depending on the type of event that occurred. Paradox for Windows generates the following types of eventInfo packets:

- event
- actionEvent
- errorEvent
- keyEvent
- menuEvent
- mouseEvent
- moveEvent

- statusEvent
- timerEvent
- valueEvent

Table 13.11 lists the type of eventInfo packets that Paradox for Windows generates on each event, and what events use that packet.

Table 13.11. Built-in events and eventInfo packets.

Event triggered	Event category
removeFocus	event
setFocus	event
open	event
close	event
pushButton	event
action	actionEvent
error	errorEvent
keyPhysical	keyEvent
keyChar	keyEvent
menuAction	menuEvent
mouseClick	mouseEvent
mouseMove	mouseEvent
mouseDown	mouseEvent
mouseUp	mouseEvent
mouseDouble	mouseEvent
mouseRightDown	mouseEvent
mouseRightUp	mouseEvent
mouseRightDouble	mouseEvent
mouseEnter	mouseEvent
mouseExit	mouseEvent
canDepart	moveEvent
depart	moveEvent
canArrive	moveEvent
arrive	moveEvent
status	statusEvent
timer	timerEvent

continues

Table 13.11. Continued.

Event triggered	Event category
changeValue	valueEvent
newValue	event

Action Events

Hidden in the list of events in table 13.11 is one important event: action. An action event occurs whenever a user edits or navigates a table or a field. The action event enables you to trap for such things as moving to the next record, locking a record, editing a field, and so on. To trap for an action event, simply add code to the action built-in method for the object in question. The particular action is identified by a Paradox for Windows constant (listed in Chapter G of the ObjectPAL reference manual). By interrogating the eventInfo packet within the built-in action method, you can determine what action event occurred.

```
method action(var eventInfo ActionEvent)
    var
        actionStr       String
        result          Logical
    endvar
    ; determine if this is a Data action
    if eventInfo.actionClass() = DataAction then
        ; convert the eventInfo.id() constant to a string
        result = constantValueToName("ActionDataCommands",
                                      eventInfo.id(),
                                      ActionStr )
        ; display the name of the action that has occurred
        msgInfo("Action Occurred", ActionStr)
    endif
endmethod
```

In this code fragment, the method constantValueToName( ) converts an event id number (which is contained in the eventInfo packet) to a string. The event id identifies the type of action event that occurred. The method constantValueToName writes the constant name into the variable actionStr.

If you were to move from one record to another, this code fragment would display a dialog box that shows *DataArriveRecord*.

The action event covers a huge list of possible internal events that you can trap for and alter. The action events can be divided into five main groups. These groups are listed in table 13.12.

Table 13.12. Action event groupings.

Grouping	Purpose
DataAction	Editing tables, locking records, navigating a table
EditAction	Field-level editing events
FieldAction	Moving from field to field events
MoveAction	Moving around within a field, especially memo fields
SelectAction	Selecting values within a field, especially memo fields

Paradox for Windows has about 140 events that fit under one of the five groupings in table 13.12. Each event has a system constant which identifies the event. Instead of typing to memorize a meaningless integer, such as 12918, to identify an action event, the constant names make your code easier to read. Some of the events you can trap for are listed in table 13.13.

Table 13.13. Some action events.

Event	Used for
Data Action	
DataBeginEdit	Entering edit mode
DataDeleteRecord	Deleting the current record
DataInsertRecord	Inserting a new record
DataLockRecord	Locking the current record
Edit Action	
EditDeleteWord	Deleting the word around the cursor
EditDeleteSelection	Deleting selected text
EditToggleFieldView	Changing the field view state
Field Action	
FieldForward	Moving to the next field in the tab order
FieldFirst	Moving to the first field in the current record
Move Action	
MoveBottom	Moving to last record or last line of a memo field
MoveBegin	Moving to the first record or the start of a memo field
Select Action	
SelectEnd	Selecting from current position to the end of the table
SelectBegin	Selecting from current position to the beginning of the table

Needless to say, learning all 140 or so events would be an arduous task. Of these events, a few are critical. These few are covered in this book. You may not have to deal with the bulk of these events. In fact, we recommend that you don't unless you absolutely have to.

Although the event model in Paradox for Windows is very sophisticated, you can reasonably ignore large portions of it and focus on the events that are important to trap. *Don't try to control every event in Paradox for Windows. Control only the exceptions to the default event handling that you or your clients need.* We can't overstate the importance of this last sentence. If you decide to trap too many events and provide your own behavior rather than the default Paradox for Windows behavior, you will never be able to develop a Paradox for Windows application rapidly.

The beauty (and the danger) of this model is that you can provide as much complexity as you want in your application. If the application requires some sophisticated handling of keystroke events, Paradox for Windows will let you control the event. If your application does not require extensive changes in the default Paradox way of doing things, you don't have to trap for and handle a large number of events.

Creating Your Own Events

Not only can you trap for and respond to all these events, you can remap the current event to another event, or you can add your events to the stream of events. This is especially useful if you either want to change the action of a key—for example, the Ctrl+Home key combination—to another action, or if you want to change one keystroke's action into several actions.

To change the current action into another action, all you have to do is use the setId( ) method for the action event you are interested in changing. The setId( ) method changes the eventInfo packet. To understand this concept, you should look at some code. The following code fragment is attached to a multi-record object and traps for the action events which correspond to a movement to the first field of the first record (the Ctrl+Home keystroke) and the last field of the last record (the Ctrl+End keystroke). The sample code swaps the two commands so that Ctrl+Home actually performs a Ctrl+End and vice versa:

```
if eventInfo.id() = DataEndLastField then
   msgInfo("Remapping","End to Begin")
   eventInfo.setId(DataBeginFirstField)
else
   if eventInfo.id() = DataBeginFirstField then
      msgInfo("Remapping","Begin to End")
      eventInfo.setId(DataEndLastField)
   endif
endif
```

In addition to this redirection of events, you can create your own events out of thin air. The Form type has two interesting methods, action( ) and postAction( ). The action( ) method takes an action id as an argument and performs the action represented by the action id. For example, the following code opens a form and edits it, without the user pressing the F9 key, which normally puts a table in edit mode:

```
var
   custForm    Form
endvar
custForm.open("Cust.fsl")
custForm.action(DataBeginEdit)
```

The action( ) method enables you to create your own action events which will be handled immediately. The postAction( ) event enables you to insert a new event into the event queue. The event you inserted will be performed after any other events for your method have been performed. It is not important to fully understand the differences between action( ) and postAction( ) right now. What is important to understand is that you can not only redirect events, but that you can create your own events; Paradox for Windows handles them as if the user created them.

Bubbling

Paradox for Windows developers will most likely be adding two terms to their vocabulary: *snippets* of code and *bubbling*. We've already explained snippets of code. You will see the term *bubbling* thrown around quite a bit. It's a simple concept, and it's important. To understand bubbling, you need to understand how Paradox for Windows dispatches events.

You have already seen examples of how to create a form and how objects can be placed on top of other objects. The fundamental layer in this design approach is the form. This is obvious because without the form, where can you place objects? What is not so obvious is that Borland has built some special intelligence into the form. The form is the central dispatcher for all events. All events, internal or external, are given to the form for dispatching.

The form is smart enough to know the intended target for the event. If you click a pushbutton, the form knows that the event is intended for the pushbutton and not the menu or some other object. The form dispatches the event to the intended target, in effect telling the object, "Hey you. Do *this*!" (in which *this* stands for the event that occurred).

Say the event was a mouse click and the target was the text on a pushbutton. Remember, a pushbutton is actually two objects, a pushbutton and a pushbutton text object. The text object sits on top of the button. When the form determines that the mouse click event occurred on the pushbutton text object, it sends the event to the text object and says: "Handle it." Now, put yourself in the place of the pushbutton. You are really a simple and rather ignorant object. All you know how to do is display yourself. When the big boss (the form) says "Do this," you might feel compelled to do something. Because you can't really handle a mouse click because this work is not part of your job description, you decide to give the work to your immediate boss: the pushbutton object.

Your boss, the pushbutton object, knows how to handle a mouse click event. It interprets the event as a request to push down the button. Your boss gleefully handles the big boss's request because it's in his or her job description. The pushbutton object passes the event off to its boss, in case that object needs to respond to the event. The event gets passed up the hierarchy, with each object getting a chance to respond to the event, until it stops at the desk of the big boss.

The form dispatches the event to the intended target. The target object either handles the event or passes the event to its immediate container. That object either handles the event, or, if it can't, it passes the event to its immediate container, and so on until one of the following three things happens:

- An object handles the event
- A built-in method explicitly terminates bubbling
- The event bubbles back up to the form, where the form handles it

Bubbling is sometimes called *fall-back*.

The most important point to remember is that external events bubble up. Internal events are dispatched to their targets and are never passed up the containership tree. This makes sense, because if it is an internal, Paradox-generated event, Paradox for Windows knows which object should handle the event.

Figure 13.11 shows the bubbling sequence for an event. The event begins with a user mouse click on the pushbutton's text object (step 1).

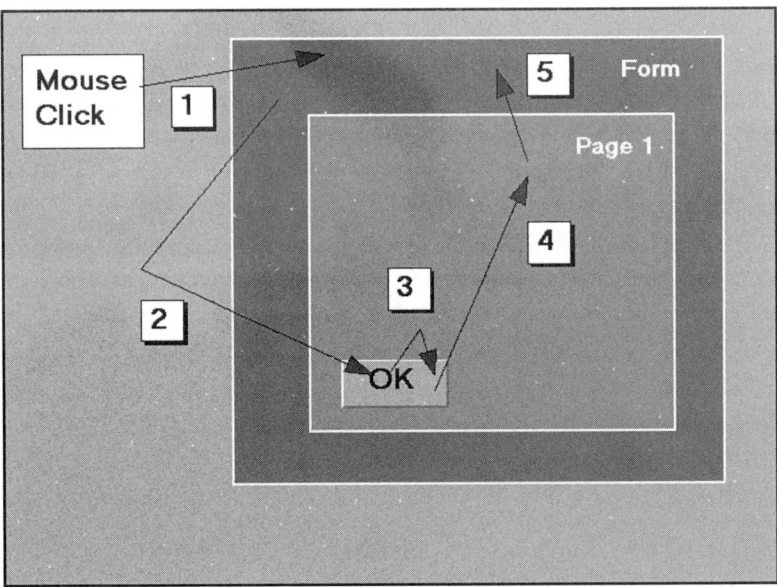

Figure 13.11. External event bubbling.

The form dispatches the event to the target (step 2). The text object, which is the target, passes the event to its container, the pushbutton (step 3). If the event was not a mouse click and it could not be handled by the pushbutton on the form, the event would bubble back up to the page (step 4) and finally to the form (step 5) where the form would handle it. Because the pushbutton knows how to respond to a mouse click, in reality the event would be handled there and no more bubbling would occur.

Summary

Paradox for Windows is a compiled, full-featured, form-based, event-driven, visual programming environment. To grasp ObjectPAL basics, developers need to know the following:

- Basic language elements
- Basic data types
- Methods, procedures, and libraries
- How to pass parameters
- The containership hierarchy
- Events

Although this list is short, it is loaded with concepts that take practice and experimentation to learn. When you understand these basic concepts, you can use more complicated, real-world application development techniques.

14

Events: Controlling User Interactions

The event model is the heart and soul of Paradox for Windows. Learning how to use it may occasionally give you grief. Mastering it, however, will enable you to do nearly anything.

Paradox for Windows has 28 built-in methods that allow you to trap for 160 or so discrete events. Many of these events are trivial, such as MouseRightDouble, but others are more significant, waiting for some creative programmer to put to creative uses. You will find many creative ways to handle events in ObjectPAL. In fact, the event model can bewilder newcomers to the event-driven world. Programmers coming from traditional environments will wonder why the event model is so chock full of different events. If you are one of those people, don't worry. With some practice and a little patience, the event-driven world is easy to understand. In fact, Paradox for Windows has a highly visual and understandable approach to event-driven programming, once you master the basics. Programmers coming from Windows or Paradox for DOS 4.0 programming backgrounds will be more at ease.

Borland endowed Paradox for Windows with a rich and sophisticated event model for a very specific reason: to make the development environment suitable for complex application development. Borland could have taken steps to make the event model simpler so that programmers can adjust to it. But this would have been a mistake because the event model is conceptually straightforward and easy to comprehend. The event model, which is intertwined with the containership model, is so powerful a metaphor for building applications that the hardest part is understanding the metaphor.

We're going to make events comprehensible, because they are. We're not going to talk about every nook and cranny of the event model, which would bore you with unimportant minutia. We will, however, show you specific examples of how to trap for the events that you will most likely use.

Internal, External Events, and Bubbling

At the end of Chapter 13, you learned the difference between internal and external events (see table 14.1). Although the words internal and external signify that perhaps external events are initiated by the user and internal events are initiated by Paradox, don't think this way because this explanation is not accurate and will only confuse you.

For example, the error and status events are clearly not instated by the user. The error event is initiated by Paradox when it cannot handle an event properly. The status event occurs when Paradox sends its message about the current event to the status bar at the bottom of the active window.

Table 14.1. Events.

Event	When the event occurs
Internal events	
open	When a form is opened, occurs for each object.
close	When a form is closed, occurs for each object.
canArrive	Can user enter an object?
arrive	After the user has entered an object.
canDepart	Can the user depart an object?
depart	After the user has left an object.
changeValue	Post changes in a field.
newValue	After a field has received a new value.
setFocus	When an object is ready for keyboard interaction.
removeFocus	When an object is no longer ready for keyboard input.
mouseEnter	When the mouse pointer moves on top of an object.
mouseExit	When the mouse pointer leaves an object.
pushButton	When a button is pushed.
timer	Whenever a set interval of time elapses.
External events	
mouseClick	Mouse left-click on an object.
mouseMove	On a mouse movement.
mouseDown	Left mouse button press.
mouseUp	Left mouse button release.
mouseDouble	Left mouse button double-click.
mouseRightDown	Right mouse button press.
mouseRightUp	Right mouse button release.
mouseRightDouble	Right mouse button double-click.

Event	When the event occurs
keyPhysical	When a key is pressed.
keyChar	After keyPhysical, when the key maps to an action.
error	Error condition.
action	When a keypress creates an internal action.
menuAction	Choosing a menu item or SpeedBar equivalent.
status	When a message is displayed on the status bar.

The difference between internal and external events is that *external events bubble. Internal events don't.*

Say these two sentences one hundred times, right now. Believe it or not, you may end up hitting your head against a wall because you forgot that *external events bubble. Internal events don't.*

Now the question is, "Why do external events bubble and internal events don't?" For a simple reason—the intended object for internal events in unambiguous. When the events occur, Paradox knows the exact target for the event. The arrive event wouldn't occur, for example, if Paradox didn't know exactly what it was arriving on. The changeValue event must, by definition, know what object's value is changing. The changeValue event is *sent to* the object *that needs changing.*

The intended target for external events, however, can be ambiguous. Paradox may not know exactly what was the intended target.

When the user clicks a field label in a form, is the target the text object that holds the field label, the field's edit region, or the container for the field edit region and the field label? When the user interacts with a form and clicks on a field, the user wants to go to that field; that field should have focus. Remember that Paradox is smart enough to know the screen coordinates where the mouse click occurred and the screen coordinates of all objects on the form. The user just happened to click on the field label rather than on the edit region. What should Paradox do—beep at the user and display the message, `Click on the Edit Region, silly fool`?

Paradox resolves this ambiguity through the concept of containership. If the external event cannot be handled by the original target, the event is passed to the target's container. In much the same way, employees pass off tasks to their boss that are beyond their capabilities or resources.

> *External events bubble. Internal events don't.*

Now that this concept is behind you, take a deeper look into bubbling.

Because external events bubble and internal events don't, you have choices when dealing with external events that you don't have with internal events. Remember that all events are bound by the following rules:

1. The form serves as the dispatcher for all events. You can trap all events before they are dispatched to their target.

2. After the target receives the event from the form, the target asks the following questions:

"Can I, the object that I am with the resources my creator gave me, respond to the event? If so, then I will respond. I will do what my programmer has told me to do—if anything—in the built-in method, *and then I will do my default behavior, if the programmer lets me.*"

"Is the event external? If I handled the event, then bubbling stops. If I cannot handle the event, pass it off to my boss, who may know how to handle it. If the event was an internal event, then the form knows I can handle it. It was an internal event meant for me to act on and no one else: no bubbling takes place."

In pseudocode, the target and any intervening object's event handling logic looks like this:

```
CallBuiltInMethod()                        ; run the built-in method
if objectCanHandleEvent then
     handleEvent()                         ; perform the default behavior
endif

if eventType = External and                ; the event was an external one
     not objectCanHandleEvent then         ; and the object can't handle it
     giveControlToContainer()              ; pass control upward - bubbling
else                                       ; the event was an internal one
     quitEventLoop()                       ; quit the event loop - no bubbling
endif
```

External events are passed off continually to each object's container until someone takes responsibility for the event and handles it. The buck finally stops at the form. When we say "takes responsibility" we mean that *the creators of Paradox endowed some object in the containership hierarchy with the capability of actually performing the event.* As ObjectPAL programmers, you may add your code to the built-in methods for the object, but we cannot make an object *smarter* than the creators made it.

The return trip for external events—the bubbling—is crucial to understand because different objects differ in intelligence. For example, the form not only dispatches all events but also handles, or takes responsibility for, a great many external events. Keystrokes and many action events can only be handled by the form. Other action events, such as record-oriented events like DataArriveRecord, can be handled by the TableFrame object and the MultiRecordObject. These objects are discussed in greater detail in Chapter 15, "UIOBjects: Controlling the User Interface."

The external events that are handled by the form therefore can be trapped twice at the form level—before the form dispatches them to the object and after the event is passed around like a cheap bottle of wine, up the containership hierarchy and back to the form. The form sees only the events handled by lower-level objects once: when the event is first dispatched.

External events get passed around, looking for someone to respond to them. External events handled by the form always have round trip tickets. External events handled by a lower-level object only get part of the way back on the return flight. Internal events know exactly where they should go and always have one-way tickets (see fig. 14.1).

Chapter 14 ■ Events: Controlling User Interactions

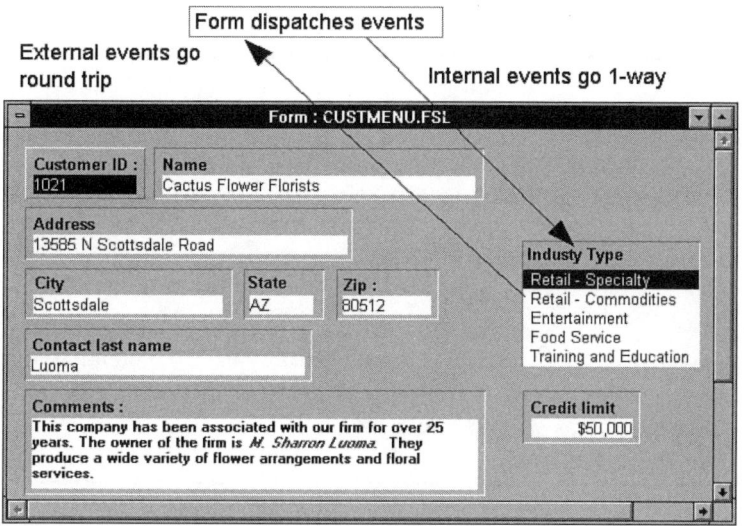

Figure 14.1. Internal and external events.

Events and eventInfo

All built-in methods have the same argument passed to them. This argument is the object, eventInfo. This object differs slightly, depending on the event. Mouse events have mouse information in eventInfo. Menu events have menu information in eventInfo. Visualize the eventInfo object as a mail pouch with different information valuable.

All eventInfo objects have, at the least, the methods listed in table 14.2.

Table 14.2. eventInfo Methods.

Method	Result
errorCode( ) LongInt	Returns 0 if no error occurred, otherwise, returns the error code. The error constants can be used to check the error code.
getTarget(var targ UIObject)	Assigns a UIObject variable the handle for the event's target so that the object can be manipulated without explicitly knowing what the object is.
isFirstTime( ) Logical	Returns true if this time is the first time the form sees the event.
isPreFilter( ) Logical	See discussion on handling form-level events.

continues

Table 14.2. Continued.

Method	Result
isTargetSelf( ) Logical	Returns true if the target of the event the same as the object that currently is handling the event. Returns false if the object handling the event wasn't the intended target. If isTargetSelf( ) = false then bubbling has occurred.
reason( ) SmallInt	For newValue events, reason reports why the event has occurred.
setErrorCode code (const id LongInt)	Allows you to manually set the errorcode. Setting the error to an on-zero value creates an error condition, which is useful to deny internal events.
setReasonCode (const reas SmallInt)	Allows you to set the reason code.

Each event has a slightly different eventInfo object. The list of eventInfo objects is listed in table 14.3.

Table 14.3. eventInfo Objects.

event	mouseEvent
actionEvent	moveEvent
errorEvent	statusEvent
keyEvent	timerEvent
menuEvent	valueEvent

Always check the built-in method header to make sure of the type of eventInfo packet you will be receiving. The mouseEvent and keyEvent packets contain many methods that interrogate the eventInfo packet and provide useful information.

Handling Form-Level Events

To trap for an event at the form level, just right-click the form title bar to get the list of properties. Select Methods, and then you can select an built-in method and attach code to it, or you can use the Properties ¦ Form ¦ Methods menu command to get to the methods dialog box, press Ctrl+space bar with the form object selected, or right-click on the form object in the object tree.

All the form level built-in methods contain the following if..else..endif statement:

```
if eventInfo.isPreFilter() then
   ; This code executes for each object on the form.
```

```
else
    ; This code executes only for the form.
endif
```

The isPreFilter( ) method enables you determine at what point you have caught this event: while the event is dispatched or when it has bubbled back up. The isPreFilter( ) method returns true [when] both 1 and 2 are true:

1. This is the first time the form object (the dispatcher) has seen the event.
2. The target of the event is an object other than the form. In other words, the event will be dispatched to some object below the form.

All code you place on the true side of the isPreFilter( ) check executes before the form has dispatched the event to some other object. All code you place on the false side of the isPreFilter( ) check executes when the event has bubbled back up to the form level for handling or *when the target of the event is the form*.

Code you place on the false side of the isPreFilter( ) check catches events at a very different time interval than code attached on the true side. The code on the false side will see external events that bubbled back up the form level after these external events have already been around. The form has already seen the event and dispatched it. Your code placed on the false side of the isPreFilter( ) check will also see events *whose target is the form, before the event is "dispatched" to the form for the first time*.

Simply, code placed on the false side of the isPreFilter( ) check will be executed when the form is the object with the smarts to handle the event.

In most cases, this kind of behavior is acceptable, because the false side of the isPrefilter( ) check frequently is used as a *buck stops here* place to handle events after all objects in the event's containership hierarchy have had a shot at handling the event but failed to do so. If the target of the event was the form, then no dispatching would occur, so no bubbling would occur either.

Understanding the isPreFilter( ) method is *extremely* important. Of all the methods and constructs that you need to understand, the isPreFilter( ) method is number one on the list. You will interact with this method frequently, and the sooner you understand how it works and whether to place your code on the true or false side of the check, the sooner your code will work.

The isPreFilter( ) method actually combines the result of two other methods: isFirstTime( ) and isTargetSelf( ). isPreFilter( ) is equivalent to the following:

```
if eventInfo.isFirstTime()=true and eventInfo.isTargetSelf()=false
```

Events Keywords

Developers can stop both internal and external events from happening. You also can physically force an event up the containership hierarchy. Denying events or pushing events upward, which is crucial to any application, is more involved than just detecting an event. Review the following four important keywords that control events:

- doDefault
- passEvent
- disableDefault
- enableDefault

The doDefault keyword will actually force the object to execute the default behavior immediately. If, in the object's built-in method, Paradox encounters a second or third doDefault keyword, they are ignored. The default behavior for a particular object/event can be triggered exactly once: either immediately following the first doDefault keyword or after the execution of the built-in method.

The passEvent keyword suspends the built-in method's code and does the following:

1. For external events, the passEvent keyword passes the event to all of the object's containers for processing. After all the object's immediate containers process the passEvent, your code continues with the statement immediately after the passEvent. If any containers initiate a bubbling sequence, this bubbling sequence also is triggered during the passEvent cycle. The passEvent can be used to *force* external events up the containership hierarchy, all the way to the form, right in the middle of a sequence of events.

2. For internal events, the passEvent keyword passes the event to the objects' immediate container. The event does not get passed further than this point up the containership hierarchy. After the container is done processing the event, your code continues with the statement immediately after the passEvent.

Intermingling passEvent with bubbling can create some unusual and confusing effects. For example, the form in figure 14.2 contains a table frame object, which is surrounded by a box object. In this example, the Record object performs the default behavior and then explicitly does a passEvent. The TableFrame object performs a passEvent *before* executing the default behavior. The box, page, and form objects do nothing but their default behavior, which—for an ArriveRecord event—is nothing.

The following code is attached to the various objects: each point in the code is marked with a number to indicate which step occurs where.

```
; Form object
method action(var eventInfo ActionEvent)
if eventInfo.isPreFilter()      then
     ; This code executes for each object on the form.
     if eventInfo.id() = DataArriveRecord then
          msgInfo("Form Object","Dispatching arrive record") ; #1
     endif

else
     ; This code executes only for the form.
     if eventInfo.id() = DataArriveRecord then
          msgInfo("Form Object","Arrive Record (passEvent)") ; #6, #12
     endif
endif
endmethod
; the Record object
method action(var eventInfo ActionEvent)
```

```
            if eventInfo.id() = DataArriveRecord then
                msgInfo("Record Object","Arrive Record, now doing default") ;#2
                doDefault          ;#2
                ; #8
                msgInfo("Record Object","Done with default, now passing the event")
                passEvent          ; #8
                msgInfo("Record Object","After passEvent") ; #14
            endif
        endmethod
        ; the TableFrame Object
        method action(var eventInfo ActionEvent)
        if eventInfo.id() = DataArriveRecord then
            ; #3, #9
            msgInfo("TableFrame Object","Arrive Record, now passing the event")
            passEvent              ;#3, #9
            msgInfo("TableFrame Object","After passEvent") ; #7, #13
        endif
        endmethod
        ; the Box object
        method action(var eventInfo ActionEvent)
        if eventInfo.id() = DataArriveRecord then
            msgInfo("Box Object","Arrive Record (passEvent)")    ;#4, #10
        endif
        endmethod
        ; the page object
        method action(var eventInfo ActionEvent)
        if eventInfo.id() = DataArriveRecord then
            msgInfo("Page Object","Arrive Record (passEvent)") ;#5, #11
        endif
        endmethod
```

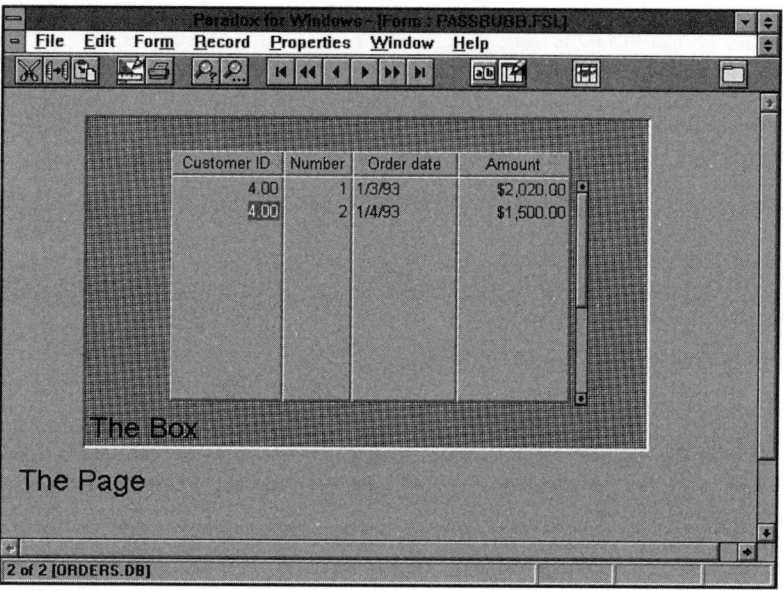

Figure 14.2. The passEvent and bubbling example.

Now follow the sequence of events. Whenever the user moves to another record, the following sequence occurs:

1. Form object dispatches the arriveRecord event to the record object.
2. The record object receives the event and prepares to perform the doDefault command, which causes the record object to pass the event to its container, the TableFrame.
3. The TableFrame receives the event and passes the event to its container, by way of passEvent.
4. The box object receives the passed event, has nothing to perform, and passes the event to its container—the Page object.
5. The Page object receives the passed event, has nothing to perform, and passes the event to its container, the Form object.
6. The form object receives the passed event, has nothing to perform, and passEvent bubbling terminates.
7. The TableFrame object resumes its built-in code immediately after the passEvent that triggered the prior bubbling. Because no more built-in code exists at this point and because no doDefault command was issued, the TableFrame performs the default behavior, which is to arrive on the next record.
8. The Record object gains control next because it started the prior chain of events with a doDefault. The Record object sends the event to its container by way of passEvent.
9. The TableFrame object receives the passed event. Because it has already performed its default behavior, nothing is done. The TableFrame object passes the event upward by way of passEvent.
10. The Box object receives the passed event, has nothing to perform and passes the event to its container.
11. The Page object receives the passed event, has nothing to perform and passes the event to its container.
12. The Form object receives the passed event, has nothing to perform and passEvent bubbling terminates.
13. The TableFrame object picks up processing after the passEvent.
14. The Record object picks up processing after the passEvent.

As you see, the passEvent keyword forces an external event to bubble. The event is passed upward until some object can handle the event. After an object handles the event, the control returns to the line of code immediately following the passEvent command.

Compared to passEvent, the other keywords—disableDefault and enableDefault—perform simple tasks. The keyword disableDefault sets a flag that is private to that object, which prevents the object from executing its default behavior after your built-in method is done. The enableDefault keyword just resets the flag so that the object will execute its default behavior. The disableDefault keyword is a key ingredient for denying events.

Denying Events

You can tell any object that handles an external event to quietly *deny*, or ignore, the event by issuing a disableDefault keyword in the object's built-in method. This addition tells the object to *not* perform its usual routine.

This procedure is good only for external events. To stop internal events from happening, you must set the eventInfo packet's if to a non-zero value (an error condition), tricking Paradox into thinking some error has occurred. For example, you can stop the user from leaving a field object by setting the error code for the canDepart event to the constant CanNotDepart. When the default behavior for the internal event executes, Paradox senses that an error occurred and doesn't allow the user to leave the object.

In effect, the following two mechanisms are available to *deny* an event:

1. Setting the event's error code and tricking Paradox into thinking that an error condition exists.

2. Explicitly disabling the object's default behavior for the event by using the disableDefault keyword.

Borland cautions you against using disableDefault on internal events. The reference manual says that disabling the default behavior for internal events can cause problems. We have found occasions where disabling the default behavior for *external* events also can cause problems. For this reason, we recommend following these rules when trying to deny an event:

1. For internal events, set the eventInfo packet's error code to a non-zero value. The object's default behavior *executes* but is *tricked* into thinking an error occurred. During an error condition, most objects' default behavior is to do nothing.

2. For external events, use the disableDefault keyword to prevent the object's default behavior from executing. If you experience problems for some external events, especially action events, set the event's error code to a non-zero value, so that the object is tricked into thinking an error occurred rather than disabling the default behavior.

The following code fragment illustrates the point 2.

```
method action(var eventInfo ActionEvent)
if eventInfo.isPreFilter()      then
    ; This code executes for each object on the form.
else
    ; This code executes only for the form.
```

```
            if ( eventInfo.id() = DataPostRecord or
                eventInfo.id() = DataUnlockRecord ) and
                if Balance.value >= Credit_limit.value then
                disableDefault
                msgInfo("Posting Message","Can't exceed credit limit")
            endif
        endif
        endmethod
```

The preceding example uses the action event, an external event, to prevent the user from increasing the customers balance if it exceeds the credit limit. The disableDefault keyword is used to deny an external event, in accordance with standard practice. This setup should work, right?

Wrong. In fact, the line of code that displays a posting message displays several times, which seems odd. Understand that the disableDefault keyword disables the default behavior for that object and for that particular event, not the stream of events. Paradox makes several attempts to post the record as part of the stream of events created by the attempt to move to another record. Therefore, the disableDefault keyword has a narrow range of effects and can stop only the default behavior for the particular object and for the particular event in question.

Setting the error code seems to have a more lasting effect than disabling the default behavior, because other events which will occur downstream will interpret the error code properly and take the appropriate action, which, in effect, denies the event. The following code example is identical to the previous one except that the event's error code is set to the constant CanNotDepart. This change fixes any problems with the prior example.

```
        method action(var eventInfo ActionEvent)
        if eventInfo.isPreFilter()    then
            ; This code executes for each object on the form.
        else
            ; This code executes only for the form.

            if ( eventInfo.id() = DataPostRecord or
                eventInfo.id() = DataUnlockRecord ) and
                if Balance.value >= Credit_limit.value then
                eventInfo.setErrorCode(CanNotDepart)
                msgInfo("Posting Message","Can't exceed credit limit")
            endif
        endif
        endmethod
```

You may be persistent and try to place this code at different levels in the containership hierarchy and on either side of the isPreFilter( ) check, but you still get exactly the same results. What happens is that the keystroke, F12, which moves to another record, is generating a series of events. As a programmer, you do not have total control over the series of events. You cannot redefine what the sequence will look like. You can, however, disable the default behavior for some of the objects the event touches and set an error code to affect how objects yet to receive the event will handle it. In addition, you can create and then insert new events into the stream.

In effect, the event model gives unprecedented capability of responding to and of creating new events by inserting them into the stream of events. This capability, however, gives only limited ability to rearrange the predestined flow of events. For all the control the event model does give, you are somewhat hampered by not knowing exactly what the default behavior for each object is and when it occurs.

For example, the push button event is peculiar because by the time code that is attached to the pushButton( ) built-in method is called, some default behavior has already occurred: the button appears depressed. Somewhere between the mouseDown event and the pushButton event, Paradox already triggered one-half of a push button's default behavior. Which means that if you want to deny a pushButton event before the button is pushed, you have to attach code to the push button's mouseDown( ) built-in method to prevent the button from appearing depressed.

Similarly, if you want the push button to appear raised before you begin any processing, you have to issue a doDefault before you begin processing, which executes the other half of a push button's default behavior.

Built-In Methods and Status Messages

Placing code in some built-in methods causes problems with status messages: the messages disappear. Status messages appear at the bottom of the active window. Paradox displays these kinds of messages as key violation errors, what keystroke to press to perform a table lookup, among others. Not being able to automatically display these messages can be disconcerting, and we hope that this problem is fixed in newer versions of the product. The two built-in methods that we have seen problems with are the action( ) and the keyPhysical( ) built-in methods. Messages originating from any problems with table-level validity checks seem to *disappear* whenever you place any code in these methods.

The work-around for this problem is simple. You must explicitly issue a doDefault command in the action( ) or keyPhysical( ) method and then do one of two things:

1. If the errorCode( ) after the doDefault returns a non-zero value, invoke the fail( ) method. This forces the method to trip the onfail side of any try..onfail blocks and, if none are defined, it causes the error message to display. The following code fragment illustrates this technique:

    ```
    doDefault
    if errorCode()<>0 then
        fail()
    endif
    ```

2. If the errorCode after the doDefault is a non-zero value, use the message( ) procedure to directly display the error message. The following code fragment illustrates this technique:

    ```
    doDefault
    if errorCode()<>0 then
        message(errorMessage())
    endif
    ```

The problem with technique 2 is that the errorMessage( ) procedure returns an error message slightly different than the error message that normally is displayed. Figure 14.3 shows a forced error message, using technique 2. In this example, the user is trying to leave the ship date field blank. The ship date field is marked as a required field, as part of the table specification.

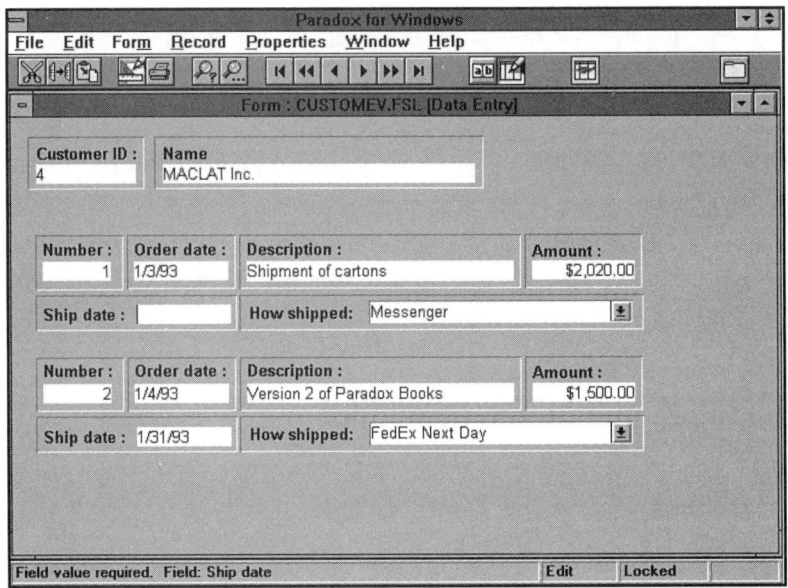

Figure 14.3. Forcing status messages with errorMessage().

Figure 14.4 shows the same error message using technique #1. Technique 1 displays the message cleanly but technique 2 doesn't.

Events—Where To Place Code

The biggest problem with handling events is learning where in the containership hierarchy to place code. All code that responds to internal events (internal events don't bubble) must be attached to the target object. You can attach external events, which do bubble up to the object that can handle them, to any object from the intended target to the object that handles the event.

For external events, we have the following suggestions:

- If the code is generic behavior and is used in several forms, place the code in a library and call the common code from the appropriate object. You will want to add a large amount of code this way. Common tasks, such as opening forms with a standard window style, displaying or logging error conditions, and standard application messaging routines are best handled this way. Using libraries to store methods that are accessed throughout the application eliminates redundant code and makes maintenance a breeze.

- If you are controlling record-level events, place the code in the record object of a multi-record object or a table frame. This code may be a one-line call to a library method. Every time you want to perform record-level event trapping, make sure that you have a multi-record object or a table frame. Both of these objects contain a record object.

- If you are controlling a list, attach the code to the list object. If you are performing a series of actions as a result of a push button event, place the code in the pushbutton object.

- In all other cases, place the code at the highest level (closest to the form) possible if you want to share the code among some of the objects within the containership hierarchy. If you want the code to apply to only a single object or to a small group of objects, place the code at lower levels in the containership hierarchy.

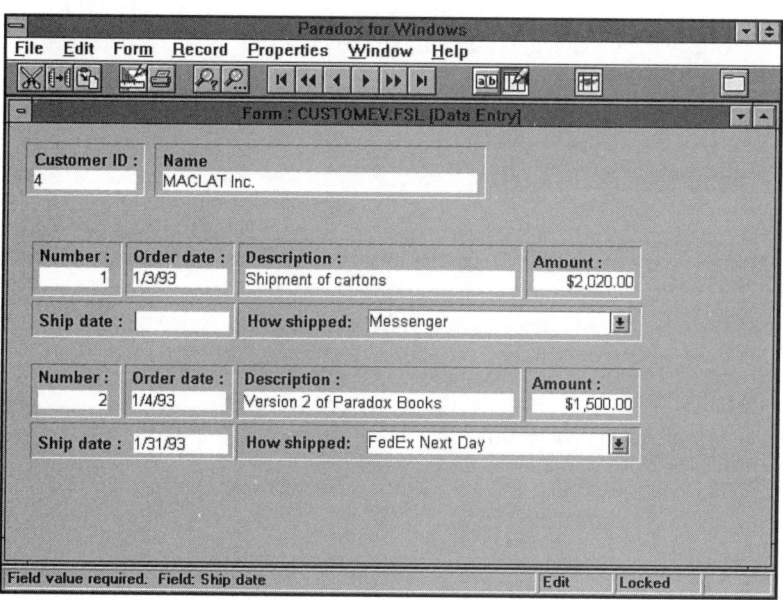

Figure 14.4. Forcing status messages with fail( ).

In real-world applications, you will find that you predominantly place code at two levels—at the form level on both sides of the isPreFilter( ) check or attached to specific objects within the form. Only infrequently do you need to place code at intermediate levels in the containership hierarchy.

Events and Placing the Code in a Library

Placing code in a library is easy. All you need to do to take the following steps:

1. Create the custom methods in a library.
2. Declare the library method in the form's (or object's) Uses window.
3. Open the library when the form is opened.
4. Invoke the library method.

To create a custom library method, you need to first create a library by using the File ¦ New ¦ Library menu sequence or by using the library SpeedBar item. Once the library is opened, you can right-click on the library window's title bar to open the methods dialog box. Once inside the methods dialog box, you can add your own methods and procedures. Remember that procedures are private to the library and cannot be accessed outside the library.

To make the form aware of the library method's existence, you need to declare the library method in the form's Uses window. The following code sample shows how to do this procedure. In this example, three library methods are declared:

```
Uses  ObjectPAL
      lKeyPhysical(var ev KeyEvent) Logical
      lArriveMessage(var ev MoveEvent) Logical
      lStatusEvent(var ev StatusEvent) Logical
endUses
```

To open the library so that the form can use the library's methods, you first need to declare a library variable in the form's Var window and then open the library when the form is opened. The following code fragments show how to declare a library variable and how to open a library:

```
Var
     lib Library
endVar
method open(var eventInfo Event)
if eventInfo.isPreFilter()    then
     ; This code executes for each object on the form.
else
     ; This code executes only for the form.
     doDefault      ; open all the form's objects first
     lib.open("UTILS.LSL",GlobalToDesktop) ; open the library
endif
endmethod
```

The only difficulty with libraries is that the doDefault keyword cannot be used from within a library method. Often, you need to either execute the object's default Paradox behavior from within a library method or disable the default behavior.

You can work around this limitation by making sure that your library method returns a true or false value and based on this value, either issue a doDefault within the form, rather than in the library, or deny the event. The following code fragment illustrates this point.

```
var
    result      Logical
endvar
; This code executes for each object on the form.
result = lKeyPhysical( eventInfo )
if result = false then
    disableDefault
else
    doDefault
    if errorCode()<>0 then
        fail()
    endif
endif
```

The beauty of libraries is that common code can be stored and maintained centrally, saving you time and maintenance headaches.

Manipulating Bubbling

You can place code that handles external events at intermediate levels in the containership hierarchy to exploit the features of bubbling. Because external events automatically bubble up to an object that can handle the event, you can place code to handle the event at the object or below the object in the containership hierarchy. Fortunately, the Form handles a large share of events including the status event. For example, you may want to change the default Paradox status messages, depending on the context. One way to accomplish this change is to place code, at the form level, on the false side of the isPreFilter check that displays a new status message. By placing code here, you catch the event as it bubbles back up to the form after the target has received it.

The following example calls a library method, lStatusEvent( ), which displays custom messages on the status bar rather than on the default messages. Don't worry about what lStatusEvent( ) does; this action is unimportant right now.

```
method status(var eventInfo StatusEvent)
if eventInfo.isPreFilter()    then
    ; This code executes for each object on the form.
else
    ; This code executes only for the form
    if lib.lStatusEvent(eventInfo) then
        doDefault
    else
        disableDefault
    endif
endif
endmethod
```

What is important is that this code fragment represents behavior that is triggered for all objects on the form that are the target of a status event. The difference is that the code is executed on the event's return trip to the handling object (the form) after the event is dispatched by the form. You can manipulate bubbling by attaching code to a lower-level object's status( ) built-in method which executes before the form object's lStatusEvent( ) method. The lower-level object can override the form's *programmed default* behavior simply by doing its own thing and then terminating bubbling by denying the event.

The following code fragment is attached to a field on the form. This code gives the field a different status message than the programmed default.

```
method status(var eventInfo StatusEvent)
    message("This message overrides the programmed default")
    disableDefault      ; this stops the event from bubbling back up
endmethod
```

Because the form dispatches all events to their intended targets and external events eventually *bubble* up the containership hierarchy until they reach their handler, this example has the programmed default behavior executing on the false side of the isPreFilter( ) check, on the event's return trip. If you place the programmed default code on the true side of the isPreFilter( ) check, then code attached to the lower-level object will occur after the programmed default code. In effect, you have no way of preventing the programmed default behavior.

Usually, you will not need to deal with all the intricacies of bubbling. But if you do, understanding exactly what happens in bubbling helps in resolving problems or handling difficult problems.

Top Events: The Big Eight

Of all the 28 built-in methods, eight stand out as perhaps the most important ones:

- open( )
- action( )
- menuAction( )
- error( )
- keyPhysical( )
- canDepart( )
- canArrive( )
- arrive( )

The following sections discuss briefly the need for each of these built-in methods and the work you probably will do with them.

open( )

The open( ) built-in method is called for each object on the form being. Objects at the lowest level in the containership hierarchy are opened first. Objects higher in the containership hierarchy are opened next. The form object is opened last.

The open method is used to perform the following tasks:

- Initialize variables declared in the object's var window
- On form objects, to display menus
- Bind any unbound fields to a field
- Initialize any objects' properties, including a lists' dataSource property
- Perform any other form- or object-level startup

The one real issue with the open method is that you should explicitly issue a doDefault *before* you perform the custom default code, which avoids any problems that frequently arise when you try to do anything before the default object code executes.

Understand that each object's open( ) is called as part of a cascade of opens. If you try to reference another object from the current object's open method, you cannot be sure that Paradox has successfully opened the object until the open event cascades to that object's container. In addition, Paradox has to perform a a large number of housekeeping chores on the open event. For this reason, always placing code after a doDefault on object's open( ) built-in method is a good idea.

action( )

The action( ) built-in method is a very busy method; 140 different events blast their way through this single built-in method, allowing excellent control over just about every data and field navigation event.

Among the most common uses of the action event are shown in the following list:

- Trap for record posting and record unlocking events.
- Trap for record locking events.
- Trap for table navigation events, such as moving to the next record, prior record, last record, first record, and so on.

One problem with the action event is that there is no event specifically tied to when the user leaves a record. Although any number of action events causes the user to leave the current record—such as moving to the next, searching for a value, moving down a set of records, and so on—there is no constant single action to signify that the user has left a record.

This problem usually is not significant when the user tries to leave a record object or a multi-record object because you can attach code to the canDepart( ) built-in method and detect when the user is moving from record to record. The problem arises when you have a multiple-page form with fields from one table on each page. Because the fields don't belong to a record object, there is no concept of trapping for a canDepart record event.

The work-around for this problem is to avoid using the record canDepart record event in these circumstances. Usually, you want to prevent the user from leaving a record because a field value is incorrect. An alternate way to check a field's validity is to do it just like Paradox does it—at the time the record gets posted. Because you can easily trap for the eventInfo.id( ) of DataUnlockRecord and DataPostRecord in the action( ) built-in method, it makes sense to do record-level validation that cannot be handled through validity and referential integrity checks there.

menuAction( )

You use this built-in method to trap for all user interactions with the menu or with Paradox's menu. This built-in method is discussed in detail in Chapter 17.

error( )

The error built-in method is useful if you want to trap for error conditions and take your own action. The top reasons that you may want to do this are shown in the following list:

- You don't like Paradox's default error messaging scheme and you don't want to use the status event to change the error message.

- You don't like Paradox's default error-handling mechanism and you want to provide your own, including the capability of saving the errors that occur in a table or a file for later reference.

- You need to take application-specific error handling action that goes beyond the scope of what Paradox provides.

The built-in error( ) method, with error handling strategies are discussed in greater detail in Chapter 19.

keyPhysical( )

Although we advise against excessive keystroke handling because this process often needlessly expands the size of your application, Paradox does allow you to trap nearly every keystroke combination. Developers often trap keystroke-level events for the following reasons:

1. To provide hot keys for push buttons or field objects.
2. To handle F1 as a help key and provide context sensitive help.
3. To override the default Paradox way of handling key events.

Although reasons 1 and 2 are legitimate reasons, we feel that reason 3 usually has suspicious origins. The most common reason developers begin to redefine many keystrokes is because the user is unfamiliar with the application's way of handling keystrokes. Because Paradox for Windows is a Windows application and Windows applications have a standard for how to handle keystrokes, the real issue is whether the application should be done in Paradox for Windows at all.

Not every developer has the luxury of telling users what to do, so from time to time, an application needs to be written that changes all the default keystrokes for an application. The good news is that ObjectPAL accommodates this easily.

Keystroke Trapping Rules

The keyPhysical( ) built-in method is called every time Windows passes a keystroke to Paradox, so certain Windows-specific keystrokes, such as Ctrl+F4, never get passed to Paradox for handling. If Windows passes the keystroke to Paradox, which is nearly every keystroke, except for Windows-specific keystrokes, the keyPhysical( ) built-in method is called.

If the keystroke maps to a Paradox-specific action, as is the case when F12 advances to the next record, then the keystroke generates an action event, and the action( ) built-in method is invoked. If the keystroke doesn't map to an action, the keyChar( ) built-in method is invoked.

The following rules explain exactly how keystroke events are handled:

1. If the keystroke is Windows-specific, Windows handles the keystroke, and Paradox has no control over it.

2. If the keystroke is not Windows-specific, Paradox invokes the keyPhysical( ) built-in method.

3. If the code in the keyPhysical( ) built-in method doesn't disable the default behavior, Paradox checks to see if the keystroke is supposed to map to an action.

4. If the keystroke maps to an action, Paradox invokes the built-in action( ) method.

5. If the keystroke doesn't map to an action, Paradox invokes the keyChar( ) built-in method.

6. If the code in the keyChar( ) built-in method doesn't disable the default behavior, Paradox handles the keystroke. If the keystroke has no meaning, it gets passed on to Windows.

Rule number 6 is interesting because by definition, certain keystrokes—such as the Alt+Tab key which normally lets the user move to another application—are not automatically handled by Windows. Instead, you can trap for the Alt+Tab key combination with the keyPhysical( ) or keyChar( ) built-in method to deny the key sequence.

The keyEvent Object

The keyPhysical event gets passed a KeyEvent eventInfo object. This object has several methods, which are listed in table 14.4.

Table 14.4. KeyEvent Methods.

Event	Result
char( )	Returns the character pressed. For Shift keypresses, uppercase letter is returned.
charAnsiCode( )	Returns an integer representing the ANSI value for the keystroke.
isAltKeyDown( )	Returns true if the Alt key is held down, otherwise returns false.
isControlKeyDown( )	Returns true if the Ctrl key is held down, otherwise returns false.
isFromUI( )	Returns true if the user created the key event (rather than a programmer generating the key event with ObjectPAL statements), otherwise returns false.
isShiftKeyDown( )	Returns true if the Shift key is held down, otherwise returns false.
setAltKeyDown( )	Changes the eventInfo packet's Alt key state to down, so that you *press* the Alt key under ObjectPAL control. Takes a logical value as an argument.
setChar( )	Changes the eventInfo packet's key value, which allows you to change or specify a character for a key event. Takes a string as an argument.
setControlKeyDown( )	Changes the eventInfo packet's Ctrl key state to down, so that you *press* the Ctrl key under ObjectPAL control. Takes a logical value as an argument.
SetShiftKeyDown( )	Changes the eventInfo packet's Shift key state to down so that you *press* the Shift key under ObjectPAL control. Takes a logical value as an argument.
SetVChar( )	Changes the eventInfo packet's key value by specifying the string which represents the Windows virtual character as an argument.
setVCharCode( )	Changes the eventInfo packet's key value by specifying the Windows virtual character constant (VK Constants).
vChar( )	Returns a Windows virtual character as a string that represents the keystroke.
vCharCode( )	Returns a Windows virtual character as an integer that represents the keystroke.

The Windows keycodes are listed in table 14.5.

Table 14.5. Windows Keycodes.

Name	Decimal Code	Description
VK_LBUTTON	1	Left mouse button
VK_RBUTTON	2	Right mouse button

Chapter 14 ■ Events: Controlling User Interactions

Name	Decimal Code	Description
VK_CANCEL	3	Used for Control-break processing
VK_MBUTTON	4	Middle mouse button (3 button mouse)
VK_BACK	8	Backspace
VK_TAB	9	Tab
VK_CLEAR	12	Clear key
VK_RETURN	13	Return
VK_SHIFT	16	Shift
VK_CONTROL	17	Control
VK_MENU	18	Menu key
VK_PAUSE	19	Pause key
VK_CAPITAL	20	Capital key
VK_ESCAPE	27	Escape
VK_SPACE	32	Space bar
VK_PRIOR	33	PgDn
VK_NEXT	34	PgUp
VK_END	35	End
VK_HOME	36	Home
VK_LEFT	37	Left arrow
VK_UP	38	Up arrow
VK_RIGHT	39	Right arrow
VK_DOWN	40	Down arrow
VK_SELECT	41	Select key
VK_EXECUTE	43	Execute key
VK_SNAPSHOT	44	Print screen key
VK_INSERT	45	Insert
VK_DELETE	46	Delete
VK_HELP	47	Help key
VK_0 .. VK_9	48 .. 57	0 through 9 key
VK_A .. VK_Z	65 .. 90	A through Z key
VK_NUMPAD0 .. VK_NUMPAD9	96 .. 105	Numeric keypad 0 through 9 key
VK_MULTIPLY	106	Multiply
VK_ADD	107	Add (+)
VK_SEPARATOR	108	Separator

continues

Table 14.5. Continued.

Name	Decimal Code	Description
VK_SUBTRACT	109	Subtract
VK_DECIMAL	110	Decimal
VK_DIVIDE	111	Divide
VK_F1 .. VK_F16	112 .. 127	F1 through F16 key
VK_NUMLOCK	144	Num lock
VK_OEM_SCROLL	145	Scroll lock
VK_OEM_PLUS	187	Plus (+)
VK_OEM_COMMA	188	Comma (,)
VK_OEM_MINUS	189	Minus (–)
VK_OEM_PERIOD	190	Period (.)

Paradox for Windows uses nearly all these Windows keycode names as constants as well, with some exceptions. The VK_A through VK_Z names are not ObjectPAL constants. To refer to these keys, use the vChar( ) method, which returns an uppercase character. The VK_0 through VK_9 also are not constants. Instead, use vChar( ) to find out what number key was pressed. The VK_OEM names also are not ObjectPAL constants.

canDepart( )

One of the most common things a developer may want to do in a data entry form is to prevent the user from leaving a field, record, or a table if certain conditions are not met. The canDepart( ) built-in method helps in this regard.

The canDepart event occurs just before the user leaves an object. Think of the canDepart event as asking for permission to leave an object. Besides the problem of trying to detect departing a record that spans multiple pages on a form, which canDepart cannot help with, the canDepart( ) method is used for the following tasks:

1. To prevent the user from leaving a field. Because field-level validity checks, although powerful, cannot do what ObjectPAL does, complex field-level checking often is done with a canDepart event. Although it makes sense to trap for the DataPostRecord and DataUnlockRecord action events to do complex field level validation, the canDepart also can be used as well.

2. To prevent the user from leaving a record.

3. To prevent the user from leaving a table frame.

4. To prevent the user from leaving a page on a form.

To prevent the user from leaving any of the preceding objects, you set the eventInfo packet's error code to a non-zero value. Because canDepart is an internal event, using disableDefault won't prevent the depart.

In the following example, the eventInfo packet's error code is set to the constant CanNotDepart:

```
method canDepart(var eventInfo MoveEvent)
if self.value = "Des Plaines" then
    msgStop("Error","This is an invalid city")
    eventInfo.setErrorCode(CanNotDepart)
endif
endmethod
```

canArrive( )

The canArrive( ) method is the inverse of the canDepart( ) built-in method. This method asks permission to arrive on an object.

```
method canArrive(var eventInfo MoveEvent)
if self.value = "Des Plaines" then
    msgStop("Error","This is an invalid city")
    eventInfo.setErrorCode(CanNotArrive)
endif
endmethod
```

In this example, you are preventing the user from arriving on a field by setting the eventInfo packet's error code to the CanNotArrive constant. When this example occurs, the user is placed at the next field or object in the tab order and is unable to arrive on the field. If the user used a mouse click to move to this field, he or she is prevented from doing so and will remain on the field he or she is in.

arrive( )

The arrive event occurs after the user has already moved to a field or an object and frequently is used to display messages, change the appearance of the object in some way, or provide other visual or auditory clues that tell the user they are on a new field or object.

The arrive event cannot be denied.

Top Events: The Little Six

We cannot leave out six other events, because although they are not the workhorse events that the big eight are, you probably will use them often.

changeValue( )

The change value event is triggered before a field's value changes. If the user changes the field's value by typing in it or if you, as a programmer, change the field's value with an ObjectPAL statement, the changeValue( ) built-in method is triggered. This built-in method is available only for field objects.

Every time the user changes a value in a field, the changeValue( ) built-in method is called when the field's value gets committed, usually when the user leaves the field. In addition, when the user changes a field's value, the changes are made in a temporary buffer, which actually is a memo type. When the field gets committed, Paradox converts the temporary buffer into the field object's underlying data type.

To prove the point, you can attach the following code to any object's changeValue( ) built-in method. This code example uses the newValue( ) method, which is available for ValueEvent eventInfo types. The change value event generates this kind of packet. As you play with this code snippet, notice that even numeric fields report the data type of the new value as Memo.

```
method changeValue(var eventInfo ValueEvent)
var
     a AnyType
endvar
a = eventInfo.newValue()
msgInfo("New Value DataType",strval(dataType(a)))   ; should be a memo!
endmethod
```

The changeValue( ) built-in method is not triggered when lookup help causes all corresponding fields to receive new values.

newValue( )

The newValue event is a bit different than the changeValue event. The newValue( ) built-in method is triggered whenever the field object's value changes, which can occur when the user scrolls through records in a multi-record object. As the user scrolls through the records, the user has not altered any field values. The newValue( ) event, however, gets invoked because the field object is reporting that it has received a new value to display.

When the user opens a form, every field in the form triggers the newValue( ) built-in method, because every field will report that a new value was received from the underlying table.

The newValue event is particularly useful for controlling undefined fields in multi-record objects. You can create an undefined field in a multi-record object and change this field's value when another field's value changes. This approach ensures that the code for the undefined field is executed only when a corresponding field's value changes.

A newValue event can occur for three reasons, which are represented by the following three constants:

StartupValue

FieldValue

EditValue

You can determine the reason by using the eventInfo packet's reason( ) method. The StartupValue constant refers to the field's new value when the form is opened. The FieldValue constant refers to the field's new value after the field is committed.

pushButton( )

The pushButton event occurs when a push button object is pressed. This event is very simple to learn and practice with. The only wrinkle to this event is that Paradox has already performed some default behavior before any code you attached to this built-in method executes: the button appears depressed, and because a push button doesn't do anything except depress itself, you cannot deny a push button event from within the pushButton( ) built-in method.

setFocus( )

The setFocus event occurs immediately after an arrive event occurs. The setFocus event prepares the field or object for user interaction. Push buttons have a rectangle drawn around their labels. Regular fields become highlighted—if field view is off—and a status message that shows the current record number and the total records is displayed.

Many developers use arrive( ) and setFocus( ) interchangeably. After all, the only difference between the two methods is largely cosmetic. If you issue a disableDefault from within a setFocus( ) built-in method (which Borland recommends against, because setFocus is an internal event), you will lose any visual indication that the field or object has focus. You will be able to edit and change the field, however. Denying a setFocus event by setting the eventInfo packet's errorCode does not stop the field from being arrived on, nor does it prevent any visual indicators that the field has focus from displaying.

Many developers frequently use the setFocus( ) built-in method to display any custom help messages or give other visual cues about which field has focus that Paradox does not or cannot display. If you explicitly issue a doDefault from within the setFocus( ) method and then display your messages, your code will execute after Paradox makes visible its visual cues.

removeFocus( )

The removeFocus event occurs just before the depart event. The default behavior for this event is to remove any cues that the field has focus. If you issue a disableDefault from within the setFocus( ) built-in method, you lose any visual indication that the field has lost focus.

Table 14.6 shows the relationship between setFocus, removeFocus, arrive, canArrive, depart, canDepart, changeValue, and newValue events, and lists them in order of occurrence and what object receives the event.

Table 14.6. Order of Events.

Order	Event	Object
1	canDepart	Current
2	canArrive	Destination
3	changeValue	Current
4	newValue	Current
5	removeFocus	Current
6	depart	Current
7	arrive	Destination
8	setFocus	Destination

timer( )

The timer event is unusual in that any UIObject can use the setTimer( ) method to designate how frequently it should receive a timer event. For example, the following code, attached to a form's open event, creates a timer for the Page1 object:

```
Page1.setTimer(5000)  ; set timer to go off every 5 seconds
```

The following code, attached to the form's close event, kills any timer set for the Page1 object:

```
Page1.killTimer()
```

Then, from within the Page1 object, you can trap for the timer event and perform whatever task you want.

The problem with the timer event is that Windows resources are used, the performance of the application will slow down, and Windows has a finite number of timers (16) available for Paradox to use. Two reasons for timers become apparent:

1. To allow Paradox to poll a table or file and perform some action, such as printing a report or performing table maintenance.

2. To poll a device, such as a communications port, on a regular basis to gather data and report the findings to the user. Applications that need to poll tank gauges for tank levels, initiate communications links to other computers or other similar tasks fall into this category.

Applications that fall into category 2 probably have to use timers because the user needs to be notified of changes in data while the application is live. Applications that fall into category 2 don't need timers because instead, these applications can use a second copy of Paradox (taking advantage of Windows multitasking capabilities) with a script or a form running the following loop:

```
while true
    if checkForRecord() then
        printRecord()
quitloop
    endif
    sleep(10000) ; sleep for 10 seconds
endwhile
```

Using this approach requires no timers and is more efficient because Paradox is suspended for the duration of the sleep. Contrast this approach with a timer, which has more overhead and consumes Windows resources.

Creating Events Out of Thin Air

In Paradox for Windows, developers can create the following events without any user interaction required:

Internal events

mouseEnter

mouseExit

External events

mouseDown

mouseUp

mouseDouble

mouseClick

mouseMove

mouseRightDown

mouseRightUp

mouseRightDouble

keyPhysical

keyChar

action

menuAction

Each of these events has a corresponding method name that may be used with Form and UIObject variables or objects. Appendix G lists these methods with the valid arguments that can be supplied. Although the Paradox reference and the Types dialog box don't show it, the keyPhysical( ) and keyChar( ) methods also can take a KeyEvent variable as an argument.

All of these methods just create an eventInfo packet of the appropriate type and send the event to the form or to UIObject's built-in method of the same name. We have already explained how action works. The others methods behave in the same way.

The action( ) method lets you direct one of the 140 or so action constants to the form or the UIObject's built-in action( ) method. The Form and UIObject postAction( ) method are similar except that postAction( ) takes the event specified by the action constant and posts the event at the end of the action queue. The action( ) method is not so kind. It executes the action event immediately, without regard for what events have not yet been executed.

Summary

This chapter just skimmed the surface of Paradox for Windows events. The event model is filled with nooks and crannies, with gems and tar pits waiting for you. We tried to illustrate as many pointers as possible to help you understand the event model and avoid any difficulties.

Fortunately, the event model is sufficiently comprehensive and open that you can work around nearly any of the shortcomings or inadequacies. As you work with Paradox for Windows, you will discover that the event model is extremely flexible and powerful.

15

UIObjects: Controlling the User Interface

The term *UIObjects* stands for User Interface Objects. Fields, radio buttons, check boxes, pushbuttons, lists, drop-down edit lists, bar and pie graphs, crosstabs, graphics, lines, circles, and boxes are all UIObjects. This is the stuff, from the perspective of the user, that applications are made of.

In Paradox for Windows you can create UIObjects interactively and set their properties. While this may seem powerful, hold on tight, because with ObjectPAL, you can change many properties on the fly while users interact with the form, all with trivial ObjectPAL code.

This chapter reviews the most important types of UIObjects and how they can be manipulated under ObjectPAL code. In addition, we review some additional aspects of the event model that you need to know in order to manipulate UIObjects.

Table Frames

Table frames are basic UIObjects that let the user view and change the records in a table. The most significant features of a table frame include: a variable number of rows (or records) to display; a variable number of fields to display; field headers; and optional vertical and horizontal scroll bars to scroll through the table's rows and fields, respectively (see fig. 15.1).

Under program control, a table frame is a useful tool because creating one and manipulating one is very easy. However, you can't change the basic structure of a table frame. Every table frame has a columnar format. In this regard, a table frame fits into a continuum of UIObjects that spreads between two extremes. One extreme represents ease of use and lack of control. The other represents more complex use and enhanced control. Figure 15.2 graphically illustrates this spectrum.

Part IV ■ Programming in ObjectPAL

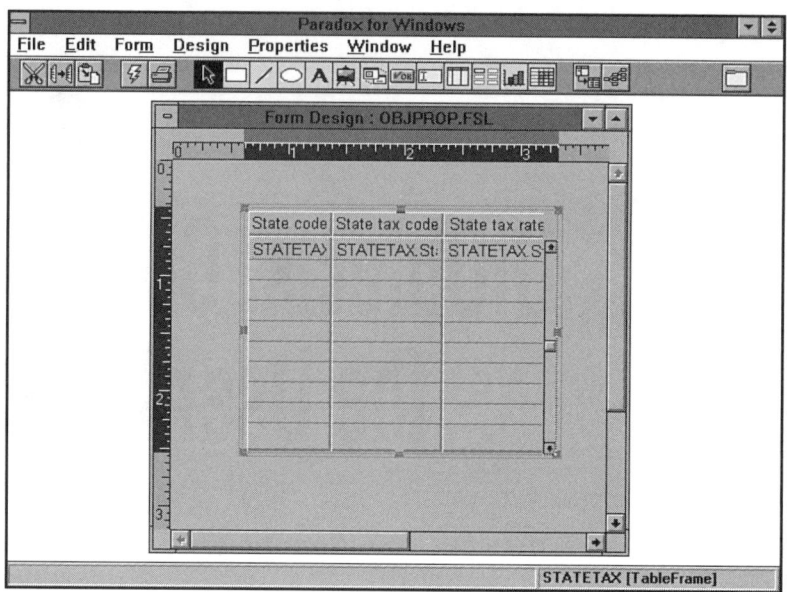

Figure 15.1. A table frame.

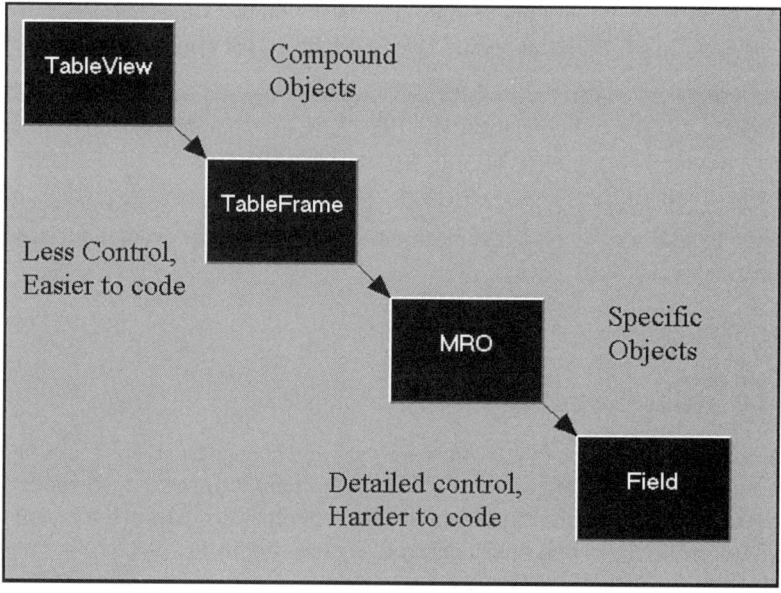

Figure 15.2. The UIObject spectrum.

Chapter 15 ■ UIObjects: Controlling the User Interface

At the top of the chart is the table view object type. A table view object lets you control the interactive viewing of a table without a form. This object type is the easiest to use because no form is needed. However, this object type lacks the programmatic control that table frames and multi-record objects possess. The next object is the table frame. Following that is the multi-record object (MRO), which gives you even greater programmatic control over a data entry session but requires more work to implement. Next is the field object, which gives you the lowest level of programmatic control and granularity. However, simulating a table frame with a series of field objects would be quite time-consuming and would involve much detailed coding.

This continuum gives you choices. Depending on the needs of the application, you can select what type of UIObject you want to use to perform the basic data entry tasks. To help you in your decision, we offer the following advice:

- UIObjects with record objects embedded in them are preferred because you can easily prevent departing from a record or handling other record-level events by attaching code to the record object's canDepart( ) built-in method. Table frames and MROs are the only UIObjects with an embedded record object.

- Table frames are good for viewing and editing simple tables that don't require a more elaborate user interface.

- MROs are suitable for most data entry tasks where a record object is required. Don't forget, it is possible to create an MRO with only one row. In fact, one of the most common uses of the MRO is to display of one record of information at a time.

- Field objects are needed to display one record of information that must span multiple pages or to display several of a table's fields where a record object is not needed.

A table frame has many properties that can be either read or changed using ObjectPAL. These properties are listed in table 15.1.

Table 15.1. TableFrame properties.

Property	*Read/Write*	*Notes*
Arrived	R	Has the object's arrive( ) method been called? (True, False) If so, then all the object's containers have been arrived on also.
BlankRecord	R	Is the current record blank? (T/F)
Class	R	What class of UIObjects does this object belong to?
Color	RW	Table frame color.
ContainerName	R	Name of the object that contains this object.
Deleted	R	Is the current record deleted? (dBASE tables only)
DeleteWhenEmpty	R	Should the object be deleted when empty?

continues

Table 15.1. Continued.

Property	Read/Write	Notes
Design.ContainObjects	R	Does the object contain other objects?
Design.PinHorizontal	RW	Lock the horizontal position.
Design.PinVertical	RW	Lock the vertical position.
Design.SizeToFit	RW	Will the object change size to fit contained objects?
First	R	Name of the first child object in the container.
FitHeight	R	Controls how the object is displayed.
FitWidth	R	Controls how the object is displayed.
FlyAway	R	Has a record moved to its sorted position in the table?
Focus	R	Does the object have focus? Set to true when the focus( ) method has been called. Set to false when the removeFocus( ) method has been called.
FullName	R	What is the object's full name?
FullSize	R	Actual size of the object (Point object).
Grid.Color	RW	Object's grid color.
Grid.Style	RW	Object's grid style.
Grid.RecordDivider	RW	Does the object have a record divide?
HorizontalScrollBar	RW	Does the object have a horizontal scrollbar?
Inserting	R	Is a record being inserted?
Locked	R	Is the table or record bound to the object locked?
Manager	R	What is the UIObject name of the form?
NCols	RW	How many columns are in the object?
NRecords	R	How many records are in the object?
NRows	RW	How many displayable rows are in the object?
Name	RW	The object's name.
Next	R	What is the next object in the same container?
Owner	R	Name of the object's logical container.
Pattern.Color	RW	Object's pattern color.
Pattern.Style	RW	Object's pattern style.
PinHorizontal	R	Is the object pinned horizontally?
PinVertical	R	Is the object pinned vertically?
Position	RW	Object's position (Point object).
Prev	R	What is the previous object in the tab order?
ReadOnly	RW	Is the object read-only?

Property	Read/Write	Notes
Recno	R	What is the current record number?
Refresh	R	Is data displayed being refreshed?
RowNo	R	What is the currently active display row number?
Scroll	RW	Scroll position (Point object).
SeqNo	RW	The sequence number of the record.
Size	RW	The lower left corner coordinates of a design object (Point object).
TableName	RW	Table name bound to the current object.
Touched	R	Has a change in the object been committed to the table?
Translucent	RW	Is the object translucent?
VerticalScrollBar	RW	Does the object have a vertical scroll bar?
Visible	RW	Is the object visible?

The key properties that make a table frame useful include:

- NCols
- NRows
- ReadOnly
- TableName
- Touched
- HorizontalScrollBar
- VerticalScrollBar

The NCols and NRow properties can dynamically change to increase or decrease the number of columns and records that are displayed at one time. Of course, the user can scroll through the records and columns at any time. These two properties only restrict what is visible at one time.

The TableName property can also be changed dynamically to reflect a new table. This means you can change the table being displayed in the table frame without having to change the design of the form.

The ReadOnly property reports True if the table frame can't be edited. This property can be set dynamically, which is a quick and effective way to prevent users from editing a table frame.

The Touched property indicates whether the table bound to the table frame has had changes committed to it. The touched property is not set to True until the user commits changes to a field (see Field and Record Posting below).

Part IV ■ Programming in ObjectPAL

The HorizontalScrollBar and VerticalScrollBar properties let you determine whether either scroll bar exists. These properties also can be set, which means you can dynamically turn scroll bars off and on.

Figure 15.3 is a test form which contains a table frame object. When pressed, the buttons on the right side of the form dynamically alter various table frame properties.

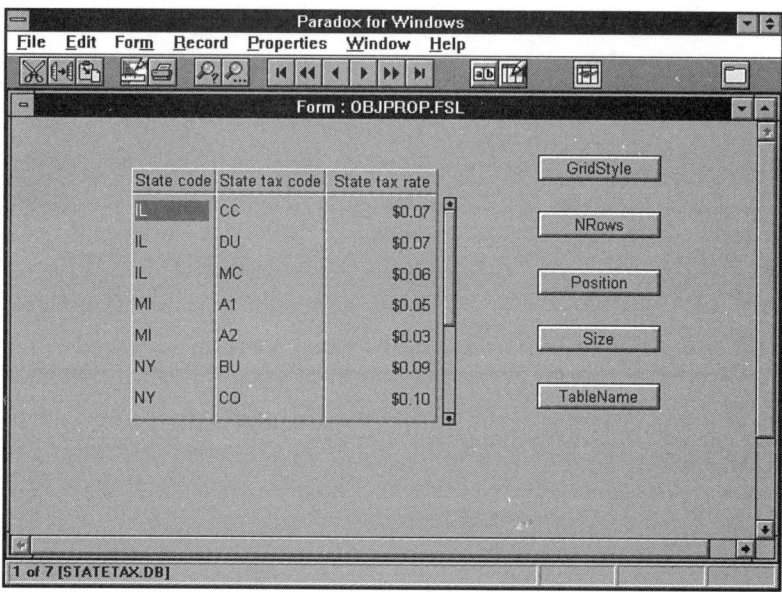

Figure 15.3. A form with property buttons.

The code for each of these buttons is listed in the following listing. As you can see, setting these properties is very easy.

GridStyle button

```
method pushButton(var eventInfo Event)
var
    p          PopUpMenu
    choice     String
endvar
p.addText("3D")
p.addText("Single line")
p.addText("Double line")
p.addText("Triple line")
p.addText("No grid")
; pop-up a menu of choices
choice = p.show()
switch
    case choice = "3D"                :
         obj.Grid.GridStyle = tf3D
```

```
            case choice = "Single line"   :
                obj.Grid.GridStyle = tfSingleLine
            case choice = "Double line"   :
                obj.Grid.GridStyle = tfDoubleLine
            case choice = "Triple line"   :
                obj.Grid.GridStyle = tfTripleLine
            case choice = "No grid"              :
                obj.Grid.GridStyle = tfNoGrid
        endswitch
    endmethod
```

NRows button

```
    method pushButton(var eventInfo Event)
    var
        p            PopUpMenu
        choice       String
    endvar
    p.addText("No change")
    p.addText("1")
    p.addText("2")
    p.addText("3")
    p.addText("4")
    p.addText("5")
    p.addText("6")
    ; pop-up a menu of choices
    choice = p.show()
    if choice <> "No change" then
        obj.NRows = SmallInt(choice)
    endif
    endmethod
```

Position button

```
    method pushButton(var eventInfo Event)
    var
        p            PopUpMenu
        choice       String
        pos          Point
    endvar
    p.addText("No change")
    p.addText("Move up")
    p.addText("Move down")
    p.addText("Move left")
    p.addText("Move right")
    ; pop-up a menu of choices
    choice = p.show()
    pos = obj.Position
    switch
        case choice = "Move left" :
            pos.setX(pos.x()-200)
        case choice = "Move right" :
            pos.setX(pos.x()+200)
        case choice = "Move up" :
            pos.setY(pos.y()-200)
        case choice = "Move down" :
            pos.setY(pos.y()+200)
    endswitch
    obj.Position = pos
    endmethod
```

Size button

```
method pushButton(var eventInfo Event)
var
    p           PopUpMenu
    choice      String
    pos         Point
endvar
p.addText("No change")
p.addText("Bigger")
p.addText("Smaller")
; pop-up a menu of choices
choice = p.show()
pos = obj.Size
switch
    case choice = "Bigger" :
        pos.setXY(pos.x()+200, pos.y()+200)
    case choice = "Smaller" :
        pos.setXY(pos.x()-200, pos.y()-200)
endswitch
obj.Size = pos
endmethod
```

TableName button

```
method pushButton(var eventInfo Event)
var
    f           String
    frec        FileBrowserInfo
endvar
frec.SelectedType = fbTable
; display a list of files
if fileBrowser(f,frec) then ; the user selected a file
    obj.tableName = f
endif
endmethod
```

Whenever you modify the TableName property, Paradox for Windows automatically adds the table, unlinked, to the data model. Just remember to use the Form method dmRemoveTable( ) to remove any unwanted tables from the data model.

Multi-Record Objects

MROs give you a finer level of control over the data entry session. The field placement is less restrictive and you have more control over the fields' visual properties (see fig. 15.4). The only major restriction for MROs is that the fields they contain must not span multiple pages. The entire MRO object must be on one page.

MROs are so useful because they give you nearly the same flexibility as using several field objects but have one big advantage: the MRO has a record object embedded in it. Although the action( ) built-in method has a DataArriveRecord event which can be trapped, the event is not deniable. It occurs after the user has arrived on a new record.

Chapter 15 ■ UIObjects: Controlling the User Interface

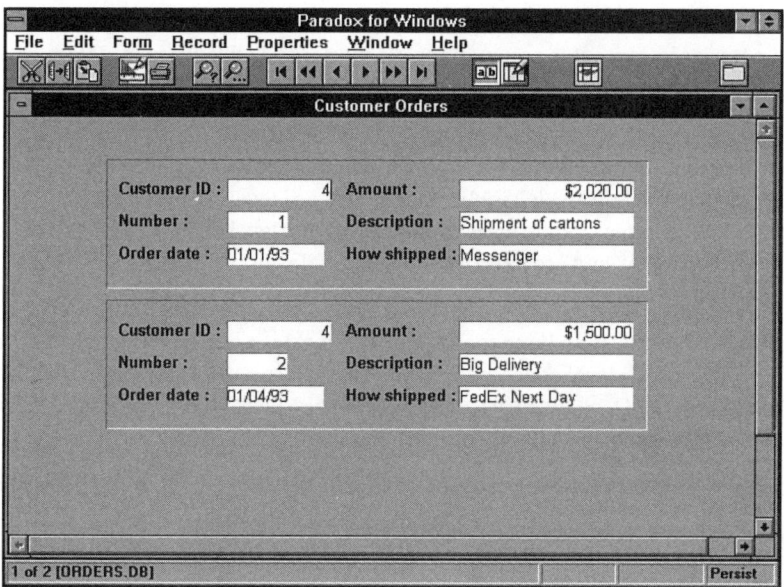

Figure 15.4. A multi-record object (MRO).

In addition, the action( ) built-in method has no DataDepartRecord event, which is sorely needed. Because of this limitation, to get a true *RecordDepart* event, you must attach code to a record object's canDepart( ) built-in method. The canDepart( ) method here is invoked whenever the user tries to leave a record. MROs also have several useful properties. MROs have many of the same properties as TableFrames (see table 15.1). Table 15.2 lists some other properties unique to MROs.

Table 15.2. Some MRO properties.

Property	Read/Write	Notes
Frame.Color	RW	What is the frame color?
Frame.Style	RW	What is the frame style?
Frame.Thickness	RW	What is the frame thickness?
Translucent	RW	Is the color of the object translucent?

Record Objects

The record object is unusual because you can never create one independent of a table frame or an MRO. The record object has many of the same properties as TableFrames and MROs (refer to tables 15.1 and 15.2).

303

The record object is crucial because you may find yourself frequently attaching code to it. The record object is also peculiar because it is common for inexperienced ObjectPAL programmers to confuse the record with its immediate container: the table frame or the MRO.

You must remember that the record object sits within a table frame or an MRO. The table frame and the MRO serve as a containing object and are not the same as the record. However, you can place code on the table frame and the MRO which is checking for record level events or properties and the code will most likely work. The reason for this is that most record-level events you might be interested in are action events. Action events are external and external events bubble.

Any time an external event occurs and you have code attached to the MRO or the table frame, the code will be invoked as part of the bubbling process. Sometimes, inexperienced ObjectPAL programmers inadvertently attach record-level code to the TableFrame or the MRO and forget that bubbling is the reason their code worked. Once they try to trap for a record-level internal event, such as canDepart, at the MRO or the table frame level, the code will not work properly.

Developers frequently need to know if a record has been changed. The Touched property will be true when a record has been modified. The unfortunate thing about the Touched property is that it gets set to true only after a field value has been committed, which usually occurs when the user leaves a field. This is often too late. You may need to know if the record has been modified before the user leaves the field object. Evaluating the touched property won't help in these cases.

If you want to trap for an event that coincides with a so-called *touch record* event, the DataLockRecord action event is one to look at. Paradox will attempt to lock any record as soon as the user presses a keystroke which will change the record. You can trap for this event and perform your own record locking or deny the event, preventing the user from making any changes.

You already saw how to use the action events DataPostRecord and DataUnlockRecord. These two events can be detected before a record gets posted. In addition, using the Form action( ) method, you can post a record with ObjectPAL.

Programming Field Objects

Fields are almost the final object standing between the user and the underlying table. Like MROs and TableFrames, fields (except for unlabeled fields) are actually composite objects; they contain one or more other objects. Not only are they composite, but they can take on several forms. One important field property, DisplayType, determines how the field looks. Table 15.3 lists the valid field display types.

Table 15.3. Field Display Types.

DisplayType Constant	Description
CheckBoxField	Field is a check box
ComboField	Field is a drop-down edit
EditField	Regular field, without a label
LabeledField	Regular field, with a label
ListField	Field is a list field
RadioButtonField	Field is a radio button

Each field type has a different containership hierarchy. Figure 15.5 shows the containership hierarchy for each field.

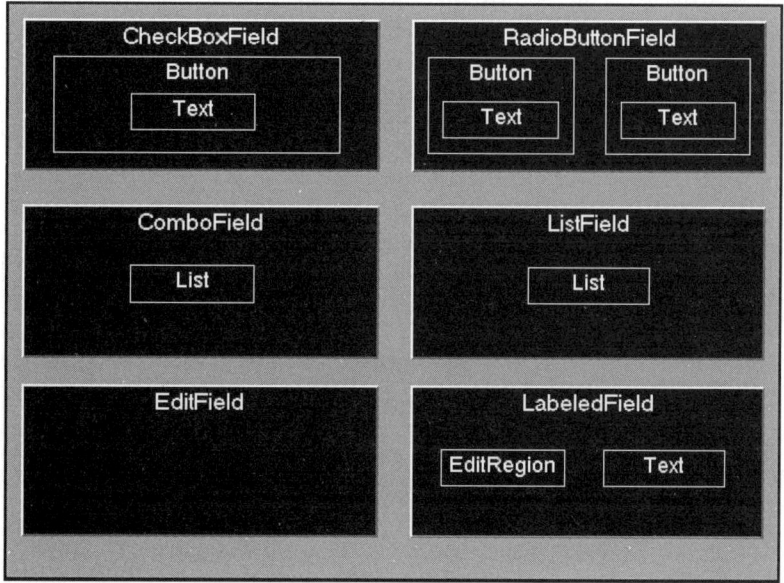

Figure 15.5. A field containership hierarchy.

Radio button and check box fields contain a button object. This button object has a ButtonType property that can be set to one of three types:

1. CheckBoxType
2. PushButtonType
3. RadioButtonType

One field can contain buttons of different types, although in most applications you will want to keep buttons in a field as the same type. The DisplayType field property can be set while the form is running. The only caveat is that when the field object is active, you can't change the field's display type. This makes sense, because Paradox has let the user arrive on a field, assuming it is a certain type of field. It wouldn't be nice to fool Paradox and suddenly switch the field type.

Like other UIObjects, fields share many of the properties listed in table 15.1. Fields have a few unique properties, however. The Editing property indicates that the user has edited the field or entered field view on the field. The Touched property indicates that the user has changed data in the field. We will discuss these properties in greater detail later.

Because of the tremendous flexibility in field properties, you can create many different effects. We will focus on what are probably the most useful and common effects you will need.

Programming a List Object

Fields created with the list or drop-down edit property enabled contain another object called the list object. For the list field type, the list object is easy to spot: the entire list is visible on the form. For drop-down edit lists, the list object is somewhat hidden. You can't tab to the list object or select it with a left mouse click, but it is there. You can click the right mouse button on the combo field's pushbutton, which is the list object. Or, if you select the field object and then display the object tree, you see a list object beneath the field object (see fig. 15.4). You can also select the drop-down edit list object from the object tree.

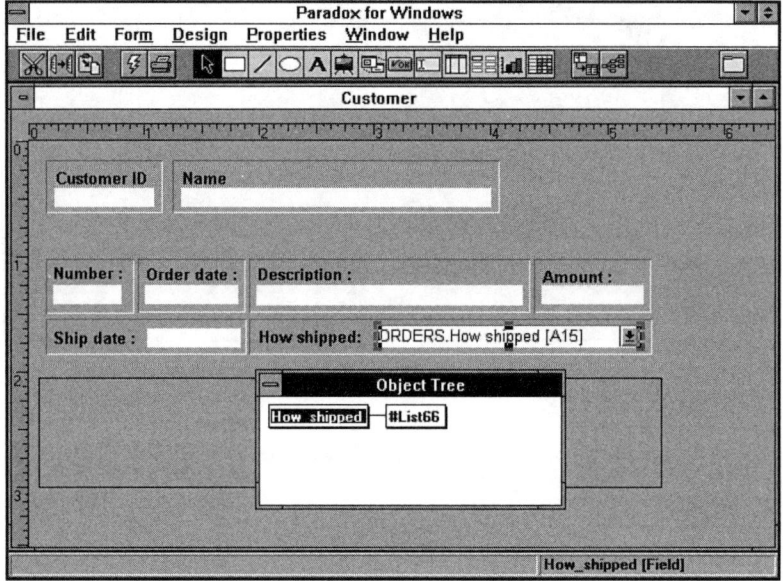

Figure 15.6. A drop-down edit list and object tree.

As we explained in Chapter 10 on designing forms, you can interactively set what should appear on the field's list. However, most of the time, the list's values reside in a table and can vary depending on the circumstances. Fortunately, the list object contains the following important properties:

- DataSource
- List.Count
- List.Selection
- List.Value

You can specify a table and field name for the DataSource property and the list will be filled with that table's field values. This technique works fine when you want to load all records from a small or medium-sized table (less than a few thousand records) into a list object. However, this won't work if you want to load the list with a range of values from the table. The List.Value and List.Selection properties come in handy here. These two properties conspire to let you stuff whatever values you want into the list.

Programming a List by Using DataSource

Programming a list by manipulating the DataSource property is extremely easy. All you need to do is place one line of code in the list object's open method. In fact, it's so easy, we wonder why Borland didn't allow interactive users to perform the same thing using menus rather than ObjectPAL code.

```
method open(var eventInfo Event)
  self.DataSource = "[shipmeth.ship method]"
endmethod
```

In this example, the SHIPMETH table holds the available shipping methods for a drop-down edit (combo) field (see fig. 15.7). The table name and field name are enclosed in quotes and square brackets. If you use the period within the table name to denote a file extension, the Borland manuals suggest that code should look like this:

```
method open(var eventInfo Event)
  self.DataSource = "[\"shipmeth.db\".ship method]"
endmethod
```

The backslash character is used to nest the quote characters within the table name string. The quote characters help resolve the ambiguity posed by the period character. However, the following code also works:

```
method open(var eventInfo Event)
  self.DataSource = "[shipmeth.db.ship method]"
endmethod
```

Also note that if you have a field with a period character in it, you will be unable to reference it within the DataSource property. You can modify the DataSource property from other events, such as the arrive event, or from another object. You can use this fact to dynamically change what table the DataSource property uses. For example, you can run a query to select certain records and change the DataSource property on the arrive event.

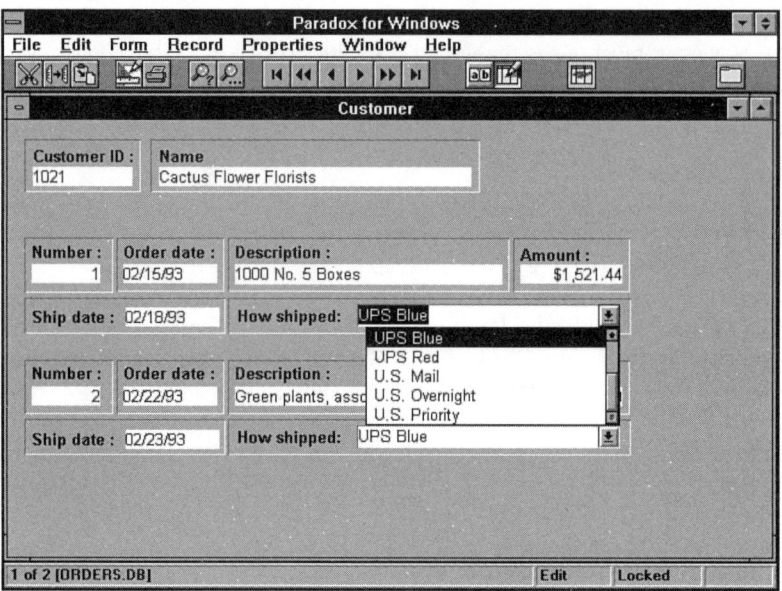

Figure 15.7. A programmed drop-down list.

The only issue with programmed lists is that you must make sure that the field which will hold the list value is wide enough to hold it. Paradox will not truncate the list entry to fit the field. Instead, it will refuse to let you select the list entry and display the message, `Data is too long for field`.

Programming a List Using List.Selection

By setting the List.Count property to 0, you can empty a list. This is easy. To load a list, you can manipulate the List.Value and List.Selection properties. The following example shows how to use them:

```
method open(var eventInfo Event)
var
     shipMeth Array[6] String
     x SmallInt
endvar
shipMeth[1] = "Courier"
shipMeth[2] = "Comp. Delivery"
shipMeth[3] = "UPS Red"
shipMeth[4] = "UPS Blue"
shipMeth[5] = "U.S. Mail"
shipMeth[6] = "U.S. Overnight"
for x from 1 to shipMeth.size()
     self.List.selection = x
     self.List.value = shipMeth[x]
endfor
endmethod
```

The List.Selection property serves as something like an array index variable. By incrementing it, you can place a new entry into the List.Value slot indicated by List.Selection. Just like the DataSource property, these properties can be set at any time and from other objects. In addition, you can use a TCursor object (which is discussed in Chapter 16) to fetch values from an invisible table and fill the list.

Remember, there is a big difference between the list field type and the drop-down edit field type. The drop-down edit field type enables the user to select from the list or type in anything they want to in the field. The list object restricts choices to what's in the list. To restrict entries in a drop-down edit field to just the contents of the list, the following code (attached to the field object's canDepart method) will help you:

```
method canDepart(var eventInfo MoveEvent)
var
     x SmallInt
endvar
for x from 1 to ShipList.List.Count
     ShipList.list.Selection = x
     ; if the field value is in the list, let the depart occur
     if self.value = ShipList.List.Value then
          doDefault
          return
     endif
endfor
eventInfo.setErrorCode(CanNotDepart)
message("Invalid field entry")
endmethod
```

Fields and the Editing Property

Field objects have an interesting property: editing. This property is set to true when the user is editing a field object. What is interesting is that the editing property has nothing to do with whether the table is in edit mode or not. In fact, the editing property can be true and the table cannot even be in edit mode. This occurs when the user enters field view while the table is not in edit mode. When this occurs, Paradox creates a text object which accepts the user's entry. The reason editing returns true is because the user is editing this temporary text object by entering field view. The changes never get committed to the record and the record never gets committed to the underlying table.

If you want to know if the underlying table is in edit mode, use the UIObject method isEdit( ). Any valid UIObject can use this method.

ObjectPAL and Calculated Fields

Calculated fields can accept custom methods and procedures in them, as long as the custom method returns a value. Any custom methods or procedures in a calculated field must be in scope or they must have some object identifier if they are outside of the calculated field's containership hierarchy. Figure 15.8 shows the field definition dialog box.

Part IV ■ Programming in ObjectPAL

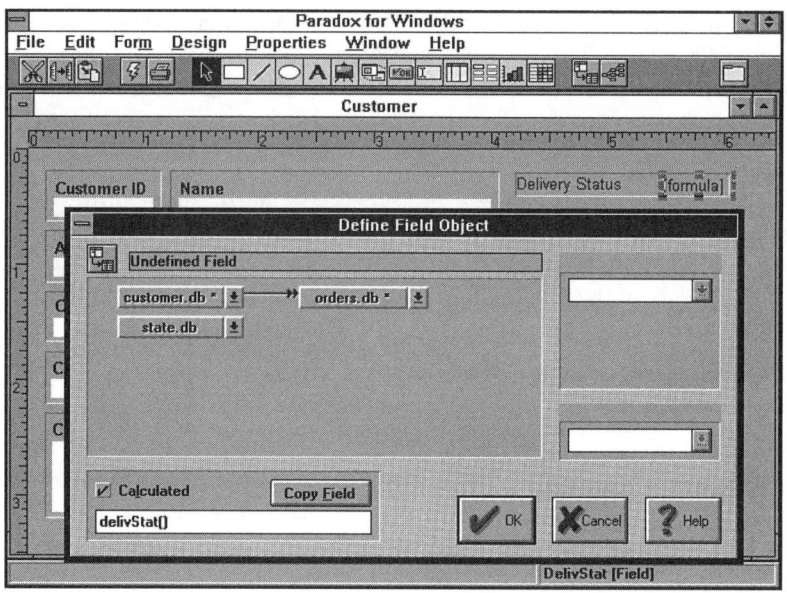

Figure 15.8. Defining a calculated field.

In this case, the calculated field is the custom method delivStat( ), which is attached to the form object and is available to all objects on the form.

Because calculated fields can't be assigned a value, as in myCalcField = "Hello," you will need to force the calculated field to evaluate its ObjectPAL method or procedure. You can use the action( ) method for this. The following code forces a recalculation of the myCalcField object, which is a calculated field:

```
myCalcField.action(DataRecalc)
```

This code can be placed in another object. It creates a DataRecalc action event and sends it to the calculated field. The ObjectPAL expression which fills the calculated field is then invoked.

Assigning a Value to Fields Not in the Form

You often may need to find or set a field's value even if the field is not on the form. At this point you have two options: place the field on the form and make it invisible, or use the dmGet( ) and dmPut( ) methods.

These two methods, and the dmAddTable( ) and dmRemoveTable( ) methods, are Form methods. They let you manipulate the form's data mode. dmGet( ) and dmPut( ) let you get and put field values directly to a table, bypassing the form. dmAddTable( ) and dmRemoveTable( ) let you add a table to and remove a table from the data model.

dmGet( ) and dmPut( ) work on the existing record. The following lines of code place "ACME General" in the Name field of the Customer table:

```
if dmPut("Customer","Name","ACME General") then
    message("Customer name changed")
else
    message("An error occurred")
endif
```

If you try to put a value into the table's field with the table in view mode, Paradox will display an error dialog box, saying that you are not in edit mode. If you place a value that is too long for a field, Paradox will display an error dialog box saying the value is too long for the field. If you place a number into an alphanumeric field, the number is converted to a string. If you try to place a string into a number field, Paradox displays an error dialog box.

One nice thing about dmPut( ) is that if you use it to place a value into a field that is already on the form, the field automatically will be updated to display the new value.

To retrieve a value from a field, the following code works:

```
var
    custName String
endvar
if dmGet("Customer","Name",custName) then
    message("Customer name is "+custName)
else
    message("Can't get the customer name")
endif
```

The following code shows how to add a table to and remove one from the data model:

```
if dmAddTable("Orders") then
    message("Orders table has been added to the data model")
else
    message("Orders table could not be added to the data model")
endif
if dmHasTable("Orders") then
    if dmRemoveTable("Orders") then
        message("Orders table has been removed from the data model")
    else
        message("Orders table could not be removed from the data model")
    endif
else
    message("Orders table is not in the data model")
endif
```

This code fragment uses the dmHasTable( ) method, which returns true if the specified table is in the data model and false if it isn't.

Graph Object Properties

Graph objects have a large number of properties that you can set under program control (see table 15.4).

Table 15.4. Graph Properties.

Arrived	LeftWall.Pattern.Color
BackWall.Color	LeftWall.Pattern.Style
BackWall.Pattern.Color	LegendBox.Color
BackWall.Pattern.Style	LegendBox.Font.Color
Background.Color	LegendBox.Font.Size
Background.Pattern.Color	LegendBox.Font.Style
Background.Pattern.Style	LegendBox.Font.Typeface
BaseFloor.Color	LegendBox.LegendPos
BaseFloor.Pattern.Color	LegendBox.Pattern.Color
BaseFloor.Pattern.Style	LegendBox.Pattern.Style
BindType	Manager
Class	MaxGroups
Color	MaxXValues
ContainerName	MinXValues
CurrentSeries	Name
CurrentSlice	Next
Design.ContainObjects	Options.Elevation
Design.PinHorizontal	Options.Rotation
Design.PinVertical	Options.ShowAxes
Design.SizeToFit	Options.ShowGrid
First	Options.ShowLabels
Focus	Options.ShowLegend
Frame.Color	Options.ShowTitle
Frame.Style	Owner
Frame.Thickness	Pattern.Color
FullName	Pattern.Style
FullSize	PinHorizontal
GraphType	PinVertical
Label.Font.Color	Position
Label.Font.Size	Prev
Label.Font.Style	Scroll
Label.Font.Typeface	Series.Color
Label.LabelFormat	Series.Graph_Title.Font.Color
Label.LabelLocation	Series.Graph_Title.Font.Size
Label.NumberFormat	Series.Graph_Title.Font.Style
LeftWall.Color	Series.Graph_Title.Font.Typeface

Series.Graph_Title.Text
Series.Graph_Title.UseDefault
Series.Line.Color
Series.Line.LineStyle
Series.Line.Thickness
Series.Marker
Series.Pattern.Color
Series.Pattern.Style
Series.TypeOverride
Size
Slice.Color
Slice.Explode
Slice.Pattern.Color
Slice.Pattern.Style
TabStop
TableName
TitleBox.Color
TitleBox.Graph_Title.Font.Color
TitleBox.Graph_Title.Font.Size
TitleBox.Graph_Title.Font.Style
TitleBox.Graph_Title.Font.Typeface
TitleBox.Graph_Title.Text
TitleBox.Graph_Title.UseDefault
TitleBox.Pattern.Color
TitleBox.Pattern.Style
TitleBox.Subtitle.Font.Color
TitleBox.Subtitle.Font.Size
TitleBox.Subtitle.Font.Style
TitleBox.Subtitle.Font.Typeface
TitleBox.Subtitle.Text
TitleBox.Subtitle.UseDefault
Touched
Translucent
Visible
XAxis.Graph_Title.Font.Color
XAxis.Graph_Title.Font.Size
XAxis.Graph_Title.Font.Style
XAxis.Graph_Title.Font.Typeface
XAxis.Graph_Title.Text
XAxis.Graph_Title.UseDefault
XAxis.Scale.AutoScale
XAxis.Scale.HighValue
XAxis.Scale.Increment
XAxis.Scale.Logarithmic
XAxis.Scale.LowValue
XAxis.Ticks.Alternate
XAxis.Ticks.DateFormat
XAxis.Ticks.Font.Color
XAxis.Ticks.Font.Size
XAxis.Ticks.Font.Style
XAxis.Ticks.Font.Typeface
XAxis.Ticks.NumberFormat
YAxis.Graph_Title.Font.Color
YAxis.Graph_Title.Font.Size
YAxis.Graph_Title.Font.Style
YAxis.Graph_Title.Font.Typeface
YAxis.Graph_Title.Text
YAxis.Graph_Title.UseDefault
YAxis.Scale.AutoScale
YAxis.Scale.HighValue
YAxis.Scale.Increment
YAxis.Scale.Logarithmic
YAxis.Scale.LowValue
YAxis.Ticks.Alternate
YAxis.Ticks.DateFormat
YAxis.Ticks.Font.Color
YAxis.Ticks.Font.Size
YAxis.Ticks.Font.Style
YAxis.Ticks.Font.Typeface
YAxis.Ticks.NumberFormat
ZAxis.Graph_Title.Font.Color
ZAxis.Graph_Title.Font.Size
ZAxis.Graph_Title.Font.Style

continues

Table 15.4. Continued.

ZAxis.Graph_Title.Font.Typeface	ZAxis.Ticks.Alternate
ZAxis.Graph_Title.Text	ZAxis.Ticks.DateFormat
ZAxis.Graph_Title.UseDefault	ZAxis.Ticks.Font.Color
ZAxis.Scale.AutoScale	ZAxis.Ticks.Font.Size
ZAxis.Scale.HighValue	ZAxis.Ticks.Font.Style
ZAxis.Scale.Increment	ZAxis.Ticks.Font.Typeface
ZAxis.Scale.Logarithmic	ZAxis.Ticks.NumberFormat
ZAxis.Scale.LowValue	

As you can see, just about everything the user can set interactively, you can set under program control, which means you have complete control over how a graph object looks, and you can easily change properties at runtime.

Object Variables

ObjectPAL has several predefined object variables that help to generically refer to a UIObject (see table 15.5).

Table 15.5. Object Variables.

Object Variable	Comments
Self	Always refers to the object which holds the current method or procedure.
Active	Refers to the last object to receive a moveTo event. This is not always the object that has focus.
Subject	Refers to the object indicated by the method call.
Container	Refers to the object's container.
LastMouseClicked	Refers to the object that was the target of the last MouseClick.
LastRightMouseClicked	Refers to the object that was the target of the last RightMouseClick.

Of these object variables, the two most useful and confusing ones are subject and self. Self is extremely useful because it always refers to the object which holds the code. For example, in a box object (named Box1) arrive built-in method, you can choose between the two statements:

a) Box1.color = Green

b) self.color = Green

Both do exactly the same thing, but b is preferred because you don't have to change the code if you give the box a new name. In addition, you can cut and paste this code to another object without having to alter it.

Use self wherever possible to reduce maintenance and improve code reusability.

Subject is a little more confusing. Subject always refers to the object indicated by the method call. For example, suppose you had the following custom method attached to an MRO:

```
method setColor()
subject.Color = Red
endmethod
```

Now suppose you had the following code attached to the arrive( ) built-in method on the MRO's record object:

```
if Amount.value < 300 then
     Amount.setColor()
endif
```

Notice that in the arrive( ) built-in method we are calling setColor( ) as if it was attached to the Amount field object. However, the Amount field object doesn't own this custom method. The MRO does. Remember, custom methods are automatically visible to the object they are attached to and all objects below it in the containership hierarchy. Paradox will run this code because the Amount field object will *see* the setColor( ) custom method because the Field Object is inside the MRO.

Using subject in the setColor( ) method lets us use setColor( ) on any object contained by the MRO. For example, suppose we had the following code attached to the depart( ) built-in method on the CustomerName field object:

```
if CustomerName.value = "Bill Clinton" then
     CustomerName.setColor()
endif
```

This code will also work just fine, because subject refers to the CustomerName object, which allows you to reuse the setColor( ) method for any objects which have a color property.

Use subject to promote code reuse among similar objects.

The active object variable is also useful because it refers to the last object to which it was moved. This is useful for writing generic code which can manipulate a table frame or an MRO. If you use the active variable, the method will be directed to the currently active table frame. With this in mind, you can see how easy it would be to program a series of push buttons to advance one record, one set of records, and to the end of the table, regardless of what form the pushbuttons are in. By using the active variable with the action( ) method, you can create these action events and have them automatically sent to the table frame or MRO the user is in.

Use active to write generic action( ) method code which can be directed to the currently active table frame or MRO.

UIObject and ObjectPAL Trivia

ObjectPAL is littered with lots of little trivial items. In fact, most ObjectPAL applications are collections of hundreds or even thousands of trivial items. Although we said we wouldn't delve into trivia in this book, we just can't resist briefly discussing some minor points.

- Object properties can be referred to as a constant or a string. The following two lines of code are both valid.

    ```
    Page.color = Green
    Page.color = "Green"
    ```

    The compiler can check for an invalid color reference with the first line of code. The second line of code will always compile, even if "Greenie" is accidentally typed in as a color. However, "Greenie" is not a valid property, so the code will not run.

- Button objects have a LabelText property which always refers to the text object contained by the button, regardless of what that text object is named. This property can be dynamically changed so that your application can change the name of the button on the fly, from the user's perspective.

- You can refer to an object's containership path dynamically. For example, the standard way to refer to an object is:

    ```
    CustForm.Page.CustTable.CustRec.Number.Color = Green
    ```

    The following line of code will also refer to the Number field object's color property:

    ```
    CustForm.(objectName()).color = Green
    ```

    In this example, objectName() is a custom method that returns the following:

    ```
    "Page.CustTable.CustRec"
    ```

As in the case of setting object properties with quoted strings, the compiler can't verify that "Page.CustTable.CustRec" is a valid containership path, so you won't get compiler error messages when a path is referred to incorrectly. You gain flexibility instead.

Form as UIObject

A form or form variable actually belongs to two types: UIObject and Form. The UIObject methods and procedures work with any UIObject and are used to manipulate the user interface in some way. This is different from the Form type which contains several methods which manipulate various parts of the form object, not any UIObject.

We saw some examples of this when we discussed dmGet() and dmPut() which manipulate the form's data model. These would be inappropriate UIObject methods because a UIObject shouldn't know how to manipulate the form's data model. Only the form should know how to do that. Other form methods let you load another form, or wait on a form so you can force the user to interact with the new form.

As you work with UIObjects and their methods and procedures, keep an important distinction in mind. A form belongs to two types: Form and UIObject.

Key UIObject Methods and Procedures

UIObjects come with a bunch of methods and procedures. You will use many of them. In this chapter, we will review the more important methods and procedures. One small reminder: it's easy to forget that the Form object has its own methods, independent of the UIObject type. Forms have different properties and behavior than UIObjects.

attach( )

This method is used to attach a UIObject to a UIObject variable. Although you don't need to declare a UIObject variable to manipulate a UIObject on a form, you need to declare a UIObject variable if you want to write code that can operate on a variety of UIObjects. This UIObject variable serves as a pointer to the real UIObject and the attach( ) method makes the connection. The following code shows an example:

```
var
     obj UIObject
endvar
obj.attach("CustomerName")
libChangeUIObject(obj)
```

In this code example, the UIObject CustomerName is attached to a UIObject variable, which is then passed to a library method, libChangeUIObject( ).

Another reason why the attach( ) method is important is that some of UIObject methods and procedures can work on forms, but only if the form is attached to a UIObject variable.

The attach( ) method is overloaded. It allows for four different sets of arguments. The following code examples show these forms:

```
var
     obj UIObject
endvar
; attach to self
obj.attach()
; attach to the form
obj.attach(CustForm)
; attach to a field in another open form
obj.attach(OtherForm,ItemNumber)
; attach to a report
obj.attach(CustRep)
; attach to a field in another report
obj.attach(CustRep,CustNumber)
```

Because you can attach to another object in another open form, you can initiate events for that form from the form that is currently active.

```
; attach to a field in another form
obj.attach(OtherForm,CustTable)
; insert a record on the other form
obj.action(DataInsertRecord)
```

copyFromArray( ), copyToArray( )

These two methods let you copy records associated with the UIObject to an array. copyFromArray( ) copies an array to an existing record. If you aren't in edit mode, the method will fail. The first element of the array corresponds to the first field in the table structure, the second array element to the second field in the table structure, and so on. If the array from which you are copying doesn't match the table structure, an error will occur. You can have more array elements than there are fields. Any extra array elements will be ignored.

copyToArray( ) will fill an array with field values. The array can be fixed or resizable and each array element must match the table's structure. You don't need to be in edit mode to use this method. The following code sample shows how to use these two methods:

```
var
      ar array[] AnyType
      ms LongInt
endvar
if active.class = "Field" then
      message("Copying records...")
      setMouseShape(MouseWait)
      active.copyToArray(ar)
      if not active.isEdit() then
            active.action(DataBeginEdit)
      endif
      active.action(DataInsertRecord)
      active.copyFromArray(ar)
      setMouseShape(MouseArrow)
      message("Record copied")
endif
```

deleteRecord( )

The deleteRecord( ) method is another way of saying:

```
action(DataDeleteRecord)
```

You will find some overlap between some UIObject methods and action event constants. Both the deleteRecord( ) and action(DataDeleteRecord) delete a record without confirmation. Both require that your form be in edit mode.

empty( )

This method is even more deadly than deleteRecord( ). It deletes all the records in a table without confirmation. In order to work, empty( ) needs to get an exclusive lock on the table bound to the UIObject variable. If the method fails for whatever reason, it returns false; otherwise it returns true. This method will work on any UIObject that is bound to a table in some way. The following code, attached to a pushbutton object on a form, shows how to use empty( ):

```
method pushButton(var eventInfo Event)
if CustName.empty() then   ; Customer name field UIObject
   msgInfo("Table Status","Customer table is empty.")
else
      msgInfo("Table Status","Customer table empty operation failed")
endif
endmethod
```

edit( ), endEdit( )

These two methods begin and end an edit session on all the tables in a form. They are also equivalent to action(DataBeginEdit) and action(DataEndEdit). Any UIObject bound to a table in some way can use these methods. If the methods succeed, they return true, otherwise they return false.

enum..( ) Methods/Procedures

The UIObject type has several enum methods that begin with enum. These methods allow you to enumerate the state of various parts of the form. Table 15.6 lists these methods.

Table 15.6. UIObject enum..( ) Methods/Procedures.

Method/Procedure Syntax	M/P
enumFieldNames(arName array[] String) Logical	M
enumLocks(tblName String) LongInt	M
enumSource(tblName String [,recurse Logical]) Logical	M
enumSourceToFile(filName String [,recurse Logical]]) Logical	M
enumUIObjectNames(tblName String) Logical	MP
enumObjectNames(arName Array[] String) Logical	MP
enumUIObjectProperties(tblName String) Logical	MP
enumUIClasses(tblName String) Logical	P

enumFieldNames( ) will load an array with all the field names in the table bound to the UIObject. If the array is resizable, the array will grow to accommodate the field names. If the array is fixed and there are more field names than array elements, the array will be filled and any extra field names will be discarded.

enumLocks( ) will create a table specified by the tblName argument listing all the locks placed on the table bound to the UIObject. This method returns the number of locks placed. This method also duplicates the File ¦ Multiuser ¦ Display Locks menu sequence functionality, giving programmers the ability to perform the same task. The table contains the following information: the user name, the lock type, the network session number, and a record number for record locks.

Session and NetSession refer to which session of Paradox and which network session of Paradox has a lock placed. The record number will display the record number for each record locked in the table.

The enumSource( ) method performs a simple task—listing out your source code in a form. The way it does it is not completely obvious. Pay attention.

- The object which holds the enumSource( ) method is the starting point for enumSource( ) to start listing code. It works downward from that object to code attached to objects it contains. So, if you want to list code for the entire form, make sure you place the enumSource( ) line of code in one of the form's built-in methods, or better still, in a form-level custom method or procedure.

- *Don't* place the enumSource( ) method in a pushbutton, unless you only want code in the pushbutton.

- The object referred to in the enumSource( ) method (on the left-hand side of the period) has nothing to do with code listed in the table. Don't let this throw you.

The enumSourceToFile( ) method works just like enumSource( ) except it writes the source code to a file rather than a table.

enumSource( ) is an extremely important method because it provides the foundations for automatic source code documentation and *backup*. If your form, which contains all those precious ObjectPAL methods, gets zapped or corrupted, those methods also get zapped or corrupted.

Enumerate your source code to tables or files on a regular basis or devise another foolproof backup scheme.

enumUIObjectNames( ) fills tables with the names of objects on a form and has the same topdown approach to listing objects. So, if you want a listing of all objects in the form, place the enumUIObjectNames( ) line of code in a method on the form. enumUIObjectNames( ) is also a UIObject procedure, so you don't need to specify an object to use. Both of the following forms will work:

```
CustomerForm.enumUIObjectNames("CUSTOBJ.DB")
enumUIObjectNNames("CUSTOBJ.DB")
```

This method/procedure will create a table with the following fields: ObjectName and ObjectClass.

enumObjectNames( ) works just like enumUIObjectNames( ) except it fills an array with the names of objects on a form. It also has the same top-down approach to listing objects on a form. So if you want a listing of all the objects on a form, place the method call in a method attached to the form. enumObjectNames is also a procedure.

enumUIObjectProperties( ) will get all the property names and values for all the objects on a form and write them to a table. This method is also a procedure, so you don't need to specify an object to use.

enumUIClasses( ) will list all objects and their available properties to the file specified by tblName.

insert..( ) Methods

ObjectPAL has three UIObject insert..( ) methods which let you insert a new record in a table. These methods are:

- insertAfterRecord( )
- insertBeforeRecord( )
- insertRecord( )

Because a record can be inserted in only two positions relative to another record, before or after, you may be wondering why there are three insert methods. As it turns out, insertRecord( ) and insertBeforeRecord( ) are equivalent. In addition, both insertRecord( ) and insertBeforeRecord( ) are equivalent to the following:

```
object.action(DataInsertRecord)
```

So you actually have four different ways to add a record to a table.

locate..( )

The six locate..( ) methods are extremely important because they give you ability to search for records in a table under program control. In addition, these methods are available for TCursor variables as well. The locate..( ) methods are:

- locate( )
- locateNext( )
- locatePattern( )
- locateNextPattern( )
- locatePrior( )
- locatePriorPattern( )

All these methods have a variable list of field name/field value pairs of arguments.

locate( ) will find the record that matches the field name, field value arguments, always beginning the search from the top of the table. For example, given an Orders table with at least two fields: [Customer number] and [Order number], to find a record with [Customer number] = 102 and [Order number] = 2131 you would do:

```
if not Orders.locate("Customer number",101,"Order number",2131) then
    msgInfo("Locate","Can't find this order")
endif
```

If [Customer number] and [Order number] are the first two fields in the Order table's structure, you could also do the following:

```
if not Orders.locate(1,101,2,2131) then
    msgInfo("Locate","Can't find this order")
endif
```

The fields don't have to be contiguous; they don't have to be primary key fields and they don't need secondary indexes on them. If Paradox can make use of the indexes to speed up the search, Paradox will use them. Keep in mind that this means it can take a long time to use any of the locate..( ) methods on a large table if you are searching on fields without any key fields or secondary indexes on them. You can specify any fields from the table you are searching. If you use any of the locate..( ) methods inside a linked detail table, locate will only search the linked records in the detail table, not the entire table. If you want to search the entire table of a linked detail table, you will need to use a TCursor variable to perform the locate instead.

locateNext( ) has the exact same argument syntax as locate( ). locateNext( ) begins the search at the next record.

locatePattern( ) operates just like locate( ). The difference is that locate Pattern allows you to use wild-card characters, also known as pattern operators, in your search criteria. For example, to find the first record with a [Customer name] field value beginning with "AC" in the Customer table, you would do

```
if not locatePattern("Customer name","AC..") then
    msgInfo("Locate","No records found")
endif
```

The .. pattern operator searches for any number of characters, including 0. Another pattern operator is the @ character, which searches for just a single character. To find the first record with a [Customer name] field value that has "AC" as the first two characters and "E" as the last with exactly one character in between you would do

```
if not locatePattern("Customer name","AC@E") then
    msgInfo("Locate","No records found")
endif
```

You can use additional pattern operators if the Session procedure advancedWildcardsInLocate(Yes) has been issued. This procedure lets you use advanced pattern operators (see table 15.7).

Table 15.7. Wild-card Operators.

Operator	Description
\	Use before special characters so it can be included in search string. (See table 15.8.)
[]	Match a set. [abd-g0-9] defines a set of characters a,b,d,e,f,g,0,1,2,3,4,5,6,7,8,9. If any of these characters are found in the string, a match is found. The "-" character denotes a range of characters.
[^]	Set negation. [^XYZ] would match any characters except X,Y,Z.
( )	Grouping operator.
^	Beginning of line.
$	End of string.
..	0 or more characters (e.g., Fred.. to match Frederick).
@	Any single character.
*	Repetition. 0 or more of the preceding character or expression. (xyz)* would find 0 or more consecutive occurrences of xyz. k* would find 0 or more consecutive occurrences of k.
+	Repetition. 1 or more of the preceding character or expression w* would find 1 or more repetitions of w.
?	None or one of the preceding character or repetition.
¦	Or operation. Keith¦Dorice would find Keith or Dorice in a string.

Table 15.8. Backslash codes.

Character	Description
\a	Bell (Ctrl-G)
\b	Backspace
\f	Form feed (Ctrl-L)
\n	New line (Ctrl-J)
\r	Carriage return (Ctrl-M)
\t	Tab (Ctrl-I)
\v	Vertical tab
\"	Double quote
\\	Backslash
\XXX	ASCII code 0-128 (\125 for the } character)

To search multiple fields with the locatePattern( ) method, you can specify field name and field value pairs just like in locate( ), with one exception: only the last field value can contain a pattern. All fields but the last one must be exact-match searches. Subsequently, the following example is an incorrect use of locatePattern( ):

```
Customer.locatePattern("Customer name","K..","Address","100..")
```

In this example, the first and the second field have patterns. The search should look like this:

```
Customer.locatePattern("Customer name","ACME","Address","100..")
```

locatePrior( ) and locatePriorPattern( ) work just like locateNext( ) and locateNextPattern( ) except they search backward in the table from the current record.

As of this writing, the locate..Pattern( ) methods have one big problem. They don't use any secondary indexes to speed up the search, if possible. For example, if you supply "G.." as a search pattern, expecting to quickly find the first record that begins with G, you won't. If the table is quite large, the search time will take longer. Hopefully, Borland will fix this problem quickly in either a maintenance release of Paradox for Windows or in a future version.

method..( )

Three method..( ) methods let you examine, add, and delete ObjectPAL code from methods on the form. These methods are:

- methodGet(methName String) String
- methodSet(methName String, methCode String) Logical
- methodDelete(methName String)

These methods let you read and modify ObjectPAL code while under ObjectPAL code. The only catch is that the form must be in design mode. To do this, you must use the Form load( ) method.

moveTo..( )

Three moveTo..( ) methods let you move around in a form or a table. These methods are:

- moveTo( )
- moveToRecNo( )
- movetoRecord( )

moveTo( ) will move the focus to the object indicated. For example, the following code moves the focus to the Amount field object:

```
Amount.moveTo()
```

moveTo is also a procedure, so the following code does the same thing:

```
moveTo("Amount")
```

If the moveTo( ) was unsuccessful, it returns false, otherwise it returns true.

The next method, moveToRecNo( ) takes a record number (LongInt) as an argument and moves to the record number indicated. It returns true if it succeeds, otherwise it returns false. This method is recommended for dBASE tables only.

moveToRecord( ) works just like moveToRecNo( ), except it is recommended for Paradox tables only. It has two forms, one takes a LongInt as an argument, the other a TCursor as an argument. If you use a TCursor as an argument, movetoRecord( ) moves to the TCursor's current record.

nextRecord( ), priorRecord( ), skip( )

nextRecord( ) and priorRecord( ) move to the next and prior records, returning True if they succeeded or false if they did not. These methods are equivalent to

```
action(DataNextRecord)
action(DataPriorRecord)
```

skip( ) takes a LongInt as an argument and will attempt to advance the number of records indicated. You can move both forward and backward. To move backward, specify a negative number as an argument:

```
CustTable.skip(-5)
```

skip( ) also returns true if it succeeded or false if it didn't.

postRecord( ), unlockRecord( )

postRecord( ) posts the current record to the table without unlocking it. It returns true if it succeeds or false if it doesn't. It is also equivalent to

```
action(DataPostRecord)
```

unlockRecord( ) posts the current record by unlocking it.

recordStatus( )

This method will tell you if a record is new, locked, or modified by passing either "New," "Locked," or "Modified" as a parameter. If the record is new, locked, or modified, recordStatus( ) returns true; otherwise it returns false.

setFilter( ), switchIndex( )

This method is another very useful method because it can be used to restrict from view only those records that meet a certain criteria. setFilter( ) works with the table's primary index. For example, to restrict the view of records in the Orders table frame to those records that belong to Customer number 1001, the following code will work:

```
if not Orders.setFilter(1001,1001) then
     msgInfo("Set Filter","Failed")
endif
```

To set a filter which restricts the Orders table to customers between the numbers of 100 and 900, the following code will work:

```
if not Orders.setFilter(100,900) then
     msgInfo("Set Filter","Failed")
endif
```

To set a filter which restricts the Orders table to Customer number 1001 and orders 242 through 353, the following code will work:

```
if not Orders.setFilter(1001,242,353) then
     msgInfo("Set Filter","Failed")
endif
```

Notice that you can set a filter for each field in the primary key. The important rule to understand is that all but the last field used in the filter must specify an exact value. You can't set a filter for two ranges on two fields.

The following code removes any filter set for that table:

```
setFilter()
```

switchIndex( ) will redisplay records in a table frame or an MRO in the order specified by a secondary index. For example, if you want to view a table sorted by state, you can use switchIndex( ), as long as the state field has a secondary index on it. Unfortunately, as of this writing, the UIObject switchIndex( ) method does not work. The good news is that the TCursor switchIndex( ) method does work properly. Until Borland fixes the UIObject switchIndex( ) method, developers have to use the following code:

```
var
     tc TCursor
endvar
; attach the TCursor to the Customer table
if tc.attach(Customer) then
     if tc.switchIndex("StateIndex") then
          ; resync the table frame to the tcursor
          if Customer.reSync(tc) then
               msgInfo("SwitchIndex","Succeeded")
               stat = true
          else
               msgInfo("Resync","Failed")
          endif
     else
```

```
            msgInfo("SwitchIndex","Failed")
        endif
    else
        msgInfo("Attach","Failed")
    endif
```

To use the TCursor switchIndex( ), you will have to attach the TCursor to the table frame or MRO you want to redisplay, use switchIndex on the TCursor, and then resynchronize the table frame or MRO with the TCursor with reSync( ). switchIndex( ) has an optional logical second argument. If a True value is supplied, the switchIndex( ) will leave the user on the current record. If no value or a false value is supplied, the table is redisplayed in the secondary index view and the cursor is positioned on the first record in the table.

You can reset the view of the table's data to the primary index by using switchIndex( ) without any arguments.

If you use setFilter( ) after a switchIndex( ), the setFilter( ) is applied to the current secondary index.

Summary

Users interact with UIObjects. Controlling each UIObject's appearance and behavior is important in building applications. Fortunately Paradox gives us some powerful tools to change nearly all aspects of an object's visual appearance, navigate table objects, and locate records within them, program list contents, and change a field's appearance among other parts of a UIObject's behavior.

In fact, exploring every property of all UIObjects (there are more than 1,500 of them) would take an extraordinary amount of time. Because so much control can be daunting, we recommend controlling only those aspects of the Paradox user interface that you absolutely have to alter. Try to use as much of Paradox as possible to do your work, otherwise you can get mired in endless detail.

16

TCursors

Forms provide the primary vehicle for users to interact with data in tables in ObjectPAL applications. But what about access to tables that you do not want the user to see? You use the TCursor! This chapter is designed to teach experienced programmers about TCursors.

Defining TCursor

A TCursor is a variable that points to the data in a table. Using a TCursor, you can manipulate a table and the table's data without displaying the table. The TCursor, not a copy or clone of a table, is a pointer to the actual data in the table and any changes you make with a TCursor are changes to the actual table and the data.

Just as changes you make to a TCursor actually change the table's data and are seen by a user viewing the table, so changes made by a user are seen by you when you access a table's data with a TCursor.

Declaring a TCursor

Because a TCursor is a variable, TCursor must be declared before use. The following code declares a TCursor, custTC:

```
var
    custTC    TCursor        ;declare the TCursor
endvar
```

After you declare a TCursor, you must associate it with a table before use.

Opening a Table

You can open an existing table with a TCursor in three ways. The first way is to use the open method, as in the following example.

```
var
    custTC         TCursor
endvar
; Open a TCursor directly on a table.
if custTC.open("customer.db") then
    msgInfo("TCursor Test", "The TCursor is open.")
else
    msgStop("TCursor Test", "Unable to open the TCursor.")
endIf
```

This example declares a TCursor—custTC—and uses the open method to open the customer table. The open method returns true or false to indicate if the TCursor was opened successfully. The TCursor now points to the first record in the table. From here on, when you use custTC, you will be working with the data in the customer table. If you use a TCursor before you associate it with a table, an error will occur just as with any other unassigned variable.

The second way to associate a TCursor with a table uses a table variable, as shown in the following example.

```
var
    custTC         TCursor
    custTable Table
endvar
; Attach the table variable to the table.
if not custTable.attach("customer.db") then
    errorShow("Customer Attach")
endIf
; Set a filter on the table.
custTable.setFilter(2000, 2999)
; Open a TCursor using the table variable.
if not custTC.open(custTable) then
    errorShow("Customer Open")
endIf
```

In this example a table variable—custTable—is declared and the attach method is used to associate this table variable with the customer table. Then, you open the TCursor custTC by using the open method and the table variable, custTable. The advantage of this technique is that the TCursor inherits the Table variable's attributes. In this case, we set a filter to restrict access to customers with numbers between 2000 and 2999, and the TCursor inherits the filter. The TCursor, therefore, now points to the first record in the range defined by the filter.

The third way to initialize a TCursor is to attach it to a UIObject that is bound to a table. Assume that a form contains a multi-record object named CUSTOMER bound to the customer table. The following code will attach a TCursor to the customer table.

```
if not custTC.attach(CUSTOMER) then
    errorShow("Customer Open")
endIf
```

> **Note:** In this case the TCursor inherits the attributes of the UIObject just as it inherited the attributes of the table object in the previous example. The TCursor now points to the current record in the multi-record object in the form.
>
> The fields and records that you have access to through a TCursor that is attached to a UIObject depend on the form's data model.

Suppose that you have a form that contains the customer and orders tables linked in a one-to-many relationship with customer as the master and orders as the detail table. When you scroll through the order records with this form, you only see the order records that belong to the current customer record. If you attach a TCursor to the orders table the TCursor inherits this restricted view.

A different restriction occurs when you have tables linked one-to-one in the form's data model. Imagine a form with two tables, employee and salary. Both tables use social security number as their primary key and are linked one-to-one with employee as the master.

If you attach a TCursor to the EMPLOYEE UIObject you are able to access only fields in the employee table, even though the fields from both tables appear as a single virtual record in the form. If you attach a TCursor to the salary table, Paradox actually attaches it to the master table and employee, and you still cannot access fields in the salary table. Fortunately, an easy solution exists. If you attach the TCursor to one of the field objects bound to the salary table, you then can access any field in the salary table with the TCursor.

Creating a Table

In ObjectPAL CREATE is a command, not a method, so you cannot use it directly with a TCursor to create a table. CREATE, however, returns the structure information to initialize a table variable and, as you have seen, a table variable can be used to open a TCursor. In the following example, we create a table and open a TCursor pointing to the table's data:

```
var
     custTC         TCursor
     custTable Table
endVar
; Create a table like customer.db.
custTable =    create "junk.db"
               like "customer.db"
               key "Customer No"
          endCreate
; Open a TCursor on the new table and display the Customer No.
if custTC.open(custTable) then
     custTC."Customer No".view()
endIf
```

Closing a TCursor

When you finish using a TCursor to work with a table, you should close the table. Closing the table does the following three things:

- Closes the table file.
- Unassigns the TCursor variable.
- Tries to commit the current record, if it is new or has been changed. Note that the table is closed and the TCursor variable is unassigned, even if the current record cannot be committed. If the record cannot be committed, the changes made to the record are lost, so it is better to post the record with the postRecord method before you close the table. By using postRecord, you retain control over what happens if the record cannot be committed.

The following code fragment uses the close method to close a TCursor. After being closed the variable custTC is unassigned.

```
var
     custTC          TCursor
     custTable Table
endVar
; Create a table like customer.db.
custTable =    create "junk.db"
               like "customer.db"
               key "Customer No"
          endCreate
; Open a TCursor on the new table and display the Customer No.
if custTC.open(custTable) then
     custTC."Customer No".view()
     custTC.close()
     msginfo("Tcursor status", custtc.isassigned()).
endIf
endmethod
```

This example is the same as the preceding example except that the call to the close method was added. Because the TCursor variable custTC is declared within the pushButton method, it automatically closes when the pushButton method ends.

The fact that closing a TCursor makes the TCursor unassigned naturally leads to the question, "How can I tell if a TCursor is assigned?" Like nearly everything else in ObjectPAL, a method exists to fill this need.

```
var
     custTC          TCursor
     x               Logical
endvar
; Open a TCursor directly on a table.
if custTC.open("customer.db") then
     ; Now custTC is assigned.
     x = custTC.isAssigned()
     x.view()
     ; After being closed custTC is not assigned.
     custTC.close()
```

```
        x = custTC.isAssigned()
        x.view()
else
    msgStop("TCursor Test", "Unable to open the TCursor.")
endIf
```

Moving Around

Moving around a table by using a TCursor is a place in ObjectPAL where DOS PAL programmers will feel right at home. There are methods with the same name and function as the commands you are used to using to move through a table. Look at a brief example:

```
var
    custTC          TCursor
    cntr            LongInt
endvar
; Open the TCursor and move to the end of the table.
custTC.open("customer.db")
custTC.end()                     ;move to the end of the table.
msgInfo("At End", "Customer No is "
            + String(custTC."Customer No"))
; Move back to the beginning
; and scan the table counting the records.
custTC.home()       ;move to the beginning of the table.

cntr = 0
SCAN custTC:                     ;scan through the table.
    cntr = cntr + 1
ENDSCAN
msgInfo("At End Again", "Table contains " + String(cntr) +
            " records.")
; Walk backwards through the records to the beginning.
while custTC.bot() = false       ;scan from bottom to top.
    custTC.priorRecord()
endWhile
msgInfo("At End", "Customer No is "
            + String(custTC."Customer No"))
custTC.close()
```

First, you open a TCursor on the customer table and move to the end by calling the end method. Next, move to the first record in the table by calling the home method.

To move quickly through all the records in the table, use a scan loop. This example uses the scan loop to count the number of records in the table. In a real application, using the TCursor method nRecords( ) is much faster.

Note that the SCAN command also is implemented as a control structure because it can enclose any number of ObjectPAL statements. The rest of the movement operations, however, are methods.

Other methods for moving through tables are atFirst( ), atLast( ), eot( ), and skip( ).

Moving to a Specific Record

Two ways are available to move to a specific record by using a TCursor. The first way is by record number and the second way is by value. To move to a specific record number, something you rarely want to do in a relational database, use the TCursor moveToRecord method.

A more useful method is locate which enables you to find a record by the value in one or more fields. The following code attaches a TCursor to the Customer multi-record object in the form then uses locate to find the record for customer 1513. If the record is found, the UIObject method moveToRecord repositions the multi-record object to the same record as the TCursor.

```
var
      custTC         TCursor
endvar
; Attach a TCursor to the Multi-Record Object in the form
; that is bound to the Customer table.
if not custTC.attach(CUSTOMER) then
      errorShow("Could not attach to Customer.")
      return
endIf
; Locate the record for Customer 1513.  If the record is
; found move the UIObject to it.
if custTC.locate("Customer No", 1513) then
      CUSTOMER.moveToRecord(custTC)
endIf
custTC.close()
```

Other methods for searching include locateNext, locatePattern, and locateNextPattern. Unlike older versions of DOS Paradox, the locateNext methods start the search from the record after the current record so that you do not need to explicitly move off of the last record that you found before executing locateNext or locateNextPattern.

Working with Records

The TCursor class has several methods that allow you to manipulate records easily. These methods are shown in the following list:

- copyFromArray( )
- copyToArray( )
- copyRecord( )
- deleteRecord( )
- initRecord( )
- insertAfterRecord( )

- insertBeforeRecord( )
- insertRecord( )

Moving records from one table to another is easy with TCursors, thanks to the copyRecord and three insert methods. To copy all records from the customer table to the junk table, for example, you can do the following:

```
var
     custTC        TCursor
     junkTC        TCursor
     tv         TableView
endvar
; Open the TCursors.
custTC.open("customer.db")
custTC.edit()
junkTC.open("junk.db")
; Empty the junk table and put it in edit mode.
junkTC.empty()
junkTC.edit()
; Move the records from customer to junk.
scan custTC:
   if junkTC.insertRecord() then
      if junkTC.copyREcord(custTC) then
           custTC.deleteRecord()
      endIf
   endIf
endScan
; End edit mode and close the TCursors.
junkTC.close()
custTC.close()
```

This example opens TCursors on both the customer and junk tables, empties the junk table and then places it in edit mode. Next, a Scan loop moves through the records in the customer table and copyRecord is used to copy the record to the junk table. Note that the destination table's copyRecord method is called and the source table is passed as a parameter, and note that copyRecord copies into the current record in the target table so insertRecord must be used to open a new record before copying. If insertRecord wasn't called, you would replace the current record in the target table, junk. Finally, deleteRecord is called to remove the record from the customer table.

Besides insertRecord, the TCursor type also provides insertBeforeRecord, which works exactly like insertRecord and insertAfterRecord, which inserts the new record after—rather than before—the current record.

The copyToArray method copies a record into a resizable array of type AnyType so that you can modify or refer to individual field values. The first field of the record is placed in the first element of the array, the second in the second element, and so on. The copyFromArray method writes the contents of the array into the current record in a table.

The last record oriented method is initRecord, which simply assigns the value blank to every field in the record. Also, if default values are set for fields, this method will initialize those fields with the default.

Accessing Fields

You can access data in any field of the current record by using a TCursor and dot notation with the field name or field number, as shown in the following example:

```
var
    tc          TCursor
    custName    String
    f           String
endVar
f = "Name"
if tc.attach(CUSTOMER) then
    ; Display the customer number and name.
    tc."Customer No".view()
    tc.(f).view()           ;A variable holds the field name.
    ; Edit the table and copy the name to field 2.
    tc.edit()
    custName = tc."Name"
    tc.(2) = custName       ;Refer to field by number.
    tc.endEdit()
    ; Close the TCursor.
    tc.close()
endIf
```

This example displays the Customer No and the contents of the field whose name is stored in the variable f, then copies the contents of the Name field to field 2. A variable that contains the field name or a field number must be in parenthesis. Note that the field name must be in quotation marks, which is different than referring to a field UIObject in a form whose name is not placed in quotes.

Also, notice that the field number is based on the table's physical structure. If you restructure the table and insert a new field between the first and second fields of the table, this code tries to assign the value of Name to the new field 2. Using field name notation is much safer because you are more likely to change the structure of a table than the name of a field within the table.

Column Calculations

Object PAL includes TCursor methods to generate several column statistics. These include cAverage, cCount, cMax, cNPV (net present value), cSamStd (sample standard deviation), cSamVar (sample variance), cStd (standard deviation), cSum, and cVar (variance). The following code determines the sum of the values in the Total Invoice field of the orders table:

```
var
    ordTC       TCursor
    amount      Number
endVar
if ordTC.open("orders.db") then
    amount = ordTC.cSum("Total Invoice")
    amount.view()
    ordTC.close()
endIf
```

These functions will include only the records visible to the TCursor, if the TCursor's view of the table has been restricted by setting a filter or by attaching the TCursor to a detail table in a form.

Table Operations

Methods also are provided to perform all of the expected table operations such as add, subtract, sort, copy, empty, and reindex. The following code, for example, adds the customer table to the junk table:

```
var
    custTC          TCursor
    junkTC          TCursor
endVar
if custTC.open("customer.db") then
    if junkTC.open("junk.db") then
        junkTC.empty()
        ; Add Customer to Junk.  Append records.
        ; Do not update existing records.
        custTC.add(junkTC, True, False)
        junkTC.close()
    endIf
    custTC.close()
endIf
```

Notice that the add method in ObjectPAL contains two parameters of type Logical. The first parameter determines if records will be appended to the destination table, and the second parameter determines if existing records in a keyed table will be updated by incoming records. In this example, because Update is False, all incoming records whose key matches an existing record is placed in a keyviol table.

These parameters provide great flexibility in add operations. For example, if Append is False and Update is true, incoming records that have the same key value as an existing record update the existing record and all other incoming records are ignored.

The sortTo method sorts one table and places the result in another table. This method, however, does not allow you to sort an unkeyed table into itself. The following example sorts the customer table, descending by Country and ascending by Name.

```
        var
           custTC    TCursor         ;TCursor for customer.db
           tv        TableView       ;TableView for sorted table.
           sortFields  Array[2] String   ;fields to sort by.
           sortOrder   Array[2] SmallInt ;Ascending/descending flags.
        endvar
        ; Initialize the sort control arrays.
        sortFields[1] = "Country"         ;Sort first by Country
        sortFields[2] = "Name"            ;and second by Name.
        sortOrder[1] = 1                  ;Sort descending by Country
        sortOrder[2] = 0                  ;and ascending by Name.
        ; Open a TCursor on the customer table and sort it.
```

Part IV ■ Programming in ObjectPAL

```
        if custTC.open("customer.db") then
            if not custTC.sortTo( "junk.db", 2,sortFields, sortOrder) then
                errorShow("Sort Failed")
            endIf
            custTC.close()
        else
            errorShow("TCursor Open Failed")
        endIf
        ; Show the junk table in tableview.
        tv.open("junk.db")         ;Open the table view.
        tv.wait()                  ;Wait for the user to close it.
        tv.close()                 ;Close the table view.
```

The arguments to the sortTo method are shown in the following list:

Argument	Result
Destination table	The name of the table the sorted records will be placed in.
Number of fields	The number of fields you are sorting by.
Field array	A string array that contains the names of the fields you want sorted by in order, or a SmallInt array that contains the field numbers of the fields you want sorted in the order you want them used.
Order	A SmallInt array the same size as the field array that indicates ascending or descending order for each field. Zero indicates ascending and one descending.

If you need to sort an unkeyed table into itself, you must sort the table as shown previously, then delete the source table and rename the table that contains the sorted records.

Generating a Unique Key

You also can use a TCursor to get the value from a field in a table or change the value in a field in a table. The following example uses a TCursor to generate a unique numeric key for a new record in the customer table on a network:

```
        var
            tc         TCursor
            n          Number
        endVar
        if eventInfo.id() = DataInsertRecord then
            ; If a new record is being inserted.
            if tc.open("tckey.db") then
                ; Go into edit mode.
                tc.edit()
                ; Lock the record.
                while (not tc.lockRecord())
                    sleep(200)
                endWhile
```

```
                ; Get the last number used, add 1 and put it back.
                n = tc."Number" + 1
                tc."Number" = n
                tc.unlockRecord()
                tc.endEdit()
                tc.close()
                ; Insert the record.
                doDefault
                ; Put the new key in the new record.
                self.Customer_No = n
          else
                errorShow("Generating Key")
          endIf
    endIf
```

This example uses a single field single record table to store the last value that was used as the key for a record in the customer table. Place this code anywhere you want to generate a key.

In a real application, you can improve performance slightly by opening the TCursor once in the form's open method and closing it in the form's close method, rather than opening and closing it each time you need to get a new key value. To do this, declare the TCursor variable in the form's Var window so that the variable is global to all of the form's methods.

Summary

TCursors provide invisible access to tables and are so useful, you will find yourself using them frequently. TCursors and UIObjects have many methods and procedures in common. You can use TCursors to manipulate fields, perform column calculations, or even perform table-level tasks such as add, subtract, and empty tables. Combined with UIObjects, TCursors enables you to solve many database programming tasks.

17

Building and Using Menus

Menus are fundamental to any application. In order to take an application beyond the simple and into the complex, developers invariably must provide some facility so that users can interact with the application easily. Menus serve to divide an application into comprehensible chunks. Behind every elegant application is an elegant menu, serving as a polite and agreeable host, showing the newcomers and regulars alike the place they want to go.

And serious applications require serious menus. Fortunately, Paradox for Windows has serious menu stuff to help you out. This chapter reviews the two types of menus you can create in Paradox for Windows pull-down menus and pop-up menus. In addition, we will cover how you can exploit Paradox for Windows to make designing and working with menus easier.

Menu Basics

Paradox for Windows has only two types of menus: pull-down menus and pop-up menus. Pop-up menus are easy to understand. They are menus that literally pop up and require that the user either accept an item off of the menu or cancel the menu selection process. Pop-up menus are modal. They are like toddlers that require your complete attention; they insist that the user interact with *them and no one else*. The user cannot interact with another window or switch to another application. Figure 17.1 shows an example of a pop-up menu.

In contrast, pull-down menus are like well-behaved adults. They sit quietly at the top of the Paradox for Windows desktop window, just below the desktop title bar. They are not modal. The user can interact with them at any time. When the user interacts with a pull-down menu, Paradox generates a menuAction event, for which you can trap. Figure 17.2 shows an example of a pull-down menu.

Although pull-down menus sit quietly and don't demand immediate user attention, no two pull-down menus can exist at the same time. The town is just not big enough for both of them. When you show a new pull-down menu, the old menu quietly disappears. In fact, when you show your own pull-down menu, the default Paradox menu disappears.

Part IV ■ Programming in ObjectPAL

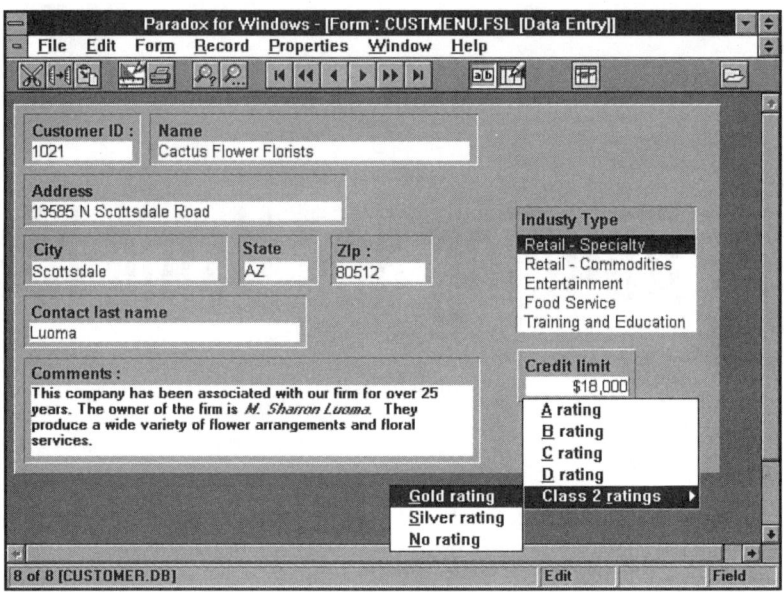

Figure 17.1. A pop-up menu.

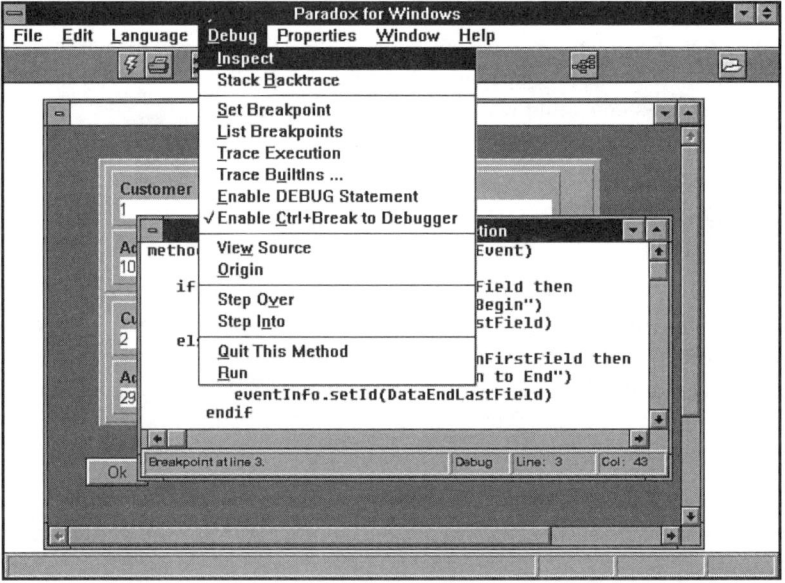

Figure 17.2. A pull-down menu.

You most likely will use pop-up menus to prompt the user for immediate feedback. Because pop-up menus look just like a list object that you place on a form, you can think of them as "lists on demand."

Pull-down menus, however, drive the application. Your application's main menu will be a pull-down menu. All other menus that drive the application's functionality probably will be pull-down menus.

Both pop-up menus and pull-down menus can cascade. That is, one menu item can have a submenu, a submenu item can have another submenu, and so on. Figure 17.1 shows a pop-up menu with one cascading pop-up.

Pop-up Menus

Building a pop-up menu is easy. First, you need to create a PopUpMenu variable. Then you need to add text items to the PopUpMenu variable. The text you add will be the actual menu items. Next, you show the menu to the user, forcing interaction. Last, you evaluate the result of the interaction and perform some action. To display a pop-up menu with a cascading menu, we need some methods from the PopUpMenu type:

1. addText( )
2. addPopUp( )
3. show( )

The following code shows how to display and interact with a pop-up menu:

```
var
      p, p2     PopUpMenu
      choice    String
endvar
; add text to the cascading popup
p2.addText("&Gold rating")
p2.addText("&Silver rating")
p2.addText("&No rating")
; add text to the main popup
p.addText("&A rating")
p.addText("&B rating")
p.addText("&C rating")
p.addText("&D rating")
; add the cascading popup to the main popup
p.addPopUp("Class 2 &ratings",p2)
; show the popup menu
choice = p.show()
; don't let the menu choice take effect
; if the user isn't editing the form
if CustForm.editing = false then
msgInfo("Error","You must be in edit mode. Press F9")
      return
endif
; based on the credit rating selected,
; set the credit_limit field
```

```
switch
    case choice = "&A rating" :
        Credit_limit = 50000
    case choice = "&B rating" :
        Credit_limit = 32000
    case choice = "&C rating" :
        Credit_limit = 18000
    case choice = "&D rating" :
        Credit_limit = 12000
    case choice = "&Gold rating" :
        Credit_limit = 8000
    case choice = "&Silver rating" :
        Credit_limit = 4000
endswitch
```

In this example, two PopUpMenu variables were declared: p and p2. The p2 variable is the cascading pop-up menu and p is the main pop-up menu. The addTLext( ) method enables you to specify a string that you want to appear in the menu. The addPopUp( ) method enables you to specify a string to display as the submenu heading and a PopUpMenu variable that contains the cascading pop-up menu.

As you see, creating pop-up menus is quite simple.

The & Character, Separators, Bars, and Breaks

In the previous example, the & character was used to precede a character in the menu string. The & character simply highlights the following character by placing an underscore beneath it. This character also becomes the keyboard character that selects the menu choice when the menu is active. The funny thing about using the & character when adding text to a PopUpMenu variable is that, when you evaluate the user's menu selection with the show( ) method, the string includes the & character.

You have more visual control over pop-up menus. You can easily add a line to separate items in a menu by using the addSeparator( ) method (see fig. 17.3).

Two other methods deserve mention: addBar( ) and addBreak( ). The addBar( ) method creates a vertical bar within the menu, and all subsequent addText( ) methods will place the text to the right of the vertical bar. The addBreak( ) method does the same thing as addBar( ), except that no vertical line gets added. Both addBreak( ) and addBar( ) let you create columns of menu choices, which is useful if you have a lot of menu choices with short text lengths. Figure 17.4 shows an example of a pop-up menu with a bar added.

Here is the code for this menu:

```
var
    p           PopUpMenu
    choice      String
endvar
p.addText("&A rating")
p.addText("&B rating")
p.addBar()
p.addText("&C rating")
p.addText("&D rating")
choice = p.show(3000,2000)
```

Chapter 17 ■ Building and Using Menus

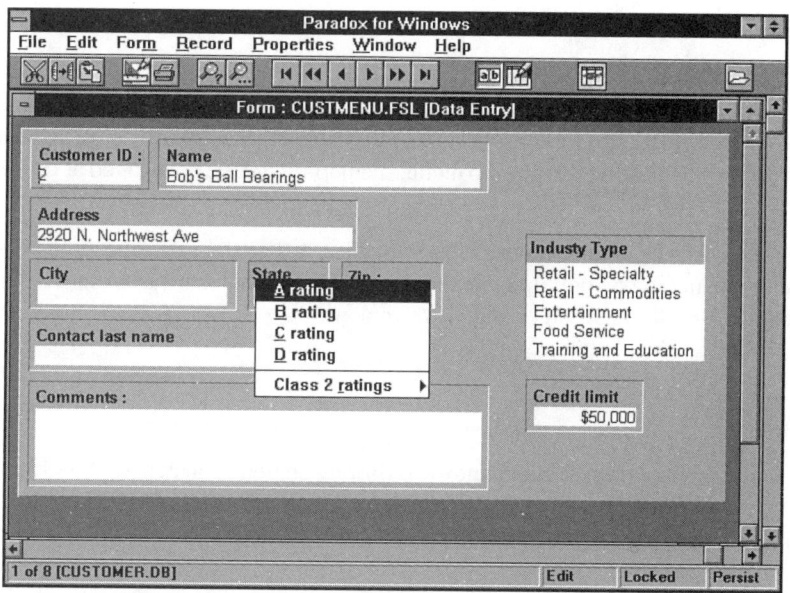

Figure 17.3. A pop-up menu with a separator.

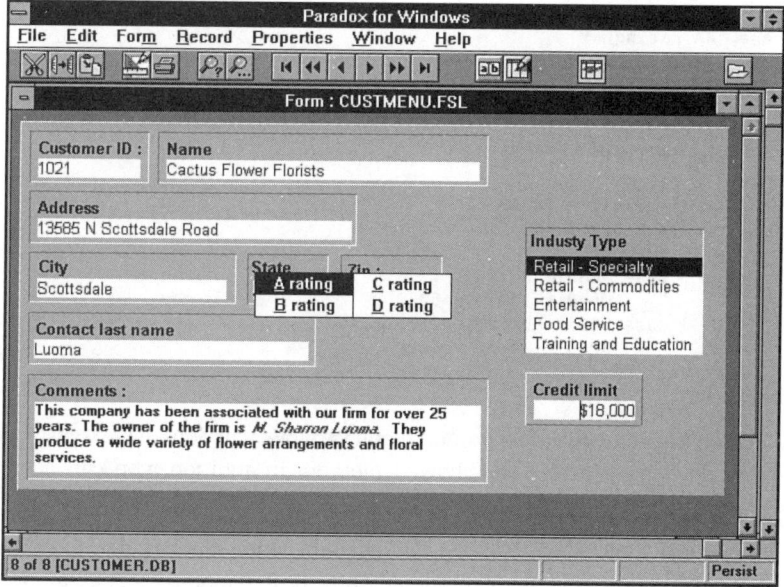

Figure 17.4. A pop-up menu with a bar.

345

Notice in this menu that we could as easily have used the addBreak( ) method to split the menu into two columns, but without displaying a vertical bar.

In this example, we use the show( ) method with two arguments supplied. The arguments specify the location of the pop-up menu in twips. A twip is 1/1440 of an inch, or 1/20 of a point. If you don't specify arguments specifically locating the pop-up menu, the pop-up menu is displayed at the mouse cursor location.

It makes sense to use the default mouse cursor location rather than specify screen coordinates in twips. Because the menu will pop up near the mouse cursor, the user has to move the mouse less distance, making menu interaction easy and convenient.

SwitchMenu

ObjectPAL has a basic language element known as the SwitchMenu construct. The advantage to using SwitchMenu is to save you lines of code. SwitchMenu automatically declares a simple pop-up menu for you and forces user interaction. It combines the functionality of the addText( ) and the show( ) methods in one construct.

The following code fragment shows how to display a simple pop-up menu with the SwitchMenu keyword:

```
switchMenu
    case "&A rating" :
        Credit_limit = 50000
    case "&B rating" :
        Credit_limit = 32000
    case "&C rating" :
        Credit_limit = 18000
    case "&D rating" :
        Credit_limit = 12000
    case "Class 2 &ratings" :
        switchMenu
            case "&Gold rating" :
                Credit_limit = 8000
            case "&Silver rating" :
                Credit_limit = 4000
        endSwitchMenu
endSwitchMenu
```

Notice that you don't need to declare a pop-up menu variable; you don't have to use the addText( ) method and you don't have to use the show( ) method. In addition, you can nest SwitchMenu statements.

SwitchMenu has some limitations. Nesting SwitchMenu statements is not the same as having cascading pop-up menus—with SwitchMenu statements, the first menu disappears before the second menu appears. Certainly not the same thing as true cascading pop-up menus! Also, you cannot use SwitchMenu to manipulate any of the menu item's attributes, which are discussed later.

However, SwitchMenu is handy when all you want to do is display a simple pop-up menu.

Using addArray( )

PopUpMenu variables come with a useful method: addArray( ). This method lets you declare all your menu items as String elements in an array. The array can then be used to create a pop-up menu.

The following code illustrates using addArray( ):

```
var
    p, p2       PopUpMenu
    a,   a2     Array[] String       ; resizable array
    choice      String
endvar
a2.grow(3)                           ; add 3 slots to the array
a2[1] = "&Gold rating"
a2[2] = "&Silver rating"
a2[3] = "&No rating"
p2.addArray(a2)                      ; add the array to p2
a.grow(4)                            ; add 4 slots to the array
a[1]="&A rating"
a[2]="&B rating"
a[3]="&C rating"
a[4]="&D rating"
p.addArray(a)                        ; add the array to p
p.addSeparator()                     ; add a separator to p
p.addPopUp("Class 2 &ratings",p2)    ; add p2 menu to p
choice = p.show()
if CustForm.editing = false then
    return
endif
switch
    case choice = "&A rating" :
        Credit_limit = 50000
    case choice = "&B rating" :
        Credit_limit = 32000
    case choice = "&C rating" :
        Credit_limit = 18000
    case choice = "&D rating" :
        Credit_limit = 12000
    case choice = "&Gold rating" :
        Credit_limit = 8000
    case choice = "&Silver rating" :
        Credit_limit = 4000
endswitch
```

The addArray( ) method is useful if you need to fill a menu with items in an array, such as field names, or field values read from a table. For example, in your application, you could use the enumFieldNames( ) method to fill an array with a table's field names. You then could display these field names in a pop-up menu, asking the user to select a field to move to, grab a value from, hide, make visible—the list goes on.

Other PopUpMenu Methods

Pop-up menus have other methods. Table 17.1 lists them and their uses.

Table 17.1. Other PopUpMenu Methods

Method	Description
addStaticText (const s String)	Adds a non-selectable item, s, in the menu. Usually used to put a title on the pop-up menu.
contains(const s AnyType)	Returns true if item s exists somewhere in the menu, false if not.
count( )	Returns a SmallInt with the total count of items in the menu, including separators, breaks, and bars. Does not, however, count items in a submenu.
empty( )	Removes all items from a menu.
remove(const s String)	Finds the first menu item that equals string s and removes it.

Creative Pop-Up Menu Uses

Pop-up menus are useful. Paradox for Windows makes extensive use of popup menus. When you right-click an object, Paradox presents you with a pop-up menu that enables you to change an object's properties.

You can add this kind of functionality in your application easily. You can place a pop-up menu code in the target object's mouseRightClick( ) built-in method. When the user right-clicks on the object, a pop-up menu appears, just as Paradox does for them interactively.

If you want to be more obtrusive, you also can use the mouseEnter( ) event to pop up a menu when the mouse cursor travels over an object. Or you can use the setFocus( ) or arrive( ) built-in method to automatically display a pop-up menu every time the user appears on a particular field or object, presenting a list to choose from. The possibilities are nearly endless.

Using Menu Attributes

Pop-up menu items have attributes that you can set. The addText( ) method takes an optional second argument that will set this particular item's attribute:

```
p.addText("A rating",MenuDisabled)
```

If you want, you can combine attributes by adding the attributes together:

```
p.addText("A rating",MenuDisabled + MenuChecked)
```

Table 17.2 lists the attributes you can set.

Table 17.2. Menu Attributes.

Method	Description
MenuChecked	Displays the item with the ✔ character preceding it.
MenuNotChecked	Displays the item without the ✔.
MenuGrayed	Displays the menu item dimmed. The menu item cannot be selected.
MenuNotGrayed	Removes the grayed attribute and displays the item normally.
MenuEnabled	Removes the disabled attribute. Menu item can be selected.
MenuDisabled	Disables the menu item. It is not dimmed, and it is unselectable. It is similar to adding a static text item.
MenuHilited	Displays the menu item highlighted. The first menu item will also appear highlighted.
MenuNotHilited	Removes the highlighted attribute and displays the item without a highlight.

You most likely will use the two attributes MenuChecked and MenuGrayed. The MenuChecked attribute lets you use a menu item as a logical toggle, indicating that a particular property is turned off or turned on. The following code sample demonstrates how to use the MenuChecked property.

A menu item, Blue Member, was added to indicate the customer is a member of a special list. The logical variable cstat is used to maintain the customers Blue Member status. The cstat variable is declared in the form's var window and was initialized to false in the form's open( ) built-in method.

The following code is attached to the Credit_limit object's mouseRightUp( ) built-in method. Each time the user right-clicks on this object in edit mode, the pop-up menu appears. Each time the user selects the Blue Member menu item, the cstat variable's value is toggled (cstat = not cstat). The cstat variable is declared global to this method in the form's var window. If it was true, it is set to false. If it was false, it is set to true.

```
var
    p, p2      PopUpMenu
    choice     String
endvar
p2.addText("&Gold rating")
p2.addText("&Silver rating")
p2.addText("&No rating")
p.addtext("&A rating")
p.addText("&B rating")
p.addText("&C rating")
p.addText("&D rating")
if cstat = true then              ; the customer is a member of Blue list
    p.addText("Blue &member",MenuChecked)
else                              ; the customer is not a member of blue list
    p.addText("Blue &member",MenuNotChecked)
endif
p.addSeparator()
p.addPopUp("Class 2 &ratings",p2)
```

```
choice = p.show()
if CustForm.editing = false then
    return
endif
switch
    case choice = "Blue &member" :
        cstat = not cstat                    ; toggle cstat
    case choice = "&A rating" :
        Credit_limit = 50000
    case choice = "&B rating" :
        Credit_limit = 32000
    case choice = "&C rating" :
        Credit_limit = 18000
    case choice = "&D rating" :
        Credit_limit = 12000
    case choice = "&Gold rating" :
        Credit_limit = 8000
    case choice = "&Silver rating" :
        Credit_limit = 4000
endswitch
```

Figure 17.5 shows the Blue Member menu item checked.

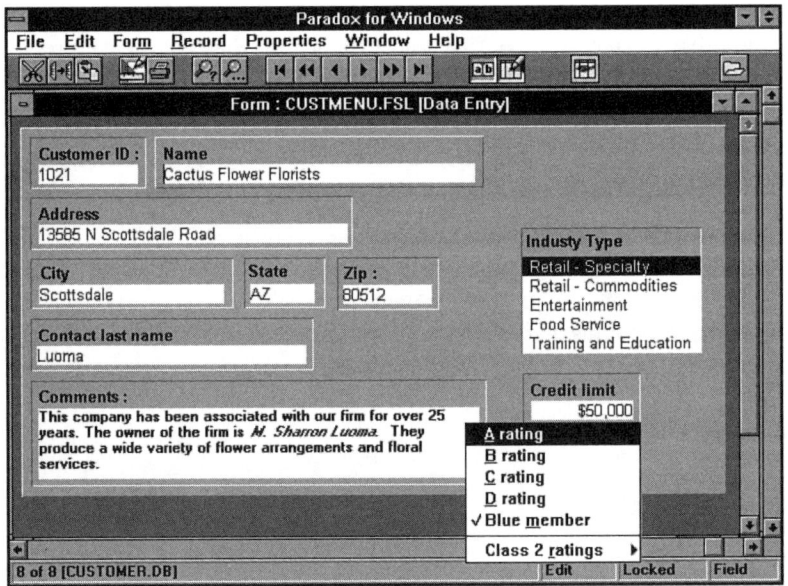

Figure 17.5. Pop-up menu item checked.

Pull-Down Menus

As discussed previously, pull-down menus will drive your application. For most applications, you will want to turn off Paradox's default pull-down menu and display your own, restricting what the user can do and giving your application a custom look and feel. All pull-down menus always appear just below the Paradox for Windows desktop window title bar. When you show your menu, it too will appear just below the desktop window title bar, replacing the Paradox menu.

The nice thing about pull-down menus is that they are composed of several pop-up menus. Therefore, all the skills you learned in creating pop-up menus directly apply to pull-down menus.

Adding and Using Menu Items

To create a pull-down menu, you need to take the following steps:

1. Create the pop-up menus.
2. Add the pop-up menus to the main menu.

It's this simple. The complexity comes when you need to refer to menu items in a pull-down menu. A pull-down menu can get very large with many cascading submenus. For this reason, just referring to the text to identify a menu can cause ambiguities. What if two menu items share the same text? In addition, in a large menu it is common to change some of the menu text. If you referred to the menu text in numerous places in your source code, you now have a maintenance headache because you have to search for and change all the references.

For this reason, the addText( ) method takes an optional third parameter: a menu id:

```
pop2.addText("&Print", MenuEnabled, 4 )
```

The menu id is a SmallInt that can uniquely identify the menu item. The menu id doesn't have to be unique, but in most cases you want it to be so that when you trap for menu events, you can determine the menu item selected.

Rather than actually typing numbers for a complex menu, we recommend using constants. Constants are easier to read. The following code listing is from a form's const window:

```
Const
      FileNew          = 1
      FileSave         = 2
      FilePrint        = 3
      FileExport       = 4
      FileExit         = 5
      EditCopy         = 6
      EditPaste        = 7
      EditNew          = 8
      EditDelete       = 9
      SearchFirst      = 10
      SearchNext       = 11
      HelpIndex        = 12
      HelpCredit       = 13
      HelpHelp         = 14
      HelpReminder     = 15
endConst
```

Part IV ■ Programming in ObjectPAL

Unfortunately, Paradox uses a large range of constants to identify its own menus. To enable you to distinguish your menus from Paradox's, Paradox defines two constants: UserMenu and UserMenuMax.

UserMenu represents the first menu id available for your menus in your applications. UserMenuMax represents the largest menu id available for your menu. In the current version, there are exactly 2000 menu id's available. When you add text to a menu, it's a good idea to add the UserMenu constant to your menu constant, which ensures that your menus are never confused with Paradox's menus.

Although this may sound strange, it makes sense when you consider how you will work with the menuAction( ) built-in method. You can add code to this method easily, trapping for any menu interaction. The menuAction( ) method gets passed a menuEvent event packet. The menuEvent packet's id( ) method returns the menu id of the selected menu. By comparing this id with your constants, you can determine which menu item was selected, as discussed in more detail in a following section of this chapter.

The following code is placed in a custom method known as a mainMenu( ), which is called from the form's open( ) built-in method:

```
method mainMenu()
var
      fileP, editP, searchP, helpP PopUpMenu
      mainM      Menu
endvar
; create the file menu
fileP.addText("&New database...", MenuEnabled, UserMenu+FileNew)
fileP.addText("&Save", MenuEnabled, UserMenu+FileSave)
fileP.addText("&Print", MenuEnabled, UserMenu+FilePrint)
fileP.addText("&Export...", MenuEnabled, UserMenu+FileExport)
fileP.addSeparator()
fileP.addText("E&xit", MenuEnabled, UserMenu+FileExit)
; create the edit menu
editP.addText("&Copy", MenuEnabled, UserMenu+EditCopy)
editP.addText("&Paste", MenuEnabled, UserMenu+EditPaste)
editP.addText("&New", MenuEnabled, UserMenu+EditNew)
editP.addText("&Delete", MenuEnabled, UserMenu+EditDelete)
; create the search menu
searchP.addText("&Search...", MenuEnabled, UserMenu+SearchFirst)
searchP.addText("Search &Next", MenuEnabled, UserMenu+SearchNext)
; create the help menu
helpP.addText("&Index", MenuEnabled, UserMenu+HelpIndex)
helpP.addText("&Credit", MenuEnabled, UserMenu+HelpCredit)
helpP.addText("&Using Help", MenuEnabled, UserMenu+HelpHelp)
helpP.addSeparator()
helpP.addText("&Reminders", MenuEnabled, UserMenu+HelpReminder)
; create the main menu
mainM.addPopUp("&File",fileP)
mainM.addPopUp("&Edit",editP)
mainM.addPopUp("&Search",searchP)
mainM.addPopUp("&Help",helpP)
; show the main menu
mainM.show()
endmethod
```

Figure 17.6 shows this menu in action.

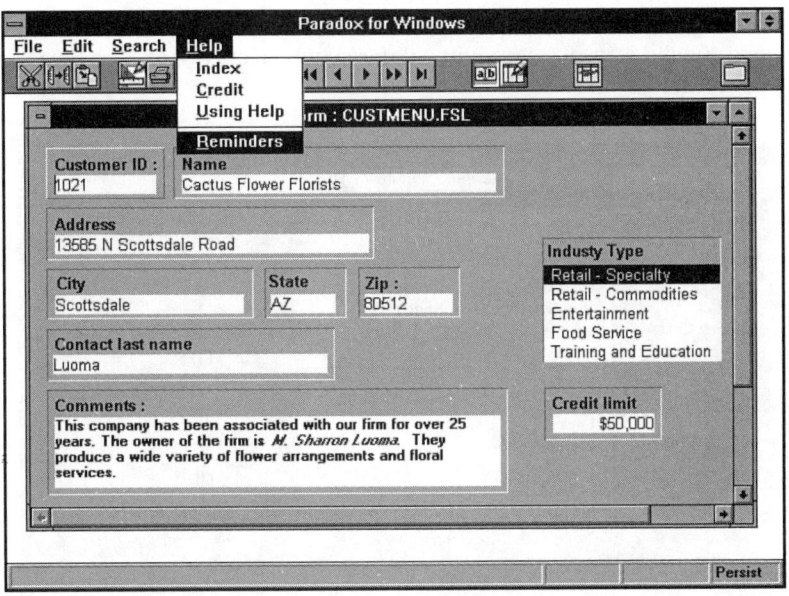

Figure 17.6. A revised pull-down menu.

Adding Accelerators

Often, you want to include right next to the menu item the keystroke equivalent of the menu command. Paradox does this on its own menus. The Record ¦ Delete menu item, for example, lists Ctrl+Del next to Delete. If you look at the entire Record menu, you see many accelerators listed (see fig. 17.7).

To add an accelerator key in your menu, you must do two things:

1. Add the key to the menu, which is a cosmetic change.

2. Trap for the key in the appropriate built-in method.

Use the \t notation when you add the pop-up menu item to tell Paradox that the following text is to appear in a column to the right of the menu item:

```
helpP.addText("&Index\tShift+F1", MenuEnabled, UserMenu+HelpIndex)
helpP.addText("&Credit\tShift+F2", MenuEnabled, UserMenu+HelpCredit)
```

In the preceding example, two keyboard accelerators are added, Shift+F1 and Shift+F2.

Adding an accelerator to a menu does absolutely nothing in terms of handling the keystroke. To handle the keystroke, you need to trap for the keystroke event at the form level or page level because menus you create most likely will persist at three levels: the application level, the form level, and the page level. Some applications require one menu for the entire application; this menu is known as an

353

application-level menu. Some applications need different menus for each form; such a menu is called a form-level menu. Finally, some forms require a different menu for each page on the form; this menu is known as a page-level menu.

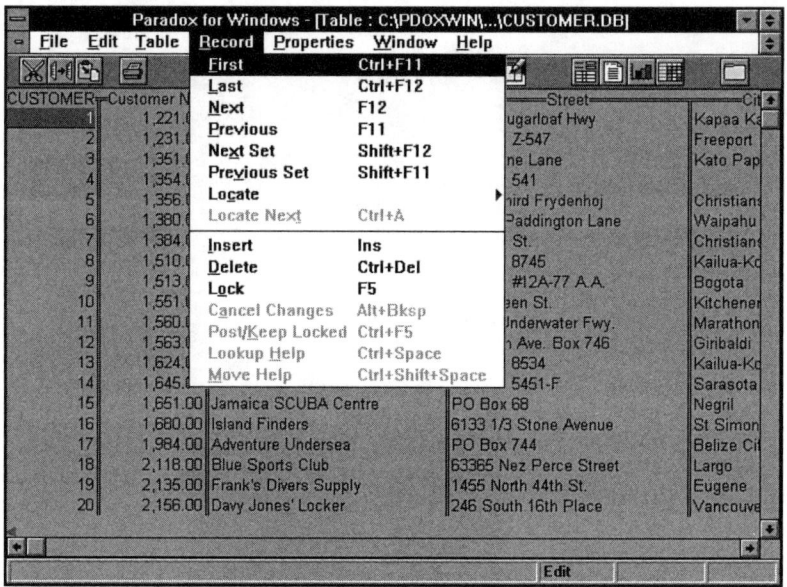

Figure 17.7. A Paradox menu with accelerators.

If you want to have keyboard accelerators, you have to trap for the keystroke at the appropriate menu level. Because no concept of application-level events exists, you have to trap the keystrokes at the form or page level. The following example is attached to the form's keyPhysical( ) built-in method.

```
        var
            keyStroke String
        endvar
        method keyPhysical(var eventInfo KeyEvent)
        if eventInfo.isPreFilter()      then
            ; This code executes for each object on the form.
            keyStroke = eventInfo.vChar()   ; get the keystroke
            disableDefault              ; prevent the keystroke from occurring

            switch
                case keyStroke = "VK_F1" and eventInfo.isShiftKeyDown() :
                    msgInfo("Help","Displaying help index...")
                case keyStroke = "VK_F2" and eventInfo.isShiftKeyDown() :
                    msgInfo("Help","Displaying credit help...")
                otherwise:
                    enableDefault       ; allow the keystroke to occur
            endswitch

        endif
        endmethod
```

The reason keyPhysical( ) is used is that you want to trap for the keystroke before Paradox does its default behavior. In this case, the Shift+F2 key, which usually is the memo view keystroke, is being redirected as an application help keystroke. To disable the default behavior for this keystroke, you must trap for the event by using the keyPhysical( ) built-in method. The keyChar( ) built-in method is invoked each time a keystroke is not handled by Paradox.

Changing Pull-Down Menu Attributes

You can change the attributes of an item on a pull-down menu easily. Two Menu procedures are useful here:

1. setMenuChoiceAttribute( )
2. setMenuChoiceAttributeById( )

The first procedure takes two arguments: a menu choice string and a SmallInt that represents a menu attribute. For example, to disable a menu item and gray it out by using the first procedure, you do the following:

```
setMenuChoiceAttribute("&Edit", MenuDisabled + MenuGrayed)
```

You use the second procedure more often, because it allows you to refer to a menu item by id, rather than by the menu item text:

```
setMenuChoiceAttributeById(MyEditMenu, MenuDisabled + MenuGrayed)
```

You can set the menu attribute when you add it to a pop-up menu to initialize it, except for the MenuChecked attribute. For some reason, this attribute doesn't check the menu item and also seems to rearrange the pop-up menu; this rearranging probably is a bug and seems to occur only with pull-down menus, not pop-up menus. The work-around to this is to just initialize the menu item's attribute as MenuEnabled and then use the setMenuChoiceAttribute( ) or setMenuChoiceAttributeById( ) procedures to change the menu item's attribute to MenuChecked.

You can always determine what attributes are set for a menu item by using the following three Menu procedures:

1. getMenuChoiceAttribute( )
2. getMenuChoiceAttributeById( )
3. hasMenuChoiceAttribute( )

The first two procedures take either a menu choice or a menu id as an argument and return a SmallInt that represents the menu item's attribute. The third procedure takes two arguments—a SmallInt that represents the current menu attribute state and a second SmallInt that represents the menu attributes to check. It returns true if the menu attributes listed are present in the set of attributes to check.

The following code shows how to check for menu attributes:

```
var
    menuAttribs          SmallInt
endvar
menuAttribs = getMenuChoiceAttributeById(UserMenu+FileNew)
if hasMenuChoiceAttribute( menuAttribs,MenuNotGrayed+MenuNotChecked ) then
    msgInfo("Menu Status","FileNew is not checked and not grayed")
endif
```

Turning Off the SpeedBar

You will probably want to turn off Paradox's SpeedBar so that you have greater control over the user interface. The following form type procedures manipulate the SpeedBar:

- hideSpeedBar( ) hides the SpeedBar, making it invisible.
- showSpeedBar( ) displays the SpeedBar, making it visible.
- isSpeedBarShowing( ) returns true if the SpeedBar is showing.

It makes sense to hide the SpeedBar when the application starts and restore it when the application closes. If, during the application's design phase, you frequently find the SpeedBar hidden, you can do two things to make it visible:

1. Play a script which contains the following code:

   ```
   if isSpeedBarShowing() = false then
       showSpeedBar()
   endif
   ```

2. Select Properties¦Desktop from the Paradox menu. Check the Floating check box, which will cause the SpeedBar to reappear. Then use either the SpeedBar's control menu to fix it in place, if you want, or use the Properties¦Desktop menu commands to do the same.

Using Paradox's Menu Ids

One little-known feature about menu ids is so useful that you may want to use the Paradox menu ids rather than creating your own. We have already shown you how to use constants to refer to a menu id that you created. This menu id distinguishes an event that involves your menu items from an event that involves a Paradox menu item.

Using a Paradox menu id rather than your own id endows your menu item with the default Paradox behavior for that menu id, which means that you can place a Delete menu item in your menu, give it the Paradox menu id that corresponds to the Record¦Delete menu item, and the menu item will be grayed out if the table is not being edited or enabled if it is being edited. When the user selects this menu item, the record will be deleted.

These menu items are automatically grayed and enabled, depending on the current mode and regardless of whether you enable or disable these menus. For example, the Record ¦ Delete menu item will appear gray when not in edit mode.

Let's look at some code:

```
method mainMenu()
var
     fileP, editP, searchP, helpP PopUpMenu
     mainM     Menu
endvar
fileP.addText("&New database...", MenuEnabled, UserMenu+FileNew)
fileP.addText("&Save", MenuEnabled, UserMenu+FileSave)
fileP.addText("&Print", MenuEnabled, UserMenu+FilePrint)
fileP.addText("&Export...", MenuEnabled, UserMenu+FileExport)
fileP.addSeparator()
fileP.addText("E&xit", MenuEnabled, UserMenu+FileExit)
; this menu uses all Paradox menu ids
editP.addText("&Copy", MenuEnabled, MenuEditCopy)
editP.addText("&Paste", MenuEnabled, MenuEditPaste)
editP.addText("Insert Customer", MenuEnabled, MenuRecordInsert)
editP.addText("Delete Customer", MenuEnabled, MenuRecordDelete)
; this menu uses all Paradox menu ids
searchP.addText("&Search...", MenuEnabled, MenuRecordLocateValue)
searchP.addText("Search Ne&xt", MenuEnabled, MenuRecordLocateNext)
searchP.addText("&Next Customer", MenuEnabled, MenuRecordNext)
searchP.addText("&Previous Customer", MenuEnabled, MenuRecordPrevious)
helpP.addText("&Index\tShift+F1", MenuEnabled, UserMenu+HelpIndex)
helpP.addText("&Credit\tShift+F2", MenuEnabled, UserMenu+HelpCredit)
helpP.addText("&Using Help", MenuEnabled, UserMenu+HelpHelp)
helpP.addSeparator()
helpP.addText("&Reminders\tF12", MenuEnabled, UserMenu+HelpReminder)
mainM.addPopUp("&File",fileP)
mainM.addPopUp("&Edit",editP)
mainM.addPopUp("&Search",searchP)
mainM.addPopUp("&Help",helpP)
mainM.show()
endmethod
```

In this example, the editP and searchP pop-up menus are filled with menu items that refer to Paradox menu commands. Because the menu id refers to Paradox menu commands, every time the user selects this menu item, the action that corresponds to this menu item executes.

Paradox for Windows has about 114 menu command constants representing all menu items. They are listed in Appendix H.

Using this technique, you can endow your application with a subset of the Paradox menus and inherit that functionality *without one line of code*. You even can rename the Paradox menu items to your own words.

However, for some reason, it seems impossible to rename the Record ¦ Delete menu item. No matter what you put in as the menu choice, if you specify MenuRecordDelete as the menu id, the menu item always displays the word `Delete` along with the Ctrl+Del key accelerator.

Building a Window Menu Item

All Window applications should have a Window menu item on the pull-down menu so that users can cascade, tile, or select a window to use. The nice thing about Paradox is that you can add a Window pop-up menu to your pull-down menu with just a few lines of code. All you have to do is add a pop-up menu called "Window" that contains a few items to your pull-down menu.

To add a full-featured Window menu to the preceding menu example, you just declare a PopUpMenu variable for the Window menu and add menu items for tile, cascade, arrange icons, and close all functions. Then just add the Window pop-up menu to the pull-down menu. The following code shows how this is done.

```
var
     WHIN, fileP, editP, searchP, helpP PopUpMenu
     mainM       Menu
endvar
; window popup menu items
WHIN.addText("&Tile",MenuEnabled,MenuWindowTile)
WHIN.addText("&Cascade",MenuEnabled,MenuWindowCascade)
WHIN.addText("Arrange &Icons",MenuEnabled,MenuWindowArrangeIcons)
WHIN.addText("Close &All",MenuEnabled,MenuWindowCloseAll)
; other popup menu addTextCode follows here
; it is ommitted for demonstration purposes
mainM.addPopUp("&File",fileP)
mainM.addPopUp("&Edit",editP)
mainM.addPopUp("&Search",searchP)
mainM.addPopUp("&Window",WHIN)
mainM.addPopUp("&Help",helpP)
mainM.show()
```

The nice thing about this process is that no code is needed to handle the window navigation, tiling, and cascading. Paradox handles all this work. To add tiling and cascading options, you will need to add a Tile and Cascade menu option in your Window pop-up menu and give these menu items the proper menu id, as the example demonstrates.

Using the menuAction() Built-In Method

To breathe life into menus and enable them to respond to user interaction, you need to trap for menu events with the built-in menuAction() method. Doing this is extremely easy. The following code example is attached to the form's menuAction() built-in method:

```
var
     choice     SmallInt
endvar
method menuAction(var eventInfo MenuEvent)
if eventInfo.isPreFilter()     then
     ; get the menu choice
     choice = eventInfo.id()
     ; this check let's us handle our own menu choices
     ; as well as Paradox menu choices
     if choice >=UserMenu and choice<=UserMenuMax then
```

```
                choice = choice - UserMenu        ; convert choice to our constant
        endif
        disabledefault
        switch
            case choice = FileNew :                ; user-defined menu id
                message("File new was selected")
            case choice = FileExport :             ; user-defined menu id
                message("File export was selected")
            case choice = MenuRecordDelete :       ; Paradox menu id
                if msgYesNoCancel("Delete", "Delete this record?")="Yes" then
                    enableDefault
                endif
            otherwise :
                enableDefault
        endswitch

    endif
endmethod
```

In case you didn't notice, the switch statement handles menu events for the Paradox menu ids as well as the menu ids we created as part of our menu. In this example, the Paradox MenuRecordDelete id is used with a pull-down menu. You can use your own menu id and then convert the menu action into the appropriate delete record action by issuing the following code:

```
switch
    case choice = FileNew :                ; user-defined menu id
        message("File new was selected")
    case choice = FileExport :             ; user-defined menu id
        message("File export was selected")
    case choice = FileDelete:              ; user-defined menu id if
        msgYesNoCancel("Delete", "Delete this record?")="Yes" then
            action(DataDeleteRecord)       ; convert to an action
        endif
    otherwise :
        enableDefault
endswitch
```

This code does the same thing except that the handling of the menu attributes, such as graying out the menu item, is entirely up to you.

When you handle menu events, you need to consider where you should handle them. If a menu is attached to a page, then you want to trap for menu actions at the page level. If a menu is attached to the form, trap for actions at the form level. You can handle menu events at any level below the page and form as well. After all, menu events are considered external events, so the event is initially handled by the form, which dispatches it to the intended target. The event then bubbles back upward, until the form finally receives the event for handling.

If you place your generic, form- or page-level menu action code on the else side of the isPreFilter( ) test, your generic form-level code can be overridden with object-level menu action code. By placing your code on the else side of the isPreFilter( ) test, your code will be called only when the event has bubbled back up to the form, or the form was the target of the event, which allows lower-level objects to handle the event first. If you place your menu trapping code on the isPreFilter( ) side, your code executes when the menu event is first dispatched to the intended target.

If you disable the default behavior from within the lower-level object with disableDefault, the event will not bubble-up to higher levels. If you don't disable the menuAction( ) default behavior in your lower-level object, the event will bubble up to higher levels in the containership hierarchy where the event can be handled. You also can use the passEvent statement to explicitly push the event off to the object's container. Because the menuAction event is an external event, the passEvent statement causes automatic bubbling. When the object's container is finished with the event, the line of code immediately following the passEvent statement is executed.

Perhaps the best way to view this kind of event behavior is through object-oriented glasses. View the form as a parent object in a hierarchy. The form has behavior defined but this behavior can be altered by attaching code to a child object. The child object's code overrides the parent's.

The event model in Paradox for Windows enables you to go a step further: you can override the parent's behavior at the child level, or you can let both levels participate in the event.

Problems with Changing Menu Attributes

If you are experiencing problems with changing menu attributes from built-in methods other than the menuAction method, try changing the menu attributes within the menuAction method, checking for an eventInfo.id( ) of MenuInit.

The MenuInit menuAction event occurs when the user presses F10 or uses the mouse to activate a pull-down menu. The MenuInit event occurs before any pop-up menu displays. All pull-down menu events have this two-phase property where a MenuInit event precedes the menu action designated by the pop-up menu attached to the pull-down menu. When the MenuInit menuAction is trapped, it is possible to change a menu attribute. The following code demonstrates this technique.

```
method menuAction(var eventInfo MenuEvent)
if eventInfo.id() = MenuInit then
    setMenuChoiceAttributeById(MyEditMenu, MenuDisabled + MenuGrayed)
endif
endmethod
```

For some reason, in certain circumstances setting menu attributes may not work. If you run into this problem, you can use this technique to work around the problem. In addition, using some of the System dialog boxes, such as msgStop( ) and msgInfo( ) during the MenuInit menuAction event can interfere with the proper display of the menu bar.

Pull-Down Menu Design Issues

The hardest part of working with pull-down menus is designing. How many menus should the application have? Should there be just one menu for the entire application? Should there be one for each form? Should several forms share a menu? How many menus does the application need? What should be on the submenus that appear in the menus? The questions can go on and on.

Perhaps the most fundamental issue is, should the application have one and only one menu?

Designing one menu for the entire application may make sense if all the application's features can fit in one menu. In addition, you can take advantage of the ability to change menu attributes by graying out items that don't make sense in one context.

You also can design a different menu for each context. Paradox for Windows does this. If you look at a table in table view, Paradox presents one menu. If you design a form for that table, Paradox presents another menu. When you attach code to an object, you see yet another menu.

If you need multiple menus in your application, you need to identify which menus need to persist across multiple forms and which may be useful for only one page of a form, for multiple-page forms. Menus that persist across forms need to be shown on the form's open( ) built-in method. Menus that change on each page of a form in multiple-page forms need to be shown on the page's arrive( ) method because the page will be opened only once, but arrived on many times.

You may want to place the menu code that is used across several forms in a library, so that the menu code is not repeated in each form's open( ) method.

There are no easy answers to menu design decisions. The answers depend on many issues. Some clients insist on a particular type of menu, thereby restricting your options as a developer. Some clients leave that decision entirely up to you. The recommendation we make is this: *Decide on a menu philosophy early and make the decision carefully.*

Menus carve up the application into recognizable chunks and if these chunks do not mirror the user's needs and requirements, the users will end up fighting with the menu structure. If menus are too *modal*—that is, if there are too many menus, with one for each context in the application—the users will be unable to remember where any menu items are located. If the menu is too *amodal*, without any changes in response to a different context, the menu may become too cluttered with useless information.

These delicate issues need to be balanced. Perhaps the best move is to evaluate how other Windows applications handle menus and see what makes sense in your environment.

Menus and Multiple Forms

If you have menus that persist across multiple forms, remember that the menu stays active until you specifically remove it. Although a menu may seem attached to a form or a page, it actually isn't. The menu is stored in a memory buffer within Paradox for Windows and its visibility and persistence properties are independent of the form, page, or any UIObject.

If you want to remove a menu item, use the menu removeMenu( ) procedure. This procedure will remove your custom menu and show Paradox's main menu.

In your multiform applications, you have to define the menu ids for the currently active menu in each form so that the form's methods can identify the menu event id.

Intercepting a Paradox SpeedBar Event

Because every Paradox SpeedBar item corresponds to a menu item, you can trap for SpeedBar events by simply trapping for the appropriate Paradox menu id. In most applications, however, you probably will hide the SpeedBar, preventing any SpeedBar event from occurring. In addition, Paradox doesn't provide a facility to create a custom SpeedBar, nor does Paradox have a SpeedBar event that traps for SpeedBar interactions exclusively. Instead, the SpeedBar rides piggyback on menu events.

This limitation is unfortunate because this kind of facility would be widely used. The limitation is easy to get around, however, through the clever use of pushbuttons and other UIObjects.

Creating Your Own Speedbar

Creating your own SpeedBar is so easy to do that you probably won't miss having a SpeedBar facility. The process goes like this:

1. Create a series of pushbuttons or other UIObjects that simulate Paradox's SpeedBar and serve as your application's SpeedBar.

2. Add code to the pushbutton( ) built-in method for each particular SpeedBar item.

The code that you add to your virtual SpeedBar can be a simple statement. In the case where the SpeedBar is synonymous with a menu item, you can just place the following in the pushbutton( ) procedure:

```
menuAction( MenuId )
```

Here the constant MenuId represents the menu item you want to invoke. The menuAction( ) procedure causes Paradox for Windows to create a menuAction event and send it to the menuAction( ) built-in method. Remember that there is a difference between the menuAction( ) built-in method and the menuAction( ) procedure.

The menuAction( ) built-in method is a place where you can add code to respond to menu action events. The menuAction( ) procedure creates a menu action event out of thin air, without the user doing anything.

The menuAction procedure does have limitations. Although you certainly can use menuAction within the context of creating a SpeedBar, you can use it to access nearly any Paradox menu item. Some menu items—including File¦New, File¦Open, File¦Import, File¦Utilities¦Export, File¦Utilities¦Import, File¦Working Directory, and File¦Private Directory—cannot be invoked.

Summary

Between pop-up menus and pull-down menus, Paradox for Windows gives developers flexibility. You have the ability to trap for events that involve your menus, and you can trap for events that involve Paradox's menu. You have the ability to invoke nearly any Paradox menu and associate any of your menus with Paradox's menus.

18
Using Dialog Boxes

Dialog boxes are a mainstay of Windows applications. These boxes *dialog*—or interact with—the user. Both Windows and Windows applications use dialog boxes to accept your input, to pause an operation until you give the "OK," or to tell you if or why a requested action is not available. Chapter 28 discusses Multiple Document Interface (MDI) in detail. For the purposes of this chapter, it is only important that you understand that dialog boxes are not confined to the physical desktop space, that they are not resizeable, and that the application's menus are not available while a dialog box is active.

As an ObjectPAL developer, you can easily access many of Paradox's own dialog boxes—such as the Locate Field Value dialog box that Paradox presents after you press Ctrl+Z and the Import/Export dialog boxes.

In addition, Paradox enables you to customize your own dialog boxes, using forms that you created, for interaction with the user. The issues involved with these dialog boxes can be quite complex, so we'll start slow and work our way up.

Using Messages

ObjectPAL comes with a relatively complete armory of basic dialog boxes. These boxes come with push-button graphics, so that they are simple to work with. These boxes are all members of the system class, and you can access them from anywhere in your application. The built-in system message methods follow:

- MsgAbortRetryIgnore
- MsgInfo
- MsgQuestion
- MsgRetryCancel

- MsgStop
- MsgYesNoCancel

Most of these message boxes return the string value contained on their buttons. The MsgYesNoCancel button returns the string Yes, No, or Cancel, depending on which button the user selects. Similarly, MsgAbortRetryIgnore returns the string value Abort, Retry, or Ignore, depending on which button the user selects. MsgRetryCancel works the same way, with the string values set to Retry or Cancel. When using any of these message boxes (MsgYesNoCancel, MsgAbortRetryIgnore, or MsgRetryCancel), pressing Esc causes the string value Cancel to be returned.

Suppose that you have a date field that defaults to the current date, but may be overridden in special circumstances. To make sure that a date other than the current date is entered intentionally, and not as a result of data-entry error, you can attach the following code to the Date field's canDepart method:

```
var
    YNC   string
endvar
if self.value<>today() then
    YNC=msgYesNoCancel("You entered "+     self.value,"Are you sure you want to
                        use a day other than today?")
    switch
        case YNC="No":
            self.value=today()
        case YNC="Cancel":
            self.value=blank()
            eventinfo.setErrorCode(canNotDepart)
    endswitch
endif
```

If you enter a different date, the dialog box shown in figure 18.1 appears.

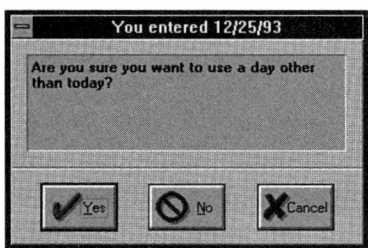

Figure 18.1. The YesNoCancel dialog box.

Keep in mind that these string values are case-sensitive. You must test for return values if *Yes*, *No*, or *Cancel*—*yes*, *no*, or *cancel* will not evaluate correctly. If you choose No from the dialog box, the field is filled with the current date; if you choose Cancel (or press Esc), the field is cleared. If you choose Yes, your code does nothing, leaving the value as entered.

MsgQuestion works much like the other message methods, except that no Cancel button is displayed on the dialog box. The returned string values are Yes and No. If the user presses Esc, the string Cancel is returned. The date field validation just shown can be performed with a MsgQuestion:

```
var
    YNC   string
endvar
if self.value<>today() then
    YNC=msgQuestion("You entered "+    self.value,"Are you sure you want to use a
                     day other than today?")
    switch
        case YNC="No":
            self.value=today()
        case YNC="Cancel":
            self.value=blank()
            eventinfo.setErrorCode(canNotDepart)
    endswitch
endif
```

MsgInfo and MsgStop do not return a value. MsgInfo just displays a text message in the dialog box for the user to see; MsgInfo pauses the application so that the user can see the message. MsgInfo is handy for telling the user that an operation has been completed successfully, or to inform the user of some value—perhaps the result of a locate or query operation. MsgStop displays a somewhat alarming dialog box (see fig. 18.2).

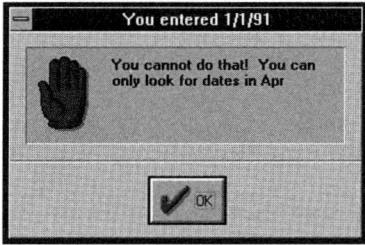

Figure 18.2. The MsgStop dialog box.

MsgStop dialog boxes are limited in how they display their text, and you cannot customize the button strings or the values they return. On the positive side, MsgStop boxes provide familiar *canned* dialog boxes to help you interact with the user. For many interactions, these boxes are just the thing to get the message across. Later in the chapter, you learn how to create your own dialog boxes, which you can customize as much as you want.

Using the View( ) Method

You can use the View( ) method to show a value to the user and extract a value in response. The View( ) syntax follows:

```
view( [const Title string])
```

Figure 18.3 shows how the optional title string appears at the top of the dialog box, with a type-in box below it. If you don't specify a title, the data type of the variable is shown on the top. Like the Msg methods, the View( ) method is good for quick-and-dirty user interaction. In other words, although it is somewhat limited, for the operations it works for, it works well.

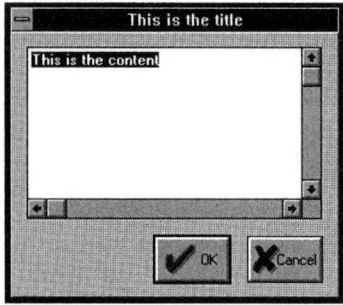

Figure 18.3. A View( ) dialog box.

View( ) is a method of the following types:

- Anytype
- Array
- Dynarray
- Record
- UIObject

Suppose that you want to use the value entered in the State field, for example, as the default value for a subsequent query. You can display this value by using the View( ) method:

```
Statefield.view("Query criterion")
```

If the State field contains the value MA, the code generates the dialog box shown in figure 18.4.

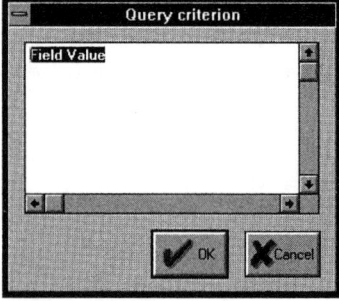

Figure 18.4. A View( ) dialog box displaying a field value.

So far, the dialog box in figure 18.4 doesn't do anything new—you could easily display a field value in a dialog box by using any of the Msg commands. This dialog box, however, is different because the viewed value is editable, so that the user can type a new value in the box. When the user types a value, the viewed variable value is also updated, which allows you to use the existing field value as the default query variable, or to change it, if necessary.

The following code sample demonstrates how the variable is changed. The first View( ) displays the value contained in the other field. The second View( ), however, displays the value that was entered into the first View( ) dialog box.

```
var
     str    string
endvar
str=State.value
str.view("Query criterion")
str.view("New criterion")
```

The View( ) method has some limitations—the biggest of which is that it doesn't work with Memo, Graphics, Binary, or OLE unbound fields except radio buttons and check boxes. Unbound field values can be displayed by the View( ) method, if the display type is set to check box or radio button. Otherwise, Paradox for Windows treats unbound fields as memos, which cannot be viewed. Although you can view the view, array, dynarray, or record data types, you cannot modify the values by using the View( ) method.

Using View( ) for Array and Dynarray data shows the entire array in the dialog box. You cannot modify the contents of these array types interactively, however, as you can with the other data types. You can get around this limitation by using a variable (usually an anytype) as an intermediate step:

```
var
     dyn   dynarray []string
     a anytype
endvar
dyn["1"]="One"
dyn["2"]="Two"
dyn["3"]="Three"
ForEach element in dyn
     a=dyn[element]       ;assign to anytype var
     a.view()             ;view the anytype var
     dyn[element]=a       ;change the dynarray
     msginfo("Dynarray value",dyn[element])
EndForEach
```

Using Paradox's Built-In Dialog Boxes

Paradox provides you with access to many of its built-in dialog boxes—the same boxes you would use if you were performing the action interactively. Some of these dialog boxes are constants that you can call from the Action method, and some are system procedures. The system procedures generate the dialog boxes that appear in response to selections from the File menu.

You can use the Action method dialog boxes if you want to cause one of these built-in dialog boxes to appear as soon as you arrive in a field, or if you want to substitute the key combination used to access a dialog box. If you are more comfortable with using F1 (used by DOS versions of Paradox) to access the Lookup Help dialog box, for example, you can disable the default Ctrl+space bar key combination and replace it with the F1 key combination. Use this syntax:

```
method keyPhysical(var eventInfo KeyEvent)
if eventinfo.vchar()="VK_F1" then
    disabledefault     ; no built-in Help
    active.action(dataLookup)
endif
endmethod
```

You use the disableDefault syntax to stop Paradox's built-in Help system from appearing. You probably want to modify your message as well, to suppress the following Paradox prompt:

```
Press Ctrl+space bar for Help with Fill-in
```

You also probably want to replace this prompt with your own prompt. You can accomplish this task by using the field's Status( ) method:

```
method status(var eventInfo StatusEvent)
    eventinfo.setReason(StatusWindow)
    eventinfo.setstatusvalue("Press F1 for Lookup Help")
endmethod
```

You can use the same technique to change the key combination used to perform a Locate operation. If you want a push button to perform a Locate operation, for example, you can use the following line in the button's pushButton( ) method:

```
action(dataSearch)
```

The system dialog box procedures are just as simple to invoke. You can recognize the procedures, because all begin with the letters, *dlg*:

Procedures	*Menu equivalents*
dlgAdd	File ¦ Utilities ¦ Add...
dlgCopy	File ¦ Utilities ¦ Copy...
dlgCreate	File ¦ New ¦ Table...
dlgDelete	File ¦ Utilities ¦ Delete...
dlgEmpty	File ¦ Utilities ¦ Empty...
dlgNetDrivers	File ¦ System Settings ¦ Drivers...
dlgNetLocks	File ¦ Multiuser ¦ Display Locks...
dlgNetRefresh	File ¦ System Settings ¦ Auto Refresh...
dlgNetRetry	File ¦ Multiuser ¦ Set Retry...
dlgNetSetLocks	File ¦ Multiuser ¦ Set Locks...
dlgNetSystem	File ¦ System Settings ¦ ODAPI...
dlgNetUserName	File ¦ Multiuser ¦ User Name...

Procedures	Menu equivalents
dlgNetWho	File ¦ Multiuser ¦ Who...
dlgRename	File ¦ UtilitiesRename...
dlgRestructure	File ¦ Utilities ¦ Restructure...
dlgSort	File ¦ Utilities ¦ Sort...
dlgSubtract	File ¦ Utilities ¦ Subtract...
dlgTableInfo	File ¦ Utilities ¦ Info Structure...

Of these procedures, the ones that operate on tables take one parameter—the table name. For example, dlgAdd (CUSTOMER.DB) brings up the Table Copy dialog box with CUSTOMER.DB filled in the Copy File From type-in area.

These dialog boxes work exactly the same way that they work interactively. Some of the dialog boxes are interactive, enabling you to enter and change values, and some are for display only. For example, the dlgTableInfo, dlgNetUserName, and dlgNetLocks dialog boxes display the table structure, the current user name, and the locks on a specified file. You cannot modify this information by using these dialog boxes.

Using Windows Built-In Dialog Boxes

Paradox for Windows allows you to access Windows dialog boxes as well as Paradox's built-in dialog boxes. This access gives you the capability to design tremendously flexible Windows-like dialog boxes. You access these dialog boxes by using Windows API calls. To call the Windows message box, include the following code in the Uses block:

```
Uses
     USER ; message routine comes from USER.EXE
     MessageBox (hwind CWORD, msgtext CPTR, msgcaption CPTR, msgtype CWORD) CWORD
endUses
```

Calling DLLs through the Uses statement is discussed in detail in Chapter 22. In a nutshell, this Uses block tells Paradox to use the MessageBox routine stored in the file USER.EXE. MessageBox takes the following four parameters:

- *hwind*: A CWORD (integer) type used to specify the window handle to receive input focus from the message box. Usually the window handle of the window that called the message.

- *msgcaption*: Indicates caption text for the message dialog box.

- *msgtext*: A pointer to the text to display within the message box.

- *msgtype*: A CWORD-type parameter that represents the result of the bitwise OR operation on a collection of flags. The integer values used for these flags stand for Windows constants representing the following:

Buttons to appear at the bottom of the dialog box.

The default button.

The icon to appear in the box.

Whether the box is application-modal or system-modal. Nearly all dialog boxes are application-modal. System-modal dialog boxes suspend all operations until the user interacts with the dialog box. The Alt+Tab and Ctrl+Esc key combinations do not work when a system-modal dialog box is displayed. This kind of dialog box is extremely rare, extremely pushy (invasive and controlling), and should be used only in extreme circumstances.

After the Uses statement is in place, you simply need to call the message box and supply values for the various parameters. The following code, for example, displays the dialog box shown in figure 18.5:

```
var
      msgtotal        SmallInt
      msgCaption      String
      msgText         String
      hwind           SmallInt
endvar
hwind = windowHandle()
msgtotal = 3
msgCaption = Strval(msgCaptionField)
msgText = Strval(msgTextField)
MessageBox(hwind,msgText,msgCaption,msgtotal)
```

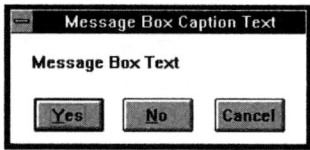

Figure 18.5. The Windows message box.

A code sample is included in the form MSGDLL.FSL on the disk provided at the back of this book. This code provides an extremely lucid display of how you can use various settings to call a message box.

Creating Your Own Dialog Boxes

Up to this point, you have seen various ways to access dialog boxes—both Paradox and Windows boxes. Now we turn our discussion to the most flexible dialog boxes of all—your own!

Custom Paradox for Windows dialog boxes are nothing more than special types of Paradox for Windows forms. Anything you can include on a form can be included in a dialog box—fields, table frames, graphics, and graphs—the possibilities are virtually limitless. Also, the same ObjectPAL code you use to call another form works with dialog boxes; only the form properties are different, as you soon will see.

To understand how to use dialog boxes, you first need to understand some important aspects of Paradox for Windows forms.

Assigning Form Properties

If you right-click on a form's title, you see a dialog box similar to the one in figure 18.6.

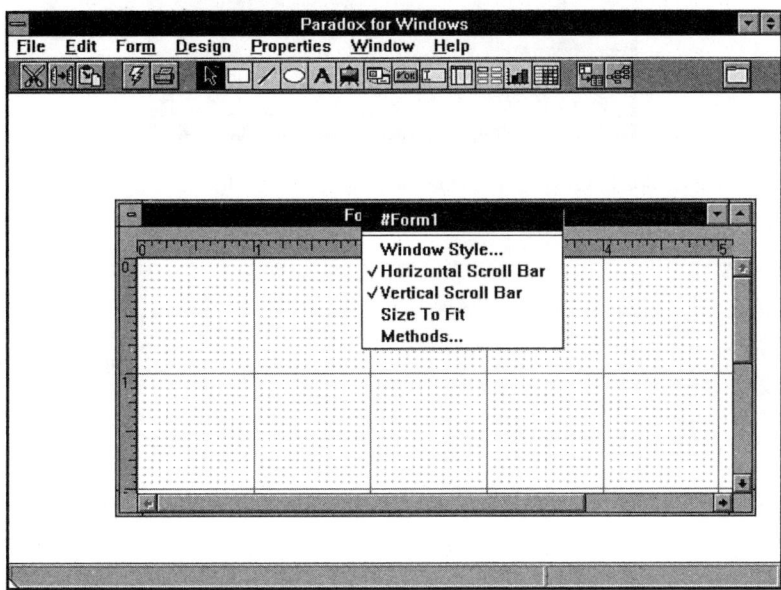

Figure 18.6. The Window Properties menu.

You use Horizontal Scroll Bar and Vertical Scroll Bar to toggle on and off the display of these bars on the form. Size to Fit tells Paradox whether to fit the form window to the size specified in the Page Layout dialog box or to use default MDI sizing. The Methods option enables you to assign methods at the form level.

The important option for our discussion, however, is the Window Style option. Choosing this option causes the dialog box shown in figure 18.7 to appear.

Many of the options shown in figure 18.7 depend on the settings in the other option boxes. The first choice in the upper right-hand corner of the Form Window Properties dialog box is Window Style, for example. Your options are Window or Dialog Box. If you select Window, for example, the Title Bar Properties options are dimmed and therefore unselectable. Title Bar Properties can be checked and unchecked only when the Window Style is set to Dialog Box. It is possible to set these properties under Style to Dialog box, uncheck the options under Title Bar Properties, and then set the Window Style back to Window, which may lead you to believe that you can display a form as a window without these Title controls, but you cannot.

Part IV ■ Programming in ObjectPAL

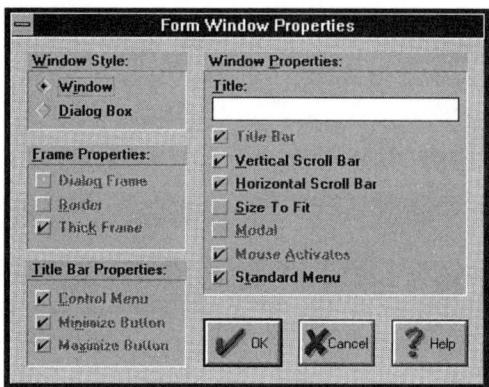

Figure 18.7. The Form Window Properties dialog box.

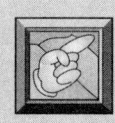 **Note:** Some of the properties you set in the Form Window Properties dialog box take effect immediately—vertical and horizontal scroll bars and title text, for example. Some properties, including many dialog box properties, do not take effect until you close, then reopen the form.

Now, look at each component of the Form Window Properties dialog box, taking each section one at a time:

- *Window Style*: This section enables you to choose whether you want to use a *Window* or *Dialog Box* style form window. Remember that dialog boxes always open on top of other windows in the center of the screen. You cannot resize dialog boxes; you can resize windows. Dialog boxes are not confined to their parent Desktop; windows are.

- *Frame Properties*: These properties are available only if you select *Dialog Box* from the Window Style section.

  Selecting *Dialog Frame* tells Paradox to use the dialog settings contained in your Windows Control Panel.

  You can prevent a form from being resized by the user by not using a frame at all. The *Border* option causes the dialog box to display with a black border. If you choose this option, you should not be able to resize the form by grabbing the border. (If you don't enable any of the frame properties, you get a dialog box that cannot be resized.) If you select Border, you should not be able to resize the form by grabbing the border. A bug in the current version of Paradox, however, enables you to do this.

  The *Thick Frame* option can be used as an alternative to Dialog Frame because both options are mutually exclusive.

374

- *Title Bar Properties*: You can set these properties only if you have selected Dialog Box from the Window Style section. You can disable the *Control Menu* check box if you want to ensure that users will not accidentally close a form. If you check the *Minimize Button* check box, when the users work with modal dialog boxes, they will be able to see an icon, but they will be unable to do anything else. You can disable the *Maximize Button* check box to prevent a user from maximizing a form so that it is no longer sized to fit.

- *Window Properties*: So far, we have dealt with properties of the window's frame and the window's title. The Window Properties are properties that apply to the window and how the window interacts with your application.

The *Title* type-in box enables you to specify a custom title for your form. The title text is also the name by which Paradox refers to the form. When you try to save a modified form named MYFORM.FSL, for example, with the title text *Order Entry*, Paradox prompts you with the message shown in figure 18.8.

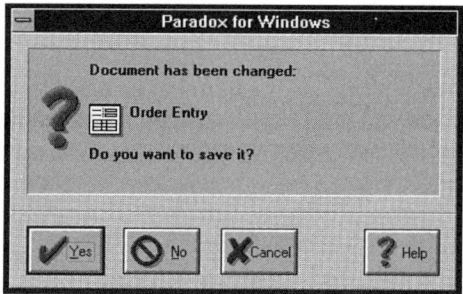

Figure 18.8. A custom form title.

The *Title Bar* check box lets you tell Paradox whether you want a title bar to appear. Even if you have text entered in the Title box, no title will appear if Title Bar is unchecked.

The *Vertical Scroll Bar* check box tells Paradox whether or not to display a vertical scroll bar on the form.

The *Horizontal Scroll Bar* check box tells Paradox whether or not to display a horizontal scroll bar on the form.

The *Size to Fit* check box tells Paradox to open the window to the exact size specified in the page layout, rather than using the Windows default.

Checking the Modal check box causes the dialog box written in an application to pause program execution to the extent that the SpeedBar and menus are not available. The next section compares modal with nonmodal dialog boxes.

The *Mouse Activates* check box tells Paradox whether to give the window focus (makes the window active) when the user clicks it. This option is available only for nonmodal dialog boxes. This feature is useful in applications that use a SpeedBar or icon sized dialog boxes as custom SpeedBars. Unchecking Mouse Activates in this situation enables you to keep a floating dialog box on top of the rest of an application. The dialog box can trap for mouse clicks on the SpeedBar windows without giving them input focus.

You also should disable Mouse Activates if you are using a dialog box solely for the purpose of displaying a status message, and the box is not a selectable window.

The *Standard Menu* check box tells Paradox whether to display the standard Paradox form menu. This option is available only for forms that have their Window Style sections set to Window. Standard Menu is dimmed and unselectable if you selected Dialog Box from the Window Style section.

If you want one form to display a custom menu for use by all other forms in your application, just attach the menu-building code to the first form and turn off the Standard Menu property for all other forms.

Disabling Standard Menu for forms also prevents the standard menu from flickering while a new form displays its custom menu.

Although some of the Form properties are purely aesthetic, such as choice of frame on the title text, other properties affect the way a dialog box or form integrates with the rest of your application. Although many of the options available in the Form Window Properties dialog box can be set in program code, as discussed in the following section, it usually is advisable to set these properties by using this dialog box.

Using Modal and Non-Modal Dialog Boxes

You can use two methods to open forms and dialog boxes—open( ) and openAsDialog( ). These methods support the following three syntax options:

1. open (const formName [, const windowStyle LongInt]) Logical
2. open (const formName String, const windowStyle LongInt, const x SmallInt, const y SmallInt, const w LongInt, const h LongInt) Logical
3. open (const openInfo FormOpenInfo) Logical

The same three syntax options are available for openAsDialog. The first syntax can be as simple as the following code:

```
var
     frm form
endvar
frm.open("FORMNAME.FSL")
```

The optional WindowStyle enables you to choose from the following window style constants:

- WinDefaultCoordinate
- WinStyleBorder

- WinStyleControlMenu
- WinStyleDefault
- WinStyleDialog
- WinStyleDialogFrame
- WinStyleHidden
- WinStyleHScroll
- WinStyleMaximize
- WinStyleMaximizeButton
- WinStyleMinimize
- WinStyleMinimizeButton
- WinStyleModal
- WinStyleThickFrame
- WinStyleTitleBar
- WinStyleVScroll

Usually, these options correspond to the options in the Form Window Properties dialog box. The only options available by using these methods that are not available interactively are WinStyleHidden, WinStyleMaximize, and WinStyleMinimize, which open the form invisible, maximized, backwards, or iconized, respectively. You can add these constants together to set more than one option.

In the Form Window Properties dialog box, you saw that some options were disabled when the window style was set to Window. The following list of constants shows you the only options available to forms not opened as dialog boxes:

- WinStyleDefault
- WinStyleMaximize
- WinStyleMinimizeVScroll
- WinStyleScroll
- WinStyleStyleHidden

You may be wondering which windows style to use: Window or Dialog Box. The answer is "one or the other, but not both." As previously mentioned, it usually is easier to use the interactive Form Window Properties dialog box to set the properties. If you have the properties set in this window, you can use the first syntax to open the form or use the second syntax of the three previously discussed syntax options by using WinStyleDefault as the window style constant.

377

You use the second syntax option to open the form with explicit coordinates and an explicit size. The x and y represent the upper left corner of the window in twips, and the w and h represent the width and height of the window, in twips. This syntax takes one or more WinStyle constants:

```
var
    frm  form
endvar
frm.openAsDialog("MYFORM.FSL", WinStyleTitleBar+
WinStyleMaximizeButton,1440,1440,2880,2880)
sleep(3000)
frm.close()
```

Using openAsDialog( ) opens the window as a *non-MDI child*, which means that it sits above other windows and can be moved anywhere on the screen; open( ), by itself, opens an MDI child window, with all the properties of MDI children. Knowing this, it makes sense that if you specify coordinates for these two methods, open( ) sets the coordinates relative to the Paradox desktop, and openAsDialog( ) sets the coordinates relative to the screen.

The third syntax—found at the beginning of this section—enables you to specify the size, position, and window style, and also enables you to specify the query to use as the basis of the form and to change the form's master.

Using Wait( ) and FormReturn( )

Any form can be made *almost* modal by waiting for it. The Wait( ) method suspends execution of the calling form until the user interacts with the called form. The called form issues a FormReturn( ) to send focus back to the form that called it.

We say *almost modal* because of the difference between dialog boxes with the modal properties checked and the boxes with their modal properties unchecked. Marking the Modal check box disables Paradox's menus and SpeedBars while the form is active.

Suppose that the form MAIN.FSL needs to know if the user wants to proceed with a given operation. To do this, MAIN.FSL can use another form, CONFIRM.FSL, as a confirmation dialog box:

```
var
  frm form
  str string
end var
 f.openasdialog("CONFIRM.FSL")
 str=frm.Wait()         ; get the returned value
 frm.close()            ; close the dialog form
 if str = "OK" then
    Continue_proc()
 endif
```

CONFIRM.FSL probably has an OK button and a Cancel button. The OK button contains only the code, formreturn("OK"); the Cancel button contains the code, formreturn("Cancel").

This simple example raises a few other important points. Notice the frm.close( ) syntax in the calling form: the user must interact with one of the buttons on the form so that the returned value can be passed back to the calling form.

The other pitfall of which you need to be aware and know the code for is the possibility that the user may click the Close icon. If this happens, the second form returns a logical value of False. When the form gets to the line that tries to assign the string variable *str* to the return value, Paradox informs you that you are trying to assign a logical value to a string variable. Here are a few solutions to this problem:

- Use True and False values for the formreturn( ) and set the str variable's type to logical instead of string. This approach works well for simple Yes/No responses but is too limited for more complex responses.
- If you don't type the variable **str**, you can convert the variable to a string and allow return values of OK, Cancel, or False.
- Create the called form (CONFIRM.FSL, in this case) without a Control menu. This method, which is the recommended solution, completely avoids the issue of the user closing the dialog box without choosing a button.

You may have noticed that you can use openAsDialog( ) or wait( ) on the called form to cause the form to behave modally. If you are working with a form designed for use as a dialog box, you should use open( ) and wait( ) to force modality and set the form properties in the Form Window Properties dialog box. You should reserve OpenAsDialog( ) for forms that need to perform double duty as both regular forms and dialog boxes.

Transferring Information between Forms

Often, a form calls and waits on another form to return a selected value from the called form. You may use this method if you want to design your own Lookup Help form. Suppose that you want to allow the user to click on a field to call a custom lookup form. You should attach the following code to the field's mouseClick( ) method:

```
var
    frm      form
    frmret   string
endvar
frm.open("cust_lkp")
frmret=frm.wait()
if frmret<>"Cancel" then
    self.value=frmret
endif
frm.close()
```

Figure 18.9 shows a custom lookup form.

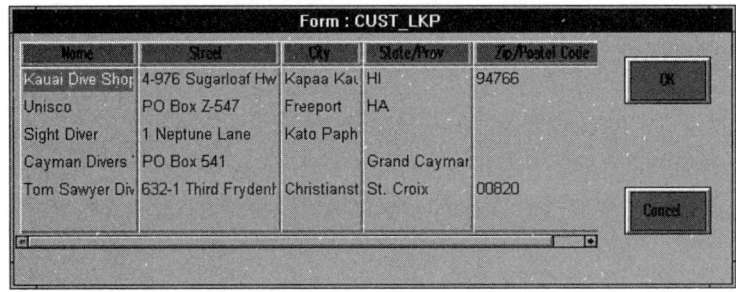

Figure 18.9. A custom lookup form.

You should place the following code segment on the OK button:

```
method push-button(var eventInfo Event)
formreturn(.name)
endmethod
```

The Cancel button returns the string Cancel.

Another way to return a value from the dialog box is to assign variables directly, including the full path to the dialog box form name from the calling form. You need to assign these variables before you close the dialog box form:

```
var
    frm         form
    frmret      string
endvar
frm.open("cust_lkp")
frmret=frm.wait()
if frmret<>"Cancel" then
    self.value=frm.name
endif
frm.close()
```

This method has the advantage of allowing you to return multiple values from the called form. You can use the values to fill in field values stored in invisible fields or assigned to variables for other purposes:

```
var
    frm         form
    frmret      string
    streetret   anytype
    cityret     anytype
endvar
frm.open("cust_lkp")
frmret=frm.wait()
if frmret<>"Cancel" then
    self.value=frm.name
    streetret=frm.Street
    cityret=frm.City
endif
frm.close()
msginfo("you selected someone from ",cityret)
```

While you are waiting on another form, you can access custom methods within the other form in the same way that you use custom methods in all open forms. Declare the method in the calling form's Uses block. This method works both ways. Suppose that you have a button on the called form, from which you wanted to access a method in the calling form. ShowYours( ) is a custom method in the calling form. The following code would be attached to the button's pushButton method in the called form. The called form can access methods from the calling form by using this technique:

```
var
    frm         form
    itsname     string
endvar
formcaller(frm)          ;get the handle of the calling form

itsname=getTitle(frm)    ;use the handle to get the title
frm.attach(itsname)      ;attach to the title
frm.showYours("This came from the calling form")
```

In the Uses block of the called form, place the following syntax:

```
Uses ObjectPAL
    showYours(str STRING)
endUses
```

Rather than a text string, you can send any variable of any type to the calling form's custom method. In fact, you can pass an entire array (or even multiple arrays). Because Paradox doesn't allow you to pass arrays and dynarrays directly, you need to define a new type with a value of type array on both forms involved:

```
Type
    myType= dynarray [] anytype
endType
```

Then, when you define the custom method, just type the variable parameter with the new type:

```
method showyours(recinfo myType)
    recinfo.view()
endmethod
```

Then, in the dialog form, assign the elements to the array and send them back to the calling form. You must declare the calling form's custom method in the Uses block of the dialog form.

The following code assigns dynarray elements based on the fields in the dialog form's data model. Notice that fields not used in the form are accessed by using dmGet:

```
var
    frm, frmhdl         form
    itsname             string
    recinfo             myType
    hourinfo            number
    billinfo            date
endvar
    dmGet("Mybills","Billed",billinfo)
    dmGet("Mybills","Hours",hourinfo)
    recinfo["Date"]=date.value
```

```
recinfo["Billing"]=billinfo
recinfo["Hours"]=hourinfo
formCaller(frm)            ;get caller's handle

itsname=gettitle(frm)      ;get caller's title
frm.attach(itsname)        ;attach to title
frm.showyours(recinfo)     ;calls the custom method
```

The preceding code segment serves as a good demonstration of gathering information into a dynarray to pass between forms in a Wait( ) relationship. A more practical approach to picking up an entire record, however, requires that the new type be an array:

```
var
    frm, frmhdl           form
    itsname               string
    recinfo               myType
    tc                    tcursor
endvar

    tc.attach(Date)
    recinfo = tc
    formCaller(frm)
    itsname=gettitle(frm)
    frm.attach(itsname)
    frm.showyours(recinfo)
```

An additional caveat of which you need to be aware when waiting on dialog boxes: you cannot have debug or any trace operations enabled when you attempt to call the dialog box.

Using Nested Waits( )

It is fairly common for dialog boxes to need additional information from a third or fourth dialog box. If you have three forms called FormOne, FormTwo, and FormThree, for example, FormOne can open and wait on FormTwo. While FormOne is waiting on FormTwo, FormTwo can open and wait on FormThree. A formReturn in FormThree returns control to FormTwo; a formReturn in FormTwo returns control to FormOne.

Under some circumstances, this flow scenario does not go as planned, and FormThree's formReturn goes directly to FormOne. This result is a function of the actions performed by the form. Those actions considered *processor intensive* require a short sleep following the open( ) or close( ) call.

Paradox uses a Windows API call to place messages in a Windows queue. Paradox needs to yield control to Windows long enough for the message to be activated. Sleep can be called with or without arguments to yield control to the operating system so that other processes can get through.

Summary

This chapter explained why dialog boxes are essential to windows programming. Paradox for Windows makes it easy to display dialog boxes to prompt the user for more information or to relay important information. Knowing how to access some of Paradox for Windows built-in dialog boxes can save you significant development time. When the built-in dialog boxes don't meet the task at hand, however, you now should understand how to create your own dialog boxes to communicate with your end users.

19
Understanding Error-Handling Strategies

Error handling in Paradox for Windows is somewhat complex. Designing an error-handling strategy is not as simple as it seems, because Paradox has a form-based and object-based interface. Each form is king over its kingdom. There simply is no single place to put error-handling code and to make this code universally applicable throughout your application.

Don't fret; Paradox gives developers plenty of built-in error support so that it is possible, but probably not desirable, to write an application without an error-handling strategy. After you understand Paradox's error mechanism, you will see why it is fairly easy and beneficial to implement good error handling.

Using an Error-Handling Manifesto

In order to discuss error handling in specifics, we need to discuss error handling in general. The following list is an error-handling manifesto that we have derived from years of working with previous versions of Paradox and in other development environments:

- The error-handling mechanism must be bulletproof. This mechanism can't fail. If the error-handling mechanism does fail, it only makes a bad situation—an error in the application—worse. If the error handler fails, the error handler should provide a graceful exit.

- An error-handling mechanism must be simple and maintainable. If overly complex, the mechanism is more likely to fail.

- An error-handling mechanism should be implemented easily so that any programmer can put it in an application with minimum effort. Otherwise, the error-handling routines become more trouble than they are worth.

- An error-handling mechanism must allow for local control over errors. The programmer should be able to detect an error close to the actual line of code that caused the error and optionally branch to another part of the offending method or procedure.

- Most important, the error-handling mechanism must enlighten users to explain not only what happened in layman's terms, but what to do about the error.

In short, you need to spend a lot of up-front time designing the error handler—coding it and testing it thoroughly. The time you spend pays off handsomely when you begin to build subsequent Paradox applications. You then can simply insert your generic error handler in all your applications.

Understanding How Paradox Handles Errors

Paradox has two kinds of error-handling mechanisms. One kind of mechanism displays status messages at the bottom of the screen and reports various general errors, such as trying to insert a record when a table is in View mode or making key violation errors. Technically, these actions represent error conditions because the events associated with them report an error code. Throughout this chapter, this mechanism is known as the *B mechanism*.

The other error mechanism grabs the error and presents a special error dialog box that gives the user some choices on what to do next. Although the first error-handling mechanism simply passes messages through to the user, the second mechanism presents a more serious message in a dialog box. We call this mechanism the *A mechanism*.

Paradox has three kinds of errors: *critical* errors, *warning* errors, and *all other* errors. Although the documentation refers to only two kinds of errors, in reality, three errors exist. We will refer to these as error types 1, 2, and 3—where 1 is a critical error, 2 is a warning error, and all the other errors are 3.

At the bottom of the severity totem pole are errors such as trying to move beyond the end or the beginning of a table, making key violation errors, trying to edit a table in View mode, and making other data-oriented errors (type 3 errors). Next in severity are warning errors (type 2 errors). These errors occur when an RTL method or procedure does not complete properly and returns false. (An RTL method or procedure is one that is supplied with Paradox, not one that you create.) One example of a warning error is trying to open a TCursor on a table that is exclusively locked. The open( ) method returns false, which is a warning error. Critical errors are more severe (type 1). These errors indicate something more serious has happened that Paradox can't handle. If you try to assign a value to a field that doesn't exist, for example, Paradox reports a critical error.

By default, Paradox's error-handling A mechanism—the one that displays a dialog box—handles all type 1 errors (critical errors). By default, Paradox ignores type 2 errors (warning errors). Neither the A nor B mechanisms handle warning errors. Your code continues with no messages displayed. All the type 3 general errors are displayed on the window's status area by way of the status event.

You can force Paradox to handle warning errors as if these errors were critical errors by using errorTrapOnWarnings(Yes). Paradox then uses the A mechanism to handle warning (type 2) errors. If you use errorTrapOnWarnings(No), Paradox ignores warning errors. After you use errorTrapInWarnings(Yes), all type 2 errors get handled by the error-handling mechanism.

You cannot use errorTrapOnWarnings( ) to force Paradox to handle general (type 3) errors, through the error-handling A mechanism. General errors are always handled through the B messaging mechanisms that the status( ) built-in method handles.

You learned in previous chapters that Paradox simply displays errors handled by the B mechanism in the status bar at the bottom of the Paradox application window. When Paradox encounters an error that goes through error-handling mechanism A, it displays the dialog box in figure 19.1.

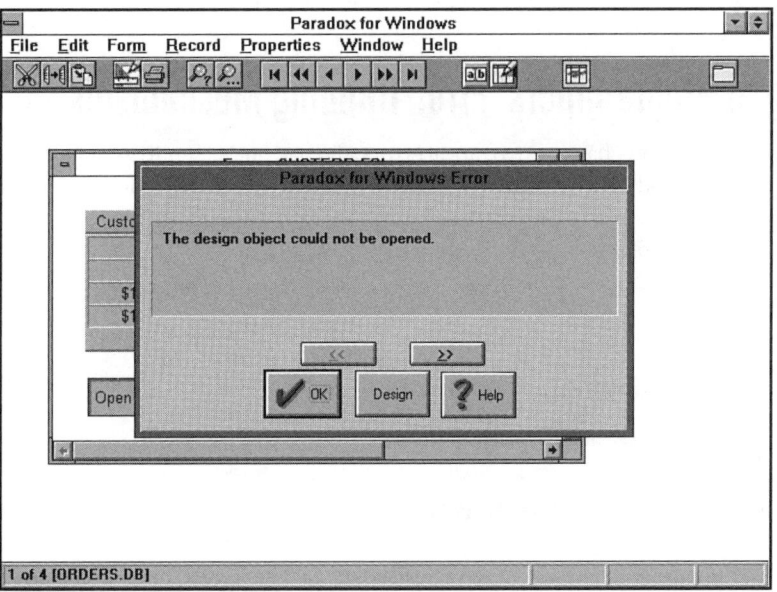

Figure 19.1. The Paradox error-handling dialog box.

As you can see, this dialog box has three buttons along the bottom: OK, Design, and Help. The dialog box also has two buttons, >> and <<. Although this dialog is helpful, it certainly is not the type of thing users should see in the middle of their applications because the Design button enables them to open the form in Design mode, which may not be prudent. Second, the two direction buttons are not intuitive to most users because some messages may make no sense to the user. Clearly, developers need to provide their own error-handling mechanisms.

You can use the >> or << button to display the next or preceding error message. These buttons are provided because one error can generate many error messages. Paradox for Windows is an application built in layers or modules. Each layer can place an error message into the *error stack*. (A *stack* is a data structure that looks and behaves just like a stack of cafeteria plates. You can place a plate only on top of the plate stack. You cannot slide a plate between the other plates. Similarly, you can take a plate off the top of the stack only.)

When an error occurs, each layer in Paradox optionally places a message onto the error stack. The Paradox error-handling dialog box simply displays this stack of errors. All errors, no matter what the type, go on the error stack. Usually, only one or two messages are on the error stack. In fact, the errorMessage( ) procedure simply displays the message on the top of the error stack.

Paradox clears the error stack when the next method or procedure executes, which means that the messages do not hang around for long. If you fail to catch some messages, they are gone forever. In addition, if you want to try to display or store the error stack, the error stack disappears as soon as you call a method to save the stack. Fortunately, a few methods and procedures are exempt from this stack-clearing behavior. If these procedures did not exist, it would be impossible to save the errors to a table or file, because the act of saving would wipe them out.

Looking at Programmers' Error-Trapping Mechanisms

Paradox gives you two mechanisms to trap all errors: the try..onFail..endtry control structure and the error( ) built-in method. The try..onFail..endtry block lets you place code between the try..onFail section. If any of the ensuing ObjectPAL statements fail, the code in the onFail..endtry portion executes. Take the following code fragment as an example:

```
var
      tc TCursor
      f    Form
endvar
errorTrapOnWarnings(Yes)]
try
      tc.open("NoTable")
      f.open("No form")
onFail
      msgStop("Error",errormessage())
endtry
```

The errorTrapOnWarnings( ) procedure ensures that the try..endtry block will trap warning errors as well as critical errors. If anything goes wrong with tc.open( ) or f.open( ), the msgStop( ) procedure executes. You can issue a retry statement from within the onFail..endtry block. This statement returns control back to the line of code that caused the error. Obviously, you should use the retry statement only on the errors where the user can actually remedy the situation. You can place a table-locking attempt around a try..onFail block and in the onFail..endtry block, for example, to display a dialog box telling users that the table is locked. You can give users a chance to find the user who has the table locked, so that the user with the table locked can unlock the table. Your dialog box can have a Retry button, so that users can try the lock again.

The other programmer's error tool—the built-in error( ) method—is called when any type 3 (general), type 2 (warning—provided errorTrapOnWarnings( ) is turned on), and type 1 (critical) error occurs. You can catch all errors at the form level on the False side of the isPrefilter( ) check, because the form is the object with enough intelligence to handle error events. Error events always are dispatched by the form to the object that created the error. The error event then bubbles its way to the form, where it is finally handled. This bubbling process is discussed in detail in Chapters 13 and 14.

The way in which an error works its way to the error( ) built-in method depends on what type of error it is (type 1, 2, or 3) and whether errorTrapOnWarnings( ) is on. If errorTrapOnWarnings( ) is on, all three error types travel through the error( ) built-in method. If errorTrapOnWarnings( ) is off, then only types 1 and 3 travel through the built-in error( ) method.

So far, you may think that the place to handle events is at the form-level error( ) built-in method. We don't think that the error( ) method is a good place to trap errors, however, for a simple reason: our error-handling manifesto says that errors should be handled locally and quite often, and you may decide on a different course of action as a result of an error. By the time an error event has occurred, it is too late to take a course of action from the method that caused the error. Paradox has yanked control from your ObjectPAL method and given it to the error( ) built-in method. You have no chance to retry the operation or take a different course of action. You can, of course, execute code in response to the error within the error( ) built-in method. The try..endTry block at least gives you the option to retry the line of code that failed or to take different action from within the same method, if the error is a critical error or errorTrappOnWarnings( ) is set to Yes.

The error( ) method may be a good place to trap some types of errors and devise a different means of displaying these errors to the user. You also may want to use the error( ) method to prevent critical errors from going to Paradox's error-handling A mechanism. Before we can discuss this, however, we need to press on with just a few more details about the error( ) built-in method.

When the built-in error( ) method is called for type 3 errors (general errors), the next event usually is a status event because Paradox will display the error message in the status bar at the bottom of the application window. Some type 3 errors, such as trying to move past the end of the table or before the first record in the table, never generate a message in the status bar. The error( ) method may be a good place to display the error message in a dialog box rather than having Paradox display the message in the status bar. If you decide to use the dialog box display method, just remember to disable the error event's default behavior so that the error message doesn't display on the status bar too.

To actually force an error, Paradox gives you the fail( ) procedure, which forces the method to fail. This procedure causes control to pass to any onFail part of an active try..onFail..endtry block. In addition, an error event is forced to occur, which triggers execution of the built-in error( ) method.

The fail method has two optional arguments—an error number and an error message. These arguments can correspond to Paradox's internal error constants and error messages, or to your own messages and constants.

The following code fragment is an example of using fail( ) from inside a try..endTry block. This code is attached to a pushbutton that tries to open a TCursor:

```
var
    tc TCursor
endvar
try
    tc.open("orders")
    if tc.nrecords() < 20 then
        fail(UserError+1,"Not enough records in the table")
    endif
onFail
    msgStop("Error",errorMessage())
endtry
```

In this example, we are creating our own error event by using fail( ) with two arguments. The first argument sets the error code to 1 plus the constant UserError. Paradox reserves a block of constants for its error constants and gives you between UserError and UserErrorMax for your own error constants. The fail( ) procedure causes control to pass to the onFail side of the try..endTry block. Here, we simply display the error message. The error does not travel further in the containership hierarchy, because the try..endTry block handled it.

If we place the fail( ) procedure immediately after the msgStop( ) procedure, some interesting things happen:

- Because the code fails out of the onFail side of the try..endTry block, Paradox generates an error event that is sent to the object.
- This event bubbles all the way back up to the form level, where the form handles it.
- If the default behavior wasn't disabled along the way, the form handles the error by invoking Paradox's error-handling A mechanism, which displays the dreaded Error Stack dialog box.

So, as you see, although you cannot use errorTrapOnWarnings( ) to force type 3 errors to the error-handling A mechanism, you can use the try..endTry block to force any user-defined error to Paradox's A mechanism. If you want to find out how to force type 3 errors through the A mechanism, read on.

You can nest try..onFail blocks in a method or procedure, which transfers control to the next try..endTry level's onFail block.

Examining Problems with action( ), keyPhysical( )

You will invariably encounter one problem that may confuse you. As soon as you place a jot of code in the keyPhysical( ) or action( ) built-in method *anywhere on the form*, an error event will not be generated for any type 3 (general) error. You must always issue a doDefault statement somewhere in these methods and check to see if the errorCode( ) is a nonzero value. If the value is nonzero, use the fail( ) method to transfer control to any onFail blocks. The onFail code then can handle the error. If no try..endTry blocks are in effect, the form dispatches an error event to the object that caused the error—where the fail( ) procedure is attached. This action forces an error event and, therefore, a status event to occur, which forces the type 3 error message to appear in the status bar. The code to handle this task looks like the following code:

```
method action(var eventInfo ActionEvent)
doDefault
if errorCode()<>0 then
    fail()
endif
endmethod
```

In this example, all type 3 error messages display properly in the status bar at the bottom of the Paradox application window. This display method solves the messaging problems with keyPhysical and action events. Apparently, Borland decided that programmers who use these methods want to control messaging, so Borland did not provide automatic messaging. Notice that this fail( ) trick does not force type 3 errors, which are predominantly caused by action and keyPhysical events, to be handled by the critical error-handling mechanism. To force type 3 errors through the A mechanism, use the following code:

```
method action(var eventInfo ActionEvent)
doDefault
if errorCode()<>0 then
    fail(errorCode(),errorMessage())
endif
endmethod
```

In this example, two arguments are used in the fail procedure—errorCode( ) and errorMessage( ), which record the error code and message that doDefault triggered. Apparently, Paradox treats this example differently than just a simple fail( ) with no arguments specified and thinks it is a critical error.

Using this example, all errors (type 1, 2, and 3) can be pushed through the critical error-handling mechanism. Although most developers consider key violations, validity check failures, and other table-oriented errors as important, perhaps more important than type 2 and even type 1 errors, Paradox doesn't. Paradox does its best to prevent table-oriented errors from ever appearing as critical errors, even if errorTrapOnWarnings( ) is on. This feature creates confusion for many developers because a host of errors never reaches the error-handling A mechanism.

The problem with action( ) and keyPhysical( ) built-in methods and error events, however, is a bit more complicated. If you have data-entry fields that are not contained within a record object, (fields on a page of a form, but not in a multi-record object or a table frame), even if you issue a fail( ) from within the keyPhysical( ) and action( ) built-in method, no error message appears in the status bar. The error code will be 0, even though a table-level error such as a key violation occurred. Apparently, the multi-record object and table frame have a certain intelligence when it comes to table-level errors, such as key violations, validity check failures, and so on.

We don't know if this lack of message display is a bug or a poor design decision. Whatever the answer, it is a bother and is inconsistent with the way all other built-in methods affect error events.

Now that we explained the theory, you can see it in practice. The following example demonstrates how action events and error events occur and also demonstrates the difference between errorCode( ) and eventInfo.errorCode( ). To clarify things, errorCode( ) is a procedure, and eventInfo.errorCode( ) is a method. Table 19.1 and the adjacent paragraphs discuss the difference between the errorCode( ) method and the eventInfo.errorCode( ) procedure.

The simple form in figure 19.2 is in Edit mode. The user has just inserted a record into a table frame and is about to post a record that has a key violation. Table 19.1 lists each action event that occurred and the status of various error codes.

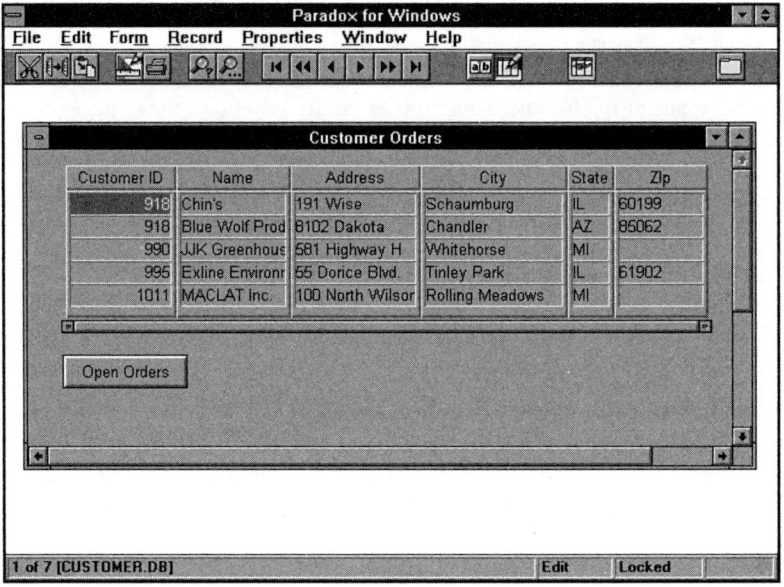

Figure 19.2. Key violation errors.

The code in the table frame's built-in Action method was designed to record the actions and events, and resembles the following code:

```
method action(var eventInfo ActionEvent)
var
     errors     Array[4] SmallInt
     evId, evClass   SmallInt
endvar
evClass = eventInfo.actionClass()
evId = eventInfo.id()
errors[1] = eventInfo.errorCode()      ; record errors
errors[2] = errorCode()                ; before default behavior
doDefault                              ; do the default behavior
errors[3] = eventInfo.errorCode()      ; record errors
errors[4] = errorCode()                ; after default behavior
endmethod
```

After the user presses the down-arrow key to move to the next record, the series of events listed in table 19.1 occurs, in the order that the events are listed.

Table 19.1. Key Violation Error Sequence.

Action Event Constant Name	Before/After doDefault	eventInfo.errorCode( )	errorCode( )
DataArriveRecord	Before	0	9729
	After	0	9729
DataUnlockRecord	Before	0	0
	After	9729	9729
DataNextRecord	Before	0	0
	After	9729	9729
MoveDown	Before	0	0
	After	9729	9729

The errorCode( ) of 9729 is equivalent to the peKeyViol error constant, which indicates a key violation error. This error code stays the same throughout the entire sequence of events. What is most interesting is that the first action event, the DataArriveRecord, which occurs when a record movement of some kind is about to occur, knows about the error condition before the default behavior has occurred and before the action event's eventInfo packet has an indication of the error. All subsequent events are ignorant of errors until after the default behavior has executed.

You now see why disabling the default behavior for an action event disables only the default behavior for the particular event that is part of a sequence. If you trap for the DataUnlockRecord action event and place a msgStop( ) error message and simply disable the default behavior, Paradox still attempts a DataNextRecord and a MoveDown event, which displays the message three times—hardly what you may expect, but entirely predictable and rational, given Paradox's event model. You must remember that the table exists independently of the form. The form initiates a sequence of events. Each event receives an error message from the ODAPI engine, telling the event whether to proceed with its own work. In the case of the user trying to leave a record with a key violation, four events are triggered.

To prevent the other two events from occurring after a key violation, you may want to set the eventInfo.errorCode( ) to a nonzero value.

```
method action(var eventInfo ActionEvent)
   dodefault
   if errorCode() = peKeyViol then
      msgStop("Error","Key violation")
      eventInfo.setErrorCode(1)
   endif
endmethod
```

The setErrorCode( ) value in the preceding example of 1 tells the form that no other events should occur. Without it, the error message would appear multiple times.

To prevent the msgStop( ) error message form displaying on-screen three times after a key violation, you can set the eventInfo.setErrorCode( ) to a nonzero value. This value tells the form that no other events should occur.

The following list summarizes the key points on how Paradox handles errors:

- Paradox has two error-handling mechanisms: one mechanism displays a dialog box displaying the error stack (mechanism A), and the other displays a status message in the status bar (mechanism B).

- Paradox has three kinds of errors: critical errors (type 1), warning errors (type 2), and general user-interaction errors (type 3).

- By default, critical errors go on the error stack and go through mechanism A. Warning errors also go on the error stack, but do not display anywhere. General user-interaction errors go on the error stack and go through mechanism B.

- Warning errors can be treated just like critical errors with errorTrapOnWarnings(Yes).

- Critical errors and user-interaction errors always create an error event dispatched by the form to the offending object. The error event bubbles back up the form's error( ) built-in method where the form makes a decision: handle it though mechanism A or mechanism B. Warning errors take the same route through the error( ) built-in methods as critical errors do if errorTrapOnWarnings( ) is on.

- The try..onFail..endtry construct enables you to control errors and prevent these errors from being dispatched as error events. You also can use this construct to retry the statement that caused the error.

- The fail( ) procedure passes control to the next onFail..endtry block, if this block is defined. Otherwise, fail( ) forces the form to dispatch an error event to the offending object. Type 3 errors (general user-interaction errors) can be forced through error-handling mechanism A (the one for critical errors), by issuing fail with two arguments: one with the current errorCode( ) and the other with errorMessage( ). You can create your own error codes and messages by using fail( ) as well. These codes and messages also get pushed through error-handling mechanism A, in the absence of a try..endTry block. This feature works independently of the errorTrapOnWarnings( ) setting.

- Any code attached to an action( ) or keyPhysical( ) built-in method causes type 3 errors to no longer create an error event with the subsequent status event. You can override this behavior by performing a doDefault, checking the result of doDefault for a nonzero errorCode( ), and issuing a fail( ) if the error code is not 0.

- The errorCode( ) procedure and the eventInfo.errorCode( ) method are not identical.

- User interactions usually map into a series of action events. Each action event tries to execute even if a prior action event failed. To prevent subsequent action events from occurring as a result of an error, use eventInfo.id( ) to set the eventInfo object's ID value to a nonzero value. Disabling the default behavior by using disableDefault will *not* prevent impending action events that are part of the same user interaction.

As you see, error handling is not simple. Because the event model is powerful and sophisticated, handling errors can be complex as well. However, as we said in our error-handling manifesto at the beginning of this chapter, error routines cannot be overly complex. We will outline a general purpose error-handling approach next, but not before we quickly review the key error-handling procedures at our disposal.

Using Error-Handling Methods and Procedures

ObjectPAL has several procedures to help you manipulate the error stack:

- `errorClear()`: Removes all errors from the error stack.
- `errorCode() SmallInt`: Displays the top error code and message on the error stack—described earlier in "Examining Problems with action( ), keyPhysical( )."
- `errorLog(const errorCode SmallInt, const errorMessage String)`: Pushes an error code and error message on the stack. Also pushes your own user-defined errors on the error stack.
- `errorMessage() String`: Displays the top error code and message on the error stack—described earlier in "Problems with action( ), keyPhysical( )."
- `errorPop() Logical`:
- `errorShow([const top String[, const bottom String] ]) Logical`: Displays an Error Stack dialog box like the dialog box shown in figure 19.1. The nice thing about errorShow( ) is that it has no Design button to allow users to bring the form into Design mode. Takes zero, one, or two arguments. The first argument specifies a string to display just above the error message, and the second string specifies a string to display just below the error message. These arguments *do not* let you change the dialog box title.
- `errorTrapOnWarnings(const YesNo Logical)`: Allows Paradox to treat warning errors as critical errors.

In addition, you can manipulate the eventInfo object for error events by using the methods that follow:

- `errorCode() LongInt`: Displays the eventInfo object's error code.
- `reason() SmallInt`: Returns a SmallInt, which evaluates to the ErrorCritical or ErrorWarning constant. Tells you whether the error is a critical or a warning error. If the eventInfo object's error code is a nonzero value and the reason is 0 (which is not ErrorWarning, 1, or ErrorCritical, 2), then the error is a type 3 general user-interaction error.
- `setErrorCode(const eCode LongInt)`: Enables you to set the eventInfo object's error code.
- `setReason(const reasonID SmallInt)`: Enables you to set the eventInfo object's reason value.

These error methods and procedures provide the tools needed to create your own error-handling routines.

Saving and Manipulating the Error Stack

You may want to save the error stack to a table or text file so that you can record the error and view it later. In addition, when you design your error-handling mechanism, some errors will pop up that you just cannot anticipate or handle gracefully. You need to catch these errors, save them, display a message to the user, and exit the application. The saved error stack can be quite helpful in diagnosing problems.

Manipulating the error stack requires gentle handling, because just about anything you do in ObjectPAL clears the error stack. The only exceptions to this fact are the error-related methods errorCode( ) and errorMessage( ), and the message-display procedures such as message( ) and beep( ). Custom methods and procedures don't affect the error stack. To save the error stack, you can use the following code:

```
method saveErrorStack(const dispMessTop String,      {dialog box title}
                     const logMess String,           {err table message}
                     const currentMethod String){method that failed}
Const
    errorTable = "ERRLOG"                ; error log table name
endconst
var
    tc          TCursor                  ; TCursor to handle error_table
    tbl         Table                    ; table var to handle error_table
    x,                                   ; loop counter variable
    numErrs     SmallInt                 ; total number of errors
    errCode     DynArray[]   SmallInt    ; error codes
    errMsg      Dynarray[]   String      ; error messages
endvar
; place the error stack into the error dynarrays.
; NOTE: this loop calls no RTL methods or procedures
; except for errorCode() and errorMessage().
; If any RTL methods or procedures, such as String() or SmallInt()
; are called from this loop, the error stack gets cleared.
numErrs = 0
while true
    numErrs = numErrs + 1
    errCode[numErrs] = errorCode()
    errMsg[numErrs] = errorMessage()
    if not errorPop() then
        quitloop
    endif
endwhile
; display each message, one after the other
for x from 1 to numErrs
    msgInfo(dispMessTop,errMsg[x])
endfor
; save the errors to a table
if not istable(errorTable) then
    tbl =
        create errorTable with
            "Date"   : "D",
            "Time"   : "A11",
            "User"   : "A20",
            "Number" : "S",
```

```
                "Error code" : "S",
                "Error message" : "A128",
                "User message" : "A64",
                "Log message" : "A64",
                "Method" : "A32"
                key "Date","Time","User","Number"
            endcreate
endif
; open the table with the tcursor
if tc.open(errorTable) then
      tc.edit()
      for x from 1 to numErrs
            tc.insertRecord()                          ; insert a record
            tc.Date = today()
            tc.Time = String(time())
            tc.User = getNetUserName()
            tc.Number = x
            tc."Error code" = errCode[x]
            tc."Error message" = errMsg[x]
            tc."User message" = dispMessTop
            tc."Log message" = logMess
            if isAssigned(currentMethod) = true then
                  tc."Method" = currentMethod
            endif
            if not tc.postRecord() then    ; make sure it can be posted
                  tc.deleteRecord()                    ; if not, delete it
                  quitloop
            endif
      endfor
      tc.endEdit()
      tc.close()
endif
endmethod
```

You can place this method in a library and call it from the form's error( ) built-in method or from an onFail..endtry block. When either of these two error-handling mechanisms call this method, a dialog box displaying each message appears, and then the messages are logged to an error file.

Designing an Error-Handling Mechanism

Because of all this complexity, you may be wondering exactly how to go about trapping errors. All developers have their own feelings, intuitions, empirical knowledge, and experience, which shapes what type of error handler they prefer. Here is a general strategy to consider:

1. Handle warning errors immediately after the method or procedure that triggers them. When opening a form or a TCursor, for example, check to make sure that the open operation succeeded. If it did not succeed, take the appropriate action right then and there. This meets the locality criterion stated in our manifesto. With this in mind, you will not need to set errorTrapOnWarnings( ) on.

2. Place a try..onFail..endtry block around a doDefault in the True side of the isPrefilter( ) check in all of the form methods, with code attached at the form level or below. If you have code attached to the pushButton( ) built-in method for the Open Orders pushbutton, for example, place a try..endtry as follows:

```
method pushButton(var eventInfo Event)
if eventInfo.isPreFilter()    then
    ; This code executes for each object on the form.
    try
        doDefault
    onFail
        saveErrorStack("Application Error","FailBlock","Form:pushbutton")
    endtry
else
    ; This code executes only for the form.
endif
endmethod
```

This code ensures that if a critical error occurs, your error-handling routine kicks in and prevents your Paradox's default error handler from taking control. This point covers the first goal of our error manifesto: all errors must be handled.

3. Make sure that all code placed in an action( ) or keyPhysical( ) built-in method issues a doDefault and checks the error code. Otherwise, as soon as you place code in these methods, type 3 errors do not display messages on the status bar. If the error code is a nonzero value, issue a fail( ) so that Paradox performs normal type 3 error messaging. The following code fragment illustrates this point:

```
method action(var eventInfo ActionEvent)
if eventInfo.id() = DataUnlockRecord or
    eventInfo.id() = DataPostRecord then
    if msgYesNoCancel("Confirm","Post this record?") = "Yes" then
        doDefault
        switch
            case errorCode()=peKeyViol :
                msgStop("Error","You cannot have two records with "+
                                "the same primary key")
            case errorCode()<>0 :
                fail()
        endswitch
    else
        ; disable the event
        eventInfo.setErrorCode(1)]
    endif
else
    ; since we have code attached to this action method,
    ; we have to always perform a doDefault and check the
    ; error code. If it is 0, we must fail() this method
    ; so that the error message displays at the bottom of
    ; the application window in the status bar
    doDefault
    if errorCode()<>0 then
        fail()
    endif
endif
```

Remember that the action( ) built-in method is called many times for a single user interaction. When you are trapping for an action event, most of the time two, three, or four action events are bundled together, one right after the other. Forgetting this and becoming confused is easy when it appears as though your code is executing many times in an action( ) method. When in doubt, use the tracer window to look at the ID for each action event. Using the Tracer window ensures that users are enlightened about any errors that occur—point 5 of our error-handling manifesto.

4. Do not use the error( ) method unless you want to catch critical errors that your error-handling scheme missed. If you forgot to place a try..onFail around each form-level built-in method, for example, a critical error eventually will bubble up back to the False side of the form's isPrefilter( ) check, where Paradox invokes its A mechanism if the error is a critical error. You can use eventInfo.reason( ) to check if the error is a critical error before you call your error-handling routine. This method meets points 1, 2, and 3 of our error-handling manifesto. All errors are trapped by our routines, not Paradox's. Because the error( ) method is hardly used at all, we limit the complexity of the error-handling code and make sure that this code is easily implemented.

5. Don't nest try..endTry blocks too much. Deeply nested try..endTry blocks are more difficult to understand and maintain, especially if the nesting involves several layers in the containership hierarchy. Properly document any nested try..endTry blocks.

Summary

Paradox has a complex and often bewildering error-handling model for a variety of reasons. First, every form is king over its own kingdom. No single entry point exists to "insert" your error-handling mechanism. Every form must be treated individually. Second, Paradox has a sophisticated event model which, when it comes to errors, behaves nothing like traditional, procedural programs. Third, Paradox's error-handling model is fairly complex.

After you become familiar with handling events and errors, developing an error-handling mechanism becomes easier.

20

Debugging Techniques

Debugging a Paradox for Windows application is different than debugging a Pascal or a C program. In those environments, when you debug the source code, you can step through each line of code, right from the first line. In ObjectPAL, the code you write is intertwined with the run-time environment. The traditional top-down debugging model shifts to an event-response model.

This event-response model means that you have to find the responses (your code) that are reacting inappropriately to events (which the Paradox run-time environment creates). Because the form contains all your code, your code is running every time you view a form. Rather than launching an EXE file to begin a debugging session, you just open a form. In some ways, the form becomes a land mine, waiting for some unsuspecting, innocent event to accidentally wander near.

Another problem with debugging in an event-driven environment is that the act of debugging creates a series of events sequences, which can add more confusion in the debugging session. Often, this process is called *quantum debugging*; the act of observing the bug sometimes changes the bug's behavior. (This rule is otherwise known as the *ObjectPAL uncertainty principle.*) Fortunately, Paradox provides enough tools to find your way in this strange new universe.

Using the Tracer Window

Perhaps the most important tool to *passively* observe your application's behavior is the Trace window (see fig. 20.1). The *Trace window* displays the events that occur and the ObjectPAL code executed. In addition, because events in Paradox occur at a fast and furious pace, it takes less time to read a Trace window than to stop your code and execute it one line at a time.

Because the Trace window is such an important debugging tool, we will step through each of the procedures that control it.

Part IV ■ Programming in ObjectPAL

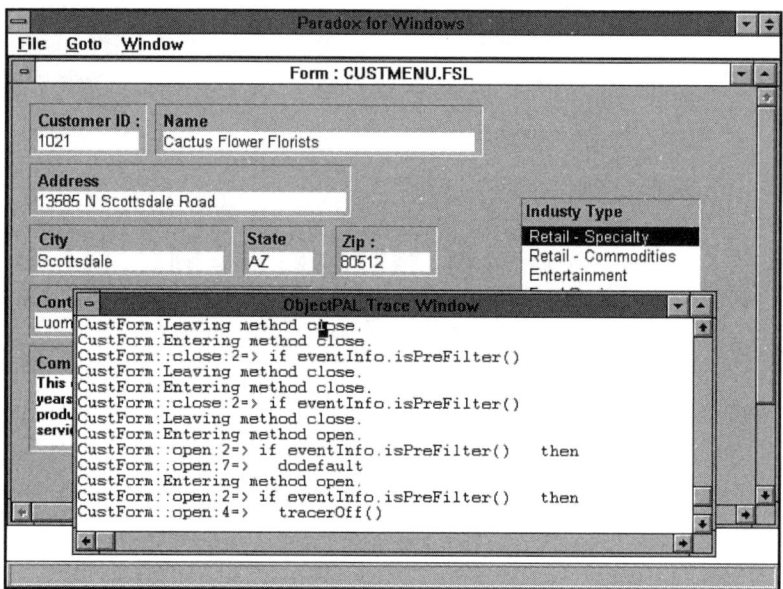

Figure 20.1. The Trace window.

tracerOn( )

The tracerOn( ) procedure turns on the tracer. Before anything is written to the tracer window, however, you must enable tracing by making sure that the Debug¦Trace Execution option is checked. Otherwise, nothing is written to the Trace window. As long as Trace Execution is checked, Paradox traces the code you have attached to any built-in methods. If you have used the Debug¦Trace Built-Ins option to select built-ins to be traced, the selected events also appear in the Trace window.

You don't have to put a tracerOn( ) call in your form just to get the Trace window to appear. As soon as the form runs, the Trace window begins to fill up. You may want to use tracerOff( ) (explained in the next section) to turn off the tracer output as the first thing in the form's open( ) built-in method. If you don't need to see all the open events (which can be numerous because one open event exists for each object on the form), you can use tracerOff( ) to turn off the tracer before all the open events occur. You can use tracerOn( ) later in your code to turn on tracing again.

tracerOff( )

You can use tracerOff( ) to stop Paradox from writing to the Trace window. Because thousands of lines may be written to the Trace window, it's a good idea to use traceOn( ) and traceOff( ) so that only a portion of the events are written to the Trace window. Otherwise, you will spend hours reading through a never-ending Trace window, looking for those events of interest.

tracerClear( )

You use tracerClear( ) to clear the Trace window. Using tracerClear( ) is the same as using the File¦Clear option while the Trace window is the active window. You use tracerClear( ) if you don't want to see any prior events and you want to erase any entries in the Trace window.

tracerHide( )

You use tracerHide( ) to hide the Trace window so that it cannot be seen while the application runs. Using tracerHide( ) is useful if you don't want to look at the Trace window and run the application at the same time. Just make sure that you save the Trace window before leaving the application.

tracerShow( )

Using tracerShow( ) simply unhides the Trace window and makes it visible again. If the Trace window is hidden, just selecting it from the Window menu doesn't make it visible. You must unhide the window by using tracerShow( ).

tracerSave( )

You should use tracerSave( ) to save the current contents of the Trace window to a file. You can specify the file name by passing tracerSave( ) a string argument, as in the following code:

```
tracerSave("CUSTFORM.TRA")
```

tracerWrite( )

You use tracerWrite( ) to write a string on a line by itself in the Trace window. For example, the following code writes `***Post record event***` on a separate line in the Trace window.

```
tracerWrite("***Post record event***")
```

This method is useful if you want to place your own comments in the Trace window. Because the Trace window fills up fast with hundreds of events, using tracerWrite( ) is a good way to document what is in the Trace window.

tracerToTop( )

Using tracerToTop( ) brings the Trace window to the top of desktop, placing it on top of all open form windows. The tracerToTop( ) method is useful if you want to make the Trace window visible because it is being obscured from view by other form windows.

Taking a Closer Look at the Tracer Window

Now that you know the tracer procedures, take a closer look at exactly what appears in the Trace window. What follows is a rather lengthy listing taken out of a real-life Trace window. The list, although long, is commented so that you can follow the chain of events. As you read this list, you will learn what appears in the Trace window, and you get a glimpse of what actually goes on during an event sequence.

To set the stage, we explain the user interaction that this tracing captures. The form contains a 1X1 *multi-record object* (MRO) (see fig. 20.2). The user is on the Customer_ID field and presses F12 to go to the next record. The user is not in Edit mode, so no data changes. A small section of code added to the form's setFocus( ) and removeFocus( ) built-in methods causes the frame style of each object to change from an inside-3D frame to an outside-3D frame to give the illusion that the object with focus appears raised.

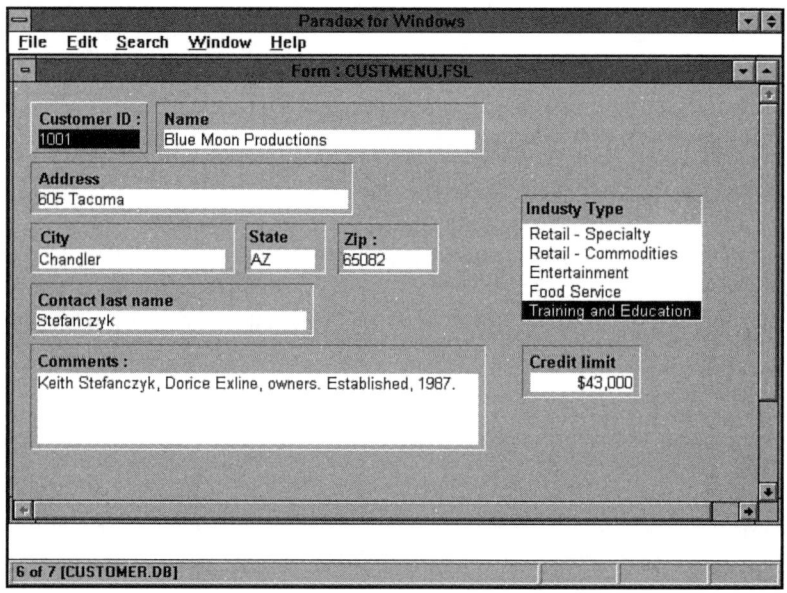

Figure 20.2. The traced form.

This sequence of events captures all the built-in events Paradox must generate to enable the user to move to the next record. Although the total time Paradox takes to execute this sequence is a fraction of a second, this interaction generates more than 77 events! Even more unbelievable, you can trap each of these events and execute your own ObjectPAL code.

As you read the tracer events, watch the *self* and *target* indicators. The self indicator always describes the object that is processing the event. The target always describes the target of the event.

Chapter 20 ■ Debugging Techniques

```
; key physical event (F12 key -- NextRecord), before it is dispatched

built-in:keyPhysical, self = "CustForm", target="Page1.CustMRO.Record.Customer_ID",
     reason=UserMove, state=, vKey=VK_F12, char='

; the form's built-in method for the keyPhysical event occurs

CustForm:Entering method keyPhysical.
CustForm::keyPhysical:7=>  if eventInfo.isPreFilter()    then
CustForm::keyPhysical:10=>     keyStroke = eventInfo.vChar()
CustForm::keyPhysical:12=>     disableDefault
CustForm::keyPhysical:14=>     switch
CustForm::keyPhysical:20=>             enableDefault
CustForm:Leaving method keyPhysical.

; The Customer_ID field receives the keyPhysical event

built-in:keyPhysical, self = "Page1.CustMRO.Record.Customer_ID",
     target="Page1.CustMRO.Record.Customer_ID", reason=UserMove, state=, vKey=VK_F12, char='

; the form generates an action event for the Customer_ID field

built-in:action(DataNextRecord), self = "CustForm", target="Page1.CustMRO.Record.Customer_ID"

; field object receives the event

built-in:action(DataNextRecord), self = "Page1.CustMRO.Record.Customer_ID",
     target="Page1.CustMRO.Record.Customer_ID"

; field object can't handle the event and passes it off to its container, the record object

Pass:action(DataNextRecord), self = "Page1.CustMRO.Record",
     target="Page1.CustMRO.Record.Customer_ID"

; record object can't handle the event and passes it off to the MRO

Pass:action(DataNextRecord), self = "Page1.CustMRO",
     target="Page1.CustMRO.Record.Customer_ID"

; the form then generates a canDepart event for the Customer_ID field

built-in:canDepart, self = "CustForm", target="Page1.CustMRO.Record.Customer_ID",
     reason = UserMove, destination="Page1.CustMRO"

; the Customer_ID field receives the canDepart event

built-in:canDepart, self = "Page1.CustMRO.Record.Customer_ID",
     target="Page1.CustMRO.Record.Customer_ID", reason = UserMove,
     destination="Page1.CustMRO"

; the form generates a canDepart event for the record object

built-in:canDepart, self = "CustForm", target="Page1.CustMRO.Record", reason = UserMove,
     destination="Page1.CustMRO"

; the record object receives the canDepart event

built-in:canDepart, self = "Page1.CustMRO.Record", target="Page1.CustMRO.Record",
     reason = UserMove, destination="Page1.CustMRO"

; the form generates a removeFocus event for the Customer_ID field

built-in:removeFocus, self = "CustForm", target="Page1.CustMRO.Record.Customer_ID"

; the built-in code for the removeFocus event at the form level executes
```

```
CustForm:Entering method removeFocus.
CustForm::removeFocus:2=> if eventInfo.isPreFilter() then
CustForm::removeFocus:5=>     eventInfo.getTarget( target )
CustForm::removeFocus:6=>     if target.name <> "CustForm" and
CustForm::removeFocus:12=>        target.frame.style = Inside3DFrame
CustForm:Leaving method removeFocus.

; the Customer_ID field receives the removeFocus event

built-in:removeFocus, self = "Page1.CustMRO.Record.Customer_ID",
    target="Page1.CustMRO.Record.Customer_ID"

; the form generates a depart event for the Customer_ID field

built-in:depart, self = "CustForm", target="Page1.CustMRO.Record.Customer_ID",
    reason = UserMove, destination="Page1.CustMRO"

; the Customer_ID object receives the depart event

built-in:depart, self = "Page1.CustMRO.Record.Customer_ID",
    target="Page1.CustMRO.Record.Customer_ID", reason = UserMove,
    destination="Page1.CustMRO"

; the form generates a removeFocus event for the record object

built-in:removeFocus, self = "CustForm", target="Page1.CustMRO.Record"

; the built-in code on the form's removeFocus event executes

CustForm:Entering method removeFocus.
CustForm::removeFocus:2=> if eventInfo.isPreFilter() then
CustForm::removeFocus:5=>     eventInfo.getTarget( target )
CustForm::removeFocus:6=>     if target.name <> "CustForm" and
CustForm:Leaving method removeFocus.

; the record object receives the removeFocus event

built-in:removeFocus, self = "Page1.CustMRO.Record", target="Page1.CustMRO.Record"

; the form generates a depart event for the record object

built-in:depart, self = "CustForm", target="Page1.CustMRO.Record", reason = UserMove,
    destination="Page1.CustMRO"

; the record object receives the depart event

built-in:depart, self = "Page1.CustMRO.Record", target="Page1.CustMRO.Record",
    reason = UserMove, destination="Page1.CustMRO"

; the form generates a series of newValue events for each field in the record object and each
    object receives the newValue event

built-in:newValue, self = "CustForm", target="Page1.CustMRO.Record.State"

built-in:newValue, self = "Page1.CustMRO.Record.State", target="Page1.CustMRO.Record.State"

built-in:newValue, self = "CustForm", target="Page1.CustMRO.Record.Zip"

built-in:newValue, self = "Page1.CustMRO.Record.Zip", target="Page1.CustMRO.Record.Zip"

built-in:newValue, self = "CustForm", target="Page1.CustMRO.Record.IndustryCode"

built-in:newValue, self = "Page1.CustMRO.Record.IndustryCode",
    target="Page1.CustMRO.Record.IndustryCode"

built-in:newValue, self = "CustForm", target="Page1.CustMRO.Record.Contact_last_name"
```

```
built-in:newValue, self = "Page1.CustMRO.Record.Contact_last_name",
    target="Page1.CustMRO.Record.Contact_last_name"
built-in:newValue, self = "CustForm", target="Page1.CustMRO.Record.Name"
built-in:newValue, self = "Page1.CustMRO.Record.Name", target="Page1.CustMRO.Record.Name"
built-in:newValue, self = "CustForm", target="Page1.CustMRO.Record.Comments"
built-in:newValue, self = "Page1.CustMRO.Record.Comments",
    target="Page1.CustMRO.Record.Comments"
built-in:newValue, self = "CustForm", target="Page1.CustMRO.Record.City"
built-in:newValue, self = "Page1.CustMRO.Record.City", target="Page1.CustMRO.Record.City"
built-in:newValue, self = "CustForm", target="Page1.CustMRO.Record.Address"
built-in:newValue, self = "Page1.CustMRO.Record.Address",
    target="Page1.CustMRO.Record.Address"
built-in:newValue, self = "CustForm", target="Page1.CustMRO.Record.Customer_ID"
built-in:newValue, self = "Page1.CustMRO.Record.Customer_ID",
    target="Page1.CustMRO.Record.Customer_ID"
built-in:newValue, self = "CustForm", target="Page1.CustMRO.Record.Credit_limit"
built-in:newValue, self = "Page1.CustMRO.Record.Credit_limit",
    target="Page1.CustMRO.Record.Credit_limit"
; the form generates a canArrive event for the record object
built-in:canArrive, self = "CustForm", target="Page1.CustMRO.Record", reason = UserMove,
    destination="Page1.CustMRO.Record.Customer_ID"
; the record object receives the canArrive event
built-in:canArrive, self = "Page1.CustMRO.Record", target="Page1.CustMRO.Record",
    reason = UserMove, destination="Page1.CustMRO.Record.Customer_ID"
; the form generates a canArrive event for the Customer_ID field
built-in:canArrive, self = "CustForm", target="Page1.CustMRO.Record.Customer_ID",
    reason = UserMove, destination="Page1.CustMRO.Record.Customer_ID"
; the Customer_ID field receives the canArrive event
built-in:canArrive, self = "Page1.CustMRO.Record.Customer_ID",
    target="Page1.CustMRO.Record.Customer_ID", reason = UserMove,
    destination="Page1.CustMRO.Record.Customer_ID"
; the form generates an arrive event for the record object
built-in:arrive, self = "CustForm", target="Page1.CustMRO.Record", reason = UserMove,
    destination="Page1.CustMRO.Record.Customer_ID"
; the record object receives the arrive event
built-in:arrive, self = "Page1.CustMRO.Record", target="Page1.CustMRO.Record",
    reason = UserMove, destination="Page1.CustMRO.Record.Customer_ID"
; the form generates a DataArriveRecord action event for the record object
built-in:action(DataArriveRecord), self = "CustForm", target="Page1.CustMRO.Record"
```

```
; the record object receives the DataArriveRecord action event
built-in:action(DataArriveRecord), self = "Page1.CustMRO.Record", target="Page1.CustMRO.Record"
; the record object can't handle the event and passes it to the MRO
Pass:action(DataArriveRecord), self = "Page1.CustMRO", target="Page1.CustMRO.Record"
; the Form generates a setFocus event for the record object
built-in:setFocus, self = "CustForm", target="Page1.CustMRO.Record"
; built-in code for the setFocus event executes

CustForm:Entering method setFocus.
CustForm::setFocus:2=> if eventInfo.isPreFilter() then
CustForm::setFocus:5=>     eventInfo.getTarget( target)
CustForm::setFocus:6=>    if target.name <> "CustForm" and
CustForm:Leaving method setFocus.

; the record object receives the setFocus event
built-in:setFocus, self = "Page1.CustMRO.Record", target="Page1.CustMRO.Record"
; the form generates an arrive event for the Customer_ID field
built-in:arrive, self = "CustForm", target="Page1.CustMRO.Record.Customer_ID", reason = UserMove,
     destination="Page1.CustMRO.Record.Customer_ID"
; the Customer_ID field receives the arrive event
built-in:arrive, self = "Page1.CustMRO.Record.Customer_ID",
     target="Page1.CustMRO.Record.Customer_ID", reason = UserMove,
     destination="Page1.CustMRO.Record.Customer_ID"
; the form generates a setFocus event for the Customer_ID field
built-in:setFocus, self = "CustForm", target="Page1.CustMRO.Record.Customer_ID"
; the built-in code for the setFocus event executes

CustForm:Entering method setFocus.
CustForm::setFocus:2=> if eventInfo.isPreFilter() then
CustForm::setFocus:5=>     eventInfo.getTarget( target)
CustForm::setFocus:6=>    if target.name <> "CustForm" and
CustForm::setFocus:13=>         target.frame.style = Outside3DFrame
CustForm:Leaving method setFocus.

; the Customer_ID field receives the setFocus event
built-in:setFocus, self = "Page1.CustMRO.Record.Customer_ID",
     target="Page1.CustMRO.Record.Customer_ID"
; the form generates a status event (to update the message areas)
built-in:status, self = "CustForm", target="Page1.CustMRO.Record.Customer_ID", reason=18826
; the Customer_ID field receives the status event and passes it to the Record object
built-in:status, self = "Page1.CustMRO.Record.Customer_ID",
     target="Page1.CustMRO.Record.Customer_ID", reason=18826
Pass:status, self = "Page1.CustMRO.Record", target="Page1.CustMRO.Record.Customer_ID",
     reason=18826
```

```
        ; the statusEvent bubbles back up to the form

        Pass:status, self = "Page1.CustMRO", target="Page1.CustMRO.Record.Customer_ID", reason=18826
        Pass:status, self = "Page1", target="Page1.CustMRO.Record.Customer_ID", reason=18826
        Pass:status, self = "CustForm", target="Page1.CustMRO.Record.Customer_ID", reason=18826

        ; the form generates three more status events, which bubble back up to the form
        ; 1
        built-in:status, self = "CustForm", target="Page1.CustMRO.Record.Customer_ID", reason=18814
        built-in:status, self = "Page1.CustMRO.Record.Customer_ID",
              target="Page1.CustMRO.Record.Customer_ID", reason=18814
        Pass:status, self = "Page1.CustMRO.Record", target="Page1.CustMRO.Record.Customer_ID",
              reason=18814
        Pass:status, self = "Page1.CustMRO", target="Page1.CustMRO.Record.Customer_ID", reason=18814
        Pass:status, self = "Page1", target="Page1.CustMRO.Record.Customer_ID", reason=18814
        Pass:status, self = "CustForm", target="Page1.CustMRO.Record.Customer_ID", reason=18814

        ;2
        built-in:status, self = "CustForm", target="Page1.CustMRO.Record.Customer_ID", reason=18802
        built-in:status, self = "Page1.CustMRO.Record.Customer_ID",
              target="Page1.CustMRO.Record.Customer_ID", reason=18802
        Pass:status, self = "Page1.CustMRO.Record", target="Page1.CustMRO.Record.Customer_ID",
              reason=18802
        Pass:status, self = "Page1.CustMRO", target="Page1.CustMRO.Record.Customer_ID", reason=18802
        Pass:status, self = "Page1", target="Page1.CustMRO.Record.Customer_ID", reason=18802
        Pass:status, self = "CustForm", target="Page1.CustMRO.Record.Customer_ID", reason=18802

        ;3
        built-in:status, self = "CustForm", target="Page1.CustMRO.Record.Customer_ID", reason=18790
        built-in:status, self = "Page1.CustMRO.Record.Customer_ID",
              target="Page1.CustMRO.Record.Customer_ID", reason=18790
        Pass:status, self = "Page1.CustMRO.Record", target="Page1.CustMRO.Record.Customer_ID",
              reason=18790
        Pass:status, self = "Page1.CustMRO", target="Page1.CustMRO.Record.Customer_ID", reason=18790
        Pass:status, self = "Page1", target="Page1.CustMRO.Record.Customer_ID", reason=18790
        Pass:status, self = "CustForm", target="Page1.CustMRO.Record.Customer_ID", reason=18790
```

As you see, this short interaction generates a long stream of Trace window lines, which is why the tracer procedures are so important. The best way to use the Trace window is to look at small sections of time within the window. The tracer methods help you *photograph* this small sliver in time, which can help you find that needle in the haystack.

Remember also that this tracer example traced every built-in method, regardless of whether or not code was added to each method. If you don't select any events from the Debug Trace Builtins dialog box, only the methods that have code attached are traced. You also can select a small subset of events to trace from the Trace Builtins dialog box, which helps you keep the tracer output to a minimum.

Debugging menuAction Events

When you debug a menuAction( ) built-in method, Paradox opens the Debugger window and gives that window focus. Your application's menu is replaced with the Debug menu, as you would expect, but to prevent the act of debugging from creating more menu events, Paradox prevents you from selecting anything from the Debugger menu at certain points in the execution of a series of menu events. If you cannot select something from the Debugger menu, you must memorize or write down the keyboard equivalents to the menu items in table 20.1.

Table 20.1. Debugger Keys.

Key	Action
F3 or Ctrl+I	Inspect variable
Shift+F3 or Ctrl+K	Stack backtrace
Ctrl+F3 or Ctrl+B	Set breakpoint
F7	Step over
Shift+F7	Step into
F8	Run
Ctrl+F5	Next warning
Ctrl+A	Search again
Ctrl+Z	Search
Ctrl+Shift+Z	Search and replace
F5 or Ctrl+G	Go to line
F9 or Ctrl+Y	Check syntax
F8	Run
F6 or Ctrl+M	Language menu

Because most applications disable the SpeedBar, you cannot use the SpeedBar to step over or step into each line of code. To help yourself out, if you invoke the debugger with a debug( ) statement, place a showSpeedBar( ) statement before it.

Examining Other Debugger Limitations

As of this writing, you cannot trace a library method from a form. If you are writing complex library methods and procedures, you may want to place a debug( ) statement in the appropriate locations in the library, or you can use many view( ), message, and msgInfo( ) methods and procedures so that you can see where errors occur.

If an error does occur in the library, Paradox displays an error dialog box, showing the offending method name and line number. If a procedure caused the error, Paradox displays the line number in the Proc window.

In addition, as you work with the Debug Step Over and Step Into features, you quickly discover that the sheer number of events that occur can make stepping through them time-consuming. Each time you step through the source code, Paradox closes the original source code window and opens a new window with the new line highlighted, slowing down things even more. For these reasons, start with a Trace window to identify a smaller time slice where the problem occurs, and then examine the Trace window output or set breakpoints in your code to narrow down your search. If you start with the Debug Step Into and Step Over features right off the bat, finding your problem may take longer.

Summary

Your best ally in debugging problem code is the Trace window. The tracer methods give you reasonable control over the Trace window, which makes debugging easier. Unfortunately, the debugger has limitations with libraries and menuAction events of which you should be aware.

Because Paradox is event-driven and object-based, debugging an application involves waiting for the proper event and watching the code respond, rather than just stepping through code in a straight-line, top-to-bottom fashion. The sooner you adjust to the event-driven world, the easier debugging becomes.

21
Delivering the Application: Putting the Pieces Together

The time comes when every application is delivered to a user. This chapter covers several miscellaneous topics that you are bound to run into as you tie up loose ends and prepare the application for delivery. Because Paradox for Windows is object-based, you often have a collection of forms, reports, and perhaps queries to bundle together and deliver.

To create a deliverable application, you will need to take the following steps:

1. Create a main form with very little on it, whose sole purpose is to display a main menu, a splash screen of some type, and launch the other forms.

2. Make sure that your libraries, if any, are opened when every form in your application is open.

3. Make sure that your tables are password protected, if required, and that the application presents the proper passwords.

4. Let your users print reports from a menu or from a pushbutton or some other UIObject.

5. Integrate all queries you may have created into the application.

6. If needed, make sure that the application can properly read and write important text files, such as the config.sys, autoexec.bat files, or Windows INI files.

7. Deliver your forms, reports, and libraries, if needed.

You review each of these issues, step by step.

Creating and Launching the Main Form

Because Paradox for Windows is form-based, you don't launch an application exactly the same way as in other application development environments, such as C or Paradox for DOS. Instead, you just create a main form, which then opens other forms in your application. This main form usually doesn't have much on it. Perhaps the form has just a splash screen, a series of buttons, or just a menu, depending on how you want to present the application to the user.

If you simulate what most Windows software products do, then you want to open a blank form with an application menu and a SpeedBar. Because Paradox doesn't give developers direct support for creating and modifying a SpeedBar, you have to design your own bar, using a form and pushbutton objects.

As with most work in Windows, you have several ways of launching a form.

You can create a small script that actually opens the form, rather than letting the user open the main form. The advantage to this approach is that you can, from the script, specify the window style as maximized, rather than trying to use the maximize( ) procedure within the form's open( ) built-in method to resize the form's window. This procedure avoids the *winking and blinking* problem when you open a form as visible and then maximize or resize the form. When you open a form in this way, users see the form in a size-to-fit size briefly and then see the form maximized.

This kind of main script can have the following code:

```
method run(var eventInfo Event)
var
      f Form
endvar
if not f.open("CUSTOMEV",WinStyleMaximize) then
     msgStop("Application Error","Can't open CUSTOMEV form")
endif
endmethod
```

You can let the user launch the application from within Paradox by selecting the main script or form from the Paradox menus, SpeedBar, or from a folder, which allows the user to work with Paradox interactively and run your application.

Alternately, you can take advantage of file extension associations in Windows, where a file-name extension is associated with an application. When the user tries to select a file name with this extension, the associated application automatically starts, loading the file. By default, form and script file extensions are associated with Paradox for Windows. You can see this process by using the Windows File Manager utility (see fig. 21.1).

Because scripts and forms are associated with Paradox for Windows, you can create an icon in a program group (or in the Startup group if you want to launch the application when Windows starts) in the user's Program Manager, as in figure 21.2. When you load an application by taking advantage of file-extension associations, make sure that Paradox for Windows is in the path, so that Windows can find all of Paradox's DLLs and other files.

Chapter 21 ■ Delivering the Application: Putting the Pieces Together

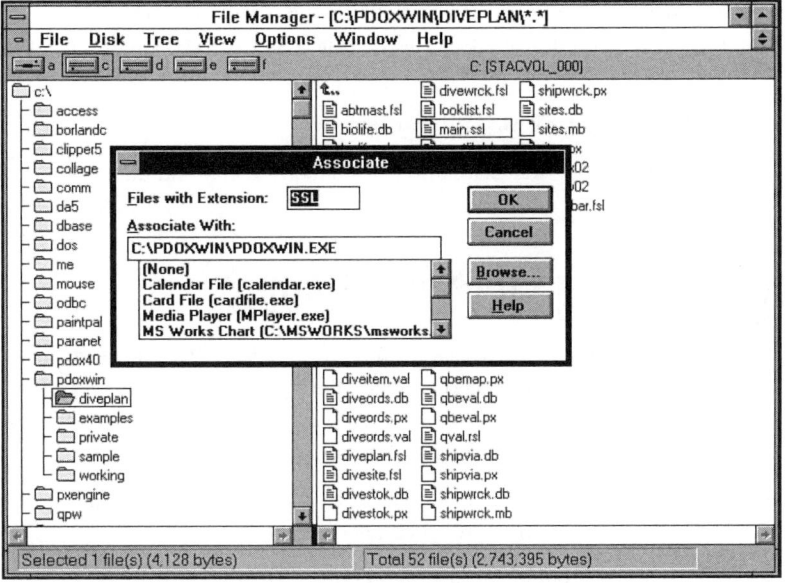

Figure 21.1. Associating script file extensions.

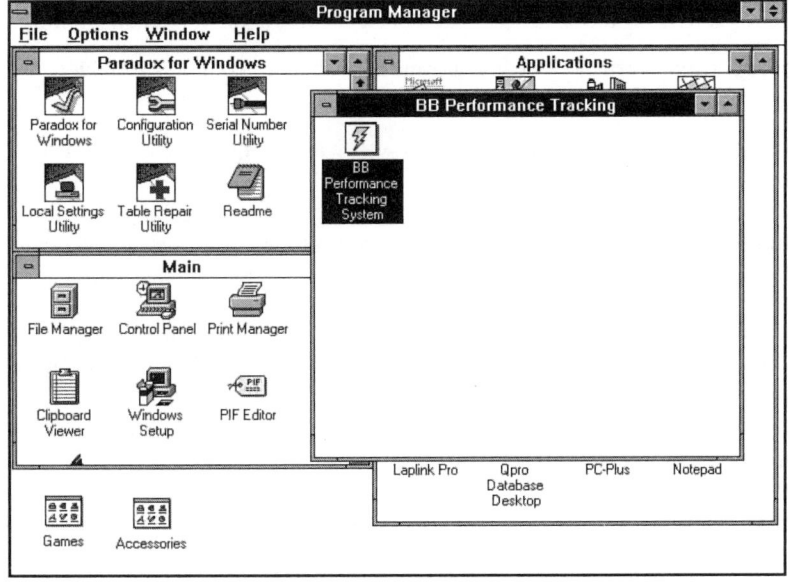

Figure 21.2. Launching a Paradox application from an icon.

415

You also can launch an application by using a command line parameter when loading Paradox. The following command line, for example, loads Paradox, which then loads the main script in the \BBAPP subdirectory:

C:\PDOXWIN\PDOXWIN.EXE\BBAPP\main.ssl

You also can enter this command line as an application icon's command line.

Opening and Using Libraries Properly

Libraries should be used when code or variables must be shared between forms in an application. Although Paradox for Windows is designed to make copying code from form to form easy, in an industrial-strength application any willy-nilly copying of code creates maintenance headaches. Coding tasks that are candidates for inclusion into a library are:

1. Common messaging utilities, such as MouseEnter and MouseExit messages, redefined StatusEvent messages, standard error messages.

2. Error handling and error logging application code.

3. Form opening and closing code. Rather than directly opening a form from a method attached to a form, using a library call is handy because you then can change the window style for all your forms just by changing a small section of code in a library.

4. Global application variable. Because Forms cannot share common variables, the library often becomes a repository for global variables.

Forms can be opened as global to the desktop or as private to the form. In most cases, you want to open the library on every form as GlobalToDesktop. If a library is opened as PrivateToForm and this form changes a global variable, then the change is not reflected to other forms. Therefore, if you have 14 forms in the application and each form uses the same library, all forms should have the following code attached after the default behavior on the form's open( ) built-in method:

```
utilLib.open("UTILS",GlobalToDesktop)
```

The utilLib variable should be declared in the form's var window or in any appropriate object's var window:

```
var
    utilLib    Library
endvar
```

Each form also must list each method used from the library in the appropriate object's Uses window. Most of the time, library methods will be declared in the form's Uses window, which becomes tedious— especially if your library holds a large number of methods that are used extensively—but must be done. The following code shows a sample Uses window:

```
uses ObjectPAL
    lMouseEnter( var eventInfo MouseEvent ) Logical
    lMouseExit( var eventInfo MouseEvent ) Logical
```

```
    lActionHandler( var eventInfo ActionEvent ) Logical
    lErrorHandler( var eventInfo ErrorEvent ) Logical
endUses
```

Table-level Password Protection

Ideally, password protection should be built early in the development of an application, which helps assure that security requirements were thoroughly tested and don't cause havoc in the application. Paradox for Windows stores security information at the table level (or ODAPI engine level), so the application usually doesn't have to supply its own security handler. Whenever you create or restructure a table, you have the opportunity to set security requirements.

Paradox can control table security at the table level and the field level. At the table level, you can restrict the user to the functions listed in table 21.1.

Table 21.1. Table-Level Security.

Functions	*Restrictions*
All	The user has all rights to the table and can add, modify, and delete records and restructure or delete tables. The user cannot change the table's master password.
Insert & Delete	The user can add and delete records, but cannot delete or restructure the table.
Data Entry	The user can add and update—but cannot delete—records in a table. The user also cannot delete or restructure the table.
Update	The user can update non-key fields only. The user cannot add records, delete records, delete the table, or restructure the table.
Read Only	The user can view the table's contents only.

At the field level, you can restrict users to the functions listed in table 21.2.

Table 21.2. Field-Level Security.

Functions	*Restrictions*
All	The user can change the field's contents.
Read Only	The user can view the field's contents only.
None	The user cannot view or change the field's contents. The field always displays a blank value.

To secure a table, you must give the table a master password (see fig. 21.3). When the table is encrypted, only the person who knows the master password can revoke security assignments. The person who knows the master password also has full rights to all aspects of the table. A table can have only one master password.

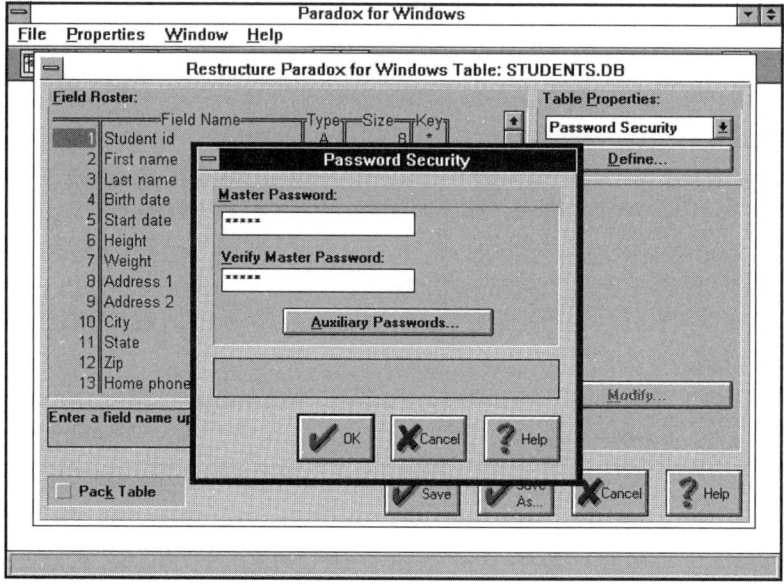

Figure 21.3. The Master password dialog box.

After the master password is defined, you can create multiple auxiliary passwords. You use the auxiliary passwords to control field and table level access rights (see fig. 21.4).

With this scheme, you can create as many auxiliary passwords as you need. You can create too many passwords, however, and the password management scheme can become difficult to maintain. The reason for this is that every time you define new auxiliary passwords, Paradox must place an exclusive lock on the table. Obviously you don't want to add or change passwords frequently.

In addition, the more tables you have, the longer it takes you to make sure that each table has the proper password security scheme. If you add a password, you have to add the password to each table. For this reason, developers often create a layer between Paradox's native password protection mechanism and the application.

In building application-level password protection systems, developers usually do the following:

1. Design a series of auxiliary passwords that implements the application's basic field level and table level security requirements. Each table in the system uses the same auxiliary passwords to reduce maintenance and complexity problems.

2. Create a STAFF table that contains a record for every user who accesses the application. This table holds each users' log-on code and an application-level password in a password field. This password is not the same as any auxiliary passwords defined for tables.

3. Map each user's application password to the appropriate table-level auxiliary password. As the user logs onto the application and knows their password, they gain access to the application. The application then invokes the Session procedure addPassword( ) to gain access to the underlying tables. The addPassword( ) procedure adds a password to the Paradox environment so that tables can be opened without prompting for a password.

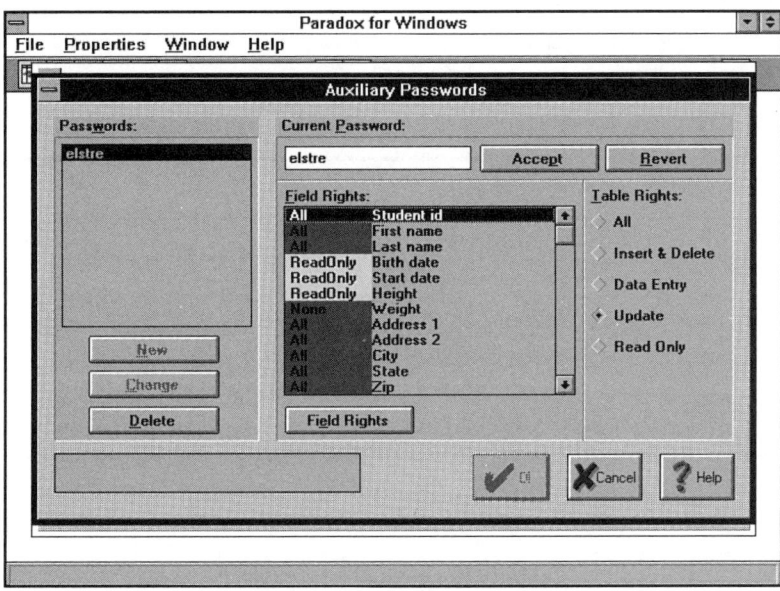

Figure 21.4. The Auxiliary Passwords dialog box.

Creating a STAFF table provides additional flexibility. You can easily allow the user to change their application-level password, and you can require that the password is changed after a set number of days. You can keep a history of passwords and make sure that the user doesn't keep reusing the same password.

You need to encrypt this STAFF table carefully so that users cannot see each other's passwords and so that a system administrator can change all passwords, which usually is accomplished by giving all users update rights to this Staff table and giving the system administrator insert and delete rights to the table. You also must make sure that all forms that use the staff table as a lookup don't allow the user to look at the password field, which you can prevent by making sure that, in these parts of the application, the application presents an auxiliary password that has password field rights set to None.

Integrating Reports into the Application

For developers new to Windows programming, controlling printing can be frustrating. Paradox, like most Windows applications, uses Windows to handle all the printing. The developer doesn't have to do anything, except make sure that the user's Windows environment is set up with the proper printers.

The advantage to the *let-Windows-handle-all-printing* scheme is that you have to write very little code to send reports to different printers. You also can take advantage of Windows fonts to print graphics and various fonts on dot matrix as well as laser printers. The disadvantage to this approach is that as a developer, you need to learn all about Windows printer management utilities.

Under ObjectPAL control, the methods in table 21.3 enable you to control printing.

Table 21.3. Report Handling Methods.

Method	Result
open( )	Displays a report to the screen
close( )	Closes a report window
print( )	Sends a report to the printer
load( )	Opens a report in design mode
design( )	Switches a report from view mode to design mode
run( )	Switches a report from design mode to view mode

Displaying Reports: Using the open( ) Method

The Report open( ) method uses the following three calling syntaxes:

```
open ( const reportName String [, windowStyle LongInt ] ) Logical
open ( const reportName String, const windowStyle LongInt, const x
      SmallInt, const y SmallInt, const w SmallInt, const h SmallInt ) Logical
open ( const openInfo ReportOpenInfo ) Logical
```

In the first example, you can use open to display a report to the screen. The following ObjectPAL code shows you how to perform this action:

```
var
     r Report
endvar
r.open("CUSTREP")
```

You can add a window style constant to control the report window:

```
r.open("CUSTREP",WinStyleMaximize)
```

The second syntax enables you to specify the upper left coordinates for the report window, in twips (1/1440-inch or 1/20-point).

```
r.open("CUSTREC",WinStyleDefault,250,300,6800,5300)
```

The third syntax enables you to specify a ReportOpenInfo record where you can set several parameters at once. The ReportOpenInfo record has the following structure:

```
type
     ReportOpenInfo = Record
          x,y,w,h              LongInt    ; starting location, width and height
          name                 String     ; report name
          masterTable          String     ; the master table name
          queryString          String     ; a query string to run
          restartOptions       SmallInt   ; a ReportPrintRestart constant
     endRecord
endType
```

You can set each of these record's fields and then just call open( ):

```
var
     r Report
     rInfo ReportOpenInfo
endvar
rInfo.name = "CUSTREC"
rInfo.x = 250
rInfo.y = 300
rInfo.w = 6800
rInfo.h = 5300
r.open(rInfo)
```

Report Restart Options

When you produce reports in a network environment, you have four options for how you want the report to handle concurrence issues. These options can be set while you are designing a report, from the Report ¦ Restart Options. These options are shown in the following list:

- *Restart report if data changes.* The default option, which tells Paradox to regenerate the report if changes occur in the data. Ensures that the report is an exact representation of the data *at the time the report was produced.* Allows other users complete access to edit the table. The drawback, of course, is if a lot of editing activity is occurring on the table, the report may take an unacceptably long time to complete.

- *Lock tables to prevent changes.* This selection favors the person generating the report at the expense of other users. After the report has begun, other users cannot modify the table until the report is complete. Conversely, Paradox needs to be able to place the lock, which it cannot do if another user already has a Record lock, Write lock, or Exclusive lock on the table.

- *Lock and copy tables, run from copies.* Behaves like the previous option, but locks the table only long enough to copy it to another, temporary table, then releases the lock immediately, so that the table is available to other users more quickly.

- *Ignore data changes and continue.* Paradox doesn't care if data changes while the report is running, which leaves open the possibility of producing a report with less than accurate results. If you are looking only for ballpark information or if you are reporting on a set of records that doesn't intersect with the set of records currently being edited, this option is the fastest.

Under ObjectPAL control, you can specify the option you want by using the proper constant in the restartOptions field in the ReportOpenInfo record. These constants are listed in table 21.4. If you look closely, you see a fifth option, PrintReturn, which cancels the report if the data changes.

Table 21.4. ReportPrintRestart Constants.

Constant	Description
PrintRestart	Restarts the report when the tables in the report's data model change.
PrintLock	Locks tables in the report's data model before printing, preventing changes until the report is complete.
PrintFromCopy	Locks the tables long enough to copy the data tables, and then prints the report from copies of the tables in the report's data model.
PrintNoLock	Prints without locking tables in the report's table model. If data changes, the report may or may not include the change, depending on the location in the table and the type of change made.
PrintReturn	Cancel the print job when data changes in tables in the report's data model.

Using the print( ) Method

The print( ) method, which enables you to send a report to a printer, also has three possible syntax's:

```
print() Logical
print(const reportName String[, const ReportPrintRestart SmallInt]) logical
print(const rInfo ReportPrintInfo) Logical
```

The first syntax brings up the report options dialog box for the report currently being displayed (see fig. 21.5). The following code uses this syntax:

```
var
     r Report
endvar
r.open("CUSTREP")
r.print()
```

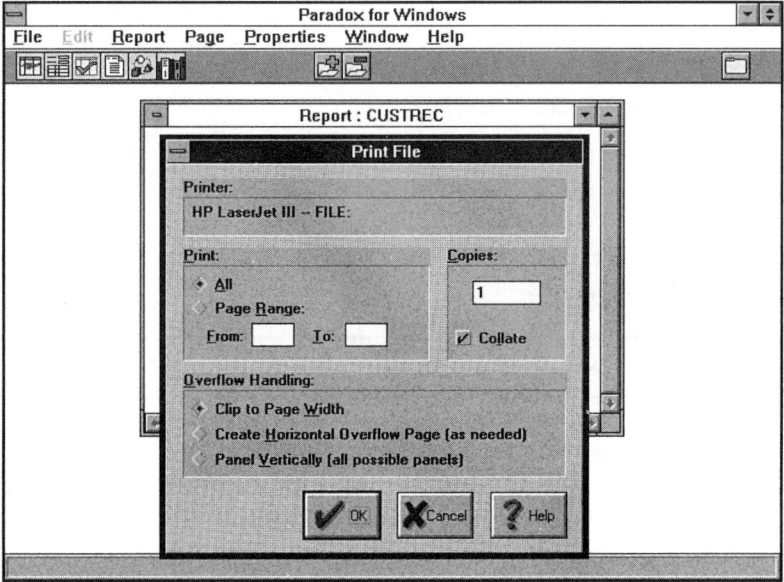

Figure 21.5. The Report Options dialog box.

The second syntax enables you to specify a report name and, if you want, restart options, which then prints the report to the currently selected Windows printer.

```
r.print("CUSTREC")
```

The third syntax, the most interesting of the three, takes a variable of type ReportPrintInfo. The record structure looks like this:

```
type
     ReportPrintInfo = Record
          name                String        ; report name, if not already open
          masterTable         String        ; the master table name
          queryString         String        ; a query string to run
          restartOptions      SmallInt      ; a ReportPrintRestart constant
          printBackwards      Logical       ; true = print backwards
                                            ; false is the default
          makeCopies          Logical       ; If true, Paradox makes the copies
                                            ; if false, printer does
          panelOptions        SmallInt      ; a ReportPrintPanel constant
          nCopies             SmallInt      ; number of copies, default = 1
          startPage           LongInt       ; starting page, default = 1
          endPage             LongInt       ; ending page
          pageIncrement       SmallInt      ; Page increment, default = 1
          xOffset             LongInt       ; horizontal page offset
          yOffset             LongInt       ; vertical page offset
          orient              SmallInt      ; a ReportOrientation constant
     endRecord
endType
```

The makeCopies field deserves some discussion because, in version 1.0 of Paradox for Windows, this field will not force Paradox to make copies. If you want multiple copies, make sure that the Windows printer driver is capable of making copies and set this field to False. Use the nCopies field to indicate how many copies you want to make.

This structure references two other report constant types: ReportPrintPanel and ReportOrientation. The ReportPrintPanel constants let you set the report options that the user can set interactively (see fig. 21.5). Table 21.5 lists these constants.

Table 21.5. ReportPrintPanel Constants.

Constant	*Description*
PintHorizontalPanel	Creates an overflow page immediately after the page that has a print line that exceeds the report width.
PrintVerticalPanel	Creates overflow pages after the report is finished printing for every page in the report, even if only one page has a print line that exceeds the report width.
PrintClipToWidth	Trims all data that doesn't fit across the page.
PrintOverFlowPages	Prints overflow pages, using the default setting.

You may have noticed that the first constant in table 21.5 is spelled PintHorizontalPanel, which is not a misspelling. The word most likely is a misspelling in Paradox because, if you mistakenly use PrintHorizontalPanel, the compiler complains that the constant, as typed, does not exist.

The report orientation constants PrintDefaultOrientation, PrintLandscape, and PrintPortait are self-explanatory.

If you want to print the report to a file, you need to add a printer in Windows that prints to a file. Unfortunately, because Paradox uses Windows printing mechanisms, the ReportPrintInfo record doesn't have an option to send the report to a file nor an option to specify a file name for a report sent to a file. Instead, Windows will interactively prompt the user for a report file name if the output for the printer is set to File.

Selecting a Printer

The only way that you, as an ObjectPAL programmer, can select the current printer is to either use the Windows Control Panel utility to select a default printer or to present the printer setup dialog box to the user so that the user can select a printer.

The Form and UIObject menuAction( ) method/Procedure makes this easy to do. All you have to do is—from a pushbutton on a form or in response to a menu item that you have designed in the menu—perform the following line of code:

```
menuAction(menuFilePrinterSetup)
```

This code brings up the Paradox printer setup dialog box, which allows the user to select a printer (see fig. 21.6).

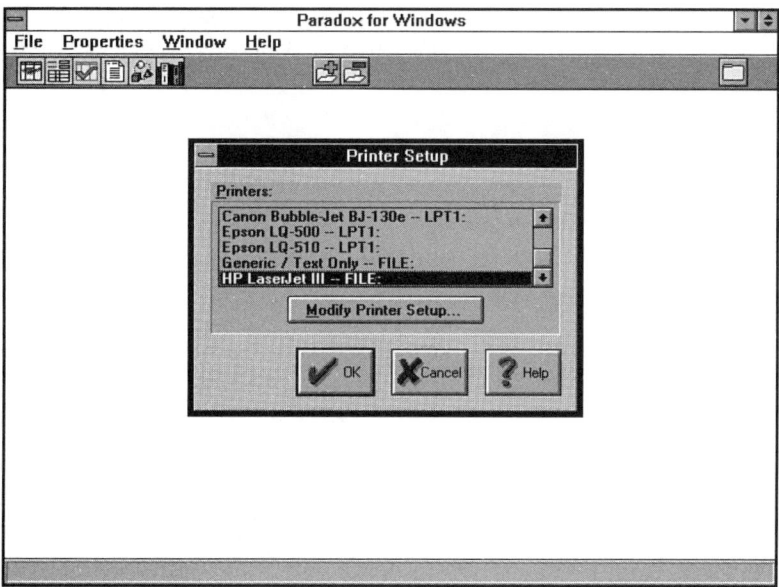

Figure 21.6. The Printer Setup dialog box.

Although you cannot change the printer under ObjectPAL control, you can determine which printers are defined and which printer is the default printer. The printers are stored in the WIN.INI file in the Windows subdirectory. With a little bit of code, you can store the printer names in an array and either display or use the names in your application. This technique is discussed in a following section, "Interacting With the Operating System."

Changing Report Properties

Report properties can be changed under ObjectPAL control, provided the report has not been delivered. To change a report, use the load( ) method, which opens the report in design mode. Then, under ObjectPAL control, you can change any report property.

If you want to load the report and prevent the user from seeing the changes taking place, you can use the following window style constant to change the report:

```
r.load("CUSTREC",WinStyleHidden)
r.RepHeader.value = "Customer Transaction Listing"
r.save()
r.run()
r.show()
```

In this example, the report is loaded as a hidden window so that the user cannot see the changes. Then the text object, RepHeader, is assigned a value. The report is then run. The last line, r.show( ), makes the report output visible so the user can view the report.

Using this technique, you can assign values to objects, even graphic objects within a report, without having to link a table in the reports data model. The following code example shows how to read a graphic file into a report.

```
var
     r Report
     PCXFile Graphic
endvar
if not PCXFile.readFromFile("LOGO.PCX") then
     PCXFile = blank()
endif
if r.load("CUSTREC",WinStyleHidden)
     r.LogoPCX = PCXFile
     r.save()
     r.print()
     r.close()
endif
```

If you cannot open the report in design mode because it is or will be a delivered report, then you have to devise some table linking scheme to place the text or graphic object in a table and then bind the table to the report. You can easily accomplish this scheme by creating a single report parameter table that holds several fields, usually a field for each report title variable and a field for a company logo graphic. This table should be keyed, so that your other tables can refer to this record. When you run your queries to retrieve records from the application's tables, make sure that you create a foreign key field with the key value from the report parameters table. This table can be placed on the data model and treated as a lookup table, in which a M:1 relationship exists between the records being printed and the report parameter table.

Integrating Queries into the Application

You also need to resolve another important issue in your applications—how to integrate queries in your application. You need queries to gather data for reports, select records for drop-down edit lists or pick lists, prepare temporary tables used in the application, or give the application *ad-hoc* query capabilities.

Perhaps the most important developer consideration in integrating queries is devising a scheme that allows for as much run-time modification of the query join criteria (joins), row selection criteria (select), field selection (project), and any other query operators. Developers frequently used such dynamic query techniques in Paradox for DOS to give applications powerful dynamic query capabilities that equaled what the user could do by using interactive Paradox, but with a user interface specific to the application. With these kinds of dynamic query schemes, the user can select and enter various field criteria and join criteria. The developer was free to manipulate the query under program control.

Paradox for Windows gives you three options to integrate queries into your application:

- Use QBE files
- Use a Query Object Type
- Use Query Strings

Each option has pros and cons, so each option is discussed in turn.

Using QBE Files

QBE files are special text files that hold query information so the query can be executed later. The query in figure 21.7, for example, results in the text file in figure 21.8.

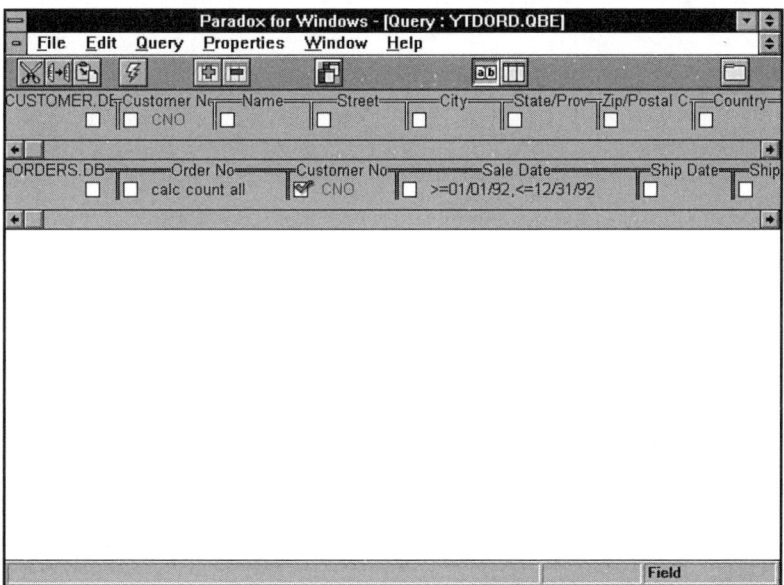

Figure 21.7. A QBE window.

As you can see from figure 21.8, the QBE file is a simple ASCII file that uses vertical bars to separate fields so that the table in the QBE file resembles the QBE window. Underscores precede join criteria, the table name is at the far left of the list of fields, and the word Check serves as a textual surrogate for the graphical check you would see in the QBE window. The name of the answer table also is written in the QBE field. In addition, if you specified any sort orders, these orders also are listed in the QBE file.

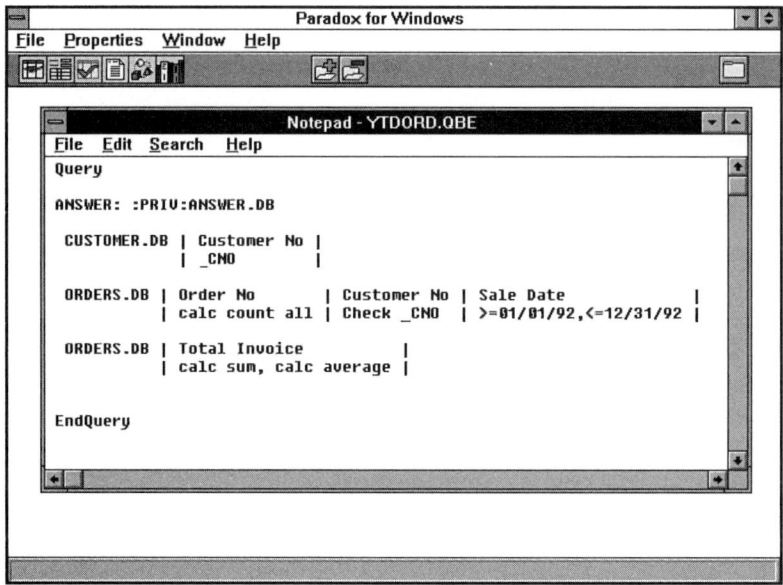

Figure 21.8. A QBE file.

QBE files are easy to create, and exist on the computers hard drive or on the network file server. If you create QBE files, therefore, users can execute and modify them. In addition, you can open forms and reports based on a QBE file. Although these features certainly are advantages in some situations, in others they are severe handicaps. If your application depends on a QBE file existing unchanged, and the user deletes or modifies your QBE file, most likely your application will bomb.

QBE files cannot be modified easily, during run time, to change their contents. You cannot reference an ObjectPAL variable from within a QBE file and you cannot easily change any selection, projection, or join criteria that were saved in the QBE file. Of course, you can use a TextStream object type to read and modify the QBE file, but the results may not be worth all this work.

You can run a QBE file easily under ObjectPAL control. You use the executeQBEFile( ) procedure:

```
if not executeQBEFile("YTDORD.QBE") then
    msgInfo("Query Error","The query file does not exist")
endif
```

Using errorShow( ) here in place of msgInfo( ) often will provide more useful information. Error handling is discussed in detail in Chapter 19.

Chapter 21 ■ Delivering the Application: Putting the Pieces Together

Using a QBE file has another disadvantage; every time the application executes the QBE file, it must be read from the disk, which is slower than if the query were compiled in with the application.

Using Query Types

The Query object type enables you to integrate a QBE file easily into your application. You only have to declare a Query variable, copy the QBE file into your ObjectPAL method, procedure, or script (using Edit¦Paste From File), and then assign the query to the variable. The following code shows how to do this:

```
var
     YTDQuery   Query
endvar
YTDQuery = Query                        ; assign the query to the variable
ANSWER: :PRIV:ANSWER.DB
 CUSTOMER.DB ¦ Customer No ¦
             ¦ _CNO         ¦
 ORDERS.DB   ¦ Order No     ¦ Customer No ¦ Sale Date              ¦
             ¦ calc count all ¦ Check _CNO ¦ >=01/01/92,<=12/31/92 ¦
 ORDERS.DB   ¦ Total Invoice ¦
             ¦ calc sum, calc average ¦
EndQuery
if not YTDQuery.executeQBE() then
     msgInfo("Query Error","Can't run query")
endif
```

Using errorShow( ) here in place of msgInfo( ) often will provide more useful information. Error handling is discussed in detail in Chapter 19.

The Query object type has three associated methods: executeQBE( ), writeQBE( ), and isAssigned( ). The method executeQBE( ) executes the query associated with the Query variable, writeQBE( ) writes the query associated with a Query variable to a QBE file, and isAssigned( ) determines if the Query variable was assigned a query.

You can invoke executeQBE( ) in four different ways. So far, executeQBE( ) was used to simply run the query as is. Another syntax is shown in the following code:

```
YTDQuery.executeQBE("YTDTBL.DB")
```

This code uses the YTDTBL.DB table as the answer table rather than the answer table designation contained within the Query variable.

The third syntax looks like the following line of code:

```
YTDQuery.executeQBE(YTDTableVar)
```

Here, YTDTableVar is a table referred to by a table variable. The query uses the table name associated with the table variable for the answer table rather than the answer table designation in the Query variable.

429

The last syntax, the most unusual one, looks like the following line:

```
YTDQuery.executeQBE(tcYTDTable)
```

Here, tcYTDTable is a TCursor variable. The TCursor variable does not have to be assigned or attached to anything. What Paradox cannot do is write the answer table to memory, rather than disk and assign the TCursor variable to the *virtual* table.

The Query object type lets you incorporate any QBE file into your application. You don't have to paste a QBE file in the application. Because the QBE file contains only ASCII characters, you can write a custom query at the keyboard.

The Query variable is even more flexible than the QBE file because you can use ObjectPAL variables within the QBE file. The following example is a valid Query variable:

```
var
     YTDQuery        Query
     param           String
endvar
param = "../../93"
YTDQuery = Query
ANSWER: :PRIV:ANSWER.DB
 CUSTOMER.DB | Customer No |
             |  _CNO       |
   ORDERS.DB | Order No        | Customer No | Sale Date |
             | calc count all  | Check _CNO  | ~param    |
   ORDERS.DB | Total Invoice            |
             | calc sum, calc average   |
EndQuery
if not YTDQuery.executeQBE() then
     msgInfo("Query Error","Can't run query")
endif
```

Notice that the param variable was placed in the Sale Date field with the tilde character preceding it. This placement is a *tilde variable*. Before Paradox executes a query associated with a Query variable, it replaces the tilde variable name with the tilde variable's current value. If you use writeQBE( ) on the YTDQuery variable, the following text is written to the query file:

```
QUERY
ANSWER: :PRIV:ANSWER.DB
 CUSTOMER.DB | Customer No |
             |  _CNO       |
   ORDERS.DB | Order No        | Customer No | Sale Date |
             | calc count all  | Check _CNO  | ../../93  |
   ORDERS.DB | Total Invoice            |
             | calc sum, calc average   |
ENDQUERY
```

You can use tilde variable for more than simple row selection criteria. Everything between the Query..EndQuery keywords can be placed in tilde variables!

Look at the following query. Everything was placed in several tilde variables.

```
var
     YTDQuery  Query
     table1, table2, field1a, field2a, field2b,
```

```
        field2c, field2d, param1a, param2a, param2b,
        param2c, param2d, ansTable String
endvar
table1 = "Customer.db"
table2 = "Orders.db"
field1a = "Customer No"
field2a = "Order No"
field2b = "Customer No"
field2c = "Sale Date"
field2d = "Total Invoice"
param1a = "_CNO"
param2a = "calc count all"
param2b = "Check _CNO"
param2c = "../../93"
param2d = "calc sum, calc average"
ansTable = "ANSWER: :PRIV:ANSWER.DB"
YTDQuery = Query
~anstable
 ~table1 | ~field1a |
         | ~param1a |
 ~table2 | ~field2a | ~field2b | ~field2c |
         | ~param2a | ~param2b | ~param2c |
 ~table2 | ~field2d |
         | ~param2d |
EndQuery
YTDQuery.writeQBE("YTD3")
if not YTDQuery.executeQBE() then
     msgInfo("Query Error","Can't run query")
endif
endmethod
```

This code executes the query successfully, but after it writes the query to a QBE file. The QBE file looks like the following code:

```
QUERY
ANSWER: :PRIV:ANSWER.DB
 Customer.db | Customer No |
             | _CNO |
 Orders.db | Order No | Customer No | Sale Date |
           | calc count all | Check _CNO | ../../93 |
 Orders.db | Total Invoice |
           | calc sum, calc average |
ENDQUERY
```

As you can see, all the tilde variables were replaced by their values. Although the vertical bars don't line up exactly, Paradox doesn't care; the query runs just fine. Perhaps the best thing about this Query variable feature is that blank tilde variables *do not contribute to the query*. They are ignored, which means that you can create an Query variable shell that has, say, 15 fields. You can leave out a field selection criteria by making sure the variable is blank before executing the query. *You cannot, however, leave a tilde variable used as a field name blank.* Paradox cannot run the query, and executeQBE( ) will fail.

Although the tilde variable and Query variable pair is useful, this scheme also suffers from limitations. You cannot, for example, add or subtract a table dynamically from the Query variable, nor can you add or remove additional fields to the Query variable to accommodate tables with different structures. To overcome these limitations, you need to use a Query string.

Using Query Strings

A *query string* is simply a Query construct stored inside a string variable. For example, the following is a valid query string:

```
var
    YTDQuery    String
endvar
YTDQuery = "Query
ANSWER: :PRIV:ANSWER.DB
 CUSTOMER.DB | Customer No |
             |   _CNO      |"+"
 ORDERS.DB | Order No        | Customer No | Sale Date              |
           | calc count all  | Check _CNO  | >=01/01/92,<=12/31/92  |
 ORDERS.DB | Total Invoice          |
           | calc sum, calc average |
EndQuery"
if not YTDQuery.executeQBEString() then
    msgInfo("Query Error","Can't run query")
endif
```

All you did here is enclose your original Query variable QBE within quotes, which made it a quoted string. Unfortunately, Paradox has a 255 character limit on quoted strings, which is why, right after the CUSTOMER.DB table in the query string you added the "+" characters. This splits the query into two quoted strings, both of which are less than 255 characters in length. As you can see, you are now using the executeQBEString( ) method, which is a String method, to execute the query.

You can write the query string like this:

```
YTDQuery = "Query\n\n"+
"ANSWER: :PRIV:ANSWER.DB\n\n"+
" CUSTOMER.DB | Customer No |\n"+
"             |   _CNO      |\n\n"+
" ORDERS.DB | Order No        | Customer No | Sale Date              |\n"+
"           | calc count all  | Check _CNO  | >=01/01/92,<=12/31/92  |\n\n"+
" ORDERS.DB | Total Invoice          |\n"+
"           | calc sum, calc average |\n\n"+
"EndQuery"
```

You also can write the query string like this:

```
YTDQuery = "Query\n\nANSWER: :PRIV:ANSWER.DB\n\n"+
" CUSTOMER.DB | Customer No |\n             |"+
" _CNO        |\n\n ORDERS.DB | Order No    |"+
" Customer No | Sale Date    |\n"+
"             | calc count all | Check _CNO |"+
" >=01/01/92,<=12/31/92 |\n\n ORDERS.DB |"+
" Total Invoice          |\n             |"+
" calc sum, calc average |\n\nEndQuery"
```

As you can see, as far as Paradox is concerned, a query string is a stream of characters, more or less formatted, which when straightened out, looks like a QBE file. The only hitch is that you cannot use tilde variables in a query string. Because a query string is just a plain old ordinary string, however, you can do string searching and substitution to change the contents of the string, and you can concatenate variables to construct a query string. With these options, you can dynamically place table names and query operators into the query string at run time.

With a query string, you can construct a query to include any number of fields, table, or query operators you want. The only problem with this approach is that you will probably need to write some string-handling custom methods to easily construct and manipulate a query string. With a library of custom methods that can build a query string, you can easily construct any type of query you want, dynamically at run time. We only wish that the next version of Paradox will include some methods to manipulate query strings so that programmers won't have to *roll their own*.

Query String Builder

Listed in the following text are all the library methods and procedures for a query string builder, in a library called QLIB. This code shows not only how to construct and manipulate a query string but also how to define variables, constants, and types in a library.

This library has several methods that you can use, which are shown in the following list:

Method	Description
qAsk( )	Puts a table in the query "window"
qCheckAll( )	Checks all fields in a table
qSetCheck( )	Places a check in a table's field
qSetFieldOrder( )	Sets the field order for the answer table structure
qSetLine( )	Specifies insert, delete, or set for a line of the query
qSetExample( )	Places an example element in a field
qSetTableName( )	Sets the answer table's name and alias
qSetStatement( )	Places an expression in a table's field
qSetSort( )	Specifies the sort order for the answer table
qSetQueryOrder( )	Makes answer table appear in table or field order
qSetTableType( )	Specifies the type of table to be created
qSetQBEInfo( )	Sets all data structures at one time
qGetQBEInfo( )	Retrieves the values of all data structures
qClearTable( )	Clears a table from the query "window"
qExecuteQBE( )	Executes the query

The basic premise is that you place a table in the query *window* with qAsk( ) and then use qSetCheck( ), qSetStatement( ), and qSetExample( ) to check fields, enter expressions, and link fields. Most of the other methods specify other query options. Each module is commented as to what task it performs.

Query String Library Variables, TypeWindow, and Const Window

```
; the library's var window
Var
    qTables         qTableType          ; holds all table names
    qChecks         qChecksType         ; holds checkmarks
    qExamples       qExamplesType       ; holds example elements
    qStatements     qStatementType      ; holds query statements
    qLines          qLineType           ; holds query line type
                                        ; i.e., "Set", "Delete"
    qOptions        qOptionsInfo        ; holds query options
    qString         String              ; holds the query string
    qSort           qSortType           ; holds sort order info
    qFieldOrder     qFieldOrdType       ; holds the field order info
endVar
; the library's type window
Type
    qOptionsInfo =
        Record
            answerTable         String
            tableType           SmallInt
            queryOrder          SmallInt
        endrecord
    qTableType      =   Array[]         String
    qChecksType     =   DynArray[]      SmallInt
    qExamplesType   =   Dynarray[]      String
    qStatementType  =   DynArray[]      String
    qLineType       =   DynArray[]      SmallInt
    qSortType       =   DynArray[]      String
    qFieldOrdType   =   DynArray[]      String
    qDynArrayType   =   DynArray[]      AnyType
    qArrayType      =   Array[]         AnyType
endType
; the library const window
Const
    ; check types
    QCheckPlus          = SmallInt(1)
    QCheckNormal        = SmallInt(2)
    QCheckDescending    = SmallInt(3)
    QCheckGroupBy       = SmallInt(4)
    QCheckNone          = SmallInt(5)
    ; query line types
    QQuerySet           = SmallInt(1)
    QQueryDelete        = SmallInt(2)
    QQueryInsert        = SmallInt(3)
    ; the separator character used in this library
    QSeparator          = "~"
    ; answer table types
    QTableParadox       = SmallInt(1)
    QTableDbase         = SmallInt(2)
    QDefaultAnswer      = "ANSWER: :PRIV:ANSWER.DB"
    ; answer table field orders
    QTableOrder         = SmallInt(1)
    QImageOrder         = SmallInt(2)
endConst
```

Library open( ) Method

```
; the library open() method
method open(var eventInfo Event)
qClearQBE()
endmethod
```

qAsk( )

```
{--------------------------------------------------
This method adds a table to the qTables dynarray.
All other methods check to make sure the table is listed
in the qTables array before doing any work.
--------------------------------------------------}
method qAsk(const tn String) Logical
if qTables.contains(tn.upper()) = false then
    ; this is a new table
    if qTables.size() = 0 then
        ; reset the query since there are no tables
        qClearQBE()
    endif
    qTables.addLast(tn.upper())
    return true
else
    return false
endif
endmethod
```

qCheckAll( )

```
{--------------------------------------------------
This method will add check entries for all fields in a table
or remove them, depending on the value of ct. ct must
be one of the check type constants.
--------------------------------------------------}
method qCheckAll(    const tn String,          {table name}
                     const li SmallInt,        {line number}
                     const ct SmallInt)        {check type}
                     Logical                   {return value}
var
    tb    Table                    ; a table variable
    flds  Array[] String           ; field name holder
    x     SmallInt                 ; temporary counter
    elem  String                   ; temp string variables
endvar
if qTables.contains(tn.upper()) = false then
    return false
endif
if not tb.attach(tn) then          ; attach the table var to
    return false                   ; the table name passed
endif
if not tb.isTable() then           ; does the table exist?
    return false
endif
if not tb.enumFieldNames(flds) then ; get the fields
    return false
```

435

```
            endif
            tb.unAttach()
            for x from 1 to flds.size()
                elem = tn+QSeparator+flds[x]+QSeparator+String(li)
                switch
                    case ct = QCheckPlus or
                         ct = QCheckNormal or
                         ct = QCheckDescending :
                        ; add the table/field/line to the check dynarray
                        qChecks[elem] = ct
                    case ct = QCheckNone :
                        ; remove the table/field/line from the check dynarray
                        if qChecks.contains(elem) then
                            qChecks.removeItem(elem)
                        endif
                endswitch
            endfor
        endmethod
```

qSetCheck( )

```
    {---------------------------------------------------
    This method sets the check type for a table/field/line.
    cType must be one of the following constants:
    QCheckPlus ¦ QCheckNormal ¦ QCheckDescending ¦
    QCheckGroupBy ¦ QCheckNone
    ---------------------------------------------------}
    method qSetCheck(       const tn String,         {table name}
                            const fn String,         {field name}
                            const li SmallInt,       {line number}
                            const cType SmallInt)    {check type}
                            Logical
        if qTables.contains(tn.upper()) = false then
            return false
        endif

        qChecks[tn+QSeparator+fn+QSeparator+String(li)] = cType
        return true
    endmethod
```

qSetFieldOrder( )

```
    {---------------------------------------------------
    This method adds an entry to the field order table, which
    determines the answer table format.
    ---------------------------------------------------}
    method qSetFieldOrder(  const tn String,
                            const ord SmallInt,
                            const fn String) Logical
        if qTables.contains(tn.upper()) = false then
            return false
        endif
        qFieldOrder[tn+QSeparator+String(ord)] = fn.upper()
        return true
    endmethod
```

qSetLine( )

```
{------------------------------------------------------
This adds the left-most query line type to the qLines
dynarray. lType must be one of the following constants:
     QQuerySet ¦ QQueryFind ¦ QQueryDelete ¦ QQueryInsert
------------------------------------------------------}
method qSetLine(        const tn String,         {table name}
                        const li SmallInt,       {line number}
                        const lType SmallInt) Logical
if qTables.contains(tn.upper()) = false then
    return false
endif

qLines[tn+QSeparator+String(li)] = lType
return true
endmethod
```

qSetExample( )

```
{------------------------------------------------------
This method adds an example element to the example dynarray.
The example element should not be preceded with an _
character, because during query string processing, it is
added there. The example dynarray is in many ways redundant,
because you can always add an example element by using
qSetStatement() with the example element embedded. This
method is just a convenience for simple queries. The example
element is always placed right after the check mark and
just before the statement.
------------------------------------------------------}
method qSetExample(     const tn String,         {table name}
                        const fn String,         {field name}
                        const li  SmallInt,      {line number}
                        const ex  String )       {example text}
                            Logical              {return type}
if qTables.contains(tn.upper()) = false then
    return false
endif

qExamples[tn+QSeparator+fn+QSeparator+String(li)] = ex
return true
endmethod
```

qSetTableName( )

```
{------------------------------------------------------
This method sets the answer table name
------------------------------------------------------}
method qSetTableName(const tPathAndName String)
qOptions.answerTable = tPathAndName
endmethod
```

qSetStatement( )

```
        {------------------------------------------------}
        This method adds a table/field/line query statement
        to the internal statements dynarray
        {------------------------------------------------}
        method qSetStatement(   const tn String,        {table name}
                                const fn String,        {field name}
                                const li SmallInt,      {line #}
                                const st String )       {statement text}
                                Logical                 {return type}
        if qTables.contains(tn.upper()) = false then
            return false
        endif

        qStatements[tn+QSeparator+fn+QSeparator+String(li)] = st
        return true
        endmethod
```

qSetSort( )

```
        {------------------------------------------------}
        This method makes an entry into the sort order table
        {------------------------------------------------}
        method qSetSort(        const tn String,        {table name}
                                const fn String,        {field name}
                                const ord SmallInt )    {sort order}
                                Logical                 {return type}
        if qTables.contains(tn.upper()) = false then
            return false
        endif
        qSort[String(ord)] = tn.upper()+QSeparator+fn
        return true
        endmethod
        method qSetQueryOrder(const qOrder SmallInt)
        if qOrder = QImageOrder then
            qOptions.queryOrder = qOrder
        else
            qOptions.queryOrder = QTableOrder
        endif
        endmethod
```

qSetTableType( )

```
        {------------------------------------------------}
        This method sets the answer table type
        {------------------------------------------------}
        method qSetTableType(const tableType SmallInt)
        if tableType = QTableDbase then
            qOptions.tableType = tableType
        else
            qOptions.tableType = QTableParadox
        endif
        endmethod
```

qSetQBEInfo( )

```
{------------------------------------------------------
This method lets the programmer prefill several arrays
with all the query string parts pre-loaded
------------------------------------------------------}
method qSetQBEInfo(          const tbls      qTableType,
                             const chks      qChecksType,
                             const exmp      qExamplesType,
                             const stmt      qStatementType,
                             const line      qLineType,
                             const sord      qSortType,
                             const ford      qFieldOrdType,
                             const opts      qOptionsInfo )

; overwrite the lib data structures with the passed ones
qTables = tbls
qChecks = chks
qExamples = exmp
qStatements = stmt
qLines = line
qSort = sord
qFieldOrder = ford
qOptions = opts
endmethod
endmethod
```

qGetQBEInfo( )

```
{------------------------------------------------------
This method will dump the current status of all the
internal data structures to the passed data types
------------------------------------------------------}
method qGetQBEInfo(          var tbls  qTableType,
                             var chks  qChecksType,
                             var exmp  qExamplesType,
                             var stmt  qStatementType,
                             var line  qLineType,
                             var sord  qSortType,
                             var ford  qFieldOrdType,
                             var opts  qOptionsInfo )

; stuff all the params with the lib data structures
tbls = qTables
chks = qChecks
exmp = qExamples
stmt = qStatements
line = qLines
sord = qSort
ford = qFieldOrder
opts = qOptions
endmethod
```

qClearTable( )

```
{----------------------------------------------------
This method will remove any references to the passed table
name from the internal data structures.
----------------------------------------------------}
method qClearTable(const tn String) Logical
var
     removeElem, parts Array[] String
     elem String
     x SmallInt
endvar
if qTables.contains(tn.upper()) = false then
     return false
endif
removeTableFromArrays(tn, qChecks)
removeTableFromArrays(tn, qExamples)
removeTableFromArrays(tn, qStatements)
removeTableFromArrays(tn, qLines)
removeTableFromArrays(tn, qFieldOrder)
; the qSort table has a different structure
; which must be handled differently
foreach elem in qSort
     qSort[elem].breakApart(parts,QSeparator)
     if parts[1].upper() = tn.upper() then
          removeElem.addLast(elem)
     endif
endforeach
for x from 1 to removeElem.size()
     qSort.removeItem(removeElem[x])
endfor
qTables.removeItem(tn.upper())
endmethod
```

qClearQBE( )

```
{----------------------------------------------------
This method will reset all internal data structures.
----------------------------------------------------}
method qClearQBE()
; empty all the dynarrays
qTables.empty()
qChecks.empty()
qExamples.empty()
qStatements.empty()
qLines.empty()
qSort.empty()
qString.blank()
; reset the options record fields to default values

qOptions.answerTable = QDefaultAnswer
qOptions.tableType = QTableParadox
qOptions.queryorder = QTableOrder
endmethod
```

qExecuteQBE( )

```
{----------------------------------------------------
This method will execute the QBE contained within the
internal data structures. Programmers can also use
qGetQBEString() to get the query string and then execute
it themselves.
----------------------------------------------------}
method qExecuteQBE() Logical
    if prepareString() then
        if qString.executeQBEString() then
            return true
        else
            return false
        endif
    else
        return false
    endif
endmethod
```

qGetQBEString( )

```
{----------------------------------------------------
This method will build a query string based on the current
data structure contents and return it.
----------------------------------------------------}
method qGetQBEString() String
    qString.blank()
    if prepareString() then
        return qString
    else
        return ""
    endif
endmethod
```

Query String Procedures

```
{----------------------------------------------------
This proc prepares a query string by examining all of the
data structures in the library and converting them to
a query string.
----------------------------------------------------}
proc prepareString() Logical
var
    elem,                             ; used for dynarray processing
    sortString,                       ; the sort command string
    x                   String        ; temporary variable
    currLine,                         ; current line of table image
    numLines,                         ; total number of query lines
    tCount,                           ; table counter variable
    y,                                ; temporary counter variable
    z                   SmallInt      ; temporary counter variable
    parts,                            ; temporary array for parts of
                                      ; dynarray indexes
    actFlds,                          ; actual fields from the table
    flds                qArrayType    ; arrays used for dynarray element
endvar
```

```
;--------------------------------------------------
; if the answerTable is blank, provide a default
;--------------------------------------------------
if qOptions.answerTable.isBlank() then
     qOptions.answerTable = QDefaultAnswer
endif
;--------------------------------------------------
; put the first line in the query string
; and build the table type line
;--------------------------------------------------
qString = "Query\n\n" + qOptions.answerTable + "\n\n"
if qOptions.tableType = QTableDbase then
     qString = qString + "TYPE: DBASE\n\n"
endif
;----------------------
; build the sort string
;----------------------
sortString.blank()
for y from 1 to qSort.size()
     if qSort.contains(String(y)) then
          if y = 1 then                              ; first time thru
               sortString = "SORT: "
          else
               sortString = sortString + ", "       ; another item coming
          endif
          elem = qSort[String(y)]
          elem.breakApart(parts, QSeparator)
          sortString = sortString + parts[1]+"->"+
                       "\""+parts[2]+"\""
     endif
endfor
if not sortString.isblank() then
     qString = qString + sortString + "\n\n"
endif
;--------------------------------------------
; process each table, beginning with table 1
;--------------------------------------------
for tcount from 1 to qTables.size()

     ; prepare flds and numLines for the new table
     actFlds.empty()
     flds.empty()
     numLines = 0
     ;----------------------------------------------
     ; get the fields that have been checked,
     ; or that have statements or examples in them
     ;----------------------------------------------
     qGetActFields(qTables[tCount], actFlds, numLines)
     ;-------------------------------------------------------
     ; setup the field order for the query string
     ; because query strings produce answer tables in
     ; the query string field order, this library lets
     ; programmers define the order or use each tables's
     ; structure for the field order
     ;-------------------------------------------------------
     if qOptions.queryOrder = QTableOrder then
          if not qGetTableOrder(qTables[tCount],flds,actFlds) then
               return false
```

```
            endif
    else
        if not qGetImageOrder(qTables[tCount],flds,actFlds) then
            return false
        endif
    endif

;-------------------------------------------
; generate the field header for the table
;-------------------------------------------
qString = qString + qTables[tCount]+" ¦ "

for y  from 1 to flds.size()
    qString = qString + flds[y] + " ¦ "
endfor

qString = qString+"\n"
;---------------------------------------
; now generate each query string line
; for the current table
;---------------------------------------
for currLine from 1 to numLines
        ;---------------------------------------
        ; add the query line operator before we
        ; start adding fields
        ;---------------------------------------
        elem = qtables[tCount]+QSeparator+String(currLine)
        if qLines.contains(elem) then
            switch
                case qLines[elem] = qQuerySet :
                    qString = qString + "Set"
                case qLines[elem] = qQueryDelete :
                    qString = qString + "Delete"
                case qLines[elem] = qQueryInsert :
                    qString = qString + "Insert"
            endswitch
        endif

        qString = qString + " ¦ "

        ;-------------------------------------------
        ; now add the field criteria and examples for
        ; each line in the table's query image
        ;-------------------------------------------
        for z from 1 to flds.size()
                ;-----------------------------------
                ; put the proper check mark in first
                ;-----------------------------------
                elem = qTables[tCount] + QSeparator + flds[z] +
                            QSeparator + String(currLine)

                if qChecks.contains(elem) then
                    switch
                        case qChecks[elem] = qCheckPlus :
                            qString = qString + "CheckPlus "
                        case qChecks[elem] = qCheckNormal :
                            qString = qString + "Check "
                        case qChecks[elem] = qCheckDescending :
```

```
                            qString = qString + "CheckDescending "
                    case qChecks[elem] = qCheckGroupBy :
                            qString = qString + "GroupBy "
                endswitch
            endif
            ;-----------------------------
            ; put in an example element next
            ;-----------------------------
            if qExamples.contains(elem) then
                qString = qString+"_"+qExamples[elem]
            endif
            ;-----------------------------
            ; now put in the statement next
            ;-----------------------------
            if qStatements.contains(elem) then
                if qExamples.contains(elem) then
                    qString = qString+", "+ qStatements[elem]
                else
                    qString = qString + qStatements[elem]
                endif
            endif

            qString = qString+" ¦ "
        endfor   ; each field
        qString = qString + "\n"
    endfor    ; each line
    qString = qString + "\n"
endfor    ; each table
qString = qString + "Endquery\n"
return true
endproc
{----------------------------------------------------------
This proc gets the fields that have been placed in the
various dynarrays for the current table and puts them in
the actFlds array.
----------------------------------------------------------}
proc qGetActFields( const tn        String,
                    var actFlds     qArrayType,
                    var numLines    SmallInt)
var
    x               String
    parts Array[]   String
endvar
;----------------------------------------------------------
; get all the fields names stuffed in the various
; arrays. There is no central data structure which holds
; all the fields. Instead, we'll examine all the
; arrays and store all the field names referenced
; (for the table tn) in the actFlds array.
;----------------------------------------------------------
; process the checks array
for each x in qChecks
    x.breakApart(parts,QSeparator)
    if parts[1].upper()<>tn.upper() then
        loop
    endif
    if actFlds.contains(parts[2].upper()) = false then
```

```
              actFlds.addLast(parts[2].upper())
        endif
        numLines = max(numLines,SmallInt(parts[3]))
endforeach
; process the examples array

for each x in qExamples
     x.breakApart(parts,QSeparator)
     if parts[1].upper()<>tn.upper() then
          loop
     endif
     if actFlds.contains(parts[2].upper()) = false then
          actFlds.addLast(parts[2].upper())
     endif
     numLines = max(numLines,SmallInt(parts[3]))
endforeach
; process the statements array
for each x in qStatements
     x.breakApart(parts,QSeparator)
     if parts[1].upper()<>tn.upper() then
          loop
     endif
     if actFlds.contains(parts[2].upper()) = false then
          actFlds.addLast(parts[2].upper())
     endif
     numLines = max(numLines,SmallInt(parts[3]))
endforeach
endproc
{---------------------------------------------------------------
This proc sets up the flds array in table order, based
on the table's structure
---------------------------------------------------------------}
proc qGetTableOrder(      const tn         String,
                          var flds         qArrayType,
                          var actFlds      qArrayType)
                          logical
var
     tbl    Table
     y      SmallInt
endvar
; get the field order from the table's structure
if not tbl.attach( tn ) then
     return false
endif
if not tbl.enumFieldNames(flds) then
     return false
endif
; remove the field from the field list
; if the field hasn't been inserted in any
; of the internal dynarrays
for y from 1 to flds.size()
     if not actFlds.contains(flds[y].upper()) then
          flds.remove(y)
          if flds.size() = 0 then
               quitloop
          endif
          y = y-1
     endif
```

```
    endfor
    return true
endproc
{------------------------------------------------------------
This proc sets up the flds array in image order, based
upon the entries in qFieldOrder.
------------------------------------------------------------}
proc qGetImageOrder( const tn        String,
                     var flds        qArrayType,
                     var actFlds     qArrayType)
                     Logical
var
    elem String
    x SmallInt
    tempFlds,
    parts Array[] String
endvar
;-----------------------------------------------------------
; Find any fields in the qFieldOrder dynarray and
; put them in the tempFlds array
;-----------------------------------------------------------
for x from 1 to qFieldOrder.size()
    elem = tn+QSeparator+String(x)
    if qFieldOrder.contains(elem) then
        tempFlds.addLast(qFieldOrder[elem].upper())
    endif
endfor
;-----------------------------------------------------------
; Any fields in the actFlds array should then be added
; in any order to the tempFlds array
;-----------------------------------------------------------
for x from 1 to actFlds.size()
    if not tempFlds.contains(actFlds[x].upper()) then
        tempFlds.addLast(actFlds[x].upper())
    endif
endfor
flds = tempFlds
return true
endproc
{------------------------------------------------------------
This proc will search all the dynarray structures in the library
and remove the table name in tn from them. This proc uses
the type qDynArray which allows us to pass any of the defined
dynarrays as a parameter, even if the dynarrays are different
------------------------------------------------------------}
proc removeTableFromArrays(const tn String, var theArray qDynArrayType)
var
    removeElem, parts Array[] String
    elem String
    x SmallInt
endvar
; find all references to the table name
; in the given array and store them in removeElem[]
for each elem in theArray
    elem.breakApart(parts,QSeparator)
    if parts[1].upper() = tn.upper() then
        removeElem.addLast(elem)
    endif
```

```
endforeach
; now remove each item from the given dynarray
; (we can't do this from within a for each loop)
for x from 1 to removeElem.size()
     theArray.removeItem(removeElem[x])
endfor
endproc
```

Interacting with the Operating System

Often, you may want your application's users to interact, in a controlled manner, with the operating system, which is done when the user needs to select a file or form to open. Also, under ObjectPAL control, you may want to read the user's AUTOEXEC.BAT, CONFIG.SYS, WIN.INI, or PDOXWIN.INI files. The good news is that Paradox has several object types that can help.

Using the fileBrowser( ) Procedure

The System fileBrowser( ) procedure displays a dialog box from which users can select one or more files. The procedure has two syntaxes:

```
fileBrowser(var selFile String[, var fInfo FileBrowserInfo]) Logical

fileBrowser(var selFiles Array[] String[,var finfo FileBrowserInfo]) Logical
```

The first syntax displays a dialog box that lets the user select *one* file. The second syntax displays a dialog box that lets the user select *many* files. Both forms let you optionally include another record structure, the FileBrowserInfo record.

```
This
Type FileBrowserInfo =
    Record
        x, y, w, h          SmallInt        ; size of Browser window in twips
        WindowStyle         LongInt         ; window style constant
        AllowableTypes      LongInt         ; file type
        SelectedType        LongInt         ; one of the AllowableTypes
        FileFilters         String          ; the filespec in edit box
        Alias               String          ; alias or drive name
        Path                String          ; path relative to Alias
    endRecord
endtype
```

If you use fileBrowser( ) without supplying a FileBrowserInfo record, the dialog box in figure 21.9 appears.

To control the appearance of the File Browser dialog, you need to supply parameters in the FileBrowserInfo record. You don't have to place a value in all the record's fields. You only need to fill in the fields that you absolutely need. The x,y,w, and h fields are self-explanatory. You can use these fields to set the position and the size of the dialog. You even can set the size to take up the entire screen. The WindowStyle field accepts the window style constants (see table 21.6).

Table 21.6. Window Style Constants.

WinDefaultCoordinate
WinStyleBorder
WinStyleControlMenu
WinStyleDefault
WinStyleDialog
WinStyleDialogFrame
WinStyleHScroll
WinStyleHidden
WinStyleMaximize
WinStyleMaximizeButton
WinStyleMinimize
WinStyleMinimizeButton
WinStyleModal
WinStyleThickFrame
WinStyleTitleBar
WinStyleVScroll

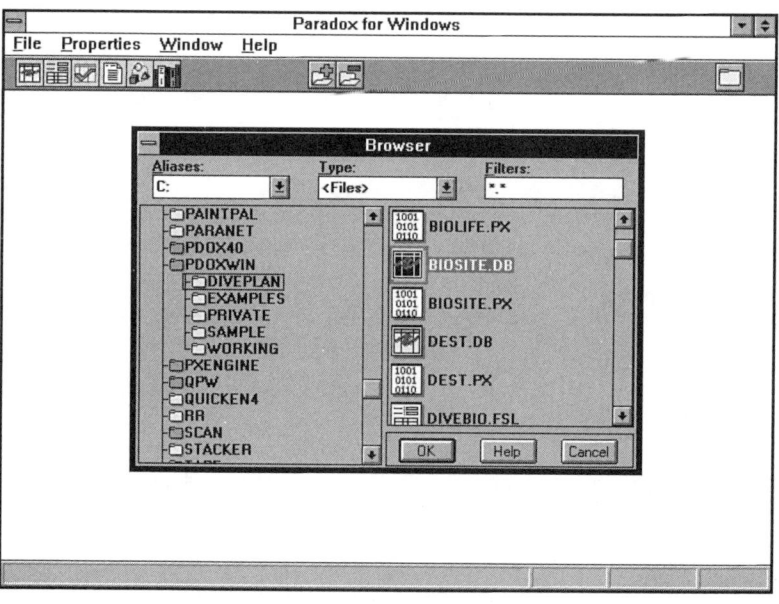

Figure 21.9. The File Browser dialog box.

The next three fields—AllowableTypes, SelectedType, and FileFilters—control the Type and Filters fields in the File Browser dialog. AllowableTypes and SelectedType accept FileBrowserFileType constants (see table 21.7). FileFilters accepts a string which is the file filter you want to appear in the Filters field.

These two fields control the Type drop-down edit field in the File Browser dialog. You can force the drop-down edit list to display multiple allowable, selectable file types by adding the constants together and placing that value in the AllowableTypes field. You can place only one constant in the SelectedType field. This field causes one of the types to appear selected. If you don't place anything in the SelectedType field, then the drop-down edit list contains the file types indicated by the AllowableTypes field, but nothing appears selected in the Type field and the FileFilters field contains only an asterisk, which causes nothing to display in the browser.

To really make the File Browser dialog work, you need to specify at least the AllowableTypes and the SelectedType fields, which cause the FileFilters field to display the file extension filter associated with the SelectedType constant (see the FileBrowserFileType constants in table 21.7). Notice that the user can change the Filters field at anytime, allowing the view and selection of any file type that matches the file filter the user entered.

Because of this user capability, you cannot *absolutely* prevent the user from selecting a file type outside the AllowableTypes list. You can only establish some default settings that make it easy for the user to select the file type you want them to select. The following code section sets up the File Browser dialog to allow selection of forms and Paradox tables, with tables as the selected item. No file filter is provided, so the File Browser displays the file extension filters for the Paradox table (*.db), because this is what you set the Selected Type to. The resulting dialog box is displayed in figure 21.10.

```
var
     fn    Array[] String
     fInfo FileBrowserInfo
endvar
fInfo.AllowableTypes = fbParadox + fbForm
fInfo.SelectedType = fbParadox
fileBrowser(fn,fInfo)
```

You can use the Alias field to specify an alias that you want displayed in the File Browser dialog. If none is supplied, the current alias (WORK) in use is displayed. In this version of Paradox, the Path field can be changed, depending on how the user interacts with the File Browser dialog. Try the following experiment in a pushButton method:

```
var
     L String
     fbi File BrowserInfo
endVar

fbi.AllowableTypes = fbParadox + fbForm
fbi.SelectedType    = fbParadox
fbi.view()
filebrowser(s,fbi)
s.view()
fbi.view()
```

Part IV Programming in ObjectPAL

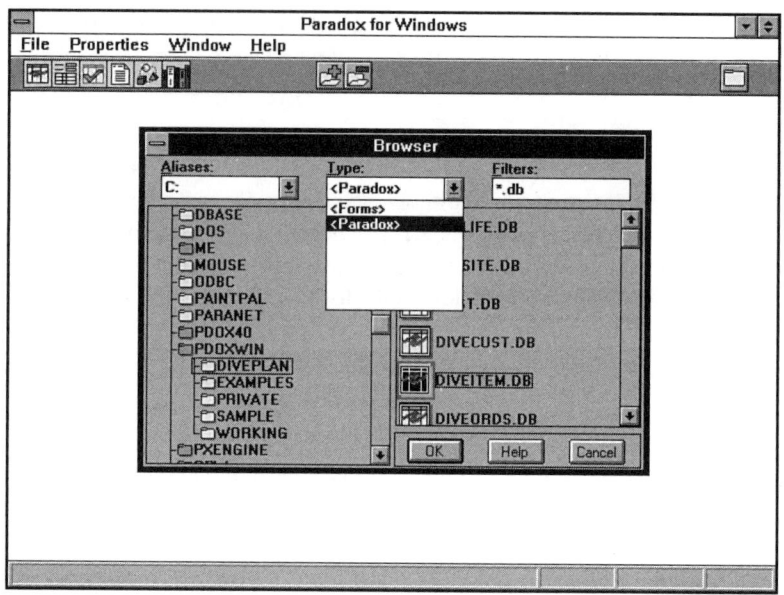

Figure 21.10. The File Browser dialog box, forms, and tables.

Notice that the string variable and FileBrowserInfo record get assigned only if you actually select a file. Notice that the FileBrowserInfo record actually can have its data changed by the fileBrowser proc. To see the path change, upon opening the File Browser change the Alias to c:, choose a subdirectory, select a file, click OK, and notice that fbi.path has been assigned.

Table 21.7. FileBrowserFileTypes Constants.

Constant	File Extensions Allowed
fbASCII	*.txt
fbAllTables	none
fbBitmap	*.bmp
fbDBase	*.dbf
fbExcel	*.xls
fbFiles	*.*
fbForm	*.fsl, *.fdl
fbGraphic	*.bmp, *.eps, *.gif, *.pcx, *.tif
fbIni	*.ini
fbLibrary	*.lsl

Constant	File Extensions Allowed
fbLotus1	*.wks
fbLotus2	*.wk1
fbMailmerge	*.msl, *.mdl
fbParadox	*.db
fbQuattro	*.wkq
fbQuattroPro	*.wq1
fbQuattroProWindows	*.wt1
fbQuery	*.qbe
fbReport	*.rsl, *.rdl
fbScript	*.ssl, *.sdl
fbTable	*.db, *.dbf
fbTableView	*.tv
fbText	*.txt

As you work with the File Browser dialog and the fileBrowser( ) procedure, notice that the Borland documentation and the constants that exist in the product are not quite the same. The ObjectPAL reference manual suggests that fbSQL and fbConfig are valid constants, whereas in the initial release of the product, they are not. In addition, the fbAllTables constant causes no files to display, and the fbTable constant displays dBASE and Paradox files, not just Paradox files.

FileSystem Type

Besides the file browser, Paradox has a FileSystem object type that lets you manipulate files and directories. The methods, listed in table 21.8, enable you to copy, delete, and rename files, set file access rights, determine disk free space, and make and remove directories, among other tasks.

Table 21.8. File System Methods and Procedures.

accessRights( )
copy( )
delete( )
deleteDir( )
drives( )
enumFileList( )
existDrive( )
findFirst( )

continues

Table 21.8. Continued.

findNext( )
freeDiskSpace( )
fullName( )
getDir( )
getDrive( )
isFixed( )
isRemote( )
isRemovable( )
makeDir( )
name( )
rename( )
setDir( )
setDrive( )
size( )
time( )
totalDiskSpace( )
getFileAccessRights( )
getValidFileExtensions( )
isDir( )
isFile( )
privDir( )
setFileAccessRights( )
splitFullFileName( )
startUpDir( )
windowsDir( )
windowsSystemDir( )
workingDir( )

Reading ASCII Text Files

Another common task you may need to perform is reading ASCII text files. With the TextStream object type, you can perform basic text file input and output operations, such as reading, writing, and searching a text file. You can use this object type to read text files such as the user's CONFIG.SYS and AUTOEXEC.BAT files or the WIN.INI or PDOXWIN.INI windows configuration files to check for certain parameters.

You may want to read, for example, the user's CONFIG.SYS file to determine the number of open files allowed, or you may want to read the AUTOEXEC.BAT file to see if SHARE is loaded. Using a TextStream object makes this procedure simple. The following code example reads the CONFIG.SYS file on the user's C drive and checks the FILES setting.

```
var
     ts                 TextStream
     line               String
     flds               Array[] String
     configFiles        SmallInt
endvar
if not ts.open("C:\\CONFIG.SYS","r") then          ; file does not exist
     return
endif
while not ts.eof()                                 ; read until eof
     if ts.readLine(line) then                     ; read one line
          line.breakApart(flds,"=")                ; look for = delimiter
          if flds.size()>1 then                    ; delimiter found
               flds[1]=flds[1].upper()             ; 1st field is left of =
                                                   ; conver and change to uppercase
               if flds[1]="FILES" then             ; if it's FILES then
                                                   ; convert right side of =
                                                   ; to a small integer
                    configFiles = SmallInt(flds[2])
                    if configFiles<70 then         ; files is too low
                         msgStop("Installation Problem",
                                 "The FILES setting in your CONFIG.SYS "+
                                 "file is too low. It is currently "+
                                 "at "+flds[2]+". You need to increase "+
                                 "it to at least 70.")
                         quitloop
                    endif
               endif
          endif
     endif
endwhile
ts.close()           ; close the TextStream file
```

This code displays the dialog box in figure 21.11. This code can be easily modified to actually write out the change. Table 21.9 lists the TextStream type methods.

Table 21.9. TextStream Methods.

advMatch( )
close( )
commit( )
create( )
end( )
eof( )
home( )

continues

Part IV ▪ Programming in ObjectPAL

Table 21.9. Continued.

open( )
position( )
readChars( )
readLine( )
setPosition( )
size( )
writeLine( )
writeString( )

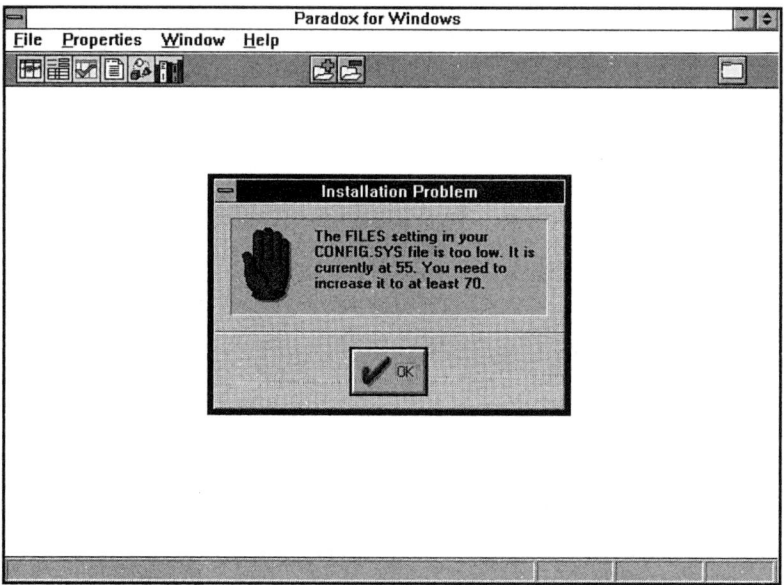

Figure 21.11. The dialog box with CONFIG.SYS files setting.

Another use for a textStream object is reading the win.ini file for entries. Although Paradox has a procedure, readProfileString( ), which finds and returns an entry in the various INI files, you may want to use a textStream object to read many lines from a system file. The following code, for example, gets both the default printer and the printers defined in the Windows win.ini file. The code uses a textStream object and the advMatch( ) method for a text stream object.

```
var
    ts              TextStream          ; text stream object
    startPos,                           ; start position for advMatch()
    endPos          LongInt             ; endPos fpr advMatch()
    line,                               ; line var to read printers
```

```
        winIni,                             ; win ini file
        defPrt          String              ; default printer string
        printOpts,                          ; printers options array
        printers  Array[] String            ; printers array
endvar
; get the location of the win.ini file
winIni = windowsDir()+"\\win.ini"
; read the default printer setting and store
; the printer name in the defPrt variable
defPrt = readProfileString("win.ini","windows","device")
defPrt = defPrt.substr(1,defPrt.search(",")-1)
; open the text stream
if not ts.open(winIni,"r") then
     return
endif
; find the [devices] line in the win.ini file
if ts.advMatch(startPos,endPos,"\\[devices\\]") then
     ; skip past the [devices] line
     ts.readLine(line)
     ; read until the end of file
     while not ts.eof()
          ; read the line next line in win.ini
          if ts.readLine(line) then
               ; did we find another [] heading in the win.ini file?
               if line.match("[..]") then
                    quitloop
               endif
               ; separate the printer name from the printer options
               line.breakApart(printOpts,"=")
               ; add the printer name to the printers array
               printers.addLast(printOpts[1])
          endif
     endwhile
endif
ts.close()
defPrt.view("Default Printer")
printers.view("Defined Printers")
```

If you need to write a value to one of the various INI files, use the ObjectPAL writeProfileString( ) procedure which sets the value for all entries in an INI file. With readProfileString( ), writeProfileString( ), and the TextSream type, you can create and manipulate your own application INI files.

Delivering Forms and Reports

Delivering forms and reports just removes any source code from them so that the user cannot change what you carefully crafted. You can manually deliver all the forms, reports, and libraries in an application by using the Language ¦ Deliver menu commands within an editor window, or you can use the Form deliver( ) method to deliver the form.

The interesting note about the deliver( ) method is that you can develop an automatic means of delivering a large number of forms and reports. The deliver( ) method can be used with a Form variable that is attached to either a report or a library and it works properly. Couple this fact with the fileBrowser( ) procedure and it's easy to prepare a utility that prompts you for a list of reports, forms, and libraries to deliver, lets you select the ones you want, and then automatically does the work.

If you need to load any forms or reports into design mode from within an application, don't deliver these forms or reports. Only nondelivered forms and reports can be opened in design mode.

Summary

This chapter demonstrated how to take your application's components, reports, queries, and libraries and glue them together into a finished application. Fortunately, Paradox for Windows provides a framework and powerful tools that make this job possible, if not simple.

V

Interoperability

22
Using DLLs To Extend ObjectPAL

A *dynamic-link library* (DLL) is a file that contains executable functions that can be called by any Windows application at runtime. A DLL is called *dynamic* because the locations (or addresses) of the functions are given (linked) to a Windows application when it is executed (*runtime*). Therefore, the actual addresses used are not determined at compile time. Linking a function at compile time is called *static linking* because the address of each function is determined when the object code is incorporated into the executable program by the compiler or linker. Traditionally, programmers have used static-link libraries from third-parties to gain additional capabilities such as serial communications, scientific and statistical computation, menuing, windowing, and so on.

Using a DLL rather than a static-linked library has a number of distinct advantages, however. A DLL is available for use by any windows application, while a static-linked library can be used only for applications that use a specific compiler. As a result, a developer who is creating a DLL must create only one version instead of one version for each compiler, or even for each version of each compiler.

In addition, a DLL is more memory efficient in a multitasking environment because it requires only one copy to be loaded in memory, regardless of how many applications (or instances of the same application) are using the DLL. A static-linked library requires that the code be incorporated into the executable, which means that there is a copy of the code loaded for each instance of each application that uses it. In fact, DLLs are so important that Windows uses them internally for much of its operation.

How can you, the Paradox-for-Windows developer, use DLLs?

- To create a custom library using another language like C or C++ when it is difficult or impossible to create an ObjectPAL function to provide the desired behavior.
- To create a custom library to optimize performance.
- To use functions from a third-party DLL.
- To create DLLs using a language like C or C++.
- To call a Windows API function to do something not provided by ObjectPAL.

Because the steps necessary to use a DLL are similar to using an ObjectPAL Library, with little effort, you should be able to use DLL functions in your ObjectPAL code, which is just a matter of specifying the DLL and its functions properly within ObjectPAL.

Declaring DLL Functions with the Uses( ) Method

Before you can use the functions contained in a DLL, you must declare them in the Uses( ) method, which is available for every object on a form. A DLL function is declared as follows:

```
Uses LibraryName
    RoutineName (Parameters) ReturnType
EndUses
```

Because a declaration made in the Uses( ) method on the Form object is visible to all objects on the form, the Form's Uses( ) method generally is the best place to declare a DLL.

Another benefit exists to declaring a DLL in the Form's Uses method. Because it takes time to load a DLL into memory for use, it is faster to declare and load the DLL only once per form, rather than once for each object that uses the DLL.

Specifying the Library Name

The *LibraryName* contains the name of the DLL to be used. The DOS filename extension is assumed to be DLL so it isn't necessary to specify it. Also, don't enclose the LibraryName in quotes. Here is an example:

```
Uses AAPLAY3
EndUses
```

If the DLL contains a function with the same name as the DLL, you must rename the DLL or you will not be able to declare the function. Paradox reports the cryptic message

```
Error: Identifier expected
```

when the syntax of the function is checked.

Specifying the Routine Name

The *RoutineName* is the name of a function in the DLL. Here's a simple example with no parameters or return type:

```
Uses AAPLAY3
    aaOpen ()
EndUses
```

If you see the message, Error: Identifier expected, when the syntax is checked, even though it appears correct, check that the RoutineName is not the same as the LibraryName. If the names are the same, you must rename the DLL to avoid this naming conflict.

Although it is only necessary to declare the functions you plan to use, it may be better to declare all of the functions anyway. If you define and test the complete capabilities of the DLL, you will reduce debugging and the need to refer to the DLL documentation later during application development.

Specifying the Routine Parameters

Most DLL functions have parameters that you also must specify. First, you must determine the correct parameters and types for the functions you plan to use. If you cannot find documentation for the parameters, we recommend that you do *not* attempt to guess. If you really must use an undocumented DLL, you can use tools provided with a product such as Borland C++ to find this information. Many DLLs are designed to be used only by programmers with intimate knowledge of the internals. Windows easily could be corrupted if an undocumented DLL were used improperly.

Caution: It is very important to correctly define the proper number of parameters and their types or you could crash or corrupt Paradox, possibly losing data in the process. Because of this, we would highly recommend that you backup your system before attempting to use a DLL from within Paradox.

Once prepared with a list of the parameter data types used for each function in the DLL, the only task is to translate the types used in the DLL to types recognized by Paradox. Because Paradox doesn't enable you to create new data types and will not be able to call directly any DLL functions that require complex structures to be passed as parameters. Although it may seem that you can create a complex data type using the Record...EndRecord construct, this technique internally creates a C++ type object, not a C style data structure. Any attempt to pass a data type other than those listed in table 22.1 probably will crash Paradox and corrupt data. You can work around this limitation by creating your own DLL functions to create internally the complex data structures necessary, assuming that you can program using a language such as C or Pascal.

ObjectPAL provides several special types to use for the parameters of a DLL: CDOUBLE, CHANDLE, CLONG, CLONGDOUBLE, CPTR, and CWORD. Table 22.1 shows how these types correspond to the C and Pascal Languages.

Table 22.1. ObjectPAL DLL Parameter Types.

ObjectPAL DLL Parameter Type	C Type	Pascal Type
CDOUBLE	double	Double
CHANDLE	handle	THandle
CLONG	long	Longint
CLONGDOUBLE	long double	Extended
CPTR	char far *	String
CWORD	int	Integer

Here are some examples of functions using parameters:

```
aaLoad(lpzFileName CPTR, hWnd CWORD, wMode CLONG, x CLONG, y CLONG, cx CLONG, cy CLONG, orgx CLONG, orgy CWORD) CWORD
aaUnload(hAa CWORD) CWORD
qeConnect (connectStr CPTR) CWORD
qeDisconnect (hdbc CWORD) CWORD
qeExecSQL (hdbc CWORD, sql_stmt CPTR) CWORD
qeEndSQL (hstmt CWORD) CWORD
qeFetchNext (hstmt CWORD) CWORD
qeValChar (hstmt CWORD, col_num CWORD, format_string CPTR, max_len CWORD) CPTR
```

In addition to declaring the parameters passed to a DLL, it is also necessary to declare the value returned from a DLL function, if there is one.

Specifying the Return Data Type

If a DLL function returns a value, you must specify the data type of this value. As with the limitations of the data type for parameters, you may use only functions that return a data type compatible with those provided by ObjectPAL. You cannot use functions that return complex data types, such as C structure variables that use the struct keyword, because no corresponding type exists in ObjectPAL.

Calling a DLL Function

You will find that it is easy to use a DLL function after you have properly declared it. You can treat the function as if it is any other ObjectPAL command. You receive a syntax error if you use an incorrect number of parameters or a data type that is different than the type declared for the function. Of course, even if you use the correct parameter and data type, you will still experience problems if you have incorrectly declared the function.

Here are some examples of using DLL functions correctly:

```
hdbc = qeConnect("DRV=QLORA;SRVR=X:ORACLESQL;UID=USER;PWD=A")
hstmt = qeExecSQL (hdbc, "SELECT * FROM CLIENT")
retVal = qeFetchNext(hstmt)
strBuf = qeValChar(hstmt, 2, "", 60)
```

Notice that no special formatting is required to distinguish a call to a DLL function from an ObjectPAL function. This is particularly helpful because the syntax remains consistent throughout your code even though you have *extended* ObjectPAL using external DLL functions.

Calling a Third-Party DLL

You probably will use a DLL most to call a third-party library to extend the capabilities of ObjectPAL. In the example in this section, we show you how to fill in a list of values in a field from a remote SQL-based Server, which demonstrates how to use the Q+E Database Library by Pioneer Software, a DLL that enables you to use SQL to access a wide variety of SQL servers and PC RDBMS file formats.

First, create a form that contains a list of values retrieved from an SQL server, which in this case is ORACLE Server for Netware.

To create a form that contains an undefined list box to hold the information you will retrieve, follow these steps:

1. Create a new form (see fig. 22.1). Do not specify any tables for the data model.

2. Select the Field tool and place a field on the form (see fig. 22.2).

3. Using the Object Inspector, right-click on the field object and choose the display type to be a list. Choose the OK button from the Define List dialog box without specifying any items to appear on the list.

4. Increase the size of the field and the list object contained inside the field to accommodate the length of the data to be placed. Make the width approximately three inches (see fig. 22.3).

5. Use the Object Inspector to change the name of the field and list objects to a better name than the default names given. Use MyListField and MyList for the names (see fig. 22.4).

    Now that the form and list are prepared for use, declare the DLL in the form's Uses method.

6. Open the Uses method of the form object and place the following code in it:

```
Uses QELIB
    qeConnect (connectStr CPTR) CWORD
    qeDisconnect (hdbc CWORD) CWORD
    qeExecSQL (hdbc CWORD, sql_stmt CPTR) CWORD
    qeEndSQL (hstmt CWORD) CWORD
    qeFetchNext (hstmt CWORD) CWORD
    qeValChar (hstmt CWORD, col_num CWORD, format_string CPTR, max_len CWORD) CPTR
endUses
```

Next, you will call the DLL functions to place the data into the list box.

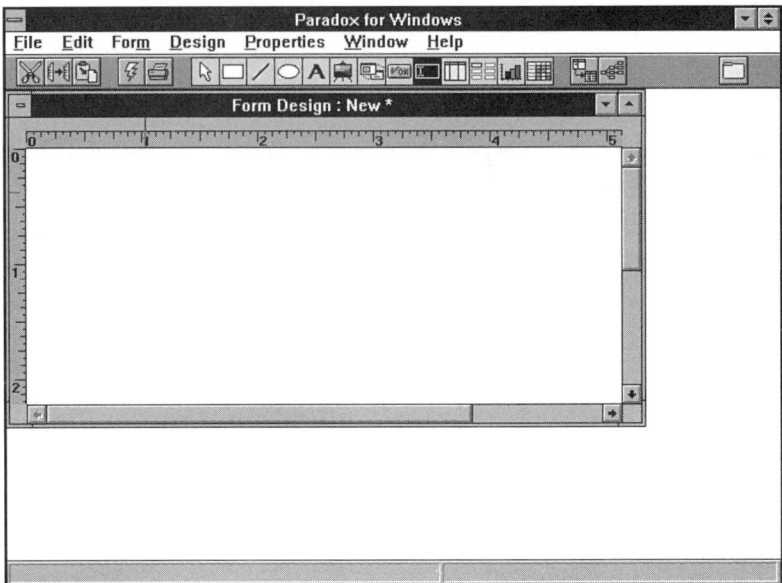

Figure 22.1. A new form.

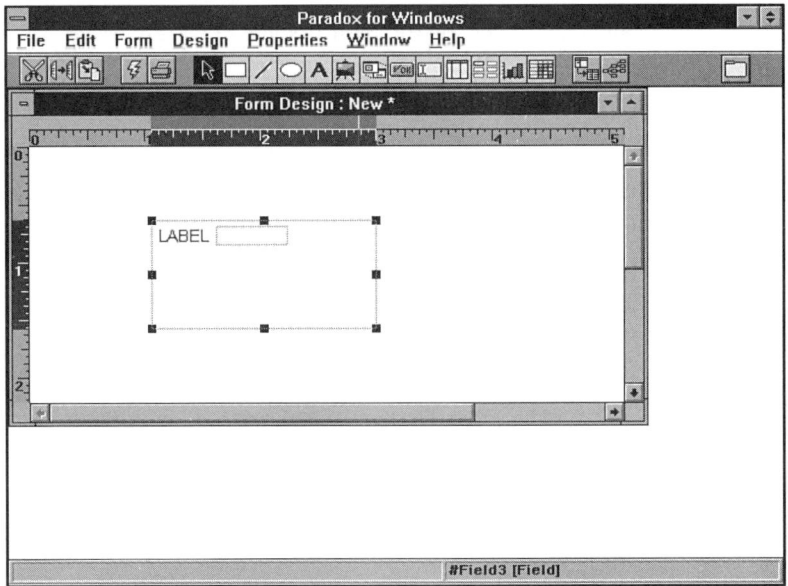

Figure 22.2. A field placed on the form.

Chapter 22 ■ Using DLLs To Extend ObjectPAL

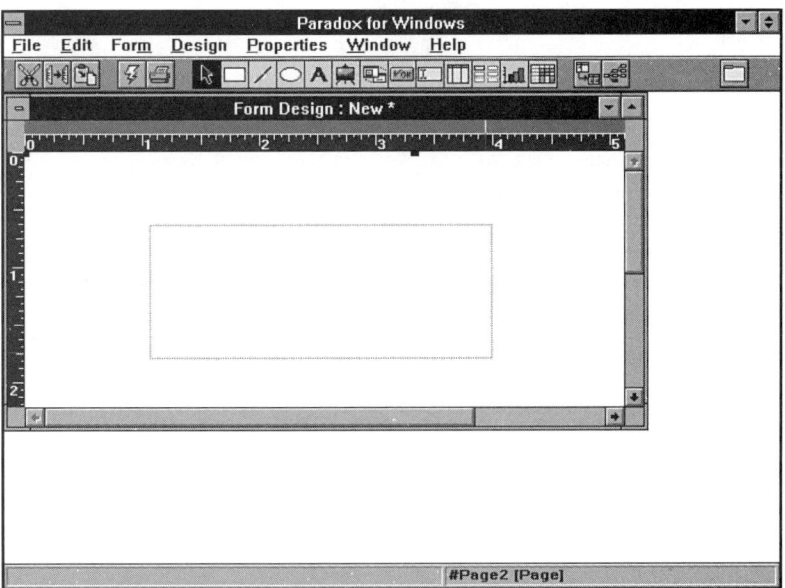

Figure 22.3. The field, increased in size to accommodate the length of the data to be placed.

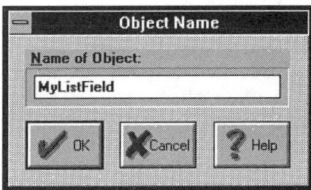

Figure 22.4. Using the Object Name dialog box to rename a form.

7. Modify the Forms Open( ) method and place the following code in it:

```
Var
    hdbc SmallInt           ; Handle to a database connection
    hstmt SmallInt          ; Handle to an SQL statement cursor
    retVal SmallInt         ; Returning value from various functions
    nRecs SmallInt          ; Counter of the records returned from SQL server
    strBuf String           ; String value retrieved from the SQL server
endVar

; Connect to ORACLE Server using Q+E Database Library
hdbc = qeConnect("DRV=QLORA;SRVR=X:ORACLESQL;UID=USER;PWD=APSWD")

; Display an error if not connected
if hdbc < 1 then
```

465

```
            MsgStop("Error","Couldn't connect to server. Error #: "+strval(hdbc))
            return
    endif

    ; Execute an SQL command to retrieve all the client names from
    ; the CLIENT table
    hstmt = qeExecSQL (hdbc, "SELECT NAME FROM CLIENT ORDER BY NAME")

    ; Empty the list of any preexisting values
    MyListField.MyList.list.count = 0

    ; Delay screen updates until the list is full
    delayScreenUpdates(Yes)

    nRecs = 0                       ; Initialize the record counter

    ; Fetch the first record returned by the SQL server
    retVal = qeFetchNext(hstmt)

    ; Fetch the remaining names in a loop
    while retVal=0
         nRecs = nRecs + 1          ; Increment the Counter

         ; Retrieve the client name from the record
         strBuf = qeValChar (hstmt, 1, "", 60)

         ; Insert the value into the list
         MyListField.MyList.list.selection = nRecs
         MyListField.MyList.list.value = strBuf

         sleep(0)  ; Let other applications do some work too
         ; Fetch the next record returned by the SQL server.
         ; retVal will be set to 0 when there are no more records
         retVal = qeFetchNext(hstmt)
    endwhile

    ; Enable screen updates now that the list has been filled
    delayScreenUpdates(No)

    retVal = qeEndSQL (hstmt)       ; Close the SQL cursor
    retVal = qeDisconnect(hdbc)     ; Close the connection to the SQL server
```

8. When the form executes, you see a list similar to the one shown in figure 22.5, assuming that you have table named CLIENT that contains the field, NAME, on the server.

Accessing data on a remote SQL server is just one of many ways to use a DLL. The techniques in this example are the same regardless of the type of DLL you plan to use.

Chapter 22 ■ Using DLLs To Extend ObjectPAL

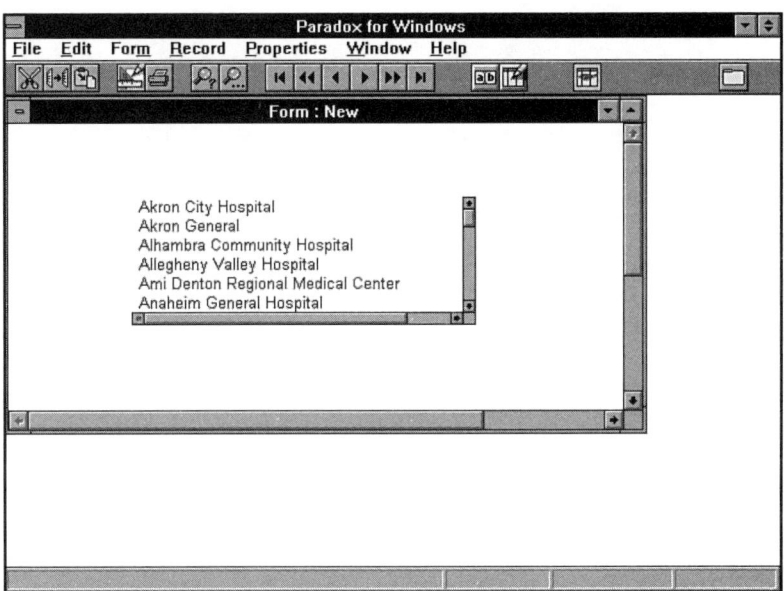

Figure 22.5. A form list, after execution.

Summary

This chapter showed you how to use a DLL in ObjectPAL and how to use a third-party DLL in an application. You learned to take great care in declaring a DLL in order to avoid computer crashes that can corrupt or lose data. After you correctly declare a DLL, it can offer you many benefits that would otherwise be unavailable to you.

As an added benefit, you can use a DLL to optimize your program's performance if you use a language such as C, C++, or Pascal.

467

23
Using DDE

Dynamic Data Exchange (DDE) is a protocol that enables Windows applications to communicate with each other and share data.

Using DDE can change how you design applications. Rather than creating an all-encompassing program from the ground up, a savvy developer can use DDE to take advantage of the many powerful Windows applications already on the market.

Because you can use DDE with Paradox for Windows, you will probably find it much easier to integrate your applications with other programs, particularly if you have used only DOS-based applications. This chapter describes DDE and explains how to use it with Paradox for Windows.

Overview of DDE

If you have ever used the Paste Link command on the Edit menu of a Windows application, you used DDE, although you may not have realized this at the time (see fig. 23.1).

Even if you have never used Paste Link, you can easily link together applications by using this command. After copying data to the Clipboard, simply choose Edit ¦ Paste Link to paste the data in another application. This technique, however, works only if the source application is a DDE Server and the destination application is a DDE Client. A *DDE Server* application has been programmed specifically to enable its data to be linked to another application by using Windows' DDE services. Similarly, a *DDE Client* has been programmed to use DDE services to initiate a conversation with a DDE Server to receive data from the server. (See fig. 23.2.)

Although the most visible use of DDE is in the Paste Link command, many programs use DDE to communicate with one another with no visible clues that DDE is used. Windows applications use DDE with the Program Manager, for example, to create icons and groups. Many Windows applications provide DDE Server commands for other applications to use. By using DDE, you can tell word processors to merge and print, spreadsheets to recalculate, and mapping programs to zoom to a particular address. Each time a new DDE Server application is released, in fact, a entire new set of applications can become possible. Paradox for Windows can use DDE to integrate with other Windows applications, because Paradox can act as both a DDE Server and a DDE Client.

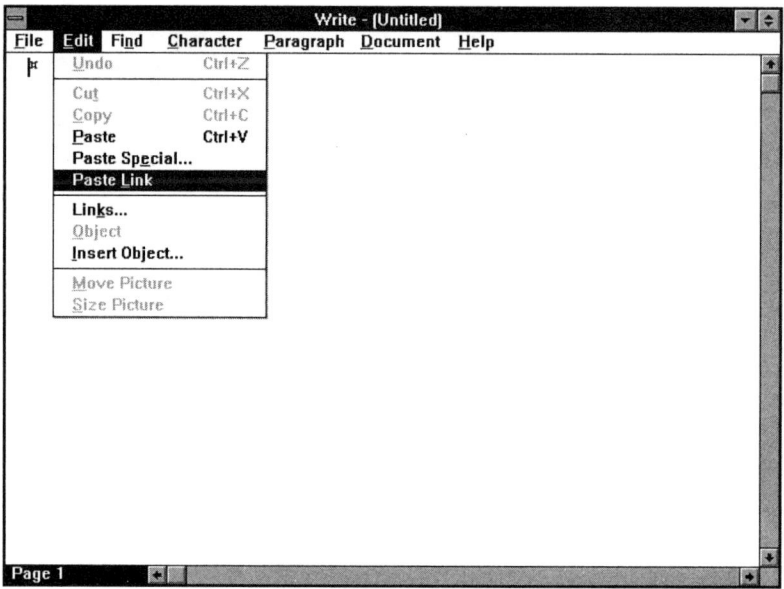

Figure 23.1. The Paste Link command.

DDE Server Capabilities

Paradox for Windows can be used as a DDE Server through its Table object feature (see fig. 23.3). Data from the Table object can be linked to other DDE Client applications. This feature can be used to transfer data from a table into a word processor document, for example, creating a boilerplate letter in which the addressee information changes with the current record.

Other applications also can access data in Paradox for Windows by using their programming language DDE commands. A caveat to this approach does exist, however: Using DDE to send a large amount of data from one application to another is quite slow; DDE, therefore, should be used to transfer only small amounts of data. The DDE Server capabilities of Paradox also are quite limited. You can obtain a field value from the current record or transfer the entire table, but you cannot move from one record to another by using DDE commands.

Chapter 23 ■ Using DDE

DDE Server Limitations

Unfortunately, the first version of Paradox-for-Windows doesn't have a full-featured DDE Server implementation. Unlike many other DDE Server applications, language elements in ObjectPAL such as methods and procedures cannot be called from other applications using DDE. Nor can you use DDE to control the Paradox-For-Windows menu system. Since this greatly limits interoperability with other products, we hope that future versions will provide greater DDE server capability.

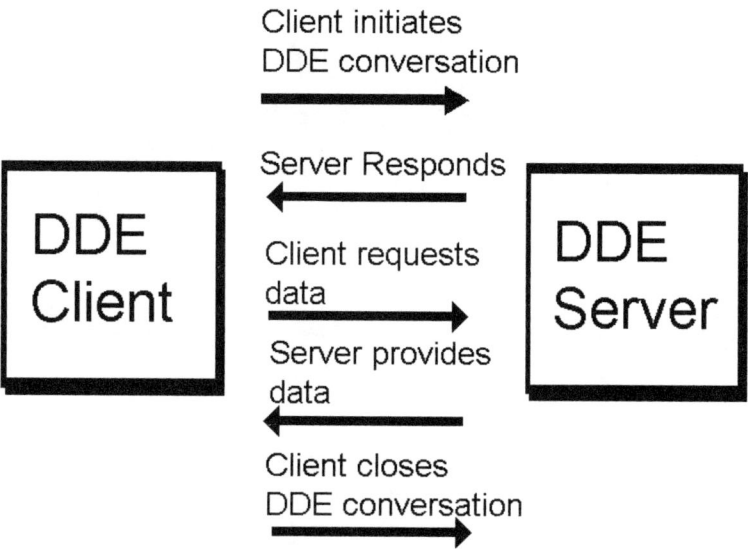

Figure 23.2. The DDE Client-Server interaction.

Interactive DDE Client Capabilities

Paradox for Windows can be used as a DDE Client interactively and through use of ObjectPAL. Data from other applications can be interactively linked to a QBE object to be used as record selection criteria. Thanks to this feature, Paradox for Windows can reexecute a query if, for example, the cell of a spreadsheet changes (see fig. 23.4.).

471

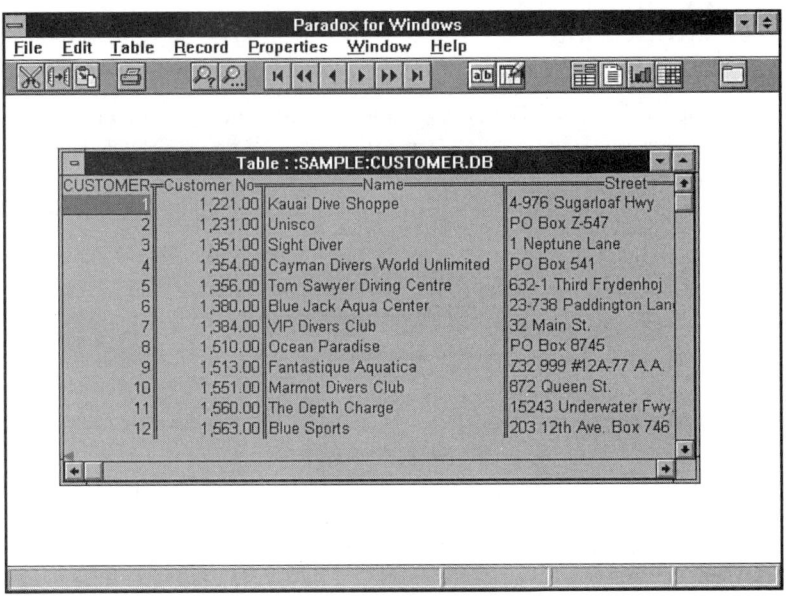

Figure 23.3. A Paradox Table object.

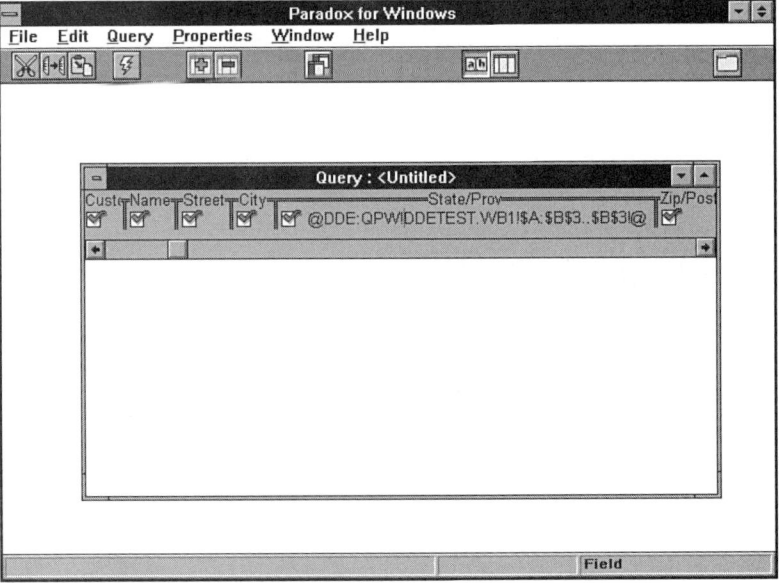

Figure 23.4. A DDE link in a query.

ObjectPAL DDE Client Capabilities

ObjectPAL gives you the capability to use DDE commands to initiate a connection to a DDE Server application by using a DDE Type variable. Not only can you send commands and data to the DDE Server, but you also can retrieve information from the server by using the DDE variable. This means that you can use DDE to send data and commands to a spreadsheet, for example, and receive information contained in its cells. The DDE Type is a very useful tool for integrating Paradox with other Windows applications.

The DDE Type provides several open( ) methods to establish a "DDE conversation" with a DDE Server application. The open( ) methods have the following syntax:

```
open(const server String) Logical
open(const server String, const topic String) Logical
open(const server String, const topic String, const item String) Logical
```

Each form of the open( ) method is distinguished solely by the number of parameters passed.

The open( ) method returns TRUE if successful and FALSE if a problem turns up in initiating the conversation with the DDE Server.

The *server* parameter defines the executable name of the server and is required to be specified in each form of the open( ) method. Although you can specify a path in the *server* parameter, the open( ) method returns false even though the DDE Server application loads without a problem. You should not, therefore, pass the path in the *server* parameter; instead make sure that the path to the DDE Server is set in the DOS PATH environment variable.

The *topic* parameter is the topic to be sent to the DDE Server, which is application specific. This topic is typically the file or document name to be opened by the application. Refer to the DDE Server's documentation to see how the topic parameter is used.

The *item* parameter is the item to be sent to the DDE Server. As with the *topic* parameter, this parameter is application specific, so you can refer to the DDE Server's documentation to see how the *item* parameter is used.

The following three examples show how to use the open( ) method:

```
; Open a DDE conversation with Quattro Pro for Windows
; sending the spreadsheet name as the topic
myDDE.open("QPW","C:\\qpw\\myspread.wb1")

; Open a DDE conversation with Word for Windows
; sending the document name as the topic
myDDE.open("WINWORD","c:\\winword\\letter.doc")

; Open a DDE conversation with Program Manager
myDDE.open("PROGMAN","PROGMAN")
```

The execute( ) method is used to send a command to a DDE Server after a connection has been established by using the open( ) method. The execute( ) method has the following syntax:

```
execute(const command String) Logical
```

The execute( ) method returns TRUE if successful and FALSE if the DDE Server has a problem executing the contents of the *command* string.

The *command* parameter contains the string for the DDE Server to execute, which is application specific. This parameter is typically the Menu Item, Macro Command, or function to be executed by the application. Refer to the DDE Server's documentation to see how the *execute* parameter is used.

The following code shows some examples of how you can use the *execute* parameter:

```
; Set the Print cell range in Quattro Pro for Windows
myDDE.execute("{Print.Block A1..D13}")

; Display the Print Preview in Quattro Pro for Windows
myDDE.execute("{Preview}")

; Print the current document in Word-for-Windows
myDDE.execute("[FilePrintDefault]")

; Exit Word-for-Windows, saving all open documents
myDDE.execute("[FileExit(1)]")

; Add a group to Program Manager
myDDE.execute("[CreateGroup(MyGroup)]")
setItem(const item String)
```

The setItem( ) method is used to specify an item with the DDE Server.

The item parameter is an application-specific string to be sent to the DDE Server. Refer to the DDE Server's documentation to see how setItem( )'s item parameter is used.

The following is an example of how the setItem( ) method is used:

```
; Open a conversation with Paradox-for-Windows and
; the City field in the table CUSTOMER.DB with the
; Alias SAMPLE.
myDDE.open("PDOXWIN",":SAMPLE:CUSTOMER.DB","City")
; Get the city from the field
aCity = myDDE
; Set the item to the State field
myDDE.setItem(" State/Prov")
; Get the state from the field
aState = myDDE
```

The close( ) method is used to close a conversation which was previously established with a DDE Server application using the open( ) method. Here is the syntax for the close( ) method:

```
close() Logical
```

As you can see, the close( ) method does not have parameter, only a return value. It returns TRUE if successful and FALSE if a problem is encountered in closing the conversation with the DDE Server.

The following is an example of how the close( ) method is used:

```
; Close the DDE conversation
myDDE.close()
```

DDE Tutorial

Now that we have shown the syntax for the DDE ObjectPAL Type, it is time to show the practical application of this relatively simple, yet powerful capability.

Controlling the Program Manager by Using DDE

After you have created an application, wouldn't it be great if you could use ObjectPAL to create an installation program to automatically add an Icon to Program Manager? This addition would enable a user to start the application just by double-clicking the icon. You can do this easily in ObjectPAL because Program Manager provides you all the DDE commands you need to create Groups (that is, windows that contain a group of related programs icons) and Items (icons that represent programs).

The following is an ObjectPAL example of how to create groups and items:

```
var
    myDDE DDE
endVar
myDDE.open("PROGMAN","PROGMAN")
myDDE.execute("[CreateGroup(MyGroup)]")
myDDE.execute("[AddItem(C:\\PDOXWIN\\PDOXWIN.EXE MYAPP.FSL,"+
    "MyApp,C:\\PDOXWIN\\PDOXWIN.EXE,13)]")
myDDE.close()
```

First, you must declare variable of DDE type. This enables you to use this variable to establish a DDE conversation with the Program Manager by using the DDE object's open( ) method.

To create the Program Manager group, use the CreateGroup command, using the name of the Group as the argument. Notice that Program Manager requires that you enclose the command to be executed in brackets (that is, [ ]). This common convention is used by Microsoft products, but be aware that other products may use different conventions.

To create the item, use the AddItem command, using the command line, Name, IconPath, and IconIndex as the arguments. In this example, the command line consists of the path to Paradox for Windows and the Form name to be automatically loaded. The Name to be displayed below the icon is MyApp. The icon specified is located in Paradox for Windows. The IconIndex is the 13th one found, which in this case is the Lightning-Bolt icon.

> **Note:** Although an icon from within the Paradox for Windows executable program is used in this example, you can use an icon from any Windows file that contains an icon resource, such as files ending in the extension DLL, EXE, or ICO. The PROGMAN.EXE file, for example, contains many icons you can use. You also can create icons by using Borland's Resource Workshop, Microsoft's SDK or AppStudio, or other Resource Editing tools.

Finally, use the DDE close( ) method to close the DDE conversation.

For more information about using DDE with the Program Manager, refer to Chapter 22 *Microsoft Windows Guide to Programming*.

If you use DDE to update a user's Program Manager configuration, you may want to consider creating a special group specifically for your application instead of updating an existing group. Users often spend much time getting their groups "just right." Seeing your application change the configuration of an existing group can be quite frustrating to such users.

Integrating with a Word Processor

Although most developers use database programs, word processors are used far more prevalently in the workplace. Most word processors, however, feature very limited database capabilities. You may be surprised, therefore, at how often word processors are used in place of database programs. Most users simply "make do" with the program they have and know instead of choosing the best tool for the job.

Using a database program to maintain lists of data, however, has many significant advantages—data integrity, manipulation, and relational capabilities, to name but a few.

Using a word processor instead of a database for document creation and editing also has its advantages, such as a word processor's capabilities for spell-checking, using style-sheets, offering multi-column support, and processing mail merges. Integrating a word processor with a database, therefore, takes advantage of the best features of each application to accomplish the task at hand.

Creating a Single Letter Boilerplate

Many companies commonly use standard boilerplate documents that must be printed on demand. Although many word processors can create such boilerplate documents, using the data directly from a database makes creating these documents even easier.

By USING DDE, you can easily link data from a table in Paradox for Windows into a word processor.

To link data from a Paradox table into a word processor, follow these steps:

1. View the table in Paradox for Windows.

2. Choose Edit ¦ Copy (or press Ctrl+Ins) to copy data from the field you want to link to the Windows Clipboard. (See fig. 23.5.)

3. Move to the word processor document.

4. Choose either Edit ¦ Paste Link or Edit ¦ Paste Special and then Paste Link to insert the value into the word processor document. (The exact menu choices presented depend on the word processor you use. See figs. 23.6 and 23.7.)

Chapter 23 ■ Using DDE

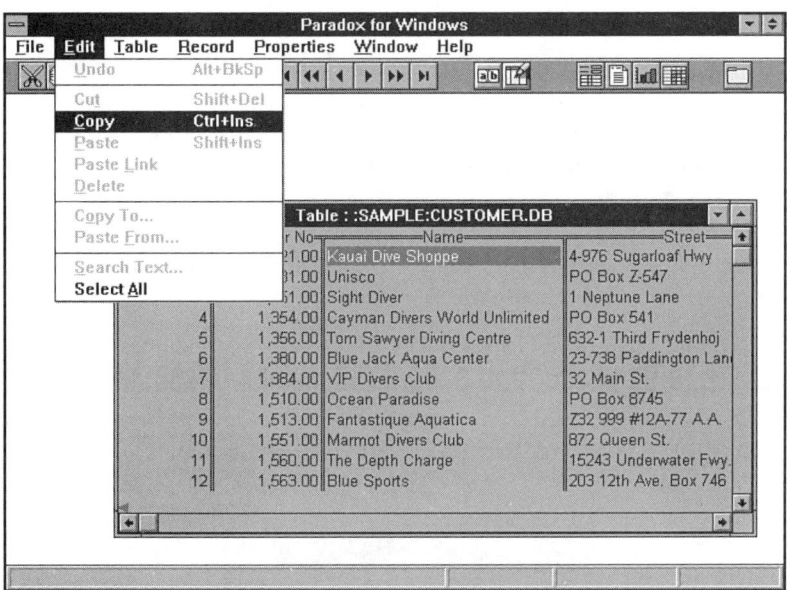

Figure 23.5. Copying a field from a Paradox table to the Clipboard by using the Edit ¦ Copy command.

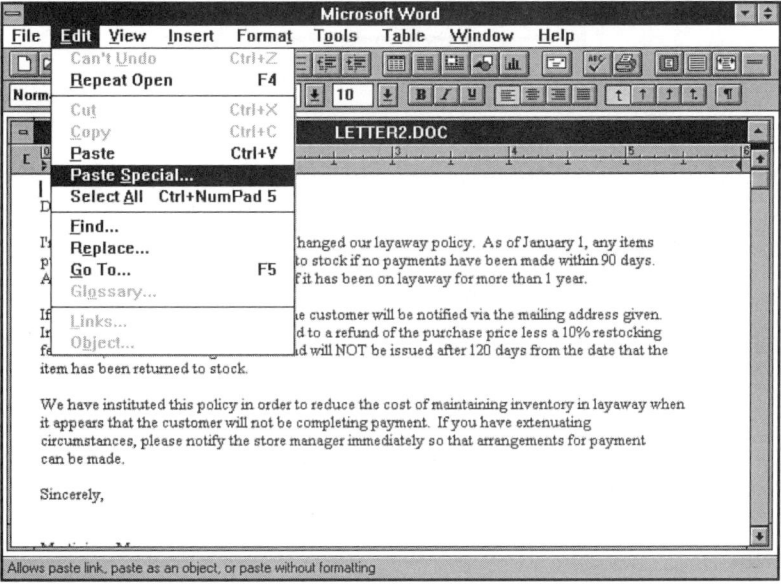

Figure 23.6. Pasting a Paradox DDE link into a word processor document by using the **E**dit Paste **S**pecial command.

477

(If your word processor does not feature either the Paste Link or the Paste Special menu option, the program does not provide DDE Client services and cannot be used in this manner.)

After completing these steps, you have a *live* link between your word processor and Paradox for Windows. To test the DDE link to determine whether it works, return to Paradox for Windows and then go to a different record in the table. If the DDE link is working, the values in the word processor are now updated to reflect the contents of the current record. (This process is easier to see if your program windows are arranged so that the word processor document and the Paradox for Windows table are both visible at the same time. A quick way to arrange the windows is to press Ctrl+Esc to access the Task List and then to choose the Tile button.)

Using ObjectPAL To Open and Print a Word Processing Document

Using the DDE Object, you can control the operation of many Windows Applications. If the application can be used as a DDE Server, you can use the DDE Object to initiate a conversation with the application and send it commands to be executed.

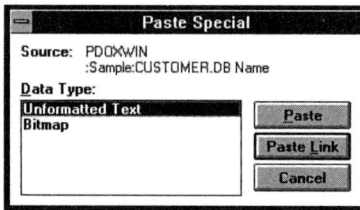

Figure 23.7. The Paste type dialog box.

To demonstrate this procedure, you can open a Word for Windows document with ObjectPAL and print it.

1. Create a new, blank form.

2. Put a button on the form (see fig. 23.8).

3. Edit the button's PushButton( ) method to include the following code:

```
var
   myDDE DDE
endvar
if myDDE.open("WINWORD","C:\\WINWORD\\LETTER2") then
   myDDE.execute("[FilePrintDefault]")
   myDDE.execute("[FileExit]")
   myDDE.close()
endif
```

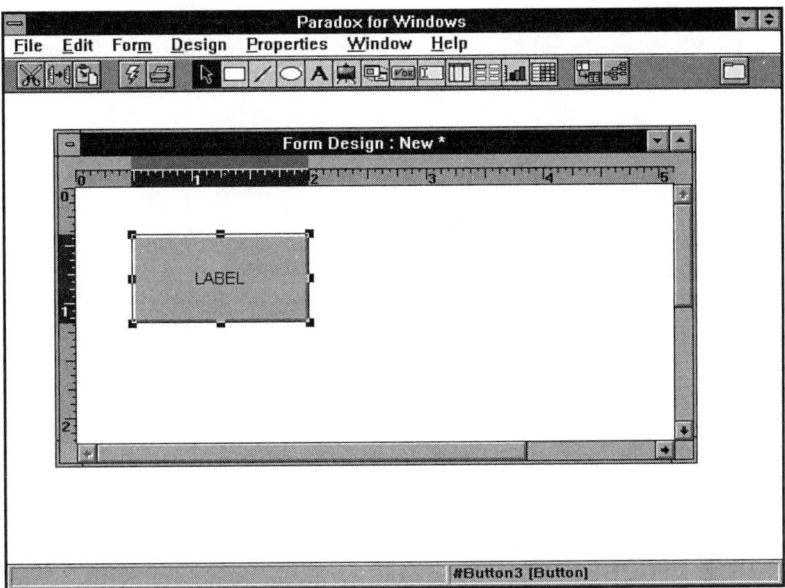

Figure 23.8. A pushbutton with DDE code.

When pushing the button, Word for Windows is executed, and the C:\\WINWORD\\LETTER2.DOC file is opened. The [FilePrintDefault] command prints the document by using the default printer setup.

Word for Windows has hundreds of commands that you can use from Paradox for Windows. Just think of many the possibilities you have to control other applications as well!

Integrating with a Spreadsheet

Companies also commonly use spreadsheets. In fact, the spreadsheet is given the credit for popularizing the use of the personal computer. With the power of the latest generation of spreadsheets such as Quattro Pro for Windows, Lotus 1-2-3, and Excel it isn't surprising to see that these products are often used to maintain lists. After all, the *2* in 1-2-3 represents the *database* part of *spreadsheet, database, graphics.*

Using Paradox for Windows with a spreadsheet can provide many benefits. Unlike most spreadsheets, Paradox for Windows permits multi-user access to data, relational Query by Example, form and reporting tools, and can handle large databases.

Because Paradox for Windows can handle large databases, it can be faster and easier to use QBE to summarize information for use in a spreadsheet. The QBE object can use a value from another application as selection criteria, and if the value is changed, the query can be automatically reexecuted by using the new value, which is accomplished by using DDE, and the application with the value to be used must therefore have DDE Server capability for this process to work.

Part V ■ Interoperability

This example will summarize the sales for a particular state, where the value for the state is in cell in a Quattro Pro for Windows spreadsheet. The resulting Answer table will be linked back to the spreadsheet by using DDE, demonstrating a two-way DDE link! Here are the steps to do this:

1. Move to the spreadsheet.

2. Choose Edit ¦ Copy (or Ctrl+Ins) from the cell in the you want to use for the query.

   The cell contains the State 'CA' (see fig. 23.9).

   You have created a QBE object using the Customer and Orders tables provided as a sample with Paradox for Windows. The tables were linked, using the Customer No field. The calculation "CALC SUM ALL" was placed in the Total Invoice field (see fig. 23.10). If you don't know how to use QBE to recreate this type of query, refer to chapter 16.

3. Move to the QBE object in Paradox for Windows.

4. Choose Edit ¦ Paste-Link to insert the value into the column used for selection.
   In this example, the column used is the State/Prov field (see fig. 23.11).

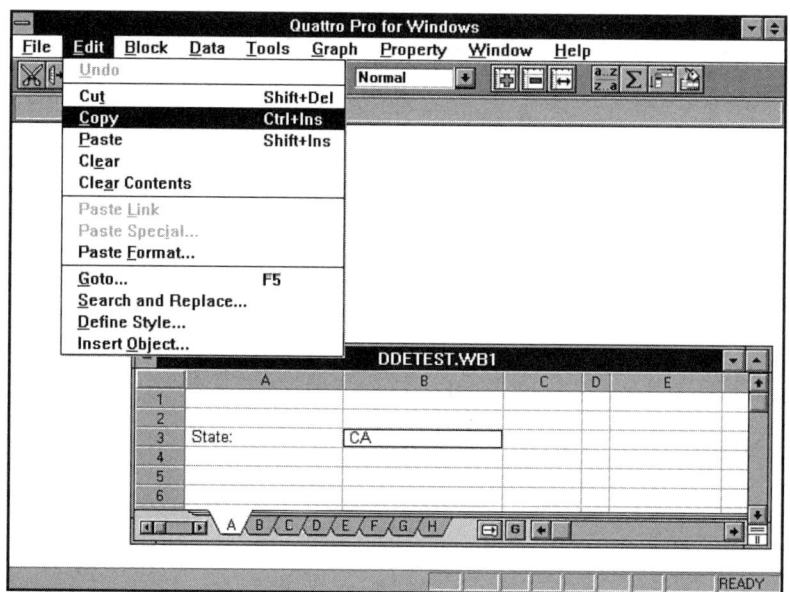

Figure 23.9. Creating a DDE link from a spreadsheet.

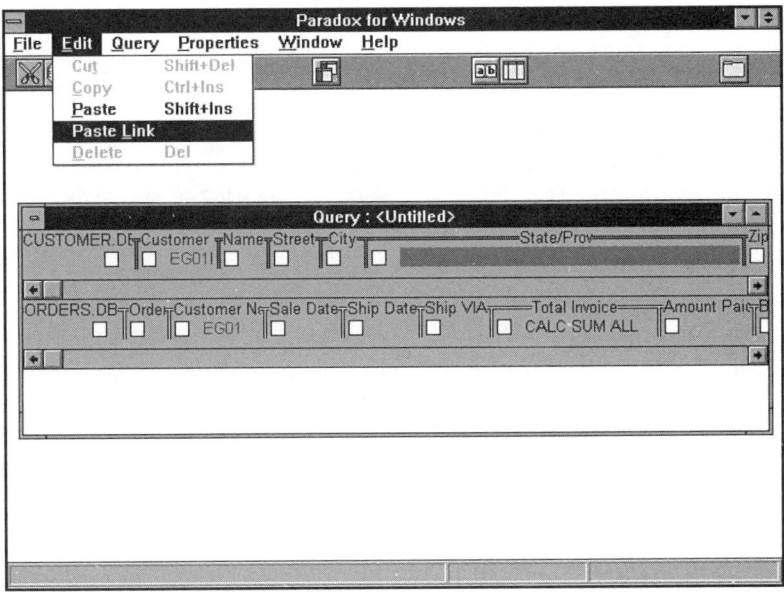

Figure 23.10. Pasting the spreadsheet link.

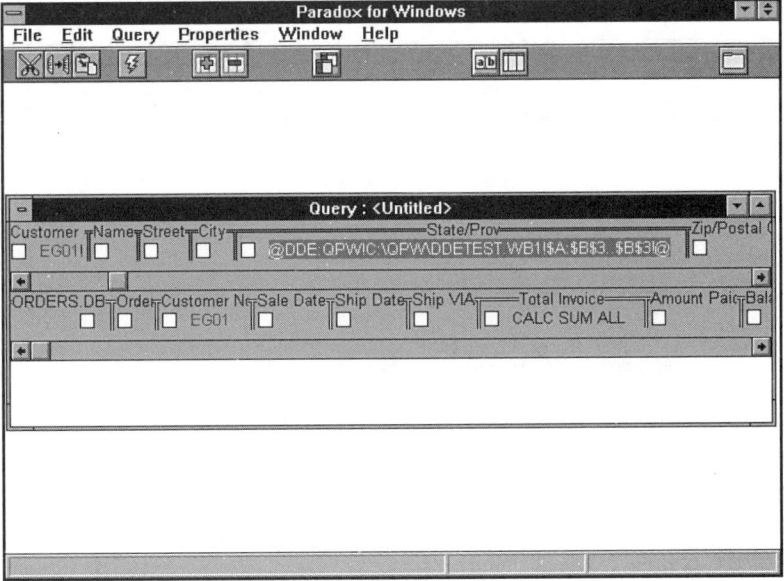

Figure 23.11. A DDE Link in a Paradox query.

Part V ■ Interoperability

If Paradox for Windows Paste-Link menu option is disabled (greyed out), then the spreadsheet doesn't have this type of DDE Server capability and can't be used in this manner.

The spreadsheet cell now should be linked to the QBE object. To test the DDE Link to see if it works, press F8 to run the query. If it is working, you should see a total reflecting the total of the invoices for customers in California, as depicted in figure 23.12. You can verify the value by removing the DDE link and then put a Check in the state column to see the total of the invoices for every state in the table.

The next step automatically reexecutes the query when the value changes.

5. Choose the Query ¦ Wait for DDE menu option (see fig. 23.13).

   Now when you change the spreadsheet value to HI (for Hawaii), the Query should display a different Answer table, as shown in figure 23.14.

   The next step is to have the answer table placed back into the spreadsheet.

6. Move to the Answer table.
7. Choose the Edit ¦ Select All menu selection (see fig. 23.15).
8. Choose Edit ¦ Copy to copy the entire contents of the table to the clipboard.
9. Move to the spreadsheet.
10. Paste-Link it into a clear area (see fig. 23.16).

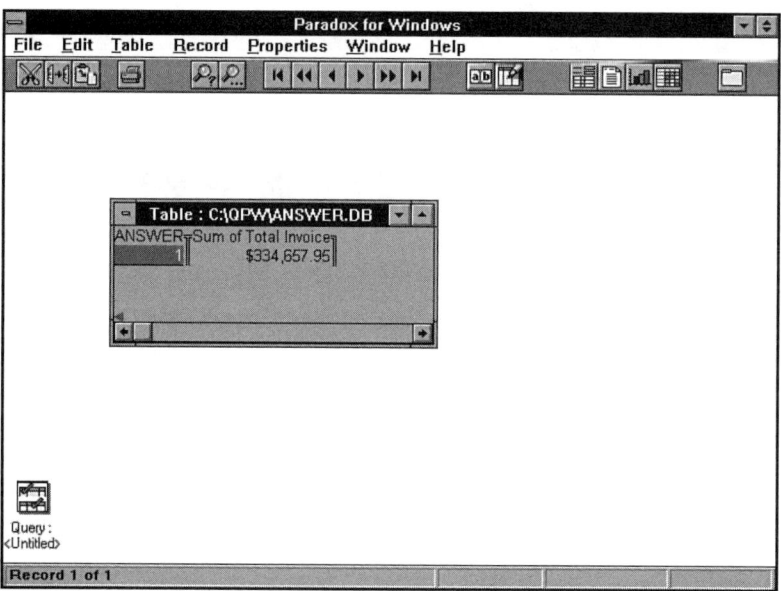

Figure 23.12. The DDE query results.

Chapter 23 ■ Using DDE

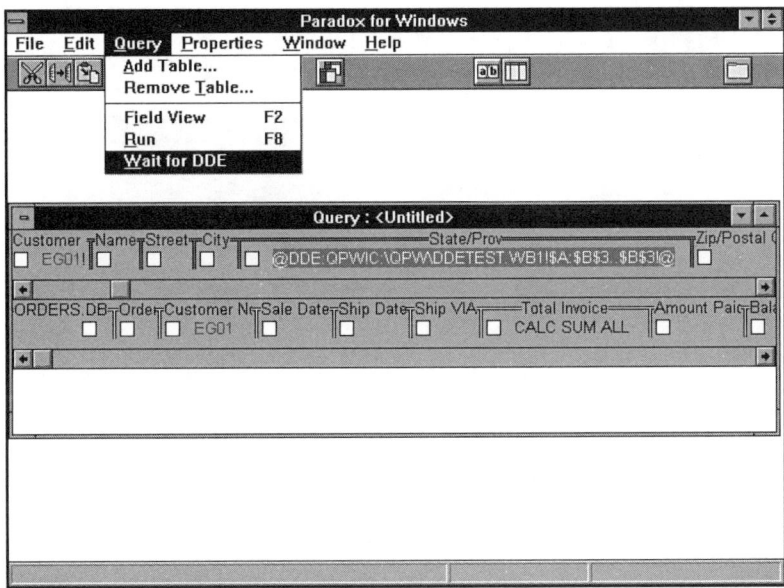

Figure 23.13. Wait for DDE menu option.

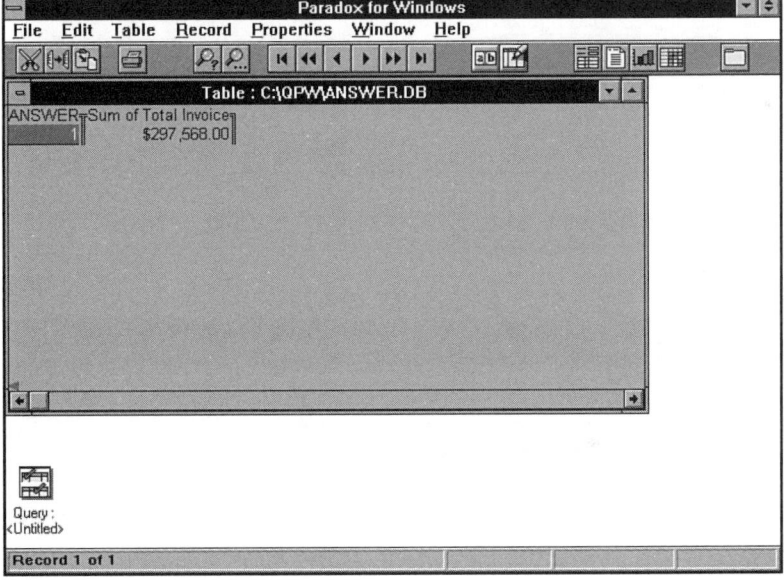

Figure 23.14. DDE Query results.

483

Part V ■ Interoperability

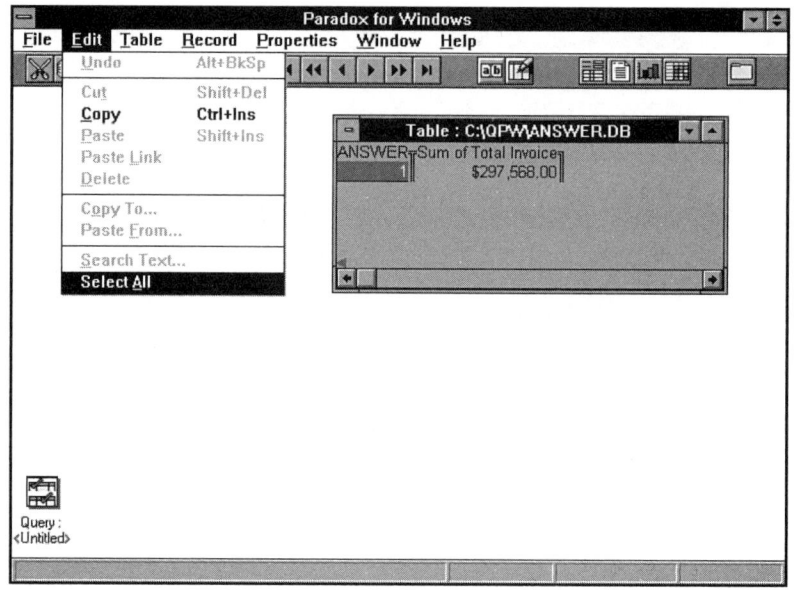

Figure 23.15. Selecting All from an Answer table.

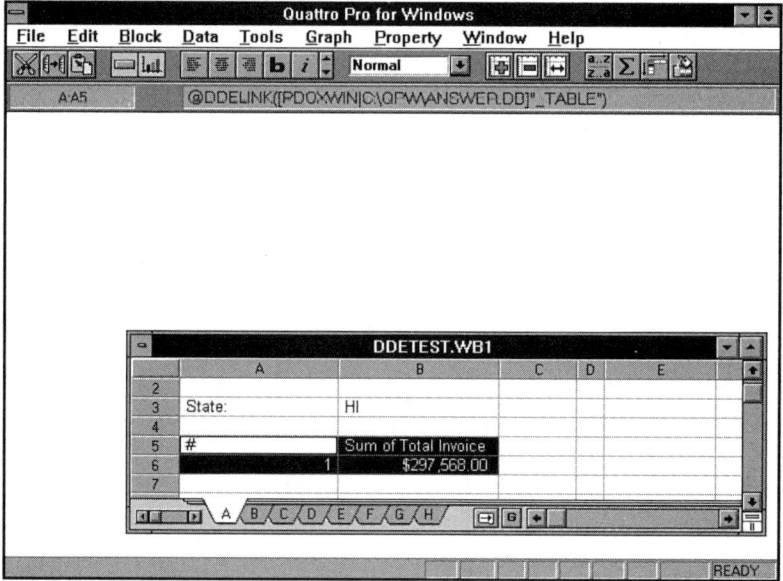

Figure 23.16. Pasting the DDE link in the spreadsheet.

When you change the cell's value now, the new Answer is displayed in the spreadsheet as a result. In the background, Paradox for Windows reexecuted the query and placed the results into the spreadsheet!

Note: If you want one value from the Answer table inserted into the spreadsheet, just move to the desired field before copying to the clipboard.

Summary

In this chapter, you have seen that you can use DDE to integrate Paradox for Windows with other applications in several ways. We demonstrated how to control a DDE Server application by using Paradox for Windows as a DDE Client. We were able to link data from a DDE Client application as selection criteria for QBE, which automatically reexecutes the query when the data changes. We linked the contents of a table into a DDE Client application, using Paradox for Windows as a DDE Server.

By using these DDE capabilities, we hope that you can take advantage of the many benefits in integrating your applications with the best Windows programs!

24
Using OLE

The object linking and embedding (OLE—pronounced "OH-lay") specification was created by Microsoft to enable a Windows application to create compound documents using objects from other applications. An OLE object could be a spreadsheet, word-processing document, bitmap, graph, sound, video, or any other type of object—even types not yet available. OLE uses the term *object* because it not only has data, but also unique functions (behavior). For example, an OLE object containing sound probably will have functions that play and edit other OLE objects in addition to the audio data.

OLE Servers and Clients

An application that has the capability of creating or editing an OLE object is an *OLE server*. An application that can use an OLE object from another application is an *OLE client*. Paradox for Windows can be used only as an OLE client, and not as an OLE server, which means that Paradox can use OLE objects but cannot create OLE objects for use by other applications. We hope that future versions of Paradox will provide OLE server capability.

Linking and Embedding an OLE Object

An OLE object can be either linked to an OLE client or embedded into it. Linking an OLE object doesn't place its data into the OLE client, only the path and other information required to find it. The actual contents of the object are stored in a file elsewhere. If the object is edited, the changes are reflected automatically in any OLE client in which the object has been linked.

When an OLE object is embedded, the related data is stored in the file of the OLE client document. If you edit the embedded object, the revised version is copied into the OLE client.

Whether an OLE object is embedded or linked, the name of the OLE server is stored internally with the object. Paradox for Windows allows an OLE object to be embedded but not linked.

Verbs

Each type of OLE object has a unique set of verbs available to the user. A verb performs some action on an object, such as edit or play, the meaning of which is determined by the OLE server. The OLE client can specify which verb to use, but the result is handled by the OLE server or its object handler. An *object handler* is a program which is usually a subset of the OLE server. An object handler is designed specifically to handle direct manipulation, display, or editing of an object without the need to load the OLE server.

When you double-click on an OLE object, the OLE client application selects its primary verb. This action might play a sound or video object, whereas a text or bitmap object might be edited. Often, an OLE object has only one verb defined for use.

Table 24.1 contains some verbs for a few common OLE servers.

Table 24.1. Verbs for common OLE servers.

Application	Type of object	Primary verb	Other verbs
Paintbrush	Bitmap	Edit	
Sound Recorder	Sound clip	Play	Edit
Word for Windows	Word-processing document	Edit	
Video for Windows	Video clip	Play	Edit
CorelDRAW!	Vector drawing	Edit	
CorelPAINT	Bitmap	Edit	

Packages

The Object Packager application in Windows 3.1 is an OLE server that enables you to create an OLE object containing one or more DOS files. Using the Object Packager, you can create an OLE object containing *any* file, not just objects created using an OLE server. Double-clicking on an OLE package calls the primary verb of the first object in the package. If the first file is not an OLE object, the file is edited using the application associated with it, as determined by the [Extensions] section in the WIN.INI file.

The Benefits of OLE in Paradox

There are many benefits to using an OLE object, including the following:

- When a new OLE object type becomes available, you can use it immediately.

- The OLE Object is easier to use than DDE because most of the work involved in using an OLE object is handled by the OLE server and the Windows OLE functions. To use DDE, the DDE client must have intimate knowledge of the DDE server and its data.

- Changes to an embedded OLE object are reflected automatically in the OLE client.

- An embedded OLE object is easier to use than other types of Binary Large Objects (BLOBS) because it incorporates behavior, not just data.

Paradox for Windows can use OLE objects in several ways:

- An OLE object is a field type that can be stored in a table and displayed using the Field UIObject (by selecting the Field tool in design mode).

- An OLE object can be directly embedded on a form or report using the OLE UIObject (by selecting the OLE tool in design mode).

- ObjectPAL has an OLE type to work with embedded OLE objects.

Using an OLE Field

The Paradox file format has a special OLE field, which enables you to embed an OLE object into a table. The OLE field type is a kind of BLOB field. A BLOB field enables you to store binary data and to move data in and out of the field. An OLE field is also stored in binary form; however, Paradox provides the additional ability to display its graphical representation and to launch the OLE server using the verbs available for it, both interactively and using ObjectPAL.

This means that it is usually much easier for users and developers to use an OLE field than a regular BLOB field, which requires you to use ObjectPAL in order to do anything with it. The only way to embed an OLE object into Paradox is to paste it from the Windows Clipboard. You must have an OLE server in order to copy an OLE object into Clipboard, or to use any of the verbs for it after it has been embedded. This is important to consider because you must know whether the user will have the applications necessary to work with the objects you embed. As described previously in this chapter, you can use the Object Packager to embed any file into an OLE field, not just objects created using an OLE Server.

In edit mode, double-clicking an OLE field launches the OLE server using the object's primary verb. You also can do this from ObjectPAL on the field by using the method action( ) with the constant EditLaunchServer as the parameter.

Because double-clicking an OLE object doesn't put it into Field View mode as with other types of fields, you must select Field View from the Table ¦ Field View menu, the SpeedBar, or F2 function key.

To access an OLE field's secondary verbs, clicking the right mouse button on the object displays a PopupMenu showing the verbs available for the OLE server. One exception is in Tableview, which requires you to be in Fieldview mode.

Don't be surprised if only one verb is displayed; it is quite common for an object to have only one verb. If there is more than one verb listed, the first one is the primary verb.

If the object's primary verb is Edit, double-clicking on the object displayed in the OLE field automatically loads the OLE server with the object prepared for editing. If the primary verb isn't Edit, you must select the Edit verb from the list of secondary verbs.

After you make changes to the object and save it, the new version is embedded into the field. When you are editing an OLE object from an OLE server, there are usually several new menu selections under the File menu—for example, Exit & Return or Update.

The OLE field has only two unique properties. The Horizontal Scroll Bar and the Vertical Scroll Bar properties enable you to use scroll bars to display hidden portions of the OLE object's graphic representation.

An OLE field also contains an Edit region, which has a Magnification property to reduce or enlarge the object's graphic display.

When you inspect an OLE Field, there are many other properties available as well. Figure 24.1 shows a sample of the properties displayed on an OLE field:

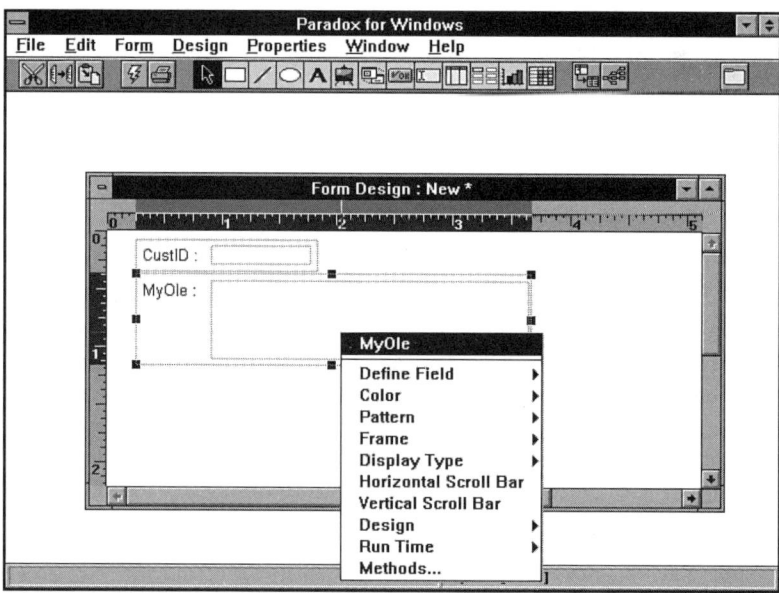

Figure 24.1. Properties of an OLE Field.

Using the OLE UIObject

In the Form and Report designers, an OLE tool is provided to create an OLE UIObject in which you can embed OLE objects. Unlike an OLE field, which embeds an OLE object into a table, the OLE UIObject is stored inside the form or report.

Instead of using the graphic tools, it is easier to use the OLE UIObject for graphical logos or other graphic elements on a Form or Report because it is simpler to edit and more flexible. However, the OLE UIObject is best used for fixed objects that will always be displayed on the form or report, such as a company logo.

For OLE objects that will change at runtime based on table contents or field position (such as video clips or sound clips in a context-sensitive help system), it is usually better to use the OLE field because it is easier to manipulate a table than an OLE UIObject. An OLE field is easier to use with other Forms and Reports because the OLE object is stored in a single location, which has the added benefit of using less disk space. Using a different OLE UIObject stores a separate copy of it each time it is used.

As with every tool provided in the Form and Report designers, the OLE tool has unique properties which you can display and modify using the Object Inspector by clicking the right mouse button.

Figure 24.2 shows a sample of the properties displayed on an OLE UIObject.

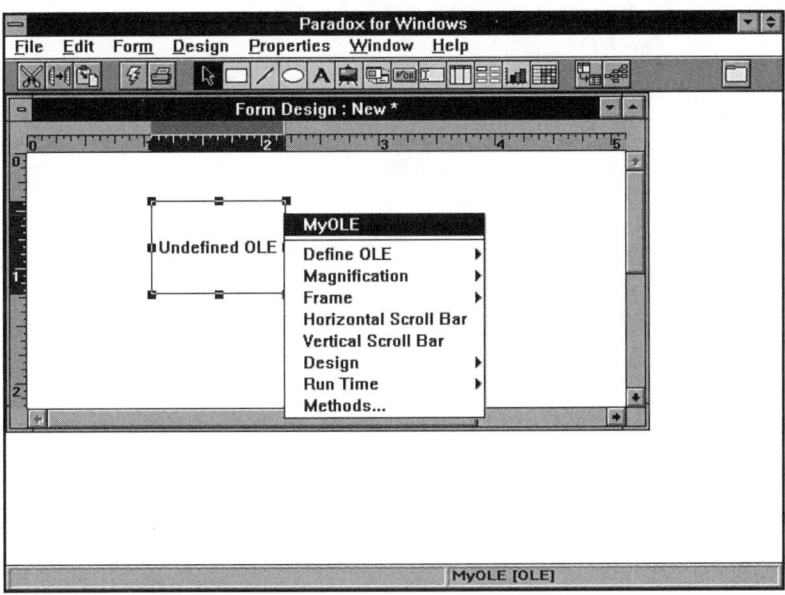

Figure 24.2. Properties of an OLE UIObject.

The Define OLE property is used to fill an OLE object using the Windows Clipboard. You use this property also to access the verbs provided by the OLE server. If you have an OLE object in the Windows Clipboard, choosing Define OLE displays a Paste function to put it into the OLE object on the form. After an OLE object has been defined, the name of the OLE server and its verbs is available for you to use.

Every OLE object contains a bitmap to visually represent it. For a non-graphic OLE object such as a sound clip or word processing document, the bitmap often is an icon that represents the type of object used. The Magnification property enables you to adjust the display of the bitmap by enlarging or reducing it. For most graphical OLE objects, you usually get a better result when you adjust the size of the object using the OLE server instead of using the Magnification property. Increasing the magnification of an OLE object does not improve the resolution or detail of the image.

From ObjectPAL, you can adjust the magnification property by setting it to one of the following constants: Magnify25, Magnify50, Magnify100, Magnify200, Magnify400, or MagnifyBestFit. You cannot adjust the magnification to other increments.

The Value property of the OLE UIObject is used to assign the object to an ObjectPAL OLE type variable. An OLE variable is used to manipulate the contents of an OLE object from ObjectPAL.

Using the OLE Type in ObjectPAL

The OLE type is used to create a variable in ObjectPAL to manipulate an OLE object, whether the OLE object was embedded in an OLE field or an OLE UIObject. There is a clear distinction between the OLE type and the OLE field and OLE UIObject. The OLE type in ObjectPAL is used to create a variable to work with an OLE object invisibly. The OLE UIObject and the OLE field are the objects placed on a Form or Report to visually display an OLE object.

Declaring an OLE Variable

You can declare an OLE variable as you do any other variable in ObjectPAL. Here is an example:

```
Var
     myOLE OLE
EndVar
```

OLE Methods

The OLE object has a number of methods for dealing with OLE objects.

The edit( ) method is used to launch the OLE server with the verb specified. The syntax for the edit( ) method is:

```
edit(const oleText String, const verb SmallInt) Logical
```

The edit( ) method returns TRUE if the OLE server was successfully launched, and FALSE if not. If the object was created using the Object Packager, edit( ) always returns TRUE if Object Packager is found, even though the application it attempts to launch for the first object isn't found. TRUE also will be returned even though an invalid verb is used. Because TRUE is returned in these situations, it is important to validate the values passed to the edit( ) method in addition to checking for a FALSE.

The *oleText* parameter is a string that is passed to the OLE server, which often displays it in the caption at the top of the window. You may want to use the name of your application for this parameter.

The *verb* parameter is a SmallInt that specifies the action to be performed by the OLE server. The meaning of the verb is determined by the OLE server.

The following are some examples of the edit( ) method:

```
; Use the Primary Verb
MyOLE.edit("My Application",0)
; Use the first Secondary Verb
MyOLE.edit("My Application",1)
; Use a DynArray to lookup the Verb using a String value
MyOLE.edit("",theVerbDynArray["&Play"])
```

The getServerName( ) method returns the name of the OLE server for the OLE object. Here is the syntax for the getServerName( ) method:

```
getServerName() String
```

The enumVerbs( ) method puts the verbs for an OLE object into a DynArray. The index values used to create the DynArray elements are strings defined by the OLE server to describe the verbs' actions. The SmallInt values put in the DynArray represent each verb that can be passed as the *verb* parameter to the edit( ) method.

```
enumVerbs(var verbs DynArray[] SmallInt) Logical
```

The enumVerbs( ) method returns TRUE if the OLE server is found, and FALSE otherwise.

The following is an example of the enumVerbs( ) method:

```
var
     anOLE      OLE
     theVerbDynArray DynArray[] SmallInt
     theVerbStrs Array[] String
     verbMenu PopUpMenu
     verbStr String
endvar
; Fill the anOLE variable using the OLE Field named MyOLE
anOLE = MyOLE.value
; Enumerate the verbs into a DynArray
anOLE.enumVerbs(theVerbDynArray)
; Put the Verb Descriptions into an Array
theVerbDynArray.getKeys(theVerbStrs)
; Create a PopUpMenu using the Verb Descriptions and show it
verbMenu.addArray(theVerbStrs)
verbStr = verbMenu.show()
; If a verb was selected
```

493

```
If verbStr<>"" Then
    ; Launch the OLE Server using the Verb Selected using
    ; the String selected as the key
    anOLE.edit("MyApplication",theVerbDynArray[verbStr])
EndIf
```

The canReadFromClipboard( ) method returns TRUE if an OLE object is in the Windows Clipboard. You should use this method prior to calling the readFromClipboard( ) method to prevent an error. You can also use this method to display or enable menu selections or other controls in your applications when an OLE object is available to be embedded.

```
canReadFromClipboard() Logical
```

The readFromClipboard method loads the OLE variable with an OLE object that is in the Windows Clipboard. TRUE is returned if the OLE object was successfully read from the Clipboard and placed into the OLE variable. The syntax of the readFromClipboard( ) method is:

```
readFromClipboard() Logical
```

The writeToClipboard( ) method copies an OLE object from an OLE variable into the Windows Clipboard. TRUE is returned if the contents of the variable are successfully placed into the Windows Clipboard. The syntax of the writeToClipboard( ) method is:

```
writeToClipboard() Logical
```

Tutorial

Now that we have defined OLE and the ObjectPAL variable type, you should be ready to see how OLE is used in practice. We show you by demonstrating in a step-by-step manner the various ways you can use OLE in your applications.

Embedding a Bitmap into an OLE Field

To embed a bitmap from Paintbrush into an OLE field in a Paradox table, perform the following steps:

1. Run Paintbrush (see fig. 24.3).
2. Open an existing bitmap or create a new one.
3. Select all or a portion of the bitmap (see fig. 24.4).
4. Copy the object to the Clipboard by selecting **C**opy from the **E**dit menu (see fig. 24.5).
5. Move to the OLE field in Paradox.
6. Go into Edit mode (if you're not editing already).
7. Choose **P**aste from the **E**dit menu to insert the OLE object from the Clipboard into the field (see fig. 24.6).

Chapter 24 ■ Using OLE

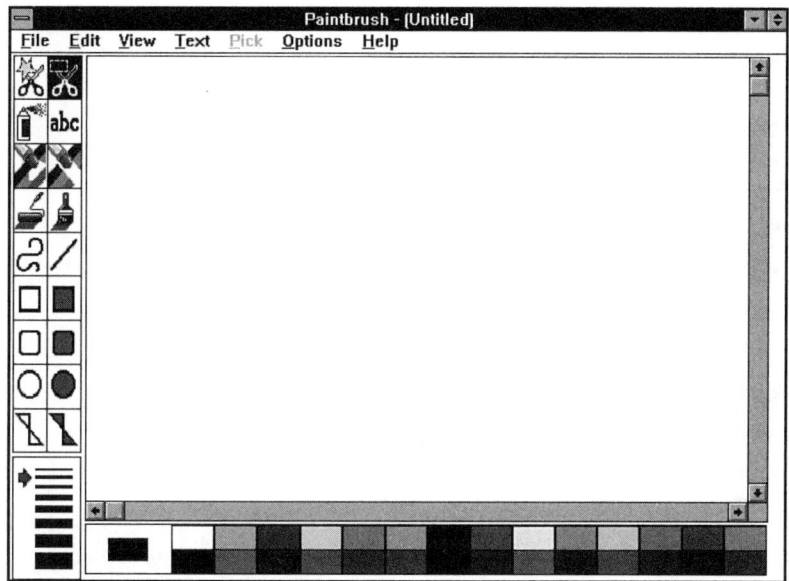

Figure 24.3. The Paintbrush screen at startup.

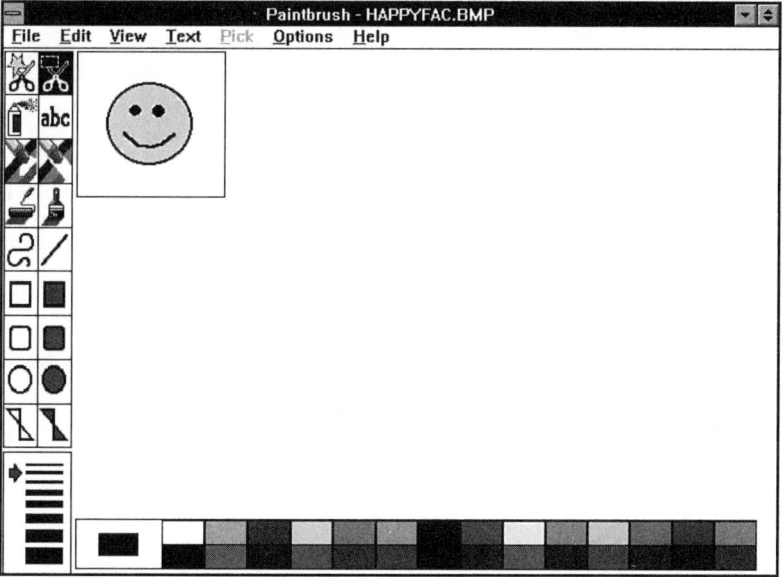

Figure 24.4. An image in Paintbrush.

495

Part V ■ Interoperability

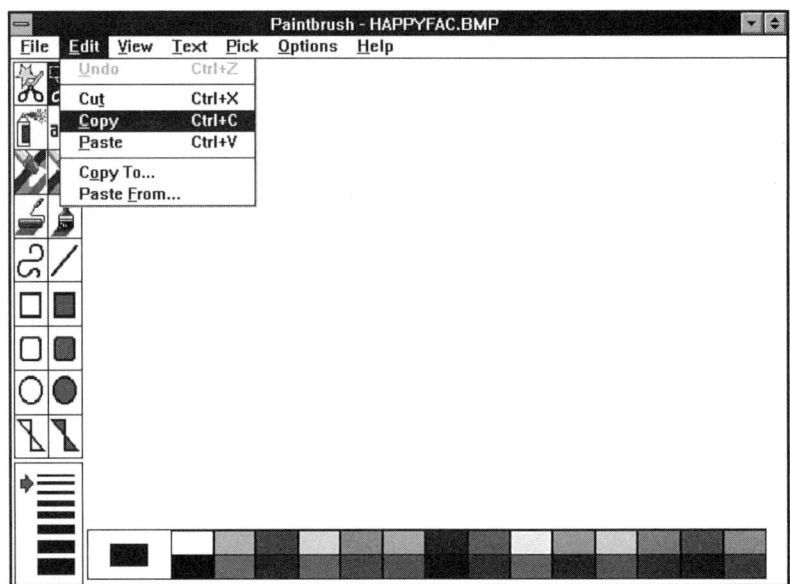

Figure 24.5. Selecting **C**opy from the **E**dit menu.

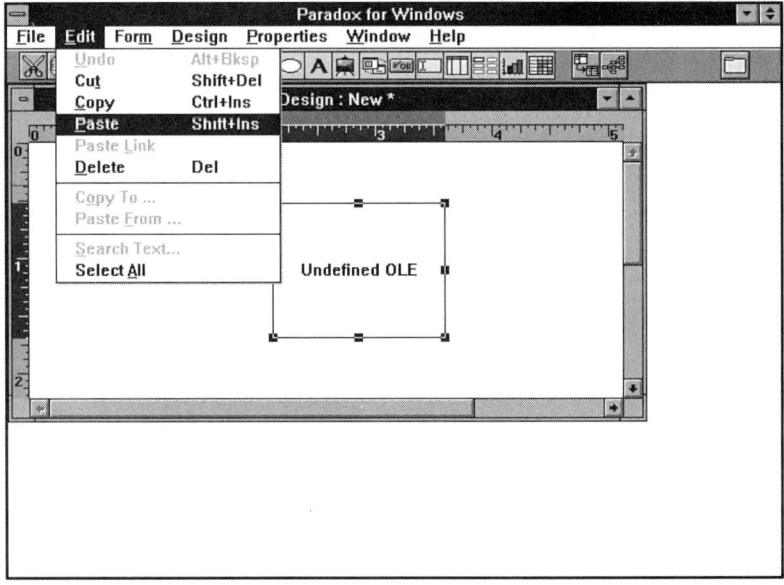

Figure 24.6. Embedding an OLE object by using Edit ¦ Paste.

Playing a Sound Clip Using the OLE Type Variable

After you place a sound clip into an OLE field, you can play the clip by placing it into an OLE type variable. The advantage is that you can play the sound clip without being in edit mode, which is required if you play it directly using the OLE field. To play a sound clip, follow these steps:

1. Create or open a form that contains an OLE field.

2. Move to a record that has a sound clip in the OLE field. Alternatively, you can create a new record and embed a new sound clip into it.

3. Create a button to play the sound clip.

4. Modify the button's pushButton( ) method to add the following code:

```
Var
      anOLE OLE
EndVar
anOLE = MyOLEField.value
anOLE.edit("My Application",0)
```

Playing a Video Clip Using the action() Method

If you attempt to use a Video Clip created with Video for Windows, you will find that using an OLE type variable to play an embedded OLE object from an OLE UIObject or OLE Field produces some unexpected results. If you attempt to play a Video Clip assigned to an OLE variable, it will be displayed in a random location on-screen because there isn't a fixed physical object that can be used to display it.

By using the action( ) method, you can play a Video Clip contained in an OLE field, which will be displayed within the rectangle of its Edit Region. You can accomplish this by passing the constant EditLaunchServer to the action( ) method. The following steps show how to do this:

1. Create or open a form that contains an OLE field.

2. Move to a record which has a Video Clip in the OLE field. Alternatively, you can create a new record and embed a new Video Clip into it.

3. Create a button to play the video clip.

4. Modify the Button's pushButton( ) method to add the following code:

```
; Must moveto the OLE Field for the action() to work
MyOLEField.moveTo()
If Not MyOLEField.IsEdit() Then
     MsgStop("Error","You must be in edit mode to play the OLE field")
Else
     MyOLEField.action(EditLaunchServer)
EndIf
```

Embedding a Windows Write Document Using the Object Packager

You can embed any file into an OLE Object by using the Object Packager in Windows 3.1. In this example, we embed a Windows Write document into an OLE field using the Object Packager. Follow these steps:

1. Run the Object Packager program.
2. Select **I**mport from the **F**ile menu.
3. Choose a file that has the extension .WRI.

   You should see the Windows Write icon displayed to the left in the Appearance window (see fig. 24.7). If not, you need to associate the .WRI file extension with Windows Write using the **A**ssociate option from the **F**ile menu in the File Manager, or by editing the [Extensions] section in your WIN.INI file.

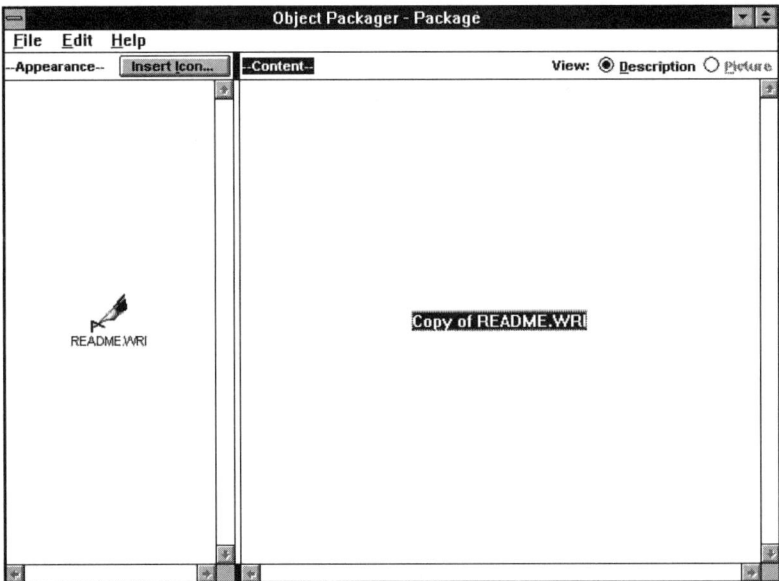

Figure 24.7. An object in the Object Packager.

4. Select Copy Pac**k**age from the **E**dit menu to copy the package to the Clipboard (see fig. 24.8).
5. Move to the OLE field in a Paradox table.
6. Go into edit mode.
7. Paste the Package, using **P**aste from the **E**dit menu (see fig. 24.9).

Chapter 24 ■ Using OLE

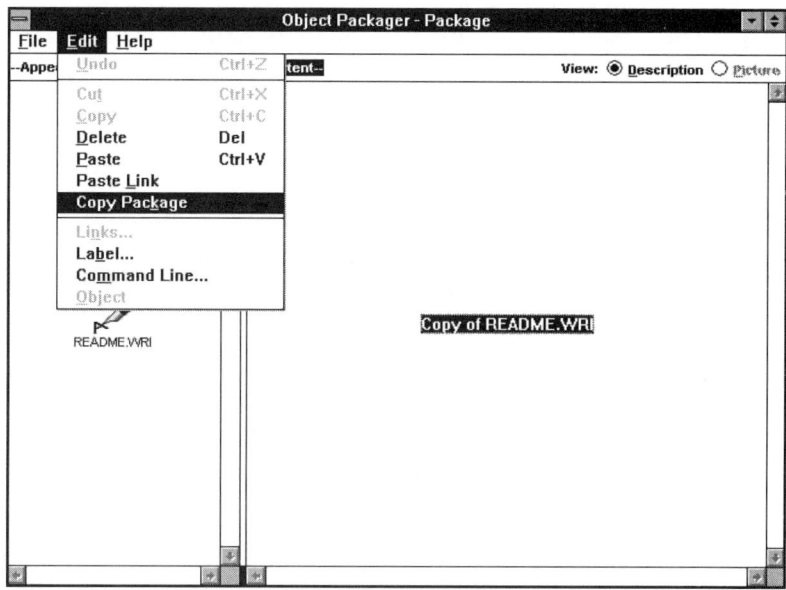

Figure 24.8. Selecting Copy Pac**k**age from the Edit menu.

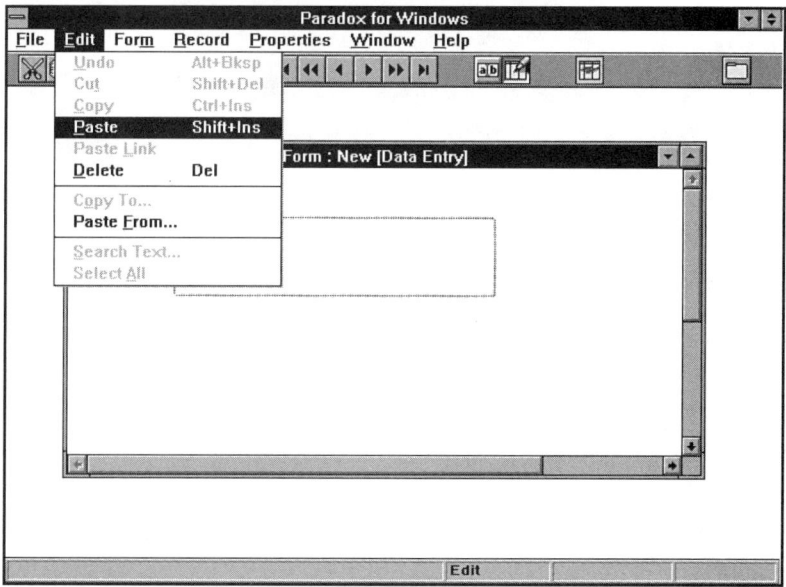

Figure 24.9. Embedding an OLE object into an OLE UIObject by using Edit ¦ Paste.

499

Embedding a CorelDRAW! Drawing into an OLE UIObject

It is very easy to embed a drawing from CorelDRAW! onto a Form or Report using the OLE UIObject. Just follow these steps:

1. Run CorelDRAW!.

2. Open an existing drawing or create a new one (see fig. 24.10).

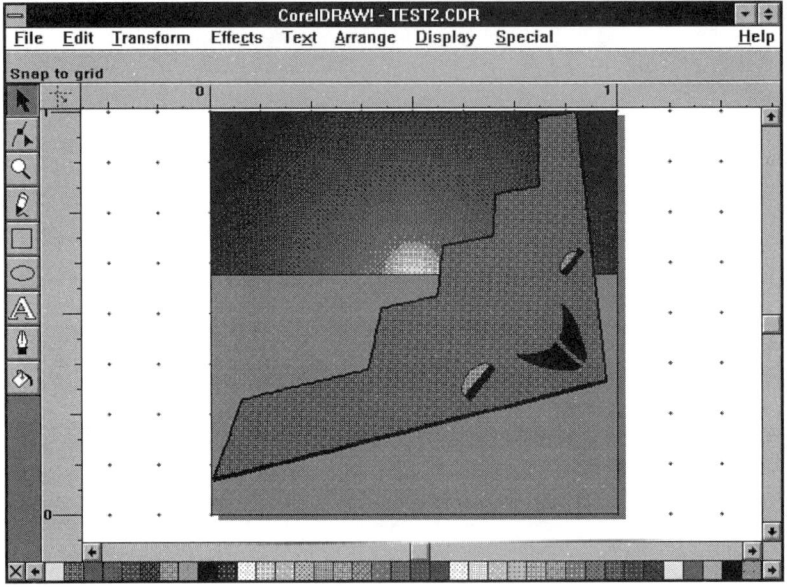

Figure 24.10. A CorelDRAW! drawing.

3. Select the objects to be embedded.

4. Copy the objects to the Clipboard using **C**opy from the **E**dit menu.

5. Move to a Form or Report in Paradox for Windows.

6. Select the OLE tool to place an OLE UIObject.

7. Drag the mouse to create the UIObject.

   Don't be concerned with the exact size of the UIObject; the object resizes anyway when you paste the OLE object.

8. Choose Paste from the Edit menu to embed the OLE object. Figure 24.11 shows the resultant embedded object.

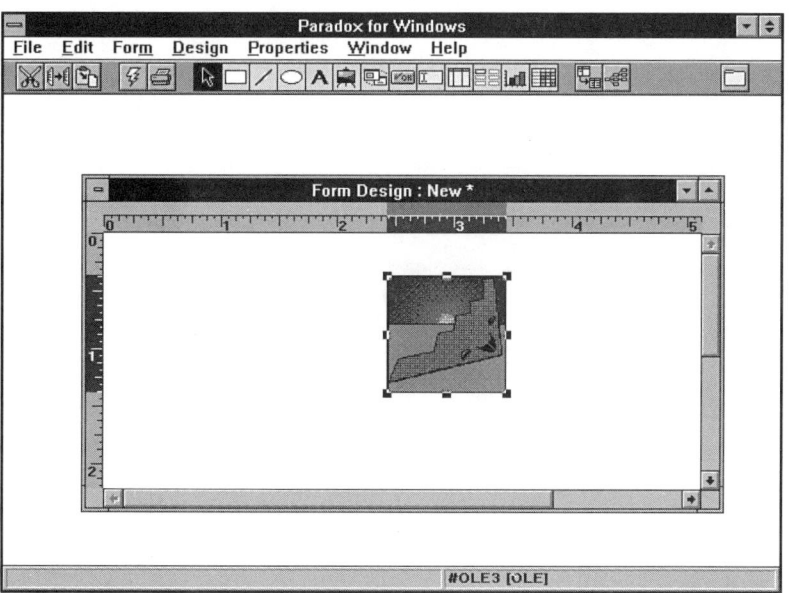

Figure 24.11. The embedded OLE object.

Summary

In this chapter, we have shown you how to use OLE with Paradox in several important ways. The OLE field type is always available when you use the Paradox file format. This availability enables you to embed an OLE object into a table. The OLE UIObject allows you to embed an OLE object directly on a Form or Report. You can use the OLE type variable in ObjectPAL to work with an OLE object. The Object Packager can create an OLE object that can embed any type of file into your applications, enabling you to automatically edit the file by launching another application.

25
Sharing Data with Other Applications

Sharing data with other applications falls into two categories: sharing data on a one-time or on an ongoing basis. Fortunately, Paradox has good interactive tools for sharing data with other applications. These tools make it easy to add or move data to and from Paradox on a one-time basis.

The bad news for programmers who need to share data on an ongoing basis under program control is that Paradox's Achilles' heel is programmatic control over exporting and importing data. No means exists under ObjectPAL to import and export tables the way interactive users can. This limitation hopefully will be addressed quickly in the next version of the product, because in the Paradox for DOS world, programmers took advantage of Paradox for DOS exporting tools, which both interactive user and programmer shared. In the new world of Windows applications, sharing data usually has a higher priority than was true in the past.

Interactive Export/Import Tools

Interactively, Paradox does nicely by supporting the following file formats for importing and exporting:

- Delimited Text
- Fixed Length Text
- Quattro, Quattro Pro for DOS, and Quattro Pro for Windows
- Lotus 2.x and 1.x
- Excel 3.0 and 4.0

To export a table, choose File | Utilities | Export from the menu. You see the dialog box in figure 25.1. To import a table, choose File | Utilities | Import from the menu. The dialog box in figure 25.2 appears.

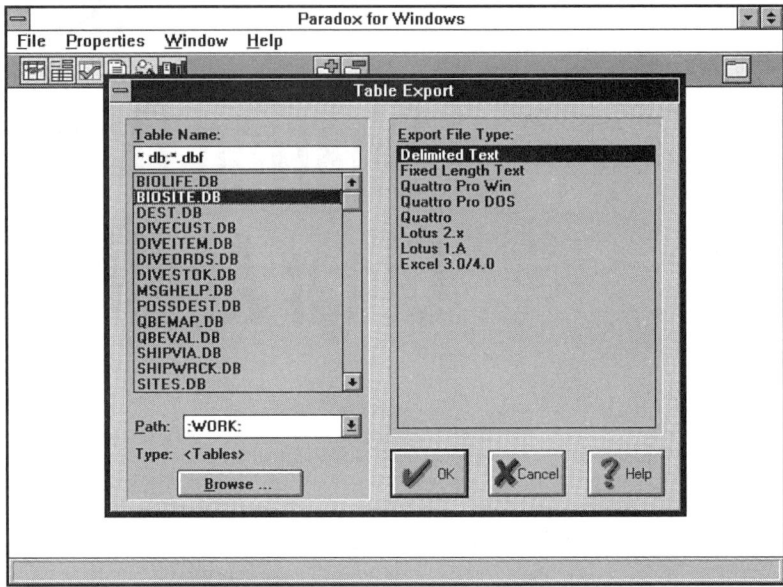

Figure 25.1. The Table Export dialog box.

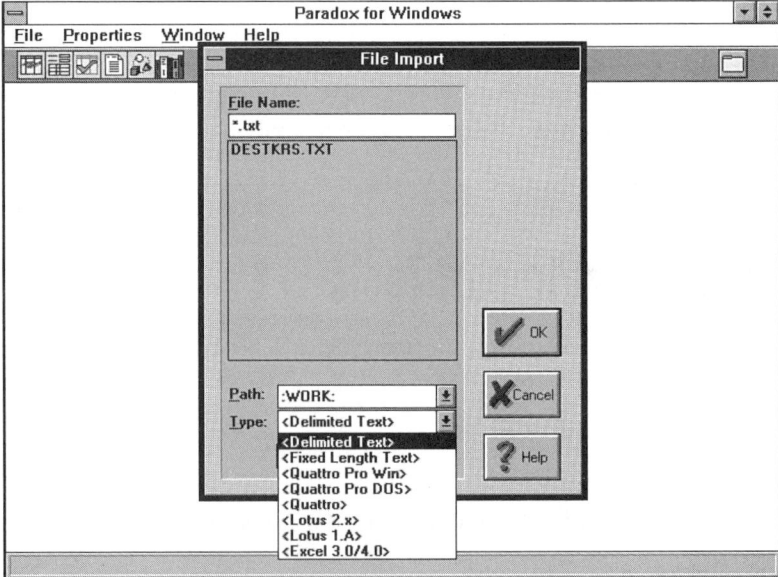

Figure 25.2. The File Import dialog box.

Delimited text files usually look like the following examples:

"VJK",8171,"Senior Consultant"

"MMN",8019,"Rehabilitation Specialist"

"STK",8327,"Programmer/Analyst"

"MRF",8762,"Actress"

"NTK",8410,"Manager, Financial Planning"

Alphanumeric fields usually are surrounded by double quotes, and fields are separated by commas. Each record is terminated with a CR/LF pair, just like standard text files. Interactively exporting or importing these files is a snap. You just choose Delimited Text from the export or import dialog box. The next dialog box has an options button where you can specify field separators and delimiters (see fig. 25.3).

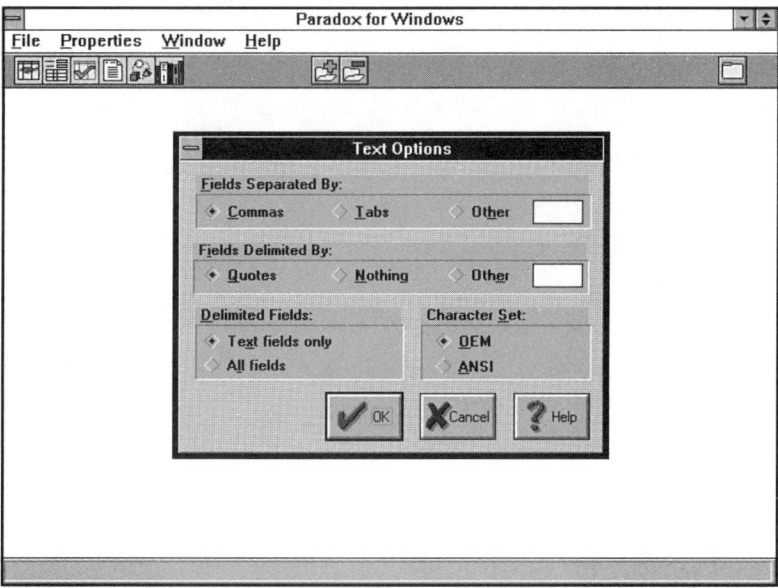

Figure 25.3. The delimited Text Options dialog box.

With this dialog box, you can choose between the comma, tab character, or other character that you can define as the field separator. You can choose between the double-quote character, your own defined delimiter character, or no field delimiter. Last, you can decide if all fields or only alphanumeric fields will have delimiters.

Fixed-length text files look like the following examples:

VJK 8171Senior Consultant

MMN 8019Rehabilitation Specialist

STK 8327Programmer/Analyst

MRF 8762Actress

NTK 8410Manager, Financial Planning

Each field occupies a certain number of characters in width. Each record is terminated with a CR/LF pair, like other text files. Importing and exporting these files also is easy. When you select a fixed-length import or export, you see the dialog box shown in figure 25.4.

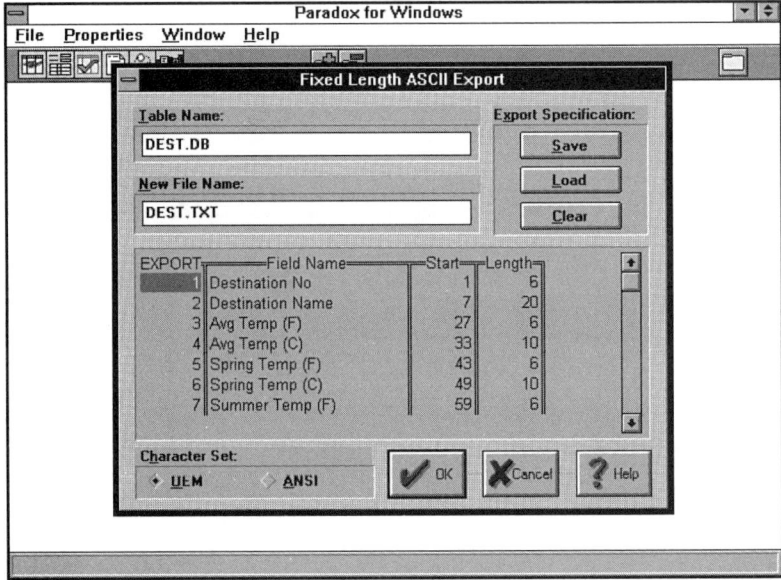

Figure 25.4. The Fixed Length Export specification dialog box.

This dialog box enables you to specify where each field should begin in the fixed-length record and how long it should be. Paradox stores this fixed-length export specification in the private directory in a table named EXPORT.DB. You can choose to save this export file to another table name and directory, or you can load another export specification table than you may have previously saved.

The spreadsheet file formats behave as you expect. If you want to bring a spreadsheet into Paradox, however, observe the following rules:

- Make sure that all numeric columns in the spreadsheet have the same data types. Spreadsheet users frequently place a space character in a cell or type **N/A** in a cell to denote that the value doesn't apply. When Paradox scans a spreadsheet before importing, if any non-numeric values are found in a column, Paradox assumes that the column is an alphanumeric field.

- Remove all excess blank lines, page breaks, and special page formatting from the spreadsheet—make it look like a database before it gets imported as one.

- The first line of the spreadsheet can be used optionally as field names rather than field values. The spreadsheet import dialog box (see fig. 25.5) enables you to specify this option, as well as others.

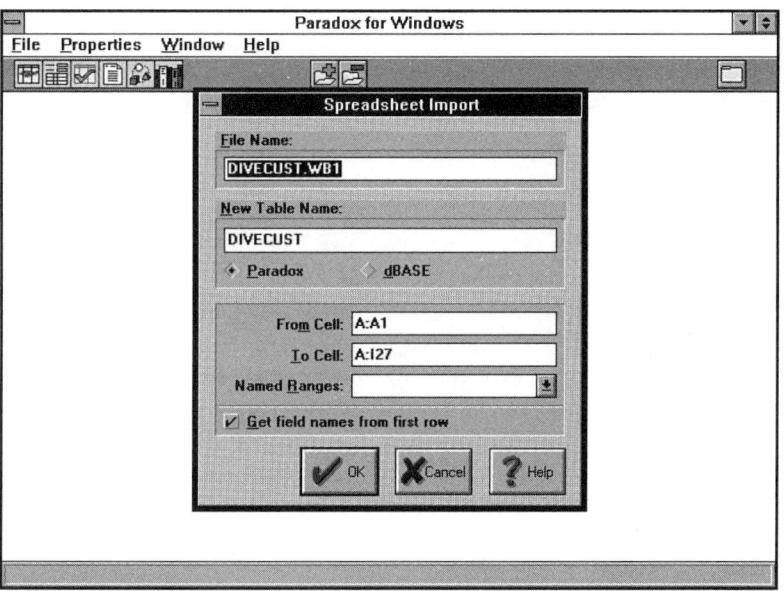

Figure 25.5. The Spreadsheet Import dialog box.

Exporting tables with memo, graphic, OLE, and BLOB fields can create problems. Paradox leaves off formatted memo, graphic, OLE, and BLOB fields because these fields cannot be converted easily to text fields. In addition, regular text memos also are not exported, because these memos can range in size from 0 bytes to megabytes of hard disk space.

Third-Party Export/Import Tools

If you need to get data in another format not supported by Paradox, you will want to explore third-party utilities. This is especially helpful when you need to either import data from or export it to a fixed-length text format and you need to do some more sophisticated date and number conversions. Two tools, Data Junction and Conduit, have been on the market for some time and both allow interactive and batch control over importing and exporting tables.

You gain several advantages in using a third-party import and export tool. First, these tools often provide conversion enhancements that are difficult to program yourself, such as several kinds of date formats, binary number conversion, and the capability of weeding out unneeded data, such as headers and footers in report print files. Second, these tools can handle project management issues that simplify the ongoing problems in tracking import and export jobs. Third, many of these third-party conversion tools export data into file formats not currently supported by Paradox.

Solutions to Problems with Sharing Data

The biggest problem for developers is importing and exporting Paradox tables under ObjectPAL control. Because—as of the first version—any control over this process is nonexistent, you can use several workarounds.

Using a TextStream Object

You can read and write text files by writing custom procedures or methods to do the job, which also is remarkably easy to do. Suppose that you had a text file that looked like the following lines:

"VJK",8171,"Senior Consultant","01/30/88"

"MMN",8019,"Rehabilitation Specialist","05/21/89"

"STK",8327,"Programmer/Analyst","10/03/88"

"MRF",8762,"Actress","03/22/90"

"NTK",8410,"Manager, Financial Planning","10/31/88"

Now, suppose that you want to place this text file in a table with the following structure:

Field	Data Type
Employee ID	A3*
Employee number	N
Title	A40
Hire date	D

The following code reads and converts such a delimited file to a table:

```
{----------------------------------------------------
This method will import an ASCII delimited file
into a table. The field delimiter is a " char and the
field separator is a , char
----------------------------------------------------}
method asciiDelimImport(      const asciiFile String,
                              const tblName String) Logical
var
    ts              TextStream              ; to read the text file
    tc              TCursor                 ; import table
    flds            Array[] String          ; fields copied to TCursor
    line,a,b,c      String                  ; temporary string variables
    x               SmallInt                ; loop counter variable
    res             Logical                 ; logical result variable
endvar
a.blank()
b.blank()
c.blank()
if not ts.open(asciiFile,"r") then      ; open the text file
    return false
endif
if not tc.open(tblName) then            ; open the import table
    return false
endif
if not tc.empty() then                  ; empty the import table
    return false
endif
if not tc.edit() then                   ; edit the import table
    return false
endif
while not ts.eof()                      ; read text file until EOF
    if ts.readLine(line) then           ; if we successfully read a line
        while not line.isblank()        ; parse the line until it is blank
            ; The above loop keeps chopping off fields at the right most
            ; end of the line. advMatch() works from right to left.
            ; The idea here is to find a field delimited with quotes
            ; at the right end of the string before looking for
            ; fields separated with commas. If the right-most field is
            ; separated with commas, then something should dangle at the end
            ; after this first advMatch()
            ; The advMatch() is decoded here:
            ; match any characters (in a),    (..)
            ; any spaces,                     [ ]*
            ; a comma,                        ,
            ; any spaces,                     [ ]*
            ; a quote char,                   \"
            ; any characters (in b),          (..)
            ; another quote char,             \"
            ; any spaces,                     [ ]*
            ; any characters (in c            (..)
            res = line.advMatch("(..)[ ]*,[ ]*\"(..)\"[ ]*(..)",a,b,c)
            ; if nothing matched or the final field c was a dangling
            ; comma separated field without quotes, then lop off the
            ; comma separated right most field
            if not res or c<>"" then
                ; lop off the comma separated right-most field
                res = line.advMatch("(..),(..)",a,b)
                ; if we can't lop off the right most field, then we
                ; have only one field, otherwise the prior statement
```

```
                        ; would have found a comma
                        if not res then
                            ; see if the field is surrounded by quotes
                            res = line.advMatch("\"(..)\"",b)
                            if not res then
                                ; the field has no quotes
                                b = line
                            endif
                        endif
                    endif
                    ; assign the line the a field
                    line = a
                    ; since we are working from last field in the record
                    ; to the first, insert the b field into the array
                    flds.insertFirst(b)

                endwhile

                tc.insertRecord()        ; insert a blank record
                tc = flds                ; copy the fields to the new record
                flds.empty()             ; empty the flds array
            endif
        endwhile
        tc.close()
        ts.close()
        return true
    endmmethod
```

The advMatch( ) method comes in handy for text processing, especially reading delimited text files. You can use this sample code with any table structure, regardless of how many fields it occupies.

Suppose that the text file looks like this:

```
VJK 8171Senior Consultant               01/30/88
MMN 8019Rehabilitation Specialist       05/21/89
STK 8327Programmer/Analyst              10/30/88
MRF 8762Actress                         03/22/90
NTK 8410Manager, Financial Planning     10/31/88
```

Importing this file into the same table as in the previous example is quite simple. All you need to do is figure out the location in the record where the fields begin and end, which is done by simply typing a ruler above one of the records:

```
0         1         2         3         4         5
1234567890123456789012345678901234567890123456789012345678
MMN 8019Rehabilitation Specialist       05/21/89
```

In this case, the fields have the following locations and lengths:

Field	Start	Length
Employee ID	1	3
Employee number	4	5
Title	9	30
Hire date	39	8

Chapter 25 ■ Sharing Data with Other Applications

The following code to import this table follows and takes three arguments: an ASCII file name, an export table name, and a markers array that holds the field starting positions and lengths. The markers array looks like the following code:

```
markers.grow(4)           ; enlarge the markers array
markers[1] = "1;3"        ; employee id field start, length
markers[2] = "4;5"        ; number field
markers[3] = "9;30"       ; title field
markers[4] = "39;8"       ; hire date field
```

To be able to pass this array to a method, however, you need to declare a type for the array and to declare the array by using the type. The following code shows type and var window declarations:

```
type
     ArrayType = Array[] String
endtype
var
     markers ArrayType
endvar
```

If the markers array is properly declared somewhere on the form, the following code can be placed in a library and called with the following syntax:

```
asciiFixedImport("Empfile.txt","Emp.db",markers)
```

The source code is listed in the following lines:

```
{------------------------------------------------------
This method will import an ASCII fixed record length
file into a table.
------------------------------------------------------}
method asciiFixedImport(    const asciiFile String,       {input file}
                            const tblName String,         {output table}
                            const markers arrayType)      {markers array}
                            Logical                       {return type}
var
     ts         TextStream       ; to read the text file
     tc         TCursor          ; import table
     markers,                    ; field start and end markers
     flds       Array[] String   ; fields copied to TCursor
     start,                      ; field start location
     length,                     ; field length
     line       String           ; line holder
     x          SmallInt         ; loop counter variable
endvar
if not ts.open(asciiFile,"r") then    ; open the text file
     return false
endif
if not tc.open(tblName) then          ; open the import table
     return false
endif
if not tc.empty() then                ; empty the import table
     return false
endif
if not tc.edit() then                 ; edit the import table
     return false
endif
```

511

```
        while not ts.eof()                  ; read text file until EOF
            if ts.readLine(line) then       ; if we successfully read a line

                ; for each entry in the markers array, starting with 1
                for x from 1 to markers.size()
                    ; get the start and length values
                    markers[x].match("..;..",start,length)
                    ; add the portion of the line to the field array
                    flds.addLast(line.substr(SmallInt(Start),SmallInt(Length)))
                endfor

                tc.insertRecord()           ; add a new record
                tc = fl ds                  ; copy the fields to the record
                flds.empty()                ; empty the fields array
            endif
        endwhile
        tc.close()
        ts.close()
        return true
        endmethod
```

This routine also is generic, and the only hard-coded piece of information is the markers array. This array can be stored easily in a table and read into an array at run time, allowing for a completely generic fixed-length record import.

Using Third-Party Batch Tools

Another option for importing and exporting data between Paradox and other applications under ObjectPAL control is to use a third-party import-and-export tool in batch mode. You can use the System execute( ) method to execute one of the following:

- an EXE or COM executable
- a BAT batch file
- a PIF file

Perhaps the best action to take is to create a PIF file for the third-party batch tool and set the display usage option to windowed, which allows you to display any message output in a window. You then have to make sure that the PIF file is in the Windows subdirectory, can be found in the path statement, or is properly referenced in the execute( ) method. The following line of code invokes the PIF file:

```
        execute("IMPORT.PIF")
```

Other Options

You have two other programming options for controlling importing and exporting under ObjectPAL: write your own DLL or purchase one and use the Windows macro recorder to control a second instance of Paradox loaded in the current Windows session.

Writing or purchasing an import/export DLL is perhaps the best way of extending the ObjectPAL environment. To write this kind of DLL, you need to be an experienced Windows programmer. To purchase one, you just need to know a little ObjectPAL. You can define the ObjectPAL method interface to any DLL method by declaring it in the form's uses window. We explained how to do this for using ObjectPAL methods in a library (Chapters 13 and 21). Unfortunately, as of this writing, we know of no such utility written expressly for Paradox tables.

Using the Windows Macro Recorder is a bit trickier. The macro recorder enables you to record keystrokes that manipulate other programs. The keystrokes can be saved in a file and played later. You can take advantage of this facility by executing it from one session of Paradox and having it control the menu choices in a second session of Paradox.

Working with Graphics

Graphics in Paradox tend to travel in one direction: into Paradox. Because Paradox is not a graphics program, you cannot design and manipulate graphic images. But because Paradox is a Windows database, you can paste graphic images into tables, forms, and reports very easily. All you need to do is use the clipboard or use Edit ¦ Paste ¦ From to bring the graphic file into the table, form, or report without using the clipboard.

You can place graphic objects (BMP, PCX, TIF, TGF, and EPS files) in tables, forms, and reports into Paradox without using the clipboard. Internally, Paradox converts each of these file formats into a BMP file.

In tables, Paradox stores graphic images in a Graphics field. This field differs from fields that hold textual information in that a graphics image can vary in size. Paradox stores these images in the .MB file, the same file that holds memo and formatted memo data. The .MB file is designed to handle varying length information.

If you are thinking of using Paradox as a repository for graphic images, you need to do some space planning to make sure that you have enough resources (hard disk space, computer memory, and processing speed) to hold and process the information. Some graphic images can take up a great deal of space. A PCX file, for example, can be anywhere from 50 to 100k in size. If you want to store a picture for each of 1000 employees in a database, you may need at least 100 megabytes of disk space just to hold the graphic images.

You have alternatives, however. Many developers use various compression utilities to reduce the stored size of each picture. This scheme requires some alteration in using graphics in Paradox. Because the graphic file is compressed, Paradox cannot display the graphic in compressed state. Also, because Paradox can't decipher a compressed graphic image, you have to store the graphic in a BLOB field rather than in a graphic field. You then need to compress the graphic file when you want to store it in a table and uncompress the file every time you want to view it.

This process can take extra processing time and slow down your application, but it can save you a lot of extra space, as much as 80 to 90 percent, which can reduce 100 megabytes of graphic storage to 10 megabytes.

Using Quattro Pro and Paradox

Paradox for Windows is a great addition to a suite of Windows application. The capability of cutting and pasting data between applications, although certainly an *ad-hoc* means of sharing data, cannot be underestimated. When you use Paradox for Windows with Quattro Pro for Windows, not only do Windows cut-and-paste facilities really shine, sharing data takes on a new meaning.

If you want to use the clipboard to share data between Quattro Pro and Paradox, just highlight a region of text from a table and copy the text to the clipboard (see fig. 25.6). You can click and drag your mouse to define the fields and rows to copy, or you can hold down the shift key and use the cursor control keys to highlight the region.

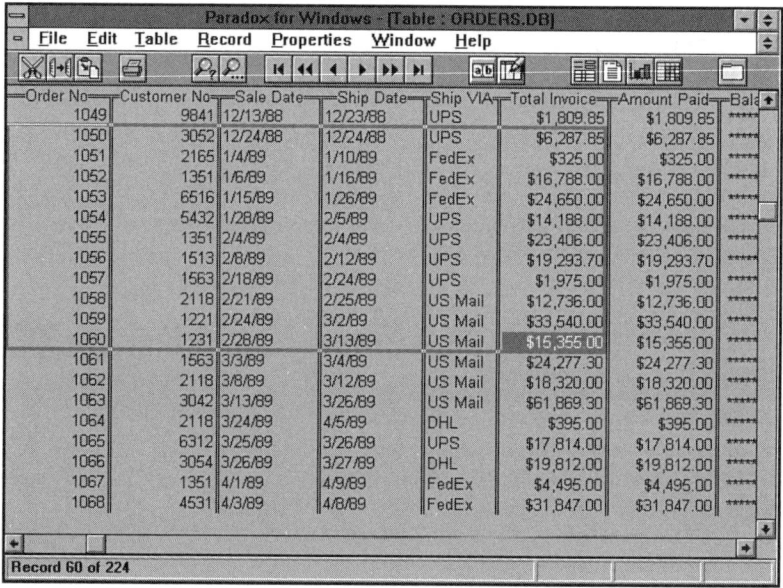

Figure 25.6. Copying a group of cells.

After the data is copied to the clipboard, you can use Edit ¦ Paste to place the data in the spreadsheet (see fig. 25.7).

The nice thing about using Quattro is that it formats the spreadsheet columns automatically, based on the table's column format. Even better, Quattro Pro for Windows comes bundled with a utility called Database Desktop. As you can see from figures 25.8 and 25.9, the Database Desktop is a stripped-down, scaled-back version of Paradox.

Chapter 25 ■ Sharing Data with Other Applications

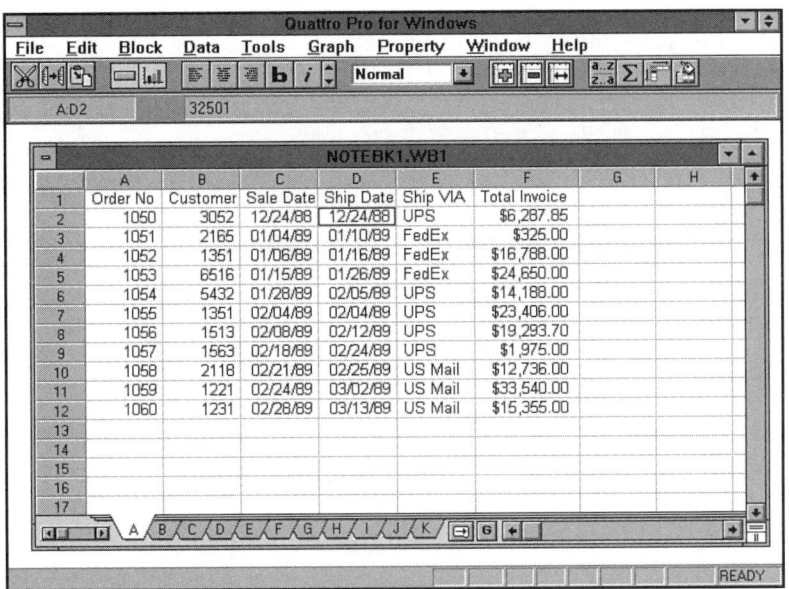

Figure 25.7. Data copied into Quattro Pro.

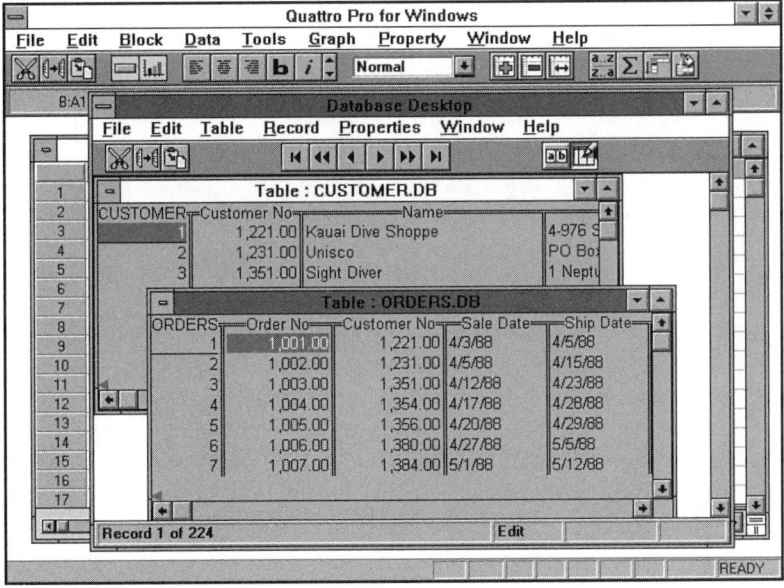

Figure 25.8. The Quattro Pro Database Desktop, editing tables.

515

Part V ■ Interoperability

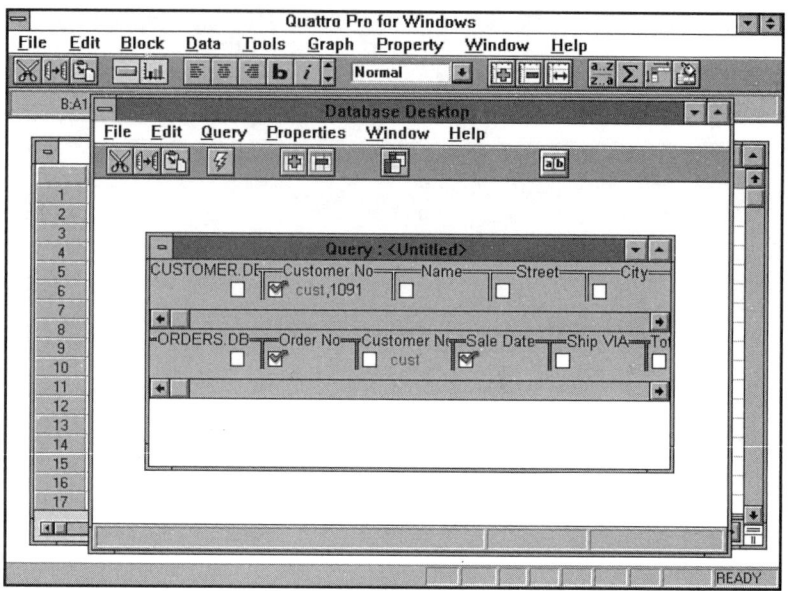

Figure 25.9. The Quattro Pro Database Desktop, querying tables.

With the Database Desktop, Quattro Pro users can edit and query Paradox tables without using Paradox. In addition, the queries and tables in the Database Desktop can be linked to the spreadsheet via DDE (see Chapter 23). The Database Desktop can act as a DDE server and a DDE client. In addition, Quattro Pro for Windows users can run a QBE file right from Quattro, without using the Database Desktop.

When you install Paradox for Windows and Quattro Pro for Windows, make sure that the ODAPI files are placed in the same directory as the Paradox for Windows ODAPI files.

Summary

When you add the import and export capabilities together with OLE and DDE, Paradox for Windows has many different ways to share data with other applications. Even though the ObjectPAL control over the importing and exporting of data is weak, the Text Stream class enables you to create your own ASCII import and export routines with a minimal amount of code.

26
IDAPI: What Is It?

As you use Paradox for Windows, you may come across the term IDAPI (or sometimes ODAPI) and then ask yourself, "What is this?"

IDAPI, which stands for Integrated Database Application Programming Interface, is a long-term plan that Borland is coordinating with several other computer companies—the major players are IBM, Novell, Inc., and WordPerfect Corporation. Before Borland joined hands with these other companies, it had a separate open database access plan called ODAPI. This is why this book often refers to the underlying data access engine in Paradox for Windows as the ODAPI engine.

The IDAPI goal is to give developers and users a simpler way to access different data on different platforms and in different file formats. Borland hopes this development will simplify the development of multi-platform database applications.

If the IDAPI plan were in place today, developers could write Paradox applications that accessed data in a variety of formats: from dBASE to Microsoft SQL Server to Oracle to Borland's Interbase server to DEC's RDB relational database product. The dream is to let developers access these disparate databases with minimal effort and changes in their applications.

Record-Oriented versus Set-Oriented Applications

The IDAPI plan divides database applications into two camps: record-oriented database applications such as Btrieve, Paradox, and dBASE; and set-oriented database applications such as Microsoft SQL Server, IBM's DB2, and other relational databases. Although end users may access either type of database application in similar ways, as in QBE or SQL (Structured Query Language), the underlying programmer's interface usually is either set-oriented or record-oriented.

Hopefully, IDAPI will be a piece of *middleware* that can bridge the gap between client-server database applications and local area-network database applications such as Paradox.

Most developers and industry pundits are somewhat skeptical of IDAPI's lofty goals, claiming that the IDAPI plan is nothing more than a hurried response to Microsoft's advances in the database market. After all, none of the vendors have produced an IDAPI product to date. Microsoft is pushing their form of database connectivity, called ODBC (for Open Database Connectivity), which is nearly as vaporous as the IDAPI plan. IDAPI, as it has been conceived so far, will be a superset of ODBC and will include ODBC protocols.

What does this mean for developers?

Depending on whether either plan becomes reality, quite a bit. One of the biggest stumbling blocks for Paradox (and any PC database application) developers is the inability to write applications which can access SQL servers and multiple platforms with the same functionality and productivity as applications that only access Paradox tables. Once vendors give developers the ability to write glitzy applications accessing multiple platforms inexpensively, the client-server marketplace will expand to encompass more potential customers and more developers.

In addition, should either plan gain corporate acceptance, there is a greater likelihood that products will be created to take advantage of that plan. In many ways, the IDAPI and ODBC plans are Borland's and Microsoft's way of trying to outmaneuver the other, while still trying to meet customers' demands for better connectivity between disparate database platforms.

Under the Hood

Now, take a closer look at the promise IDAPI holds.

Suppose you could create a Paradox for Windows form and have the form access a number of SQL relational database products, existing on any number of hardware platforms with the same code, the same event model, the same power that Paradox gives you in Paradox or dBASE tables?

You could perform multi-table queries linking data from three, four, or five platforms transparently. You could create a sophisticated form with some complex code peculiar to the Paradox event model and use the form against data on a different platform. You could start the application on a PC and move it to a local area network that uses Paradox tables. You then could move the data to a SQL Server running on a computer under UNIX. If the number of records and tables in the application grew to monstrous sizes, you could then move the application to a mainframe or some kind of super-server—all with little or no change in your application's code.

This power sounds too good to be true, and it may be. The IDAPI plan is ambitious because different database environments have different ways of doing the same thing. Right now, Paradox tables don't support a time data type, although several SQL servers do. Many SQL platforms provide support for triggers and stored procedures, which have no identical counterparts in Paradox.

Paradox tables are closely intertwined with the form's event model. Most SQL tables would have no idea how to talk to forms as fluently and efficiently as Paradox does. How would different servers communicate and cooperate to determine the most efficient way to perform a multi-platform database query? Building a relational query optimizer is quite a trick in just a single-platform environment.

In addition, even if multi-platform database access were a reality, it is likely that the developer still would need to make performance decisions rather than relying on the underlying database platforms to make the decisions. When you construct a query that accesses three tables—a table in Paradox, a table in an IBM mainframe relational database, and a table in a Sybase SQL server—which platform should perform the join? The IBM mainframe? The UNIX machine running Sybase's SQL server? Paradox?

The answer to this question depends on how many records are where, which machine can join data the fastest, and which network topology can ship records most efficiently across a wire. These questions are not easy to answer, especially for a piece of middleware that doesn't yet exist. Although an IDAPI plan certainly does allow *casual* access to data, high performance, multi-platform access still needs to be tailored to each database platform.

An IDAPI plan certainly can provide an additional layer that insulates an application from each database's API, but this plan is not a panacea.

Summary

If fulfilled, the IDAPI plan would provide numerous benefits by letting developers leverage their investment in PC application software (like Paradox) by enabling the developer to access more data on more platforms and by providing developers with a consistent programming interface across platforms. In turn, a cross-platform capability would enable the developer to create database applications that deal easily with a variety of data platforms. For the end user, this capability would be a real advantage.

Will you see any significant IDAPI products within the coming year? Almost assuredly, no. Will the IDAPI plan affect developers in the short run? Probably not. Do Paradox developers need to be concerned with what's happening with IDAPI? A little bit.

Are IDAPI or IDAPI-like plans the way of the future? If not, they should be. As soon as developers can get their hands on a robust piece of middleware that makes possible or greatly simplifies multi-platform database access, client-server may be able to take off. Until then, we can only hope.

27

Sound and Video

Paradox for Windows begs a big question: can you stuff your application full of sound and video, or does all this multimedia mumbo jumbo signify nothing?

One of the promises Windows holds is the capability of incorporating sound and video images in database applications. Because Paradox has the capability of displaying a variety of graphic formats and can hold graphics, binary objects, and OLE information in fields, you should be able to use it for sound and video as well.

This chapter explores some developer issues you need to confront if you want your application to use these new media.

Video

Of all the media that have potential, video certainly is the most prevalent. Video cameras are within the price range of just about any developer and most users as well. They have become extremely commonplace, and everyone knows a little about them. Using video images with Paradox is a natural extension of this curiosity.

Application Ideas for Video

Using video in applications falls into two basic categories: using still video images and using full-motion video images. Because the still video image is just a different form of the graphic image and full-motion video extends this camera metaphor, many application ideas come to mind:

1. Using a video camera to record employee's pictures for storage in a personnel table.
2. Using a video camera to record pictures of houses for a real-estate application.

3. Recording a piece of equipment, showing component parts or installation or implementation procedures.

4. Using video images in an athletic performance database to record optimal performance postures, techniques, or movements.

5. Using full-motion video in a training database to demonstrate a sequence of actions.

With this approach, the video camera can be used not only for full-motion photography, but anywhere you may use a traditional camera for still pictures.

Video images needn't be stored in Paradox tables to be used in conjunction with Paradox applications. The source for the video image may be a live feed from a video camera, or from a tape or CD-ROM with video image included. In addition, computer screens, computer artwork, and computer data may be outputted to a video recording device. Rather than using Paradox as a repository for video information, Paradox can be used to generate computer images which then are merged with video images to produce, for example, a training tape on how to use an application.

Some of these ideas seem a bit out of the realm of many traditional database applications, but with the advent of the graphical user interface, multimedia, and Windows, it is only a matter of time before developers find clever uses for the new technology.

Still Video Issues

To use still video images in a Paradox application, a great many issues must be examined, and most of these issues have nothing to do with Paradox. Most video capture cards require sufficient hardware, including the items in the following list:

- Six or more megabytes of memory (in some cases, no more than 15M. Many video cards use the 15M to 16M memory address area for a frame buffer).

- Plenty of hard disk space (50-100M or more, depending on the volume of images).

- A VGA card with a feature connector. (Most VGA cards have a feature connector, which is a connection at the top of the video card to which you can attach a cable. Occasionally, the connection is on the side of the card.)

- A VGA monitor.

- A video camera or some form of television input.

- Software that stores or *presents* the video image (here, the software is Paradox).

Installing a video card is easy, but getting it to work is not. Depending on the hardware configuration, you may encounter interrupt and base address conflicts, as well as strange interactions between your PC's VGA card and the video-TV card. The basic concepts behind these kinds of hardware are shown in the following list:

- Use the video-TV card's software to display and *freeze* the video image.
- Save the video image to a common graphic format, such as a BMP or PCX format.
- Bring the graphic image into a Paradox table or form.

Many problems exist with this approach. The graphic quality of the image quality usually is poorer than using a good 35mm camera to take a photo and then scanning the photo with a scanning device. Usually, the image quality is worse. Also, remember that using images taken from cable television or free television sources is illegal. You, however, can freely use your own video images.

Still video images occupy a fair amount of space—from 60K to 400K per image. If you have a database with 1,000 records that needs to store a 100K graphic image in each record, you need 100 megabytes just to hold the video images. You can get around the storage space problem by using a compression utility, which can reduce the space required to around 25M, which is certainly more manageable. Then, however, you have to compress and uncompress the image every time you want to write and view the image. Because Paradox can display only uncompressed graphic images in forms, you need to uncompress the graphic image, which takes a second or so, and then display the image in a graphic field on a form.

Perhaps the most important issue is that, while using a video-TV card may be a cheap alternative, getting the card and the software to work properly on a wide variety of machines is often difficult. For Paradox applications that need to distribute this sort of functionality across several hardware platforms, this variation can be a problem.

Still-Image Cameras

As an alternative to using a video camera for a still image, some camera and electronics manufacturers are now producing small, pocket-sized cameras that take a digital picture and store it in memory rather than on film. As of this writing, these cameras fall into the same price range as video cameras but are smaller and resemble film cameras.

These still-image cameras can hold around 25 pictures and usually let you store the files on a special-format floppy disk. The files then can be transferred to your computer through a special camera-to-PC cable.

This alternative may be much handier than using a video camera to capture still images.

Understanding Graphic File Formats

Most video-TV cards enable you to freeze—and then save to disk—the video image. Most cards also give you options on how to store the graphic file. A variety of graphic formats exist, some of which Paradox can store and display. All graphic file formats are either bit-map or vector files.

Bit-Map Formats

Bit maps store the graphic image as a series of dots, or pixels. Bit maps can be black and white, gray-scale, or color. In a black-and-white bit map, a pixel represents either a black dot or a white dot. In a gray-scale bit map, each pixel can represent one of 256 shades of gray. Color bit-map images can store a variety of colors, depending on how many bits are needed to represent the pixel. A 4-bit pixel can represent 16 colors, an 8-bit pixel can represent 256 colors, and a 24-bit pixel can represent 16.7 million colors. Of course, the more bits needed to represent the pixel, the bigger the file. A large 24-bit color bit map can take a megabyte or so of space. 24-bit color formats also require special hardware for viewing and editing. Standard VGA *cannot* be used with 24-bit color images.

Format	*Description*
BMP	The format Windows uses. Paradox also automatically converts other bit maps to this format in graphic fields. BMPs can be 4-, 8-, or 24-bit color or monochrome image files.
PCX	The PC Paintbrush format. Also one of the earliest file formats and is very popular and available on most PC software packages. PCX files can be 4- or 8-bit color, monochrome, and gray-scale.
EPS	The encapsulated PostScript format can contain a bit-map image, a vector file, or both. Bit maps in EPS files cannot be edited and usually take more space than other formats.
TIF	Tagged Image File can be black and white, gray-scale, and color from 4 to 24-bit. Also can include a compression scheme as part of the format, so compressed TIF files take less space than uncompressed files. Some applications cannot read compressed TIF files.
TGA	Short for Targa, a file format developed by TrueVision. Supports color formats up to 16-bit.
GIF	Graphics Interchange File is used by many shareware and public domain software packages and is used on CompuServe and other bulletin boards.
JPG	Short for the Joint Photographic Experts Group. This file format supports high compression ratios, up to 100:1, because of the *lossey* compression scheme in which some data is lost during compression. Compression programs like PKZIP use a lossless compress algorithm in which no data is lost during compression.

Vector Formats

Vector graphic files are composed of shapes that you can resize with no loss of image clarity. These files are inherently more complex than bit maps but because of their excellent resizeability, the vector graphic files are more useful. These files are always created by drawing and graphics programs.

Format	Description
DRW	The Micrografx Designer/Draw graphic file format.
CGM	The Computer Graphics Metafile format is one of the most popular vector graphic file formats. Many Windows applications accept CGM files.
EPS	The encapsulated PostScript format.
HPGL	(Hewlett-Packard Graphics Language) designed so that pen plotters can draw pictures.
PIC	The graphics format for Lotus 1-2-3 graphs.

Paradox for Windows can accept BMP, EPS, PCX, TIF, and GIF graphic file formats.

Full-Motion Video Issues

The database storage issues for full-motion video make still-image storage requirements seem positively trivial. Full-motion video is captured, usually, at 15 frames per second. A few seconds of video can consume your entire hard disk. In addition, 15 frames per second appears jerky, like old silent movies.

Microsoft's Video for Windows software, which is designed to capture full-motion video images from a VCR or a video camera, saves the images in an .AVI file format, where each frame captured can be edited and manipulated. Just a dozen frames can occupy more than a megabyte of space.

In addition, Windows just cannot keep up with the video display image. Full-screen, real-time full-motion video requires displaying 30 frames per second at 640 by 480 pixels, with 24 bits per pixel (to represent all the colors), which translates to over 27 megabytes per second of uncompressed data. The Microsoft AVI (for audio video interleave) compresses and stores the video image with the audio information in one file. Uncompressed, 30 seconds of full-motion color video would require more than 500M of storage space.

You can use one of several full-motion video boards to capture and store full-motion video. You then could store this video image in a Paradox table and, using either OLE or the Microsoft Media Player software, display the video images. With compression, the AVI file can get down to a few megabytes of data for several seconds.

In many ways, capturing full-motion video in a Paradox table is like a dog walking on hind legs. It's a wonder it can be done at all. The real question to ask about full-motion video: is the quality good enough to add value to an application?

As of today, we feel the answer is no, unless you are interested in spending far more than the $500 to $1,000 for lower-priced video cameras and video boards. When you jump to the $3,000 to $10,000 price range, the hardware quality improves substantially. So does the cost, however.

Part V ■ Interoperability

Sound

Adding sound to an application is fairly straightforward. Buy a sound card and microphone, and you're in business. The most important part of the puzzle is to use Paradox as a client application that invokes a sound player.

You can store the sound files (usually .WAV files) in a Paradox OLE field. By clicking on this field, your application can invoke a sound player. WAV files are smaller than full-motion video files—usually between 10-100K in size for sound bites that run from one to five seconds. Longer sound bites cost more disk space.

To bring a sound file into a Paradox table, take the following steps:

1. Create a table with an OLE field.
2. Edit a WAV file in Sound Recorder (see fig. 27.1).
3. Use Edit ¦ Copy to copy the WAV file to the clipboard.
4. Edit the Paradox table.
5. Move to the OLE field and use Edit ¦ Paste to paste the WAV file in the OLE field.
6. Double-click the OLE field or press Shift+F2 to play the sound (see fig. 27.2).

The sound file then plays.

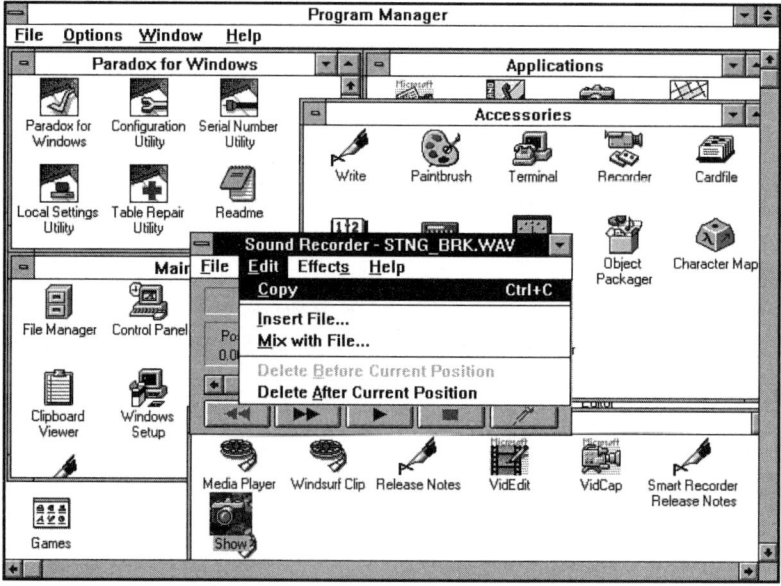

Figure 27.1. The Windows Sound Recorder.

526

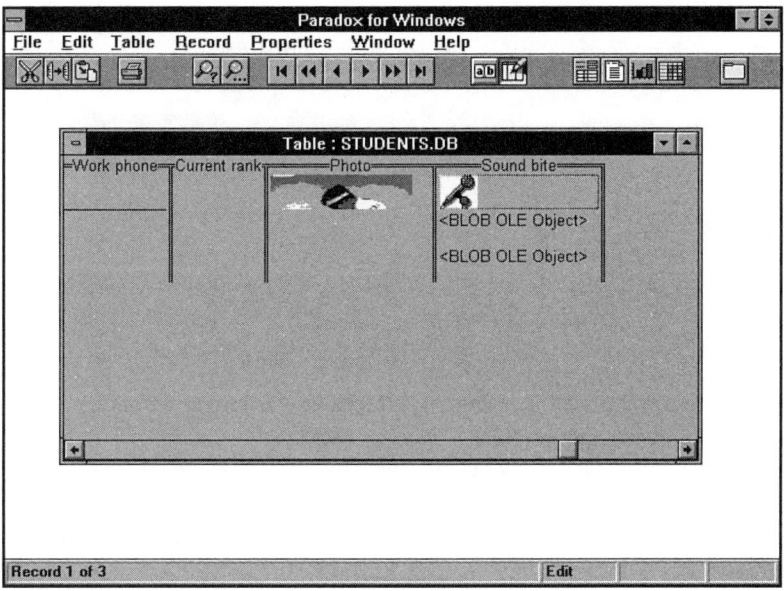

Figure 27.2. A Paradox table with the Windows sound file embedded.

For most business applications, sound falls into two categories: human speech or special effects. Training applications in which a human voice is added to the application is now certainly possible with Paradox for Windows. Also, because many of the sound boards are achieving better quality sound, using sound is practical.

Sound annotations can be used in help systems (to provide a friendly hint) or added to mail messages, letters, and other documents that can be stored within Paradox tables. You also can use Paradox to store messages, speeches, synthesized music, and other audio objects, but again you can run into a space problem. One minute of sound occupies about a megabyte of space.

An Example: Using Still Video Images

Now that we have explained the down side of using video images with Paradox, we will demonstrate an example. Still video images seem like such a natural extension of the graphic image. For this reason, we have used several different still video cards (all under $400 each) to process video images.

The approach each card takes is fairly similar—most attach to your VGA card and force you to attach your monitor cable to a VGA port on their card. Some of these cards use the memory address range between 15M and 16M to store and process the video frame buffer. This frame buffer then is mapped to your monitor, where the image can be viewed. In fact, if you try to print your screen or capture your video screen with screen-shot software, you see either a big black square or magenta square where the video image should be because the video card doesn't store the full-motion video image in the VGA card's video buffer. The screen shot software cannot access where the video image is stored.

Usually, this part of the package works just fine, provided you don't have any hardware interrupt or base address conflicts. Where these cards fall down is in capturing a video image to a file. Several of these cards produced unusable graphic images. If you plan on purchasing a video-TV card, make sure that the vendor has a no-questions, money-back policy. You probably will be back, returning or exchanging your video-TV card.

Some of these cards come with TV tuners built-in. All you have to do is supply a cable feed or an antenna. Some cards allow multiple video inputs, some cards allow audio inputs at the same time, and other cards don't. Intel, for example, produces the Intel Smart Video Recorder, which doesn't require a video card with a feature connector and uses a microprocessor to handle the video image so that the CPU can relax a little. This card doesn't have an audio input but instead uses the Microsoft Video for Windows program to capture and edit video images. The Microsoft Video for Windows program can take advantage of several sound cards, if you have one installed. Unlike the other cards, this card displays all video images to the regular VGA screen buffer, so the images can be captured.

Figure 27.3 displays a still video picture from a martial-arts database application developed for a client. We will let you judge the quality of the image.

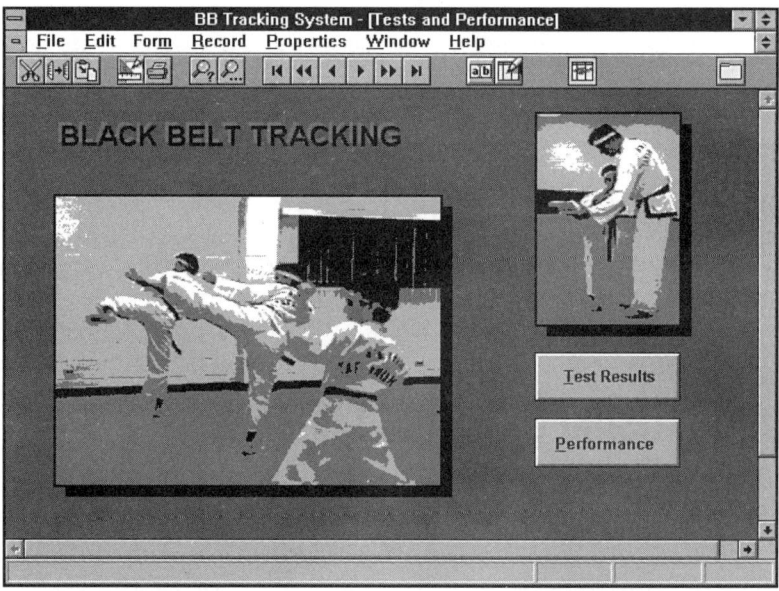

Figure 27.3. A video frame on a form.

Summary

Paradox can easily accommodate full- and still-motion video and sound in tables. It's very easy to do, thanks to Windows OLE and DDE capabilities. However, the road is fraught with hardware difficulties, storage space requirements, and image quality problems.

Using sound and video in Paradox is a whole new frontier in database applications. In many ways, the software is willing, but the inexpensive hardware available today is weak and struggles to perform quickly and precisely what the software wants. Nonetheless, if you brave the elements in this frontier, you may find yourself creating applications like no other. Besides, with the rate of technological advances, high-quality sound and video may be closer than you think.

28

The Multiple Document Interface (MDI)

The Multiple Document Interface (MDI) is a specification and set of functions created by Microsoft to manage multiple windows *within* an application. The most apparent implementation of MDI is in Program Manager and File Manager, in which it is used internally for the management of the windows displayed in each application. The interaction with multiple windows and menus was carefully designed to maintain a consistent and easy user interface. Although MDI's use is common, reference to the term MDI is intentionally avoided in many cases because it would only serve to confuse users. For Windows programmers, however, understanding MDI and how to use it in an application is essential.

Because Paradox for Windows is an MDI application, Paradox developers also must understand MDI and how an application can use it. Fortunately, all the tools you need are provided to easily create an MDI application using ObjectPAL.

The Application Window

The main application window is the primary component of a Windows application and contains all the components used to work with the application, such as menus, button bars, toolbars, and so on. After launching Paradox for Windows, the application window displays a menu and a SpeedBar for you to begin working with objects. These components are not unique to an MDI application, however, and can be used in any Windows application.

The special nature of MDI is that any window displayed in the application is confined to a particular region within the window known as the workspace. Additional features also are added to the application's menu to let the user arrange and move to the windows in the workspace. You also should be aware that the workspace is also known as the MDI frame or the Client Frame in some cases, but each term refers to the same thing.

By containing all an application's windows within the workspace, MDI applications reduce clutter and confusion because this clear visual boundary is provided between applications. Without this boundary, distinguishing between the various windows used by each application would be difficult.

Because Paradox for Windows is an MDI application, all that you do in Paradox for Windows is displayed within workspace. In an MDI application, the application window—such as the example shown in figure 28.1—can be resized or moved and any windows contained in the workspace will be clipped rather than being displayed outside of it. In this case, the workspace displays no scroll bars, which are used to see the parts of windows hidden from view.

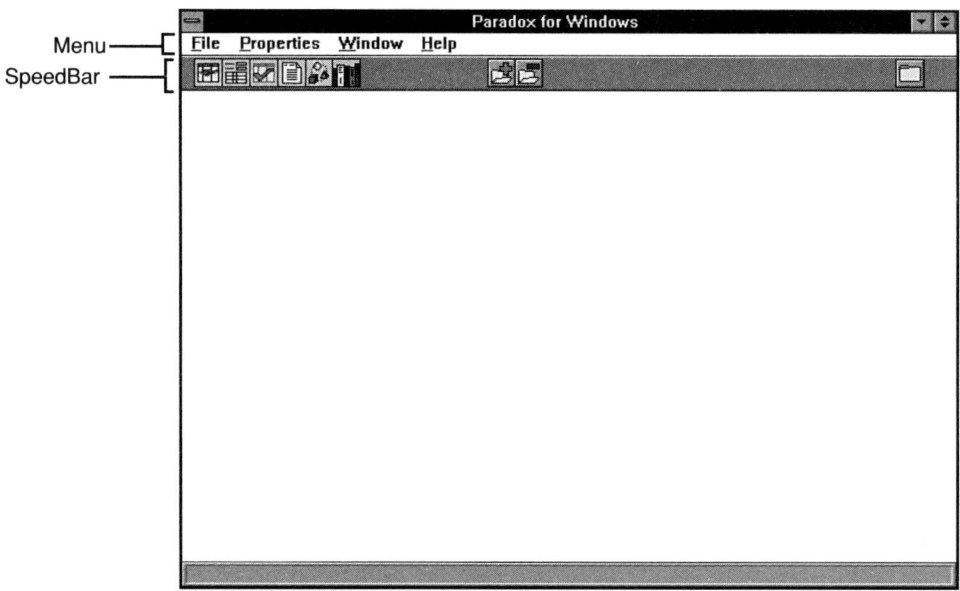

Figure 28.1. The Paradox for Windows application window.

Usually, the only items that aren't confined to the MDI workspace are dialog boxes that require immediate interaction—for example, in the event of fatal application error. These dialog boxes generally cannot be confined to the workspace because the user must be notified even though the application is minimized or inactive.

The Document Window

Although the term *document* usually refers to a word processing document, here the term has a broader meaning. In an MDI application, a document is any object represented in a window within the application and usually is given a more descriptive name. A document window is used to display multiple objects or multiple views of the same object. Program Manager, for example, displays groups of applications (represented as icons) in its windows. When you create a Group in Program Manager, you are creating a document window that is managed by using MDI.

Paradox for Windows also uses MDI to manage documents, which here are tables, forms, reports, scripts, queries, and libraries. The behavior of the windows that contain these objects within the workspace is controlled through MDI, although the contents displayed inside the window are managed by the application and not by MDI.

Other terms, such as Child Window or MDI Child, also are used to refer to the document window. In this context, the *Parent* is the application workspace. This terminology indicates that the Parent Window must closely keep track of the related Child Windows. As a practical example, before the application window is closed, each Child window must first be checked individually to see if the Child window can be closed.

A document window also can be moved and resized but exhibits slightly different behavior than other windows when minimized to an icon and when maximized.

Minimized Document Window

When minimized, a document window is displayed as an icon in the application's workspace, usually at the bottom of the application's workspace rather than the bottom of the Windows main workspace (see fig. 28.2). The following two sections describe this difference.

Maximized Document Window

When maximized, the contents of the document window fills only the application's workspace, not the entire screen as with other windows (see fig. 28.3). The document window's control box and restore button are displayed to the left and right of the Application's menu, respectively. Also, the title of the document displayed in its caption is appended to the application's caption at the top of the window while it is maximized. Scroll bars appear along the right side and bottom of the window.

The window is *restored* to the original position by pressing the restore button or by choosing the Restore menu item on the control box.

You also should be aware that a subtle difference exists in the behavior of a maximized window in an MDI application. Maximizing a non-MDI window has no effect on any other window and will remain maximized until restored, closed, or minimized. Maximizing an MDI document window differs in that it puts the workspace in a maximized *state* in which the window remains until it is restored. As you switch to other document windows, each is displayed maximized in turn. Restoring the currently active child window turns off the maximized state. In other words, when one document window is maximized, you must view every document as maximized until the restore button is clicked.

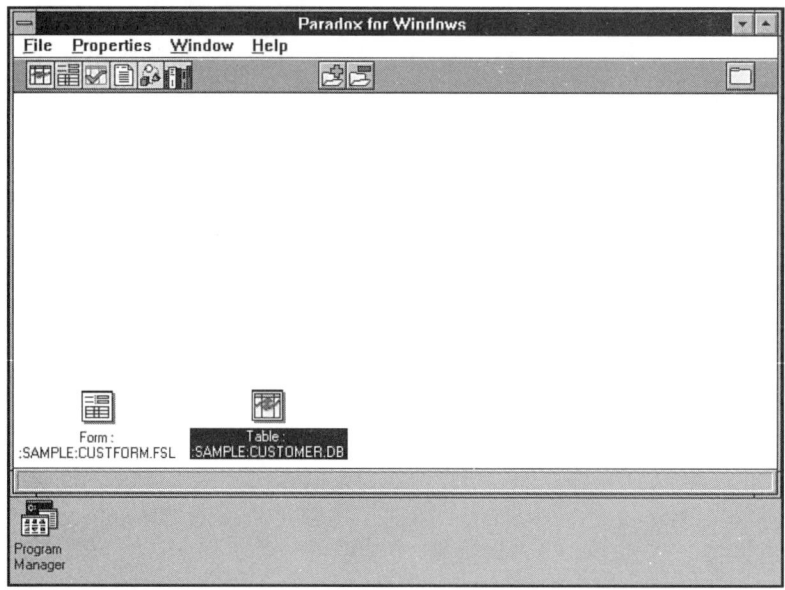

Figure 28.2. Minimized document windows.

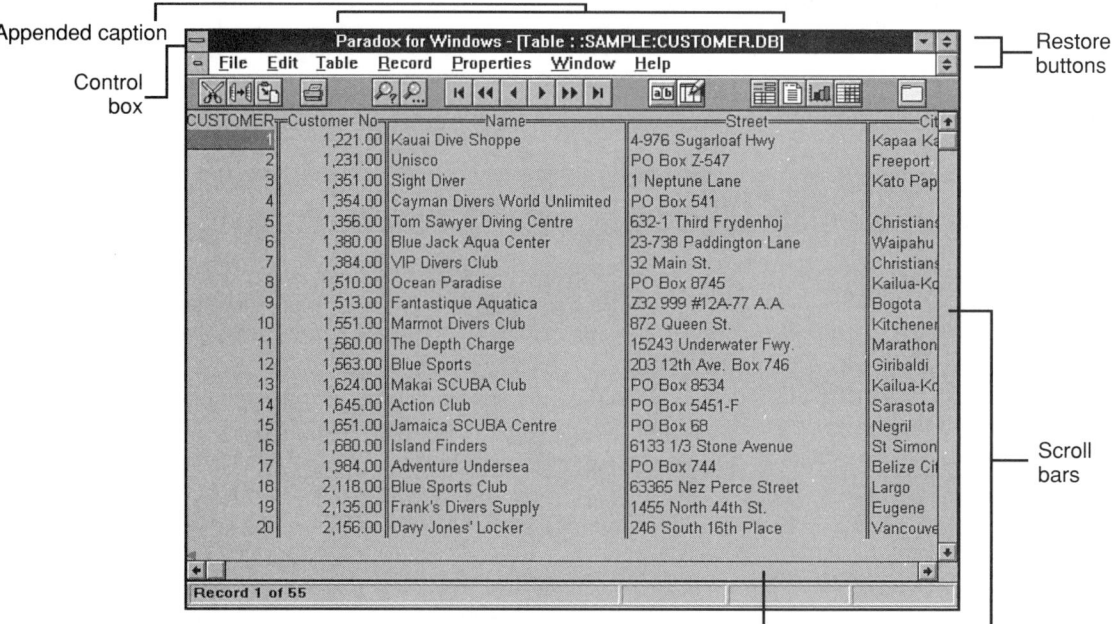

Figure 28.3. A maximized document window.

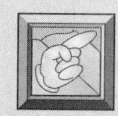 **Tip:** A quick way to maximize a document window is to double-click on the caption with the mouse.

The Window Menu

The Window drop-down menu displayed on the application window's menu bar provides a number of features to make work with MDI document windows easier (see fig. 28.4).

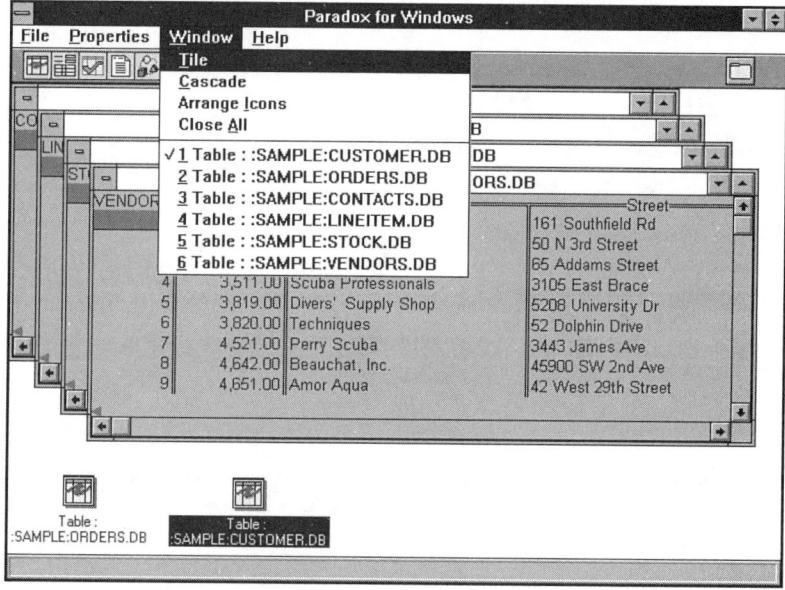

Figure 28.4. The Window pull-down menu, over Cascaded windows.

Tile

The Tile menu selection resizes and arranges all the document windows by using the entire workspace in a tiled manner, giving about the same amount of space to each window (see fig. 28.5).

Tiling the windows also rearranges all icons to the bottom of the workspace.

Cascade

The Cascade menu selection arranges all the document windows from the top left corner to the bottom right corner of the workspace, overlaying everything but the captions (see fig. 28.6).

Part V ■ Interoperability

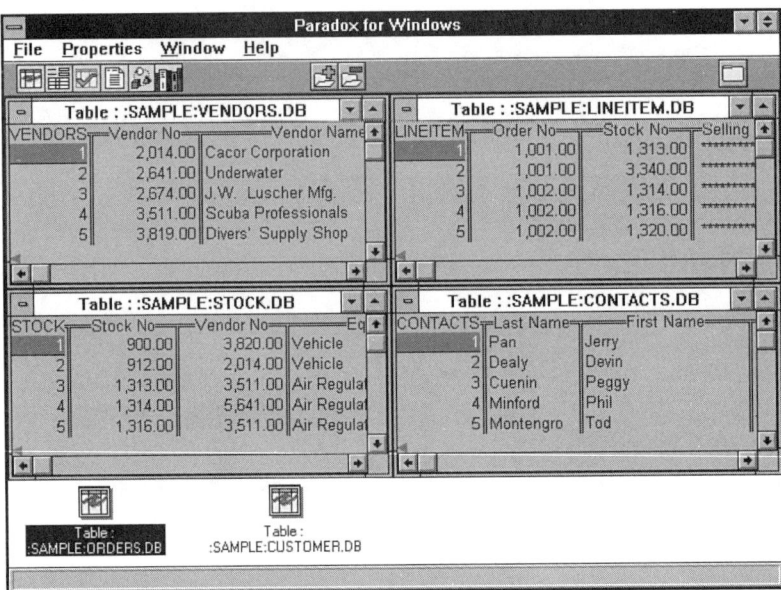

Figure 28.5. Tiled windows.

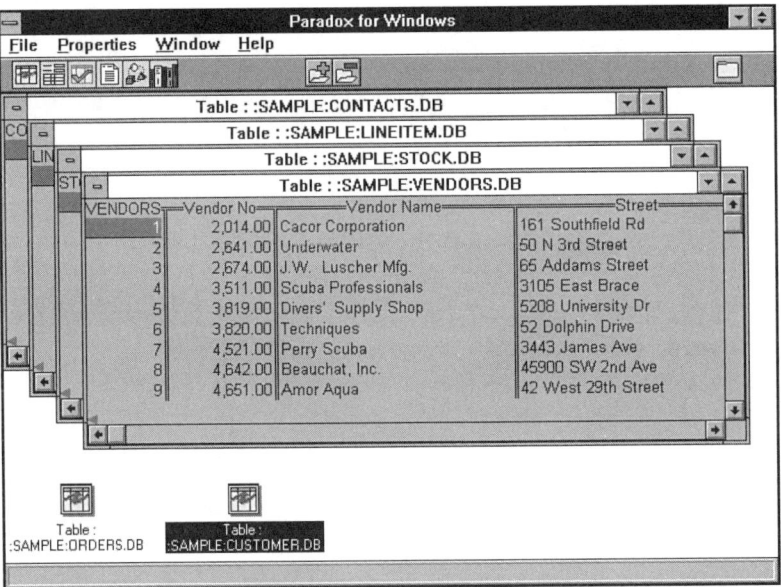

Figure 26.6. Cascaded windows.

Cascading the windows also rearranges any icons to the bottom of the workspace.

Arrange Icons

This menu selection rearranges the icons to the bottom of the workspace, from left to right.

Close All

Close All is a quick way to close every window currently being used. If something wasn't saved, a dialog box displays, allowing you to save the contents or not, or to cancel the Close All process.

Document Window List

Separated by a bar at the bottom of the Window drop-down menu is a numbered list of the document windows currently open on the workspace. Choosing one window listed will activate and bring the window into view on top of all other windows. When working with many windows, this option usually is the easiest way to get to a window hidden from view.

Keyboard Shortcuts

The keyboard shortcuts used with MDI document windows are different than for application windows. The following list compares many of the common shortcuts:

MDI Shortcut	*Function*	*Application shortcut*	*Function*
Ctrl+F4	Close Document Window	Alt+F4	Close Application Window
Ctrl+Tab	Move to the next document	Alt+Tab	Move to the next application
Ctrl+Shift+Tab	Move to the previous document	Alt+Shift+Tab	Move to the previous application
Alt+Hyphen	Display the document control box	Alt+Space	Display the application control box
Ctrl+F6	Move top document to the bottom of the stack	Alt+Esc	Move the top application to the bottom of the stack
Ctrl+Shift+F6	Move bottom document to the top	Alt+Shift+Esc	Move the bottom application to the top

Controlling the Application Window

In order to create an MDI application, a developer must control the look of the application with ObjectPAL by changing the title of the caption, the menus, the display of the SpeedBar, and the contents of the status bar.

Changing the Title

To change the title of the application window in ObjectPAL, you use the Application object's setTitle( ) method. To use this function, you first must declare a variable of type Application as shown in the following example:

```
Var
    . myApp      Application
EndVar
myApp.setTitle("My Application")
```

This code changes the title from Paradox for Windows to My Application, as shown in figure 28.7.

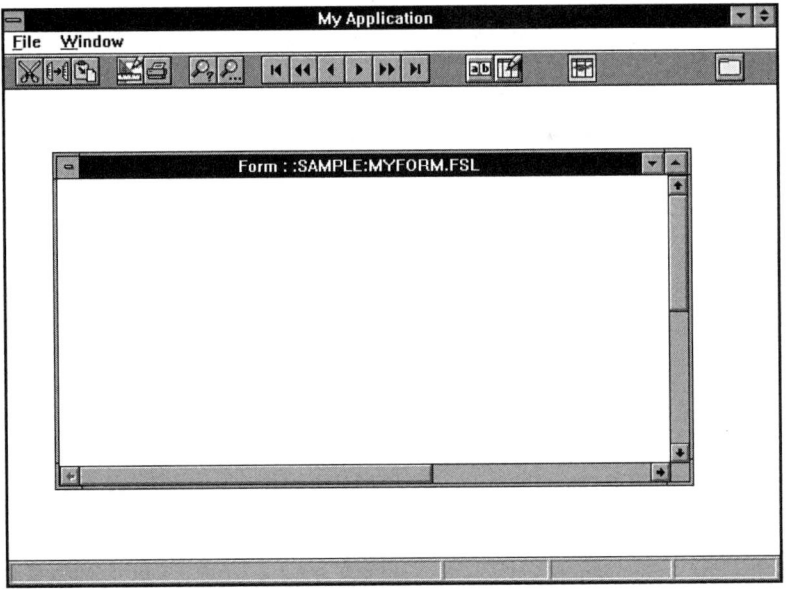

Figure 28.7. Changing the Paradox application window title.

The setTitle( ) method doesn't change the behavior of Paradox for Windows in any other way, it just changes the name displayed at the top of the window.

 **Note:** It's a good idea to get the current title with the getTitle( ) method and save it before you make changes. You then can reset the title to the original value when your application is finished.

When a document window is maximized in an MDI application, its caption is automatically appended to the application's caption.

Changing the Menu

In an MDI application, you need to display a Window menu to provide certain functions necessary to access and manipulate the document windows.

To change the menu displayed by the application window, you use the Menu and PopUpMenu objects.

First you should declare a variable of type Menu, and a variable for each PopUp menu to be displayed.

Next, you use the methods of the Menu and PopUpMenu to add items to display. You also can add separators, bars, and breaks to menus.

Finally, you call the Menu's show( ) method to display the menu, which will replace the Paradox menu.

The following example displays the standard menus that most applications have, including the Window menu required for an MDI application:

```
myFileMenu.addText("&New")
myFileMenu.addText("&Open...")
myFileMenu.addText("&Save")
myFileMenu.addText("Save &As...")
myFileMenu.addSeparator()
myFileMenu.addText("&Print...")
myFileMenu.addText("P&rint Setup...")
myFileMenu.addSeparator()
myFileMenu.addText("E&xit")
myEditMenu.addText("&Undo\tCtrl+Z")
myEditMenu.addSeparator()
myEditMenu.addText("Cu&t\tCtrl+X")
myEditMenu.addText("&Copy\tCtrl+C")
myEditMenu.addText("&Paste\tCtrl+V")
myEditMenu.addText("&Delete\tDel")
myWindowMenu.addText("&Tile")
myWindowMenu.addText("&Cascade")
myWindowMenu.addText("Arrange &Icons")
myWindowMenu.addText("Close &All")
myMyMenu.addText("&MyMenuItem")
myHelpMenu.addText("&Contents")
myHelpMenu.addText("&Search for Help On...")
myHelpMenu.addText("&How to Use Help")
myHelpMenu.addSeparator()
myHelpMenu.addText("&About MyApp...")
myMainMenu.addPopUp("&File", myFileMenu)
```

```
myMainMenu.addPopUp("&Edit", myEditMenu)
myMainMenu.addPopUp("&MyMenu", myMyMenu)
myMainMenu.addPopUp("&Window", myWindowMenu)
myMainMenu.addPopUp("&Help", myHelpMenu)
myMainMenu.show()
```

The preceding code displays the menu shown in figure 28.8.

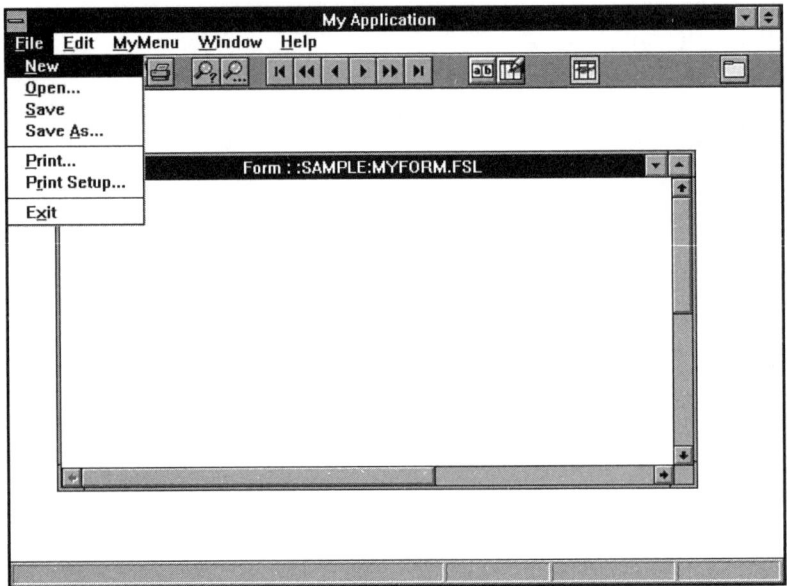

Figure 28.8. A Paradox custom menu.

When you create a Window menu in your application, Paradox for Windows automatically handles the numbered list of windows to be displayed in it, which makes it much easier for you because you don't have to maintain your own list internally and constantly revise the menu choices. You still have to handle the other menu choices such as Tile and Cascade, but this process is easy to do.

Besides the menu required for MDI applications, some other conventions that the developer should know are used by Windows applications.

Menus Displaying Dialog Boxes and Forms

Add Ellipses (...) to any menu selection that displays a dialog box or a form to receive user input. This addition allows the user to see a visual distinction between menu items that have an immediate effect or not. In an MDI application, any menu that displays a form, for example, should have ellipses appended to it.

Creating Short-Cut Keys

Putting an ampersand (&) before a letter of a menu item underlines the letter and automatically makes it a keyboard shortcut. Otherwise, to indicate a short-cut key that isn't one of the letters of the menu, you should append the keystroke description to the menu item separated by a Tab (\t). Use Alt, Ctrl, and Shift as descriptions for the shortcuts, with the plus (+) symbol to separate keystrokes. For example, describe the short cuts as Ctrl+A, Ctrl+Shift+Z. In particular, don't use the caret (^) symbol for the Ctrl key.

In an MDI application, be extremely careful when assigning shortcut keys. Using a shortcut such as Alt+W can be very confusing when the user expects it to display the Window menu and can be frustrating when a user gets unexpected results when using shortcut keys that are standard throughout Windows and MDI applications. Be careful to follow Windows standards when creating short-cut keys. If you're not sure, look at applications such as Program Manager or File Manager, or better yet, read *The Windows Interface: An Application Design Guide* by Microsoft Press for guidance. You also can use the previous menu example as a guideline.

Because you also can implement shortcut keys in forms, you can avoid ambiguous and conflicting keys if you maintain a comprehensive list of the shortcut keys used in an application.

Removing the SpeedBar

To further customize the appearance of your MDI application, you can remove the SpeedBar displayed by Paradox for Windows. You then can create your own SpeedBar or toolbox by using a form.

The Form object contains the hideSpeedBar( ) procedure to remove the SpeedBar.

Note: Using the isSpeedBarShowing( ) procedure to save the state of the SpeedBar before removing it is good form and will permit you to return it to the original state when your application is finished.

Changing the Status Bar

To change the contents of the status bar, you can use the Message( ) procedure, which is a member of the System object. One way the status bar is commonly used is to display a description of an object as the mouse moves over it. This use can be particularly helpful for fields and graphical buttons or any other object that needs further clarification.

Summary

In this appendix, we described MDI and how you can take advantage of its features in your applications. Using MDI gives your applications the same windowing features as other Windows applications, providing a consistent user interface design.

VI

Special Topics

29
Multiuser Strategies

Prior versions of Paradox always handled multiuser issues well and Paradox for Windows is no different. It comes out of the box with built-in network support, ready for multiuser access. In fact, ObjectPAL programs that don't explicitly control multiuser access may run just fine in multiuser environments because Paradox for Windows implicitly handles all multiuser access issues. This news may sound good, but it isn't always. For many kinds of applications, especially critical network applications, we still recommend that ObjectPAL developers take multiuser access matters into their own hands rather than trust them entirely to Paradox for Windows.

The good news is that ObjectPAL gives you plenty of installation options and methods and procedures to control multiuser issues. This chapter discusses multiuser configuration issues, multiuser table manipulation issues, and how to control multiuser issues in ObjectPAL.

Configuration Issues

Paradox for Windows handles nearly all multiuser locking issues by itself. It does not rely on DOS or the network operating system to ensure that tables and records are properly locked. The benefit of this approach is that Paradox for Windows can provide better multiuser functionality than would normally be feasible if it relied exclusively on DOS. There are a few features that rely heavily on Paradox's own multiuser support. Automatic refresh of data updates all users' screens with new information. Referential integrity locking ensures that child records cannot be orphaned by other users changing their parent's key fields. Query restart automatically restarts queries when data in a table changes.

The downside to this approach is that you must configure Paradox for Windows properly to have any meaningful multiuser access support. The other downside is that Paradox for Windows must create some resources to hold multiuser access information. These resources must not be subverted by other applications, otherwise clean multiuser access won't be possible.

Part VI ■ Special Topics

How Paradox Locks Tables

When Paradox for Windows accesses a table on a network or a shared device (a hard disk running under Windows with multiple copies of Paradox or Borland ODAPI engines running can be a shared device), it will access at least two and most likely three resources: network control files, directory locking files, and a private directory. Each of these resources plays an important part in Paradox's multiuser access control mechanism.

NET Files

In order to maintain locking integrity, Paradox for Windows requires two network control files: PDOXWIN.USR and PDOXUSRS.NET. These files are created in the directory configured as the network control file directory with the ODAPI configuration utility (see fig. 29.1).

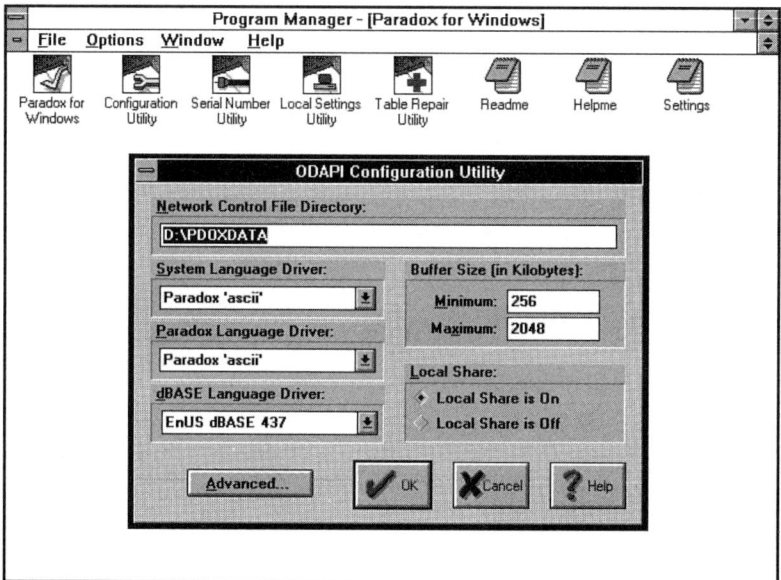

Figure 29.1. The ODAPI Configuration Utility.

To allow multiple instances of Paradox to peacefully access the same tables simultaneously, each user or multiple instance of Paradox must have the network control file directory configured identically. *All users of Paradox on a network must share the same physical PDOXWIN.USR and PDOXUSRS.NET files.* If you do not ensure that these two files are available to all network or simultaneous users, sharing data will become impossible. Each user must also have read, write, create, and delete rights to this directory, because Paradox needs to create the NET files and write to them.

The PDOXWIN.USR file keeps track of all Paradox for Windows users on the network. The PDOXUSRS.NET file is used to control simultaneous access to tables. Paradox for Windows can share tables with Paradox for DOS 4.0 users. However, neither Paradox for Windows users nor Paradox for DOS 4.0 users can share data with earlier versions of Paradox. This does not mean that Paradox for Windows cannot read tables created by earlier versions of Paradox. It can. What it does mean is that a Paradox for Windows user and a Paradox for DOS 3.5 or earlier user cannot both be looking at tables in the same directory at the same time.

With Paradox for DOS 4.0, Borland revamped the table and record locking mechanism to provide superior performance. The cost of this benefit is the inability to provide concurrent access to tables with prior versions of Paradox.

The bottom line to the whole issue is this:

1. When installing Paradox for Windows on a network, make sure all users have the exact same drive and path specified for the network control file directory.

2. When running multiple copies of Paradox for Windows or other Borland ODAPI applications under Windows or other multitasking software, make sure each application has the exact same drive and path specified for the network control file directory.

Private Directory

Paradox for Windows needs to have exclusive use of at least one directory for each user. Paradox uses this directory, called the private directory, to store temporary tables, such as answer tables, struct tables, and error tables, as well as intermediate files it creates when sorting, indexing, and accessing tables. All the files it creates are considered temporary and are deleted from the private directory when Paradox for Windows is exited normally.

The private directory must remain just that: *private*. Each copy of Paradox must ensure that no other Paradox for Windows or Borland ODAPI user can access anyone else's private directory. Because a lot of temporary tables are written to this directory, it makes good sense to put it on a fast device, preferably a local hard drive, that has plenty of room available. Otherwise, Paradox for Windows may run out of disk space during certain queries or reports.

It also makes good sense to create a private directory for each user and make sure that the private directory is properly set up during the Paradox for Windows Local Settings Utility (see fig. 29.2). If no private directory is configured, Paradox sets the working directory as the private directory.

Always explicitly declare every user's private directory.

As a programmer, you can exploit the fact that each user's private directory is inaccessible to other users by creating or using tables on the user's private directory. These tables do not need to be checked for concurrent access conflicts, because there cannot be any. Therefore, you don't need to worry about locking any tables in the private directory. In addition, Paradox can access tables in the private directory faster than tables in a shared directory because Paradox doesn't have to worry about concurrent access in the private directory.

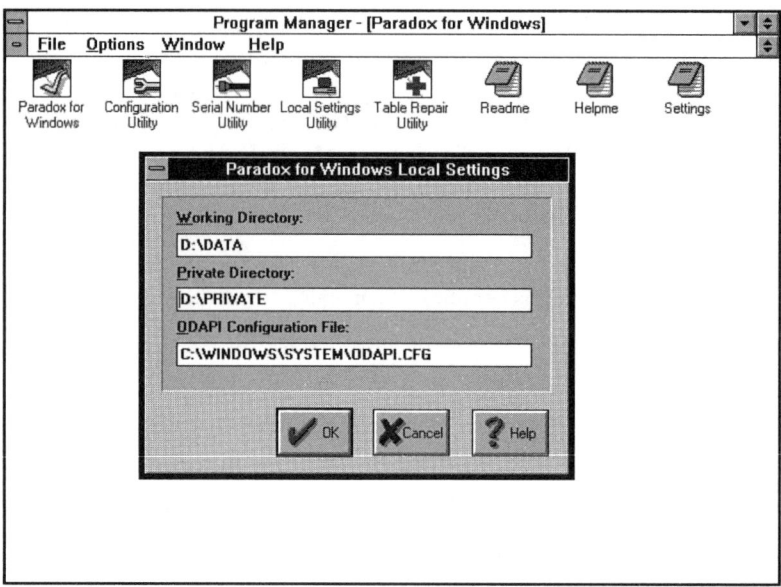

Figure 29.2. The Local Settings Utility.

LCK Files

Besides the network control files, Paradox for Windows creates two files in each directory that contain tables it is accessing: PDOXUSRS.LCK and PARADOX.LCK. The PARADOX.LCK file ensures that others cannot make into their private directory a directory that contains a PARADOX.LCK file and also prevents users from accessing tables in another user's private directories. These measures are necessary to keep private directories the sanctum they need to be.

The PDOXUSRS.LCK file holds entries that track which tables and records are locked. Every simultaneous copy of Paradox for Windows examines this file to make sure that it can access a table and a record. In fact, one of the few places Paradox for Windows uses DOS to control multiuser access is when it accesses this file.

When a copy of Paradox needs to lock a record, it accesses the PDOXUSRS.LCK file and locks a portion of the file by using DOS locking controls. If another copy of Paradox for Windows attempts to access the same record at the exact same time, one of the copies of Paradox is blocked until the other has safely accessed and written locking information in the LCK file. After one copy has completed this process, the other can proceed. In other words, access to the PDOXUSRS.LCK file is controlled with DOS locking mechanisms, which is analogous to access to Paradox tables, which is controlled by Paradox locking mechanisms.

These two locking files should not be deleted, renamed, or written to by file utilities or program editors while any copies of Paradox are running. Otherwise, the users running the copy of Paradox that created the locking files may experience strange and unexpected things.

Single and Multiple File Server Issues

When installing and using Paradox for Windows in a single file server environment, the number one configuration issue is making sure that each copy of Paradox is configured to access one and only one PDOXWIN.NET and PDOXUSRS.NET file. Searching the file server volumes for stray NET files is often a good idea. Paradox for Windows will not automatically create a NET file if run on a shared device without a network control file directory specified.

For multiple file server environments, the same *one NET file* principle holds. All Paradox for Windows users (or Borland ODAPI application users) wanting to share data with other Paradox for Windows users should access the same physical NET files, which means that you will have to dedicate a directory on one file server, and give all users full access to this directory so that Paradox can read and write the two network control files.

If you are setting up a Paradox for Windows application in a multiple file server environment you have only two choices when sharing tables concurrently:

1. Place all sharable data on one server and place the NET files in a subdirectory on the server. All users then attach to this server and map a common drive letter to the application data and another common drive to the NET files subdirectory.

2. Place the NET files in a shared subdirectory on one server. All users must attach to this server and map a common drive letter to the NET files subdirectory. All sharable application data is kept on separate file servers.

Multiuser Table Issues

After the configuration schemes are determined, you need to devise a scheme for the next level of concurrency granularity—table locking and record locking. Fortunately, this area is where Paradox for Windows really shines.

At first glance, it may seem unnecessary to lock tables explicitly, because Paradox handles all locking implicitly. Although this action makes sense for interactive use of the product, you may want to impose a stricter locking mechanism than what Paradox usually enforces. Usually, Paradox for Windows locks tables with a type of lock that gives the most amount of concurrency as close to the time when the resource is expected to be needed. When displaying a form, for example, all the tables in the form's data model are locked appropriately when the form is opened. When a query is run, all the tables in the query are locked before the query begins.

Frequently, under ObjectPAL control, you may want to lock a table well before Paradox for Windows normally locks it or you may want to keep the table locked longer for any batch jobs that cannot or should not get interrupted by another user. This kind of *tightening up* of concurrency controls is one of the most important actions that developers take when building custom applications. They often want the application to detect locked tables sooner and take more graceful actions when any tables are not available.

Table Locks

Paradox for Windows supports four types of table locks that users can set interactively by using the File¦Multiuser¦Set Locks menu items: open, read, write, and exclusive.

The exclusive lock is the most restrictive lock the user can place on a table. It prevents any other users from doing anything at all with the table. They cannot even view the table. The user who places the lock has exclusive access to this table and only the person who places the exclusive lock can remove it. Of course, if anyone is doing anything with a table on which you want to place an interactive exclusive lock, the exclusive lock operation will fail. It must have the table to itself.

The write lock is less restrictive and lets you read and write to the table, allows others to read the table, but prevents others from writing to the table. This lock ensures that you can write, uninterrupted, to a table. You cannot prevent others from reading the table just by placing a write lock. You have to use an exclusive lock to perform this lock. Other users cannot put a read, write, or exclusive lock on a table that you have write-locked.

The read lock works just like a write lock, except that multiple users can place read locks on a table, whereas only one user can place a write lock on a table. A read lock, like the write lock, also ensures that you are always able to read the table. The write lock goes further and prevents others from editing the table. Other users also will be able to read the table, but are prevented from placing a write or exclusive lock on the table.

The open lock, the least restrictive, ensures that others cannot place an exclusive lock on the table. Other users can place open, read, and write locks on the table, and other users can edit a table you have open locked. Paradox automatically places an open lock on any table opened.

If you read closely, you may notice a subtle difference between the read and the write lock. Both locks prevent other users from editing data. The write lock, however, prevents other users from placing a read lock on the table. Table 29.1 lists each lock and what affect it has on other user's ability to edit the table and place locks on it.

In addition, if a user already is editing a table with a record locked, you are prevented from placing any lock except for an open lock. If the user is editing the table, but has no records locked, then an open, read, and write lock can be placed (see table 29.2).

Table 29.1. Interactive Locking Chart.

If you have the table locked as:	Can other users edit table?	Can other users place these locks?			
		Excl.	Write	Read	Open
Open	Y	N	Y	Y	Y
Read	N	N	N	Y	Y
Write	N	N	N	N	Y
Exclusive	N	N	N	N	N

Table 29.2. Table Status and Lock Availability.

If other users have the table in following status:	Can you place these locks?			
	Excl.	Write	Read	Open
Edit mode, records locked	N	N	N	Y
Edit mode, no records locked	N	Y	Y	Y
View mode	N	Y	Y	Y

Under ObjectPAL control, you can place read, write, and full locks. The read, write, and full locks correspond to the read, write, and exclusive locks that you can set interactively. No equivalent to the interactive open lock exists in ObjectPAL. Using locks under program control is discussed in "ObjectPAL Issues," a following section of this chapter.

Paradox for Windows and Paradox for DOS Table Locks

Paradox for Windows has a different locking scheme than Paradox for DOS 4.0. Both Paradox for DOS and Paradox for Windows can understand and react to each others' locks. Tables 29.3 and 29.4 show how Paradox for Windows interprets Paradox for DOS' locks and vice versa.

Table 29.3. How Paradox for Windows Sees Paradox for DOS Locks.

Locks Placed By Paradox for DOS (v4.01):	Paradox for Windows Sees as:
Prevent Full Lock (PFL)	Open Lock
Prevent Write Lock (PWL)	Unknown Lock
Write Lock (WL)	Read Lock
Full Lock (FL)	Exclusive Lock

Table 29.4. How Paradox for DOS Sees Paradox for Windows Locks.

Locks Placed By Paradox for Windows:	Paradox for DOS (v4.01) Sees as:
Open Lock	Prevent Full Lock
Read Lock	Write Lock
Write Lock	Prevent Write Lock + Write Lock
Exclusive Lock	Full Lock

As you can see from these tables, the two variant locks are the read lock and the write lock. Paradox for Windows considers Paradox for DOS' PWL as an unknown lock, which can create some problems. If you have existing Paradox for DOS applications that use PWLs, Paradox for Windows applications won't be able to place write or read locks on these tables. Because both the read and write lock are WLs in Paradox for DOS, this makes sense but is unexpected behavior if you are used to the Paradox for DOS locking schemes.

The following table is similar to table 29.1, except that it shows what you can do with tables in Paradox for Windows that Paradox for DOS has locked.

Table 29.5. DOS and Windows Locking Interactions.

If you have a table locked in Paradox for DOS:	Can you place the following locks in Paradox for Windows?			
	Open	Read	Write	Full
Prevent Full Lock	Y	Y,N*	Y,N*	N
Prevent Write Lock	Y	N	N	N

If you have a table locked in Paradox for DOS:	Can you place the following locks in Paradox for Windows?			
	Open	Read	Write	Full
Write Lock	Y	Y	N	N
Full Lock	N	N	N	N

* *If you have a table open and a record locked in Paradox for DOS, both read and write locks will fail, which makes sense because Paradox for DOS treats both of these locks as write locks (WL).*

Record Locks

After a user gains access to a table and is allowed to edit a record, Paradox for Windows locks the record automatically, preventing any other users from editing the record. If one user tries to edit a record that another user has locked, Paradox displays a message that says the record is locked by another user.

Paradox does not lock the record as soon as the user arrives on it. Rather, Paradox waits until the user presses a key that would change a record. Paradox even allows users to enter field view (on memo fields, too) and doesn't attempt to lock the record. Not until the user actually attempts to change the record does Paradox attempt to lock the record, which means that no record is locked before its time.

In most cases and in data-entry applications, this kind of strong concurrency is desirable. You may be tempted to use a more restrictive record-locking scheme, but rarely is one necessary. With record locking occurring at the last possible moment and released as soon as the user leaves the record, and with automatic refresh capabilities, every user can be assured they are seeing the latest version of the record. In addition, users are never denied access to a record for an unnecessary length of time.

There are cases where you may want to employ more active record-locking schemes. If you access a table under ObjectPAL control by using TCursors or any other means, you should perform explicit record locking so that your code runs correctly. If you use a TCursor, for example, to access a table that holds an incrementing number that contributes to a record's key field, you must make sure that you have exclusive access to this record before changing it. Otherwise, the number may not be a unique number. Explicit record locking is appropriate in this case.

The other case where explicit record locking may be appropriate is when you want to display a different message. If so, you can trap for the status event and check the message being displayed by using the statusValue( ) method. If the message displayed is the message you want to change, you can set the error message with setStatusValue( ). The following example is a multi-record object's built-in status( ) method:

```
method status(var eventInfo StatusEvent)
var
    s String
endvar
```

```
if eventInfo.reason() = StatusWindow then
    s = eventInfo.StatusValue()
    if s.search("locked") <> 0 then
        eventInfo.setStatusValue("My own message")
    endif
endif

endmethod
```

Alternatively, you can add code to an object's built-in method to trap for the error when the error occurs and redisplay with a dialog box. The following example traps for a locked record error (peLocked constant), and, if it finds one, a new error message is displayed.

```
method error(var eventInfo ErrorEvent)

if eventInfo.errorCode()=peLocked then
    msgStop("No!","Record is already locked by another user")
endif

endmethod
```

Query Restart Options

When Paradox for Windows runs a query on a network, concurrency issues arise. What happens when the data in the table changes while the query is running? What should Paradox for Windows do?

Three options are available:

1. Ignore all changes. Let the query run, accumulating totals or gathering information, even though it may have changed since the query started. Worse, a record may have been added or deleted and the query may or may not reflect the change.

2. Lock all the tables and prevent changes from occurring, which gives a clean read of data but prevents users from changing the data. If the query takes a long time to complete, the users will be unable to enter or change any data until the query finishes.

3. Restart the query should any changes occur. This allows users change data, but the query may continually restart itself if many changes are occurring, which may cause the query to take a long time to complete.

The nice thing about Paradox for Windows is that you can choose from these three options interactively. When you or the user is about to run the query, you can select Properties ¦ Restart Options from the menu (see fig. 29.3).

Retry Period

The retry period becomes a factor when you are running queries that attempt to lock tables interactively or under program control, or are locking records interactively or under program control.

The retry period specifies the length of time that Paradox for Windows will take in retrying a locking operation. Paradox for Windows defaults to a retry period of zero seconds, which means no retry.

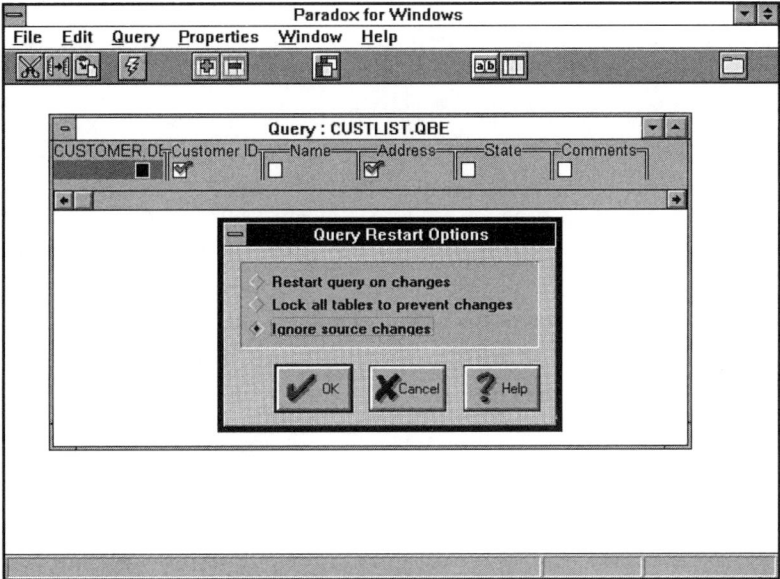

Figure 29.3. The Query Restart Options dialog box.

You can increase this amount to whatever you feel appropriate, but be forewarned: when Paradox for Windows goes into a retry cycle, everything in Paradox stops. The user can get confused because it looks like the computer has locked up. It is wise to keep the retry period as low as possible.

The retry period is useful in very busy networks in which locks are placed frequently but held for very short periods of time. In these cases you can let Paradox automatically retry the lock. Some developers specifically set the retry period to zero and put all explicit locks into a loop which is performed a certain number of times with a pause between tries. This lets the developer display a message to the user as the lock is being retried. When Paradox performs a retry, no message is displayed; if the retry period is too long, the user often thinks the machine has locked up.

In most applications, the retry period can be kept at zero or set to some small number like 1 or 2 seconds. We recommend that you keep the default setting of zero and only adjust it if the application warrants it.

The only exception to this occurs when you run concurrent batch jobs unattended which need to restrict a table's or a series of tables' availability. Using a large retry period will keep one Paradox for Windows application alive, while waiting for another application to finish.

Refresh Rate

The refresh rate is another important component in multiuser access. The refresh rate determines how frequently Paradox for Windows will poll all the tables on the desktop for changes. Paradox for Windows is configured for a five second refresh rate, which is fast enough to display changes on a user's screen quickly, yet infrequent enough to keep the network from being overloaded with several copies of Paradox continually polling the tables on the file server.

In extremely active data entry applications where a large number of users are entering data, you may notice some slowdown as Paradox pauses and attempts to read the table on the file server. If this slows down data entry speed, you can set the refresh rate to a higher number, perhaps 15 or 20 seconds, with the File¦System Settings¦Auto Refresh menu items. These will bring up the auto refresh dialog box (see fig. 29.4). Please note that setting the refresh rate too high can cause problems for some networks.

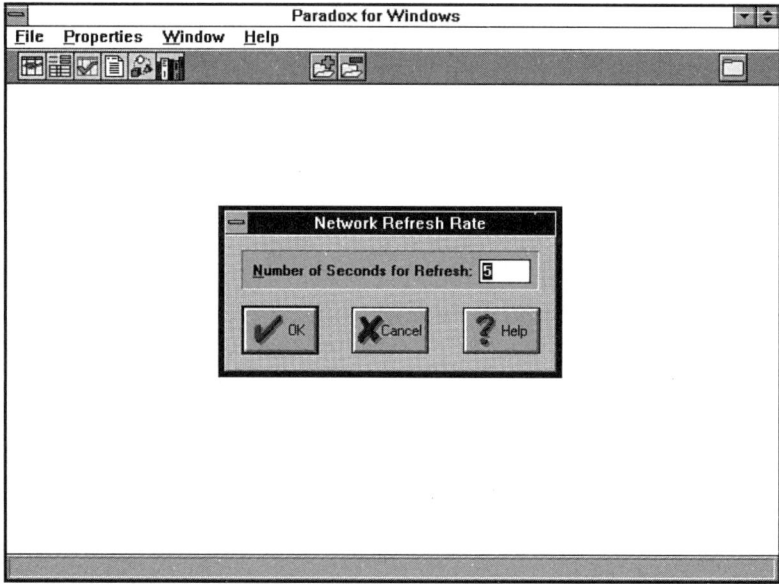

Figure 29.4. The Network Refresh Rate dialog box.

ObjectPAL Issues

So far we have discussed how Paradox for Windows handles locking issues interactively. The ObjectPAL issues are identical. The only issue is knowing which ObjectPAL method or procedure to use. In addition, there are some subtleties and complexities in using ObjectPAL locking issues that don't arise from using the interactive facilities.

Locking Tables in ObjectPAL

The most important concurrency issue in ObjectPAL is locking tables correctly. You may often need to ensure access to a table and prevent interactive users or other application users from exclusively locking a table or temporarily writing to a table. Although Paradox automatically places implicit locks appropriate for the action, whether under program or interactive control, sometimes these implicit locks are not strong enough.

As you place explicit locks (with the various lock( ) procedures and methods) in your application, Paradox for Windows will automatically place implicit locks as well. This is not a bad thing, because Paradox can keep straight how many locks have been placed. It doesn't matter that you have full-locked a table under ObjectPAL control and Paradox for Windows has full-locked it as well (which you may do before reindexing a table). Paradox allows duplicate locks on the same table. Paradox keeps a count of how many locks are placed and removes each one whenever an unlock method or procedure is invoked, or when Paradox is finished with the operation that placed the lock.

As programmers, we have options when locking tables. Paradox for Windows provides one lock( ) procedure and two lock( ) methods.

Session lock( ) Procedure

The real workhorse will be the lock( ) procedure found in the Session type. This procedure can take a variable amount of arguments, letting you lock several tables at once. This has a tremendous advantage over locking tables one at a time: it automatically prevents deadlock. Deadlock occurs when two processes attempt to access a sequence of tables in a different order. One process may have locked the orders table exclusively and is just about to lock the customer table exclusively when another process, which has just locked the customer table exclusively, tries to lock the orders table. Both processes are waiting to lock a table that the other has locked. Keep in mind that the time differences between these interleaving sequences of locks may be milliseconds.

To lock tables, you can simply invoke the lock( ) procedure as follows:

```
lock( "Customer.db", "FULL", "Orders.db", "FULL" )
```

In this example, we are locking two tables using a quoted string to identify the table. The file extension .db is not required. You only need it to distinguish between Paradox and dBASE tables.

The lock( ) procedure can take three identifiers for a table:

1. A quoted string
2. A Table variable
3. A TCursor variable

The three types can be mixed within the same lock procedure. The following example is a valid lock procedure:

```
var
    tc    TCursor
    tb    Table
```

```
          ts    String
       endvar

       ; open the TCursor
       if not tc.open("CUSTOMER.DB") then
          msgInfo("TCursor Open", "Failed")
          return
       endif

       ; attach the table variable to a table
       if not tb.attach("CUSTOMER.DB") then
          msgInfo("Table Attach","Failed")
          return
       endif

       ; lock the table 3 times
       if lock(tb,"READ",tc,"READ","CUSTOMER.DB","READ") then
          msgInfo("Lock","Succeeded")
       else
          msgInfo("Lock","Failed")
       endif

       ; unlock the table 3 times
       if unlock(tb,"READ",tc,"READ","CUSTOMER.DB","READ") then
          msgInfo("Unlock","Succeeded")
       else
          msgInfo("Unlock","Failed")
       endif
```

Notice that before you can lock a TCursor or a Table variable, you must have a table associated with it. Otherwise, the lock will fail. The attach( ) method for Table variables attaches a specified table to the variable, whereas the open( ) method binds a table with the TCursor. The TCursor attach( ) method binds a TCursor to an exiting UIObject, another TCursor or a TableView object.

Always check the result of a lock( ) or unlock( ) procedure. Otherwise you will not know if the lock succeeded.

You can use either a quoted string, a TCursor variable, or a Table variable to place read, write, and full locks. The example above could be modified to use "WRITE" or "FULL" in place of "READ".

TCursor, Table lock( ) Methods

The TCursor class has a lock method which behaves just like the Session lock( ) procedure. If you have an opened TCursor variable, tc, the following line of code locks the table:

```
       if not tc.lock("FULL") then
          msgInfo("Lock","Failed")
       endif
```

Likewise, if you have a Table variable, tb, already attached to a table, the following line of code will lock the table:

```
       if not tb.lock("FULL") then
          msgInfo("Lock","Failed")
       endif
```

Should you use the Session lock( ) procedure or the Table or TCursor lock method? If you want to lock multiple tables, always use the Session lock( ) procedure. If the lock succeeds, then all the tables will be locked. If the lock fails, then none of the locks get placed. If you're just locking one table, then use the TCursor or the Table method, whichever is more convenient.

Listing Table/Record Locks

Very often, especially while you are debugging your application, you may want to know what locks are actually out there on your table or records. The File¦Multiuser¦Display Locks menu choices will create a LOCKS.DB table in your private directory. In addition, you can use the UIObject or TCursor enumLocks( ) method to do the same thing (shown below).

This table contains some interesting things. Not only does it list all the table locks for the selected table currently in effect, it lists what records in this table are locked. The LOCKS.DB table will list the type of lock in effect, the name of the user who placed the lock, the session number and the record number locked, if applicable.

The TCursor enumLocks( ) method accepts a table name as a quoted string as an argument and returns the number of locks in effect as a LongInt and creates the table with locking information passed as the argument.

```
var
    tc TCursor
    numLocks LongInt
endvar

tc.open("Cusomtomer.db")
numLocks = enumLocks("Lcks.db")
```

Unfortunately, this facility works only with Paradox tables. Because the dBASE file format and locking mechanisms are different and don't maintain this information, the enumLocks( ) method will create a locks table that lists only the lock you have asserted. It will not list any other users' locks.

Table Locking Schemes

The weakest point in ObjectPAL table locking is the inability to place open locks under program control. In the majority of cases, the implicit locking support Paradox for Windows provides will be enough. But there will always be some applications where the need for more locking control will be great.

If you absolutely need to secure an open lock under program control well in advance of the actual physical opening of the table, the solution is simple: open a TCursor. This will place an implicit open lock on the table, preventing users from gaining exclusive access to the table.

Detecting Locks You Placed with lockStatus( )

If you want to know how many locks you have placed on a table, the TCursor and the UIObject lockStatus( ) method will tell you. This method will not tell you how many locks other users have on the table. For this, you can use the TCursor or UIObject enumLocks( ) method, which creates a table listing all the locks on a table.

Because you can have multiple locks on a table, lockStatus( ) returns a SmallInt number representing the number of locks you have placed. If no locks have been placed, lockStatus( ) returns zero. The following examples list checks how many read, write, and full locks have been placed. The last lockStatus( ) example checks how many total locks have been placed.

```
var
    tc    TCursor
    rl, wl, fl, totl SmallInt
endvar

; open the TCursor
if not tc.open("CUSTOMER.DB") then
    msgInfo("TCursor Open", "Failed")
    return
endif

rl = tc.lockStatus("READ")
wl = tc.lockStatus("WRITE")
fl = tc.lockStatus("FULL")
totl = tc.lockStatus("ANY")
```

Locking and Unlocking Records

Compared with locking tables, locking records is easy. This is because a record lock is binary: either a record is locked or it isn't. If it is locked, no one else can lock this record. If it isn't, the record is fair game to be locked. As we have already discussed, it is a good idea to keep the same record-locking scheme Paradox employs as default behavior. This locking scheme makes sure that records are locked only when they need to be and unlocked as soon as the user leaves the record.

If you want to detect when Paradox locks records for the user, you can add code to the built-in action( ) method for the appropriate record or table frame object. The particular event you want to trap for is the DataLockRecord, which is triggered whenever Paradox needs to lock a record. This occurs when the user presses a key which may change a record, or when they press F5 to lock a record.

Also remember that when the user begins typing on a new record, the DataLockRecord event is not triggered, even though the status window shows the record is locked. If the user presses the F5 key on a new record, the DataLockRecord event will be triggered. However, this isn't really a problem. A new record does not exist in the table yet, so other users cannot see it. Therefore, locking a new record is superfluous and unnecessary.

Within the action( ) method, you may be tempted to check to make sure the record is available by attempting to lock the record. You may want to issue a doDefault and check the eventInfo.errorCode( ) to see what happened, or you may be tempted to use the UIObject lockRecord( ) method to explicitly lock it (the lockRecord( ) method returns true if the lock succeeded or false if it failed).

Using the action( ) method to explicitly lock a record is the wrong approach, because the action method will call the built-in method as part of the locking process. Remember, there is a difference between the UIObject action( ) method and the built-in action method on your form. The UIObject action( ) method takes a constant as an argument and causes an event to occur. The built-in action( ) method has an eventInfo object as an argument and responds to an event.

If you invoke lockRecord( ) from within the action method, lockRecord( ) does its thing by sending a DataLockRecord event to the target's action method, which means that you will be caught in an infinite loop as each occurrence of the action method attempts to issue a lockRecord( ), which in turn, calls the action method with the DataLockRecord event id. You wouldn't actually be caught in an infinite loop. Paradox would perform the action DataLockRecord about 30 times and then stop.

Although you can explicitly lock records, the main question arises: where or on which event do you trap to explicitly lock records? You may want to use a push button to lock a record. By letting the user press a button, you can, behind the scenes, lock the record and take the appropriate action should the lock fail. A record lock can fail for the following three reasons:

- Someone else has the record locked.
- Someone else has the table locked so that no records can be locked.
- The record no longer exists and the refresh rate was not fast enough to redisplay the table on the screen.

When you attempt to lock a record, keep these conditions in mind. You can use errorCode( ) and errorMessage( ) to determine why a record lock failed and who has the record locked.

Unlocking and Posting Records

Unlocking a record posts it to the table. The user can post a record by taking the following actions:

1. Moving off of the current record and on to another record.
2. Pressing Shift+F5 to post the record.
3. Pressing Ctrl+F5 which posts the record but leaves it locked.

The user can prevent a changed record from being posted by pressing Alt+Backspace, which cancels the record changes and leaves the record in an unlocked state.

Under ObjectPAL program control, you have access to the same tools. You can post a record by invoking the UIObject or TCursor unlockRecord( ), or you can use the UIObject or TCursor method, postRecord( ). The two methods post records differently.

Issuing an unlockRecord( ) unlocks the record and posts the record to the table. If the record's key fields have changed, the record will be positioned into the proper place in the table. The user, however, will not be positioned on this record, but on the location the changed record previously occupied. This situation is known as *fly-away* and is a problem for many users.

Issuing a postRecord( ) will post the current record, keeping it locked and keeping the user on the record, even if the record's key field has changed. Both postRecord( ) and unlockRecord( ) invoke the action( ) method for the intended object, with eventInfo IDs of DataPostRecord and DataUnlockRecord.

New Records and TCursors

Whenever you work with UIObjects such as table frames, multi-record objects, and TCursors, you must understand that neither the TCursor or the UIObject can see each other's new, unposted records.

Although this situation at first may be confusing, the process makes sense because a new record is not yet posted to a table and cannot be seen by anyone else.

Other ObjectPAL Issues

You need to consider several other issues when programming for multiuser access in Paradox for Windows. These issues include the use of aliases, semaphores, locking and the data model, controlling access with setReadOnly( ) and setExclusive( ), controlling the network retry period, and controlling query restart options, of Windows and networks, and dBASE.

Aliases

Aliases are powerful ways to refer to various objects within your application. The purpose of aliases is to avoid having to explicitly code a directory or drive letter names in your application. For this reason, using aliases makes good sense. An *alias* is a name that refers to a directory.

You can use an alias almost everywhere. In referring to the location of forms, tables, and other objects, you need to decide on some set alias names and remember to always use the alias to refer to the object. One useful alias is the :PRIV: alias, which always points to the user's private directory. Tables and objects in the :PRIV: alias will never be concurrently accessed by other users.

Of course, if your entire application fits neatly into one subdirectory, then you don't have to worry about aliases. If it doesn't, you need to spend some time learning about and using aliases.

Semaphores: Locking Nonexistent Tables

Developers often need to lock nonexistent tables for two reasons: to prevent anyone from exclusively locking a table that has just been created; and to use the lock as a semaphore, communicating between applications and coordinating their activities.

The semaphore lock is a useful one because it can serve as a flag that alerts other instances of the application, or sessions, to potential conflicts. For example, you can associate a lock on a nonexistent file, say "$#UPDATE", with a particular update process.

You may want to prevent multiple instances of the application from running an update routine at the same time, yet still let data-entry people edit and enter data. Rather than exclusively locking the tables and preventing data-entry people from working, you can lock a nonexistent table from within the update routine. If it cannot get exclusive access to the semaphore, then some other instance of the application has it. This ensures that only one process can be running the update routine at a time.

The only limitation to this scheme is that you can only place full locks on nonexistent tables. Paradox for DOS enables to you place any type of lock on a nonexistent table. Having the ability to place multiple semaphore read locks gives developers some added flexibility. Because this is not possible in Paradox for Windows, developers who need this capability will need to create dummy tables with the semaphore's name. Although this adds overhead because now you have to both properly create and remove these dummy tables, it is possible to do.

Locking and the Data Model

When you work with forms in your applications, you must be aware that Paradox locks tables through the data model where appropriate. If you change a key field in a master table, the dependent child records must be locked so that all child records can have their foreign keys changed. This is standard behavior for Paradox forms, making it easy for the developer, who never needs to worry about orphaning dependent records.

In a multiuser environment, however, Paradox will attempt to lock from the top of the data model hierarchy downward. If the appropriate locks can be secured, then Paradox will lock the requested record. If the appropriate locks cannot be secured, then an error message will be displayed.

If you lock a record, Paradox must make sure that another user cannot change your record's linking key fields. It will lock all parent tables, starting with the top parent table downward. This works the same way, whether you manipulate the data interactively or use ObjectPAL methods or procedures.

Opening a Table Exclusively or Read-Only

Two table methods, setReadOnly( ) and setExclusive( ) perform an interesting service. The setReadOnly( ) method operates on a Table variable which has been attached to but not yet opened by a TCursor. When the TCursor opens the table indicated by the Table variable, the table will be in read-only mode.

The other method, setExclusive( ), works in a similar manner, except it ensures that when the TCursor opens the table indicated by the Table variable, the table will be opened exclusively, preventing other users from viewing or editing the table.

Both methods can optionally take the logical constants Yes or No as an argument. If Yes is specified, the table is opened as either exclusive or read-only. If No is specified, the table opens as shared or read-write. If no argument is supplied, Yes is assumed.

Setting the Retry Period

Two useful methods let you determine the current retry period setting and change it: the Session methods/procedures retryPeriod( ) and setRetryPeriod( ). retryPeriod( ) will return a SmallInt representing the retry period in seconds. setRetryPeriod( ) takes a SmallInt representing the retry period in seconds as an argument and returns true if the operation succeeded or false if it failed.

Query Restart Options

Two very useful procedures let you determine the current query restart setting and change it. These Database procedures are setQueryRestartOptions( ) and getQueryRestartOptions( ). These procedures are not documented in the manuals or in on-line help, but are documented in the README file that comes with Paradox for Windows and in the Language¦Types dialog box.

getQueryRestartOptions( ) returns a SmallInt representing the current query restart setting. This SmallInt can be compared with the following constants:

Constraint	*Result*
QueryLock	Paradox locks the tables before running the query, thus preventing any changes to the tables.
QueryNoLock	Paradox lets the query continue, ignoring any changes.
QueryRestart	Paradox will restart the query if any table changes are detected while the query is running.

To set the query restart options, you can pass setQueryRestartOptions( ) one of the three constants as an argument, or a fourth constant, QueryDefault which will restore the default restart option the session of Paradox started with. If the operation was successful, the procedure will return true; otherwise, it will return false.

With these two procedures, you can set the query restart options on the fly, in one instance ignoring changes (called *dirty reads*), and in another restarting the query whenever the query's tables change.

Windows and Networks

For experienced Paradox for DOS users, Paradox for Windows may seem a little strange when it comes to networks. In DOS versions of Paradox, you had the ability to set the user name as part of each user's configuration profile. In addition, on certain networks, Paradox for DOS automatically detected the user's network log-on name.

Paradox for Windows is dependent on the network support provided in your Windows environment. This is why in Paradox for Windows you won't find any place where you can set the user name. You can register a user name with the serial number utility, but this only displays who owns the software licensed, not the user's name.

Check with your network manuals and see what support Windows provides for your network. Novell and Microsoft LAN Manager networks both have a series of Windows utilities which provide good networking support.

dBASE Issues

Although Paradox supports both dBASE and Paradox file format, the Paradox file format provides greater functionality than the dBASE file format. For example, no read locks are possible on a dBASE file. dBASE files do not keep detailed locking information in a special lock file. Paradox does.

Originally, dBASE files performed all file and record locking using standard DOS interrupts to lock files and regions in files. In order to allow Paradox to access all dBASE-type files, the ODAPI engine cannot assume that these files have the same intelligence that Paradox tables have.

If you have a choice in picking a file format for multiuser applications, choose the Paradox file format. It provides better multiuser support.

Summary

Paradox for Windows provides good networking support. It gets this ability by taking control of nearly all multiuser locking issues, rather than using standard DOS or network operating system services. Developers have the ability to set table and field level locks both interactively and under program control. In addition, developers can detect what types of locks they have placed and what locks others have placed.

Embedding highly concurrent yet robust and safe access to tables is an extremely critical service that developers provide. We recommend using locking schemes that follow the Paradox for Windows locking model whenever possible because this promotes a higher level of concurrent access with less code. If you need to have more restrictive multiuser schemes, spend the time to learn the locking and configuration issues and plan your strategy wisely.

30 Using Indexes

Indexes provide a variety of benefits in Paradox. Many operations, including querying and locating, happen faster when tables are keyed. Keys provide a way to sort your data. Key fields can also be used to uniquely identify records in a table. Much of the literature on database design uses the terms "key" and "index" interchangeably; the distinction is that a key is the field or field(s) used to make up the index. Paradox stores indexes as files on disk.

Primary versus Secondary Indexes

Broadly speaking, Paradox uses two types of indexes: primary and secondary. The field(s) that are used to make up the primary index are used to uniquely identify records in a table; duplicate primary keys are not allowed. If you attempt to enter a record with the same primary key value as an existing record, Paradox kicks the record out to a table called KEYVIOL.DB. The primary index defines the table's default sort order. A Paradox requirement (although not a requirement of relational databases in general) is that the field or fields comprising the primary key appear as the first fields in the table's structure. Primary indexes are designated by an asterisk (*) in the Key column of the table structure (see fig. 30.1). There are three ways to enter the asterisk:

- Move to the column and type it in.
- Position the cursor in the column, then press the space bar.
- Double-click in the Key column.

Although the primary key can include as many fields as you want, you'll only want to key as many fields as necessary to uniquely identify each record. When more than one field is used as the table's key, it is referred to as a *composite key*. As we'll see in the discussion of how Paradox stores indexes, the less data (i.e., fewer and shorter fields), the greater advantage you'll be able to derive from your tables' indexes. Often, a sequence number is a unique ID; sequence numbers are especially handy if no logical field(s) emerge as the appropriate keys, or if the number of fields required to uniquely identify a record is too large.

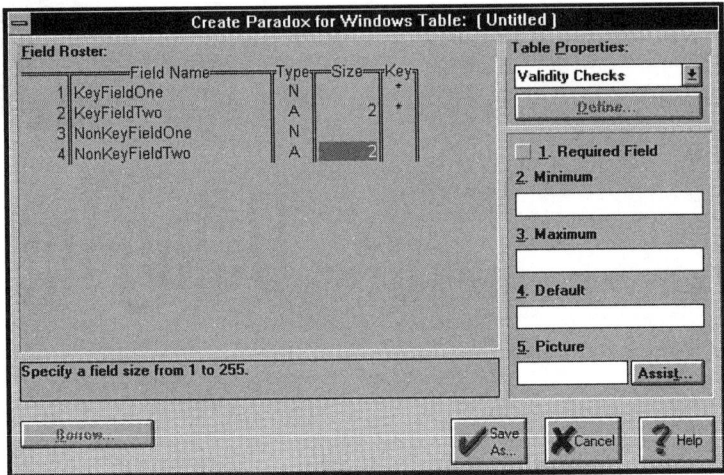

Figure 30.1. The Create Table dialog box showing keyed fields.

Secondary indexes can be used for sorting, querying, or linking tables. For instance, you might want to use a Social Security Number field as a table's primary key to avoid duplicates, or you might want to display the table sorted by customer/client/patient name. In contrast to the fields used for primary keys, the fields used to define a secondary index can appear anywhere in the table's structure. They are not required to be consecutive. Also in contrast to primary keys, you can have multiple secondary indexes for each table.

The keys used to define a secondary index do not need to make up a unique combination. However, a secondary index with less duplication offers more benefit than one with a lot of redundancy. Fields like Sex (M/F) or Marital Status (M/S/D/W) that only have a few possible values are not good candidates for secondary indexes, whereas Name fields frequently are.

If you have a field in your table that can contain a variety of values (such as Country), but usually does not (the Country usually is USA), it doesn't make much sense to put a secondary index on that field. On the other hand, a field with a high ratio of unique values to number of records, especially one that requires frequent searches, is a prime candidate for a secondary index.

Creating a Secondary Index

To create a secondary index, access the table through either the Create or Restructure dialog box. From the Table Properties drop down list, select Secondary Indexes. Click on the Define button to invoke the Define Secondary Index dialog box (see fig. 30.2).

Notice that the Notes field in the figure is dimmed; Paradox does not allow you to build secondary indexes based on any of the extended field types (M, B, O, G, or F).

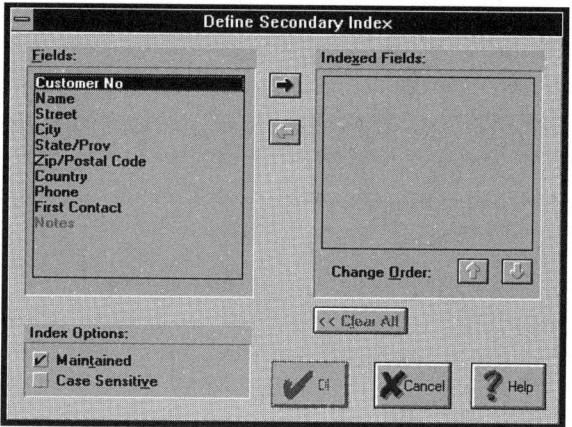

Figure 30.2. The Define Secondary Index dialog box.

The index options are shown in the lower left corner of this dialog box. Maintained indexes are updated whenever a change occurs in the table that affects the index. Non-maintained indexes are not updated until they are needed—to perform a query, for instance. Until the index is updated, it is seen as "out-of-date." If the table undergoes frequent changes, then a maintained index is significantly faster than a non-maintained index, since the entire non-maintained index needs to be rebuilt for an operation that uses it. In almost all cases, you will want your indexes maintained. Maintained is the default setting in Paradox for Windows.

The Case Sensitive option tells Paradox whether to treat capital and lowercase letters as having the same or different values. Case-sensitive indexes sort capital letters before lowercase letters, placing "Zigfield" before "au Berge," for instance. A case-insensitive index would place these values in the opposite order. It would treat "Jones," "JONES," and "jones" as identical values. The default setting for this option is case-insensitive.

Case-sensitive, single-field secondary indexes are given the same name as the field they use. Case-insensitive secondary indexes require a user-defined name.

For the most part, you won't need to create an index on the field or fields in the primary key. The exception, however, is if you want to sort the values in the primary index in case-insensitive order. The primary key uses a case-sensitive sort.

Multi-Field Secondary Indexes

Paradox allows you to create secondary indexes based on more than one field. These multi-field secondary indexes use the values in each of the included fields to sort their values. Values are sorted on the values in the first field of the index; if there are duplicates in the first field, the values in the second field are used as tie-breakers; if there are duplicates in the second field, the third field is used; and so on. Although you can use all the fields in a table as the basis for a secondary index, it is advisable to keep the number of fields to a minimum.

To create a multi-field secondary index, open the Define Secondary Index dialog as you did with single field indexes, then use the right-arrow key to add as many fields as you need to the Indexed Fields list. Multi-field secondary indexes must be given a user-defined name. The default Option settings for multi-field indexes are maintained and case-insensitive.

Indexes with ObjectPAL

After you see it done, using ObjectPAL to generate indexes is simple. For a primary index, the approach is shown in the following text:

```
INDEX "tablename.db"
    PRIMARY
    on "field1", "field2",...
ENDINDEX.
```

Where "field1" ... must be consecutive starting with the first field of the table.

To create a maintained secondary index you can use the following:

```
INDEX "tablename.db"
    MAINTAINED
    on "field1","field2",...
    to "Indexname"
ENDINDEX
```

In addition to the MAINTAINED keyword, there is a CASE SENSITIVE keyword to create a case-sensitive secondary index.

How Paradox Uses Indexes

We mentioned a few times that Paradox uses secondary indexes for speeding up queries, locates, and zooms, and linking tables. In the following sections, you see a little more closely how and when they are used in various situations.

Sorting/Viewing

A frequent use for indexes is to allow you to view your table sorted in an order other than the primary index order. Interactively, select the Order/Range menu selection under the Table or Form menu, while viewing a table or form, respectively. The Order/Range dialog box (see fig. 30.3) allows you to select from existing indexes.

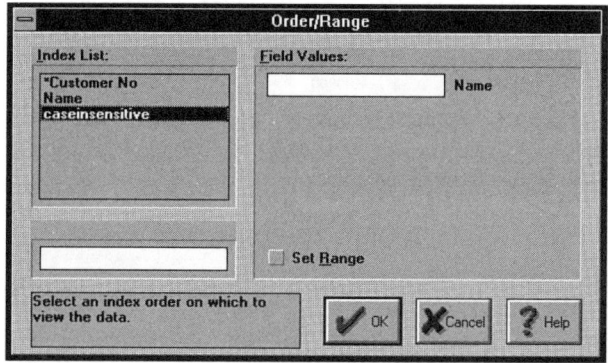

Figure 30.3. The Order/Range dialog box.

Besides forcing a sort on the selected index, you can use this dialog box to display either a range of records or only records with a specified index value. Suppose that you have an index on the Zip Code field. You select the index from the list of indexes in the Index List. Then, to only display indexes in Zip Code 90210, you type the exact value into the Field/Values area (see fig. 30.4).

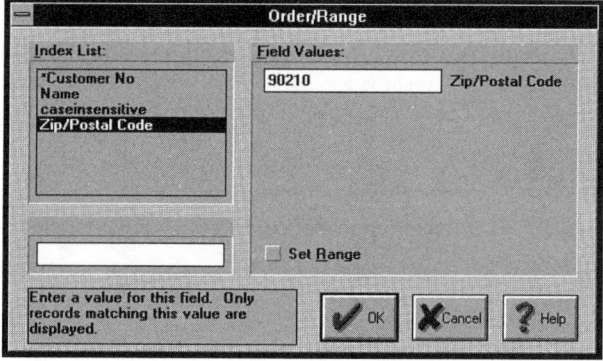

Figure 30.4. A completed Order/Range dialog box specifying an exact value.

This filters the data to only show the records in the selected Zip Code.

If you wanted to use the Zip Code secondary index to show all the area codes in southern California, you would use the range feature. To do this procedure, check the Set Range box at the bottom of the dialog box. In response, Paradox opens another type-in area for you to set the high range value. The low range value goes in the upper type-in area (see fig. 30.5).

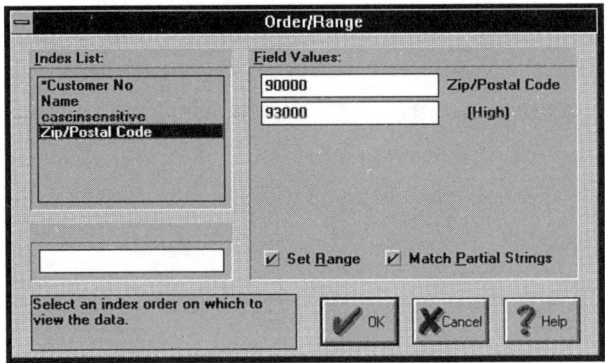

Figure 30.5. A completed Order/Range dialog box specifying a range.

Multi-field indexes work a little differently. If you choose to sort on a multi-field index, when you select a composite primary or secondary index, all the fields in the index appear in the Index List area. You can specify exact values for any combination of fields in the index *as long as you start from the first and work down*. In other words, if you had an index on State and City, with the state field as the first field in the index, you can look for a specific state, without giving a city value, but you cannot enter a city value without indicating a state.

Likewise, you can perform range matches on multi-field indexes. If you want to set a range on the second field in a two field index, you need to first fill in a value for the first field; for a three-field index, the first field's value must be supplied before you can look for a range on the second field, and the first and second field values must be supplied before you can look for a range on the third field, and so on.

After you have set a range of records to display, the record numbers correspond to the subset of data. There is no indication of a record's position in the tables, only in the selected view.

The ObjectPAL command to use an alternate index is SwitchIndex:

```
var
     tc    tcursor
endvar
tc.open("Customer.db")
tc.switchindex("StateCity")
Customer_No.resync(tc)
```

Customer_No in the above is a field name. Any UIObject should suffice.

After you select the index using SwitchIndex, the SetFilter command allows you to do the equivalent of a range definition. SetFilter works on the active index.

```
var
     tc    tcursor
endvar
tc.open("Customer.db")
tc.switchindex("StateCity")
tc.setFilter("CA","San Jose","San Jose")
Customer_No.resync(tc)
```

With no parameters, tc.setFilter( ) clears filters that have been set. For more information about SetFilter and SwitchIndex, refer to Chapter 15.

Querying

If there is a secondary index on a field, Paradox uses it to speed up queries. However, Paradox always performs case-sensitive searches, regardless of whether or not the index is sensitive. If you do a wild-card search, Paradox uses a case-insensitive search to speed up the index; it will not use a case-sensitive index if you include wild cards in the query.

Zoom/Locating

There are a few ways to invoke the Paradox for Windows Locate Value dialog box:

1. By pressing Ctrl-Z.
2. By selecting Record/Locate from the menus.
3. By using ObjectPAL's action(DataSearch).

There is also a locate method available for TCursors.

A somewhat surprising fact is that wild-card searches don't use existing indexes. The Locate method does not use indexes under any circumstances.

If you want to search using an index use tc.setfilter, locate the desired value. The locate will then only need to look at the filtered subset of data.

There are situations when an Advanced Pattern Match search will happen more quickly than a wild-card search. Although Advanced Pattern Matches do not use existing indexes, Advanced Pattern Matches use a different search engine, which means they will frequently produce faster results.

Linking

Paradox uses indexes to link tables. When you link two tables using a Data Model, Paradox presents you with a list of existing indexes on the detail table that are available for linking. Note that you can only use Order/Range to tell Paradox how to display records in the master record; the detail records are confined by the settings of the master table. The index that you use to link determines both the filter and the order of the records in the linked detail.

The other situation where Paradox uses secondary indexes for linking is when you define referential integrity. Although the linking field or fields in the child table do not need to be keyed to establish RI, a maintained secondary index must exist there. If you haven't already defined an index, Paradox will automatically do it for you.

How Paradox Stores Indexes

In Chapter 8, we discussed how Paradox stores a table's records in uniform block sizes. When it runs out of space for records in any given block, it opens a new (typically 2K or 4K) block. If a new record is added to a keyed table it is placed in its proper position relative to existing key values. If the added record belongs between two existing records, and if there is no room within the block that contains them, a new block is opened and the records are split between the blocks. Thus, Paradox uses a record-sequential method of storing records. Each block of records points forward to the next block and backwards to the previous block.

We also mentioned throughout this chapter that Paradox uses indexes to speed up various table operations. Rather than storing its values sequentially, it uses a B-tree system of storage and retrieval for index files. Each record in the primary index contains information on an entire block of records. The index grows; not necessarily when a new record is added to the table, but when the new record causes a new block to open up. The detail level of the B-tree index file (i.e., the outermost or lowest branches) keeps track of the number of records in the block, the key value of its first record, and the block's position relative to the block within the table.

Each higher level in the tree is used to navigate, or narrow down, the choices Paradox uses to find the detail information on the table block—it acts as a sort of switching station. Paradox begins its broadest search at the top and uses the records in the higher level blocks to determine which branch to pursue. This fine tuning can save a significant amount of time, its value increasing with the size of the table. The next level up in the tree is used to store information on the blocks comprising the lower level. If ever a picture is worth a million words, it's figure 30.6.

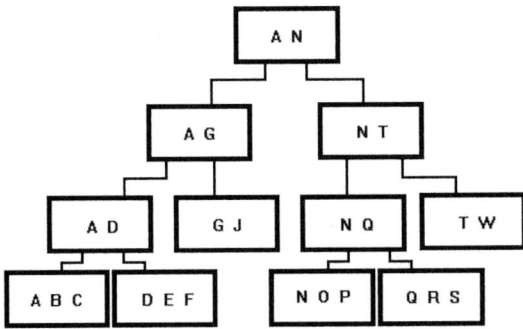

Figure 30.6. A schematic of the B-tree structure.

Paradox uses these indexes in sequence: it uses the B-tree to quickly locate the primary index, then, with the information it finds there, locates the record in the table. Together, this method of accessing data is referred to as a B-tree.

Secondary indexes for keyed tables relate information about the secondary keyed field(s) to the primary key. Secondary indexes for non-keyed tables use the block number of the associated record instead of the key field. All secondary indexes create two files on disk—one with the .X?? extension, one with the .Y?? extension, both with the same first name as the table.

Secondary indexes (.X??) are essentially tables that contain the secondary index fields plus either the primary key or block number information. The .Y?? files serve the same purpose as the .PX file except they point to the .X?? instead of the DB. As a matter of fact, the best way to understand how Paradox stores index information is to rename the .X?? files to .DB files and view them in Paradox.

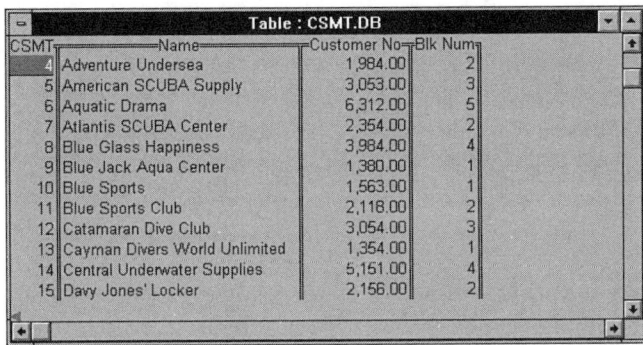

Figure 30.7. A table containing a case-sensitive secondary index value.

This index was built on the Name field. The Name field is the field used to generate the index, the Customer No field contains the values of the key field in the indexed table. The BLK NUM field tells Paradox the block number of the table that contains this record. You should be able to see that the larger Customer Number values are stored in larger block number—they are closer to the end of the table.

You should also see that it was created as a case-sensitive index because all the values are not stored as capitals. Contrast this index to the following index file (renamed as a .DB file):

Name	Street	Customer N	Name	Blk Nu
ACTION CLUB	PO BOX 5451-F	1,645.00	Action Club	2
ACTION DIVER SUPPLY	BLUE SPAR BOX #3	3,158.00	Action Diver Supply	3
ADVENTURE UNDERSEA	PO BOX 744	1,984.00	Adventure Undersea	2
AMERICAN SCUBA SUPPLY	1739 ATLANTIC AVENUE	3,053.00	American SCUBA Supp	3
AQUATIC DRAMA	921 EVERGLADES WAY	6,312.00	Aquatic Drama	5
ATLANTIS SCUBA CENTER	42 AQUA LANE	2,354.00	Atlantis SCUBA Center	2
BLUE GLASS HAPPINESS	6345 W. SHORE LANE	3,984.00	Blue Glass Happiness	4
BLUE JACK AQUA CENTER	23-738 PADDINGTON LANE	1,380.00	Blue Jack Aqua Center	1
BLUE SPORTS	203 12TH AVE. BOX 746	1,563.00	Blue Sports	1
BLUE SPORTS CLUB	63365 NEZ PERCE STREET	2,118.00	Blue Sports Club	2
CATAMARAN DIVE CLUB	BOX 264 PLEASURE POINT	3,054.00	Catamaran Dive Club	3
CAYMAN DIVERS WORLD U	PO BOX 541	1,354.00	Cayman Divers World U	1

Figure 30.8. A table containing case-insensitive secondary index values.

A few things should become apparent from this index. The first is that the original table has been restructured to use both the Customer No field and the Name field as the primary key—the entire primary key is used in the secondary index. This is another strong argument in favor of keeping the primary index as small as possible: extra space is required to repeat the contents of the primary index for every secondary index used by the table.

The other thing that you should see in the second table is that it is case-insensitive. Paradox sees all of the values in the index as capitals, even though they are stored in mixed case in the table.

Finally, this index is a multi-field index, based on both the Name and the Street fields.

Some general rules for working with indexes should be apparent from the preceding discussion. The first is the importance of only using fields as part of both the primary and secondary key that are necessary for uniqueness, viewing, or locating your data. Each key field is stored both with the index and with the table. It is advisable to limit the number of indexes you use as well, since each file needs to be updated when corresponding changes to the table occur. These considerations need to be weighed against the benefits that result from the index.

Index Names

We saw that secondary indexes generate two files—one with a .X?? suffix and one with a .Y?? suffix. You might be wondering what's contained in the "??"s. Paradox uses some predictable conventions for naming case-sensitive single-field indexes—they correspond to the hex number equivalent to the index field's position in the table. Therefore, if you create a case-sensitive secondary index on the third field in the table, the index file extensions will be .X03 and .Y03; a case-sensitive secondary index on the 16th field in the table will have the extensions .X10 and .Y10. Case-insensitive, or composite indexes are sequentially numbered starting at .XG0 and YG0.

Summary

Using indexes correctly enables you to speed up many operations, including searches and queries. Primary indexes are used as a primary sort order; and also ensure uniqueness in the involved fields. Paradox uses secondary indexes to link tables in your data model. Secondary indexes are also valuable for sorting and filtering your data. Understanding how they work, how they are used, and how they are stored on disk enables you to put both primary and secondary indexes to optimal use.

31
Performance Tuning

Paradox is an ambitious Windows program that requires plenty of hardware resources and patience when it comes to performance tuning. There are several reasons for this. First, Paradox gives programmers tremendous power without programming. The form and report designers are full of tools that require no coding to create. The database engine handles referential integrity, table lookups, record-level validity checking, full multi-user table and record locking, and many other critical tasks—all without requiring the developer to write code. All of this power comes at a cost, however: computer resources.

Second, database applications stress the PC architecture like no other application. When word processors operate, they usually work on files that range in size from 3K or 4K to several hundred kilobytes. It is not uncommon for Paradox to query megabytes of data. A good portion of this data must be shuttled between the computer's hard disk and the PC's memory. Database applications also have full multi-user concurrent access, which enables many users to edit the same table simultaneously. Paradox continually refreshes each user's screen so that they see the latest changes. Spreadsheet and word processing applications don't even come close to this sort of multi-user complexity and data volume.

In short, because database applications push the envelope of the PC architecture, they will expose memory shortages, network conflicts, or hard disk problems more frequently than any other type of application. Performance tuning and troubleshooting take hard work, determination, and a willingness to explore.

PC Configuration

To run Paradox, you need appropriate hardware. Table 31.1 lists our recommended *minimum* figures. These figures are higher than the official recommended minimum values; however, we feel that the higher values are necessary for reasonable performance.

Table 31.1. Recommended minimum hardware requirements.

Hardware	Requirements
CPU	386DX, 386SL, or better
Memory	6M available to Windows
Hard disk	Three times the size of the largest table as free space available to the drive that holds the user's private directory.
Mouse	Paradox is very cumbersome to use without one
Video	VGA or better
Windows	Version 3.1

If you want your ObjectPAL applications to run well under Paradox for Windows, we strongly recommend 8M of main memory. Even 8M of memory is rather sparse for serious Windows use. If the user has your application running, plus three other applications, and each consumes between 2M and 4M, it's easy to see that 8M can be eaten up quickly.

Perhaps the biggest problem with poor Paradox for Windows performance is Windows' virtual memory management scheme. Windows allows users to run several applications at the same time, even if there isn't enough system memory to hold all the applications. Windows uses the PC's hard disk for memory management. When Windows runs out of memory, Windows writes current memory contents to a special file, called a *swap file*, saving memory contents and freeing up more space in main memory.

Although this enables users to run more applications than they otherwise could, it comes at a cost: performance. Reading and writing that swap file takes much more time than reading and writing directly to main memory. We have seen new computers with the latest and fastest CPUs—but with insufficient memory (4 megabytes or less)—absolutely crawl whenever virtual memory management needs to swap memory to disk.

In addition, future Windows software will be even more ambitious, requiring even more resources. If you want to enter the Windows generation, come with 8M of memory.

We also recommend that you use a 386DX chip or better, rather than a 386SX chip. Although Windows runs on a 386SX chip, a DX chip is significantly faster. In fact, given the low cost of 486 chips, we recommend that platform, if you can afford it. However, given a choice between buying a new CPU or getting more memory, if you already have a 386DX chip, buy more memory.

Be careful with SMARDRV.EXE when using Paradox in low memory situations. If you have a PC with 6M of memory, with SMARTDRV taking up 1.5M and Windows consuming about another 1.5M, you now have only 3M available for Paradox. In these cases, reduce the amount of memory SMARTDRV.EXE consumes to 512K or less.

Perhaps one of the most important things you can do to improve Windows system performance is to create a permanent swap file. Use 32-bit file access, if possible, and make it large enough (at least 4M or 5M, preferably as much memory as you have available). Windows documentation warns against using 32-bit file access on certain laptop computers. If your machine works properly with 32-bit file access, use it. So if you have 8M of memory, create a swap file 8M in size. Windows reports different recommended swap file sizes depending on how much disk space you have available, so take the recommendations with a large grain of salt. If you want Paradox to run well, give it a big permanent swap file.

Disk compression utilities, such as the one in DOS 6.0 and STACKER, cause a small performance degradation. However, you will gain twice the amount of disk space, which will help Paradox during queries and reports. A general rule of thumb is that the user's private directory needs about 3 to 5 times the size of the largest table in the application. This rule, however, is only a best guess. Some queries require 10 to 15 times the amount of disk space as the table on which they are working; others require far less than 2 times the largest table size.

Network Performance

If you want the best performance for your application, install both Windows and Paradox locally on each machine. Don't try to run Windows or Paradox from a network drive, unless you have an unusually fast network topology. The Paradox *Getting Started* documentation describes three network installation types: local-only, combined, and server-only. For best performance, use the local-only installation setting.

In addition, you must think carefully about where to place the user's private directory. The private directory is where Paradox writes many temporary files during queries, reports, table sorting, and other file management tasks. The best choice, in terms of performance, is usually a directory on the user's local hard drive.

However, two issues complicate matters. First, users often have little free space on their local drives. If you don't give the private directory ample free space, you will run out of disk space during certain queries. Sometimes you will be forced to move the private directory to a network drive. Second, we have run into some older hard drives that are not terribly fast. In these cases, you can actually improve Paradox performance by moving the private directory to a network drive. You should compare how your application performs when the private directory is local to how the application performs when it is on the server.

If your users are installing a new network topology, influence them to get a fast one. Database applications stress network topologies in ways that most PC applications don't. Many network installation consultants, if they are unaware of the demands that Paradox and other database application software make on a network, can severely underestimate network throughput requirements. Perhaps the single biggest determinant of network performance is the type of network topology chosen. If you or your users try to save money and forgo purchasing the better-performing network topology, you might be sacrificing the database application's performance.

Table Access Performance

All developers must find ways to make their applications run faster without relying exclusively on hardware improvements. In fact, you can achieve the most significant improvements in speed by examining two areas in your application: table design and program logic.

Using Secondary Indexes Wisely

As part of building every application, you will have to decide which fields in which tables will need secondary indexes. Secondary indexes substantially improve the performance of certain queries. For example, if you have a date field in a customer table, placing a secondary index on it speeds any queries and exact-match locates on that field. If the table is large and the number of records you need to find is small, secondary indexes provide a big performance boost.

Usually, the best thing to do is build the application by taking your best guesses, based on user interviews or the application's design, and pick the fields that would be best served with secondary indexes. Then install the application and observe how users *actually* use the application. Based on these observations, add or revise the secondary indexes. Very often, this post-delivery tweaking can result in significant performance improvements in key areas.

Using Queries and TCursors Properly

With the advent of TCursors, developers now have some choices when it comes to accessing tables. Traditional programmers may feel more at home with the record-at-a-time access that TCursors provide. Paradox for DOS developers will feel at home in Paradox for Windows' set-oriented QBE. Both tools have their place, and both tools overlap each other to some degree. Knowing which to use, and when, separates the Paradox masters from the novices.

The following example illustrates the point. It demonstrates timing differences between using a TCursor to insert records into a table and using a query. This code was used against the LINEITEM.DB table each copy of Paradox has as part of the SAMPLE subdirectory. In one test case, just over 1,000 records were copied. In the second case, only 8 records were copied. Table 31.2 lists the timing results. The source code is presented here:

TCursor versus Query Performance Test

```
var
     tc1, tc2 TCursor
     q Query
     start, end array[2] LongInt
endvar
q = Query
ANSWER: :PRIV:ANSWER.DB
```

```
            LINEITEM.DB ¦ Order No ¦ Stock No ¦ Selling Price ¦ Qty   ¦ Total ¦
                        ¦ _EG01    ¦ _EG02    ¦ _EG03         ¦ _EG04 ¦ _EG05 ¦
            LINETEST.DB ¦ Order No ¦ Stock No ¦ Selling Price ¦ Qty   ¦ Total ¦
            Insert      ¦ _EG01    ¦ _EG02    ¦ _EG03         ¦ _EG04 ¦ _EG05 ¦
EndQuery
start[1] = cpuClockTime()                       ; start the clock
if not q.executeQBE() then                      ; run the query
    msgStop("Error","In QBE")
    return
endif
end[1] = cpuClockTime()                         ; stop the clock
if not tc2.open("linetest") then                ; open the table
    msgStop("Error","In TC2")
endif
tc2.empty()                                     ; empty it
tc2.close()                                     ; close the table
start[2] = cpuClockTime()                       ; start the clock
if not tc1.open("lineitem") then                ; open table 1
    msgStop("Error","In TC1")
endif
if not tc2.open("linetest") then                ; open table 2
    msgStop("Error","In TC2")
endif
tc2.edit()                                      ; edit table 2
scan tc1:
    tc2.insertRecord(tc1)                       ; add record
endscan
tc2.endedit()                                   ; end the edit
tc1.close()                                     ; close table 1
tc2.close()                                     ; close table 2
end[2] = cpuClockTime()                         ; stop the clock
if not tc2.open("linetest") then                ; open the table
    msgStop("Error","In TC2")
endif
tc2.empty()                                     ; empty the table
tc2.close()                                     ; close it
msgInfo("Timing","The elapsed time for Query was "+
           String(end[1]-start[1])+" milliseconds. "+
           "The elapsed time for TCursor was "+
           String(end[2]-start[2])+" milliseconds.")
```

Table 31.2. TCursor versus query performance.

Table size	Query	TCursor
1,000 records	22.1 seconds	32.5 seconds
8 records	3.2 seconds	2.4 seconds

As you can see from table 31.2, a simple insert query is faster on large amounts of data, whereas TCursors are faster when handling smaller numbers of records. Our advice is as follows: use queries whenever possible, except for adding or copying a small number of records from one table to another.

In the TCursor timing on copying eight records, nearly two seconds were consumed just opening and closing the TCursor. Every time you execute a query, the query engine has to open and close each table in the query image. For simple record copying, a TCursor might be in order, especially if you can keep the TCursor open for several iterations of the copy.

In applications that use TCursors to access tables, you can gain a big boost in performance by opening and closing a TCursor as little as possible. Instead, open the TCursor when the form is opened and close it when the form is closed. While the form is running, use the TCursor to access the tables.

Using Multi-Step Queries

Many Paradox programmers make the mistake of trying to have one query do it all. In some queries, this can result in slower performance than using multi-step queries. The Paradox query engine, although smart enough to find the best way to run most types of queries, is not omniscient.

In some circumstances, multi-step queries can also drastically reduce the amount of time it takes to execute a query, especially if the size of the tables is quite large. In these cases, it is best to sequence the queries so that the first query has a selection criteria which uses a secondary index, and that the selection criteria reduces the number of records returned.

ObjectPAL Performance

Tweaking ObjectPAL code is perhaps the most difficult way to optimize an application, because this optimization technique is the least likely to improve the performance of the entire application. Instead, examining ObjectPAL code usually improves the performance of only the object and the form changed. Still, users have much to gain if you improve the performance of your code.

Perhaps the cardinal rule of ObjectPAL performance tuning is this:

Use the least expensive event to accomplish your goal.

In the Paradox for Windows event model, there are many ways to accomplish the same thing. More often than not, we have a choice about when and where we want to perform our ObjectPAL code. Because hundreds of events occur each second, you have to make sure that your code is being executed only when it absolutely needs to execute.

For example, you can place code in a record object's canDepart( ) built-in method that evaluates the current record and prevents the user from leaving the record if certain values are not what they should be. Or you can place the code in the record object's action( ) built-in method to trap for the DataUnlockRecord event or DataPostRecord event and check the record before it is posted.

Which is the better place to put this sort of record-validation code? It depends on how ambitious your record-checking code is. If the code is doing some fairly complex and involved things which slow down the record object's depart event cycle, you might want to place the code in the action( ) built-in method. This ensures that your code won't be executed when users scroll through the records in the table without making changes. If users frequently scroll through records without making changes, the application's performance will be improved from their perspective.

Other ObjectPAL performance improvement alterations you can make include:

- Explore implementation alternatives. Don't assume that the code you wrote during the development cycle is the best-performing code. Test other ways of achieving what you want.

- Be careful about how frequently you open or close tables and files. The preceding TCursor example shows that the overhead in opening a table is quite high. Accessing any file, including text files and Paradox locking files, takes time, especially on a network. In general, try to avoid excessively or needlessly opening and closing resources.

- Reduce file and table accesses. Next to opening a table or a file, accessing one is the most expensive. Avoid needlessly writing, inserting, or posting records. Every time you change a table under ObjectPAL control, Paradox has to write the changes to the table. Each time Paradox accesses a table, it checks to see if the table cache in memory is up to date with the table. If not, Paradox has to refresh the cache. If tables change needlessly, all users can experience degraded performance.

- Take advantage of compile-time binding. Because ObjectPAL is compiled, Paradox runs faster if the compiler can reference all variables. If you forget to declare a variable in a var..endvar statement, the compiler assumes the variable is an AnyType variable.

- Consider using multi-page forms instead of using multiple forms. Opening a form is a more expensive operation than simply switching to another page of an already open form. You could place several data entry screens all in one form, but on different pages. You will notice a significant improvement in speed when the user is simply switching pages in a form.

- Watch your form size. Forms that get too big (over 150 to 200K or too many fields or tables in the data model) can't be debugged and also run the risk of corruption.

- Maintain performance records. Keep a history of the different tests you've put your application through. Use these records to identify performance bottlenecks and to record your attempts to improve the bottleneck. Past performance records are frequently valuable when a new version of Paradox becomes available, because you can find out if Borland has made performance gains in areas that affect your application. Performance records also force you to quantify your reasons for tweaking your code.

- Analyze your algorithms. Although you can tweak your code, improve your table structure, and add hardware to your machine, you can't completely overcome bad algorithms. The basic algorithm you chose in parts of your application has a bigger impact on performance than most other issues. Be aware that analysis of algorithms is a well-established computer science discipline. Grab some books on algorithm performance analysis and read them. They can help you distinguish between a fast approach and a slow approach to a problem.

Summary

Performance tuning in the world of Windows can get wacky. There are hundreds of pieces of software and hardware built by all sorts of different manufacturers. It is downright difficult, at times, to find the source of a performance problem. In this chapter, we've tried to highlight those issues over which you, as a Paradox programmer, have control. These issues include some basic Windows and hardware configuration issues, Paradox configuration issues, and most importantly, ObjectPAL programming issues.

If you exhaust the possibilities discussed here, you will need to explore further into network performance issues (if the application is on a network), Windows, and PC hardware configuration issues. Don't give up. Our experience has been that Paradox runs fast enough when the machine, Windows, and the application are set up properly.

32
Neat Tricks and Bad Traps

This chapter contains several little tricks and traps that we have encountered from working with applications, while teaching classes on ObjectPAL, and from participating in PDOXWIN—a forum on CompuServe. These tricks and traps are dealt with quickly and are not in-depth discussions of topics. After you become familiar with ObjectPAL, this chapter is a good place to look for little tidbits that can save you time and effort. Some of these topics are discussed in greater length in later chapters throughout the book.

How do I run multiple copies of Paradox for Windows on one machine?

1. Create a second private directory, C:\PDOXWIN\PRIVATE2.
2. Make another copy of the Paradox for Windows icon within the Paradox for Windows group.
3. Change the icon's command line by using the File ¦ Properties menu choice. Add the following to the end of the command line:

    `-pC:\PDOXWIN\PRIVATE2`

    The `-p` parameter tells Paradox to use a different private directory, other than the default one. You can add a second parameter with the following line:

    `-iPDOXWIN2.INI`

    This line tells Paradox to load using the PDOXWIN2.INI file rather than the default one.

The second copy of Paradox loads quickly because the code is *reentrant*—each copy of Paradox shares the same DLLs in memory. With two copies of Paradox running, interesting things become possible. You can use DDE, for example, to communicate between the two copies, or you can use a shared file as a communications resource. One copy of Paradox—the background copy—would use a timer event to poll the shared table. As soon as this copy found a certain record that you predefined to mean something, the background task performs some action.

I created and placed a crosstab in a form. How do I get the crosstab in a Paradox table?

You can create a pushbutton on the form and use the pushbutton built-in method (or use the form's arrive event or open event after a doDefault), and place the following line of code there:

```
xtabname.action(DataSaveCrosstab)
```

This code creates a table, CROSSTAB.DB, in your private directory.

How much memory should I have for Paradox for Windows?

In our estimation, you cannot have *enough memory* in a Windows environment. Because Windows allows you to run multiple applications concurrently, the more memory the merrier. A good baseline Windows configuration should have at least 8 megabytes of memory or more. Paradox can actually load with 2 megabytes, but only if you are into pain. Better still, consider 4 megabytes a minimum amount of memory. By the way, Paradox is more memory intensive than CPU intensive. If you have a choice between a faster CPU and more memory, choose more memory (provided you are using at least a 386DX processor).

Does Paradox for Windows run with Stacker or other disk compression utilities?

Paradox runs just fine in these environments.

How do I get the same table onto my data model twice. The data model only lets me select a table once?

Create an alias that points to the same directory as the table you want to load twice. Next, add the table to the data model by referencing the second alias rather than the default alias or no alias.

Is there any way to place unlinked tables onto a form?

Yes, just use the TableFrame or Multi-Record SpeedBar item to add a table frame or an MRO. Then, right click on the new object and define the table. In addition, you can just place a table in the data model without linking it to another table.

How can I change the background colors on my lists and edit lists in forms?

Use the Windows Control Panel utility and change the Windows background to the color you want. It would be nice to change the color of the background in the list just like you change any other object's color; but alas, you have to wait for the next version of Paradox for Windows.

When do tables actually get saved to disk?

The answer to this question depends on whether or not the table is on what Paradox considers a shared device. If the table is shared, such as a table on a network file server or a table on your local hard drive with Paradox configured as local share on, then Paradox writes the changes to the disk every time the user leaves or posts a record. If the table is not shared, such as tables in your private directory, Paradox doesn't write changes to disk immediately. In addition, if you have a disk caching utility, like SMARTDRV.SYS or SMARTDRV.EXE (which comes with DOS 5.0) and this disk cache has write caching enabled, Paradox writes the changes to tables to the disk, but the disk cache intercepts the data, caching it, and may write it out later.

We strongly advise that you turn off write caching whenever you use Paradox for Windows to access data on your local drive. To turn write caching off, just list the drive letter at the end of the SMARTDRV.EXE command line, without a colon. Because the default for SMARTDRV is to have write caching enabled, this turns off write caching. Also, check how much memory SMARTDRV consumes. If SMARTDRV is consuming, say, 2M on a 4 or 8M machine, consider reducing to 1M or less. Paradox for Windows also can use this memory.

How do I deny a pushbutton event before it occurs? The reason is that as soon as the user pushes the button, it depresses. I don't want the button to depress if I want to deny the push button event.

Trap for the mouse down event and the keyphysical event that can occur on the pushbutton. It is obvious that the user can use the mouse to push a button, but they can also tab to the button and press the enter key. Deny these two events rather than denying the pushbutton event.

Can table family objects be placed in separate directories?

No. All of a table's .DB, .MB, .PX, .X??, .SET, .VAL,.FAM, and .TV files must reside in the same directory.

I just found out how to set up and save my SpeedBar properties so that every time I create a new form, I get the look I want. The problem is that when I create a quick report, the report looks like the forms, which is what I don't want. Can I have two different SpeedBar settings, one for reports and one for forms?

Unfortunately, after Paradox finds a .FT file, it uses the file for the session. You have to change your default setting.

I want to create dialog boxes with forms that look just like the Borland dialog boxes. What is the pattern for the hatched area, the color of the depressed area where fields are placed, the color of the fields and frames around the fields, and the font for the field labels?

The hatched area uses a pattern style of VeryHeavyDotPattern. The depressed area where fields are placed uses a Gray color, the frame style of Inside3DFrame and the font is MS Sans Serif 8 point or Helvetica and the font style is FontAttribBold. In addition, to get the 3-D button with the fancy graphics that Borland uses on OK, Cancel and other buttons, you need to download a file, BORBTN.ZIP from library 9 in the PDOXWIN forum on CompuServe.

How do I change properties for several fields at once in a form?

You can select multiple objects by pressing and holding down Ctrl and left-clicking on the objects. After you select multiple objects, hold down Ctrl and right-click. You then can change properties for all the objects selected. If you selected one object, and the object contains other objects, if you hold down Ctrl and right-click, the object selected and all the objects it contains are included so that you can change all the properties at once.

What are "noise names"?

Noise names are the names of objects that Paradox gives when it creates the objects. Noise names begin with the number (#) character. When you need to reference objects in the containership hierarchy with dot notation, you can ignore any noise names in your dot notation.

How do I build a list on the fly, without using the DataSource = "[tableName.fieldName]" method?

Assuming that you had an array, shipMethod, that holds the available shipping methods for an order, you can place the shipping methods in a list with the following code:

```
for x from 1 to shipMeth.size()
   self.List.selection = x
   self.List.value = shipMeth[x]
endfor
```

You must attach this code to the list object, not the field object, so that self will refer to the list and not to the field.

How many timer events can I have going at one time?

Windows has a limit of 32 timer events. But before you program 32 timer events, check all other applications in Windows that may use timer events and test thoroughly.

Does Paradox for Windows have a counter type that I can use when creating tables?

No, Paradox doesn't have a counter type, although you can program one easily in ObjectPAL. In this book, check Chapter 16 on TCursors.

What actually happens when delivering forms?

The source code statements are stripped from the form, reducing the size of the form and making it impossible for the users to edit any of the forms methods.

Do methods and procedures get copied to the clipboard when I cut or paste an object to the clipboard?

Yes, all methods and procedures are copied to the clipboard as well. In addition, whenever you save desktop properties, all objects that were copied to the SpeedBar that also have code attached are written to the .ft file.

I just imported a table from Microsoft Access into Paradox for Windows, and I noticed that the file takes up much more space in Paradox. Why?

This can happen. What can also happen is that some Paradox tables, when imported into Access can grow significantly in size as well. The reason is that Access and Paradox store data differently. Access stores all tables in a database in a single file, using variable-length field and record structures to conserve space. Some tables, depending on how many alphanumeric fields they have, grow when exported to a Paradox table. Conversely, Paradox uses a fixed-length record format and when some tables are imported to Access, they grow significantly because Access has some additional overhead it uses for every Paradox record.

What files can I safely remove from my Paradox for Windows directory? My user is short on disk space and needs to conserve space.

The following files can be deleted:

- All *.doc and *.txt files.
- Any *.cfg files, except for ODAPI.CFG.
- The pwlocal.exe file, if you don't need to set local settings.
- The odapicfg.exe file, if you don't need to edit the odapi.cfg file.
- The pwupdate.exe file, which enables you to add serial numbers to your configuration.
- All TUTILITY.* files, if you don't want to run TUTILITY, which fixes files.
- Any *.hlp files, if you don't need to access on-line help.
- Any of the sample and DIVEPLAN application files.

What graphic file formats can I import into Paradox forms and reports:

The following file formats are supported: BMP, EPS, PCX, GIF, TIF, and TLE formats. All graphics are stored as BMP files, unless you import the graphic into a Blob field, in which case the file is not converted, just stored.

Does a way exist to switch indexes from within a form, so that the user can look at records in a different order?

Interactively, you can use the Form ¦ Order/Range menu items. Under program control, attach a TCursor to a field on the form, use the switchIndex( ) method on the TCursor, and then use the resync( ) method to resynchronize the object with the TCursor. Check out Chapter 15 on UIObjects.

What's the difference between the errorCode( ) procedure and the errorCode( ) functions?

The errorCode( ) procedure is used after a method and procedure were invoked to determine what went wrong if the invocation failed. The errorCode( ) method is always available to eventInfo and eventInfo-derived types to determine what went wrong during an event.

I designed a form on one computer (with an 800 x 600 display resolution), and when I run it on another computer (with a normal VGA display, 640 x 480 resolution), the size has changed. How can I design forms that work on all displays?

The problem with designing forms for multiple screen display types is that you have to consider a few design questions. Do you want higher resolution displays to be able to view more of the form or a larger form? Do you want higher resolution displays to display more forms? Because larger resolution displays have more *real estate* with which to work, forms that you design on a standard display and run on a higher resolution display appear to shrink and *vice versa*.

If all your forms are designed within a 6-by-4-inch maximum size, they will be seen on all displays. The higher the resolution, the smaller the form window. If you want all forms to occupy the same amount of space on screen displays, you have to determine what kind of screen display the user has and resize the form image appropriately. You also can just maximize all form windows, which is a less desirable solution.

What's the difference between the two following quoted strings which refer to a field in a table:

`"[customer.city]"` and `"[\"customer.db\".city]"` ?

The first reference makes sense. The second example, however, is a little more confusing. To see why the second form is often required, you need to look at the second example the way you might want to incorrectly use it:

`"[customer.db.city]"`

If you need to explicitly distinguish between dBASE and Paradox tables within a quoted string such as this one, using the `.db` will confuse the compiler, because the compiler doesn't know whether or not `.db` is a field name. To solve the problem, you can place quotes around the customer name:

`"["customer.db".city]"`

This code, however, also confuses the compiler because it treats everything between double quotes as the quoted string. The compiler can't handle nested quote characters. So, to tell Paradox that the inside quote characters have no semantic meaning, you place the backslash (\) character in front, which changes the code in the following manner:

`"[\"customer.db\".city]"`

Why can't I use Paradox as a DDE Server from a form or report?

Unfortunately, as of now, Paradox can be a DDE server only from within a table view.

When I use the File ¦ Utilities *menu command to display a table's structure, the fields are listed in a dialog box. How do I print this structure of a table?*

With some ObjectPAL and the enumFieldStructure( ) TCursor method, you can easily print a table's structure. You can use the following code in a script, or on the pushbutton method of a form:

```
var
    tc TCursor
    tb, structTb String
    viewStruct tableView
endvar
tb = "Customer.db"
structTb = "Tstruct.db"
if tc.open(tb) then
    tc.enumFieldStructure(structTb)
    viewStruct.open(structTb)
endif
```

Also, whenever you restructure a table, Paradox creates a STRUCT.DB table in your private directory. You can view and print an instant report from this table.

I placed some code at the form level in the open built-in method. I noticed that when I ran the form, I didn't get the SpeedBar that I expected. What went wrong?

If you place code in the form's open built-in method, issue a doDefault first, then perform the stuff you need to do. The open method is akin to a constructor in C++: it initializes a lot of internal data structures that Paradox for Windows uses. Let Paradox complete the open before you assign variables or perform your own code. Placing the doDefault before your code forces Paradox to complete the open process. This same line of reasoning also holds true for taking action at each object's open method. Issue a doDefault first.

I have referential integrity set between two tables that have a one-to-many relationship. In the master table, when I change the linking field, all the child record's linking fields also change. When I blank out the master linking field, all the child records' linking field also are blanked out. When I change the master linking field from blank back to a non-blank value, however, none of the child records change. Why?

Because of the way referential integrity is designed, this is a known problem. The solution is to never allow a linking field's value to become blank by setting the required validity check to On for the field, or to change all the blank child records, either with a query or interactively.

Paradox seems to be "eating" certain keystrokes, like Ctrl+Shift+M. Why?

Check your other concurrently running Windows applications. Some applications, such as screen savers (After Dark 2.0) seem to cause these keyboard problems. Removing these applications sometimes helps.

Are forms really DLLs?

Yes, all FSL, FDL, RSl, and RDL files are Windows DLLs (Dynamic Link Libraries), with the suffixes renamed. All the ObjectPAL source code is compiled down to what is known as *pcode*, similar to Clipper and FoxPro. DLLs are part of the Windows run-time environment and are similar to Windows EXE files. Both Windows EXE and DLL files are not stand-alone, and require plenty of other Windows services, which are found in other DLL files.

In the DOS, non-Windows world of programming, compilers and linkers needed to create a single stand-alone EXE file so that the application can run. In Windows, this need no longer is true.

In fact, DLLs not only save space by allowing multiple applications to share code dynamically at run time, but they also allow multiple copies of the same code to share the same area of memory. Because Paradox for Windows is written to be reentrant, you can load a second copy of Paradox in memory at a fraction of the memory cost of the first copy in memory.

I noticed that I can use the ( ) characters inside a containership path portion of an ObjectPAL statement. Do these characters have special meaning?

The ( ) characters serve to reference the expression contained within the containership path.

For example:

```
var
   s String
   x SmallInt
endvar
s = "Page1.CustMRO.Record"
; this:
x = TheForm.(s).Amount.value
; is the same as this:
x = TheForm.Page1.CustMRO.Record.Amount.value
```

Part VI ■ Special Topics

If you place the containership path in a variable, the compiler cannot check to make sure that you referenced a valid object.

I would like to have my forms opened maximized. How can I do this?

You can use the form open( ) method to do this:

```
formVar.open("Formname",WinStyleMaximize)
```

You also can set the form size to fit property on, in which case the form always opens to the size of the page.

I have trouble running Stacker and Paradox for Windows. What's the proper configuration?

If you run Stacker with the /EMS switch, add the /NB switch to your Stacker command line. If you also have QEMM with the Stealth features on, use the DBF=2 option on the QEMM command line. In addition, try to run Stacker in high memory with LOADHI.

I am using SMARTDRV with Paradox for Windows and Stacker. What are the issues?

First, don't let SMARTDRV take too much memory. Limit memory use from 512K to 1M of memory for small and moderate memory configurations (4 to 8M). Also, make sure that SMRTDRV only caches the original non-STACKER drive, which holds the STACKER volume. Disable caching on any of the STACKER volumes. Also, disable any write-behind caching to prevent SMARTDRV from delaying writes to the disk.

How can I execute other Windows applications from within Paradox?

Just use the execute( ) procedure. During development, for example, you may want to use the Windows Notepad or Paint. You only have to create a form with a button on it. Add the following code to the pushbutton's pushButton( ) built-in method:

```
execute("NOTEPAD.EXE "+fileName,Yes,WinStyleDefault)
```

The variable, *fileName*, is the name of the file you want to edit. The second argument, a logical parameter, makes the Notepad application active. If you specify No, Notepad launches but is inactive. The last parameter is a WindowStyle constant.

How do I calculate someone's age from their birthday?

Use the following code:

```
year(today()-birthDay+1)-1
```

When you subtract two date variables, the result is another date variable. If the person is under a year old, then the above formula returns a date that represents the number of days old the person is since 01/01/01. To count the number of days correctly, one day is added to the birthday. Otherwise, a person born on January 1 is considered 1 year old on December 31. Next, a year is subtracted from the year( ) procedure to correctly count the years from 0, not 1.

I am unable to launch Paradox by running the form from the Windows File Manager. What am I doing wrong?

Make sure that Paradox for Windows is in your path before trying to run the form from within File Manager.

I was looking at another developer's computer screen and noticed that the method dialog box on his computer was different than mine. Is there more than one version of Paradox?

Look at figures 32.1 and 32.2. The two dialog boxes are different, yet the same version of Paradox created both. This is possible; all the dialog boxes in Paradox are resource objects. You can use Borland's Resource Workshop utility, which is sold with Borland language products, to edit any resources in the Paradox DLLs. This practice is not recommended because you are messing with the internals to Paradox's DLLs, but it is so easy to do, and fun! All you have to do is open the proper DLL, find the appropriate dialog box, and use the resource editor to visually redesign the box. The Resource Workshop has designer tools similar to Paradox's form designer, so Workshop is easy to use. When you are done, save the DLL you modified and run Paradox. This technique was used to make figure 32.1 look as it does.

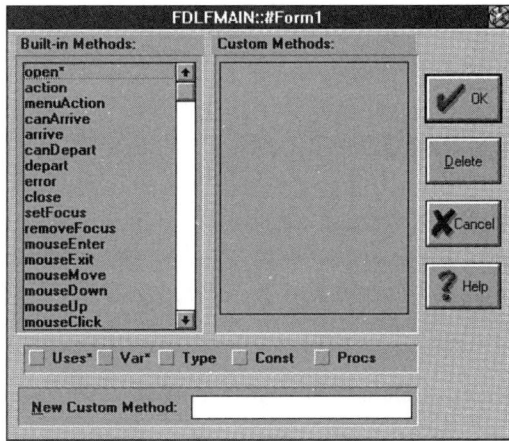

Figure 32.1. The modified Methods dialog box.

How do I convert a Paradox table to a dBASE table? I don't see that option on the Export and Import menu items.

Use File | Utilities | Copy to select the Paradox table, and make sure that you type a .DBF extension for the destination file name. Paradox automatically converts the table as part of the copy. Remember that dBASE tables are a native file format for Paradox.

What does the thicker vertical arrow mean when you point it at the border of a selected object?

The thick vertical arrow means that you can change the size of the object.

Why does Paradox beep when I trap for and deny Alt+key combinations?

If you have a sound board, a sound driver, or both installed in Windows, for some reason this occurs. If you remove the sound driver, you can deny the Alt+key combination and no beep is heard. Apparently, with the sound driver loaded, Windows thinks that the Alt+key combination is an attempt to access an invalid menu shortcut key and beeps.

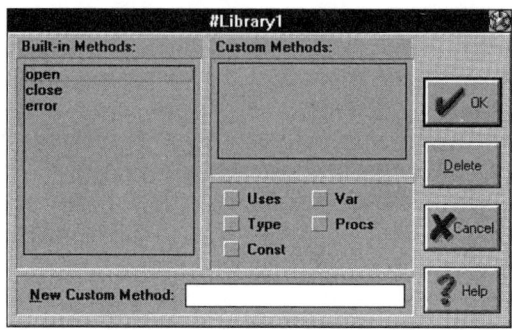

Figure 32.2. The standard Methods dialog box.

Is there any way to change printers in an application without user intervention?

No ObjectPAL method exists that will do the trick. Although you can change the WIN.INI file to indicate a new default printer, this setting is read only when Paradox is started. Until Borland gives us an ObjectPAL method to change the printer, there is nothing you can do.

Is there any way to prompt the user to change the printer?

Yes, use menuAction(menuFilePrinterSetup) from within a pushButton or add it to a custom menu.

Weird things keep happening when I try to open forms when using the form.open( ) method. It almost seems like the open is not succeeding. Sometimes Paradox crashes.

Try using sleep( ), sleep(200) or sleep(500) right after the open. Windows is a multitasking environment and your ObjectPAL code will continue to execute while the form is opening. The sleep command stops the ObjectPAL code momentarily until the window is opened. To Windows programmers, the open( ) is considered a posted event. Other similar methods are close( ), run( ), and design( ) form and report methods.

Is there any way to change the color of messages on the status bar?

No.

How many tables can I put in a data model?

Some users have gotten as many as 60 tables in a data model. However, when the form gets this many tables in the data model, or when the form exceeds a certain size, you can lose the ability to reload your form.

 **Caution:** When your forms begin to exceed 100 to 150K in size, watch for this problem.

What do the terms OEM and ANSI stand for?

OEM refers to the characters supported by DOS drivers and your keyboard.. *ANSI* refers to the set of characters that Windows supports.

Is there anyway to speed searches that have a known first character and then trailing wild cards, as in SM..?

Paradox doesn't use indexes when performing wild-card searches. This limitation may be changed in future versions of the product, because it is an important performance feature. You can use switchIndex( ) and setFilter( ) to restrict the search criteria and then locate on the restricted view, which can provide significant performance improvements for trailing wild-card searches on large tables.

Can I export memo fields to an ASCII file using the File | Utilities | Export *menu item?*

No. You can export memo fields using ObjectPAL, however. Check out the Memo object type for readFromFile( ) and writeToFile( ) and review the TextStream object type's methods and procedures.

I created a field called Shipped&Signed in a table, and I keep getting error messages when I try to refer to the field.

Don't use the ampersand (&) or the period (.) characters in field names. This use tends to confuse Paradox when evaluating ObjectPAL statements.

Where does Paradox store the custom pictures I create when creating or restructring tables?

The custom pictures are found in your PDOXWIN.INI file in the Windows directory.

How can I dial a modem from ObjectPAL code?

The Windows USER DLL file contains some communications functions that you can call from ObjectPAL. First, you need to declare the proper functions in a Uses window:

```
Uses USER
    OpenComm(CommString CPTR, In CWORD, Out CWORD) CWORD
    WriteComm(CommID CWORD, Buffer CPTR, Size CWORD) CWORD
    CloseComm(CommID CWORD) CWORD
enduses
```

Then you need to access these functions in an ObjectPAL method:

```
method DialModem( NumberToDial String, cPort SmallInt )
var
      cstring, dstring String
      size, commID SmallInt
endvar
cstring = "COMM"+String(cPort)+":"
commID = OpenCOmm(cstring,32,32)
dstring = "ATDT"+NumberToDial"+chr(13)
size = dstring.size()
WriteComm(commID,dstring,size)
CloseComm(commID)
endmethod
```

Summary

This chapter touched on many small but often important issues that other programmers have encountered. We strongly encourage you to seek out support services, such as the PDOXWIN forum on CompuServe, which are designed to encourage programmers and users to share their neat tricks and bad traps.

VII

Appendixes

Paradox for Windows Installation and Configuration

Windows software products typically require more attention to installation and configuration than their older DOS counterparts. Luckily, Paradox for Windows provides several tools and good documentation to help users get setup properly.

Unfortunately, given the complexity and interaction between products nowadays, finding an optimal configuration often is difficult. Often developers must experiment with different configurations to find the best results. This appendix discusses the configuration options and the impact these options have on the system.

System Requirements

As a minimum, Paradox for Windows requires an 80386 PC with 4M of RAM memory, running Microsoft Windows 3.1. However, you will find that a more realistic requirement is a 33MHz machine with 8M RAM. For applications that display a lot of graphic images you will want to beef up the video display of the system. While EGA is supported, you will want to have at least a VGA monitor and driver. An interlaced monitor with video cache will provide the best display performance.

The entire Paradox system, including sample files, will require 15MB of hard disk space. The optional sample files take up approximately 3.5MB of disk space. There are a number of .CFG files in the PDOXWIN program file directory, that correspond to several foreign language drivers, that you could also remove. However, these files only take 4K of space and if you ever need to switch to a different character set and sort order you will have to reinstall Paradox.

Appendix A

The minimum required free disk space is 5M, but the amount of free disk space needed will depend on the size of your database tables. A general rule of thumb for calculating hard disk requirements is to have three times the size of your largest database table as free disk space. Paradox when performing some operations will automatically create and delete temporary processing files. Certain operations, like sorting and reporting, can require significant amounts of free disk space.

Installing Paradox for Windows

To install Paradox for Windows, insert Program Disk 1 in drive A, select File ¦ Run from the Windows Program Manager and type **a:\install**. The Paradox for Windows Installation dialog box is then presented.

This dialog box enables you to enter a name and company, which appear on-screen when you start Paradox. You also need to specify the serial number, from and to directory destinations, and the drive where the ODAPI drivers are located. ODAPI stands for Object Database Architecture Programming Interface. The database engine allows other software products to access the same files. Currently, ODAPI also is used in the Database Desktop of Quattro Pro for Windows. Borland is developing and promoting ODAPI technology as a standard set of API access routines. If you have other products that use ODAPI, specify the same directory where these ODAPI drivers are stored in this dialog box.

 **Note:** Quattro Pro for Windows doesn't check for the existence of ODAPI files when installed and will overwrite any ODAPI configuration files that already may have been written by Paradox for Windows. If possible, install Quattro Pro for Windows before you install Paradox for Windows or run the Paradox Configuration Utility described in the following text to re-create the configuration file.

Besides the preceding settings, several check boxes enable you to select which components of Paradox for Windows to install. Several sample files and applications are included with the product. The SubDirectories button displays a dialog box that enables you to specify the directories in which to install these sample files. After you enter the selections and click the Install button, Paradox for Windows provides a clever visual representation of a car driving down the road to display installation progress.

Installing Paradox for Windows on a network uses the same installation program as previously described. You need to enter the correct drive and path specification of your network in the Install To accept box. You also need to increase the number of user counts that use the Serial Number Utility, and specify the correct location of the PDOXUSRS.NET and PDOXWIN.USR files, explained in Chapter 29.

To have users access Paradox for Windows from a network directory, you need to modify their Paradox for Windows Program Item group files to point to the network drive and directory. For performance reasons, we recommend that you install and run Paradox for Windows from local hard drives, rather than in a server configuration from a network drive and directory.

If you are running other applications that access Paradox data, such as Quattro Pro, Paradox for DOS, Paradox Engine applications, or running multiple instances of Paradox in separate windows, you need to add the DOS Share command to your AUTOEXEC.BAT or CONFIG.SYS startup files. Some types of networks also require Share to be loaded. The recommended settings for Share are shown in the following line:

    SHARE /F:4096 /L:400

The /F parameter specifies the amount of DOS disk space to store file sharing information. The default is 2048 bytes. The /L parameter specifies the total number of files that can be locked at one time. The default for the setting is only 20.

You also want to make sure you have at least FILES=60 in the CONFIG.SYS, and probably higher if you have many windows open at the same time. Set BUFFERS=40 if you do not have a disk cache program like SMARTDRV.EXE loaded, and set to 10 if you do. A good disk-caching program is recommended to increase the performance of your machine. The Microsoft Windows SMARTDRV.EXE disk cache usually allocates a large amount of RAM to itself during the Microsoft Windows installation program. You may want to reduce the amount of RAM allocated to it in a low memory configuration.

If you encounter problems when installing Paradox, try to eliminate possible sources of conflicts. REM out all lines of your AUTOEXEC.BAT and CONFIG.SYS files except the following bare bones configurations:

AUTOEXEC.BAT

    PATH=C:;C:\DOS;C:\WINDOWS;

    SET TEMP=C:\WINDOWS\TEMP

CONFIG.SYS

    FILES=60

    BUFFERS=40

    DEVICE=C:\WINDOWS\HIMEM.SYS

    SHELL=C:\DOS\COMMAND.COM C:\DOS /p /e:2048

    STACKS=9,256

In addition, run the Microsoft Windows Setup program and remove all OEM device drivers that may be installed in place of the standard Microsoft device drivers. Replace these drivers with the standard device drivers that come with Microsoft Windows.

If you are in a low memory situation, try running Windows with the /S parameter to start in Standard, rather than Enhanced, mode. Windows in Enhanced mode reports virtual memory in the Program Manager Help ¦ About box, which doesn't report the true amount of memory. By starting in standard mode, you can get an accurate idea of the actual amount of free memory. You need at least 2500 bytes free to run Paradox for Windows. The more memory you have, the better off you will be. After you optimize your memory configuration in standard mode, switch back to virtual mode to operate Paradox.

You may need to modify the Windows initialization file WIN.INI for certain font characteristics. If you notice fonts that are hard to read when operating Paradox, check the WIN.INI file for the following minimum setting:

> [Font Substitutes]
>
> Helv = MS Sans Serif

You also need to have the MS Sans Serif assigned to a specific font file in the [Fonts] section of the WIN.INI file. If Paradox for Windows cannot find a Helvetica fixed size font it will default to using a TrueType font which will cause problems viewing certain areas on-screen, like the status line messages. Certain programs, like PageMaker, will modify your fonts selection that will cause this problem.

You must also make sure that you have defined printer drivers in the Windows Control Panel. It has been reported that Paradox may hang when loading as it tries to access the assigned printer driver. The printer driver selected affects the fonts used when designing and previewing reports.

Startup Processing

When you start Paradox, it reads configuration files in a certain order and establishes the settings within. The following outline indicates the order and the setting that is established.

1. The WIN.INI file is scanned for the [ODAPI] section for a statement like:

    ```
    "CONFIGFILE01=C:\WINDOWS\SYSTEM\ODAPI.CFG"
    ```

    This statement establishes the directory the ODAPI.CFG file is in.

2. The ODAPI.CFG file is read and several settings are defined. The settings that are defined are created by running the ODAPI configuration utility (discussed in a following section of this appendix).

3. The WIN.INI file is read again to set the working and private directories defined in the [PDOXWIN] section.

4. The PDOXWIN.INI file is used to set the default properties and preferences of Paradox windows.

5. PDOXWORK.INI defines default settings for the working directory. The main purpose is to define the properties of a folder. PDOXWORK also can be used to override many of the settings of the PDOXWIN.INI that define the properties of windows.

The various settings allowed in the WIN.INI and PDOXWIN.INI files are explained in the SETTINGS.TXT file located in the Paradox program file directory.

The ODAPI Configuration Utility

When you install Paradox for Windows, Paradox creates a Microsoft Windows program group and places several icons in it. One of the icons is the Configuration Utility. Selecting this icon presents a dialog box used to set ODAPI configuration settings stored in the file, ODAPI.CFG (see fig. A.1).

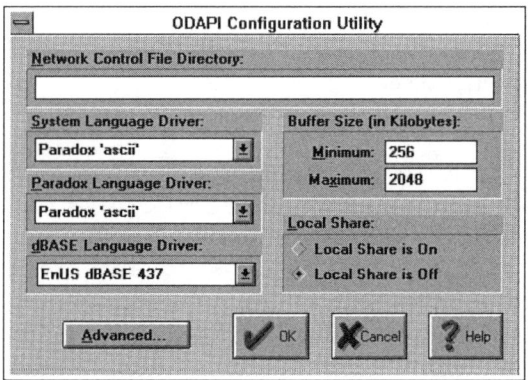

Figure A.1. The ODAPI Configuration Utility dialog box.

A read only version of this same dialog box is displayed in the Paradox for Windows File ¦ System Utilities menu. The Network Control File Directory should be set to the full drive, path, and directory where the PDOXUSRS.NET file is located. Each user on a network that shares common data must have the same setting specified, which includes all DOS Paradox users, setting the same directory that uses the Custom Configuration Program. They also must have read, write, and create access rights to the network directory.

Language Drivers

The Language Driver Pull Downs show the available language drivers that determine the character set and sort order of data. The driver defined in the System Language Driver will be used if the Paradox or dBASE drivers are not defined. Paradox for Windows, being a Windows product, uses the Windows ANSI character set. However, because Paradox for Windows data can be accessed by DOS versions, and DOS uses a different OEM code page character set, Paradox stores OEM character data in tables. Paradox translates the ANSI characters into the OEM characters when it saves the data. Not all ANSI characters translate into an OEM code page, and by default, the character will be set to OEM character 254 as a □. Some diacritical characters and accent marks may be lost in the translation from ANSI to OEM code page characters.

Appendix A

You can prevent this character translation by setting the Strict Translation option from the Table or Form menus within Paradox. If you do, Paradox issues the warning message, Character{s} not supported by Table Language, and does not allow you to save the character.

Each of the language drivers in the drop down lists correspond to particular OEM code pages. You should use the language driver appropriate to the OEM code page. The on-line help system for the ODAPI configuration shows which language drivers correspond to which OEM code pages. When you install Paradox, it looks in the CONTROL.INI file to find the International language driver that is set for Windows. Paradox initially selects an ODAPI language driver depending on the setting in the CONTROL.INI file at installation time.

Note: If you change the International setting in the Windows Control Panel after you have installed Paradox, run the ODAPI Configuration Program and select the corresponding language drivers. Otherwise, certain operations in Paradox, such as queries linking tables on date and number fields, may not perform as expected because the formats of dates and numbers can change between different language drivers.

Table Buffer and Local Share

The Minimum and Maximum Buffer Size settings specify the amount of RAM Paradox will use for the table buffer, which controls how many records can be read into memory at one time. As a general rule, we suggest setting the maximum amount of RAM to 2/3, and the minimum to 1/3 of your total. If you run many different windows programs at the same time, you may want to decrease the maximum amount. If you are running only Paradox, you may want to change this setting to the maximum amount of available RAM. The minimum setting guarantees that Paradox reserves some RAM for working with table data.

If Local Share is checked On, Paradox performs network type locking of files on your local hard disk. If you have non-ODAPI programs that access Paradox data, you can turn Local share on. You also will need to have the DOS Share command loaded before running Windows, as described previously.

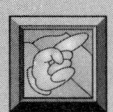

Note: If you plan not to run other applications at the same time as Paradox, make sure that you set Local Share Off. You will get better performance because Paradox doesn't have to go through the file locking routines.

Advanced ODAPI Settings

The Advanced ODAPI settings allow the user to set more specific configurations. When you select the Advanced button from the ODAPI Configuration dialog, you are presented with the ODAPI Full Tree Editor dialog box (see fig. A.2).

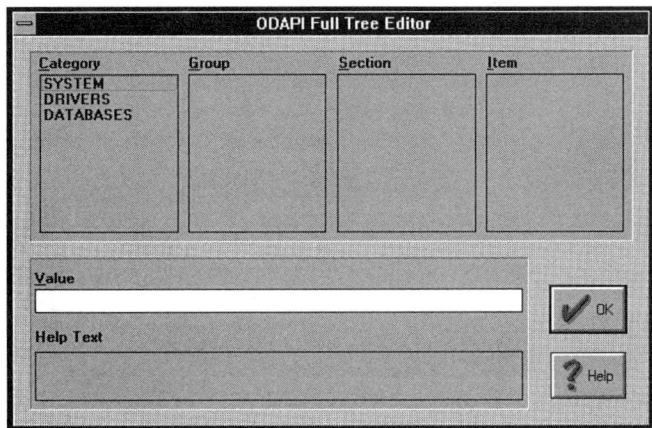

Figure A.2. The ODAPI Full Tree Editor dialog box.

This dialog box is divided into four main sections: Category, Group, Section, and Item. Presently, there are only three categories: System, Drivers, and Databases. When you click on a Category, the Groups for the category then are displayed. If you select a Group, the Sections for this group appear, unless there are no Sections for the Group. The final column for Items are the specific configuration items that you can change. When you select an item, the current value for this item is displayed in the Value accept area, and a Help message describing the item is displayed (see fig. A.3).

Many System categories correspond to the settings established using the International Windows Control Panel. If you change the settings in the Windows Control Panel, you will want to change the corresponding ODAPI configuration. The System Init group Items display the same settings defined in the initial ODAPI Configuration dialog box. Some of these items are reserved for internal use by Paradox and should not be changed, such as SYSFLAGS (see fig. A.4).

Currently, only two Drivers category groups exist—Paradox and dBASE. The Table Create Section has Items that can affect performance and system resources (see fig. A.5).

Appendix A

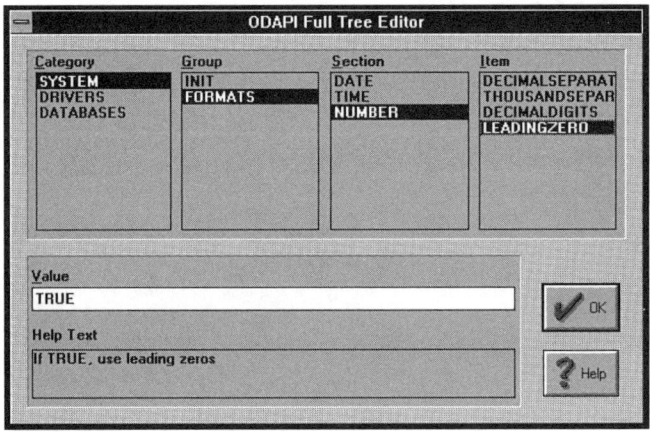

Figure A.3. Changing items in the ODAPI Full Tree Editor.

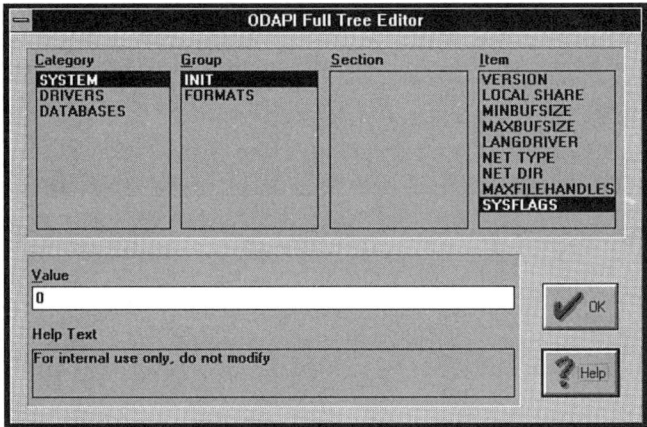

Figure A.4. Configuration items for internal use.

The Fill Factor is the percentage of an index disk block, that when reached, Paradox will create a new disk block. A higher percentage creates indexes that take less disk space; lower percentages may increase performance by allowing indexes to be updated without having to create new disk blocks.

The Block Size item determines the physical disk block size that Paradox for Windows uses when creating tables. This item can be set to 1024, 2048, 3072, or 4096 bytes, and the default is 2048. Paradox tries to fit as many records as possible into a physical disk block. For tables defined with large record sizes, it may be beneficial to increase the block size to reduce wasted disk space.

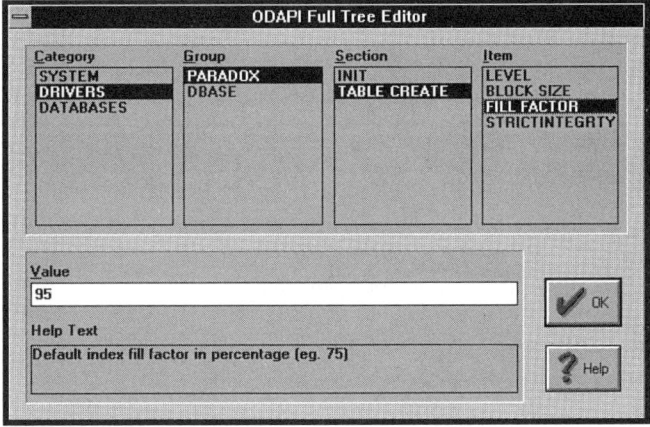

Figure A.5. Index Fill Factor configuration.

The Databases category is used to display any Aliases defined in Paradox for Windows. If an Alias exists, the Group will display the name of the Alias. The item Path shows the drive and directory to which the Alias points (see fig. A.6).

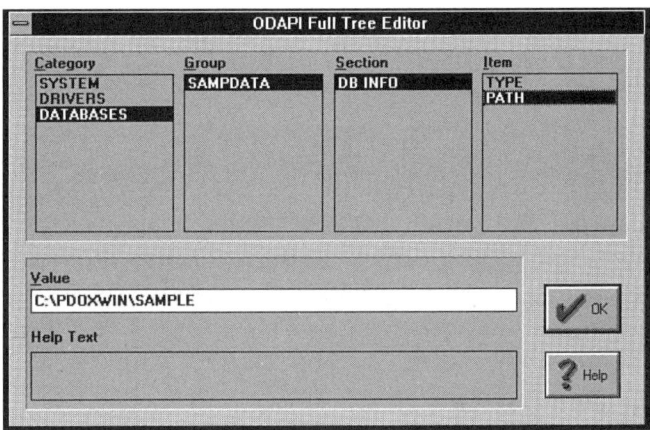

Figure A.6. Alias information in the ODAPI Full Tree Editor.

 **Note:** Changing the Alias Path by using the ODAPI Full Tree Editor dialog box is not recommended. To change Aliases, select the File ¦ Aliases menu option from the Paradox menu.

Appendix A

The ODAPI Full Tree Editor has an extensive on-line help system to explain all the Items that can be reconfigured (see fig. A.7).

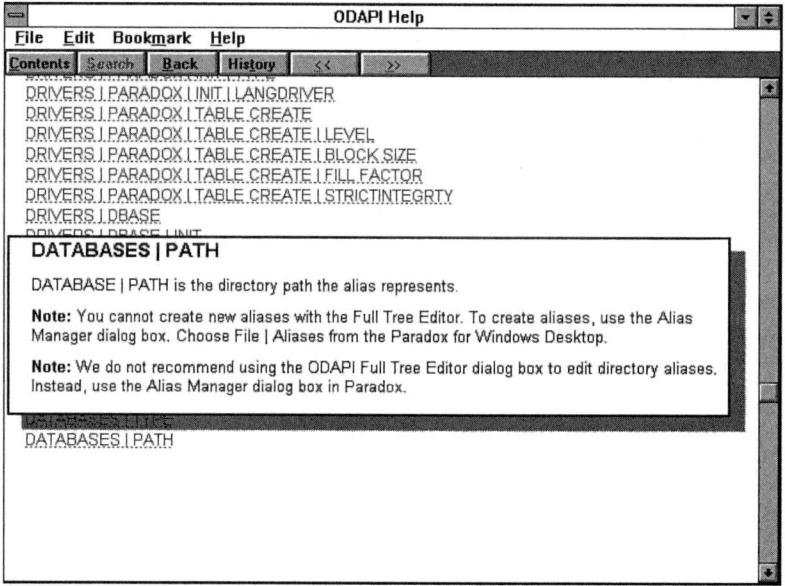

Figure A.7. The ODAPI Full Tree help system.

This on-line help system provides a hypertext link to all Items in the ODAPI Full Tree Editor. When you select a help item, a glossary box displays information about the item.

As Borland develops the ODAPI standard, the ODAPI Full Tree Editor probably will be expanded with new items. As Borland develops the SQL Link technology for Paradox for Windows the Database and Drivers section probably will be expanded to include links to SQL server databases.

Serial Number Utility

The Serial Number Utility program is used to add user counts to a network by adding multiple serial numbers (see fig. A.8). Serial numbers entered are verified for legitimacy.

Just type a serial number and click the Add button to add serial numbers to the list. Valid serial numbers entered will increase the Total User Count. The user count is maintained in the PDOXUSRS.NET file, which does not allow more users to access Paradox than there are user counts.

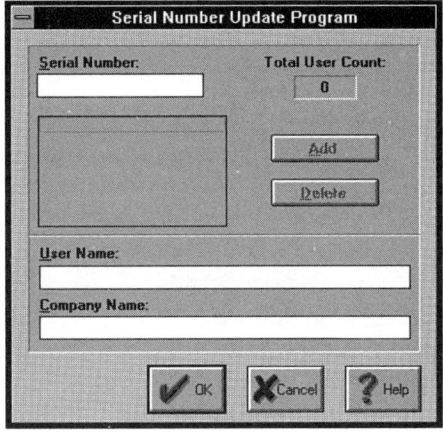

Figure A.8. The Serial Number Utility program's Serial Number Update Program dialog box.

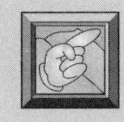 **Note:** You can have multiple instances of Paradox running under Windows without having to have multiple serial numbers. This technique is described in a following section, "Command Line Options."

Local Settings Utility

The Local Settings Utility dialog box enables you to change the directories that Paradox sets for the Working, Private, and ODAPI.CFG when you start Paradox (see fig. A.9).

Changing these settings changes the corresponding section of the WIN.INI file which is read when Paradox starts. The Working and Private directories can be changed from within Paradox using the Files menu. You can override each of these settings by using a command line argument when starting Paradox, described in the following section. The Private directory cannot point to a floppy disk drive and must have adequate disk space available to hold private tables, such as Answer tables from the result of queries.

All the Configuration utilities require the presence of a DLL file called BWCC.DLL, which stands for Borland Windows Custom Control (see fig. A.10). This file must be located in the Windows/System directory and if it cannot be found, Paradox issues an error message.

Appendix A

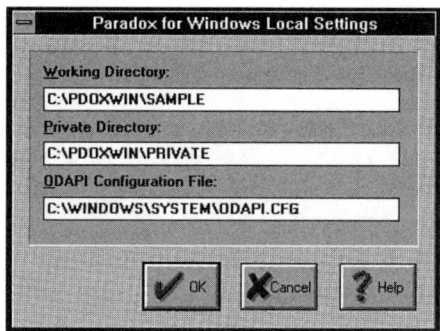

Figure A.9. The Local Settings Utility dialog box.

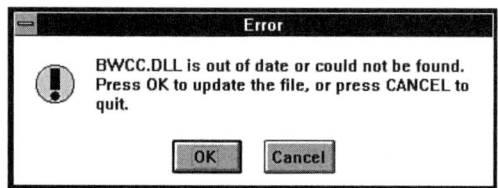

Figure A.10. The BWCC.DLL Error dialog box.

Selecting OK reinstalls the BWCC.DLL file from the PDOXWIN program file directory into the Windows/System directory. If you are running Windows from a network directory you must make sure that you have access to the Systems directory.

Command Line Options

Several command line arguments are available that you can use to change configurations when Paradox is started. To start Paradox with one or more of the command line options, pull down the File menu and choose Run from the Windows Program Manager, type PDOXWIN and add the options you want. If you use more than one option, separate each with a blank space. If Paradox for Windows is not on your DOS Path, you need to specify the full drive and directory of the location of PDOXWIN.

If you find that you run the same command line options often, you probably will want to make your own Program Item and add it to the Paradox for Windows group (see fig. A.11).

The -N option tells Paradox to write no changes to the WIN.INI file when it exits. The -P option tells Paradox to override the Private directory specification in the WIN.INI file. This configuration is useful for starting a second instance of Paradox under Windows. If you do not specify a different Private directory, you see the error message shown in figure A.12.

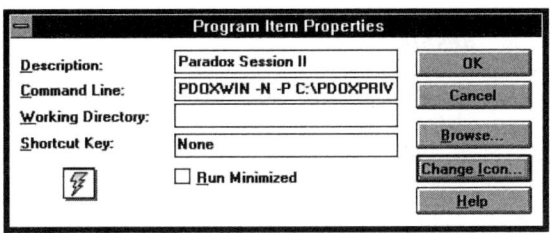

Figure A.11. Defining command line options.

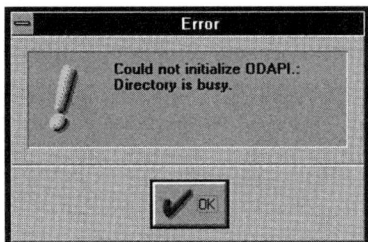

Figure A.12. An ODAPI initialization error, when pointing to the same Private directory.

The first instance of Paradox creates a lock file in the Private directory. When you try to load the second instance of Paradox, pointing to the same Private directory, you get the error message that the directory is busy.

The following list shows the command line options and a description of what each option does. Each of these command line options can be placed in the Flags= setting of the [PDOXWIN] section of the WIN.INI file. If placed in this section, they become the global default configuration options for Paradox. Some of the following options are used to override the defaults established in the Flags= section:

Option	*Result*
-C	Clears the Paradox desktop at startup time. Usually, any windows open when you exit Paradox are restored the next time you start Paradox.
-D *Filename*	*Filename* specifies an alternate PDOXWORK.INI file. Useful for creating different folders for different users. The PDOXWORK.INI file contains information on the contents of folders.
-E	Prevents Paradox from writing changes to the PDOXWORK.INI and PDOXWIN.INI. These files contain default window attributes and designer properties. Developers may create several files to help create different looks and feels to their applications.

Appendix A

Option	Result
-F	Overrides the -E option and allows changes to PDOXWORK.INI and PDOXWIN.INI.
-I *Filename*	*Filename* specifies an alternate PDOXWIN.INI file.
-M	Starts Paradox as a minimized application. It loads and then minimizes Paradox so you can work with other Windows applications and quickly switch back to it.
-N	Will not write changes to the WIN.INI file, as discussed previously.
-O *Filename*	*Filename* specifies an alternate ODAPI.CFG file to use. Useful if you need to create data tables using different foreign language drivers.
-P *Directory*	*Directory* specifies a different directory location to use as the Private directory.
-Q	Tells Paradox not to display the title screen when loading, which includes the percent complete status bar that indicates how fast Paradox is loading.
-S	To keep users from being able to resize the Paradox Desktop you can use this option. ObjectPAL applications still can adjust the size of the Desktop.
-T	Allows you to resize the Desktop and will override the -S option if set in the Flags= section of [PDOXWIN] in the WIN.INI file.
-Y	Allows you to override the -N option and write changes to the WIN.INI file when you exit Paradox.
Startfile	If you give the name of a specific Paradox object, this object will be used at startup time with its default behavior. For example, if you specify the name of a QBE query file, Paradox starts and then runs the query. If you give it the name of an FSL Form file, Paradox runs the form.

When you specify an alternate configuration file to use, make sure that you clearly specify the location of the file. If Paradox cannot find the alternate file you specify, it will use the regular configuration file. If you give just a relative directory and file name, Paradox starts from the Working directory to try and find the file. When in doubt, use the full drive, directory, and file name specification.

Paradox for Windows offers a lot of flexibility in how you can configure it. There are several configuration files, including both Paradox and Windows INI files, that you can adjust for specific needs. Three utility programs exist to help ease the configuration process. Several Command Line Options are available to override settings and specify different configuration files. Using all these different options allows you to customize the database in many ways.

An Overview of ObjectPAL for the PAL Programmer

If you're a pro with PAL, you will feel like a novice with ObjectPAL, but only for a short while. You may have heard that Paradox for Windows has a steep learning curve. It only seems steep when you first encounter it. As you work more with Paradox for Windows, it becomes clear that you can do useful things in ObjectPAL sooner than you thought. ObjectPAL is a strange new world, but when you understand the Paradox for Windows model, you will find that writing ObjectPAL code is easy and usually error-free.

Experienced PAL programmers will have some advantages in learning ObjectPAL. The designers of ObjectPAL have tried to use PAL terms wherever possible. Perhaps this is the reason that PAL programmers will feel a bit strange in ObjectPAL: the language is just familiar enough that you think you should know what to do, yet this language is clearly different enough that you don't know exactly what to do. It's kind of like a dream in which you are in a strange land, yet the landscape seems vaguely familiar.

This appendix is designed to make this strange world seem more friendly by directing you to study the areas with which you are probably least familiar, and to skim over the areas where you are strongest. If you are like most experienced PAL programmers, you know Paradox for DOS's interactive environment very well. You are versed in how to use queries and reports. You can design some great looking forms, and you can write code to work with forms easily. You may have coded some dialog boxes in Paradox 4.0 and have added this ability to your repertoire of skills. You probably have become familiar with Paradox 4.0's event-driven Wait command.

You probably haven't had to do any Windows development. You probably had some experience with other languages, such as Pascal and C, but PAL is probably your strongest language. If this description describes you, this chapter will be very illuminating.

What To Study First

To get up to speed in ObjectPAL, you are going to have to understand the following concepts inside and out as soon as possible:

- Forms, as reports and as dialog boxes
- The containership hierarchy
- Event bubbling

These three features are the heart and soul of Paradox for Windows. Master these concepts and the rest is easy. Not that these concepts are horrendously difficult; they're not. They're clear, concrete, useful concepts that give Paradox for Windows a distinct flavor. But they do require some thought and some experimentation.

Although you might be very familiar with using and creating forms in Paradox for DOS, Paradox for Windows has a powerful new forms designer. For this reason, we suggest you pay close attention to Chapter 10, "Designing and Using Forms." We also recommend that you pay close attention to the discussion of the containership hierarchy and event model in Chapter 13, and to all of Chapter 14 on controlling events. Work with the ideas in these chapters. Create your own examples and start playing with the concepts discussed there.

The following concepts also are important, but are clearly secondary to the first three:

Using the ObjectPAL editor

Creating data models

Creating tables

Designing Windows applications

Using the ObjectPAL Editor

Paradox for Windows comes with an editor that is much more powerful and useful than the one that came with previous versions of Paradox. Until a great third-party editor becomes available, you need to know this editor well.

The ObjectPAL editor is very different than the editors in previous versions of Paradox. You can do such things as set breakpoints; trace your code in a separate window; view ObjectPAL methods, properties, and constants; edit code from multiple objects at the same time; and check your syntax as you go along. If you master the interactive uses of the editor, you will be able to write code quickly, and you'll feel better about ObjectPAL. If you don't master the editor, you will be less productive than you were in PAL. Needless to say, you won't like ObjectPAL.

Creating Data Models

Paradox for Windows has a powerful mechanism, the data model, that enables you to create some hot forms. Your first tendency in Paradox for Windows may be to try and create a form without thinking about a data model. We feel that this route is a mistake; forms are easy, and you will pick them up quickly. Creating a data model also is easy, but it is something you never had to do in Paradox for DOS. In addition, you can use the data model tool when you create queries. Spend some time learning this fantastic new tool, which can make you more productive. Chapters 8 and 9 should be high on your list of chapters to read.

Creating Tables

One of the biggest improvements for developers in Paradox for Windows is the improvement in the underlying database engine that manages tables. In Paradox for Windows, you can set referential integrity rules, validity checking rules, pictures, and other properties when you create the table. In addition, all these constraints are active all the time. It doesn't matter if the user is using a form to put data in, running an insert query, or using the Paradox for Windows menus to add one table to another. If any record violates any of the constraints you set up when creating or restructuring the table, the record will not be added. How many lines of your old PAL code does *this* procedure replace?

Because Paradox for Windows now enforces more aspects of the relational model, it's a good idea to brush up on relational database theory. Chapter 2 can help you in this area.

Although you already know how to create tables, Paradox for Windows has significant enhancements in this area that you don't want to miss, which is why we think that you should put creating tables high on your list of Paradox for Windows skills.

Designing Windows Applications

We believe that designing Windows applications is perhaps the most critical area for experienced PAL programmers. You have most likely resisted Windows, use of the mouse, graphics, and Common User Access (CUA) style interfaces as much as possible. Well, in Paradox for Windows, you have no choice but to become master of a new universe: Windows programs.

Maybe the best way to learn how to write good Windows applications is not just to read about it (although Chapter 3 is a must-read), but to become fluent in actually using Windows applications on a regular basis. You can do this by using Paradox for Windows or by buying other Windows software. As you work with Windows software, take a critical look at how the software handles keystrokes, mouse clicks, and menu accessing. What types of user interface elements (radio buttons, combo boxes, edit lists, check boxes, and push buttons) are used most often and where? Every Windows application interacts with the user in slightly different ways. Examine the possibilities and choose an approach that makes sense for you and your clients.

We also recommend that you seek out books on user interface design in Windows. After all, now that you are on your way to becoming a Paradox for Windows programmer, you need to become an informed Windows programmer.

What To Get Out of Your Head First

The first thing to purge from your mind is the PAL Menu command. Ah, what an island of security and stability was the PAL Menu command! As a PAL programmer, it was easy to use the PAL Menu command to do all kinds of things, from exporting data to other file formats to changing a report grouping on-the-fly.

Those days are gone. In ObjectPAL, no equivalent to the Menu command exists. Moreover, there is not a concept of recording or playing back keystrokes. Purging this tremendously useful habit from both your mind and your fingers will be difficult, but hang in there.

The second concept you have to let go of is the concept of writing code independent of forms. In previous versions of Paradox, you usually wrote code in scripts, which ultimately were placed in procedure libraries. Your data entry code, although often tailored for a specific form, existed independent of the form; you could edit the code without editing the form.

In Paradox for Windows, the form is the container for the data entry code. When you write code tailored for a form, you open the form, select the object on the form, and attach code. Granted, Paradox for Windows has a *library*, which lets you put common or generic code in one place. For the most part, you will be placing code that you tailored for a form on the actual object. This concept can be disconcerting at first, especially to programmers used to using a third-party editor to manage the source code. These third-party editors help you compress the cognitive space your application occupies by providing sophisticated searching and cataloging features. These editors enable you to manage megabytes of source code easily and quickly.

What was reassuring about Paradox for DOS was that all your source code existed in separate DOS text files. In Paradox for Windows, your source code will be scattered about in your ocean of objects. You will manage your source code by managing your objects, which is easy to do in Paradox for Windows. But it is different from Paradox for DOS. Many traditional programmers find this change troublesome.

Similarities between PAL and ObjectPAL

Paradox for Windows can be hauntingly familiar to PAL programmers. When you begin writing your first "snippets" of code, you will be amazed at how easy it is to write them and how error-free they seem to be. This is by design, because Borland has tried to preserve as many language elements from Paradox for DOS in Paradox for Windows as possible.

An Overview of ObjectPAL for the PAL Programmer

The following control structures are identical in the two languages:

```
If <condition> Then
    <statements>
Else
    <statements>
Endif
Switch
    Case <condition> :
        <statements>
    Case <condition> :
        <statements>
    ...
    Otherwise:
        <statements>
EndSwitch
While <condition>
    <statements>

EndWhile
For <variable> from <Start> to <Stop> Step <increment>
    <statements>
endfor
```

The Loop, QuitLoop, and Return language elements behave the same. ObjectPAL has a Scan..Endscan construct that behaves the same as the PAL Scan..Endscan, but has a slightly different syntax. In addition, ObjectPAL has several run-time library (RTL) procedures and methods that are similar to the PAL counterparts. Table B.1 lists some common functions/methods or procedures between ObjectPAL and PAL.

Table B.1. Common PAL/ObjectPAL functions/methods or procedures.

dateVal( )
strVal( )
numVal( )
substr( )
search( )
match( )
upper( )
lower( )
isBlank( )

ObjectPAL also has several *compatibility procedures* designed to make life easier for the PAL programmer. Compatibility procedures operate on tables in the same way as the corresponding PAL function or PAL command. Each compatibility procedure has a corresponding method or procedure which performs the same thing, but in an object-based way. Table B.2 lists the compatibility procedures.

617

Appendix B

Table B.2. Compatibility procedures.

add( )
cAverage( )
cCount( )
cMax( )
cMin( )
cNpv( )
copy( )
cSamStd( )
cSamVar( )
cStd( )
cSum( )
cVar( )
delete( )
empty( )
familyRights( )
fieldName( )
fieldNo( )
fieldType( )
isEmpty( )
isEncrypted( )
isShared( )
isTable( )
nFields( )
nKeyFields( )
nRecords( )
protect( )
rename( )
subtract( )
tableRights( )

As you can see, Borland has tried, wherever possible, to provide ObjectPAL methods and procedures with the same name as their cousins in the PAL language.

Paradox 4.0 programmers also have an edge in Paradox for Windows and ObjectPAL when it comes to events. If you have done some heavy PAL Wait command or ShowDialog command programming, taking full advantage of the event-driven programming paradigm which PAL provides, you will drool over the power of Paradox for Windows event model. If you thought the PAL Wait command was powerful and complicated, you haven't seen anything yet.

Paradox for Windows creates a furious blizzard of events, compared to Paradox 4.0's light snow flurries. ObjectPAL, like PAL, gives you fantastic control over nearly every aspect of events. Hard-core PAL event programmers will need to adjust to the sheer number of events available and the level of control that is possible over them; however, they will feel very much at home in the world of events.

Differences between PAL and ObjectPAL

Just about everything else between the two programming environments and languages is different. Objects are king in ObjectPAL. Because of this, there are lots of new terms and concepts that have absolutely no counterparts in PAL.

PAL applications, for the most part, are modal. When you enter coedit mode on one table, all other tables on the workspace are in coedit mode also. When you are designing a form or report, you can't edit a table at the same time.

Paradox for Windows and ObjectPAL have no such limitations. It is now possible to create modeless applications based on the Windows model. You can be editing one table in one window, reporting on another table in another window, and creating a form in a third window. PAL programmers will have a hard time remembering that Paradox for Windows is modeless. Your first reaction will be to create modal applications because, after all, that is what you have been used to. Being able to create successful modeless applications in Paradox for Windows and ObjectPAL requires creative thought, experimentation, and the setting aside of old habits.

Other differences leap out. ObjectPAL code is attached to objects and embedded in forms, whereas PAL code is placed in scripts. ObjectPAL is strongly typed, and PAL is not. ObjectPAL uses static scoping based on the containership hierarchy. PAL uses dynamic scoping based on the procedure stack. ObjectPAL uses dot notation to resolve naming conflicts between methods in the containership hierarchy. In PAL, duplicate procedure names are just not allowed. PAL is an interpreted language. ObjectPAL is compiled. PAL has commands, whereas ObjectPAL does not. PAL has a few hundred functions and commands. ObjectPAL has about 1,000 methods and procedures. ObjectPAL methods and procedures are divided into about 45 groups, known as *types*. PAL commands and functions are not as rigorously subdivided.

ObjectPAL allows three options when passing parameters:

- *Pass by value*, in which a copy of the argument is passed to the child procedure or method
- *Pass by reference*, in which the child procedure or method can change the argument's value and the change is reflected in the parent method or procedure
- *Pass by constant*, in which the argument is passed to the child procedure and method and can't be modified there.

PAL only passes variables by value, except for Arrays and DynArrays, which are passed by reference.

Experienced PAL programmers familiar with DynArrays will be surprised to find that ObjectPAL does not allow Arrays or DynArrays to be passed as arguments unless the Array or DynArray is converted to a programmer-defined type. Although this is a minor inconvenience, ObjectPAL has two advantages over PAL when it comes to Arrays. First, after they are converted to types, Arrays can be returned from methods or procedures. Second, you can copy the entire contents of one Array to another simply by assigning one Array variable to another, as in the following:

```
var
     a,b  DynArray
endvar
a["name"] = "Liz Donnelly"
a["id"] = 4345
b = a     ; copy a[] to b[]
```

Paradox for DOS has three reserved system variables: autolib, errorproc, and retval. ObjectPAL does not have comparable reserved system words, but does have some system variables that are used to refer to UIObjects. These are the following: self, container, active, subject, target, lastMouseClicked, and lastMouseRightClicked. These are discussed more fully in Chapters 13, 14, and 15.

Earlier versions of Paradox also had commands such as Setswap, and command-line parameters to configure Paradox's memory allocation scheme. In Paradox for Windows and ObjectPAL, Windows automatically provides memory management. The table-locking commands have different names and slightly different meanings. Don't plunge into Paradox for Windows development thinking you can use the same locking commands, because you can't. A quick look at Chapter 29, which covers locking issues, is probably in order.

One of the most significant differences between PAL and ObjectPAL is that ObjectPAL allows you to manipulate a table without the table ever being visible or on the desktop. This is accomplished through the TCursor type. PAL has no equivalent construct. Chapter 16 is devoted exclusively to this important new construct.

Finally, Paradox for Windows has a new error-handling scheme that gives the programmer more power and flexibility in creating error-handling routines. Error handling is discussed in Chapter 19.

Summary

In all, ObjectPAL and Paradox for Windows are significantly different than PAL and Paradox for DOS. However, Borland has taken measures to make the transition as easy as possible by retaining key language syntax similarities.

Experienced PAL programmers should make sure they understand the new form model, events, and the containership hierarchy before creating applications. In addition, most PAL programmers should carefully study Windows user interface designs. Perhaps what will be most challenging for PAL programmers is trying to "unlearn" several key concepts that served them well in previous versions of Paradox.

An Overview of ObjectPAL for Non-PAL Programmers

If you are new to Paradox but not to programming, you should find Paradox for Windows and ObjectPAL easier to understand than you may think. ObjectPAL is similar in many ways to languages such as C, C++, and Pascal. If you are experienced with object-oriented programming, you already have a good head-start in learning Paradox, because Paradox for Windows exhibits a strong object-oriented flavor.

What You May Find That Is Easy

All programmers should find sections of Chapter 13, "ObjectPAL Basics," easy to understand. This chapter discusses ObjectPAL's basic language elements: control structures, variables, dot notation, methods, and procedures—all the usual nuts-and-bolts issues of programming languages. Because ObjectPAL is strongly typed and supports three methods of passing arguments (by value, by reference, and by constant), traditional programmers should feel right at home.

Object-oriented programmers should find Chapter 1, "Objects and Properties," an easy read, and experienced database programmers and SQL programmers will find Chapter 2 similarly easy. If you are an experienced Windows programmer and understand the Windows user interface, Chapter 3 also can be covered quickly.

What To Study First

Understanding Paradox for Windows interactive capabilities and its event model may be the program's biggest challenge for experienced programmers. A solid understanding of these features, however, is critical to programmers. To develop applications in Paradox for Windows, you must be familiar with Paradox's interactive tools. Forms and reports, for example, are created interactively, and to create complex forms you must learn the tricks and traps involved.

After you can create forms interactively, you need to understand two important concepts:

- The containership hierarchy
- The event model

The *containership hierarchy* is a tree-like representation of the form. This representation enables programmers to view their forms in a more abstract way. The containership hierarchy also encompasses several rules that govern the visibility and persistence of methods and data. How you organize code depends entirely on the form's containership hierarchy (or *object tree*).

After you learn the program interactively, your number-one priority is to understand the object tree. The object tree is what gives Paradox its uniqueness. You learn, too, that the event model and the containership hierarchy are intertwined concepts. The event model is the set of rules Paradox uses to propagate user interactions up and down the containership hierarchy.

Events come fast and furious in Paradox for Windows. Most programmers, however, are not accustomed to event-driven programming. If event-driven programming is new to you, make sure that you thoroughly read Chapters 13 and 14. Even if you are a pro at event-driven programming, read these chapters, which explain how Paradox manages—and enables you to manage—events. You probably will find the sections on events in Chapter 13 easy, but Chapter 14 may challenge even those among you who are experienced at event-driven programming.

What To Get Out of Your Mind

Experienced programmers must selectively purge old habits from both their memories and fingers. ObjectPAL may then seem relatively easy. You may experience some trouble remembering how to code the basic constructs: if, switch, and while statements. Fortunately, the Paradox for Windows programmer's editor features the Language ¦ Keywords menu choice that displays these basic language elements. This menu choice can even type the keyword into your method automatically.

If you have solid C++ or object-oriented experience, you may be disappointed that ObjectPAL doesn't allow the programmer to create true class hierarchies or implement object-oriented techniques directly through ObjectPAL code. ObjectPAL is not an object-oriented language. However, you can employ some object-oriented-style traits in limited ways, such as inheritance and data-hiding, by understanding the form, its containership hierarchy and libraries. Because you attach code to objects on a form, and because all the objects in the form fit into a treelike structure, you must organize your application around those objects, not around ObjectPAL methods or procedures, code placed in objects at lower levels of the object tree can *inherit* code from objects at higher levels in the tree or can override the higher level default behavior.

Programmers not yet exposed to object-oriented programming also may feel out of place because the containership hierarchy and its visual organization of code is unique to Paradox. All programmers, therefore, must remember that ObjectPAL code is not organized in a hierarchy of modules, but in a hierarchy of objects.

There is a big difference between an application organized as a hierarchy of modules and one organized as a hierarchy of objects.

If you, as a programmer, are new to Paradox, you may not like the quality of the debugger, especially if you are accustomed to the Borland language debuggers. The debugging environment in the current version of Paradox for Windows is not yet up to the same standard as other Borland language products. If you are one of these disgruntled programmers, be sure that you read Chapter 20, "Debugging Techniques," which offers valuable tips that may save you headaches.

ObjectPAL and C

C programmers will discover that Paradox's basic language elements—the conditional and looping structures—are constructed slightly differently than are the elements of C. C's `for()` construct, for example, has three arguments: a beginning statement, a loop invariant conditional test, and a statement that is executed each time the loop occurs. In ObjectPAL, however, the `for` statement displays an English-like syntax:

```
for x from 1 to 100 step 2
    y = x + 1
endfor
```

All of Paradox's basic language elements have the same flavor. C programmers also are used to the `{` character referring to blocks of code, usually between an `if` statement and the `else` clause. In ObjectPAL, however, the `{` character begins a comment block.

Aside from these superficial differences in the basic language elements, the real difference for C programmers—and for most other programmers—working in Paradox is in resolving variable and method visibility within the containership hierarchy. Usually, C programmers expect strict static scoping rules that clearly govern if a variable and a function are visible.

In Paradox for Windows, however, the containership hierarchy within the form determines method and variable visibility. C programmers may at first find these rules a bit fast and loose.

ObjectPAL and C++

Many of the same comments in the preceding section for C programmers apply to C++ programmers. C++ programmers, however, are accustomed to creating reusable class hierarchies and may try to do the same in Paradox for Windows. If, however, you do try this tactic, you may be disappointed.

ObjectPAL is not a true object-oriented language. In fact, the primary model behind ObjectPAL and Paradox for Windows is a prototyping model. In this model, you create a reusable object, attach all the code to the object that modifies the object's behavior, and then copy the object to all the forms that need it. Changing the behavior of the generic object, therefore, can prove profoundly disturbing, because you must recopy the new object onto all your applications forms.

To help you create truly reusable code, you may want to read as much as you can about libraries and the containership and event models. Appendix E (concerning the development of large applications) was written with code reuse in mind.

C++ provides a tractable means of understanding and coming to grips with a class hierarchy. In general, in C++ you study the class declarations. In Paradox for Windows, you do not look first at source code to understand an application. You look instead at the various forms in the application and how the forms are constructed. Because the source code usually is scattered throughout the form, you must get comfortable with the object tree tool to avoid feeling lost.

ObjectPAL and dBASE Dialects

Moving from dBASE to ObjectPAL, you find the environments quite different. Perhaps the biggest difference is how applications are built. In most dBASE environments, such as Clipper, the application is built by writing code. Code generators may be employed, but the code itself makes up the entire application.

In Paradox for Windows, the code you write fits into a predefined application development environment. Your ObjectPAL code is attached to an object on a form. Paradox for Windows opens the form and begins processing events for the form. Your code, which is attached to an object, responds to these events. Because your code is closely intertwined with the form, compiled code does not produce an EXE file. Instead, compiled ObjectPAL code produces a Windows DLL file which requires Paradox for Windows to run. Borland has or soon will have a run-time version of Paradox that developers can distribute with their applications so that their users won't need to purchase a copy of Paradox to run the application.

Another difference between ObjectPAL and dBASE is that, when you write ObjectPAL code, you add code directly to a form. The form takes a central role in Paradox. In dBASE, the form is just a tool for displaying data and obtaining user input. In Paradox for Windows, the form is the start, middle, and end of the application. To start an application, you open a form. To query data, you attach query code to an object on a form. To print a report, you open a report (which is actually a type of form).

Paradox for Windows has a more complex event model than do the dBASE dialects. Understanding the Paradox event model should be a high priority for dBASE developers who want to work with Paradox.

The basic language elements—if, switch, while, and for—are somewhat different in ObjectPAL and require some memorization. ObjectPAL has a greater variety of basic data types, such as DateTime, SmallInt, LongInt, Number, Currency, and Memo. The scoping rules for variables is intertwined with the containership model, which means that—if you want to know what variable is visible (and where)—you must know all about the containership hierarchy and forms design.

ObjectPAL has two terms that refer to programmer modules: *methods* and *procedures*. Methods and procedures are quite distinct from each other, and dBASE developers must understand the precise difference between the two in order to work with ObjectPAL. Chapter 13 discusses methods and procedures.

ObjectPAL includes a library of more than 1,150 methods and procedures that programmers can use. Learning all these methods and procedures in detail is impossible. Getting an overview of them so that you know what is available, however, *is* possible but takes time.

Summary

Learning Paradox for Windows and ObjectPAL can be frustrating for programmers fluent in other languages. The biggest problem such developers face is in abandoning previously learned procedures and learning the new paradigms. The following recommendations, therefore, are offered:

- *Do not attempt to tackle the ObjectPAL language first.* Instead, become a productive interactive user of the product before writing any ObjectPAL code. Create a few simple tables, forms, and reports, and then use them. Create some more tables, and then create multi-table forms and reports.

- *Learn the containership hierarchy and the event model thoroughly.* Work with small examples first. Do not undertake a real world application until you believe you understand the following concepts: how to create tables and table validity checks, referential integrity, external events, internal events, bubbling, the `error()` method, error handling, the `action()` method, action constants, libraries, how to create dialog boxes, and how to manipulate object properties.

- *Do not be concerned about ObjectPAL syntax, declaring variables, and passing arguments to methods and procedures.* These are the least of your worries, because such concepts should be familiar to you already. ObjectPAL implements these concepts in a manner similar to the concepts of other traditional programming languages.

A Brief Discussion of Containership and the Object-Oriented Paradigm

For developers familiar with object-oriented programming, it may seem disappointing that Paradox for Windows doesn't provide much support for OOP in ObjectPAL. In fact, even the name ObjectPAL seems misleading considering its lack of inheritance and user defined classes.

To understand how ObjectPAL has taken advantage of OOP, you must look beyond the missing elements to see how Paradox for Windows has addressed the underlying needs that resulted in the development of OOP principles. Upon close examination, we think that you will find that ObjectPAL provides many of the benefits of OOP with few of the disadvantages. And yes, there are disadvantages to OOP which are often overlooked or dismissed by OOP purists. Having spent many months or years becoming familiar with OOP, it's easy for a developer to forget that the learning phase is a significant barrier to most programmers, particularly when the demands of the job leave few with the luxury of taking time away from the work that users and management expect.

Borland designers recognized this when creating ObjectPAL. ObjectPAL doesn't require the programmer to spend a lot of time learning complex concepts yet still provides many of the benefits. It provides a powerful set of objects which combine data and behavior, as well as OOP concepts like encapsulation and polymorphism. Paradox for Windows also has innovative features such as containership that provides a hierarchy for handling events and the scoping of objects via a visual metaphor.

In this appendix we will show the features of ObjectPAL that are related to object-oriented principles.

Objects Smobjects... What's the Scoop on OOP?

The term *object-oriented* has been abused so often, it has little real meaning anymore other than as marketing hype. Many products became Object-Oriented overnight by simply changing the brochures to use the "in" terminology. This has merely served to make it more difficult for OOP developers to discern which products really make it easier to employ OOP techniques and principles.

Will the Real OOP Program Please Stand Up?

To help distinguish the real OOP products from the rest, it is easiest to define what is NOT object-oriented.

Many application development products claim to be object-oriented because they have been programmed using an OOP language and principles. *The language or principles used to create a development product make it no more object-oriented than a word processor or spreadsheet programmed using C++.*

Another common mistake is to presume that a product is object-oriented because it uses things called objects. Is a word processor object-oriented simply by using the term *object* instead of *document*? Is a spreadsheet object-oriented when a cell is referred to as an object? How about when the spreadsheet has a cell with properties and behavior that can be individually changed? The answers are No, No, and No. *The reason that products with "objects" aren't necessarily object-oriented is because the concept of an object (Object Identity) is only one aspect of object-orientation.*

In actuality, *a development language or product is not object-oriented unless it allows the developer to use object-oriented principles to create an application with explicit support for object identity, encapsulation, classes and inheritance, and polymorphism.* If it doesn't, it might be a great program, but it isn't object-oriented.

The object-oriented programming model was developed to solve some of the inherent problems in application development, centering around these issues:

- Object Identity to better model real-world objects.

- Classes and inheritance to allow the reuse of code and data.

- Encapsulation to improve the maintenance and reliability by reducing internal code dependencies.

- Polymorphism to improve the ability to use objects by allowing the creation of an abstract class which has the common behavior of similar objects. This is helpful because it provides the flexibility to use objects created later without changing code.

Paradox for Windows isn't object-oriented because it doesn't support inheritance and classes, but it is much closer than similar products because it addresses many of the underlying object-oriented issues in a manner that provides most of the benefits. It is for this reason that it is proper to refer to Paradox for Windows as Object-based, a term used in OOP texts for products that support object identity but only the other OOP principles in a different or limited way. You'll also notice that the Paradox for Windows manuals also use the term Object-based as well.

Object Identity...Crisis?

Object identity is the notion of an object comprised of both data (properties and attributes) and programs (behavior). This is a good way to organize computer programs because it better models the way we organize everything in the world around us.

We learn about something by examining its behavior as well as its properties. This way of learning is enforced in early childhood development and is the natural way we use to classify and distinguish objects as we encounter them. As children we learned that a dog is not only a furry four-legged animal (attributes), but that it is different from many other animals in that it barks, fetches, runs, and other doggy-type behavior. OOP can model a dog by allowing the developer to create a class which combines the attributes and behavior of a dog relevant to the program. For a developer creating a game, the dog object might play a sound clip when the bark( ) method is called, or perhaps display animation of a dog running when the run( ) method is executed.

Traditional programming languages which isolate data from programs do so primarily because this is how computer hardware is organized. Using languages such as COBOL, Pascal, or C, the programmer must continually separate the data and functional aspects instead of modeling the objects as they exist in the real world. When creating large and complex programs, it is a constant battle to model real world objects in a computer hardware modeled language.

Object Identity is arguably the most important principle of OOP because it is the most significant conceptual difference with traditional languages. *ObjectPAL takes advantage of Object Identity by incorporating data and behavior in its objects.* Without Object Identity, it would be difficult and confusing to program in ObjectPAL because of the number of objects and methods would be overwhelming without this type of organization. Even so, it is quite a challenge to master it all!

Classes and Inheritance—Trickle Down Programming

Most developers know that reusing code is the key to creating programs faster and with fewer bugs. Completely rewriting the code for each new program is a waste of time, particularly when applications often perform the same tasks but with different data. Putting a large amount of effort in crafting tools and libraries allows a developer to spend much less time in creating each application.

Classes and inheritance incorporate the concept of reusability into formal language constructs. A *class* is an abstract definition which represents the common data and operations used by a set of similar objects. A class is a model used to create an object. When an object is created from a class it is called an *instance* of the Class. An object differs from other objects of the same class by having different values for its properties. The primary distinction between an object and a class is that an object represents a unique, physical entity while a class is an abstract definition that describes the properties and behavior of similar objects.

Inheritance allows the data and behavior of a particular class to be reused by more specialized versions of the class. The common behavior and data of a class need only be defined once in a higher level class for it to be reused.

ObjectPAL has classes which define the behavior and data of similar objects. The term *type* is used by ObjectPAL for its classes, which is a term more familiar to programmers. Regardless of the term used, as programmer you create an instance of one of these types when you create any object in ObjectPAL. Creating a new form creates a new instance of the Form type. To declare a variable you must use a type. *Unfortunately, ObjectPAL doesn't permit you to create new types, much less inherit one type from another.* Don't be fooled by the TYPE...ENDTYPE, which allows you to use a different name for a type, not create a new type. It would be a natural extension to allow the creation of new types in ObjectPAL and we hope that Borland will add this capability in future versions.

Delegation—Passing the Buck

ObjectPAL uses *delegation* to improve reusability. The objects provided each have a powerful set of properties and behavior for you to use. When you create an object, it isn't necessary to completely redefine behavior or properties, only change the parts that you want to be different.

With delegation, you don't necessarily need classes. Instead, you simply clone the prototype and add the "inherited" code. Unfortunately, in Paradox for Windows, delegation is achieved by creating a prototype object and copying the object to the appropriate forms and "tweaking" the code to override default behavior. There is no automatic code inheritance feature in this scheme. This leads to code proliferation, which in many ways defeats one of the important goals of object-oriented programming: reduced code maintenance.

Encapsulation—Maybe It's Best To Mind Your Own Business

Encapsulation means data hiding. The purpose is to hide the internal operation and data of an object to allow it to be changed without affecting other objects that use it. The proper use of encapsulation prevents the "ripple-effect" caused when a program changes in ways that break other parts of it. A language that has encapsulation provides a formal way of creating functions and data of an object that are inaccessible by others.

Paradox doesn't formalize encapsulation. It does let you put procedures in libraries that cannot be accessed by any other forms. Whenever you place a procedure in a library, no other form can see or call that procedure. The same holds true for any variables in forms. These parts of the application are hidden from other programmers and can only be accessed indirectly through methods.

However, this is not in the same league as the encapsulation options possible in C++ or other object-oriented languages. In these languages, there exists a formal notation for identifying what parts of an object ought to be visible and what parts ought not to be visible.

Containership—Propagation of Events

The containership hierarchy serves two purposes. The first is to provide some visual hierarchy to organize objects on a form. The second is to provide control over the propagation of events. External events get dispatched to their targets and then bubble up in the containership hierarchy until they reach the object with the intelligence to handle them.

While you can exploit this propagation technique to ensure that some code will be executed at lower levels in the containership hierarchy instead of higher levels in the containership hierarchy, the intent of the event model and containership hierarchy is not truly object oriented.

Some people refer to the containership hierarchy as the inheritance hierarchy because methods are automatically visible to all objects lower in the containership tree. Lower level objects "inherit" these methods and can call them as if these methods were attached to them and not their parents or great-grandparents.

Calling this inheritance in the strictly object-oriented way is stretching the term a bit. Grady Booch, in his book, *Object-Oriented Design with Applications*, defines inheritance as:

> "... a relationship among classes, wherein one class shares the structure or behavior defined in one or more other classes. Inheritance defines a 'kind of' hierarchy among classes in which a subclass inherits from one or more superclasses; a subclass typically augments or redefines the existing structure and behavior of its superclasses."

In Paradox for Windows, the inheritance of methods and data is between objects, not classes. Objects are bound in a hierarchy based on purely visual or functional requirements, not on the application's logical design. The "inheritance" found in Paradox for Windows, while extremely useful in its own right, is a limiting form of inheritance.

Summary

Paradox for Windows is clearly object-based, not object-oriented. Is this bad? Of course not. As one experienced C programmer told us: "I wish Paradox had inheritance like C, and I wish C++ had containership like Paradox for Windows."

Paradox for Windows does not need to be object-oriented. It provides plenty of power with little code that object-oriented programming techniques probably won't be needed to control an application's size and maintainability. In addition, developers are freed from the complex programming and design issues which object-oriented environments often demand.

Issues in Developing Large Applications

Paradox for Windows is a significant departure from traditional ways of building software. The usual standbys that served us well in the past will need some rethinking. This appendix discusses some of these issues and proposes solutions to problems Paradox's object-based environment poses.

Construction Tools, Techniques

The way you build Paradox for Windows applications differs from building systems in Paradox for DOS or traditional programming languages like C, COBOL, or Pascal. A fundamental problem with Paradox for Windows application development is that applications are form based, source code and all. Although this kind of programming gives developers great flexibility and increased ability to understand the problem at hand, form-based applications create problems when trying to reliably construct software.

Source Code Version Control

One of the greatest challenges for serious ObjectPAL application development is controlling source code versions. In Paradox for DOS and most traditional languages, developers can purchase source code version control systems. These systems let programmers keep a complete revision history of the application's source code. If the current version goes berserk, the programmer can check out a prior version and compare to see what changes were made. If the programming team needs to coordinate multiple programmers, version control systems prevent two programmers from working on the same program. If the software requires concurrent construction of two or more versions of the software, version control systems come to the rescue.

Version Control Problems

A key advantage of a version control system is it can report changes in source code. Because source code text files have a basic structure—each line ends in a CR/LF and each character in the source code document is within a certain ASCII range—the version control system can detect which lines have changed and report the changes. This report of changes has semantic meaning.

In Paradox for Windows, because code is attached to a binary object (a form), analyzing the form for changes doesn't provide meaningful reports. A version control system needs intimate knowledge about the form and the various objects and source code contained, which version control systems to date don't have.

A solution to this problem involves creating a custom source code version control system, written in ObjectPAL, that checks-out and checks-in methods and procedures attached to objects. Each version of each method and procedure would be stored in a Paradox table.

Writing this kind of routine would be possible by (using the various enum..( ) and method..( ) methods), but the routine would suffer from one major weakness, a crucial one in a team programming environment: the source version control system can be subverted by anyone with a copy of Paradox. In addition, two programmers would not be able to work on the same form. Because objects within a form cannot be locked like records in a table, only one programmer at a time can edit a form.

For multiple programmer applications, system designers have to keep form sizes small enough so that two programmers don't need to edit the same form, which means that complex forms that span multiple pages, which may be a suitable design for one-person teams, probably will be out for teams.

Source Code Backup

Because source code version control doesn't seem feasible for now, developers need a means of protecting their source code from damage. Because all code is stored in a form and the form is a binary object (a DLL), when a form becomes corrupted, retrieving the source code may be impossible. If the form's corruption was undetected for some time, the corrupted form may have infiltrated deeply into your system backups and may require a great deal of effort to find a version of the form that isn't corrupt.

We recommend that you dump your source code, on a routine basis, to a table or a file, using the Browse Sources menu item or the various enum..( ) methods. If you have a listing of your source code, you can at least type the source code by hand, or you can write an ObjectPAL routine that reads the source code table, determines which object the method or procedure belongs to, and—using the various method..( ) methods—places the dumped method into the form. You then avoid retyping all your source code by hand.

In addition, we recommend that you routinely save your source code while you are working on it, especially before running a form. Due to the many complex interactions between the numerous pieces of hardware and software available, Windows is not a 100 percent rock-solid, stable environment. You can find that your PC locks up or that you have to restart Paradox or Windows, or you may even have to reboot your PC. If these problems occur and you have not saved your source code to disk (you must use the File ¦ Save command), you can lose minutes, if not hours of work.

Multi-Form Search and Replace

Another area of weakness in developing large, multi-form applications is making simple substitutions across forms. Most good programmers' editors allow search and replace capabilities to span multiple source code files. Writing this kind of routine also is possible by using ObjectPAL. Again, the various enum..( ) and method..( ) methods can come in handy because these methods can be used to list the objects in a form and retrieve the source code. The String methods also are useful because they let you perform string substitution.

Without such a tool, however, making changes across multiple forms can become tedious, which is why libraries are so convenient. Any common source code used in several forms gets put into a library where one change is reflected in all forms that use the library.

Object Version Control

So far, we have talked about only source code version control, because this is where the complexity lies. Should you also have object version control? You could use a version control scheme for binary objects that various document management systems employ where the entire form is evaluated, byte for byte, for changes. If the object version control system finds changes, a copy of the form is marked with a version number and stored. This scheme can provide automatic code and object version control, without any semantic reporting or understanding of the changes.

You also could use the enumSource( ) and enumUIObjectProperties( ) Form procedures to create a table listing each object, its current properties, and any source code attached. This route certainly would provide the basis for object version control because this data can be stored and used to re-create the form at any time.

The only problem with this approach is performance. A simple form has dozens of objects and hundreds, if not thousands of properties. The enumUIObjectProperties( ) procedure creates a table with nearly three thousand records for a simple form that has one table frame and three pushbuttons. The nice thing about this approach is that you can, with a some hard work, use the UIObject and Form create( ) methods in a routine that creates a form from these tables. ObjectPAL also converts the property settings from strings so that the following line of code will always assign the proper point property setting:

```
button.position = "(1500,231)"
```

This approach is much simpler than using the setX( ) and setY( ) methods and a point variable to set an object's position. Setting an object's properties, stored in a table, is possible.

Using Paradox for Version Control

If you could live with the limitation that only one developer can work on a form at a time, you could use Paradox as a version control database. Each form is stored in a record in a Blob field. Other fields in the record would include a description for the form, who has the form checked out, when it was last checked out, and other information that would aid in tracking the form.

An application could then be written to *check-in* and *check-out* each form. When checking a form out, the application would simply extract the form (perhaps even stored as compressed by a compression utility such as PKZIP) to the appropriate location on the network or the hard disk. To check a form back in, the form would be compressed and copied into the version control record, and then the form would be delivered, preventing anyone else from changing the form.

Reusable Objects and Utility Forms

Paradox for Windows was designed to promote code and object reuse through two means: by copying an object to the clipboard and pasting it into another form and by using libraries. We discussed libraries in Chapters 13 and 21, and we have briefly mentioned using generic objects.

Because ObjectPAL has object variables (self, subject, active, container, lastMouseClicked, and lastMouseRightClicked), creating an object that can respond to or create events, no matter where the object is placed, is rather easy. Placing these objects into a *reusable objects* form makes good sense. These objects then can be copied to other forms.

The following objects may make good generic objects or generic code:

- Video controller buttons (for navigating a table)
- SpeedBar buttons
- Menu skeleton code
- Graphic field objects, such as company logos or other artwork

The one problem with the generic object approach is that you begin to populate your application with objects that have the same code attached. If the original object's source code changes (which all forms in the application also must have), you need to copy the object to all the forms again. But you may have altered some of the copied objects' code slightly, which means that you cannot just recopy the object everywhere. You have to make all the code alterations, by hand, in each object that requires them.

At some point, you will need to decide whether the code in the generic object needs to be placed in a library. If the code is truly shared and identical in all instances of the object, then you probably should place the code in a library, which will ease the maintenance headache that code proliferation causes.

Utility forms are forms on which various buttons or other widgets have been placed that provide the programmer with services, enhancing the application development environment. You can use a utility form to provide the following services:

- Print a table structure
- Print a report of all the source code in a form or forms
- Display or print a report that lists all of an object(s) properties
- Print a report that shows the containership hierarchy for a form
- Print a report that lists all the objects on a form

Utility forms are a great time-saver, and we're sure that many developers will *roll their own* to enhance the application development environment. In addition, as time passes, you may see some utility forms popping up on computer bulletin boards or on on-line services, such as CompuServe.

Code and Object Generation

Code generation was a little-used but helpful technique in Paradox for DOS. The basic idea went something like this: You used PAL (Paradox for DOS's programming language) to automatically create source code. The code generator utility algorithmically wrote a text file that contained PAL source code. This file, saved as a script, then was compiled into a procedure library.

This technique was useful for creating modules which were, from a programmatic perspective, highly repetitive or easily created through algorithms. Because source code files in this and other environments are not attached to any user-interface object, the process is easy.

Paradox for Windows creates some problems here. Source code is attached to an object, so any code generation tool must attach the code to an existing object or create a new object with the code attached. Because it also is so easy to create an object interactively and because most objects contain small amounts of source code, you may wonder if Paradox for Windows needs a source code generator at all.

A few cases exist where this technique may be useful, such as developing an on-line help system, *without* using the Windows help system. Although most developers may choose the Windows help system to make their application behave more like a Windows application, some developers may want to create their own help systems.

In these cases, you may want to place all the help text in a Paradox table, where you then can modify the help contents independent of the application. This table then can be scanned, under program control, and the help text can be converted into some ObjectPAL data structure, such as an array of strings or a field object. This kind of task can be automated easily under ObjectPAL control. In addition, because the help text can be bound to the forms at compile time, the help system does not have to read a table and access a disk, which slows down the help system.

Software Quality Issues

Paradox for Windows begs a multitude of quality questions. Anyone delivering large, multi-person programming team projects needs to adjust to the new object-based paradigm. Old software quality control standbys once again need examining.

Product Measurement Issues

In order to assess a Paradox application's quality, you must first measure quality. Otherwise, you have only a bag full of amorphous terms, such as *bullet-proof*, *superb*, and *looks good*. For many applications, such terms are inadequate. Measurements, while not a panacea, are extremely valuable to managers of large applications. Because ObjectPAL is object-based, many typical software measurements need reconsidering.

For example, what is the best measure of the size of a Paradox for Windows application? The number of forms in the application? The number of tables? The number of ObjectPAL lines of code? The size of the form in bytes? Because the lines of code in an ObjectPAL application is only a partial indication of size, lines of ObjectPAL code probably is not a good indication of size. Likewise, a simple count of forms and tables does not take form or table complexity into account.

In addition, when measuring a Paradox application's size, you may want to compare it with applications in other environments, even to Paradox for DOS applications. For this reason, restricting your size measurements to something that is translatable across platforms is a good idea.

Fortunately, function point analysis (FPA), in which an application is measured for functionality from the consumer (user) perspective, is a general-purpose measuring scheme that may work well with Paradox for Windows. One of the authors of this book has conducted research in this area with Paradox for DOS. In that environment, using FPA to assess the overall size of an application met with some success. The preliminary assessment is that FPA may be suitable for Paradox for Windows for several reasons. Paradox for Windows extends the form-based application development metaphor in Paradox for DOS. In fact, measuring different aspects of each Paradox for Windows form may be an even better indicator of size than Paradox for DOS forms because in Paradox for Windows, unlike Paradox for DOS, nothing exists without a form. In addition, Paradox for Windows gives developers some good tools to document and count how many objects each form contains.

Developers interested in FPA should consult the texts or articles listed in the bibliography at the end of this appendix.

Other important measures have to do with code complexity. For example, developers frequently want to evaluate source code modules to see if these modules exceed some complexity threshold. If so, the module then is examined for possible decomposition or redesign.

One measure, the McCabe cyclomatic complexity measure, examines the number of different linear paths a program can take. The number of if and switch statements will impact the score. ObjectPAL methods tend to be very short, and those that aren't probably do not have a high cyclomatic complexity score because these methods will be performing linear tasks, such as running a query and printing a report. Some methods benefit from this measurement, but many methods will not.

Another set of measures concerns the localization of variables. How long is a variable active? How far away from its declaration is it referenced. These measures are tied to code that is partitioned into modules that are based on some source document without an object intervening.

Measuring variable life span in ObjectPAL code is difficult because the span of the variable is determined by the containership hierarchy and the persistence of objects such as fields, table frames, and multi-record objects. Measuring variable life by lines of code between its declaration and the last use does not accurately indicate the *psychological* span. Measuring the span by evaluating the number of intervening objects might. However, many composite objects in Paradox have trivial intervening objects that sit between the variable declaration and the variable's use in a line of code. Objects would have different *span* values, depending on their complexity.

Schemes that attempt to measure code complexity, variable life span, levels of coupling between modules, or other code-based measures, have to contend with the containership hierarchy. The containership hierarchy and the event handling containership provides determines the complexity and coupling of methods. Just looking at the code is insufficient. You must evaluate and quantify the code's visual organization. How deeply nested is the containership hierarchy? How wide is it? Where is the code attached within the containership hierarchy? How many levels in the hierarchy have code attached? Some forms may have a great deal of code at the form level. Other forms may have code sprinkled at all levels. Certainly the relationship between ObjectPAL code and the containership hierarchy will say a lot about the complexity of the application.

In time, as enough people gain experience in working with form-based application development, new measurement techniques will be applied. For now, we can say only that it's a new world; use your best judgment when applying traditional product counting schemes, but don't overlook new ways of evaluating applications.

Process Measurement Issues

Not only can you measure the size and complexity of a Paradox application, you also can measure different aspects of construction process. For example, one burning question arises: how fast is application development in ObjectPAL? Will programmers be more productive in this environment than others?

Answering these kinds of questions accurately is difficult. Intuitively and from unmeasured or not well-measured experience, many developers are saying that Paradox for Windows application development is more productive than traditional environments and more productive than Paradox for DOS simply because Borland packed a lot of power in the product's interactive features. Developers are freed from writing many lines of code.

However, unless you have hard numbers stating how big each application is and how much time went into building it, comparisons are more or less just testimonials. Measuring the process of building Paradox for Windows applications is not possible without measuring what is being built.

After you get a handle on measuring an application's size, however, and you accurately measure how long it takes to construct an application, you can start to measure things such as programmer productivity, compare Paradox productivity with C++ productivity, or compare a project's productivity with other projects.

In addition, Paradox for Windows also should fit in well with software defect measurement systems. Because defect measurement doesn't measure an application's code or logical organization—only its effects—no special consideration needs to be made. If anything, reviewing any categories you might have for a defect's source or cause may be wise. Make sure that the types of causes or sources mirror Paradox for Windows object-based nature.

Managing Complexity: Philosophical Issues

A large application's greatest enemy is complexity. Excessive complexity can frustrate even the most gifted and experienced developers, delaying an application's delivery, or riddling it with too many defects. Practitioners and researchers have expended great effort trying to provide tools and approaches that attempt to manage an application's complexity. These approaches have met with limited success over the past decade or so.

Several issues converge to make complex systems difficult to deal with. These issues are not limited to the following list:

- The inherent difficulty in mapping nonformal user requirements into a formal mathematical model or a collection of algorithms. Computer programs are completely deterministic, with clear rules and boundaries. Applications often are based on user requirements or user expectations that have not or cannot be so clearly defined.

- The lack of sufficient abstraction in computer languages to easily map the user requirements, as informal as they may be, into a working system.

- The lack of software adaptability to accommodate changes in design and implementation.

- The inherent limited abilities of the human mind to grasp all of an application's logical interrelationships at one time.

- The inherent difficulties in explaining to other programmers an application's structure and logic.

Paradox for Windows presents a very different way to abstract, organize, partition, and describe an application. Paradox helps you deal with these complexity issues in the following ways:

- Paradox's functionality in its database engine enables you to work with an application at a higher level of abstraction. Through referential integrity, validity checks, table lookups, and other facilities—which do their work at the database engine layer—the amount of code you have to write is greatly reduced.

- Paradox's forms enable you to control much of the user interface without code, which decreases the amount of code you write, which in turn reduces the application's complexity.

- Paradox's visual, form-based environment enables you to work with concrete, visual metaphors that make understanding the application easier. Human minds are better equipped to comprehend sophisticated visual objects rather than logical or algorithmic languages.

- Paradox's forms partition an application into smaller, more cohesive modules, where each module performs a small, discrete task. Because each module is smaller, understanding and fixing problems that arise is easier.

- Paradox's event model, although sophisticated, is clearly grounded in a highly visual and kinesthetic metaphor. Because the event framework is visual, mastering it involves recruiting visual, not logical, linguistic, or mathematical skills. Because of this grounding, the event model is *teachable*, even to less experienced programmers.

- The containership model enables you to group objects into hierarchical groups, increasing your ability to visually abstract and understand an application. You can ignore lower layers in the containership hierarchy and analyze an application's behavior at higher levels of organization, which frees you from dealing with too many details.

This new approach, however, is not without flaws, but the approach is a substantial improvement over traditional programming environments. This approach lets us build complex applications with less code and more comprehensibility and lets you partition the world into concrete user-interface objects, which, for the vast majority of business and database applications, is an important step in a new and right direction.

Underestimating or quickly dismissing the importance vision has on cognition is easy. Human beings are designed by nature to process an intense amount of visual information. Some cognitive scientists and philosophers are beginning to realize how dependent our consciousness and our cognition—including language and logic—is indebted to the vast amount of brain real estate devoted to processing visual information. Paradox takes a bold step towards completely and clearly intertwining an application's logic with a visual organization. If anything has a chance of letting us better understand and manage an application's complexity, it is this approach.

Design Issues

Paradox for Windows gives developers many ways to perform the same task. The possibilities for different design approaches are enormous. We expect to see a great number of different ways to construct similar applications. Developers building large applications, however, will continually trip over the same issues: "How can I reduce maintenance? What's the most inexpensive, yet reliable way to construct this application?"

In many ways, Paradox for Windows gives developers two fundamental approaches to deal with large programming issues.

Prototyping: The Borland Way

Paradox for Windows was built with prototyping in mind. The form designer gives developers the ability to create smart objects with code, and then to cut and paste these objects from form to form. The containership hierarchy enables these smart objects to quietly fit in another form's world. The object variables active, subject, and self make this easy to do.

In this approach, a smart object is created and code is attached. This object then is copied to other forms where the code is tweaked. You soon will have proliferated various versions of this object throughout your application.

In addition, any not-so-reusable objects handle their events with code attached as well. In this scheme, the library is a bit of an afterthought. The primary place to add code is to the form at hand. If you look closely, the library user interface wasn't designed to handle large amounts of procedures or forms.

Extensive Use of Libraries: An Alternate Way

Prototyping creates code proliferation, which is a problem because it introduces redundancy, which in turn frustrates maintenance efforts. An alternate approach places all code in a library. Some developers feel uncomfortable with their code scattered throughout various objects on a form and like the idea of placing all code in one place. The only code that gets attached to an object is a one-line call to a library method (or two or three, depending on whether the target is the form and how the developer wants to handle doDefault issues). The library does all the work.

Obviously, the two approaches represent two ends of a continuum. Developers can decide how much code to place in a library and how much code to place in the object. The following factors may help in your decision:

- Eliminating all code redundancy is not necessarily a good thing. Some objects begin with identical code, except one class of users owns one object and another class of users owns the other. Although the objects may be identical at birth, the demands on their lives may force independent modifications. You have two choices—separate them and endow them with their own code or continue to modify one set of code for both objects. The latter approach increases the level of coupling between objects and increases the complexity of code, but decreases the amount of code. The former approach decreases the coupling and hopefully complexity between modules, but increases the lines of code to maintain in the application. In many ways, this situation is a classic size versus complexity tradeoff.

- Excessive proliferation of copies is a seductive habit. You can easily compromise the future to expedite things in the present. Unless you clearly identify, beforehand and at each maintenance pass, which objects should share code and which should not, simply copying objects is not the answer any more than simply placing all code in a library.

- In this version of Paradox, the library manager was not designed to handle large numbers of procedures. Unfortunately, the only way to view your procedures in a library is to check the Proc check box. One window will pop up. In this window you place each procedure, one after the other, just like writing C source code or Paradox for DOS source code, which is hardly an improvement over traditional programming environments. In fact, this way is worse because the ObjectPAL editor, unlike other programmer's editors, was not designed to handle large amounts of code in one window.

- Developers tend to hate a product's warts and expend a great deal of effort to devise schemes around them. ObjectPAL is sufficiently open-ended that any developer can completely redefine all events.Trying to control everything in Paradox for Windows is a mistake. Many developers who control everything leverage time and effort by making all the changes generic and placing the changes in a library. While this method certainly is possible, we recommend that wherever possible, you try to design your application the way Windows and Paradox are designed to handle them. Deviations from the Windows and Paradox application models cost more money, require more code, and take more time. Besides, if you don't like the way Windows or Paradox handles applications, the target application may need to be constructed in another environment.

Excessive code proliferation and excessive code centralization without good reason are two evils to avoid. Knowing what code should be in a library and what code should be in the object requires some planning as well as experimentation.

Minimizing Naming Dependencies

A key issue in developing large applications is knowing if, when, and what to name something. The basic idea is insulate your code so that renaming an object in the physical world (file names, directory names, object names) will not upset the logical arrangements you've set up.

The following tips help you minimize naming dependencies:

- Use the object variables, self, active, subject, container, lastMouseClicked, and lastMouseRightClicked wherever possible. By using the object variables properly, you can rename files, fields, and UIObjects without affecting your code. In addition, you improve the chances that your code can be copied around without ill effects.

- Take advantage of the fact that UIObjects are *bound* to tables or fields and can be named *independently* of the table or field name. When a field object or other table-bound UIObject is created, it gets its name from the underlying table or field name. The UIObject can be renamed without upsetting the relationship to the table or field. Now the reverse is not true. If a table or field name is deleted or changed, the UIObject will be unbound. Although you do have to rebind the object to the table or field, you don't need to rename it.

- Don't name every UIObject. Paradox creates UIObjects with noise names. These names begin with the # character. Noise names can be totally ignored in a containership reference. Because noise names are always unique, Paradox can always locate objects with noise names in their containership path.

- Remember that you need to change field names or field object names in calculated fields every time the referred field or object changes.

Aliases

Aliases are a way to refer to a directory without having to use the actual DOS path name in your application. You can add aliases under program control with the Session addAlias( ) method/procedure or interactively with the File ¦ Aliases menu commands. Aliases added under program control are temporary. As soon as the session ends, the alias disappears. Aliases added interactively can be either temporary or permanent. Aliases are stored with the Paradox for Windows ODAPI configuration file.

The nice thing about aliases is that your source code can use an alias name in place of a DOS file path anywhere in ObjectPAL where a Paradox object is referenced. You can also use aliases to refer to tables in forms, reports, and queries.

You even can refer to an alias when assigning lookup tables to fields in the restructure table dialog box (see fig. E.1). Although the full path appears in the lookup table's path name (in the restructure dialog), the alias is actually stored in with the lookup table name, not the full path name, which means that you can move an application from one directory to another without having to change the application. You just have to make sure that you have the proper aliases set up.

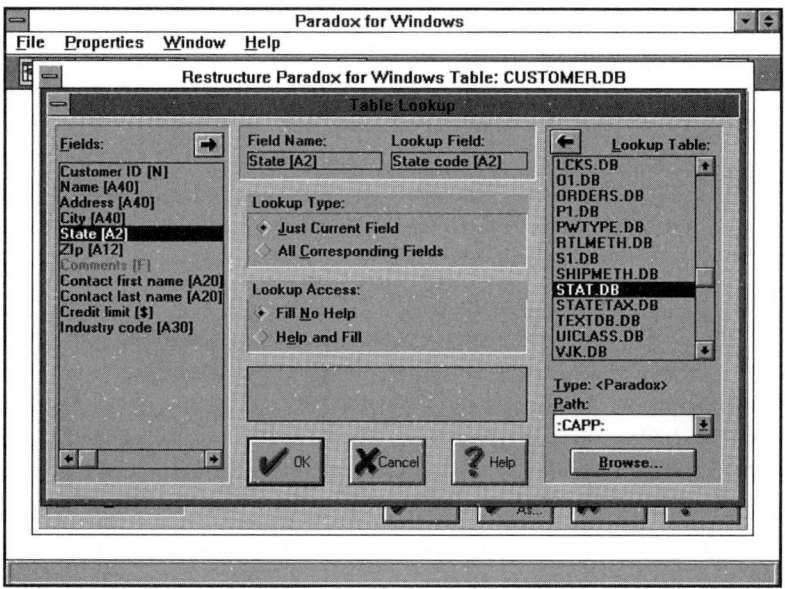

Figure E.1. The Lookup Table Definition dialog box.

Although this capability sounds great, there are some limitations in Paradox that limits aliases' usefulness. The concept behind aliases is that objects within an application can be located anywhere seamlessly. The rub is that one key feature cannot use aliases: referential integrity. All tables defined in a referential integrity relationship must reside in the same directory, which means than any tables linked by referential integrity cannot be split between two physical subdirectories.

Because of these current limitations, you must plan carefully where you want to place tables. In Paradox for DOS, it was common for an application to have multiple subdirectories, with each subdirectory holding a different group of tables. Each subdirectory was contained by the application's main directory, so that an application directory structure looked like the following example:

C:\APP	; application "home" directory
C:\APP\DATA	; main data tables subdirectory
C:\APP\REPORTS	; report tables subdirectory
C:\APP\LOOKUP	; lookup tables subdirectory
C:\APP\QUERY	; query tables subdirectory

This kind of directory scheme is known as *relative directory addressing*, or RDA. However, because of the limitations with aliases and referential integrity, in the current version of Paradox for Windows (1.0), this scheme is difficult, if not impossible to manage, unless of course, your application does not have extensive referential integrity requirements.

Instead, we recommend that you use aliases as much as possible and work around the referential integrity relationship issue by keeping tables that share a relationship in the same directory.

Multi-Forms versus Multi-Pages

If you are designing an application with dozens and dozens of forms, you have an alternative: use multiple pages in a form rather than multiple forms. There are, however, pros and cons to this approach. In the defense of this approach are the following arguments:

- *Better performance.* Switching to another page within an open form is much faster than opening another form.

- *No need to deal with the complexities of using the wait( ) method to specifically wait on another form.* Instead, as programmer, you force the user to interact with the page by controlling movement to the page, or you can let the user select the page interactively with the Shift+F3 and Shift+F4 keys.

In the prosecution of this approach are the following arguments:

- *Forced modality.* Pages cannot be interacted with simultaneously, so the user cannot work with the pages like they can work with multiple forms. Forms can be tiled, cascaded, and put side by side. Pages cannot. Of course, the defense also can use this argument, claiming that forced modality is often good for inexperienced Windows users.

- *Forms should be limited as to the number of objects that it can contain.* This action reduces complexity in the data model, reduces coupling between objects, and keeps the form DLL size to a reasonable number.

Appendix E

These arguments are good both for and against such an approach. We believe that both approaches have value, depending on the clients' needs, and both approaches will be used.

Maintenance Issues

A penny of time spent in designing an application is worth a dollar spent in maintaining one. Nonetheless, after an application is shipped, maintenance begins. In keeping with its DOS ancestry, Paradox for Windows shines when it comes to maintenance. Fixing and altering Paradox for Windows applications should be as easy as changing Paradox for DOS applications and applications built with traditional tools, for several reasons.

- Forms and tables are less coupled than Paradox for DOS forms and tables. This means that changes in a table don't have drastic consequences in your form or report. Code will not disappear. Instead, objects bound to the field or table become unbound objects. You can then define new fields for the field objects in the form or report.

- Paradox for Windows has powerful data modeling capabilities that let you redesign your form quickly. The only catch is that if you change the data model, Paradox will inform you if any objects will be adversely affected. The way to prevent an object, and all its code, from being removed as part of a data model change is to copy the object (or objects) to the clipboard, make the changes, and then reinsert your saved objects. You can use a third-party clipboard utility which lets you cut and paste several items at once to help you.

- Paradox makes using a form or report with several tables easy. All you have to do is open the form or report and select another master table. If you want to add a table to a form or report, you just add the table to the form's data model, add the appropriate object (a table frame, a multi-record object or fields) to the form, and bind the object and the related fields to the table. If you have built the form with multiple tables in mind, then none of your ObjectPAL code should need changing.

- Paradox methods tend to be small and highly cohesive. Built-in methods respond to discrete and specific events. The code that responds to these events usually inherits this modularity. Fixing problems in these areas is *usually* easy because the change doesn't ripple through a lot of other objects. If, however, you used library methods extensively, then making a change does ripple through a lot of objects, which can be a good thing. As long as the library method is highly cohesive, then changing individual modules should be easy.

Paradox's object-based, visual programming environment automatically encourages highly cohesive modules, which are easy to understand, which should make for easy maintenance. The only problem with ObjectPAL code maintenance is that the Paradox event model encourages a higher level of coupling between methods than do conventional languages.

Because the scope and visibility of variables, procedures, and methods is determined by the containership hierarchy, any particular method or procedure may depend on a variable declared elsewhere in the containership hierarchy. Changes in this *elsewhere* location can cause code that depends on this object to blow up. For this reason, ObjectPAL code tends to be highly cohesive and modestly coupled. We see no easy way around this problem in pursuit of the highly cohesive, loosely coupled ideal. The more that objects need to work together, the more coupling is needed to coordinate their activities.

Because Windows is a semi-concurrent, messaging operating environment, coupling between various parts of an application is bound to be higher than in more procedure-oriented application languages. You need to keep this fact in mind and design the containership hierarchy—which determines the scope and visibility for variables, procedures, and methods—clearly and carefully.

Problem Areas and Solutions

Paradox for Windows is an excellent application development tool. However, when it comes to large applications with multi-person programming teams building them, there are some problem areas we previously discussed that you can avoid. This section summarizes these areas and proposes alternatives that would be welcome in future versions of the product.

No Layer Above the Form

Although many people decry the use of global variables, many developers love and use them. Developers have compelling arguments for and against global variables. In ObjectPAL, through the use of libraries, you can have global variables. The method for declaring and accessing these variables, however, is indirect and quite different from handling other variables. In addition, having certain objects persist that rested above the form within the containership hierarchy would help developers.

Having a layer above the form would extend the containership hierarchy and design principles to all aspects of an application and simplify many design decisions.

No Concept of a True "Record" Object

Because record objects are found only in table frames and multi-record objects, in order to handle all record-level events properly, your fields must reside in these two objects. The key limitation is that a record object cannot span two form pages. Larger applications tend to have more complex form designs where it may be impossible to keep all a table's fields on one page. These applications will have to design some more cumbersome workarounds to get the concept of a record object.

Having a record object that can span multiple pages will greatly simplify complex code associated with fields that span multiple pages.

Import/Export Problems

A key area for developers of applications that must deal with data in a variety of formats is programmatic control over importing and exporting data. Unfortunately, as of this writing, the only way to achieve this under ObjectPAL is to display the appropriate export and import Paradox dialog boxes.

Without programmatic control over exporting and importing without user intervention, ObjectPAL developers need to either access DLLs (dynamic link libraries) that perform the import and export task or use the Microsoft Macro recorder and DDE to manipulate a second copy of Paradox running under Windows to perform the export. Fortunately, if you need to import and export straight text files, the TextStream object type and the String object type come in handy because they have the necessary methods to manipulate a text file so that it can be converted to and from a Paradox or dBASE table.

Hopefully this problem will be solved in a future version of the product.

Summary

Although Paradox for Windows gives developers many tools to tackle large applications, it is not without some weaknesses. Fortunately, each of these weaknesses can be overcome with extra effort. The point to remember is that the object-based paradigm that Paradox presents will cause you to rethink your methods for designing, building, and controlling large applications. The old standbys don't always work. In many ways, Paradox for Windows is a forward-looking product that poses as many challenges as opportunities.

Bibliography

Albrecht, A. "Measuring Application Development Productivity," *Proceedings of the Joint SHARE/GUIDE/IBM Application Development Symposium,* October, 1979, pp. 83-92.

Albrecht, A. and Gaffney, J. "Software Function, Source Lines of Code and Development Effort Prediction: A Software Science Validation," *IEEE Transactions on Software Engineering,* Vol. SE-9, No. 6, November 1983 pp. 639-648.

Jones, C. *Applied Software Measurement,* McGraw-Hill, Inc. 1991.

Kemerer, C. and Porter, B. "Improving the Reliability of Function Point Measurement: An Empirical Study," *IEEE Transactions on Software Engineering,* Vol. 18, No. 11, November, 1992, pp. 1011-1024.

Symons, C. "Function Point Analysis: Difficulties and Improvements," *IEEE Transactions of Software Engineering,* Vol 14, No. 1, January, 1988, pp. 2-11.

Object Type Reference

An *Object Type* is a category that classifies objects according to similar attributes. An object type determines the properties and methods that are available for that type. Some object types actually provide the underlying base for other object types. For example, ActionEvent and ErrorEvent types inherit the properties and methods of the Event object type. ObjectPAL further classifies Object Types into six broad categories, Data Types, Data Model Objects, Events, System Objects, Design Objects, and Display Managers.

To learn what methods are available for the different object types, see Appendix G. You also may select Language ¦ Types from any ObjectPAL editor window. The on-line ObjectPAL Help Reference system provides a description of all the object types along with sample code using those types.

ActionEvent

An ActionEvent inherits any Event type methods. An ActionEvent is an event that is dispatched to a form's built-in action( ) method. Through this built-in method, you can trap for about 140 different events, most of them related to table and field navigation.

The methods in this type enable you to determine the type of action event that occurred and the event's id. These methods interrogate and set data values in the eventInfo packet that is sent to the action( ) built-in method. Action constants define what the event was and allow you to accept the event or to initiate a different one. This type has only three methods or procedures.

AnyType

Anytype serves as the basis for several other object types with the mission to evaluate and manipulate the basic data types, including: arrays, binary numbers, currency, dates, date/time, dynarrays, graphic, logical, longint, memo, number, OLE, point, record, smallint, string, and time.

An AnyType variable takes on the characteristics of the value assigned to it—Dates when a date value, Logical when logical values, and so on. Anytype cannot be used to represent complex object types such as Tables, TCursors, Queries, Reports, and so on. You can use AnyType data objects for variables whose type may be unknown at compile time or changes over time.

This type contains methods to determine the data type of any variable, determine if the variable is blank, make it blank, unassign it, and view it. This type has seven methods or procedures.

Application

This data type enables you to control the desktop window of the application. This method contains no methods or procedures, but inherits several form methods and procedures that serve to manipulate a window's title, size, visibility, and position.

Under Windows, you can have multiple Applications running. A variable defined as an Application data type refers to the current Paradox Desktop only.

Array

The Array data type enables you to create variables with a predefined number of elements that contain the same type of values. The values can be any of the basic data types, such as smallint, number, currency, date, and so on. These are one-dimensional memory areas that can be used to quickly locate and access specific elements and values. Access is performed by addressing elements of the array through numeric indexes, or subscripts.

Arrays in Paradox for Windows can be resized. Arrays inherit the methods from the AnyType object type and also have 21 additional methods.

Binary

Binary data types, also known as BLOBs (Binary Large Objects), contain complex data values such as sound and video files. Three methods are associated with Binary objects to read and write from a file and to determine the size in bytes. This type also inherits the methods from the AnyType object type.

Currency

The Currency data type is a numeric value displayed in a money display format. The format displayed is set in the International settings dialog in the Windows Control Panel. Internally Paradox stores currency values to six decimal places in tables. The same methods as the Numeric, and AnyType types can be used with a Currency type. A Currency type has only one method.

Database

The Database data model type enables you to specify variables to use as handles to Aliases or directories. For applications that must reference files in several subdirectories, Database can help simplify coding and make it easier to maintain.

By default, Paradox starts up applications in the working directory. By assigning an Alias to a different subdirectory, and using the open method, you can access tables not in the current working directory. Nine different methods and procedures are associated with Database types.

Date

Date data type objects hold date information in one of three different formats, *month/day/year*, *day.month.year*, or *day-month-year*. You can control the format with the formatSetDateDefault method (System Type) or ObjectPAL formatting statements. The valid range of date values allowed in Paradox tables is Jan. 1, 100 to Dec. 31, 9999.

Date variables must be *cast* (explicitly declared) before use. You can perform date calculations on Date data type variables and fields. Methods defined for the AnyType and DateTime object types are available for the Date data type. In addition, three methods are specific to Date types.

DateTime

These data types are only available in ObjectPAL calculations, no support exists for DateTime in Paradox tables. A DateTime variable is formatted as, *hour:minute:second:millisecond* (am or pm) *year/month/day*. You can use the following characters as separators: blank, tab, space, comma (,), hyphen (-), slash (/), period (.), colon (:), and semicolon (;). DateTime values are formatted using the formatSetDateTimeDefault method (System type), or by ObjectPAL formatting statements.

You must cast (explicitly declare) DateTime variables before using these variables in calculations. You must declare all parts of the DateTime format or enter zero for parts not specified. Methods for the AnyType object type is available for DateTime types. Thirteen methods are defined for DateTime objects, which also can be used by the Date and Time types.

DDE

The Dynamic Data Exchange (DDE) system type is a standard Windows convention for the transfer of data that establishes a link between one data source and another. With DDE, you can pass data to and from Paradox for Windows and other Windows software, such as spreadsheets and word processors, that are DDE-capable. DDE also can be used to establish links between different Paradox for Windows data sources, such as between a Table and a Query. Four Methods exist to establish the links and pass data and commands back and forth.

DynArray

A DynArray data type is a dynamically structured array. Values in the elements of this array type can be of any other data type. You do not have to define the number of elements of the DynArray before using it, you can add to and remove elements of the DynArray at any time. Unlike regular arrays, which use numeric indexes to access elements, DynArrays can be any valid expression that evaluates to a String.

Methods are available to access, view, remove elements, and determine the size of a DynArray. The DynArray type also uses methods defined for the AnyType type.

ErrorEvent

The ErrorEvent type is built on top of the Event type and provides methods for obtaining error information that may occur from ObjectPAL code. ErrorEvent can be used to find out if the error was a Critical, irrecoverable error, or if it was just a Warning message of possible run-time problems.

The result of an error generates a packet of information that then triggers the built-in method error. Several methods from the Event type are available for use with the ErrorEvent type.

Event

The Event type forms the core of other event types such as ActionEvents and ErrorEvents. When events occur, a packet of information is generated that methods can interrogate to find out what event just occurred. Eight basic methods exist for Events.

FileSystem

This system type provides information about a system's drive, directories, and files. FileSystem types contain several methods for accessing, copying, deleting, and listing files in a directory. FileSystem variables can be beneficial as handles that represent files or directories. Use the findFirst method to determine if a file exists and initialize FileSystem variables.

Form

The Form type forms the base type for other Display Manager types—such as Reports—and TableViews. Form variables are convenient as handles for working with forms in Paradox. Sixty-one different methods are available for Form objects that enable you to manipulate forms in many ways, some of which are shown in the following list:

- Open and close—as well as position and maximize or minimize—forms

- Start form design sessions and save the designs
- Attach to an open form
- Change the data model of a form by adding or deleting tables
- List object names, properties, and source code for methods
- Send events, such as a mouseUp or keyPhysical, to a form

Graphic

Paradox stores graphic images as bit mapped pictures (BMP) files. It can read in other file formats including (GIF) graphic interchange format, (PCX) Paintbrush files, (EPS) encapsulated PostScript, and (TIF) tagged information file format. Methods associated with the Graphic data type provide for reading and writing bit maps from tables, forms, reports, files, and the Clipboard. The Graphic data type has four methods and also inherits methods from the AnyType object type.

KeyEvent

Keystroke events create packets of information stored as KeyEvent object types. The Event type forms the base of a KeyEvent object type. These events trigger the keyChar and keyPhysical built-in methods. Methods associated with this type can help determine the keyboard state when a key event occurs, such as whether or not the Ctrl, Alt, or Shift keys were pressed. KeyEvents also return the key character or virtual key that was pressed.

Library

A Library system object type is used to store custom methods, procedures, variables, and constants. A Library is a convenient place to maintain generic routines that even can be shared between different forms. Rather than having to track a custom method or procedure attached to many objects in many forms to make a change, you just call the custom routine stored in one place in a library.

Working with a Library is similar to working with Forms. You add code to Libraries just like in Forms, using the Methods dialog box and the ObjectPAL editor windows. Libraries also have built-in methods to perform open, close, and listing functions.

Logical

Variables declared as Logical data types can have two possible values, True or False. Paradox Table objects do not support Logical data types. A Logical variable can substitute Yes or On for True, and No or Off for False values. Three logical operators are available in calculations, in order of precedence

NOT, AND, and OR. Logical variables occupy only one byte of memory storage. Many ObjectPAL methods and procedures return logical values to inform the developer of the success or failure of an operation. Only one method exists for this type for casting logical values; however, it does inherit the methods of the AnyType object type.

LongInt

Long integer data types can have values that range from –2,147.483,648 to 2,147,483,647. These data types require only four bytes of storage. Paradox Tables support LongInt data type fields. Methods available for Number and AnyType data types also are available for LongInt types. In addition, LongInt has methods for performing logical bitwise operations on values.

Memo

The Memo data type provides for text and text formatting information. Paradox allows both Memo and Formatted Memo fields in tables. Both fields use the base Memo data object type. Memos, however, are maintained in separate .MB files that are linked to the Paradox tables. Methods exist to read and write text from disk files and to transfer memos between forms, reports, and tables.

You can assign Memo or String variables the value of a memo field. String variables assigned memo values don't maintain the text formatting information. No arithmetic or comparison operators can be used on memo variables. Wild-card searches in a Paradox Query can scan memos for the occurrence of text values. Three methods plus the ones inherited from the AnyType object type.

Menu

A Menu is a Design Object type that contains a list of the items that appear in the application menu bar. ObjectPAL programmers can create custom menus that replace Paradox's menus when running a form. By default, menus do not persist between forms. If your form calls another form and you want the same custom menu for each form, set the *StandardMenu* form property off for each form. To restore Paradox's menus, use the removeMenu Run-Time Library Method.

Methods available to Menu objects enable you to dynamically add or remove items and to disable and gray out items. Sixteen methods are available for working with menus.

MenuEvent

An event that selects an item from a menu triggers the built-in menuAction method. By trapping for this event, you can determine what menu item was selected and define the action taken. Many constants are defined for common menu items such as File ¦ Open or File ¦ Exit. This type takes several methods from the base Event type plus has eight of its own methods.

MouseEvent

The MouseEvent object type contains information on mouse events. The built-in methods that get activated when mouse events occur are: mouseDown, mouseUp, mouseDouble, mouseRightUp, mouseRightDown, mouseRightDouble, mouseMove, mouseEnter, and mouseExit. Like other high level event types, this type inherits the methods of the base Event type. Twenty other methods are specific to working with MouseEvents.

MoveEvent

The built-in methods—arrive, canArrive, canDepart, and depart—are triggered by MoveEvents. Using the methods associated with the MoveEvent type, you can determine why a movement occurred and where to find the destination of the movement. Using this information, you can deny or redirect movements.

Number

Number data types are floating point values that can have 18 digits of significands, in other words, decimals multiplied by a power of 10 that can range from $\pm 3.4*10^{-4930}$ to $\pm 1.1*10^{4930}$. Methods for numbers also work with the LongInt and SmallInt data types. The AnyType object type forms the base for Number types, which have 31 associated methods.

OLE

Object Linking and Embedding (OLE) is a standard protocol developed for Windows applications to share data. This technology enables one application to be quickly opened from within another application and make a change to an object. Paradox is an *OLE Client* application, one that can open other applications only and cannot be opened by others. *OLE Servers* are applications that create an OLE object that is shared between applications. To launch the OLE Server applications from within an OLE Client, the OLE Server must be installed on the user's system.

Six methods are associated with an OLE object type, which also inherits methods from the AnyType type.

Point

Point variables contain the grid coordinates of the screen. The screen is a two dimensional grid of x and y values, which are measured in twips. A twip is 1/1440 inch. The origin of an object on-screen begins at the upper left corner with x values extending right, and y values down. An object's origin is relative to the object in which the first object is contained.

This data type inherits methods from the AnyType type and includes 11 of it's own methods.

PopUpMenu

A PopUpMenu type holds information about a vertically displayed menu of items, which typically are assigned to items from regular horizontal menu design objects. When users select a menu item, the built-in menuAction method isn't triggered unless the pop-up menu is attached to a custom menu.

This design object has nine methods and inherits the methods of the Menu object.

Query

You can create and execute queries from ObjectPAL just like from regular interactive Paradox. Queries can be created from a query file, a string variable, or an ObjectPAL query statement. Methods for working with Queries also are defined by the Database type.

Record

A Record data type is a user-defined data structure much like programming languages like Pascal or C allow. You define the field names and the field types of the structure. The field types can be any valid ObjectPAL data type. The logical comparison operators = and <> can be used to compare records and make assignments.

The only methods defined for a Record type are the methods that are inherited from the AnyType type.

Report

Report design objects are used to manipulate, display, and print information. Like Forms, Reports are complex objects that contain other display objects. Unlike Forms, Reports can have no methods attached to the objects of the report. A Report object has 11 methods available and can use several methods from Form objects.

Session

The Session system type provides access to the Paradox database engine. Running a Paradox application opens one Session, and developers can open multiple Sessions by using ObjectPAL. Each Session opened uses one user count, which requires a valid Paradox serial number. Using Paradox interactively manages the default Session, and using any of the 32 methods does not require opening a separate Session with ObjectPAL. All locks explicitly declared with ObjectPAL work just like locks placed implicitly with interactive Paradox.

SmallInt

The Small Integer data type represents integer values from –32,768 to 32,768. A SmallInt variable takes up only two bytes of storage and is commonly used as the data type for sequencing fields of a table. If you assign a SmallInt data type a value outside of the possible range, an error occurs. Paradox cannot store a SmallInt variable assigned the value –32,768 because it interprets this value as a blank. You can use this value in calculations or store the value in a dBASE table.

The SmallInt methods are the same methods used by the LongInt data type. SmallInt types also can use the methods associated with Number and AnyType data types.

StatusEvent

Events that change the Desktop status bar result in the generation of StatusEvent types. Each of the design objects has a built-in status method triggered by status events. Using the four methods available with this type, along with the base methods from the Event type, you can control information displayed in the status bar, which includes determining what is displayed, blocking the display, or displaying the information elsewhere on-screen.

String

String data types can contain values of up to 32,767 characters, 255 characters for quoted strings. Using double quotes ("") represents an empty String value. Strings occupy one byte of storage for each character assigned. For text values longer than the limit, use Memo data objects. The 28 different methods of this type provide string manipulation such as searching, returning sub strings, formatting, and character conversion procedures.

System

The 94 different methods of a System type provide access to many of the user interface and file management routines of interactive Paradox. For example, you can use the Paradox Files ¦ Utilities dialog boxes, which prompt users for copying, deleting, and restructuring files. Several standard pop-up message display routines are available. You can control the default display formats of data types and list names of object types. Being able to access these System type methods allows developers to build applications with a user interface consistent with Paradox's.

Table

Table objects contain information describing tables. Do not confuse Table with TableFrame and TableView objects which control display of data. Fifty-three methods allow table level operations such as adding, copying, and creating indexes. You also can perform many statistical calculations on fields of the table.

A Table object cannot be used to edit data. To edit data of a table, you can use a TableFrame or TableView object and enter edit mode. Table data can be changed with ObjectPAL code by using the TCursor, a table cursor that points to a table's data.

TableView

TableView is a display manager object that shows data of a table in a separate window, and inherits many of the methods of a form that can control the display properties, size, and position. Do not confuse TableView with a TableFrame UIObject, which displays data in an area on a Form. You can start and end Edit mode on a TableView; however, you cannot use ObjectPAL to change the data. The wait method on a TableView keeps the table displayed until the user closes the window.

TCursor

One of the most welcome new features of Paradox for Windows is the introduction of the TCursor data model type. A TCursor is a pointer to data in a table, which allows you to change data without actually having to view the table on screen. All edits or locks placed on a TCursor actually change or restrict access to data in the table to which they point. Using the method attach, you can establish a link between a TCursor and a UIObject, like a TableFrame or TableView. This link respects the restricted view of a linked detail table on a form.

Over 103 methods are available to TCursors to perform data management functions, such as the functions shown in the following list :

- Add, copy, delete, and change records
- Create indexes and lock records
- Locate values and list table information
- Perform various statistical calculations on columns of data

TextStream

The TextStream system object enables you to read and write sequence of characters to text files. A TextStream can contain only ANSI characters, including carriage returns and line feeds, and cannot contain formatting information, such as different fonts, bold face print, or italic print like you can have in a Formatted Memo field. Paradox maintains a pointer into a TextStream to tell you how many characters from the beginning you are positioned. The 15 methods of this type allow you to read, write, and position the cursor inside of a TextStream.

Time

A Time data object contains time information in the format of hours:minutes:seconds:milliseconds. You can use any one of the following separators between components: blank, colon, comma, hyphen, period, semicolon, slash, and space. Paradox tables do not have a Time field available, these values must be stored in an alphanumeric field. Time variables must be explicitly declared by using the only available method, time. This type also can use the base methods defined for the DateTime and AnyType types. Paradox allows time values to be interpreted in either a 12- or 24-hour format. Use the system type method formatSetTimeDefault to change the format.

TimerEvent

UIObjects have built-in timer methods that use information contained in TimerEvent event objects. This type has no methods of it's own but uses the methods defined by its base type Event. Using UIObject's setTimer and killTimer methods, you can program your own tasks to be executed in the built-in timer method at a specific time.

UIObject

A UIObject (User Interface Object) display type is any one of the different objects you can place on a form, including bitmap, box, button, crosstab, ellipse, field object, form, graph, line, multi-record object, OLE object, page, record object, table frame, and text box objects. The UIObject methods that operate on tables work on the table through the visible portion of the UIObject, which means that actions directed to UIObjects, that are bound to a table, will immediately be shown through the UIObject.

UIObjects behave much like TCursors and Form types. In many cases, when performing table operations, using a TCursor type rather than a UIObject type is quicker because TCursors work with data behind the scenes and refresh the screen when done. UIObjects refresh the screen as each change is being made.

ValueEvent

A ValueEvent event type is triggered each time the value of a field is about to change. The changeValue built-in method is triggered by a ValueEvent. You can use this event to determine if the value of a field is changing from its previous state and execute an appropriate task. This event occurs before the changed value is posted, so—if needed—you can deny the change. Two methods are available for this type to determine the new value and set it to some other value.

Do not confuse these methods and the ValueEvent event with the built-in method newValue, which is triggered by just the Event type. The newValue method reports when a field has a new posted value.

G

Methods by Type

Paradox has more than one thousand methods organized into groups called types. This chapter lists each method, the arguments the method expects, if any, and the type of variable the method returns, if any.

ActionEvent Methods

```
actionClass() SmallInt
errorCode() LongInt
getTarget(var target UIObject)
id() SmallInt
isFirstTime() Logical
isPreFilter() Logical
isTargetSelf() Logical
reason() SmallInt
setErrorCode(const errorId LongInt)
setId(const actionId SmallInt)
setReason(const reasonId SmallInt)
```

AnyType Methods

```
blank()
dataType() String
isAssigned() Logical
isBlank() Logical
isFixedType() Logical
unAssign() Logical
view()
view(const title String)
```

AnyType Procs

```
blank() AnyType
```

Application Methods

```
bringToTop()
getPosition(var x LongInt, var y LongInt, var w LongInt, var h LongInt)
getTitle() String
hide()
isMaximized() Logical
isMinimized() Logical
isVisible() Logical
maximize()
minimize()
setPosition(const x LongInt, const y LongInt, const w LongInt, const h LongInt)
setTitle(const text String)
show()
windowClientHandle() SmallInt
windowHandle() SmallInt
```

Array Methods

```
addLast(const value AnyType)
append(const newArray Array[] AnyType)
contains(const value AnyType) Logical
countOf(const value AnyType) LongInt
empty()
exchange(const index1 LongInt, const index2 LongInt)
fill(const value AnyType)
grow(const increment LongInt)
indexOf(const value AnyType) LongInt
insert(const index LongInt)
insert(const index LongInt, const numberOfElements LongInt)
insertAfter(const keyItem AnyType, const insertedItem AnyType)
insertBefore(const keyItem AnyType, const insertedItem AnyType)
insertFirst(const value AnyType)
isResizeable() Logical
remove(const index LongInt)
remove(const index LongInt, const numberOfElements LongInt)
removeAllItems(const value AnyType)
removeItem(const value AnyType)
replaceItem(const keyItem AnyType, const newItem AnyType)
setSize(const size LongInt)
size() LongInt
view()
view(const title String)
```

Binary Methods

```
readFromFile(const fileName String) Logical
size() LongInt
writeToFile(const fileName String) Logical
```

Currency Methods

```
view()
view(const title String)
```

Currency Procs

```
currency(const value AnyType) Currency
```

DDE Methods

```
close() Logical
execute(const command String) Logical
open(const server String) Logical
open(const server String, const topic String) Logical
open(const server String, const topic String, const item String) Logical
setItem(const item String)
```

Database Methods

```
close() Logical
delete(const tableName String [, const tableType String]) Logical
delete(const tableVar Table) Logical
executeQBE(const qbeVar Query) Logical
executeQBE(const qbeVar Query, const ansTbl String) Logical
executeQBE(const qbeVar Query, const ansTbl Table) Logical
executeQBE(const qbeVar Query, var ansTbl TCursor) Logical
executeQBEFile(const fileName String) Logical
executeQBEFile(const fileName String, const ansTbl String) Logical
executeQBEFile(const fileName String, const ansTbl Table) Logical
executeQBEFile(const fileName String, var ansTbl TCursor) Logical
executeQBEString(const qbeString String) Logical
executeQBEString(const qbeString String, const ansTbl String) Logical
executeQBEString(const qbeString String, const ansTbl Table) Logical
executeQBEString(const qbeString String, var ansTbl TCursor) Logical
getQueryRestartOptions() SmallInt
isAssigned() Logical
```

```
isTable(const tableName String[, const tableType String]) Logical
isTable(const tableVar Table) Logical
open() Logical
open([const databaseName String,] [const ses Session]) Logical
setQueryRestartOptions(const qryRestartType SmallInt) Logical
writeQBE(const qbeVar Query, const fileName String) Logical
writeQBE(const str String, const fileName String) Logical
```

Database Procs

```
delete(const tableName String[, const tableType String]) Logical
delete(const tableVar Table) Logical
executeQBE(const qbeVar Query) Logical
executeQBE(const qbeVar Query, const ansTbl String) Logical
executeQBE(const qbeVar Query, const ansTbl Table) Logical
executeQBE(const qbeVar Query, var ansTbl TCursor) Logical
executeQBEFile(const fileName String) Logical
executeQBEFile(const fileName String, const ansTbl String) Logical
executeQBEFile(const fileName String, const ansTbl Table) Logical
executeQBEFile(const fileName String, var ansTbl TCursor) Logical
executeQBEString(const qbeString String) Logical
executeQBEString(const qbeString String, const ansTbl String) Logical
executeQBEString(const qbeString String, const ansTbl Table) Logical
executeQBEString(const qbeString String, var ansTbl TCursor) Logical
getQueryRestartOptions() SmallInt
isTable(const tableName String[, const tableType String]) Logical
isTable(const tableVar Table) Logical
setQueryRestartOptions(const qryRestartType SmallInt) Logical
writeQBE(const qbeVar Query, const fileName String) Logical
writeQBE(const str String, const fileName String) Logical
```

Date Methods

```
day() SmallInt
daysInMonth() SmallInt
dow() String
dowOrd() SmallInt
doy() SmallInt
isLeapYear() Logical
month() SmallInt
moy() String
view()
view(const title String)
year() SmallInt
```

Date Procs

```
date([const value AnyType]) Date
dateVal(const value AnyType) Date
today() Date
```

DateTime Methods

```
day() SmallInt
daysInMonth() SmallInt
dow() String
dowOrd() SmallInt
doy() SmallInt
hour() SmallInt
isLeapYear() Logical
milliSec() SmallInt
minute() SmallInt
month() SmallInt
moy() String
second() SmallInt
view()
view(const title String)
year() SmallInt
```

DateTime Procs

```
dateTime([const value AnyType]) DateTime
```

DynArray Methods

```
contains(const value AnyType) Logical
empty()
getKeys(var keyNames Array[] String)
removeItem(const value AnyType)
size() LongInt
view()
view(const title String)
```

ErrorEvent Methods

```
errorCode() LongInt
getTarget(var target UIObject)
isFirstTime() Logical
```

```
isPreFilter() Logical
isTargetSelf() Logical
reason() SmallInt
setErrorCode(const errorId LongInt)
setReason(const reasonId SmallInt)
```

Event Methods

```
errorCode() LongInt
getTarget(var target UIObject)
isFirstTime() Logical
isPreFilter() Logical
isTargetSelf() Logical
reason() SmallInt
setErrorCode(const errorId LongInt)
setReason(const reasonId SmallInt)
```

FileSystem Methods

```
accessRights() String
copy(const srcName String, const dstName String) Logical
delete(const name String) Logical
deleteDir(const name String) Logical
drives() String
enumFileList(const fileSpec String, const tableName String)
enumFileList(const fileSpec String, var Array[] String)
existDrive(const driveLetter String) Logical
findFirst(const pattern String) Logical
findNext() Logical
freeDiskSpace(const driveLetter String) LongInt
fullName() String
getDir() String
getDrive() String
isFixed(const driveLetter String) Logical
isRemote(const driveLetter String) Logical
isRemovable(const driveLetter String) Logical
makeDir(const name String) Logical
name() String
rename(const oldName String, const newName String) Logical
setDir(const name String) Logical
setDrive(const name String) Logical
size() LongInt
time() DateTime
totalDiskSpace(const driveLetter String) LongInt
```

FileSystem Procs

```
getFileAccessRights(const fileName String) String
getValidFileExtensions(const objectType String) String
isDir(const dirName String) Logical
isFile(const fileName String) Logical
privDir() String
setFileAccessRights(const fileName String, const rights String) Logical
splitFullFileName(const fullFileName String, var driveName String, var pathName
     String, var fileName String, var extensionName String)
splitFullFileName(const fullFileName String, var fileNameParts DynArray[]
     String)
startUpDir() String
windowsDir() String
windowsSystemDir() String
workingDir() String
```

Form Methods

```
action(const actionId SmallInt) Logical
attach() Logical
attach(const formName String) Logical
bringToTop()
close()
create() Logical
deliver() Logical
design() Logical
dmAddTable(const tableName String) Logical
dmGet(const tableName String, const fieldName String, var datum AnyType)
     Logical
dmHasTable(const tableName String) Logical
dmPut(const tableName String, const fieldName String, const datum AnyType)
     Logical
dmRemoveTable(const tableName String) Logical
enumSource(const tableName String [, const recurse Logical]) Logical
enumSourceToFile(const fileName String [, const recurse Logical]) Logical
enumTableLinks(const tableName String) Logical
enumUIObjectNames(const tableName String) Logical
enumUIObjectProperties(const tableName String) Logical
getFileName() String
getPosition(var x LongInt, var y LongInt, var w LongInt, var h LongInt)
getTitle() String
hide()
isMaximized() Logical
isMinimized() Logical
isVisible() Logical
keyChar(const aChar SmallInt, const vChar SmallInt, const state SmallInt)
     Logical
keyChar(const characters String) Logical
keyChar(const characters String, const state SmallInt) Logical
keyPhysical(const aChar SmallInt, const vChar SmallInt, const state SmallInt)
     Logical
load(const formName String) Logical
```

Appendix G

```
maximize()
menuAction(const menuId SmallInt) Logical
methodDelete(const methodName String) Logical
methodGet(const methodName String) String
methodSet(const methodName String, const methodText String) Logical
minimize()
mouseDouble(const x LongInt, const y LongInt, const state SmallInt) Logical
mouseDown(const x LongInt, const y LongInt, const state SmallInt) Logical
mouseEnter(const x LongInt, const y LongInt, const state SmallInt) Logical
mouseExit(const x LongInt, const y LongInt, const state SmallInt) Logical
mouseMove(const x LongInt, const y LongInt, const state SmallInt) Logical
mouseRightDouble(const x LongInt, const y LongInt, const state SmallInt)
     Logical
mouseRightDown(const x LongInt, const y LongInt, const state SmallInt) Logical
mouseRightUp(const x LongInt, const y LongInt, const state SmallInt) Logical
mouseUp(const x LongInt, const y LongInt, const state SmallInt) Logical
moveTo() Logical
moveTo(const objectName String ) Logical
moveToPage(const pageNumber SmallInt) Logical
open(const formName String, [const windowStyle LongInt, [const x LongInt, const
     y LongInt, const w LongInt, const h LongInt]]) Logical
open(const openInfo FormOpenInfo) Logical
openAsDialog(const formName String, [const windowStyle LongInt, [const x
     LongInt, const y LongInt, const w LongInt, const h LongInt]]) Logical
openAsDialog(const openInfo FormOpenInfo) Logical
postAction(const actionId SmallInt)
run() Logical
save([const newFormName String]) Logical
setPosition(const x LongInt, const y LongInt, const w LongInt, const h LongInt)
setTitle(const text String)
show()
wait() AnyType
windowClientHandle() SmallInt
windowHandle() SmallInt
```

Form Procs

```
action(const actionId SmallInt) Logical
bringToTop()
close([const returnValue AnyType])
delayScreenUpdates(const yesNo Logical)
disableBreakMessage(const yesNo Logical) Logical
dmAddTable(const tableName String) Logical
dmGet(const tableName String, const fieldName String, var datum AnyType)
     Logical
dmHasTable(const tableName String) Logical
dmPut(const tableName String, const fieldName String, const datum AnyType)
     Logical
dmRemoveTable(const tableName String) Logical
enumSource(const tableName String [, const recurse Logical]) Logical
enumSourceToFile(const fileName String [, const recurse Logical]) Logical
enumTableLinks(const tableName String) Logical
formCaller(var caller Form) Logical
formReturn()
```

```
formReturn(const returnValue AnyType)
getFileName() String
getPosition(var x LongInt, var y LongInt, var w LongInt, var h LongInt)
getTitle() String
hide()
hideSpeedBar()
isMaximized() Logical
isMinimized() Logical
isSpeedBarShowing() Logical
isVisible() Logical
maximize()
menuAction(const menuId SmallInt) Logical
minimize()
moveToPage(const pageNumber SmallInt) Logical
setPosition(const x LongInt, const y LongInt, const w LongInt, const h LongInt)
setTitle(const text String)
show()
showSpeedBar()
windowClientHandle() SmallInt
windowHandle() SmallInt
```

Graphic Methods

```
readFromClipboard() Logical
readFromFile(const fileName String) Logical
writeToClipboard() Logical
writeToFile(const fileName String) Logical
```

KeyEvent Methods

```
char() String
charAnsiCode() SmallInt
errorCode() LongInt
getTarget(var target UIObject)
isAltKeyDown() Logical
isControlKeyDown() Logical
isFirstTime() Logical
isFromUI() Logical
isPreFilter() Logical
isShiftKeyDown() Logical
isTargetSelf() Logical
reason() SmallInt
setAltKeyDown(const yesNo Logical)
setChar(const char String)
setControlKeyDown(const yesNo Logical)
setErrorCode(const errorId LongInt)
setReason(const reasonId SmallInt)
setShiftKeyDown(const yesNo Logical)
setVChar(const char String)
setVCharCode(const VKCode SmallInt)
vChar() String
vCharCode() SmallInt
```

Library Methods

```
close()
enumSource(const tableName String [, const recurse Logical]) Logical
enumSourceToFile(const fileName String [, const recurse Logical]) Logical
execMethod(const methodName String)
open(const libName String) Logical
open(const libName String, const scopeType SmallInt) Logical
```

Logical Methods

```
view()
view(const title String)
```

Logical Procs

```
logical(const value AnyType) Logical
```

LongInt Methods

```
bitAND(const value LongInt) LongInt
bitIsSet(const value LongInt) Logical
bitOR(const value LongInt) LongInt
bitXOR(const value LongInt) LongInt
view()
view(const title String)
```

LongInt Procs

```
longInt(const value AnyType) LongInt
```

Memo Methods

```
readFromFile(const fileName String) Logical
writeToFile(const fileName String) Logical
```

Memo Procs

```
memo(const value AnyType, ... ) Memo
```

Menu Methods

```
addArray(const items Array[] String)
addBreak()
addPopUp(const menuName String, const cascadedPopUp PopUpMenu)
addStaticText(const item String)
addText(const menuName String)
addText(const menuName String, const attrib SmallInt)
addText(const menuName String, const attrib SmallInt, const id SmallInt)
contains(const item String) Logical
count() SmallInt
empty()
remove(const item String)
show()
```

Menu Procs

```
getMenuChoiceAttribute(const menuChoice String) SmallInt
getMenuChoiceAttributeById(const menuId SmallInt) SmallInt
hasMenuChoiceAttribute(const menuAttribute SmallInt, const testAttributes
     SmallInt) Logical
removeMenu()
setMenuChoiceAttribute(const menuChoice String, const menuAttribute SmallInt)
setMenuChoiceAttributeById(const menuId SmallInt, const menuAttribute SmallInt)
```

MenuEvent Methods

```
data() LongInt
errorCode() LongInt
getTarget(var target UIObject)
id() SmallInt
isFirstTime() Logical
isFromUI() Logical
isPreFilter() Logical
isTargetSelf() Logical
menuChoice() String
reason() SmallInt
setData(const menuData LongInt)
setErrorCode(const errorId LongInt)
setId(const actionId SmallInt)
setReason(const reasonId SmallInt)
```

MouseEvent Methods

```
errorCode() LongInt
getMousePosition(var p Point)
getMousePosition(var xPosition LongInt, var yPosition LongInt)
getObjectHit(var target UIObject) Logical
getTarget(var target UIObject) Logical
isControlKeyDown() Logical
isFirstTime() Logical
isFromUI() Logical
isInside() Logical
isLeftDown() Logical
isMiddleDown() Logical
isPreFilter() Logical
isRightDown() Logical
isShiftKeyDown() Logical
isTargetSelf() Logical
reason() SmallInt
setControlKeyDown(const yesNo Logical)
setErrorCode(const errorId LongInt)
setInside(const trueFalse Logical)
setLeftDown(const yesNo Logical)
setMiddleDown(const yesNo Logical)
setMousePosition(const p Point)
setMousePosition(const xPosition LongInt, const yPosition LongInt)
setReason(const reasonId SmallInt)
setRightDown(const yesNo Logical)
setShiftKeyDown(const yesNo Logical)
setX(const xPosition LongInt )
setY(const yPosition LongInt )
x() LongInt
y() LongInt
```

MoveEvent Methods

```
errorCode() LongInt
getDestination(var dest UIObject)
getTarget(var target UIObject)
isFirstTime() Logical
isPreFilter() Logical
isTargetSelf() Logical
reason() SmallInt
setErrorCode(const errorId LongInt)
setReason(const reasonId SmallInt)
```

Number Methods

```
abs() Number
acos() Number
asin() Number
```

```
atan() Number
atan2(const x Number) Number
ceil() Number
cos() Number
cosh() Number
exp() Number
floor() Number
fraction() Number
fv(const interestRate Number, const periods Number) Number
ln() Number
log() Number
mod(const modulus Number) Number
pmt(const interestRate Number, const periods Number) Number
pow(const exponent Number) Number
pow10() Number
pv(const interestRate Number, const periods Number) Number
round(const places SmallInt) Number
sin() Number
sinh() Number
sqrt() Number
tan() Number
tanh() Number
truncate(const places SmallInt) Number
view()
view(const title String)
```

Number Procs

```
max(const x1 AnyType, const x2 AnyType) AnyType
min(const x1 AnyType, const x2 AnyType) AnyType
numVal(const value AnyType) Number
number(const value AnyType) Number
rand() Number
```

OLE Methods

```
canReadFromClipboard() Logical
edit(const name String, const verb SmallInt) Logical
enumVerbs(var verbs DynArray[] SmallInt) Logical
getServerName() String
readFromClipboard() Logical
writeToClipboard() Logical
```

Point Methods

```
distance(const p Point) Number
isAbove(const p Point) Logical
isBelow(const p Point) Logical
```

```
isLeft(const p Point) Logical
isRight(const p Point) Logical
setX(const newXValue LongInt )
setXY(const newXValue LongInt, const newYValue LongInt)
setY(const newYValue LongInt )
view()
view(const title String)
x() LongInt
y() LongInt
```

Point Procs

```
point(const newPoint Point ) Point
point(const x LongInt, const y LongInt ) Point
```

PopUpMenu Methods

```
addArray(const items Array[] String)
addBar()
addBreak()
addPopUp(const menuName String, const cascadedPopUp PopUpMenu)
addSeparator()
addStaticText(const item String)
addText(const menuName String)
addText(const menuName String, const attrib SmallInt)
addText(const menuName String, const attrib SmallInt, const id SmallInt)
contains(const item String) Logical
count() SmallInt
empty()
remove(const item String)
show() String
show(const xTwips SmallInt, const yTwips SmallInt) String
```

Query Methods

```
executeQBE() Logical
executeQBE(const ansTbl String) Logical
executeQBE(const ansTbl Table) Logical
executeQBE(var ansTbl TCursor) Logical
isAssigned() Logical
writeQBE(const fileName String) Logical
```

Record Methods

    view()
    view(const title String)

Report Methods

    attach(const reportName String) Logical
    bringToTop()
    close()
    create() Logical
    currentPage() SmallInt
    design() Logical
    enumUIObjectNames(const tableName String) Logical
    enumUIObjectProperties(const tableName String) Logical
    getPosition(var x LongInt, var y LongInt, var w LongInt, var h LongInt)
    getTitle() String
    hide()
    isMaximized() Logical
    isMinimized() Logical
    isVisible() Logical
    load(const reportName String) Logical
    maximize()
    minimize()
    moveToPage(const pageNumber SmallInt) Logical
    open(const openInfo ReportOpenInfo) Logical
    open(const reportName String, [const windowStyle LongInt, [const x LongInt,
         const y LongInt, const w LongInt, const h LongInt]]) Logical
    print() Logical
    print(const reportName String [, const refresh SmallInt]) Logical
    print(const ri ReportPrintInfo) Logical
    run() Logical
    save([const newReportName String]) Logical
    setPosition(const x LongInt, const y LongInt, const w LongInt, const h LongInt)
    setTitle(const text String)
    show()

Session Methods

    addAlias(const alias String, const type String, const path String) Logical
    addPassword(const password String)
    blankAsZero(const yesNo Logical)
    close() Logical
    enumAliasNames(const tableName String) Logical
    enumDatabaseTables(const tableName String, const databaseName String, const
         fileSpec String) Logical
    enumOpenDatabases(const tableName String) Logical
    getAliasPath(const aliasName String) String
    getNetUserName() String
    isAssigned() Logical

```
isBlankZero() Logical
open([const name String]) Logical
removeAlias(const alias String) Logical
removeAllPasswords()
removePassword(const password String)
retryPeriod() SmallInt
saveCFG([const fileName String]) Logical
setAliasPath(const aliasName String, const aliasPath String) Logical
setRetryPeriod(const period SmallInt) Logical
```

Session Procs

```
addAlias(const alias String, const type String, const path String) Logical
addPassword(const password String)
advancedWildcardsInLocate([const yesNo Logical])
blankAsZero(const yesNo Logical)
enumAliasNames(const tableName String) Logical
enumDatabaseTables(const tableName String, const databaseName String, const
    fileSpec String) Logical
enumDriverCapabilities(const DrvCap_TblName String, const TblCap_TblName
    String, const FldCap_TblName String)
enumDriverInfo(const tableName String) Logical
enumDriverNames(const tableName String) Logical
enumDriverTopics(const tableName String) Logical
enumEngineInfo(const tableName String) Logical
enumFolder(const tableName String [, const fileSpec String]) Logical
enumFolder(var result Array[] String [, const fileSpec String]) Logical
enumOpenDatabases(const tableName String) Logical
enumUsers(const tableName String) LongInt
getAliasPath(const aliasName String) String
getNetUserName() String
ignoreCaseInLocate([const yesNo Logical])
isAdvancedWildcardsInLocate() Logical
isBlankZero() Logical
isIgnoreCaseInLocate() Logical
lock(const tableName {Table | TCursor}, const lockType String, ... ) Logical
removeAlias(const alias String) Logical
removeAllPasswords()
removePassword(const password String)
retryPeriod() SmallInt
saveCFG([const fileName String]) Logical
setAliasPath(const aliasName String, const aliasPath String) Logical
setRetryPeriod(const period SmallInt) Logical
unlock(const tableName {Table | TCursor}, const lockType String, ... ) Logical
```

SmallInt Methods

```
bitAND(const value SmallInt) SmallInt
bitIsSet(const value SmallInt) Logical
bitOR(const value SmallInt) SmallInt
bitXOR(const value SmallInt) SmallInt
```

```
view()
view(const title String)
```

SmallInt Procs

```
int(const value AnyType) SmallInt
smallInt(const value AnyType) SmallInt
```

StatusEvent Methods

```
errorCode() LongInt
getTarget(var target UIObject)
isFirstTime() Logical
isPreFilter() Logical
isTargetSelf() Logical
reason() SmallInt
setErrorCode(const errorId LongInt)
setReason(const reasonId SmallInt)
setStatusValue(const statusValue AnyType)
statusValue() AnyType
```

String Methods

```
advMatch(const pattern String, ... ) Logical
breakApart(var tokenArray Array[] String, [const separators String])
isSpace(const string String) Logical
lTrim() String
lower() String
match(const pattern String, ... ) Logical
rTrim() String
search(const str String) SmallInt
size() SmallInt
substr(const startIndex SmallInt) String
substr(const startIndex SmallInt, const numberOfChars SmallInt) String
toANSI() String
toOEM() String
upper() String
view()
view(const title String)
```

String Procs

```
ansiCode(const char String) SmallInt
chr(const ansiCode SmallInt) String
chrOEM(const oemCode SmallInt) String
```

```
chrToKeyName(const char String) String
fill(const fillCharacter String, const numberOfRepetitions SmallInt ) String
format(const formatSpec String, const value AnyType) String
ignoreCaseInStringCompares(const yes_no Logical)
isIgnoreCaseInStringCompares() Logical
keyNameToChr(const keyName String) String
keyNameToVKCode(const keyName String) SmallInt
oemCode(const char String) SmallInt
space(const numberOfSpaces SmallInt ) String
strVal(const value AnyType) String
string(const value AnyType) String
string(const value AnyType, ...) String
vkCodeToKeyName(const vkCode SmallInt) String
```

System Procs

```
beep()
close([const returnValue AnyType])
constantNameToValue(const constantName String) AnyType
constantValueToName(const groupName String, const value AnyType, var constName
      String) Logical
cpuClockTime() LongInt
debug()
dlgAdd(const tableName String)
dlgCopy(const tableName String)
dlgCreate(const tableName String)
dlgDelete(const tableName String)
dlgEmpty(const tableName String)
dlgNetDrivers()
dlgNetLocks()
dlgNetRefresh()
dlgNetRetry()
dlgNetSetLocks()
dlgNetSystem()
dlgNetUserName()
dlgNetWho()
dlgRename(const tableName String)
dlgRestructure(const tableName String)
dlgSort(const tableName String)
dlgSubtract(const tableName String)
dlgTableInfo(const tableName String)
enumDesktopWindowNames(const tableName String) Logical
enumDesktopWindowNames(var windowNames Array[] String)
enumFonts(const tableName String) Logical
enumFormNames(var formNames Array[] String)
enumRTLClassNames(const tableName String) Logical
enumRTLConstants(const tableName String) Logical
enumRTLMethods(const tableName String) Logical
enumReportNames(var reportNames Array[] String)
enumWindowNames(const tableName String) Logical
enumWindowNames(var windowNames Array[] String)
errorClear()
errorCode() SmallInt
errorLog(const errorCode SmallInt, const errorMessage String)
```

```
errorMessage() String
errorPop() Logical
errorShow() Logical
errorShow(const topHelp String, const bottomHelp String) Logical
errorShow(const topHelp) Logical
errorTrapOnWarnings(const yesNo Logical)
execute(const programName String ) Logical
execute(const programName String, const wait Logical) Logical
execute(const programName String, const wait Logical, const displayMode
     SmallInt ) Logical
exit()
fail()
fail(const errorNumber SmallInt, const errorMessage String )
fileBrowser(var selectedFile String) Logical
fileBrowser(var selectedFile String, var browserInfo FileBrowserInfo) Logical
fileBrowser(var selectedFiles Array[] String) Logical
fileBrowser(var selectedFiles Array[] String, var browserInfo FileBrowserInfo)
     Logical
formatAdd(const formatName String, const formatSpec String) String
formatDelete(const formatName String) Logical
formatExist(const formatName String) Logical
formatSetCurrencyDefault(const formatName String) Logical
formatSetDateDefault(const formatName String) Logical
formatSetDateTimeDefault(const formatName String) Logical
formatSetLogicalDefault(const formatName String) Logical
formatSetLongIntDefault(const formatName String) Logical
formatSetNumberDefault(const formatName String) Logical
formatSetSmallIntDefault(const formatName String) Logical
formatSetTimeDefault(const formatName String) Logical
getMouseScreenPosition() Point
helpOnHelp() Logical
helpQuit(const helpFileName String) Logical
helpSetIndex(const helpFileName String, const indexId LongInt ) Logical
helpShowContext(const helpFileName String, const helpId LongInt ) Logical
helpShowIndex(const helpFileName String ) Logical
helpShowTopic(const helpFileName String, const topicKey String ) Logical
helpShowTopicInKeywordTable(const helpFileName String, const keyTableLetter String,
     const topicKey String ) Logical
message(const message String, ... )
msgAbortRetryIgnore(const caption String, const text String) String
msgInfo(const caption String, const text String)
msgQuestion(const caption String, const text String) String
msgRetryCancel(const caption String, const text String) String
msgStop(const caption String, const text String)
msgyesNoCancel(const caption String, const text String) String
pixelsToTwips(const pix Point ) Point
play(const scriptName String) AnyType
readEnvironmentString(const key String) String
readProfileString(const fileName String, const section String, const key
     String) String
setMouseScreenPosition(const mousePosition Point)
setMouseScreenPosition(const x LongInt, const y LongInt)
setMouseShape(const mouseShapeId LongInt) LongInt
sleep()
sleep(const numberOfMilliSecs LongInt)
sound(const freqHertz LongInt, const durationMilliSecs LongInt )
sysInfo(var info DynArray[] AnyType)
tracerClear()
```

```
tracerHide()
tracerOff()
tracerOn()
tracerSave(const fileName String )
tracerShow()
tracerToTop()
tracerWrite(const message String, ... )
twipsToPixels(const twips Point) Point
version() String
winGetMessageId(const msgName SmallInt ) SmallInt
winPostMessage(const hWnd SmallInt, const msg SmallInt, const wParam      SmallInt,
    const lParam LongInt) Logical
winSendMessage(const hWnd SmallInt, const msg SmallInt, const wParam      SmallInt,
const lParam LongInt) LongInt
writeEnvironmentString(const key String, const value String) Logical
writeProfileString(const fileName String, const section String, const key String,
    const value String) Logical
```

TCursor Methods

```
add(const destTCursor TCursor [, const append Logical [, const update
    Logical]]) Logical
add(const destTable Table [, const append Logical [, const update Logical]])
    Logical
add(const destTableName String [, const append Logical [, const update
    Logical]]) Logical
atFirst() Logical
atLast() Logical
attach(const object UIObject) Logical
attach(const srcTCursor TCursor) Logical
attach(const tv TableView) Logical
attachToKeyViol(const oldTC TCursor) Logical
bot() Logical
cAverage(const fieldName String) Number
cAverage(const fieldNum SmallInt) Number
cCount(const fieldName String) Number
cCount(const fieldNum SmallInt) Number
cMax(const fieldName String) Number
cMax(const fieldNum SmallInt) Number
cMin(const fieldName String) Number
cMin(const fieldNum SmallInt) Number
cNpv(const fieldName String, const discRate Number) Number
cNpv(const fieldNum SmallInt, const discRate Number) Number
cSamStd(const fieldName String) Number
cSamStd(const fieldNum SmallInt) Number
cSamVar(const fieldName String) Number
cSamVar(const fieldNum SmallInt) Number
cStd(const fieldName String) Number
cStd(const fieldNum SmallInt) Number
cSum(const fieldName String) Number
cSum(const fieldNum SmallInt) Number
cVar(const fieldName String) Number
cVar(const fieldNum SmallInt) Number
cancelEdit() Logical
```

```
close() Logical
compact([const regIndex Logical]) Logical
copy(const tableName String) Logical
copy(const tableVar Table) Logical
copyFromArray(const ar Array[] AnyType) Logical
copyFromArray(const ar DynArray[] AnyType) Logical
copyRecord(const cursor TCursor) Logical
copyToArray(var ar Array[] AnyType) Logical
copyToArray(var ar DynArray[] AnyType) Logical
currRecord() Logical
deleteRecord() Logical
didFlyAway() Logical
dropIndex(const indexName String [, const tagName String]) Logical
edit() Logical
empty() Logical
end() Logical
endEdit() Logical
enumFieldNames(var fieldArray Array[] String) Logical
enumFieldNamesInIndex([const indexName String, [const tagName String,]] var
    fieldNames Array[] String) Logical
enumFieldStruct(const tableName String) Logical
enumIndexStruct(const tableName String) Logical
enumLocks(const tableName String) LongInt
enumRefIntStruct(const tableName String) Logical
enumSecStruct(const tableName String) Logical
enumTableProperties(const tableName String) Logical
eot() Logical
familyRights(const rights String) Logical
fieldName(const fieldNum SmallInt) String
fieldNo(const fieldName String) SmallInt
fieldRights(const fieldName String, const rights String) Logical
fieldRights(const fieldNum SmallInt, const rights String) Logical
fieldSize(const fieldName String) SmallInt
fieldSize(const fieldNum SmallInt) SmallInt
fieldType(const fieldName String) String
fieldType(const fieldNum SmallInt) String
fieldUnits2(const fieldName String) SmallInt
fieldUnits2(const fieldNum SmallInt) SmallInt
fieldValue(const fieldName String, var result AnyType) Logical
fieldValue(const fieldNum SmallInt, var result AnyType) Logical
getLanguageDriver() String
getLanguageDriverDesc() String
home() Logical
initRecord() Logical
insertAfterRecord() Logical
insertAfterRecord(const cursor TCursor) Logical
insertBeforeRecord() Logical
insertBeforeRecord(const cursor TCursor) Logical
insertRecord() Logical
insertRecord(const cursor TCursor) Logical
isAssigned() Logical
isEdit() Logical
isEmpty() Logical
isEncrypted() Logical
isRecordDeleted() Logical
isShared() Logical
isShowDeletedOn() Logical
isValid(const fieldName String, const value AnyType) Logical
```

```
isValid(const fieldNum SmallInt, const value AnyType) Logical
locate(const fieldName String, const exactMatch String, ...) Logical
locate(const fieldNum SmallInt, const exactMatch String, ...) Logical
locateNext(const fieldName String, const exactMatch String, ...) Logical
locateNext(const fieldNum SmallInt, const exactMatch String, ...) Logical
locateNextPattern([const fieldName String, const exactMatch AnyType, ...] const fieldName
     String, const pattern String) Logical
locateNextPattern([const fieldNum SmallInt, const exactMatch AnyType, ...]
     const fieldNum smallInt, const pattern String) Logical
locatePattern([const fieldName String, const exactMatch AnyType, ...] const
     fieldName String, const pattern String) Logical
locatePattern([const fieldNum SmallInt, const exactMatch AnyType, ...] const
     fieldNum smallInt, const pattern String) Logical
locatePrior(const fieldName String, const exactMatch String, ...) Logical
locatePrior(const fieldNum SmallInt, const exactMatch String, ...) Logical
locatePriorPattern([const fieldName String, const exactMatch AnyType, ...] const fieldName
     String, const pattern String) Logical
locatePriorPattern([const fieldNum SmallInt, const exactMatch AnyType, ...]
     const fieldNum smallInt, const pattern String) Logical
lock(const lockType String) Logical
lockRecord() Logical
lockStatus(const statusType String) SmallInt
moveToRecNo(const recordNum LongInt) Logical
moveToRecord(const recordNum LongInt) Logical
nFields() LongInt
nKeyFields() LongInt
nRecords() LongInt
nextRecord() Logical
open(const tableName String [, const db Database] [, const indx String])
     Logical
open(const tableVar Table) Logical
postRecord() Logical
priorRecord() Logical
qLocate(const exactMatch String, ...) Logical
reIndex(const IndexName String[, const TagName String]) Logical
reIndexAll() Logical
recNo() LongInt
recordStatus(const statusType String) Logical
seqNo() LongInt
setFieldValue(const fieldName String, const value AnyType) Logical
setFieldValue(const fieldNum SmallInt, const value AnyType) Logical
setFilter([const exactMatch AnyType, ...] const minValue AnyType, const
     maxValue AnyType) Logical
setFlyAwayControl([const yesNo Logical])
showDeleted([const yesNo Logical]) Logical
skip() Logical
skip(const nRecords LongInt) Logical
sortTo(const destTable Table, const NumField SmallInt, const sortFields Array[]
     String, const sortOrder Array[] SmallInt) Logical
sortTo(const tableName String, const NumField SmallInt, const sortFields
     Array[] String, const sortOrder Array[] SmallInt) Logical
subtract(const destTCursor TCursor) Logical
subtract(const destTable Table) Logical
subtract(const destTablename String) Logical
switchIndex([const indexName String [,const indexTagName String]] [, const
     stayOnRecord Logical]) Logical
tableName() String
tableRights(const rights String) Logical
```

```
type() String
unDeleteRecord() Logical
unlock(const lockType String) Logical
unlockRecord() Logical
updateRecord() Logical
updateRecord(const moveTo Logical) Logical
```

Table Methods

```
add(const destTable Table [, const append Logical [, const update Logical]])
    Logical
add(const destTableName String [, const append Logical [, const update
    Logical]]) Logical
attach(const tableName String) Logical
attach(const tableName String, const dB Database) Logical
attach(const tableName String, const tableType String) Logical
attach(const tableName String, const tableType String, const dB Database)
    Logical
cAverage(const fieldName String) Number
cAverage(const fieldNum SmallInt) Number
cCount(const fieldName String) Number
cCount(const fieldNum SmallInt) Number
cMax(const fieldName String) Number
cMax(const fieldNum SmallInt) Number
cMin(const fieldName String) Number
cMin(const fieldNum SmallInt) Number
cNpv(const fieldName String, const discRate AnyType) Number
cNpv(const fieldNum SmallInt, const discRate AnyType) Number
cSamStd(const fieldName String) Number
cSamStd(const fieldNum SmallInt) Number
cSamVar(const fieldName String) Number
cSamVar(const fieldNum SmallInt) Number
cStd(const fieldName String) Number
cStd(const fieldNum SmallInt) Number
cSum(const fieldName String) Number
cSum(const fieldNum SmallInt) Number
cVar(const fieldName String) Number
cVar(const fieldNum SmallInt) Number
compact([const regIndex Logical]) Logical
copy(const destTable Table) Logical
copy(const destTableName String) Logical
delete() Logical
dropIndex(const indexName String [, const tagName String]) Logical
empty() Logical
enumFieldNames(var fieldArray Array[] String) Logical
enumFieldNamesInIndex([const indexName String, [const tagName String,]] var
    fieldNames Array[] String) Logical
enumFieldStruct(const tableName String) Logical
enumIndexStruct(const tableName String) Logical
enumRefIntStruct(const tableName String) Logical
enumSecStruct(const tableName String) Logical
familyRights(const rights String) Logical
fieldName(const fieldNum SmallInt) String
fieldNo(const fieldName String) SmallInt
```

Appendix G

```
fieldType(const fieldName String) String
fieldType(const fieldNum SmallInt) String
isAssigned() Logical
isEmpty() Logical
isEncrypted() Logical
isShared() Logical
isTable() Logical
lock(const lockType String) Logical
nFields() LongInt
nKeyFields() LongInt
nRecords() LongInt
protect([const password String]) Logical
reIndex(const indexName String[, const tagName String]) Logical
reIndexAll() Logical
rename(const destTableName String) Logical
setExclusive([const yesNo Logical])
setFilter([const exactMatch AnyType, ...] const minValue AnyType, const
    maxValue AnyType) Logical
setIndex(const indexName String) Logical
setIndex(const indexName String, const indexTagName String) Logical
setReadOnly([const yesNo Logical])
showDeleted([const yesNo Logical]) Logical
subtract(const destTable Table) Logical
subtract(const destTableName String) Logical
tableRights(const rights String) Logical
type() String
unAttach() Logical
unProtect() Logical
unProtect(const password String) Logical
unlock(const lockType String) Logical
usesIndexes(const indexName String, ...) Logical
```

Table Procs

```
add(const tableName String, const destTableName String) Logical
add(const tableName String, const destTableName String, const append Logical,
    const update Logical) Logical
cAverage(const tableName String, const fieldName String) Number
cAverage(const tableName String, const fieldNum SmallInt) Number
cCount(const tableName String, const fieldName String) Number
cCount(const tableName String, const fieldNum SmallInt) Number
cMax(const tableName String, const fieldName String) Number
cMax(const tableName String, const fieldNum SmallInt) Number
cMin(const tableName String, const fieldName String) Number
cMin(const tableName String, const fieldNum SmallInt) Number
cNpv(const tableName String, const fieldName String, const discRate AnyType)
    Number
cNpv(const tableName String, const fieldNum SmallInt, const discRate  AnyType)
    Number
cSamStd(const tableName String, const fieldName String) Number
cSamStd(const tableName String, const fieldNum SmallInt) Number
cSamVar(const tableName String, const fieldName String) Number
cSamVar(const tableName String, const fieldNum SmallInt) Number
cStd(const tableName String, const fieldName String) Number
cStd(const tableName String, const fieldNum SmallInt) Number
```

```
cSum(const tableName String, const fieldName String) Number
cSum(const tableName String, const fieldNum SmallInt) Number
cVar(const tableName String, const fieldName String) Number
cVar(const tableName String, const fieldNum SmallInt) Number
copy(const tableName String, const destTable Table) Logical
copy(const tableName String, const destTableName String) Logical
delete(const tableName String [, const tableType String]) Logical
empty(const tableName String) Logical
familyRights(const tableName String, const rights AnyType) Logical
fieldName(const tableName String, const fieldNum SmallInt) String
fieldNo(const tableName String, const fieldName String) SmallInt
fieldType(const tableName String, const fieldName String) String
fieldType(const tableName String, const fieldNum SmallInt) String
isEmpty(const tableName String) Logical
isEncrypted(const tableName String) Logical
isShared(const tableName String) Logical
isTable(const tableName String) Logical
nFields(const tableName String) LongInt
nKeyFields(const tableName String) LongInt
nRecords(const tableName String) LongInt
protect(const tableName String) Logical
protect(const tableName String, const password String) Logical
rename(const tableName String, const destTableName String) Logical
subtract(const tableName String, const destTableName String) Logical
tableRights(const tableName String, const rights AnyType) Logical
unProtect(const tableName String) Logical
unProtect(const tableName String, const password String) Logical
```

TableView Methods

```
action(const actionId SmallInt) Logical
bringToTop()
close()
getPosition(var x LongInt, var y LongInt, var w LongInt, var h LongInt)
getTitle() String
hide()
isMaximized() Logical
isMinimized() Logical
isVisible() Logical
maximize()
minimize()
moveToRecord(const tc TCursor) Logical
open(const tableViewName String) Logical
open(const tableViewName String, const windowStyle LongInt) Logical
open(const tableViewName String, const windowStyle LongInt, const x LongInt,
     const y LongInt, const w LongInt, const h LongInt) Logical
setPosition(const x LongInt, const y LongInt, const w LongInt, const h LongInt)
setTitle(const text String)
show()
wait()
windowHandle() SmallInt
```

TextStream Methods

```
advMatch(var startIndex LongInt, var endIndex LongInt, const pattern String)
     Logical
close() Logical
commit()
create(const fileName String) Logical
end()
eof() Logical
home()
open(const fileName String, const mode String) Logical
position() LongInt
readChars(var string String, const nChars SmallInt) Logical
readLine(var stringArray Array[] String) Logical
readLine(var value String) Logical
setPosition(const offset LongInt)
size() LongInt
writeLine(const value AnyType, ...) Logical
writeString(const value AnyType, ...) Logical
```

Time Methods

```
hour() SmallInt
milliSec() SmallInt
minute() SmallInt
second() SmallInt
view()
view(const title String)
```

Time Procs

```
time([const value AnyType]) Time
```

TimerEvent Methods

```
errorCode() LongInt
getTarget(var target UIObject)
isFirstTime() Logical
isPreFilter() Logical
isTargetSelf() Logical
reason() SmallInt
setErrorCode(const errorId LongInt)
setReason(const reasonId SmallInt)
```

UIObject Methods

```
action(const actionId SmallInt) Logical
atFirst() Logical
atLast() Logical
attach() Logical
attach(const form Form) Logical
attach(const form Form, const objectName String) Logical
attach(const object UIObject) Logical
attach(const report Report) Logical
attach(const report Report, const objectName String) Logical
broadcastAction(const actionId SmallInt)
cancelEdit() Logical
convertPointWithRespectTo(const otherUIObject UIObject, const oldPoint  Point,var
    convertedPoint Point)
copyFromArray(const ar Array[] AnyType) Logical
copyToArray(var ar Array[] AnyType) Logical
create(const objectType SmallInt, const x LongInt, const y LongInt, const w
    LongInt, const h LongInt)
create(const objectType SmallInt, const x LongInt, const y LongInt, const w
    LongInt, const h LongInt, const container UIObject)
currRecord() Logical
delete()
deleteRecord() Logical
edit() Logical
empty() Logical
end() Logical
endEdit() Logical
enumFieldNames(var fieldNames Array[] String) Logical
enumLocks(const tableName String) LongInt
enumObjectNames(var objectNames Array[] String) Logical
enumSource(const tableName String [, const recurse Logical]) Logical
enumSourceToFile(const fileName String [, const recurse Logical]) Logical
enumUIObjectNames(const tableName String) Logical
enumUIObjectProperties(const tableName String) Logical
execMethod(const methodName String)
getBoundingBox(var topLeft Point, var bottomRight Point)
getPosition(var x LongInt, var y LongInt, var w LongInt, var h LongInt)
getProperty(const propertyName String) AnyType
getPropertyAsString(const propertyName String) String
hasMouse() Logical
home() Logical
insertAfterRecord() Logical
insertBeforeRecord() Logical
insertRecord() Logical
isEdit() Logical
isEmpty() Logical
isRecordDeleted() Logical
keyChar(const ansiKeyValue SmallInt) Logical
keyChar(const ansiKeyValue SmallInt, const vChar SmallInt, const state
    SmallInt) Logical
keyChar(const characters String) Logical
keyChar(const characters String, const state SmallInt) Logical
keyPhysical(const ansiKeyValue SmallInt, const vChar SmallInt, const state
    SmallInt) Logical
killTimer()
locate(const fieldName String, const exactMatch AnyType, ...) Logical
```

```
locate(const fieldNum SmallInt, const exactMatch AnyType, ...) Logical
locateNext(const fieldName String, const exactMatch AnyType, ...) Logical
locateNext(const fieldNum SmallInt, const exactMatch AnyType, ...) Logical
locateNextPattern([const fieldName String, const exactMatch AnyType, ...],
     const fieldName String, const pattern String) Logical
locateNextPattern([const fieldNum SmallInt, const exactMatch AnyType, ...],
     const fieldNum SmallInt, const pattern String) Logical
locatePattern([const fieldName String, const exactMatch AnyType, ...], const
     fieldName String, const pattern String) Logical
locatePattern([const fieldNum SmallInt, const exactMatch AnyType, ...], const
     fieldNum SmallInt, const pattern String) Logical
locatePrior(const fieldName String, const exactMatch AnyType, ...) Logical
locatePrior(const fieldNum SmallInt, const exactMatch AnyType, ...) Logical
locatePriorPattern([const fieldName String, const exactMatch AnyType, ...],
     const fieldName String, const pattern String) Logical
locatePriorPattern([const fieldNum SmallInt, const exactMatch AnyType, ...],
     const fieldNum SmallInt, const pattern String) Logical
lockRecord() Logical
lockStatus(const statusType String) SmallInt
menuAction(const menuId SmallInt) Logical
methodDelete(const methodName String) Logical
methodGet(const methodName String) String
methodSet(const methodName String, const methodText String) Logical
mouseClick() Logical
mouseDouble(const x LongInt, const y LongInt, const state SmallInt) Logical
mouseDown(const x LongInt, const y LongInt, const state SmallInt) Logical
mouseEnter(const x LongInt, const y LongInt, const state SmallInt) Logical
mouseExit(const x LongInt, const y LongInt, const state SmallInt) Logical
mouseMove(const x LongInt, const y LongInt, const state SmallInt) Logical
mouseRightDouble(const x LongInt, const y LongInt, const state SmallInt)
     Logical
mouseRightDown(const x LongInt, const y LongInt, const state SmallInt)    Logical
mouseRightUp(const x LongInt, const y LongInt, const state SmallInt) Logical
mouseUp(const x LongInt, const y LongInt, const state SmallInt) Logical
moveTo() Logical
moveToRecNo(const recordNum LongInt) Logical
moveToRecord(const recordNum LongInt) Logical
moveToRecord(const tc TCursor) Logical
nFields() LongInt
nKeyFields() LongInt
nRecords() LongInt
nextRecord() Logical
pixelsToTwips(const pix Point) Point
postAction(const actionId SmallInt)
postRecord() Logical
priorRecord() Logical
pushButton() Logical
reSync(const tc TCursor) Logical
recordStatus(const statusType String) Logical
setFilter([const exactMatch AnyType, ...] const minVal AnyType, const maxVal
     AnyType) Logical
setPosition(const x LongInt, const y LongInt, const w LongInt, const h LongInt)
setProperty(const propertyName String, const propertyValue AnyType)
setTimer(const milliSeconds LongInt)
setTimer(const milliSeconds LongInt, const repeat Logical)
skip(const nRecords LongInt) Logical
switchIndex([const indexName String [, const indexTagName String]] [, const
stayOnRecord Logical]) Logical
```

```
twipsToPixels(const twips Point) Point
unDeleteRecord() Logical
unlockRecord() Logical
view()
view(const title String)
wasLastClicked() Logical
wasLastRightClicked() Logical
```

UIObject Procs

```
enumObjectNames(var objectNames Array[] String) Logical
enumUIClasses(const tableName String) Logical
enumUIObjectNames(const tableName String) Logical
enumUIObjectProperties(const tableName String) Logical
execMethod(const methodName String)
getRGB(const rgb LongInt, var red SmallInt, var green SmallInt, var blue
    SmallInt)
isContainerValid() Logical
isLastMouseClickedValid() Logical
isLastMouseRightClickedValid() Logical
moveTo(const objectName String) Logical
rgb(const red SmallInt, const green SmallInt, const blue SmallInt) LongInt
```

ValueEvent Methods

```
errorCode() LongInt
getTarget(var target UIObject)
isFirstTime() Logical
isPreFilter() Logical
isTargetSelf() Logical
newValue() AnyType
reason() SmallInt
setErrorCode(const errorId LongInt)
setNewValue(const newValue AnyType)
setReason(const reasonId SmallInt)
```

Constants and Properties

Paradox has thousands of constants and hundreds of properties. Constants are a name for a number, usually an error code or a number to represent some action. Constants make programs easier to read and maintain. Properties are object attributes which you can read or, in many cases, set. By changing object properties, you can change an object's appearance or behavior. This chapter lists all of Paradox's constants and properties.

Constants

ActionClasses	Type	Value
DataAction	SmallInt	12
EditAction	SmallInt	10
FieldAction	SmallInt	11
MoveAction	SmallInt	8
SelectAction	SmallInt	9

ActionDataCommands	Type	Value
DataArriveRecord	SmallInt	3111
DataBegin	SmallInt	3076
DataBeginEdit	SmallInt	3078
DataBeginFirstField	SmallInt	3105
DataCancelRecord	SmallInt	3082
DataDeleteRecord	SmallInt	3085
DataDesign	SmallInt	3102
DataDitto	SmallInt	3098
DataEnd	SmallInt	3077
DataEndEdit	SmallInt	3079
DataEndLastField	SmallInt	3106
DataFastBackward	SmallInt	3101
DataFastForward	SmallInt	3100
DataHideDeleted	SmallInt	3096
DataInsertRecord	SmallInt	3084

DataLockRecord	SmallInt	3080
DataLookup	SmallInt	3086
DataLookupMove	SmallInt	3099
DataNextRecord	SmallInt	3072
DataNextSet	SmallInt	3074
DataPostRecord	SmallInt	3094
DataPrint	SmallInt	3103
DataPriorRecord	SmallInt	3073
DataPriorSet	SmallInt	3075
DataRecalc	SmallInt	3110
DataRefresh	SmallInt	3104
DataRefreshOutside	SmallInt	3112
DataSaveCrosstab	SmallInt	3107
DataSearch	SmallInt	3089
DataSearchNext	SmallInt	3090
DataSearchReplace	SmallInt	3091
DataShowDeleted	SmallInt	3095
DataTableView	SmallInt	3087
DataToggleDeleteRecord	SmallInt	3109
DataToggleDeleted	SmallInt	3097
DataToggleEdit	SmallInt	3088
DataToggleLockRecord	SmallInt	3083
DataUnDeleteRecord	SmallInt	3108
DataUnlockRecord	SmallInt	3081

ActionEditCommands	Type	Value
EditCommitField	SmallInt	2574
EditCopySelection	SmallInt	2570
EditCopyToFile	SmallInt	2579
EditCutSelection	SmallInt	2569
EditDeleteBeginLine	SmallInt	2564
EditDeleteEndLine	SmallInt	2565
EditDeleteLeft	SmallInt	2560
EditDeleteLeftWord	SmallInt	2562
EditDeleteLine	SmallInt	2567
EditDeleteRight	SmallInt	2561
EditDeleteRightWord	SmallInt	2563
EditDeleteSelection	SmallInt	2568
EditDeleteWord	SmallInt	2566
EditDropDownList	SmallInt	2585
EditEnterFieldView	SmallInt	2583
EditEnterMemoView	SmallInt	2588
EditEnterPersistFieldView	SmallInt	2591
EditExitFieldView	SmallInt	2584
EditExitMemoView	SmallInt	2589
EditExitPersistFieldView	SmallInt	2592
EditHelp	SmallInt	2581
EditInsertBlank	SmallInt	2571
EditInsertLine	SmallInt	2572
EditLaunchServer	SmallInt	2586
EditPaste	SmallInt	2573
EditPasteFromFile	SmallInt	2580
EditProperties	SmallInt	2577
EditReplace	SmallInt	2576
EditTextSearch	SmallInt	2593
EditToggleFieldView	SmallInt	2582
EditUndoField	SmallInt	2575

ActionFieldCommands	Type	Value
FieldBackward	SmallInt	2817
FieldDown	SmallInt	2824
FieldEnter	SmallInt	2820
FieldFirst	SmallInt	2821
FieldForward	SmallInt	2816
FieldGroupBackward	SmallInt	2819
FieldGroupForward	SmallInt	2818
FieldLast	SmallInt	2822
FieldLeft	SmallInt	2825
FieldNextPage	SmallInt	2827
FieldPriorPage	SmallInt	2828
FieldRight	SmallInt	2826
FieldRotate	SmallInt	2829
FieldUp	SmallInt	2823

ActionMoveCommands	Type	Value
MoveBegin	SmallInt	2058
MoveBeginLine	SmallInt	2054
MoveBottom	SmallInt	2057
MoveBottomLeft	SmallInt	2061
MoveBottomRight	SmallInt	2063
MoveDown	SmallInt	2051
MoveEnd	SmallInt	2059
MoveEndLine	SmallInt	2055
MoveLeft	SmallInt	2048
MoveLeftWord	SmallInt	2052
MoveRight	SmallInt	2049
MoveRightWord	SmallInt	2053
MoveScrollDown	SmallInt	2067
MoveScrollLeft	SmallInt	2064
MoveScrollPageDown	SmallInt	2075
MoveScrollPageLeft	SmallInt	2072
MoveScrollPageRight	SmallInt	2073
MoveScrollPageUp	SmallInt	2074
MoveScrollRight	SmallInt	2065
MoveScrollScreenDown	SmallInt	2071
MoveScrollScreenLeft	SmallInt	2068
MoveScrollScreenRight	SmallInt	2069
MoveScrollScreenUp	SmallInt	2070
MoveScrollUp	SmallInt	2066
MoveTop	SmallInt	2056
MoveTopLeft	SmallInt	2060
MoveTopRight	SmallInt	2062
MoveUp	SmallInt	2050

ActionSelectCommands	Type	Value
SelectBegin	SmallInt	2314
SelectBeginLine	SmallInt	2310
SelectBottom	SmallInt	2313
SelectBottomLeft	SmallInt	2317
SelectBottomRight	SmallInt	2319
SelectDown	SmallInt	2307
SelectEnd	SmallInt	2315
SelectEndLine	SmallInt	2311

Appendix H

Name	Type	Value
SelectLeft	SmallInt	2304
SelectLeftWord	SmallInt	2308
SelectRight	SmallInt	2305
SelectRightWord	SmallInt	2309
SelectScrollDown	SmallInt	2323
SelectScrollLeft	SmallInt	2320
SelectScrollPageDown	SmallInt	2331
SelectScrollPageLeft	SmallInt	2328
SelectScrollPageRight	SmallInt	2329
SelectScrollPageUp	SmallInt	2330
SelectScrollRight	SmallInt	2321
SelectScrollScreenDown	SmallInt	2327
SelectScrollScreenLeft	SmallInt	2324
SelectScrollScreenRight	SmallInt	2325
SelectScrollScreenUp	SmallInt	2326
SelectScrollUp	SmallInt	2322
SelectSelectall	SmallInt	2332
SelectTop	SmallInt	2312
SelectTopLeft	SmallInt	2316
SelectTopRight	SmallInt	2318
SelectUp	SmallInt	2306

ButtonStyles	Type	Value
BorlandButton	SmallInt	0
WindowsButton	SmallInt	1

ButtonTypes	Type	Value
CheckboxType	SmallInt	2
PushButtonType	SmallInt	0
RadioButtonType	SmallInt	1

Colors	Type	Value
Black	LongInt	0
Blue	LongInt	711680
Brown	LongInt	32896
DarkBlue	LongInt	388608
DarkCyan	LongInt	421376
DarkGray	LongInt	421504
DarkGreen	LongInt	32768
DarkMagenta	LongInt	388736
DarkRed	LongInt	128
Gray	LongInt	12632256
Green	LongInt	65280
LightBlue	LongInt	16776960
Magenta	LongInt	16711935
Red	LongInt	255
Translucent	LongInt	-16777216
Transparent	LongInt	-1
White	LongInt	16777215
Yellow	LongInt	65535

Constants and Properties

CompleteDisplay	Type	Value
DisplayAll	SmallInt	1
DisplayCurrent	SmallInt	0

ErrorReasons	Type	Value
ErrorCritical	SmallInt	1
ErrorWarning	SmallInt	2

Errors	Type	Value
peARYFixedSizeArray	SmallInt	-30589
peARYIndexOutOfBounds	SmallInt	-30588
peARYNoMemory	SmallInt	-30591
peARYRangeTooLarge	SmallInt	-30590
peARYTooLarge	SmallInt	-30592
peAccessError	SmallInt	-31721
peActiveIndex	SmallInt	10035
peAliasInUse	SmallInt	-30391
peAliasNotDefined	SmallInt	-30393
peAlias_X_Db	SmallInt	-30411
peAllFieldsReadOnly	SmallInt	-31184
peAlreadyLocked	SmallInt	10247
peArgumentNumber	SmallInt	-30400
peBOF	SmallInt	8705
peBad1Sep	SmallInt	-31980
peBad1TSep	SmallInt	-31970
peBad2Sep	SmallInt	-31979
peBad2TSep	SmallInt	-31969
peBad3Sep	SmallInt	-31978
peBad3TSep	SmallInt	-31968
peBad4Sep	SmallInt	-31977
peBad4TSep	SmallInt	-31967
peBad5Sep	SmallInt	-31976
peBad5TSep	SmallInt	-31966
peBad6TSep	SmallInt	-31965
peBadAMPM	SmallInt	-31971
peBadAlias	SmallInt	-31731
peBadArgument	SmallInt	-30397
peBadArrayResize	SmallInt	-30379
peBadBlobHeader	SmallInt	-31662
peBadDate	SmallInt	-31986
peBadDay	SmallInt	-31983
peBadField	SmallInt	-31699
peBadFileFormat	SmallInt	-31722
peBadHandle	SmallInt	-32482
peBadHour	SmallInt	-31974
peBadLogical	SmallInt	-31975
peBadMinutes	SmallInt	-31973
peBadMonth	SmallInt	-31984
peBadRecordTag	SmallInt	-32496
peBadSeconds	SmallInt	-31972
peBadTable	SmallInt	-31700
peBadTime	SmallInt	-31985
peBadTypeArray	SmallInt	-30390
peBadVersion	SmallInt	-31697

Appendix H

peBadWeekday	SmallInt	-31982
peBadXtabAction	SmallInt	-31664
peBadYear	SmallInt	-31981
peBad_FieldType	SmallInt	-30423
peBigXtab	SmallInt	-31728
peBlankField	SmallInt	-31220
peBlankTableName	SmallInt	-30418
peBlankValue	SmallInt	-30703
peBlobFileMissing	SmallInt	8714
peBlobModified	SmallInt	13058
peBlobNotOpened	SmallInt	10755
peBlobOpened	SmallInt	10754
peBlobReaderror	SmallInt	-31707
peBlobVersion	SmallInt	12037
peBracketMismatch	SmallInt	-31995
peBreak	SmallInt	-30672
peBufferSizeError	SmallInt	-32488
peBufferTooSmall	SmallInt	-31998
peCFunction	SmallInt	-30383
peCancel	SmallInt	-31705
peCannotArrive	SmallInt	-31646
peCannotClose	SmallInt	10034
peCannotCopy	SmallInt	-31724
peCannotCopyTo	SmallInt	-31172
peCannotCut	SmallInt	-31725
peCannotCutTo	SmallInt	-31173
peCannotDelete	SmallInt	-31174
peCannotDeleteLine	SmallInt	-31179
peCannotDepart	SmallInt	-31647
peCannotDitto	SmallInt	-31694
peCannotEdit	SmallInt	-31739
peCannotEditField	SmallInt	-31203
peCannotEditRefresh	SmallInt	-31675
peCannotExitField	SmallInt	-31227
peCannotExitRecord	SmallInt	-31226
peCannotInsert	SmallInt	-31730
peCannotInsertText	SmallInt	-31169
peCannotLoadDriver	SmallInt	15877
peCannotLock	SmallInt	-31740
peCannotLookupFill	SmallInt	-31209
peCannotLookupFillCorr	SmallInt	-31208
peCannotLookupMove	SmallInt	-31207
peCannotMakeQuery	SmallInt	-31666
peCannotOpenClip	SmallInt	-31716
peCannotOpenTable	SmallInt	-31206
peCannotOrderRange	SmallInt	-31167
peCannotPaste	SmallInt	-31723
peCannotPasteFrom	SmallInt	-31171
peCannotPasteLink	SmallInt	-31175
peCannotPerformAction	SmallInt	-31170
peCannotPutField	SmallInt	-31743
peCannotPutRecord	SmallInt	-31742
peCannotRotate	SmallInt	-31695
peCannotUndelete	SmallInt	-31669
peCantSearchField	SmallInt	-31192
peCantSetFilter	SmallInt	-30367
peCantShowDeleted	SmallInt	-30381
peCatalogCountError	SmallInt	-32484

peCatalogSizeError	SmallInt	-32483
peCfgCannotWrite	SmallInt	8453
peCfgMultiFile	SmallInt	8454
peClientsLimit	SmallInt	9486
peCompatERR	SmallInt	-30454
peConversion	SmallInt	-30701
peCorruptLockFile	SmallInt	8966
peCreateERR	SmallInt	-30455
peCreateWarningRange	SmallInt	-30364
peCursorLimit	SmallInt	9478
peDBLimit	SmallInt	9489
peDDEAllocate	SmallInt	-30557
peDDEExecute	SmallInt	-30553
peDDEInitiate	SmallInt	-30558
peDDENoLock	SmallInt	-30556
peDDENotOpened	SmallInt	-30559
peDDEPoke	SmallInt	-30555
peDDERequest	SmallInt	-30554
peDDETimeOut	SmallInt	-30552
peDDEUnassigned	SmallInt	-30560
peDataLoss	SmallInt	-31734
peDatabaseERR	SmallInt	-30461
peDeliveredDocument	SmallInt	-31665
peDetailRecordsExist	SmallInt	9734
peDiffSortOrder	SmallInt	13313
peDifferentTables	SmallInt	10020
peDirBusy	SmallInt	10244
peDirLocked	SmallInt	10246
peDirNoAccess	SmallInt	9219
peDirNotPrivate	SmallInt	11269
peDriverLimit	SmallInt	9491
peDriverNotLoaded	SmallInt	10762
peDriverUnknown	SmallInt	-30368
peEOF	SmallInt	8706
peEditObjRequired	SmallInt	-31686
peEmptyClipboard	SmallInt	-31668
peEmptyTable	SmallInt	-31223
peEndOfBlob	SmallInt	8711
peEnumERR	SmallInt	-30453
peFAILEDMETHOD	SmallInt	-30403
peFailedStdDB	SmallInt	-30429
peFamFileInvalid	SmallInt	8967
peFieldIsBlank	SmallInt	9740
peFieldLimit	SmallInt	9492
peFieldNotCurrent	SmallInt	-31204
peFieldNotInEdit	SmallInt	-31687
peFieldValueERR	SmallInt	-30378
peFileBusy	SmallInt	10243
peFileCorrupt	SmallInt	8962
peFileDeleteFail	SmallInt	9220
peFileExists	SmallInt	13057
peFileLocked	SmallInt	10245
peFileNoAccess	SmallInt	9221
peFileOpenError	SmallInt	-32490
peFileReadError	SmallInt	-32494
peFileWriteError	SmallInt	-32492
peFixedType	SmallInt	-30697
peFmlMemberNotFound	SmallInt	8713

Appendix H

peForeignKeyErr	SmallInt	9733
peFormClosed	SmallInt	-30541
peFormCompileError	SmallInt	-31685
peFormInvalidName	SmallInt	-30539
peFormInvalidOptions	SmallInt	-30540
peFormNotAttached	SmallInt	-30542
peFormOpenFailed	SmallInt	-30533
peFormReadError	SmallInt	-31720
peFormTableOpen	SmallInt	-31718
peFormTableReadonly	SmallInt	-31735
peFormWriteError	SmallInt	-31719
peFormatError	SmallInt	-32493
peGENERICERR	SmallInt	-30404
peGroupLocked	SmallInt	10250
peHasOpenCursors	SmallInt	10765
peHeaderCorrupt	SmallInt	8961
peIllFormedCalcField	SmallInt	-31706
peIllegalConversion	SmallInt	-30699
peIllegalIndexName	SmallInt	-30376
peIllegalOperator	SmallInt	-30717
peIllegalXtabSpec	SmallInt	-31689
peInUse	SmallInt	-31684
peInappropriateFieldType	SmallInt	-31214
peInappropriateSubType	SmallInt	-31213
peIncompatibleDataType	SmallInt	-30366
peIncompatibleDataTypes	SmallInt	-30428
peIncompleteExponent	SmallInt	-31990
peIncompletePictureMatch	SmallInt	-31667
peIncompleteSymbol	SmallInt	-31992
peIncompleteXtab	SmallInt	-31729
peIndexCorrupt	SmallInt	8965
peIndexERR	SmallInt	-30457
peIndexExists	SmallInt	10027
peIndexFailed	SmallInt	-30421
peIndexLimit	SmallInt	9487
peIndexNameRequired	SmallInt	10010
peIndexOpen	SmallInt	10028
peIndexOutOfdate	SmallInt	12034
peIndexStartFailed	SmallInt	-30419
peInfiniteInsert	SmallInt	-31663
peInterfaceVer	SmallInt	12033
peInternal	SmallInt	-30718
peInternalError	SmallInt	-32510
peInternalLimit	SmallInt	9482
peInvalidBlobHandle	SmallInt	10030
peInvalidBlobLen	SmallInt	10029
peInvalidBlobOffset	SmallInt	9998
peInvalidBookmark	SmallInt	10021
peInvalidCallbackBuflen	SmallInt	10017
peInvalidCfgParam	SmallInt	12550
peInvalidChar	SmallInt	-31994
peInvalidColumn	SmallInt	-31231
peInvalidDBSpec	SmallInt	12545
peInvalidDataBase	SmallInt	-30438
peInvalidDataTypeCompare	SmallInt	-30427
peInvalidDesc	SmallInt	10004
peInvalidDescNum	SmallInt	9999
peInvalidDir	SmallInt	10018

peInvalidFieldDesc	SmallInt	10001
peInvalidFieldName	SmallInt	10038
peInvalidFieldType	SmallInt	10000
peInvalidFileExt	SmallInt	10042
peInvalidFileName	SmallInt	9987
peInvalidFormat	SmallInt	-31999
peInvalidHandle	SmallInt	9990
peInvalidIndexDesc	SmallInt	10023
peInvalidIndexName	SmallInt	10022
peInvalidIndexStruct	SmallInt	10005
peInvalidKey	SmallInt	10026
peInvalidLinkExpr	SmallInt	10040
peInvalidMode	SmallInt	10033
peInvalidModifyRequest	SmallInt	9996
peInvalidOperationForTableType	SmallInt	-30365
peInvalidOptParam	SmallInt	11522
peInvalidOption	SmallInt	9989
peInvalidParam	SmallInt	9986
peInvalidPassword	SmallInt	10015
peInvalidPrefferedFile	SmallInt	-31224
peInvalidProperty	SmallInt	-31212
peInvalidQuery	SmallInt	-30439
peInvalidRecStruct	SmallInt	10003
peInvalidRecordNumber	SmallInt	-31673
peInvalidRestrTableOrder	SmallInt	10008
peInvalidRow	SmallInt	-31225
peInvalidSession	SmallInt	-30408
peInvalidSysData	SmallInt	12547
peInvalidTCursor	SmallInt	-30441
peInvalidTableName	SmallInt	10039
peInvalidTableVar	SmallInt	-30436
peInvalidTranslation	SmallInt	10019
peInvalidUserPassword	SmallInt	10036
peInvalidValChkStruct	SmallInt	10006
peKeyFieldTypeMismatch	SmallInt	9995
peKeyOrRecDeleted	SmallInt	8708
peKeyViol	SmallInt	9729
peLDNotFound	SmallInt	8715
peLOCATEFAILED	SmallInt	-30402
peListTooBig	SmallInt	-31671
peLocateERR	SmallInt	-30458
peLockInvalid	SmallInt	-30388
peLockTimeout	SmallInt	10249
peLocked	SmallInt	10241
peLookupTableErr	SmallInt	9736
peLostExclusiveAccess	SmallInt	10252
peLostTableLock	SmallInt	10251
peMasterExists	SmallInt	9741
peMasterTableOpen	SmallInt	9742
peMatchNotFound	SmallInt	-31714
peMathError	SmallInt	-30688
peMaxValErr	SmallInt	9731
peMemoCorrupt	SmallInt	8963
peMinValErr	SmallInt	9730
peMisMatchedOperands	SmallInt	-30698
peMultiLevelCascade	SmallInt	10037
peMultipleInit	SmallInt	10759
peMultiplePoints	SmallInt	-31993

Appendix H

peMultipleSigns	SmallInt	-31996
peNA	SmallInt	10756
peNameNotUnique	SmallInt	10009
peNameReserved	SmallInt	10041
peNan	SmallInt	-31989
peNeedRestructure	SmallInt	10032
peNetFileLocked	SmallInt	11268
peNetFileVersion	SmallInt	11267
peNetInitErr	SmallInt	11265
peNetMultiple	SmallInt	11270
peNetUnknown	SmallInt	11271
peNetUserLimit	SmallInt	11266
peNo1Sep	SmallInt	-31948
peNo1TSep	SmallInt	-31938
peNo2Sep	SmallInt	-31947
peNo2TSep	SmallInt	-31937
peNo3Sep	SmallInt	-31946
peNo3TSep	SmallInt	-31936
peNo4Sep	SmallInt	-31945
peNo4TSep	SmallInt	-31935
peNo5Sep	SmallInt	-31944
peNo5TSep	SmallInt	-31934
peNo6TSep	SmallInt	-31933
peNoAMPM	SmallInt	-31939
peNoArguments	SmallInt	-30401
peNoAssocIndex	SmallInt	10764
peNoCallback	SmallInt	10016
peNoConfigFile	SmallInt	8452
peNoCurrRec	SmallInt	8709
peNoDay	SmallInt	-31951
peNoDayOrMonthSpec	SmallInt	-31987
peNoDestRecord	SmallInt	-30424
peNoDetailRoom	SmallInt	-31727
peNoDiskSpace	SmallInt	9475
peNoFamilyRights	SmallInt	10499
peNoFieldRights	SmallInt	10497
peNoFieldRoom	SmallInt	-31726
peNoFile	SmallInt	-32487
peNoFileHandles	SmallInt	9474
peNoHour	SmallInt	-31942
peNoHourSpec	SmallInt	-31988
peNoKeyField	SmallInt	-31691
peNoLogical	SmallInt	-31943
peNoLookup	SmallInt	-31733
peNoLookupMove	SmallInt	-31182
peNoMemoView	SmallInt	-31732
peNoMemory	SmallInt	9473
peNoMinutes	SmallInt	-31941
peNoMonth	SmallInt	-31952
peNoNumber	SmallInt	-31991
peNoPage	SmallInt	-31702
peNoPictureMatch	SmallInt	-31738
peNoProperty	SmallInt	-31679
peNoRecordNos	SmallInt	-31191
peNoRecords	SmallInt	-31704
peNoSearchField	SmallInt	-31715
peNoSeconds	SmallInt	-31940
peNoSelect	SmallInt	-31701

peNoSelection	SmallInt	-31717
peNoSeqnums	SmallInt	-31703
peNoSession	SmallInt	-31708
peNoSoftDeletes	SmallInt	-31185
peNoSortField	SmallInt	-30417
peNoSrcRecord	SmallInt	-30425
peNoSuchFile	SmallInt	9988
peNoSuchIndex	SmallInt	9997
peNoSuchTable	SmallInt	10024
peNoTableName	SmallInt	-30430
peNoTableRights	SmallInt	10498
peNoTempFile	SmallInt	-31711
peNoTempTableSpace	SmallInt	9476
peNoWeekday	SmallInt	-31950
peNoWorkPrivAlias	SmallInt	-30387
peNoYear	SmallInt	-31949
peNotABlob	SmallInt	10753
peNotAValidField	SmallInt	-30380
peNotAllowedFieldType	SmallInt	-30389
peNotCoEdit	SmallInt	-30444
peNotEnoughtRights	SmallInt	-30394
peNotField	SmallInt	-30446
peNotFieldNum	SmallInt	-30445
peNotImplemented	SmallInt	12290
peNotInEditMode	SmallInt	-31736
peNotInRunMode	SmallInt	-31659
peNotIndexed	SmallInt	10757
peNotInitialized	SmallInt	10758
peNotLocked	SmallInt	10248
peNotNumericField	SmallInt	-30448
peNotOleField	SmallInt	-31696
peNotOnThatNet	SmallInt	12549
peNotOpenIndex	SmallInt	-30396
peNotSameSession	SmallInt	10760
peNotSupported	SmallInt	12289
peNotValidSearchField	SmallInt	-30375
peNullFieldName	SmallInt	-31709
peOSAccessDenied	SmallInt	11013
peOSArgListTooLong	SmallInt	11028
peOSBadFileNo	SmallInt	11014
peOSCrossDevLink	SmallInt	11030
peOSExecFmt	SmallInt	11029
peOSFileExist	SmallInt	11043
peOSInvalidAccCode	SmallInt	11020
peOSInvalidArg	SmallInt	11027
peOSInvalidData	SmallInt	11021
peOSInvalidEnviron	SmallInt	11018
peOSInvalidFormat	SmallInt	11019
peOSInvalidFunc	SmallInt	11009
peOSInvalidMemAddr	SmallInt	11017
peOSLockViol	SmallInt	11059
peOSMathArg	SmallInt	11041
peOSMemBlocksDestroyed	SmallInt	11015
peOSNetErr	SmallInt	11109
peOSNoDevice	SmallInt	11023
peOSNoFATEntry	SmallInt	11010
peOSNoMemory	SmallInt	11016
peOSNoMoreFiles	SmallInt	11026

Appendix H

peOSNoPath	SmallInt	11011
peOSNotSameDev	SmallInt	11025
peOSOutOfRange	SmallInt	11042
peOSRemoveCurDir	SmallInt	11024
peOSShareViol	SmallInt	11058
peOSTooManyOpenFiles	SmallInt	11012
peOSUnknown	SmallInt	11047
peObjImplicitlyDropped	SmallInt	12801
peObjImplicitlyModified	SmallInt	12803
peObjMayBeTruncated	SmallInt	12802
peObjectNotFound	SmallInt	-30646
peObjectTreeTooBig	SmallInt	-31670
peOk	SmallInt	0
peOldVersion	SmallInt	12035
peOleActivateFailed	SmallInt	-32485
peOpenBlobLimit	SmallInt	9494
peOpenTableLimit	SmallInt	9483
peOperatorNotAllowed	SmallInt	-30700
peOutOfHandles	SmallInt	-32491
peOutOfMemory	SmallInt	-32511
peOutOfRange	SmallInt	9985
peOverFlow	SmallInt	-30702
pePart1Sep	SmallInt	-31916
pePart1TSep	SmallInt	-31906
pePart2Sep	SmallInt	-31915
pePart2TSep	SmallInt	-31905
pePart3Sep	SmallInt	-31914
pePart3TSep	SmallInt	-31904
pePart4Sep	SmallInt	-31913
pePart4TSep	SmallInt	-31903
pePart5Sep	SmallInt	-31912
pePart5TSep	SmallInt	-31902
pePart6TSep	SmallInt	-31901
pePartAMPM	SmallInt	-31907
pePartDay	SmallInt	-31919
pePartHour	SmallInt	-31910
pePartLogical	SmallInt	-31911
pePartMinutes	SmallInt	-31909
pePartMonth	SmallInt	-31920
pePartSeconds	SmallInt	-31908
pePartWeekday	SmallInt	-31918
pePartYear	SmallInt	-31917
pePasswordLimit	SmallInt	9490
pePasteNeedPage	SmallInt	-31692
pePastePage	SmallInt	-31693
pePathNonExistant	SmallInt	-30392
pePdx10Table	SmallInt	13061
pePdxDriverNotActive	SmallInt	10761
pePictureErr	SmallInt	-31200
pePrecisionExceeded	SmallInt	-31997
pePrimaryKeyRedefine	SmallInt	9993
pePropertyAccess	SmallInt	-31677
pePropertyBadValue	SmallInt	-31678
pePropertyGet	SmallInt	-30652
pePropertyNotFound	SmallInt	-30650
pePropertySet	SmallInt	-30653
peQBEbadFileName	SmallInt	-30416
peQryAmbOutPr	SmallInt	11780

peQryAmbSymAs	SmallInt	11781
peQryAmbigJoAsy	SmallInt	11777
peQryAmbigJoSym	SmallInt	11778
peQryAmbigOutEx	SmallInt	11779
peQryAseToPer	SmallInt	11782
peQryAveNumDa	SmallInt	11783
peQryBadExpr1	SmallInt	11784
peQryBadFieldOr	SmallInt	11785
peQryBadFormat	SmallInt	11885
peQryBadVName	SmallInt	11786
peQryBitmapErr	SmallInt	11787
peQryBlobErr	SmallInt	11896
peQryBlobTerm	SmallInt	11895
peQryBuffTooSmall	SmallInt	11888
peQryCalcBadR	SmallInt	11788
peQryCalcType	SmallInt	11789
peQryCancExcept	SmallInt	11880
peQryChNamBig	SmallInt	11797
peQryChgTo1ti	SmallInt	11790
peQryChgToChg	SmallInt	11791
peQryChgToExp	SmallInt	11792
peQryChgToIns	SmallInt	11793
peQryChgToNew	SmallInt	11794
peQryChgToVal	SmallInt	11795
peQryChkmrkFi	SmallInt	11796
peQryChunkErr	SmallInt	11798
peQryColum255	SmallInt	11799
peQryConAftAs	SmallInt	11800
peQryDBExcept	SmallInt	11881
peQryDel1time	SmallInt	11801
peQryDelAmbig	SmallInt	11802
peQryDelFrDel	SmallInt	11803
peQryEgFieldTyp	SmallInt	11804
peQryEmpty	SmallInt	11886
peQryExaminOr	SmallInt	11805
peQryExprTyps	SmallInt	11806
peQryExtraCom	SmallInt	11807
peQryExtraOro	SmallInt	11808
peQryExtraQro	SmallInt	11809
peQryFatalExcept	SmallInt	11883
peQryFind1Att	SmallInt	11810
peQryFindAnsT	SmallInt	11811
peQryGrpNoSet	SmallInt	11812
peQryGrpStRow	SmallInt	11813
peQryIdfPerli	SmallInt	11815
peQryIdfinlco	SmallInt	11814
peQryInAnExpr	SmallInt	11816
peQryIns1Time	SmallInt	11817
peQryInsAmbig	SmallInt	11818
peQryInsDelCh	SmallInt	11819
peQryInsExprR	SmallInt	11820
peQryInsToIns	SmallInt	11821
peQryIsArray	SmallInt	11822
peQryLabelErr	SmallInt	11823
peQryLinkCalc	SmallInt	11824
peQryLngvName	SmallInt	11825
peQryLongExpr	SmallInt	11878
peQryLongQury	SmallInt	11826

peQryMemExcept	SmallInt	11882
peQryMemVProc	SmallInt	11827
peQryMisSrtQu	SmallInt	11830
peQryMisngCom	SmallInt	11828
peQryMisngRpa	SmallInt	11829
peQryNIY	SmallInt	11884
peQryNamTwice	SmallInt	11831
peQryNoAnswer	SmallInt	11856
peQryNoChkmar	SmallInt	11832
peQryNoDefOcc	SmallInt	11833
peQryNoGroups	SmallInt	11834
peQryNoPatter	SmallInt	11836
peQryNoQryToPrep	SmallInt	11887
peQryNoSuchDa	SmallInt	11837
peQryNoValue	SmallInt	11838
peQryNonsense	SmallInt	11835
peQryNotHandle	SmallInt	11890
peQryNotParse	SmallInt	11889
peQryNotPrep	SmallInt	11857
peQryOnlyCons	SmallInt	11839
peQryOnlySetR	SmallInt	11840
peQryOutSens1	SmallInt	11841
peQryOutTwic1	SmallInt	11842
peQryPaRowCnt	SmallInt	11843
peQryPersePar	SmallInt	11844
peQryProcPlsw	SmallInt	11845
peQryPwInsrts	SmallInt	11846
peQryPwModrts	SmallInt	11847
peQryQbeFieldFound	SmallInt	11848
peQryQbeNoFence	SmallInt	11849
peQryQbeNoFenceT	SmallInt	11850
peQryQbeNoHeaderT	SmallInt	11851
peQryQbeNoTab	SmallInt	11852
peQryQbeNumCols	SmallInt	11853
peQryQbeOpentab	SmallInt	11854
peQryQbeTwice	SmallInt	11855
peQryQuaInDel	SmallInt	11858
peQryQuaInIns	SmallInt	11859
peQryQxFieldCount	SmallInt	11892
peQryQxFieldSymNotFound	SmallInt	11893
peQryQxTableSymNotFound	SmallInt	11894
peQryRagInIns	SmallInt	11860
peQryRagInSet	SmallInt	11861
peQryRefresh	SmallInt	11879
peQryRegister	SmallInt	11877
peQryRestartQry	SmallInt	11897
peQryRowUsErr	SmallInt	11862
peQrySQLg_Alpho	SmallInt	11902
peQrySQLg_Avera	SmallInt	11915
peQrySQLg_BadPt	SmallInt	11917
peQrySQLg_Chini	SmallInt	11907
peQrySQLg_Cntln	SmallInt	11906
peQrySQLg_Count	SmallInt	11914
peQrySQLg_DateA	SmallInt	11916
peQrySQLg_Dateo	SmallInt	11903
peQrySQLg_FndSu	SmallInt	11920
peQrySQLg_IDcco	SmallInt	11922
peQrySQLg_IfDcs	SmallInt	11921

peQrySQLg_Liken	SmallInt	11901
peQrySQLg_MDist	SmallInt	11899
peQrySQLg_NoAri	SmallInt	11900
peQrySQLg_NoQuery	SmallInt	11925
peQrySQLg_OTJvr	SmallInt	11910
peQrySQLg_Onlyc	SmallInt	11905
peQrySQLg_Onlyi	SmallInt	11923
peQrySQLg_Patrn	SmallInt	11919
peQrySQLg_Quant	SmallInt	11912
peQrySQLg_RegSo	SmallInt	11913
peQrySQLg_RelPa	SmallInt	11918
peQrySQLg_Relop	SmallInt	11904
peQrySQLg_SQLDialect	SmallInt	11924
peQrySQLg_SlfIn	SmallInt	11909
peQrySQLg_StRow	SmallInt	11911
peQrySQLg_Union	SmallInt	11908
peQrySetExpec	SmallInt	11863
peQrySetVAmb1	SmallInt	11864
peQrySetVBad1	SmallInt	11865
peQrySetVDef1	SmallInt	11866
peQrySumNumbe	SmallInt	11867
peQrySyntErr	SmallInt	11891
peQryTableIsWP3	SmallInt	11868
peQryTokenNot	SmallInt	11869
peQryTwoOutr1	SmallInt	11870
peQryTypeMIsM	SmallInt	11871
peQryUnknownAnsType	SmallInt	11898
peQryUnrelQ1	SmallInt	11872
peQryUnusedSt	SmallInt	11873
peQryUseInsDe	SmallInt	11874
peQryUseOfChg	SmallInt	11875
peQryVarMustF	SmallInt	11876
peQueryERR	SmallInt	-30459
peREGExpressionTooLarge	SmallInt	-30622
peREGInvalidBracketRange	SmallInt	-30616
peREGNestedSQP	SmallInt	-30617
peREGOperandEmpty	SmallInt	-30618
peREGSPQFollowsNothing	SmallInt	-30613
peREGTooManyParens	SmallInt	-30621
peREGTrailingBackSlash	SmallInt	-30612
peREGUnmatchedBrackets	SmallInt	-30615
peREGUnmatchedParens	SmallInt	-30620
peReadAccessError	SmallInt	-32495
peReadErr	SmallInt	9217
peReadOnlyDB	SmallInt	10501
peReadOnlyDir	SmallInt	10500
peReadOnlyProperty	SmallInt	-31681
peRecAlreadyLocked	SmallInt	-30407
peRecDeleted	SmallInt	8708
peRecLockLimit	SmallInt	9485
peRecMoved	SmallInt	8707
peRecNotFound	SmallInt	8710
peRecTooBig	SmallInt	9477
peRecordAlreadyLocked	SmallInt	-31737
peRecordIsDeleted	SmallInt	-31165
peRecordIsNotDeleted	SmallInt	-31164
peRecordNotLocked	SmallInt	-30377
peReqOptParamMissing	SmallInt	11521

peReqSameTableTypes	SmallInt	-30386
peReq_WLock_TC	SmallInt	-30413
peReqdErr	SmallInt	9732
peRequiredField	SmallInt	-31741
peRequiresPDOXtable	SmallInt	-30399
peSerNumLimit	SmallInt	9481
peSessionERR	SmallInt	-30460
peSessionsLimit	SmallInt	9488
peShareNotLoaded	SmallInt	11273
peSharedFileAccess	SmallInt	11272
peSortERR	SmallInt	-30456
peSortFailed	SmallInt	-30422
peSortStartFailed	SmallInt	-30420
peSysCorrupt	SmallInt	8451
peSysFileIO	SmallInt	8450
peSysFileOpen	SmallInt	8449
peTCursorAttach	SmallInt	-30382
peTCursorERR	SmallInt	-30463
peTableClose	SmallInt	-30508
peTableCopy	SmallInt	-30510
peTableCreate	SmallInt	-30512
peTableCursorLimit	SmallInt	9484
peTableERR	SmallInt	-30462
peTableExists	SmallInt	13060
peTableFull	SmallInt	9479
peTableInUse	SmallInt	-31672
peTableMismatch	SmallInt	-31690
peTableOpen	SmallInt	10031
peTableProtected	SmallInt	-30395
peTableReadOnly	SmallInt	10763
peTableRename	SmallInt	-30511
peTableRights	SmallInt	-30509
peTableSQL	SmallInt	12291
peTableViewTableReadOnly	SmallInt	-31187
peTablelockLimit	SmallInt	9493
peTooFewSeries	SmallInt	-31674
peTooManyTables	SmallInt	-31710
peToolsRead	SmallInt	-31683
peToolsWrite	SmallInt	-31682
peUnassigned	SmallInt	-30704
peUnboundXtab	SmallInt	-31712
peUnknownDB	SmallInt	10014
peUnknownDBType	SmallInt	12546
peUnknownDataBase	SmallInt	-30433
peUnknownDriver	SmallInt	10013
peUnknownExtension	SmallInt	-31698
peUnknownFieldName	SmallInt	-31215
peUnknownFieldNum	SmallInt	-31216
peUnknownFile	SmallInt	9992
peUnknownIndex	SmallInt	-30384
peUnknownNetType	SmallInt	12548
peUnknownSQL	SmallInt	13059
peUnknownTableType	SmallInt	9991
peUnlockFailed	SmallInt	10242
peUpdateNOIndex	SmallInt	-30405
peUseCount	SmallInt	10025
peValFieldModified	SmallInt	12805
peValFileCorrupt	SmallInt	8968

Constants and Properties

peValFileInvalid	SmallInt	12036
peValidateData	SmallInt	12804
peWriteAccessError	SmallInt	-32489
peWriteErr	SmallInt	9218
peWriteOnlyProperty	SmallInt	-31680
peWrongDriverName	SmallInt	15873
peWrongDriverType	SmallInt	15876
peWrongDriverVer	SmallInt	15875
peWrongObjectVersion	SmallInt	-32486
peWrongSysVer	SmallInt	15874
peWrongTable	SmallInt	-31713
peXtabAnswerError	SmallInt	-31688
pecantOpenTable	SmallInt	-30435
EventErrorCodes	Type	Value
CanNotArrive	SmallInt	-31646
CanNotDepart	SmallInt	-31647
Can_Arrive	SmallInt	0
Can_Depart	SmallInt	0
ExecuteOptions	Type	Value
ExeHidden	SmallInt	0
ExeMinimized	SmallInt	6
ExeShowMaximized	SmallInt	3
ExeShowMinimized	SmallInt	2
ExeShowMinimizedNoActivate	SmallInt	7
ExeShowNoActivate	SmallInt	4
ExeShowNormal	SmallInt	1
FieldDisplayTypes	Type	Value
CheckBoxField	SmallInt	4
ComboField	SmallInt	1
EditField	SmallInt	0
LabeledField	SmallInt	5
ListField	SmallInt	2
RadioButtonField	SmallInt	3
FileBrowserFileTypes	Type	Value
fbASCII	LongInt	8192
fbAllTables	LongInt	512
fbBitmap	LongInt	8388608
fbDBase	LongInt	4096
fbExcel	LongInt	1048576
fbFiles	LongInt	1
fbForm	LongInt	8
fbGraphic	LongInt	128
fbIni	LongInt	2097152
fbLibrary	LongInt	4194304
fbLotus1	LongInt	524288
fbLotus2	LongInt	262144
fbMailmerge	LongInt	32
fbParadox	LongInt	2048

fbQuattro	LongInt	131072
fbQuattroPro	LongInt	65536
fbQuattroProWindows	LongInt	32768
fbQuery	LongInt	4
fbReport	LongInt	16
fbScript	LongInt	64
fbTable	LongInt	2
fbTableView	LongInt	1024
fbText	LongInt	256

FontAttributes	Type	Value
FontAttribBold	SmallInt	2
FontAttribItalic	SmallInt	4
FontAttribNormal	SmallInt	1
FontAttribStrikeOut	SmallInt	8
FontAttribUnderline	SmallInt	16

FrameStyles	Type	Value
DashDotDotFrame	SmallInt	4
DashDotFrame	SmallInt	3
DashedFrame	SmallInt	1
DottedFrame	SmallInt	2
DoubleFrame	SmallInt	6
Inside3DFrame	SmallInt	10
NoFrame	SmallInt	5
Outside3DFrame	SmallInt	11
ShadowFrame	SmallInt	9
SolidFrame	SmallInt	0
WideInsideDoubleFrame	SmallInt	8
WideOutsideDoubleFrame	SmallInt	7

General	Type	Value
No	Logical	False
Off	Logical	False
On	Logical	True
PI	Number	3.141593
Yes	Logical	True

GraphBindTypes	Type	Value
Graph1DSummary	SmallInt	2
Graph2DSummary	SmallInt	3
GraphTabular	SmallInt	1

GraphLabelFormats	Type	Value
GraphHideY	SmallInt	0
GraphPercent	SmallInt	2
GraphShowY	SmallInt	4

GraphLabelLocation	Type	Value
LabelAbove	SmallInt	2

Constants and Properties

LabelBelow	SmallInt	4
LabelBottom	SmallInt	7
LabelCenter	SmallInt	0
LabelLeft	SmallInt	1
LabelMiddle	SmallInt	6
LabelRight	SmallInt	3
LabelTop	SmallInt	5

GraphLegendPosition	Type	Value
LegendBottom	SmallInt	0
LegendRight	SmallInt	1

GraphMarkers	Type	Value
MarkerBoxedCross	SmallInt	11
MarkerBoxed_Plus	SmallInt	9
MarkerCross	SmallInt	10
MarkerFilledBox	SmallInt	0
MarkerFilledCircle	SmallInt	4
MarkerFilledDownTriangle	SmallInt	2
MarkerFilledTriangle	SmallInt	6
MarkerFilledTriangles	SmallInt	12
MarkerHollowBox	SmallInt	1
MarkerHollowCircle	SmallInt	5
MarkerHollowDownTriangle	SmallInt	3
MarkerHollowTriangle	SmallInt	7
MarkerHollowTriangles	SmallInt	13
MarkerHorizontalLine	SmallInt	14
MarkerPlus	SmallInt	8
MarkerVerticalLine	SmallInt	15

GraphTypeOverRide	Type	Value
GraphArea	SmallInt	3
GraphBar	SmallInt	1
GraphDefault	SmallInt	0
GraphLine	SmallInt	2

GraphTypes	Type	Value
Graph2DArea	SmallInt	3
Graph2DBar	SmallInt	1
Graph2DColumns	SmallInt	21
Graph2DLine	SmallInt	5
Graph2DPie	SmallInt	20
Graph2DRotatedBar	SmallInt	9
Graph2DStackedBar	SmallInt	6
Graph3DArea	SmallInt	14
Graph3DBar	SmallInt	11
Graph3DColumns	SmallInt	23
Graph3DPie	SmallInt	22
Graph3DRibbon	SmallInt	12
Graph3DRotatedBar	SmallInt	26
Graph3DStackedBar	SmallInt	24
Graph3DStep	SmallInt	13

Appendix H

Graph3DSurface	SmallInt	17
GraphXY	SmallInt	19

GraphicMagnification	Type	Value
Magnify100	SmallInt	100
Magnify200	SmallInt	200
Magnify25	SmallInt	25
Magnify400	SmallInt	400
Magnify50	SmallInt	50
MagnifyBestFit	SmallInt	-1

IdRanges	Type	Value
UserAction	SmallInt	0
UserActionMax	SmallInt	2047
UserError	SmallInt	0
UserErrorMax	SmallInt	2047
UserMenu	SmallInt	8000
UserMenuMax	SmallInt	10000

KeyBoardStates	Type	Value
Alt	SmallInt	128
Control	SmallInt	8
LeftButton	SmallInt	1
RightButton	SmallInt	2
Shift	SmallInt	4

Keyboard	Type	Value
VK_ADD	SmallInt	107
VK_BACK	SmallInt	8
VK_CANCEL	SmallInt	3
VK_CAPITAL	SmallInt	20
VK_CLEAR	SmallInt	12
VK_CONTROL	SmallInt	17
VK_DECIMAL	SmallInt	110
VK_DELETE	SmallInt	46
VK_DIVIDE	SmallInt	111
VK_DOWN	SmallInt	40
VK_END	SmallInt	35
VK_ESCAPE	SmallInt	27
VK_EXECUTE	SmallInt	43
VK_F1	SmallInt	112
VK_F10	SmallInt	121
VK_F11	SmallInt	122
VK_F12	SmallInt	123
VK_F13	SmallInt	124
VK_F14	SmallInt	125
VK_F15	SmallInt	126
VK_F16	SmallInt	127
VK_F2	SmallInt	113
VK_F3	SmallInt	114
VK_F4	SmallInt	115
VK_F5	SmallInt	116

Constants and Properties

VK_F6	SmallInt	117
VK_F7	SmallInt	118
VK_F8	SmallInt	119
VK_F9	SmallInt	120
VK_HELP	SmallInt	47
VK_HOME	SmallInt	36
VK_INSERT	SmallInt	45
VK_LBUTTON	SmallInt	1
VK_LEFT	SmallInt	37
VK_MBUTTON	SmallInt	4
VK_MENU	SmallInt	18
VK_MULTIPLY	SmallInt	106
VK_NEXT	SmallInt	34
VK_NUMLOCK	SmallInt	144
VK_NUMPAD0	SmallInt	96
VK_NUMPAD1	SmallInt	97
VK_NUMPAD2	SmallInt	98
VK_NUMPAD3	SmallInt	99
VK_NUMPAD4	SmallInt	100
VK_NUMPAD5	SmallInt	101
VK_NUMPAD6	SmallInt	102
VK_NUMPAD7	SmallInt	103
VK_NUMPAD8	SmallInt	104
VK_NUMPAD9	SmallInt	105
VK_PAUSE	SmallInt	19
VK_PRINT	SmallInt	42
VK_PRIOR	SmallInt	33
VK_RBUTTON	SmallInt	2
VK_RETURN	SmallInt	13
VK_RIGHT	SmallInt	39
VK_SELECT	SmallInt	41
VK_SEPARATOR	SmallInt	108
VK_SHIFT	SmallInt	16
VK_SNAPSHOT	SmallInt	44
VK_SPACE	SmallInt	32
VK_SUBTRACT	SmallInt	109
VK_TAB	SmallInt	9
VK_UP	SmallInt	38

LibraryScope	Type	Value
GlobalToDesktop	SmallInt	2
PrivateToForm	SmallInt	1

LineEnds	Type	Value
ArrowBothEnds	SmallInt	2
ArrowOneEnd	SmallInt	1
NoArrowEnd	SmallInt	0

LineStyles	Type	Value
DashDotDotLine	SmallInt	4
DashDotLine	SmallInt	3
DashedLine	SmallInt	1
DottedLine	SmallInt	2
NoLine	SmallInt	5

SolidLine	SmallInt	0
LineThickness	**Type**	**Value**
LWidth10Points	SmallInt	200
LWidth1Point	SmallInt	20
LWidth2Points	SmallInt	40
LWidth3Points	SmallInt	60
LWidth6Points	SmallInt	120
LWidthHairline	SmallInt	5
LWidthHalfPoint	SmallInt	10
LineTypes	**Type**	**Value**
CurvedLine	SmallInt	2
StraightLine	SmallInt	0
MenuChoiceAttributes	**Type**	**Value**
MenuChecked	SmallInt	1
MenuDisabled	SmallInt	64
MenuEnabled	SmallInt	128
MenuGrayed	SmallInt	32
MenuHilited	SmallInt	512
MenuNotChecked	SmallInt	2
MenuNotGrayed	SmallInt	16
MenuNotHilited	SmallInt	1024
MenuCommands	**Type**	**Value**
MenuCanClose	SmallInt	7102
MenuControlClose	SmallInt	-4000
MenuControlKeyMenu	SmallInt	-3840
MenuControlMaximize	SmallInt	-4048
MenuControlMinimize	SmallInt	-4064
MenuControlMouseMenu	SmallInt	-3952
MenuControlMove	SmallInt	-4080
MenuControlNextWindow	SmallInt	-4032
MenuControlPrevWindow	SmallInt	-4016
MenuControlRestore	SmallInt	-3808
MenuControlSize	SmallInt	-4096
MenuEditCopy	SmallInt	132
MenuEditCopyTo	SmallInt	140
MenuEditCut	SmallInt	131
MenuEditDelete	SmallInt	134
MenuEditPaste	SmallInt	133
MenuEditUndo	SmallInt	130
MenuFileAliases	SmallInt	124
MenuFileAutoRefresh	SmallInt	1501
MenuFileExit	SmallInt	108
MenuFileExport	SmallInt	1006
MenuFileImport	SmallInt	1005
MenuFileMultiBlankZero	SmallInt	15009
MenuFileMultiUserDrivers	SmallInt	15007
MenuFileMultiUserInfo	SmallInt	15006
MenuFileMultiUserLock	SmallInt	15004

MenuFileMultiUserLockInfo	SmallInt	15001
MenuFileMultiUserRetry	SmallInt	15005
MenuFileMultiUserUserName	SmallInt	15002
MenuFileMultiUserWho	SmallInt	15003
MenuFilePrint	SmallInt	7401
MenuFilePrinterSetup	SmallInt	120
MenuFilePrivateDir	SmallInt	112
MenuFileTableAdd	SmallInt	1104
MenuFileTableCopy	SmallInt	1102
MenuFileTableDelete	SmallInt	1105
MenuFileTableEmpty	SmallInt	1106
MenuFileTableInfoStructure	SmallInt	4001
MenuFileTablePasswords	SmallInt	1108
MenuFileTableRename	SmallInt	1103
MenuFileTableRestructure	SmallInt	1001
MenuFileTableSort	SmallInt	1101
MenuFileTableSubtract	SmallInt	1107
MenuFileWorkingDir	SmallInt	111
MenuFolderOpen	SmallInt	1305
MenuFormDesign	SmallInt	7520
MenuFormEditData	SmallInt	7409
MenuFormFieldView	SmallInt	7704
MenuFormNew	SmallInt	7871
MenuFormOpen	SmallInt	7851
MenuFormOrderRange	SmallInt	7446
MenuFormPageFirst	SmallInt	7451
MenuFormPageGoto	SmallInt	7455
MenuFormPageLast	SmallInt	7452
MenuFormPageNext	SmallInt	7453
MenuFormPagePrevious	SmallInt	7454
MenuFormShowDeleted	SmallInt	7447
MenuFormTableView	SmallInt	7426
MenuHelpAbout	SmallInt	176
MenuHelpContents	SmallInt	170
MenuHelpKeyboard	SmallInt	173
MenuHelpSpeedBar	SmallInt	172
MenuHelpSupport	SmallInt	175
MenuHelpUsingHelp	SmallInt	174
MenuInit	SmallInt	7462
MenuLibraryNew	SmallInt	7875
MenuLibraryOpen	SmallInt	7855
MenuPasteFrom	SmallInt	142
MenuPasteLink	SmallInt	136
MenuPropertiesCurrent	SmallInt	7212
MenuPropertiesDesigner	SmallInt	7329
MenuPropertiesDesktop	SmallInt	123
MenuPropertiesExpandedRuler	SmallInt	7319
MenuPropertiesFormRestoreDefaul	SmallInt	7327
MenuPropertiesFormSaveDefaults	SmallInt	7322
MenuPropertiesHorizontalRuler	SmallInt	7309
MenuPropertiesVerticalRuler	SmallInt	7310
MenuPropertiesZoom100	SmallInt	7303
MenuPropertiesZoom200	SmallInt	7304
MenuPropertiesZoom25	SmallInt	7301
MenuPropertiesZoom400	SmallInt	7305
MenuPropertiesZoom50	SmallInt	7302
MenuPropertiesZoomBestFit	SmallInt	7308
MenuPropertiesZoomFitHeight	SmallInt	7307

Appendix H

MenuPropertiesZoomFitWidth	SmallInt	7306
MenuQueryNew	SmallInt	1303
MenuQueryOpen	SmallInt	1304
MenuRecordCancel	SmallInt	7449
MenuRecordDelete	SmallInt	7432
MenuRecordFastBackward	SmallInt	7421
MenuRecordFastForward	SmallInt	7424
MenuRecordFirst	SmallInt	7420
MenuRecordInsert	SmallInt	7431
MenuRecordLast	SmallInt	7425
MenuRecordLocateNext	SmallInt	7444
MenuRecordLocateRecordNumber	SmallInt	7445
MenuRecordLocateSearchAndReplace	SmallInt	7434
MenuRecordLocateValue	SmallInt	7433
MenuRecordLock	SmallInt	7430
MenuRecordLookup	SmallInt	7460
MenuRecordMove	SmallInt	7461
MenuRecordNext	SmallInt	7423
MenuRecordPost	SmallInt	7448
MenuRecordPrevious	SmallInt	7422
MenuReportNew	SmallInt	7872
MenuReportOpen	SmallInt	7852
MenuSave	SmallInt	106
MenuSaveAs	SmallInt	107
MenuScriptNew	SmallInt	7874
MenuScriptOpen	SmallInt	7854
MenuSearchText	SmallInt	141
MenuSelectAll	SmallInt	138
MenuTableNew	SmallInt	3001
MenuTableOpen	SmallInt	3002
MenuWindowArrangeIcons	SmallInt	152
MenuWindowCascade	SmallInt	151
MenuWindowCloseAll	SmallInt	153
MenuWindowTile	SmallInt	150

MenuReasons	Type	Value
MenuControl	SmallInt	2
MenuDesktop	SmallInt	1
MenuNormal	SmallInt	0

MouseShapes	Type	Value
MouseArrow	LongInt	32512
MouseCross	LongInt	32515
MouseIBeam	LongInt	32513
MouseUpArrow	LongInt	32516
MouseWait	LongInt	32514

MoveReasons	Type	Value
PalMove	SmallInt	2
RefreshMove	SmallInt	5
ShutDownMove	SmallInt	4
StartupMove	SmallInt	3
UserMove	SmallInt	1

PatternStyles	Type	Value
BricksPattern	SmallInt	50
CrosshatchPattern	SmallInt	17
DiagonalCrosshatchPattern	SmallInt	21
DottedLinePattern	SmallInt	66
EmptyPattern	SmallInt	0
FuzzyStripesDownPattern	SmallInt	22
HeavyDotPattern	SmallInt	78
HorizontalLinesPattern	SmallInt	1
LatticePattern	SmallInt	54
LeftDiagonalLinesPattern	SmallInt	9
LightDotPattern	SmallInt	70
MaximumDotPattern	SmallInt	86
MediumDotPattern	SmallInt	74
RightDiagonalLinesPattern	SmallInt	13
ScalesPattern	SmallInt	34
StaggeredDashesPattern	SmallInt	58
ThickHorizontalLinesPattern	SmallInt	6
ThickStripesDownPattern	SmallInt	18
ThickStripesUpPattern	SmallInt	14
ThickVerticalLinesPattern	SmallInt	10
VerticalLinesPattern	SmallInt	5
VeryHeavyDotPattern	SmallInt	82
WeavePattern	SmallInt	46
ZigZagPattern	SmallInt	2

QueryRestartOptions	Type	Value
QueryDefault	SmallInt	0
QueryLock	SmallInt	2
QueryNoLock	SmallInt	1
QueryRestart	SmallInt	3

RasterOperations	Type	Value
MergePaint	LongInt	12255782
NotSourceCopy	LongInt	3342344
NotSourceErase	LongInt	1114278
SourceAnd	LongInt	8913094
SourceCopy	LongInt	13369376
SourceErase	LongInt	4457256
SourceInvert	LongInt	6684742
SourcePaint	LongInt	15597702

ReportOrientation	Type	Value
PrintDefaultOrientation	SmallInt	0
PrintLandscape	SmallInt	2
PrintPortrait	SmallInt	1

ReportPrintPanel	Type	Value
PintHorizontalPanel	SmallInt	3
PrintClipToWidth	SmallInt	0
PrintOverflowPages	SmallInt	1
PrintVerticalPanel	SmallInt	2

Appendix H

ReportPrintRestart	Type	Value
PrintFromCopy	SmallInt	1
PrintLock	SmallInt	0
PrintNoLock	SmallInt	2
PrintRestart	SmallInt	3
PrintReturn	SmallInt	4

StatusReasons	Type	Value
ModeWindow1	SmallInt	1
ModeWindow2	SmallInt	2
ModeWindow3	SmallInt	3
StatusWindow	SmallInt	0

TableFrameStyles	Type	Value
tf3D	SmallInt	3
tfDoubleLine	SmallInt	1
tfNoGrid	SmallInt	4
tfSingleLine	SmallInt	0
tfTripleLine	SmallInt	2

TextAlignment	Type	Value
TextAlignBottom	SmallInt	6
TextAlignCenter	SmallInt	1
TextAlignJustify	SmallInt	3
TextAlignLeft	SmallInt	0
TextAlignRight	SmallInt	2
TextAlignTop	SmallInt	4
TextAlignVCenter	SmallInt	5

TextDesignSizing	Type	Value
TextFixedSize	SmallInt	0
TextGrowOnly	SmallInt	2
TextSizeToFit	SmallInt	1

TextSpacing	Type	Value
TextDoubleSpacing	SmallInt	2
TextDoubleSpacing2	SmallInt	3
TextSingleSpacing	SmallInt	0
TextSingleSpacing2	SmallInt	1
TextTripleSpacing	SmallInt	4

UIObjectTypes	Type	Value
BoxTool	SmallInt	1
ButtonTool	SmallInt	7
ChartTool	SmallInt	11
EllipseTool	SmallInt	3
FieldTool	SmallInt	8

Constants and Properties

GraphicTool	SmallInt	5
LineTool	SmallInt	2
OleTool	SmallInt	6
RecordTool	SmallInt	10
TableFrameTool	SmallInt	9
TextTool	SmallInt	4
XtabTool	SmallInt	12

ValueReasons	Type	Value
EditValue	SmallInt	1
FieldValue	SmallInt	0
StartupValue	SmallInt	3

WindowStyles	Type	Value
WinDefaultCoordinate	SmallInt	-32768
WinStyleBorder	LongInt	8388608
WinStyleControlMenu	LongInt	524288
WinStyleDefault	LongInt	8192
WinStyleDialog	LongInt	-2147483648
WinStyleDialogFrame	LongInt	4194304
WinStyleHScroll	LongInt	1048576
WinStyleHidden	LongInt	16384
WinStyleMaximize	LongInt	16777216
WinStyleMaximizeButton	LongInt	65536
WinStyleMinimize	LongInt	536870912
WinStyleMinimizeButton	LongInt	131072
WinStyleModal	LongInt	2
WinStyleThickFrame	LongInt	262144
WinStyleTitleBar	LongInt	12582912
WinStyleVScroll	LongInt	2097152

Properties

Property	Type or Constant Group	ReadOnly?
Alignment	TextAlignmnent	
Arrived	Logical	RO
BlankRecord	Logical	RO
Border	Logical	
Breakable	Logical	
ButtonType	ButtonTypes	
Caption	Logical	
CenterLabel	Logical	RO

Appendix H

Property	Type or Constant Group	ReadOnly?
Class	String	
Color	Colors	
CompleteDisplay	Logical	
ContainerName	String	RO
CurrentRecordMarker.Color	Colors	
CurrentRecordMarker.LineStyle	LineStyles	
CurrentRecordMarker.Show	Logical	
CursorColumn	LongInt	
CursorLine	LongInt	
CursorPos	LongInt	
DataSource	String	
DateFormat	String	
Default	String	RO
DefineGroup	Logical	
Deleted	Logical	RO
Design.ContainObjects	Logical	
Design.PinHorizontal	Logical	
Design.PinVertical	Logical	
Design.SizeToFit	Logical	
DesignSizing	TextDesignSizing	
DesktopForm	Logical	
DialogForm	Logical	
DisplayType	FieldDisplayTypes	
Editing	Logical	RO
End	Point	
FieldName	String	
FieldNo	SmallInt	RO
FieldRights	String	RO
FieldSize	SmallInt	RO
FieldType	String	RO
FieldUnits2	SmallInt	RO
FieldValid	Logical	RO
FieldView	Logical	RO
First	String	RO

Property	Type or Constant Group	ReadOnly?
FitHeight	Logical	
FitWidth	Logical	
FlyAway	Logical	RO
Focus	Logical	RO
Font.Color	Colors	
Font.Size	SmallInt	
Font.Style	FontAttributes	
Font.Typeface	String	
Format.DateFormat		
Format.LogicalFormat		
Format.NumberFormat		
Format.TimeFormat		
Format.TimeStampFormat		
Frame.Color	Colors	
Frame.Style	FrameStyles	
Frame.Thickness	SmallInt	
FullName	String	RO
FullSize	Point	RO
Grid.Color	Colors	
Grid.GridStyle	TableFrameStyles	
Grid.RecordDivider	Logical	
GridLines.Color	Colors	
GridLines.ColumnLines	Logical	
GridLines.HeadingLines	Logical	
GridLines.LineStyle	LineStyles	
GridLines.RowLines	Logical	
GridLines.Spacing	TextSpacing	
Heading.Color	Colors	
Heading.Font.Color	Colors	
Heading.Font.Size	SmallInt	
Heading.Font.Style	FontAttributes	
Heading.Typeface	String	
Heading.Justification	TextAlignment	
Headings	String	

Appendix H

Property	Type or Constant Group	ReadOnly?
HorizontalScrollBar	Logical	
IndexField	Logical	RO
Inserting	Logical	RO
Justification	TextAlignment	
KeyField	Logical	RO
LabelText	String	
Line.Color	Colors	
Line.LineStyle	LineStyles	
Line.Thickness	SmallInt	
LineEnds	LineEnds	
LineSpacing	TextSpacing	
LineStyle	LineStyles	
LineType	LineTypes	
List.Count	SmallInt	
List.Selection	SmallInt	
Locked	Logical	RO
LookupTable	String	RO
LookupType	String	RO
Magnification	GraphicMagnification	
Manager	String	RO
MarkerPos	LongInt	
MaximizeButton	Logical	
Maximum	String	RO
MemoView	Logical	RO
MinimizeButton	Logical	
Minimum	String	RO
Modal	Logical	
MouseActivate	Logical	
NCols	SmallInt	
NRecords	LongInt	RO
NRows	SmallInt	
Name	String	
Next	String	RO
NoEcho	Logical	

Property	Type or Constant Group	ReadOnly?
OverStrike	Logical	
Owner	String	RO
Pattern.Color	Colors	
Pattern.Style	PatternStyles	
PersistView	Logical	RO
Picture	String	RO
PinHorizontal	Logical	
PinVertical	Logical	
Position	Point	
PrecedePageHeader	Logical	
Prev	String	RO
PrintOn1stPage	Logical	
RasterOperation	RasterOperations	
Readonly	Logical	
RecNo	LongInt	RO
Refresh	Logical	RO
Required	Logical	RO
RowNo	SmallInt	RO
Scroll	Point	
SelectedText	String	
SeqNo	LongInt	RO
Shrinkable	Logical	
Size	Point	
SizeToFit	Logical	
SortOrder	Logical	
StandardMenu	Logical	
Start	Point	
Style	ButtonStyle	
TabStop	Logical	
TableName	String	
Text	String	
ThickFrame	Logical	
Thickness	LineThickness	
Title	String	

Property	Type or Constant Group	ReadOnly?
TopLine	LongInt	
Touched	Logical	
Translucent	Logical	
Value	String	
VerticalScrollBar	Logical	
Visible	Logical	
WordWrap	Logical	

Graph Object Properties

Property	Type or Constant Group
BackWall.Color	Colors
BackWall.Pattern.Color	Colors
BackWall.Pattern.Style	PatternStyles
Background.Color	Colors
BackGround.Pattern.Color	Colors
BackGround.Pattern.Style	PatternStyles
BaseFloor.Color	Colors
BaseFloor.Pattern.Color	Colors
BaseFloor.Pattern.Style	PatternStyles
BindType	GraphBindTypes
CurrentSeries	SmallInt
CurrentSlice	SmallInt
GraphType	GraphTypes
Label.Font.Color	Colors
Label.Font.Size	SmallInt
Label.Font.Style	FontAttributes
Label.Font.Typeface	String
Label.LabelFormat	GraphLabelFormats
Label.LabelLocation	GraphLabelLocation
Label.NumberFormat	

Property	Type or Constant Group
LeftWall.Color	Colors
LeftWall.Pattern.Color	Colors
LeftWall.Pattern.Style	PatternStyles
LegendBox.Color	Colors
LegendBox.Font.Color	Colors
LegendBox.Font.Size	SmallInt
LegendBox.Font.Style	FontAttributes
LegendBox.Font.Typeface	String
LegendBox.LegendPos	GraphLegendPosition
LegendBox.Pattern.Color	Colors
LegendBox.Pattern.Style	PatternStyles
MaxGroups	SmallInt
MaxXValues	SmallInt
MinXValues	SmallInt
Options.Elevation	SmallInt
Options.Rotation	SmallInt
Options.ShowAxes	Logical
Options.ShowGrid	Logical
Options.ShowLabels	Logical
Options.ShowLegend	Logical
Options.ShowTitle	Logical
Series.Color	Colors
Series.Graph_Title.Font.Color	Colors
Series.Graph_Title.Font.Style	SmallInt
Series.Graph_Title.Font.Typeface	FontAttributes
Series.Graph_Title.Text	String
Series.Graph_Title.UseDefault	Logical
Series.Line.Color	Colors
Series.Line.LineStyle	LineStyles
Series.Line.LineThickness	LineThickness
Series.Marker	GraphMarkers
Series.Pattern.Color	Colors
Series.Pattern.Style	PatternStyles
Series.TypeOverride	GraphTypes

Property	Type or Constant Group
Slice.Color	Colors
Slice.Explode	Logical
Slice.Pattern.Color	Colors
Slice.Pattern.Style	PatternStyle
TitleBox.Color	Colors
TitleBox.Graph_Title.Font.Color	Colors
TitleBox.Graph_Title.Font.Size	SmallInt
TitleBox.Graph_Title.Font.Style	FontAttributes
TitleBox.Graph_Title.Font.Typeface	String
TitleBox.Graph_Title.Text	String
TitleBox.Graph_Title.UseDefault	Logical
TitleBox.Pattern.Color	Colors
TitleBox.Pattern.Style	PatternStyle
TitleBox.Subtitle.Font.Color	Colors
TitleBox.Subtitle.Font.Size	SmallInt
TitleBox.Subtitle.Font.Style	FontAttributes
TitleBox.Subtitle.Font.Typeface	String
TitleBox.Subtitle.Text	String
TitleBox.Subtitle.UseDefault	Logical
XAxis.Graph_Title.Font.Color	Colors
XAxis.Graph_Title.Font.Size	SmallInt
XAxis.Graph_Title.Font.Style	FontAttributes
XAxis.Graph_Title.Font.Typeface	String
XAxis.Graph_Title.Text	String
XAxis.Graph_Title.UseDefault	Logical
XAxis.Scale.AutoScale	Logical
XAxis.Scale.HighValue	Number
XAxis.Scale.Increment	Number
XAxis.Scale.Logarithmic	Logical
XAxis.Scale.LowValue	Number
XAxis.Ticks.Alternate	Logical
XAxis.Ticks.DateFormat	
XAxis.Ticks.Font.Color	Colors
XAxis.Ticks.Font.Size	SmallInt
XAxis.Ticks.Font.Style	FontAttributes

Property	Type or Constant Group
XAxis.Ticks.Font.TypeFace	String
XAxis.Ticks.NumberFormat	
YAxis.Graph_Title.Font.Color	Colors
YAxis.Graph_Title.Font.Size	SmallInt
YAxis.Graph_Title.Font.Style	FontAttributes
YAxis.Graph_Title.Font.Typeface	String
YAxis.Graph_Title.UseDefault	Logical
YAxis.Scale.AutoScale	Logical
YAxis.Scale.HighValue	Number
YAxis.Scale.Increment	Number
YAxis.Scale.Logarithmic	Logical
YAxis.Scale.LowValue	Number
YAxis.Ticks.Alternate	Logical
YAxis.Ticks.DateFormat	
YAxis.Ticks.Font.Color	Colors
YAxis.Ticks.Font.Size	SmallInt
YAxis.Ticks.Font.Style	FontAttributes
YAxis.Ticks.Font.TypeFace	String
YAxis.Ticks.NumberFormat	String
ZAxis.Graph_Title.Font.Color	Colors
ZAxis.Graph_Title.Font.Size	SmallInt
ZAxis.Graph_Title.Font.Style	FontAttributes
ZAxis.Graph_Title.Font.Typeface	String
ZAxis.Graph_Title.UseDefault	Logical
ZAxis.Scale.AutoScale	Logical
ZAxis.Scale.HighValue	Number
ZAxis.Scale.Increment	Number
ZAxis.Scale.Logarithmic	Logical
ZAxis.Scale.LowValue	Number
ZAxis.Ticks.Alternate	Logical
ZAxis.Ticks.Font.Color	Colors
ZAxis.Ticks.Font.Size	SmallInt
ZAxis.Ticks.Font.Style	FontAttributes
ZAxis.Ticks.Font.TypeFace	String

Glossary

4GL Fourth-generation language. An application-development environment in which each language construct performs many 3GL language constructs, allowing programmers to develop more complex applications with less code.

alias A name given as a shortcut to a directory and/or drive.

application window An MDI window containing the application menu. Also called an MDI child, the Paradox Desktop is an example of an application window.

argument Variables, constants, or literal values listed in the procedure or methods declaration. Using arguments allows unrelated procedures or methods to share information.

attribute Another word for a column.

bitmap An image stored as a pattern of dots, commonly used for Windows graphics.

check box A box that can be checked to set its value on or off. Depending on whether you use a Borland- or Windows-style button, the check box will either contain a check mark or an X when the button is selected.

Clipboard An area used by Windows as a temporary storage area. Items copied to the Clipboard can be pasted into the same application or into other Windows applications.

column A field of a table; for example, the customer table has a column which holds phone numbers.

compilation The process of turning source code entered by a programmer into instructions the computer can understand.

containership hierarchy The tree-like representation of every item on its form. Each object, starting with the top level object (the form), is considered the parent of all the objects it contains.

crosstab   A UIObject used to analyze data in one field based on values in another field or fields. The result is a spreadsheet-like display.

DDE   See *dynamic data exchange*.

DDE client   The application that receives data from the other (server) application.

DDE server   The application that sends the data to the other (client) application.

DLL   See *dynamic link library*.

desktop   The main application window in Paradox for Windows, containing the menu bar, SpeedBar, and status bar.

dialog box   A special type of window used to interact with the user. The dialog can either provide information to the user, or extract information from the user.

display manager   A UIObject used to display Paradox data and other objects. Paradox forms and reports are display managers.

document window   A document window is an MDI child window. Each table, query, form, and report opens into its own document window.

dynamic data exchange (DDE)   A way for Paradox to communicate information between Windows applications. DDE links can be active or passive (hot or cold). Windows applications need to be DDE-capable in order to set up a DDE link.

dynamic link library (DLL)   Code libraries that are linked at runtime.

encapsulation   Data-hiding. Keeping hidden from view details about an object, including either its data or methods or both.

entity integrity rule   The rule states that no primary key field can have a null value. All primary key fields must have some value.

event   Something that occurs in a programmed application that was not initiated by the programming logic but by some external cause, such as a mouse click or a database-error condition.

event-driven   An environment where programmers write methods and procedures which respond to events, rather than controlling all events in a linear fashion.

folder   Folders use icons to represent both Paradox objects (forms, reports, tables, scripts, and queries) and non-Paradox objects. These icons are used as a convenient way to access their object's properties.

form-based   An environment where application development occurs primarily on forms which contain objects.

formatted memo   An extended field type that allows text to be sized, colored, and aligned within the field.

grid   The lines used to separate rows and columns in table view. In form or report design, the grid is the background pattern of dots and lines used to help size and space objects in the document.

header   In table view, the header is the text that appears at the top of each column, describing the field. In a form or report, the header is the material that is printed at the beginning of the document.

inheritance   The capability of one class to share the data and methods of another class.

library   A special type of form which serves as a repository of ObjectPAL methods and procedures.

MDI   See *multiple document interface*.

MDI child   A window owned by its parent or application window. Child windows must reside within their parent window. They do not contain their own menu or SpeedBar; instead, they use these items from their parent window.

MDI parent   In contrast to an MDI child, parent windows contain their own menu and SpeedBar. They contain the open child windows for the current application. The Desktop is the MDI parent in Paradox for Windows.

MRO   See *multi-record object*.

maximize   To open a window to its largest size. For an MDI parent window, the maximum size is the size of the screen; for an MDI child, the maximum size is limited to the size of its parent window.

minimize   To display a window as an icon. An MDI parent window is minimized to an icon at the bottom of the Windows desktop. An MDI child window is minimized to an icon at the bottom of the Application window.

modal   An application environment in which only one process or task can be done at a time.

modeless   An application environment where multiple processes or tasks can be active simultaneously, allowing the user or developer to switch seamlessly between tasks.

multiple document interface (MDI)   A Microsoft specification for working with multiple windows in a Windows application.

multi-record object (MRO)   A UIObject used to display multiple records—either vertically, horizontally, or both.

noise name   The default name given to an object on a form or report. Noise names always begin with a pound sign (#), and are numbered sequentially as they are placed on the form.

non-modal   See *modeless*.

object   A discrete entity, such as a table, form or report. An object is an instance of a class. A programming construct composed of data and methods, or state and behavior.

object-based   An environment where application development is tied to objects that belong to some class without the concepts of inheritance and polymorphism. Paradox for Windows is object-based.

object inspector   The result of pressing the right mouse button to bring up the properties associated with the current object.

object linking and embedding (OLE)   OLE is used to transfer data between Windows applications.

object-oriented   An environment where application development is tied to objects, which belong to some class and whose classes allow for inheritance, polymorphism, encapsulation, and object identity.

object tree   The object tree is a graphical representation of the concept of the containership hierarchy.

ODAPI   See *open database application program interface*.

OLE   See *object linking and embedding*.

open database application program interface (ODAPI)   The database engine used by Paradox for Windows.

parameter   Another word for *argument*.

paste   Copy the current Clipboard contents into the active object.

paste link   Copy the current contents of the Clipboard to the active object, maintaining a link to the original document. Using Paste Link, the connection information, not the value, is stored to the source document.

pixel   The smallest unit of measurement for working with screen position.

polymorphism   The ability of related but different objects to respond appropriately to the same message.

private directory   The directory, or Alias, where your temporary files are stored. Each user in a multiuser environment needs a private directory.

procedure   Code which is not attached to any object, but exists independent of any object. A procedure may manipulate an object, but it does not need an object to exist.

property   Attributes or values which describe an object.

query by example (QBE)   A method of getting information out of a database using visual cues rather than linguistic or mathematical ones to convey the meaning of the question.

radio button   A user-interface control that can be set to either an on or an off value. When radio buttons are used together, they represent a list of mutually exclusive options.

relation   A specific type of mathematical set used in set theory. Informally used as another term for a table.

row   Another word for a record.

scoping   Refers to the various rules which determine the visibility of variables, constants, methods, and procedures.

secondary index   An index other than the primary index, used for viewing the data in a different order, linking tables, and speeding up operations such as queries.

session   A channel to the database engine. Each session utilizes one user count.

SpeedBar The icon bar displayed (by default) at the top of the Windows Desktop, providing shortcuts to common menu actions.

status bar The area at the bottom of the Paradox Desktop used to display status messages.

STRUCT.DB The table created when you perform an Info Structure. It contains information on the fields in the table, and any validity checks set.

surrogate key A programmer-defined primary key value which gives a record identity. Incrementing numbers assigned as key values under program control are surrogate keys.

table An informal term used to describe a relational database file. A table is composed of records with identical structures. Each record has fields or columns where information is stored.

TableFrame The UIObject used to display a table in a form or report.

table view The view of the table that you see when you select File/Open. The table independent of any display manager.

TCursor An invisible pointer to a table. TCursors are used to perform table operations behind the scenes.

tuple A tuple is the formal relational term which is often used to refer to a record.

twip 1/1440th of an inch. Twips are used to precision place objects.

type A type is an abstract categorization of variables or objects. All number variables belong to the number type. All date variables belong to the date type, and so on.

UIObject (user interface object) Any of the objects that can be placed on a form or report. Examples include, fields, boxes, ellipses, crosstabs, graphs, and lines.

validity checks A check or rule used to limit the data entered into a field. Validity checks include picture masks, minimum and maximum values, and default values.

variable A variable is an instance of a type which can be evaluated and manipulated by a programmer.

working directory The directory or Alias that contains the files that you are working with. Files in this directory can be accessed without any other directory or alias specification.

Index

Symbols

! (exclamation mark)
    as inclusion operator, 201, 210, 213
    in picture strings, 121
(number sign) in picture strings, 121
& (ampersand)
    as character, 344
    in menus, 541
    in picture strings, 121
( ) (parentheses) characters, 591-592
... ellipses in menus, 540
* (asterisk) in picture strings, 121
+ (plus sign) concatenation operator, 206
... (ellipses), 57
; (semicolon)
    in ObjectPAL code, 239
    in picture strings, 121
? (question mark) in picture strings, 121
~ (tilde) variables (in Ch.21), 430, 431
@ (at sign) in picture strings, 121
[ ] (brackets) in picture strings, 121
{ } (braces) in picture strings, 121
1-D summary graphs, 177
2-D summary graphs, 177-178
4GL (Fourth-generation language) environment, 727

A

abs( ) method, 229
accelerator keys, 353-355
accessing
    DLL functions, 462-463
    fields, 336
    methods, 249
    program editor, 75-78
    QBE, 199
    tables, 580
action events, 258-260
Action method dialog boxes, 370
action( ) method, 260-261, 277, 283-284, 294, 302-306, 398-399, 560-562, 582
    errors, 390-395
    ObjectPAL launching OLE server, 489
    video clips, 497
ActionClasses constants, 691
ActionDataCommands constants, 691-692
ActionEditCommands constants, 692
ActionEvent methods, 661
ActionEvent object type, 649
ActionFieldCommands constants, 693
ActionMoveCommands constants, 693
ActionSelectCommands constants, 693-694
Active object variable, 315
ad-hoc data sharing, 514
ad-hoc queries in applications, 426
addArray( ) method, 347
addBar( ) method, 344
addBreak( ) method, 344
addLast( ) method, 233
addPassword( ) procedure, 419
addPopUp( ) method, 344
addSeparator( ) method, 344
addStaticText( ) method, 348

addText( ) method, 351
addTLext( ) method, 344
adjusting table block size, 132
Advanced level Methods dialog box, 67
advanced methods options (ObjectPAL), 68
Advanced Pattern Match search, 573
advMatch( ) method, 232, 454-455, 510
Alias feature, 139
aliases, 71, 72, 562, 644-645, 727
aligning
    column totals in reports, 193
    objects, 160
    text, 170
All Records, 186
    see also bands
Alpha field types, 129
alphanumeric fields, 120
Alt+key combinations, 593
alternate keys, 28
amodal
    applications, 55
    menus, 361
anomalies, 37
ANSI character set, 595
Answer tables, 201-202, 480
AnyType
    methods, 661
    object type, 649-650
    procedures, 662
    variables, 238
Application menu, 414
Application methods, 662
Application object type, 650
application window, 61, 531-532, 538-539, 727
application-level
    menus, 354
    password protection, 418-419
applications
    ad-hoc queries, 426
    amodal applications, 55
    debugging, 401-403
    design, 51-55
        hot keys, 55
        platform behavior, 53-54

        window movement, 54-55
        Windows interface model compatibility, 54
    integrating
        queries, 426-447
        reports, 420-426
    MDI, 61-62
    passive observation, 401-403
    password protection, 418-419
    sharing data, 503
    starting, 414-416
    user-ready, 413
    video, 521-522
AppStudio (Microsoft), 475
arguments, 243, 727
Array methods, 662
Array object type, 650
arrays
    copying, 234
    dynamic, 233-234, 242
    multidimensional, 234
    passing, 381-382
    resizeable, 233
    return capacity, 242
    static, 232-233
arrive events, 291
arrive( ) method, 240, 289, 315-317
arriving on objects, *see* entering objects
arrow mouse pointer, 49
ASCII files
    as QBE files, 427
    exporting to memo fields, 595
    reading, 452-455
assigning
    field values, 310-311
    form properties, 373-376
    object properties, 104-105
assignment checks with TCursors, 332-333
associating forms/reports with tables, 135
asymmetrical outer joins, 210
atFirst( ) method, 333
atLast( ) method, 333
atomic fields, 24-25
attach( ) method, 317-318, 558
audio interleave (AVI), 525

AUTOEXEC.BAT file, 601
auxiliary passwords, 418-419
Auxiliary Passwords dialog box, 419
average group operator, 214
AVI (audio interleave), 525

B

B-tree index files, 574
Background Bitmaps, 66-67
backing up source code, 634
backslash codes, 232, 323
bands, 190-191
    properties, 188
    resizing, 187
    types, 186-187
base classes, 10
batch tools, 512
BCNF (Boyce-Codd normal form), 40
Beginner level Methods dialog box, 67
beginner methods option (ObjectPAL), 68
benefits of OLE objects, 489
binary
    methods, 663
    object type, 650
Binary large object field, *see* Blob fields
binding (ObjectPAL), 250
bitmap file formats, 524
bitAND( ) method, 230
bitIsSet( ) method, 230
bitmaps, 494-496, 727
bitOR( ) method, 230
bitXOR( ) method, 230
Blob field (Binary large object), 33, 129, 489, 513
blocks (memory), 131-132
BMP files, 524
bookmarks, 87-88
bordering dialog boxes, 374
borders (objects), 593
Borland Dialog boxes, 587
borrowing table structures, 128
Boyce-Codd normal form, *see* BCNF
Breakable property (bands), 188
breakApart( ) method, 232

breaking objects in forms, 190
Breakpoint dialog box, 80
breakpoints, 80
Breakpoints command (Debugger menu), 95-96
bubbling, 261-263
    events, 262, 267-269
    manipulating, 281-282
    menu events, 359
    passEvent keyword, 272-275
buffers
    frame buffer (video), 527
    table, 604
building
    popup menus, 343-350
    pull-down menus, 350-362
    queries, 142-144
    tables, 117-118, 128
    Window menu items, 358
built-in
    dialog boxes
        Paradox, 369-371
        Windows, 371-372
    events, 257-258
    methods, 90, 240, 282-293
        action( ), 283-284, 294, 302-306
        arguments, 269
        arrive( ), 289, 315-317
        canArrive( ), 289
        canDepart( ), 288-289
        changeValue( ), 290
        error( ), 284
        for events, 255-256
        keyChar( ), 285-288
        keyPhysical( ), 284-288
        libraries, 251
        menuAction( ), 284
        newValue( ), 290-291
        open( ), 282-283
        pushButton( ), 291
        removeFocus( ), 291-292
        setFocus( ), 291
        status message problems, 277-278
        timer( ), 292-293

735

button objects, 172-173, 305-306, 316
ButtonStyles constants, 694
ButtonTypes constants, 694
BWCC.DLL file, 609

C

C programming language, 623
C++ programming language, 624
calc query operator, 205
calculated fields, 162-163, 192, 309-310
calculations, 205-206
calling
   methods by reference, 241
   Windows message box, 371
cameras, *see* video
canArrive( ) method, 289
canDepart( ) method, 283, 288-289, 297, 309, 366, 582
canReadFromClipboard( ) method, 494
capacity of DDE servers, 473-474
capture cards, 522
capturing video in tables, 525
cardinality (tables), 23
cascade option (referential integrity), 31
Cascading Deletes, 146
cascading
   menus, 343
   windows, 47, 535-536
Cascading Update capability, 146, 208-210
case-sensitive indexes, 126, 569
casting procedures (data types), 237
ceil( ) method, 229
center tabs, 171
CGM (Computer Graphics Metafile) file format, 525
Change To queries, 148, 207-208
changeValue( ) method, 290
char( ) method, 286
character support (tables), 142
charAnsiCode( ) method, 286
Check Box fields, 166, 305
Check Box Values dialog box, 166
check boxes, 50, 727

child
   records, 146
   tables, 141
   windows, 61, 62, 533, 728-729
classes, 628-630
   base classes, 10
   TCursor, 558
   UIObject class, 10
classes (objects), 9
Client frame, *see* MDI frame
clients
   DDE, 469, 728
      Database Desktop, 516
      interactive capabilities, 471-472
      linking Table objects, 470
   OLE, 487
Clipboard, 588, 727
close( ) method, 251, 474, 476
close( ) procedure, 240
closing
   TCursors, 332-333
   windows, 537
code placement in events, 278-282
code statements (ObjectPAL), 238-239
codes
   inheriting, 623
   libraries, 416, 642-643
   prototyping, 641-642
   source, 633-637
Color command (Grid menu), 108
Color menu, 106
color properties, 106-108
Colors constants, 694
column calculations with TCursors, 336
column totals alignment, 193
columnar menu choices (popup menus), 344
columns, 727
combo boxes, 50
ComboField, 305
command lines, 416, 610-612
command parameter, 474
command string, 473

commands
    CREATE, 331
    Debugger menu
        Breakpoints, 95-96
        Enable Debug, 97-98
        inspect, 94-95
        List Breakpoints, 96
        Origin, 98
        Quit This Method, 98
        Run, 98
        Stack backtrace, 95
        Step Into, 98
        Step Over, 98
        Trace BuiltIns, 96-97
        Trace Execution, 96-97
        View Source, 98
    doDefault, 277
    Edit menu
        Copy, 476, 480, 482, 494, 500
        Copy Package, 498
        Paste, 494, 498, 500
        Paste Link, 469, 476, 480
        Paste Special, 476
        Select All, 482
    File menu
        Export, 504
        Import, 498, 504
    Grid menu
        Color, 108
        Grid Lines, 108
    Language menu, Deliver, 455
    menu command constants, 357
    ObjectPAL
        SetFilter, 572
        SwitchIndex, 572
    Properties menu, Show Grid, 180
    Query menu, Wait, 482
    Report menu, Restart Options, 421
    SCAN, 333
    Table menu
        Field View, 489
        Order/Range, 570
    Utilities menu, Info Structure, 195

comments in ObjectPAL code, 239
Common User Access, *see* CUA
comparing records, 214-218
compatibility procedures, 617-618
compiler (ObjectPAL), 250
compiling source code, 727
CompleteDisplay constants, 695
composite key, 567
compressing
    disks, 586
    files, 513, 524
concatenation, 206
condition evaluation (ObjectPAL), 226-227
Conduit, 508
CONFIG.SYS file, 601
configuration files, 602
CONFIRM.FSL form, 378
Constant dialog box, 91
constants
    ActionClasses, 691
    ActionDataCommands, 691-692
    ActionEditCommands, 692
    ActionFieldCommands, 693
    ActionMoveCommands, 693
    ActionSelectCommands, 693-694
    ButtonStyles, 694
    ButtonTypes, 694
    Colors, 694
    CompleteDisplay, 695
    declaring, 238
    EditLaunchServer, 497
    ErrorReasons, 695
    Errors, 695-707
    EventErrorCodes, 707
    ExecuteOptions, 707
    FieldDisplayTypes, 707
    FileBrowserFileTypes, 450-456, 707-708
    FontAttributes, 708
    FrameStyles, 708
    General, 708
    GlobalToDesktop constant, 253
    GraphBindTypes, 708
    GraphicMagnification, 710

GraphLabelFormats, 708
GraphLabelLocation, 708-709
GraphLegendPosition, 709
GraphMarkers, 709
GraphTypeOverRide, 709-710
GraphTypes, 709-710
IdRanges, 710
in pull-down menus, 351
Keyboard, 710-711
KeyBoardStates, 710
LibraryScope, 711
LineEnds, 711
LineStyles, 711-712
LineThickness, 712
LineTypes, 712
menu command constants, 357
MenuChoiceAttributes, 712
MenuCommands, 712-714
MenuReasons, 714
MouseShapes, 714
MoveReasons, 714
passing, 241
PatternStyles, 715
peKeyViol error constant, 393
PrivateToForm constant, 253
QueryRestartOptions, 715
RasterOperations, 715
ReportOrientation, 715
ReportPrintPanel, 424, 715
ReportPrintRestart, 422, 716
StatusReasons, 716
TableFrameStyles, 716
TextAlignment, 716
TextDesignSizing, 716
TextSpacing, 716
UIObjectTypes, 716-717
ValueReasons, 717
WindowStyles, 447-48, 717
Constants dialog box, 87
Contain Objects (UIObject property), 159
containership, 12, 158-159, 243-244, 267
    hierarchy, 245-246, 622, 631, 727
    method & procedure scope, 249-250
    variable scope, 247-249

contains( ) method, 348
control files (networks), 546-547
control structures (ObjectPAL), 223-227
    for, 223-224
    foreach, 223-225
    if, 225
    if-else, 223
    switch, 224-225
    try-onFail, 226
    while, 224, 226
converting
    data types (ObjectPAL), 237
    tables, 593
Copy command (Edit menu), 476, 480, 482, 494, 500
Copy Package command (Edit menu), 498
copyFromArray( ) method, 318, 335
copying arrays, 234
copyRecord( ) method, 335
copyToArray( ) method, 318, 335
CorelDRAW!, 500-501
count( ) method, 348
counter types, 588
CREATE command, 331
Create dialog box, 119-122, 128
Create Table dialog box, 568
critical errors, *see* type 1 errors
cross-hair mouse pointer, 49
crosstables, 586
crosstabs, 178-179, 728
cstat variable, 349
CUA (Common User Access), 61
currency
    data type, 229
    field types, 129
    methods, 663
    object type, 650
    procedures, 663
Custom Color dialog box, 107
custom
    dialog boxes, 372-376
    events, 260-261
    library methods, 280
    lookup form, 379-380

methods, 90, 249, 381
procedures, 240, 250
SpeedBars, 362-363

D

Data Dependent Properties dialog box, 109, 110
data input elements, 50-51
Data Junction, 508
Data Model dialog box, 138-144, 194, 200
data models, 138-144
    building queries, 142-144
    changing, 144
    creating queries, 199-201
    locking tables, 563
    ObjectPAL, 615
    tables, 586, 594
data normalization, 34-44
data properties, 109-113
data types, 227-229
    array type, 232-234
    converting, 237
    currency, 229
    date and time, 230-231
    numeric, 229-230
    object type, 236-237
    record type, 234-236
    string type, 231-232
        backslash codes, 232
        capacity, 231
        creating, 231
    values, 462
DataAction grouping, 259
database applications, 517-518
Database Desktop, 514, 516
Database methods, 663-664
Database object type, 651
Database procedures, 664
databases, 22
    fields, 25
    integrating with word processors, 476-479
    records, 23-25
    relational databases, 21, 29-32, 517
        data normalization, 34-44
        entity integrity rule, 29-30
        extensions, 33-34
        integrity, 26-29
        joining tables, 210-213
        operators, 33
        referential integrity, 145-150
        referential integrity rule, 30-32
        terminology, 21-34
        views, 33
    spreadsheets, 479-485
    tables, 23, 28-29
    tuples, 23
    see also tables
DataSource property, 307-308
date and time data types, 230-231
dates
    fields, 129, 169-170
    methods, 231, 664
    object type, 651
    procedures, 665
DateTime methods, 665
DateTime object type, 651
DateTime procedures, 665
day( ) method, 231
dBASE
    converting Paradox tables, 593
    field types, 118
    locking files, 565
    programming language, 624-625
    table properties, 119
DDE (dynamic data exchange), 469-474, 728
    capabilities, 475-485
    clients, 469-472, 516
    controlling Program Manager, 475-476
    conversations with Program Manager, 475
    links
        Answer tables, 480
        tables and word processors, 476-478
        Table objects, 470
        tests, 478

methods, 663
object type, 651
servers, 469-470
    capabilities, 473-474
    Database Desktop, 516
    limitations, 471
    Paths, 473

type variables, 473
Debug Trace BuiltIns dialog box, 409
debug( ) statement, 410
Debugger
    commands
        Breakpoints, 95-96
        Enable Debug, 97-98
        Inspect, 94-95
        List Breakpoints, 96
        Origin, 98
        Quit This Method, 98
        Run, 98
        Stack backtrace, 95
        Step Into, 98
        Step Over, 98
        Trace BuiltIns, 96-97
        Trace Execution, 96-97
        View Source, 98
    keyboard shortcuts, 99-100
    menu
        accessing, 94
        breakpoint options, 95-96
        keyboard equivalents, 410
        quitting, 98
        speedbar, 99
        stepping through source code, 98
        trace options, 96-97
debugging
    applications, 401-403
    limitations, 410-411
    menuAction( ) methods, 409-410
    object-based programming, 93-94
    quantum, 401
decimal tabs, 171
declaring
    constants (ObjectPAL), 238
    custom library methods, 280

external methods, 252
OLE variables, 492
TCursors, 329
default
    printers, 424
    tabs, 170
default validity checks, 120
Default Value field, 134
Define Crosstab dialog box, 179
Define Data Model dialog box, 142
Define Field dialog box, 192
Define Field Object dialog box, 162
Define Group dialog box, 191
Define Link dialog box, 141-142
Define List dialog box, 165, 463
Define Multi-Record Object dialog box, 174
Define OLE property, 492
Define Secondary Index dialog box, 125, 568-569
Define Table Object dialog box, 175-176
degree (tables), 24
Delete menu items, 356
Delete queries, 148, 208-210
deleteRecord( ) method, 318
DeleteWhenEmpty property (Table Frames), 189
deleting
    dependent Child records, 146
    fields, 128
    forms, 144
    records
        active referential integrity, 146-148
        in reports, 189
    SpeedBar, 541
    tables, 144
delimited text files
    converting to tables, 509-510
    exporting/importing, 505
Deliver command (Language menu), 455
delivering forms/reports, 183, 455-456
denying events, 275-277
Design Layout dialog box, 152-155, 174
design objects, 13
Designer Properties dialog box, 181

designing
    applications, 51-55
        hot keys, 55
        platform behavior, 53-54
        window movement, 54-55
        Windows interface model compatibility, 54
    error handling mechanisms, 397-399
    forms, 151-156
        layout options, 153-156
        Page Layout dialog box, 152-153
        Quick Forms, 151-152
        UIObjects, 156-167
    pull-down menus, 360-361
    reports, 185-190
        aligning column totals, 193
        bands, 186-188
        breaking objects, 190
        calculated fields, 192
        deleting records, 189
        displaying records, 189
        grouping, 190-191
        header placement, 189
        MROs, 188-190
        page breaks, 193
        Page Layout dialog box, 185-186
        Quick Report option (SpeedBar), 195
        query based, 194
        shrinking objects, 190-192
        summary calculations, 192
        Table Frames, 188-190
desktop, 61-63, 728
    menus
        File menu, 68
        menu selections, 68-73
        MultiUser menu, 71
        New menu, 69
        Password menu, 70
        Utilities menu, 69
    properties, 66-67
        changes, 14
        Background Bitmaps, 66-67
        SpeedBar, 67
        Title text box, 66

SpeedBar, 64-65
status bar, 65
system setting options, 71
Desktop Properties dialog box, 66
Detach Header property (Table Frames), 189
diagonal mouse pointer, 49
dialog boxes, 57, 62, 365-367, 540, 728
    Action method, 370
    Advanced level Methods, 67
    aliases, 72
    Auxiliary Passwords, 419
    Beginner level Methods, 67
    bordering, 374
    Borland, 587
    Breakpoint, 80
    built-in
        Paradox, 369-371
        Windows, 371-372
    Check Box Values, 166
    Constant, 91
    Constants, 85
    Constants dialog box, 87
    Create, 119, 122, 128
    Create Table, 568
    custom, 372-376
    Custom Color, 107
    Data Dependent Properties, 109, 110
    Data Model, 138-144, 194, 200
    Debug Trace Builtins, 409
    Define Crosstab, 179
    Define Data Model, 142
    Define Field, 192
    Define Field Object, 162
    Define Group, 191
    Define Link, 141-142
    Define List, 165, 463
    Define Multi-Record Object, 174
    Define Secondary Index, 125, 568-569
    Define Table Object, 175-176
    Design Layout, 152-155, 174
    Designer Properties, 181
    Desktop Properties, 66
    Error, 410

error-handling, 387-388
field definition, 309
File Browser, 447, 449
File Import, 504
File¦Open, 89
Fixed Length Export, 506
focus control, 375
Form Properties, 182
Form Window Properties, 373-377
Grid Settings, 180
International dialog box (Windows), 167
Language¦Types, 564
Link, 141
Local Settings Utility, 609-610
Locate Value, 573
Lookup Help, 370
Lookup Table Definition, 644
MessageBox routine, 371-372
Methods, 76, 89-92, 280
modal, 62, 376-378
modality, 372
mouse, 375
MsgStop, 367
nested Waits( ), 382
Network Refresh Rate, 556
New Query, 144
non-modal, 376-378
Object Name, 158
ODAPI Configuration Utility, 603
ODAPI Full Tree Editor, 605-608
Open Document, 135, 194
Order/Range, 570-572
Page Layout, 152-155, 185-186, 195
Password Security, 126-127
Picture Assist, 122
Picture Assistance, 121
Printer Setup, 425
Private Directory, 73
procedures, 370-371
Properties, 85
Query Select File, 143
Record Layout, 174-175, 188
Referential Integrity, 145
Report Options, 422
Restructure, 71, 122, 128
Restructure Warning, 123
returning values, 380
Save Picture, 122-123
scroll bars, 375
Search and Replace, 104-105
Select Date Format, 169
Select Fields, 155
Select File, 199
Select Number Format, 168–169
Serial Number Update Program, 609
Sort Answer, 202
Spreadsheet Import, 507
Structure Information, 132-133
Table Export, 504
Table Lookup, 124, 125
Table Properties, 201-202
Table Type, 117-118
Text Options, 505
title bars, 375
Trace Builtins, 96, 409
Types, 84-85
value handling with View( ) method, 367-369
View( ), 368
window style constants, 376-377
Working Directory, 73
YesNoCancel, 366
directories
 aliases, 71-72, 644-645
 private, 547-548, 559, 730
 removing files, 588-589
 working, 731
disableDefault keyword (event control), 275-276
disabling SpeedBar, 356
disk compression utilities, 586
dispatching events, 261-263
display manager, 728
displaying
 multiple records, 174-175
 popup menus, 343-344
 video, 525

DLLs (dynamic-link libraries), 459-460, 728
    accessing remote servers, 463-466
    forms, 591
    functions, 460-462
        accessing, 462-463
        calling, 463-466
        routine parameters, 461-462
        value data types, 462
    import/export, 512-513
    parameter types (ObjectPAL), 462
dmAddTable( ) method, 310
dmGet( ) method, 310
dmHasTable( ) method, 311
dmPut( ) method, 310-311
dmRemoveTable( ) method, 302, 310
document window, 61, 533-537, 728
    keyboard shortcuts, 537
    listing open windows, 537
    maximizing, 533-535
    minimizing, 533-534
documents
    mail merges, 195
    Windows Write, 498
    Word for Windows, 478-479
    word processing, 478-479
doDefault command, 277
doDefault keyword (event control), 272, 280
domains, 26-27
DOS access, 16
DOS PATH environment variable, 473
dot notation, 249
double Inclusive links, 213
dow( ) method, 231
doy( ) method, 231
drawings in OLE UIObjects, 500-501
drivers
    language, 603-604
    ODAPI, 600
Drop-Down Edit fields, 165
DRW (Designer/Draw) file format, 525
duplicate records, 24
duplicating objects, 160-161
dynamic arrays, 233-234, 242
dynamic data exchange, *see* DDE

DynArray methods, 665
DynArray object type, 652

E

Edit menu commands
    Copy, 476, 480, 482, 494, 500
    Copy Package, 498
    Paste, 494, 498, 500
    Paste Link, 469, 476, 480
    Paste Special, 476
    Select All, 482
Edit mode, 551
edit( ) method, 319, 492-493
EditAction grouping, 259
EditField, 305
editing
    lists, 586
    menus, 539-541
    resources, 593
editing keys, 77-78
Editing property, 309
EditLaunchServer constant, 497
Editor
    accessing, 75-78
    Edit menu, 82-83
    File menu, 82
    Help, 87-89
    Language menu, 83-85
    menu items, 82-87
    Property menu, 85-86
    SpeedBar, 78-81
    Window menu, 86-87
Editor Window, 77
editors (ObjectPAL), 614
embedding
    bitmaps in OLE fields, 494-496
    CorelDRAW! drawings, 500-501
    files into OLE objects, 498-499
    OLE objects, 487-488
    Windows Write documents, 498
empty( ) method, 319, 348
Enable Debug command (Debugger menu), 97-98

enableDefault keyword (event control), 275
encapsulation, 9, 253, 628-631, 728
endEdit( ) method, 319
enhancing popup menus, 348
entering objects, 289
entities
   integrity rules, 29-30, 728
   properties, 22
   relationships, 22, 43
   tables, 23
   tuples, 23
enumFieldNames( ) method, 320, 347
enumFieldStructure( ) method, 590
enumLocks( ) method, 320
enumObjectNames( ) method, 321
enumSource( ) method, 320
enumSource( ) procedure, 635-648
enumSourceToFile( ) method, 320
enumUIClasses( ) method, 321
enumUIObjectNames( ) method, 320
enumUIObjectProperties( ) method, 321
enumUIObjectProperties( ) procedure, 635
enumVerbs( ) method, 493-494
eot( ) method, 333
EPS (Encapsulated PostScript) file format, 525
EPS files, 524
Error dialog box, 410
error events, 17, 389
error( ) method, 284, 388-389, 399
error-handling dialog box, 387-388
Error: Identifier expected message, 460
errorClear( ) procedure, 395
errorCode( ) method, 269, 391, 395-396, 561, 589
errorCode( ) procedure, 395, 589
ErrorEvent methods, 665-666
ErrorEvent object type, 652
errorLog( ) procedure, 395
errorMessage( ) method, 396, 561
errorMessage( ) procedure, 278, 388, 395
errorPop( ) procedure, 395
ErrorReasons constants, 695

errors
   action( ) method, 390-395
   error stacks, 388, 396-397
   error( ) method, 388
   forcing, 389-391
   handling, 385, 394-395
      A mechanism, 386
      B mechanism, 386
      mechanism design, 397-399
      methods and procedures, 395
      recommendations, 389
      reliability factors, 385-386
   key violation, 392-393
   keyPhysical( ) method, 390-395
   onFail..endtry block, 388
   severity, 386
   trapping, 388-390, 397-399
   try..onFail..endtry control structure, 388
   types, 386
Errors constants, 695-707
errorShow( ) procedure, 395
errorTrapOnWarnings( ) method, 387, 389
errorTrapOnWarnings( ) procedure, 388, 395
Event methods, 666
event model, 265-278, 622
   bubbling, 261-263
   events, 254-257
      action, 258-260
      custom, 260-261
Event object type, 652
event-driven environments, 728
EventErrorCodes constants, 707
eventInfo packets, 256-258, 269-270
events, 17-18, 254-258, 618, 622, 728
   action events, 259-260
   arrive events, 291
   bubbling, 267-269, 281-282
   built-in
      events, 257-258
      methods, 255-256
   code placement, 278-282
   containership, 267
   creating, 293-294
   denying, 275-277

disableDefault keyword, 275, 276
dispatching, 261-263
doDefault keyword, 272
enableDefault keyword, 275
error events, 17, 389
eventInfo packets, 256-258, 269-270
external events, 256, 266
    bubbling, 262, 267-269, 272-275
    denying, 275-277
    forcing, 272
    passEvent keyword, 272-275
handling objects, 281
internal events, 255, 266
    bubbling, 262, 267
    denying, 275
    disableDefault keyword, 275, 276
    passing, 272
key events, 17
keyPhysical, 285-294
keywords, 271-275
menu events, 17, 358-360
methods, 277-278
mouse events, 17
occurrence, 266-267
order of events, 292
passEvent keyword, 272
push button, 291, 587
push button events, 277
selecting, 77
SpeedBar intercepts, 362
terminating, 271-275
timer events, 292-293, 588
touch record events, 304
trapping, 260, 270-271
Every set comparison operator, 216
Exactly set comparison operator, 216
example elements (queries)
    Change To queries, 207-208
    calculations, 205-206
    concatenating fields, 206
    insert queries, 206-207
    placing, 203
    search conditions, 203-205
Exclusive Links, 211, 213
exclusive table lock, 550, 552

execute parameter, 474
execute( ) method, 473
execute( ) procedure, 592
ExecuteOptions constants, 707
executeQBE( ) method, 429
executeQBEFile( ) procedure, 428
executeQBEString( ) method, 432
exiting objects, 288-289
explicit locks, 557
Export command (File menu), 504
EXPORT.DB table, 506
exporting
    delimited text files, 505
    fields, 595
    files, 503-508
    fixed-length text files, 506
    spreadsheets, 506-507
    tables, 504
extended fields, 170
extensions (relational databases), 33-34
external events, 256, 266
    bubbling, 262, 267-269, 272-275
    code placement, 278-279
    creating, 293
    denying, 275-277
    forcing, 272
    passEvent keyword, 272-275
    terminating, 271-275
external methods, 252

F

fail( ) method, 277, 398
fail( ) procedure, 389-390
fall-back, *see* bubbling
FAM file extension, 136
family objects, 587
FDL file extension, 135, 183
field definition dialog box, 309
field level function restriction, 417
Field tool, 489
Field UIObject, 489
Field View command (Table menu), 489
FieldAction grouping, 259
FieldDisplayTypes constants, 707

fields, 24, 595
  accessing with TCursors, 336
  action events, 258-260
  assigning values, 310-311
  atomic, 24-25
  BLOBs, 489, 513
  button objects, 305-306
  calculated fields, 162-163, 192, 309-310
  concatenating, 206
  containership hierarchy, 305
  controlling, 290-291
  date, 169-170
  deleting, 128
  display types, 165-167, 305
  Editing property, 309
  exporting, 595
  extended fields, 170
  foreign keys, 28-29
  format property, 167-170
  Graphics, 513
  list object programming, 306-309
  memo fields, 171, 728
    formatted, 170
    Runtime¦Complete Display property, 170
    size considerations, 130
    word-wrap property, 170
  navigating, 283-284
  number format, 167-168
  OLE, 489-490
  primary keys, 28
  programming, 304-311
  properties, 164, 587
  rearranging, 176
  reordering, 119
  repeating groups, 25
  sizes, 129-130
  sound files, 526
  special fields, 161-162
  summary calculations, 192
  summary fields, 163-164
  table lookups, 124-125
  Table structure, 133-134
  tables, 590
  types, 118-119
  unbound fields, 161
  undefined fields, 290
  unordered lists, 25
  validity checks, 120-124
  values
    changing, 290
    manipulation, 338
    retrieving, 311
fifth normal form, 42-43
File Browser dialog box, 447-448
File Import dialog box, 504
File Manager
  Paradox, 593
  Windows, 414
File menu, 68
  Export command, 504
  Import command, 498, 504
  program editor, 82
file servers, 549
File System object type methods/procedures, 451-452
File¦Open dialog box, 89
fileBrowser( ) procedure, 447-451
FileBrowserFileTypes constants, 450-456, 707-708
FileBrowserInfo record, 447
files
  ASCII, 427, 452-455
  AUTOEXEC.BAT, 601
  AVI (audio interleave), 525
  BWCC.DLL, 609
  compressing, 524
  CONFIG.SYS, 601
  dBASE, 565
  deleting, 588-589
  delimited text, 505, 509-510
  embedding into OLE objects, 498-499
  exporting, 503-508
  FAM extension, 136
  FDL extension, 183
  fixed-length text, 506
  form file extensions, 135
  FSL extension, 183
  graphics, 426, 523-525
  importing, 503-512, 589

index files, 135
MB files, 135
network control, 546-547
PARADOX.LCK, 548-549
PC Paintbrush, 524
PDOXUSRS.LCK, 548-549
PDOXUSRS.NET, 546-547, 600, 603
PDOXWIN.INI, 595
PDOXWIN.USR, 546-547, 600
printing reports to, 196
PROGMAN.EXE, 475
PX file extension, 135
QBE, 427-429
report file extensions, 135
resizing, 176
SMARDRV.EXE, 578
sound, 526
starting, 414
swap, 578-579
table associated, 134-136
temporary, 547-548
transfers, 523
TV files, 136
USER.EXE, 371
VAL files, 136
video, 523
WIN.INI, 602, 610
FileSystem methods, 666
FileSystem object type, 652
FileSystem procedures, 667
first normal form, 34-37
Fixed Length Export dialog box, 506
fixed-length text files, 506
Flags= section (WINI.INI file), 611-612
Flicker-Free Draw, 181
floor( ) method, 229
focus control (dialog boxes), 375
folders, 728
Font menu, 106
fonts
   properties, 106
   substitution, 153
FontAttributes constants, 708
for control structure (ObjectPAL), 223-224
forcing errors, 389-391

foreach control structure (ObjectPAL), 223-225
foreign keys, 28-29, 142, 210
Form action( ) method, 304
Form menu commands, Order/Range, 570
form open( ) method, 592
Form Properties dialog box, 182
Form variables, 236
Form Window Properties dialog box, 373-377
form-level
   event traps, 270-271
   menus, 354
form.open( ) method, 594
format property, 167-170
format( ) method, 232
formatted memo fields, 129-130, 170, 728
FormReturn( ) method, 378-379
forms, 12, 134-135
   accessing custom methods, 381
   almost modal, 378-379
   as UIObjects, 316-317
   Close icon input, 379
   CONFIRM.FSL, 378
   containership hierarchy, 622
   crosstabs, 586
   custom lookup form, 379, 380
   Data Model dialog box, 138-144
   data models, 144
   delivering, 183, 455-456, 588
   designer properties, 181
   designing
      layout options, 153-156
      Page Layout dialog box, 152-153
      Quick Forms, 151-152
      UIObjects, 156-167
   designing for multiple screen displays, 589
   dialog boxes, 587
   DLLs (Dynamic Link Libraries), 591
   event models, 622
   FDL file extension, 183
   field properties, 587
   file extensions, 135
   FSL file extension, 183

graphic images, 523
indexes, 589
library access, 253
lists, 586
main, 414-416
MAIN.FSL, 378
manipulating data mode, 310
maximizing, 592
menus, 316, 540
methods, 250, 667-668
Multi-Record layout, 155-156
multi-valued dependency, 42
multiple, 645-646
objects, 13, 652-653
   aligning, 160
   containership, 158-159
   duplicating, 160-161
   grouping, 159
   multiple object selection, 159
   noise names, 157-158
   overlaping, 159-160
   pinning, 160
   placement, 180-182
passing arrays, 381-382
procedures, 668-669
properties, 113, 182, 373-376
resizing prohibition, 374
running, 79
Scroll Bar properties, 182
search/replace, 635
Size To Fit property, 182
SpeedBars, 587, 590
table deletions
tabular layout, 156
transferring information between forms, 379-382
UIObjects, 156-167, 171
   aligning, 160
   button objects, 172-173
   calulated fields, 162-163
   containership, 158-159
   crosstabs, 178-179
   duplicating, 160-161
   field display types, 165-167
   field properties, 164
   graphics objects, 172
   graphs, 176-178
   grouping, 159
   MROs, 173-175
   multiple object selection, 159
   noise names, 157-158
   OLE Objects, 179-180
   overlapping, 159-160
   pinning, 160
   special fields, 161-162
   summary fields, 163-164
   Table Frames, 175-176
   text objects, 171-172
   unbound fields, 161
   word wrap, 165
unlinked tables, 586
utility, 636, 637
Forms Open( ) method, 465-466
fourth normal form, 41-42
frame buffer (video), 527
frames (tables), 175-176
FrameStyles constants, 708
freezing video, 522
FSL file extension, 135, 183
Full Tree Editor (ODAPI), 132
full-motion video, 521, 525
function point analysis (FPA), 638
functional dependency, 34
functions
   DDL, 460-461
      accessing, 462-463
      calling third-party libraries, 463-466
      value data types, 462
   restrictions, 417

G

General constants, 708
generating
   crosstabs, 179
   objects, 637
   source code, 637
   unique numeric keys, 338-339
getMenuChoiceAttribute( ) procedure, 355
getMenuChoiceAttributeById( ) procedure, 355

Index

getQueryRestartOptions( ) method, 564
getServerName( ) method, 493
getTarget( ) method, 269
getTitle( ) method, 539
GIF (Graphics Interchange Files), 524
global variables, 253
GlobalToDesktop
   constant, 253
   libraries, 416
graph
   objects, 311-314
   types, 177
GraphBindTypes constants, 708
Graphic field types, 129
Graphic methods, 669
Graphic object type, 172, 653
graphical user interface, *see* GUI
GraphicMagnification constants, 710
graphics, 513
   compression utilities, 513
   file formats, 416, 523-525, 589
      bit map, 524
      BMP files, 524
      CGM (Computer Graphics Metafile), 525
      DRW (Designer/Draw), 525
      EPS (Encapsulated PostScript), 524,525
      EPS files
      GIF (Graphics Interchange Files), 524
      HPGL (Hewlett-Packard Graphics Language), 525
      JPG (Joint Photographics Experts Group) files, 524
      PCX files, 524
      PIC (Lotus 1-2-3), 525
      TGA (Targa) files, 524
      TIF (Tagged Image Files), 524
      vector formats, 524
   tables, 523
   video images, 523
Graphics fields, 513
graphics format support, 66

GraphLabelFormats constants, 708
GraphLabelLocation constants, 708-709
GraphLegendPosition constants, 709
GraphMarkers constants, 709
graphs, 176-178
GraphTypes constants, 709-710
GraphTypes procedures, 710
grayed menu items, 356, 357
Grid menu commands
   Color, 108
   Grid Lines, 108
grid properties, 108-109
Grid Settings dialog box, 180
grids, 728
group bands, 190-191
grouping
   objects, 159
   reports, 190-191
groups
   ObjectPAL, 475
   Program Manager, 475, 533
grow( ) method, 233, 239
GUI (graphical user interface), 47

H

handling
   errors, 385, 394
      A mechanism, 386
      B mechanism, 386
      mechanism design, 397-399
      methods and procedures, 395
      recommendations, 389
      reliability factors, 385-386
   form-level events, 270-271
   keystrokes, 284-288, 353
   menu events, 359
   objects, 281
hardware requirements, 577-579
hasMenuChoiceAttribute( ) procedure, 355
header placement in reports, 189
headers, 729
heading properties (tables), 105-108

Help, 87-89
    bookmark, 87-88
    Lookup Help dialog box, 370
    opening second help file, 89
hideSpeedBar( ) procedure, 356, 541
horizontal mouse pointer, 49
horizontal Scroll Bar, 373, 490
hot keys, 55
hourglass mouse pointer, 49
HPGL (Hewlett-Packard Graphics Language) file form, 525

I

I-Beam mouse pointer, 49
icons, 475
    MDI, 537
    starting applications, 414
IDAPI (Integrated Database Application Programming Interface), 517-519
IdRanges constants, 710
if control structure (ObjectPAL), 225
if statement, 622
if-else control structure (ObjectPAL), 223
Import command (File menu), 498, 504
import/export DLL, 512-513
importing
    delimited text files, 505
    files
        formats, 503-507, 589
        third-party utilities, 507-508
        to tables, 510-512
    fixed-length text files, 506
    spreadsheets, 506-507
    tables, 504
inclusion operator (!), 201, 210, 213
Inclusive Links, 210-211, 213
index files, 135
indexes
    forms, 589
    names, 576
    options, 126
    primary
        comparison to secondary, 567-568
        created with ObjectPAL, 570

secondary, 125-126, 568-569, 730
    accessing tables, 580
    multi-field, 569-570
storing, 574-576
tables
    linking, 573
    querying, 573
    searching, 573
    sorting/viewing, 570-573
indicators
    self, 404
    target, 404
Info Structure command (Utilities menu), 195
inheritance, 10-11, 628-630, 729
inheriting code, 623
initRecord( ) method, 335
insert queries
    example elements, 206-207
    referential integrity, 148
insert..( ) method, 321
inserting
    Delete menu items, 356
    records, active referential integrity, 146-148
inspect command (Debugger menu), 94-95
inspectors (objects), 729
installing Paradox for Windows, 600-602
instances of Class, 629
integer bit-level methods, 230
integrating
    reports in applications, 420-426
    word processors and databases, 476-479
integrity of relational databases, 26-32
    alternate keys, 28
    domains, 26-27
    entity integrity rule, 29-30
    foreign keys, 28-29
    primary keys, 27-28
    referential integrity rule, 30-32
interacting with operating system, 447-455
interactive capabilities of DDE clients, 471-472
intercepting SpeedBar events, 362

internal events, 255, 266
    bubbling, 262, 267
    creating, 293
    denying, 275
    disableDefault keyword, 275-276
    occurrence, 266
    passing, 272
    terminating, 271-275
International dialog box (Windows), 167
Invariant Field ID (STRUCT table), 134
isAltKeyDown( ) method, 286
isAssigned( ) method, 429
isControlKeyDown( ) method, 286
isEdit( ) method, 309
isFirstTime( ) method, 269, 271
isFromUI( ) method, 286
isLeapYear( ) method, 231
isPreFilter( ) method, 269, 271
isShiftKeyDown( ) method, 286
isSpeedBarShowing( ) procedure, 356
isTargetSelf( ) method, 270-271
item parameter, 473-474
items (ObjectPAL), 475

J–K

joining tables, 210-213
JPG (Joint Photographics Experts Group) files, 524
key events, 17
Key field (STRUCT table), 133
key properties in Table frames, 299-300
key violation errors, 392, 393
keyboard
    editing keys, 77-78
    shortcut keys
        Copy command (Ctrl+Ins), 476, 480
        debugger, 99-100
        document windows, 537
        Task List (Ctrl+Esc), 478
        Windows, 55
Keyboard constants, 710-711
KeyBoardStates constants, 710
keyChar( ) method, 285-288
keycodes (Windows), 286-288

keyed tables, 28
KeyEvent methods, 669
KeyEvent object type, 653
keyPhysical event, 285-294
keyPhysical( ) method, 277, 284-288, 354-355, 398
    errors, 390-395
keys, surrogate, 731
keystroke handling, 284-288
keystrokes
    disappearing, 591
    handling, 353
    trapping, 354
keywords (events), 271-275

L

labeled fields, 165
LabeledField, 305
Language¦Types dialog box, 564
language drivers, 603-604
Language menu
    Deliver command, 455
    program editor, 83-85
        Constants dialog box, 85
        Keywords option, 84
        Properties dialog box, 85
        Types dialog box, 84-85
languages (programming)
    module tree, 245
    object tree, 246
    ObjectPAL, 11, 221-222
        binding, 250
        compiler, 250
        condition evaluation, 226-227
        constants, 238
        containership, 243-250
        control structures, 223-227
        data types, 227-229
        event model, 254-263
        formatting and commenting code, 238-239
        level, 67-68
        libraries, 251-253
        method notation, 222-223

methods, 239-240
Methods dialog box, 89-92
passing parameters, 240-243
procedures, 239-240
returning values, 241-242
variables in reports, 197
launching OLE servers, 489
left tabs, 171
libraries, 13, 642-643, 729
   coding tasks, 416
   creating, 280
   debugging limitations, 410
   global variables, 253
   GlobalToDesktop, 253, 416
   ObjectPAL, 251-253
      built-in methods, 251
      calling methods, 252
      creating, 251
      encapsulation, 253
      scope, 253
   opening, 416-417
   PrivateToForm, 253, 416
   QLIB methods, 433
   Query String variables, 434
   third-party calling with DLL functions, 463-466
Library methods, 670
Library object type, 653
Library open( ) method, 435
LibraryNames, 460
LibraryScope constants, 711
limitations of debugging, 410-411
LineEnds constants, 711
LineStyles constants, 711-712
LineThickness constants, 712
LineTypes constants, 712
Link dialog box, 141
linking
   Answer tables with DDE, 480
   objects, 730
   OLE objects, 487-488
   static, 459
   tables
      with indexes, 573
      with word processors, 476-478

links
   DDE, testing, 478
   relationships (TCursors), 331
   tables, defining, 141-142
list boxes, 50
List Breakpoints command (Debugger menu), 96
List fields, 166
list objects, 306-309
   programming
      Data Source property, 307-308
      List Selection property, 308-309
   properties, 307
List Selection property
   programming list objects, 308-309
   setting, 309
ListField, 305
lists
   background colors, 586
   building on the fly, 588
   document windows, 537
live links, 478
ln( ) method, 229
load( ) method, 425
Local Settings Utility dialog box, 609-610
Locate operations, 370
Locate Value dialog box, 573
locate( ) method, 322
locateNext( ) method, 322
locatePattern( ) method, 322-324
locatePrior( ) method, 324
locatePriorPattern( ) method, 324
lock( ) procedure
   Session type, 557-558
   Table variable, 558
   TCursor class, 558
locking
   files (dBASE), 565
   records
      with ObjectPAL, 560-562
      with Paradox for Windows, 553-554
   tables
      comparison of Paradox for DOS and Windows, 551-553
      data models, 563

nonexistent, 562-563
   with ObjectPAL, 557-560
   with Paradox for Windows, 546-551
lockRecord( ) method, 561
LOCKS.DB table, 559
lockStatus( ) method, 560
log( ) method, 229
Logical methods, 670
Logical object type, 653-654
Logical procedures, 670
logical variables (cstat variable), 349
LongInt methods, 670
LongInt object type, 654
LongInt procedures, 670
Lookup Help dialog box, 370
Lookup Table Definition dialog box, 644
lookups (tables), 124-125
Lossey file compression, 524
lower( ) method, 232

M

Magnification property (OLE UIObjects), 492
mail merges, 195
mailing labels, 195
main form
   application menu, 414
   creating, 414-416
   SpeedBar, 414
main script coding example, 414
MAIN.FSL form, 378
Maintained indexes, 126
manipulating field values with TCursors, 338
manipulating bubbling in events, 281-282
manipulating windows, 54-55
many view( ) method of debugging libraries, 410
master passwords, 126
   securing tables, 418
Max Value field (STRUCT table), 134
maximize( ) procedure, 414
maximizing
   forms, 592
   windows, 533-535, 729

MB files, 132, 135
McCabe cyclomatic complexity measure, 638
MDI (Multiple Document Interface), 61-62, 531, 729
   application window, 531-532
   child window, 729
   document window, 533-537
      keyboard shortcuts, 537
      listing open, 537
   frame, 532
   icons, 537
   menus
      editing, 539-541
      SpeedBar, 541
   parent windows, 729
   Program Manager groups, 533
   status bar contents, 541
   Window menu, 535-537
   windows
      cascading, 535-536
      closing all, 537
      maximized, 533
      tiling, 535
MDI Child, 533
measuring programs
   construction process, 639
   size, 637-639
Media Player software, 525
memo fields, 170-171
   exporting to ASCII files, 595
   formatted, 130, 170, 728
   Runtime¦Complete Display property, 170
   size considerations, 130
   types, 129
   word-wrap property, 170
Memo methods, 670
Memo object type, 654
Memo procedures, 671
memory
   block sizes, 131-134
   field type requirements, 129-130
   record sizes, 130-131
   requirements, 586
   video (still images), 523

753

menu access keys (Windows), 57
menu attributes
   popup menus, 348-350
   pull-down menus, 355-356
      determining, 355-356
      resetting, 360
Menu command (PAL), 616
menu events, 17
menu items (program editor), 82-87
Menu methods, 671
Menu object type, 654
Menu procedures, 671
menu selections, 68-73
menuAction( ) method, 284, 352, 358-360, 409-410
menuAction( ) procedure, 362, 425
MenuChoiceAttributes constants, 712
MenuCommands constants, 712-714
MenuEvent object type, 654
MenuEventmethods, 671
MenuReasons constants, 714
menus, 341
   & (ampersand), 541
   (...) ellipsis, 540
   across multiple forms, 361
   application-level menus, 354
   building Window menu items, 358
   cascading, 343
   command constants, 357
   Debugger menu
      accessing, 94
      breakpoint options, 95-96
      Enable Debug, 97-98
      Inspect, 94-95
      Origin, 98
      quitting, 98
      Run, 98
      SpeedBar, 99
      Stack Backtrace, 95
      stepping through source code, 98
      trace options, 96-97
      View Source, 98
   Delete menu items, inserting, 356
   dialog boxes, 540
   disabling SpeedBar, 356
   form-level menus, 354
   forms, 540
   grayed menu items, 356-357
   MDI (Multiple Document Interface)
      editing, 539-541
      SpeedBar, 541
   menu events, 359
   menu id, 351, 356-357
   object inspector, 104
   pinning, 106
   popup, 341-343
      addArray( ) method, 347
      attributes, 348-350
      building, 343-350
      columnar menu choices, 344
      displaying, 343-344
      enhancing, 348
      methods, 347-348
      separating menu items, 344
      structure, 344-346
      SwitchMenu construct, 346
      twips, 346
      vertical bars, 344
   pull-down, 341-343
      accelerator keys, 353-355
      attributes, 355-356, 360
      building, 350-362
      constants use, 351
      design issues, 360-361
      menu items, 351-353
   removing items, 361
   short-cut keys, 541
   SpeedBar
      custom, 362-363
      intercepting events, 362
   trapping menu events, 358-360
   types, 341
   unpinning, 106
   Window menu, 535-537
message method of debugging libraries, 410
message( ) procedure, 240, 277, 541
MessageBox routine parameters, 371-372

messages
    Error: Identifier expected, 460
    status bars, color, 594
method clutter, 250
method notation (ObjectPAL), 222-223
method..( ) method, 324
methods, 588, 617, 625
    accessing with dot notation, 249
    action( ), 260-261, 277, 390-395,
        398-399, 560-562, 582
        video clips, 497
    ActionEvent, 661
    addArray( ), 347
    addBar( ), 344
    addBreak( ), 344
    addPopUp( ), 344
    addSeparator( ), 344
    addStaticText( ), 348
    addText( ), 351
    addTLext( ), 344
    advMatch( ), 454-455, 510
    AnyType, 661
    Application, 662
    Array, 662
    arrive( ), 240
    atFirst( ), 333
    atLast( ), 333
    attach( ), 317-318, 558
    Binary, 663
    built-in, 90, 240, 282-293
        action( ), 283-284, 294, 302-306
        arguments, 269
        arrive( ), 289, 315-317
        canArrive( ), 289
        canDepart( ), 288-289
        changeValue( ), 290
        error( ), 284
        for events, 255-256
        keyChar( ), 285-288
        keyPhysical( ), 284-288
        libraries, 251
        menuAction( ), 284
        newValue( ), 290-291
        open( ), 282-283
        pushButton( ), 291
        removeFocus( ), 291-292
        setFocus( ), 291
        status message problems, 277-278
        timer( ), 292-293
    calling by reference, 241
    canDepart( ), 283, 297, 309, 336, 582
    canReadFromClipboard( ), 494
    char( ), 286
    charAnsiCode( ), 286
    close( ), 251, 474, 476
    compared to procedures, 239
    contains( ), 348
    copyFromArray( ), 318, 335
    copyRecord( ), 335
    copyToArray( ), 318, 335
    count( ), 348
    Currency, 663
    custom, 90, 249
        accessing in forms, 381
        library methods, 280
    Database, 663-664
    Date, 664
    date methods, 231
    DateTime, 665
    DDE, 663
    deleteRecord( ), 318
    dmAddTable( ), 310
    dmGet( ), 310
    dmHasTable( ), 311
    dmPut( ), 310-311
    dmRemoveTable( ), 302, 310
    DynArray, 665
    edit( ), 319, 492, 493
    empty( ), 319, 348
    endEdit( ), 319
    enumFieldNames( ), 320, 347
    enumFieldStructure( ), 590
    enumLocks( ), 320
    enumObjectNames( ), 321
    enumSource( ), 320
    enumSourceToFile( ), 320
    enumUIClasses( ), 321
    enumUIObjectNames( ), 320
    enumUIObjectProperties( ), 321
    enumVerbs( ), 493-494

eot( ), 333
error handling, 395
error( ), 388-389, 399
errorCode( ), 269, 391, 395-396, 561, 589
ErrorEvent, 665-666
errorMessage( ), 396, 561
errorTrapOnWarnings( ), 387-389
Event, 666
eventInfo, 269-270
execute( ), 473
executeQBE( ), 429
executeQBEString( ), 432
fail( ), 277, 398
File System object types, 451-452
FileSystem, 666
Form, 667-668
Form action( ), 304
Form deliver( ), 455
form open( ), 592, 594
FormReturn( ), 378-379
Forms Open( ), 465-466
getQueryRestartOptions( ), 564
getServerName( ), 493
getTarget( ), 269
getTitle( ), 539
Graphic, 669
grow( ), 239
initRecord( ), 335
insert..( ), 321
integer bit-level methods, 230
isAltKeyDown( ), 286
isAssigned( ), 429
isControlKeyDown( ), 286
isEdit( ), 309
isFirstTime( ), 269, 271
isFromUI( ), 286
isPreFilter( ), 269
isPreFilter( ) method, 271
isShiftKeyDown( ), 286
isTargetSelf( ), 270-271
KeyEvent, 669
keyPhysical( ), 277, 354-355, 390-395, 398
libraries, 251-253

built-in, 251
calling, 252
creating, 251
encapsulation, 253
scope, 253
Library, 670
Library open( ), 435
load( ), 425
locate( ), 322
locateNext( ), 322
locatePattern( ), 322-324
locatePrior( ), 324
locatePriorPattern( ), 324
lockRecord( ), 561
lockStatus( ), 560
Logical, 670
LongInt, 670
m( ), 246, 247
many view( ), 410
Memo, 670
Menu, 671
menuAction( ), 352, 358-360, 425
    debugging, 409-410
MenuEven, 671
message, 410
method..( ), 324
mouseClick( ), 379
MouseEvent, 672
mouseRightUp( ), 349-350
MoveEvent, 672
moveTo( ), 324
moveToRecNo( ), 325
moveToRecord( ), 325, 334
msgInfo( ), 410
nextRecord( ), 325
nRecords( ), 333
Number, 672-673
number methods, 229
ObjectPAL, 239-240
OLE, 492-494, 673
open( ), 12, 251, 376, 378, 414, 416, 420-421, 473
openAsDialog( ), 376, 378-379
passing parameters, 240-243
Point, 673-674

PopUpMenu, 674
postAction( ), 260-261
postRecord( ), 325, 561-562
print( ), 422-424
priorRecord( ), 325
pushButton( ), 277, 362, 398, 478, 497
qCheckAll( ), 435-436
qClearQBE( ), 440
qClearTable( ), 440
qExecuteQBE( ), 441
qGetQBEInfo( ), 439
qGetQBEString( ), 441
QLIB library, 433
qSetCheck( ), 436
qSetExample( ), 437
qSetFieldOrder( ), 436
qSetLine( ), 437
qSetQBEInfo( ), 439
qSetSort( ), 438
qSetStatement( ), 438
qSetTableName( ), 437
qSetTableType( ), 438
Query, 674
readFromClipboard, 494
reason( ), 270, 395
Record, 675
recordStatus( ), 325
Report, 675
resync( ), 589
retryPeriod( ), 564
returning values, 241-242
scope (ObjectPAL), 249-250
Session, 675-676
setAltKeyDown( ), 286
setChar( ), 286
setControlKeyDown( ), 286
setErrorCode( ), 270, 395
setExclusive( ), 563
setFilter( ), 326-327
setId( ), 260
setItem( ), 474
setQueryRestartOptions( ), 564
setReadOnly( ), 563
setReason( ), 395

setReasonCode, 270
setRetryPeriod( ), 564
SetShiftKeyDown( ), 286
setStatusValue( ), 553
setTitle( ), 538
SetVChar( ), 286
setVCharCode( ), 286
setX( ), 635
setY( ), 635
show( ), 344, 539
skip( ), 325, 333
SmallInt, 676-677
sortTo method( ), 337-338
status( ), 281, 370, 553
StatusEvent, 677
statusValue( ), 553
String, 677
string methods, 232
switchIndex( ), 326-327, 589
System execute( ), 512
Table, 683-684
TableView, 685
TCursor, 680-683, 731
TextStream, 685-686
TextStream object types, 453-454
Time, 686
TimerEvent, 686
UIObjects, 317-327, 686-689
unlockRecord( ), 325, 561-562
Uses( ), 460-463
ValueEvent, 689
vChar( ), 286
vCharCode( ), 286
View( ), 367-369
Wait( ), 378-379
writeQBE( ), 429
writeToClipboard( ), 494
Methods dialog boxes, 76, 89-92, 280
  built-in methods, 90
  Constant dialog box, 91
  custom methods, 90
  Proc check box, 91
  Type window, 90
  Uses window, 90

Microsoft
  AppStudio, 475
  ODBC (for Open Database
    Connectivity), 518
  SDK, 475
Microsoft Access tables, 588
middleware, 517
minimizing windows, 533-534, 729
modal dialog boxes, 62, 376-378
modal environment, 729
modal menus, 341, 361
modeless environment, 729
modems, 595
modes
  Edit, 551
  View, 551
module tree, 245
mouse
  dialog box operations, 375
  events, 17
  pointer shapes, 49
mouseClick( ) method, 379
MouseEvent methods, 672
MouseEvent object type, 655
mouseRightUp( ) method, 349-350
MouseShapes constants, 714
MoveAction grouping, 259
MoveEvent methods, 672
MoveEvent object type, 655
MoveReasons constants, 714
moveTo( ) method, 324
moveToRecNo( ) method, 325
moveToRecord( ) method, 325, 334
moy( ) method, 231
MROs (multi-record objects), 103, 173-175,
    302-303, 404, 729
  advantages, 302
  mailing labels, 195
  properties, 303
  report design, 188-190
  report limitations, 189
  Show All Records property, 189
MsgAbortRetryIgnore system message, 365
MsgInfo system message, 365, 367

msgInfo( ) method of debugging libraries,
    410
MsgQuestion system message, 365, 367
MsgRetryCancel system message, 365
MsgStop dialog box, 367
MsgStop system message, 366-367
msgStop( ) error message, 393
msgStop( ) procedure, 388
MsgYesNoCancel system message, 366
multi-field secondary indexes, 569-570
Multi-Record layout (forms), 155, 156
multi-record objects, *see* MROs
Multi-Record tool (SpeedBar), 174
multi-step queries, 582
multi-table queries (IDAPI), 518
multi-user environment
  ObjectPAL, 556-565
  Paradox for Windows, 545-556, 579
multi-valued dependency, 42
multi-valued relationships (tables), 138
multidimensional arrays, 234
Multiple Document Interface, *see* MDI
multiple instances, 63
multiple menu design, 361
multiple objects, 9
  aligning, 160
  selecting, 159
multiple records, 174-175
MultiUser menu, 71

N

naming
  indexes, 576
  objects, 158, 643
navigating
  fields, 283-284
  tables with TCursors, 333
nested Waits( ), 382
nesting try..endTry blocks, 399
Netware ORACLE Server, 463
network control files, 546-547
Network Refresh Rate dialog box, 556

networks
    ObjectPAL, 556-565
    Paradox for Windows
        accessing records/tables, 545-556
        performance, 579
    serial numbers, 608-609
New menu, 69
New Query dialog box, 144
newValue( ) method, 290-291
nextRecord( ) method, 325
No set comparison operator, 216
noise names, 157-158, 729
"noise names", 587
non-modal dialog boxes, 376-378
nRecords( ) method, 333
null values, 29
number fields
    custom formats, 168
    default formats, 167
    memory usage, 129
Number methods, 229, 672-673
Number object type, 655
Number procedures, 673
Number( ) procedure, 238
numeric data types (ObjectPAL), 229-230

O

object data types (ObjectPAL), 236-237
Object Database Architecture Programming Interface, *see* ODAPI
object handler, 488
Object Identity, 628-629
Object Inspector, 463, 491, 729
Object Linking and Embedding, *see* OLE
Object Name dialog box, 158
object-oriented programming, *see* OOP
Object Packager
    embedding files into OLE objects, 498-499
    embedding Windows Write documents into OLE fields, 498
    OLE server, 488
    Windows 3.1, 488

Object Trees, 80-81, 157-158, 246, 622-623, 730
object types, 731
    ActionEvent, 649
    AnyType, 649-650
    Application, 650
    Array, 650
    Binary, 650
    Currency, 650
    Database, 651
    Date, 651
    DateTime, 651
    DDE, 651
    DynArray, 652
    ErrorEvent, 652
    Event, 652
    File System
        methods, 451-452
        procedures, 451-452
    FileSystem, 652
    Form, 652-653
    Graphic, 653
    KeyEvent, 653
    Library, 653
    Logical, 653-654
    LongInt, 654
    Memo, 654
    Menu, 654
    MenuEvent, 654
    MouseEvent, 655
    MoveEvent, 655
    Number, 655
    OLE, 655
    Point, 655-656
    PopUpMenu, 656
    Query, 429-431, 656
    Record, 656
    Report, 656
    Session, 656-657
    SmallInt, 657
    StatusEvent, 657
    String, 657
    System, 657
    Table, 658

TableView, 658
TCursor, 658
TextStream, 659
    code listing, 453
    methods, 453-454
textStream code listing, 454-455
Time, 659
TimerEvent, 659
UIObject, 659
ValueEvent, 660
object variables, 314-315
    Active, 315
    Self, 314-315
    Subject, 315
object-based environment, 729
object-based programming, 11-18, 93-94
Object-Oriented Design with Applications, 631
ObjectPAL, 11, 221-222, 613, 621-623
    application window title, 538-541
    binding, 250
    class inheritance, 629-630
    commands
        SetFilter, 572
        SwitchIndex, 572
    commenting code, 238-239
    comparison
        with C, 623
        with C++, 624
        with dBASE, 624-625
    compiler, 250
    condition evaluation, 226-227
    constants, 238
    containership, 243-250
        method scope, 249-250
        procedure scope, 249-250
        variable scope, 247-249
    control structures, 223-227
        for, 223, 224
        foreach, 223-225
        if, 225
        if-else, 223
        switch, 224, 225
        try-onFail, 226
        while, 224, 226

data models, 615
data types, 227-229
    array type, 232-234
    converting, 237
    date and time, 230-231
    numeric, 229-230
    object type, 236-237
    record type, 234-236
    string type, 231-232
DDE Types, 473-474
delegating properties, 630
designing Windows programs, 615-616
DLLs parameter types, 462
editor, 614
encapsulation, 630-631
event model, 254-263
    action events, 258-260
    bubbling, 261-263
    custom events, 260-261
    events, 254-258
formatting code, 238-239
groups, 475
items, 475
level, 67-68
libraries, 251-253
    built-in methods, 251
    calling methods, 252
    creating, 251
    encapsulation, 253
    scope, 253
messages, 365-367
method notation, 222-223
methods, 239-240
Methods dialog box, 89-92
    built-in methods, 90
    Constant dialog box, 91
    custom methods, 90
    Proc check box, 91
    Type window, 90
    Uses Window, 90
objects, 245
opening documents, 478-479
PAL comparison, 616-620
passing parameters, 240-243

printing
    control methods, 420
    Word for Windows documents, 478-479
procedures, 65, 239-240
    HideSpeedBar( ), 65
    IsSpeedBarShowing( ), 65
    ShowSpeedBar( ), 65
programs, optimizing performance, 582-583
properties, 15
returning values, 241-242
SwitchMenu construct, 346
tables, 615
    locking, 557-559
trivia, 316
using OLE types, 492-494
variables
    OLE objects, 492
    reports, 197
ObjectPAL uncertainty principle, 401
objects, 8-9, 12-13, 487, 729
    aligning, 160
    base classes, 10
    borders, 593
    breaking in forms, 190
    classes, 9
    containership, 12, 158-159, 243-250
        hierarchy, 631
        variable scope, 247-249
    cutting/pasting, 588
    design objects, 13
    DOS access, 16
    duplicating, 160-161
    entering, 289
    event model, 254-263
        action events, 258-260
        bubbling, 261-263
        custom events, 260-261
        events, 254-260
    eventInfo, 270
    eventInfo packets, 256-258
    events, 17-18
    exiting, 288-289

family, placing in tables, 587
forms, 12, 13
generating, 637
grouping, 159
libraries, 13
linking, 730
list objects, 306-309
    Data Source property, 307-308
    List Selection property, 308-309
    properties, 307
MROs, 103
multiple objects, 9
    aligning, 160
    selecting, 159
names, 158
naming dependencies, 643
noise names, 157-158
object inspection, 104
ObjectPAL code, 245
OLE, 179-180
    benefits, 489
    embedding, 487-488
    linking, 487-488
    methods, 492-494
    verbs, 488
overlapping, 159-160
pasting, 730
penetrating properties, 158
pinning, 160
placement in forms, 180-182
properties, 14-15, 85, 103-105
    assigning, 104-105
    delegating, 630
QBE, 479
queries, 12
referring to, 316
reports, 12
reusable, 636-637
scripts, 12
shrinking in forms, 190-192
source-code based, 15-16
system-level objects, 16
table control, 16

761

tables, 12, 105-113
    color properties, 106-108
    data properties, 109-111
    font properties, 106
    grid properties, 108-109
    heading properties, 105-108
    saving properties, 112-113
    setting properties, 112
text objects, 103
types, 84-85
UIObjects, 10, 171, 295
    button objects, 172-173
    Contain Objects property, 159
    crosstabs, 178-179
    field, 304-311
    forms, 316-317
    graphics objects, 172
    graphs, 176-178, 311-314
    in forms, 156-167
    methods and procedures, 317-327
    MROs, 173-175, 302-303
    object variables, 314-315
    OLE Objects, 179-180
    records, 303-304
    Table Frames, 175-176, 295-302
    text objects, 171-172
ungrouping, 159
user interface, 16
version control, 635-637
visibility, 246
see also UIObjects
ODAPI (Object Database Architecture Pro-gramming Interface) drivers, 517, 600, 730
    configuration settings, 603
ODAPI Configuration utility, 546-547
    dialog box, 603
    files, 516
    Full Tree Editor, 132, 605-608
ODBC (for Open Database Connectivity), 518
OLE (Object Linking and Embedding), 33, 487, 729
    clients, 487
    fields, 489-490
        BLOB fields, 489
        embedding bitmaps, 494-496
        Horizontal Scroll Bar property, 490
        memory usage, 129
        properties, 490
        sound files, 526
        Vertical Scroll Bar property, 490
    methods, 492-494, 673
    object type, 655
    Objects, 179-180
        benefits, 489
        embedding, 487-488
        embedding files with Object Packager, 498-499
        linking, 487-488
        methods, 492-494
        ObjectPAL variables, 492
        verbs, 488
    servers, 487
        launching with ObjectPAL, 489
        Object Packager, 488
    tool, 489
        changing properties with Object Inspector, 491
        OLE UIObjects, 491-492
    type variables, 492-494, 497
    UIObject, 489-492
        Define OLE property, 492
        embedding CorelDRAW! drawings, 500-501
        Magnification property, 492
        Value property, 492
    variables, 492
oleText parameter, 493
one-dimensional crosstabs, 179
one-to-many relationships (entities), 43
one-to-one relationships (entities), 43
onFail..endtry block, 388
Only set comparison operator, 215
OOP (object-oriented programming), 8-11, 628-630, 730
    encapsulation, 9
    inheritance, 10-11
    objects, 8-9
    polymorphism, 10

Open Document dialog box, 135
  Change Table button, 194
open table lock, 550, 552
open( ) method, 12, 236, 251, 282-283, 376, 378, 473
  built-in, 414
  reports, displaying, 420-421
openAsDialog( ) method, 376-379
opening
  document windows, listing, 537
  libraries, 416-417
  second help file, 89
  tables, exclusive/read-only, 563
  Word for Windows documents with ObjectPAL, 478-479
  tables, TCursors, 330-331
operating system, 447-455
operators
  average group operator, 214
  calc query operator, 205
  inclusion operator (!), 201, 210, 213
  relational databases, 33
  set comparison operators, 215-216
  summary operators, 163
  wild-cards, 323
ORACLE Server (Netware), 463
order of events, 292
Order/Range command (Table menu), 570
Order/Range dialog box, 570-572
Origin command (Debugger menu), 98
outer joins, 210-211
Outlined Move display, 181
overlapping, 159-160

P

Page bands, 186
  see also bands
page breaks in reports, 193
Page Layout dialog box, 152-155, 185-186, 195
pages, multiple, compared to multiple forms, 645-646

PAL
  commands, 616
  ObjectPAL
    differences, 619-620
    similarities, 616-619
Paradox for DOS, 551-553
Paradox for Windows
  compatibility with disk compression utilities, 586
  configuring access to tables and records, 545-556
  directories, deleting files, 588, 589
  field type support, 118-119
  hardware requirements, 577-579
  installing, 600-602
  main form, 414-416
  memory requirements, 586
  network environment performance, 579
  networks, 564-565
  running multiple copies on one computer, 585
  starting with configuration files, 602
  system requirements, 599-600
  table locks, compared to Paradox for DOS, 551-553
  table properties support, 120
  troubleshooting, 647-648
Paradox Informant magazine, 218
PARADOX.LCK file, 548-549
parameters, 730
  command, 474
  execute, 474
  item, 473-474
  oleText, 493
  passing, 619
  routines
    DLL functions, 461-462
  server, 473
  topic, 473
  types, 462
  verb, 493
parent tables, 141
parent windows, 533, 729
passEvent keyword, 272-275

passEvent keyword (event control), 272
passing
    arrays in forms, 381-382
    constants, 241
    internal events, 272
    parameters, 619
        ObjectPAL, 240-241
        performance, 243
Password menu, 70
Password Security, 126-127
    dialog box, 126-127
    levels, 127
    master passwords, 126
passwords
    application-level protection, 418-419
    auxiliary, 418-419
    encrypting in STAFF tables, 419
    master, securing tables, 418
    table-level protection, 417-419
Paste command (Edit menu), 494, 498, 500
Paste Link command (Edit menu), 469, 476, 480
Paste Special command (Edit menu), 476
pasting objects, 730
Paths (DDE Servers), 473
PatternStyles constants, 715
PC Paintbrush files, 524
pcode, 591
PCs, configuring for maximum performance, 577-579
PCX files, 524
PDOXUSRS.LCK file, 548-549
PDOXUSRS.NET file, 546-547, 600, 603
PDOXWIN.INI file, 595
PDOXWIN.USR file, 546-547, 600
peKeyViol error constant, 393
penetrating properties, 158
PIC files (Lotus 1-2-3), 525
Picture Assistance dialog box, 121, 122
Picture Value field (STRUCT table), 134
picture values, validity checks, 120-123
pictures, 595
pinning objects, 160
pinning menus, 106
Pioneer Software (Q+E Database Library), 463

pixels, 730
placing
    code in events, 278-282
        external, 278-279
        libraries, 280-281
    example elements, 203
    objects in forms, 180-182
    UIObjects on forms, 156
Point methods, 673-674
Point object type, 655-656
Point procedures, 674
pointer shapes (mouse), 49
polymorphism, 10, 628, 730
popup menus, 341-343
    addArray( ) method, 347
    attributes, 348-350
    building, 343-350
    columnar menu choices, 344
    displaying, 343-344
    enhancing, 348
    methods, 347-348
    separating menu items, 344
    structure, 344-346
    SwitchMenu construct, 346
    twips, 346
    vertical bars, 344
PopUpMenu methods, 674
PopUpMenu object type, 656
postAction( ) methods, 260-261
posting records, 561-562
postRecord( ) method, 325, 561-562
PostScript file formats, 524
pow( ) method, 229
pow10( ) method, 229
preventing form resizing, 374
primary indexes
    comparison to secondary, 567-568
    created with ObjectPAL, 570
    names, 576
    storing, 574-576
primary keys, 27-28
    keyed tables, 28
    null values, 29
    surrogate keys, 28

print( ) method, 422-424
Printer Setup dialog box, 425
printers, 594
   default, 424
   selecting, 424-425
printing
   constants for ReportOpenInfo record, 422
   form letters, 193
   ObjectPAL control methods, 420
   reports
      Quick Report, 195
      to files, 196
   tables, 590
   Word for Windows documents, 478-479
priorRecord( ) method, 325
PRIV: alias, 72
private directories, 547-548, 559, 730
Private Directory dialog box, 73
PrivateToForm constant, 253
PrivateToForm libraries, 416
Proc check box, 91
procedures, 588, 617, 625, 730
   addPassword( ), 419
   AnyType, 662
   close( ), 240
   compared to methods, 239
   compatibility, 617-618
   Currency, 663
   custom, 240
   custom procedures, 250
   Database, 664
   Date, 665
   DateTime, 665
   dialog boxes, 370-371
   enumSource( ), 635-648
   enumUIObjectProperties( ), 635
   error handling, 395
   errorClear( ), 395
   errorCode( ), 395, 589
   errorLog( ), 395
   errorMessage( ), 278, 388, 395
   errorPop( ), 395
   errorShow( ), 395

errorTrapOnWarnings( ), 388, 395
execute( ), 592
executeQBEFile( ), 428
fail( ), 389-390
File System object types, 451-452
fileBrowser( ), 447-451
FileSystem, 667
Form, 668-669
getMenuChoiceAttribute( ), 355
getMenuChoiceAttributeById( ), 355
GraphType, 710
hasMenuChoiceAttribute( ), 355
hideSpeedBar( ), 356, 541
isSpeedBarShowing( ), 356
lock ( ), 557-558
Logical, 670
LongInt, 670
maximize( ), 414
Memo, 671
Menu, 671
menuAction( ), 362, 425
message( ), 240, 277, 541
msgStop( ), 388
Number( ), 238, 673
passing parameters, 240-243
Point, 674
query strings, 441-447
readProfileString( ), 454
removeMenu( ), 361
returning values, 241-242
Session, 676
setMenuChoiceAttribute( ), 355
setMenuChoiceAttributeById( ), 355
showSpeedBar( ), 356
SmallInt, 677
String, 677-678
System, 678-680
Table, 684-685
Time, 686
tracerClear( ), 403
tracerHide( ), 403
tracerOff( ), 402
tracerOn( ), 96, 402
tracerSave( ), 403

tracerShow( ), 403
tracerToTop( ), 403
tracerWrite( ), 403
UIObject, 689
UIObjects, 317-327
writeProfileString( ), 455
progamming languages, ObjectPAL, 629-631
PROGMAN.EXE file, 475
Program Manager
   conversations with DDEs, 475
   DDE control, 475-476
   groups, 533
      creating, 475
      MDI, 533
   starting applications, 414
programming
   data input elements, 50-51
   Debugger menu
      accessing, 94
      breakpoint options, 95-96
      Enable Debug, 97-98
      Inspect, 94-95
      Origin, 98
      quitting, 98
      Run, 98
      SpeedBar, 99
      Stack Backtrace, 95
      stepping through source code, 98
      trace options, 96-97
      View Source, 98
   dialog boxes, 62
   editor, 75-78
      editing keys, 77-78
      menu items, 82-87
      SpeedBar, 78-81
   encapsulation, 9
   fields, 304-311
      assigning values, 310-311
      button objects, 305-306
      calculated fields, 309-310
      containership hierarchy, 305
      display types, 305
      Editing property, 309
      list objects, 306-309

   inheritance, 10-11
   object-based, 11-18
   object-oriented, 8-11, 730
   objects, 8-9, 12-13
      events, 17-18
      forms, 13
      properties, 14-15
      source-code based, 15-16
   polymorphism, 10
programming languages
   ObjectPAL, 11, 67-68, 221-238, 613, 621-623
      comparison with C, 623
      comparison with C++, 624
      comparison with dBASE, 624-625
      data models, 615
      designing Windows programs, 615-616
      differences from PAL, 619-620
      editor, 614
      similarities with PAL, 616-619
      tables, 615
programs
   complexity, 640-641
   maintenance, 646-647
   measuring
      processes, 639
      size, 637-639
   ObjectPAL, 582-583
   saving, 79
   Serial Number Utility, 608-609
   SMARTDRV, 592
   Windows, designing with ObjectPAL, 615-616
prohibit option (referential integrity), 31-32
properties, 717-722, 730
   Answer table properties
      controlling, 201-202
      sorting, 202
   bands, 188
   DataSource property
      modifying, 307
      programming list objects, 307-308

delegating, 630
desktop, 14, 66-67
    Background Bitmaps, 66-67
    SpeedBar, 67
    Title text box, 66
entities, 22
fields, 164, 167-170, 587
forms, 113, 182
    assigning, 373-376
    Scroll Bar properties, 182
    Size To Fit property, 182
graph objects, 312-314
group bands, 191
Horizontal Scroll Bar (OLE field), 490
list objects, 307
List Selection property
    programming list objects, 308-309
    setting, 309
MROs, 189, 303
objects, 14-15, 103-105
OLE fields, 490
OLE tool, 491
property buttons, 300
    GridStyle, 300-301
    NRows, 301
    Position, 301
    Size, 302
    TableName, 302
records, 304
reports, 425-426
Table Frames, 297-299
    DeleteWhenEmpty, 189
    Detach Header property, 189
    Show All Records property, 189
tables, 24-25, 105-113, 119-120
    data properties, 109-111
    direct manipulation, 112
    grid properties, 108-109
    heading properties, 105-108
    Password Security, 126-127
    saving, 112-113
    Table language, 127-132
text objects, 172
use in ObjectPAL, 15
Vertical Scroll Bar (OLE fields), 490

Properties menu (Windows), 373
    Show Grid command, 180
property buttons, 300
    GridStyle, 300-301
    NRows, 301
    Position, 301
    Size, 302
    TableName, 302
Property menu program editor, 85-86
protecting passwords at table-level, 417-419
prototyping, 641-642
psychological span, 638
pull-down menus, 341-343
    accelerator keys, 353-355
    application-level menus, 354
    attributes, 355-356
        resetting, 360
    building, 350-362
    constants use, 351
    design issues, 360-361
        amodal, 361
        modal, 361
        multiple menus, 361
    determining attributes, 355-356
    form-level menus, 354
    menu items, 351-353
    UserMenu constant, 352
pushbutton events, 277, 587
pushButton( ) method, 277, 291, 362, 398, 478, 497
PX file extension, 135

Q

Q+E Database Library (Pioneer Software), 463
QBE (Query By Example), 21, 730
    accessing, 199
    files
        as ASCII files, 427
        integrating queries in applications, 427-429
    objects, 479
    views, 33

qCheckAll( ) method, 435-436
qClearQBE( ) method, 440
qClearTable( ) method, 440
qExecuteQBE( ) method, 441
qGetQBEInfo( ) method, 439
qGetQBEString( ) method, 441
QLIB library methods, 433
qSetCheck( ) method, 436
qSetExample( ) method, 437
qSetFieldOrder( ) method, 436
qSetLine( ) method, 437
qSetQBEInfo( ) method, 439
qSetSort( ) method, 438
qSetStatement( ) method, 438
qSetTableName( ) method, 437
qSetTableType( ) method, 438
quantum debugging, 401
Quattro Pro for Windows, 514-516
    ODAPI files, 516
    spreadsheets, 480
queries, 12
    ad-hoc, 426
    Answer table properties
        controlling, 201-202
        sorting, 202
    building in data models, 142-144
    calc query operator, 205
    Change To queries, 207-208
    creating from data models, 199-201
    Delete queries, 208-210
    example elements, 203-208
        Change To queries, 207-208
        concatenating fields, 206
        in calculations, 205-206
        in insert queries, 206-207
        in search conditions, 203-205
        placing, 203
    Exclusive Links, 211, 213
    Inclusive Links, 210-213
    insert queries, 206-207
    integrating in applications
        with QBE files, 426-447
        with Query object types, 429-431
    multi-step, 582
    multi-table, 518

networks
    restart options, 554-555, 564
    retry periods, 554-555
outer joins, 210-211
reports based on, 194
Set queries, 214-218
tables with indexes, 573
Query By Example, *see* QBE
Query menu Wait command, 482
Query methods, 674
Query object types, 429-431, 656
Query Select File dialog box, 143
Query String Library variables, 434
query strings, 432-433
    code listing, 432
    procedures, 441-447
Query variables, code listing, 430
querying tables, 580
QueryRestartOptions constants, 715
Quick Form icon, 151
Quick Forms, 151-152
Quick Report option (SpeedBar), 195
Quit This Method command (Debugger menu), 98
quoted strings, 231

R

Radio Button fields, 166
radio buttons, 50, 730
RadioButtonField, 305
RAM table buffers, 604
RasterOperations constants, 715
RDA (relative directory addressing), 645
read table lock, 550, 552
read-only tables, 141
readFromClipboard method, 494
reading ASCII text files, 452-455
ReadOnly property, 299
readProfileString( ) procedure, 454
rearranging fields in tables, 176
reason( ) method, 270, 395
record data type (ObjectPAL), 234-236
Record Layout dialog box, 174-175, 188
Record methods, 675

Record object type, 656
record-oriented database applications, 517-518
records, 303-304
    attributes, 23-24
    comparing, 214-218
    date field formats, 169-170
    deleting/inserting, 146-148, 189
    duplicates, 24
    extended fields, 170
    fields, 24
        accessing with TCursors, 336
        atomic, 24-25
        calculated fields, 162-163
        controlling, 290-291
        display types, 165-167
        field properties, 164
        format, 167-170
        navigating, 283-284
        special fields, 161-162
        summary fields, 163-164
        unbound fields, 161
        value changes, 290
        word wrap, 165
    FileBrowserInfo, 447
    locking
        with ObjectPAL, 560-562
        with Paradox for Windows, 553-554
    manipulating with TCursors, 334
    memo fields, 170-171
    moving to with TCursors, 334
    number fields
        custom, 168
        default formats, 167
    posting after unlocking, 561-562
    record numbers, 25
    ReportOpenInfo, 421-422
    ReportPrintInfo, 423
    scanning, 333
    sizes, 130
    Touched property, 304
    unordered lists, 25
    see also tuples

recordStatus( ) method, 325
referential integrity, 125, 145-150, 591
    Cascading Update capability, 208-210
    defining on preexistent tables, 146
    deleting/inserting records, 146-148
    self referential integrity, 149-150
    Strict, 148-149
Referential Integrity dialog box, 145
referential integrity rule, 30-32
referring to objects, 316
refresh rates of networks, 556
relational databases, 21, 517
    data normalization, 34-44
        functional dependency, 34
        first normal form, 34-37
        second normal form, 37-38
        third normal form, 38-40
        fourth normal form, 41, 42
        fifth normal form, 42-43
        avoiding problems, 43-44
    databases, 22
    entities, 22
    extensions, 33-34
    integrity, 26-32
        alternate keys, 28
        domains, 26-27
        entity integrity rule, 29-30
        foreign keys, 28-29
        primary keys, 27-28
        referential integrity rule, 30-32
    joining tables, 210-213
    operators, 33
    referential integrity, 145-150
        defining on preexistent tables, 146
        deleting/inserting records, 146-148
        self referential integrity, 149-150
        Strict, 148-149
    table properties, 24-25
        duplicate records, 24
        fields, 24-25
        records, 25
    views, 33

relationships, 730
    entities, 22
    Foreign key relationships, 142
    tables, 138-142
        Alias feature, 139
    see also tables
relative directory addressing (RDA), 645
remote servers, accessing with DLLs, 463-466
removeFocus( ) method, 291-292
removeMenu( ) procedure, 361
removing menu items, 361
renaming tables, 70
reordering fields, 119
repeating groups, 25
Report bands, 186
    see also bands
Report Header, 188
Report menu Restart Options command, 421
Report methods, 675
Report object type, 656
Report Options dialog box, 422
ReportOpenInfo record, 421-422
ReportOrientation constants, 715
ReportPrintInfo record, 423
ReportPrintPanel constants, 424, 715
ReportPrintRestart constants, 422, 716
reports, 12, 134-135
    aligning column totals, 193
    bands
        resizing, 187
        types, 186-187
    calculated fields, 192
    Data Model dialog box, 138-144
    data models, changing, 144
    delivering, 455-456
    designing, 185-190
        band properties, 188
        breaking objects, 190
        deleting records, 189
        displaying records, 189
        header placement, 189
        MROs, 188-190
        shrinking objects, 190-192
        Table Frames, 188-190

displaying with open( ) method, 420-421
file extensions, 135
grouping, 190-191
header placement, 189
integrating in applications, 420-426
mail merges, 195
mailing labels, 195
MROs, 189
page breaks, 193
printing to files, 196
properties, 425-426
query based, 194
Quick Report option (SpeedBar), 195
reading graphic files, 426
restart options, 196, 421-422
SpeedBars, 587
summary calculations, 192
tables, deleting, 144
variables in, 197
required fields validity checks, 120
Required Value field (STRUCT table), 134
resetting menu attributes, pull-down menus, 360
resizeable arrays, 233
resizing
    bands (reports), 187
    files, 176
Resource Workshop (Borland), 475, 593
resources, editing with Resource Workshop, 593
restart options (reports), 196, 421-422
Restart Options command (Report menu), 421
restoring windows, 533
restricting functions, 417
Restructure dialog box, 71, 122, 128
Restructure Warning dialog box, 123
restructuring tables, 128
resync( ) method, 589
retrieving values from fields, 311
retryPeriod( ) method, 564
returning values
    from dialog boxes, 380
    ObjectPAL, 241-242

reusable objects, 636-637
right tabs, 171
routine parameters (DLL functions), 461-462
RoutineNames, 460-461
Run command (Debugger menu), 98
running
    forms, 79
    multiple instances of Paradox, 63
runtime, 459
Runtime¦Complete Display property, 170

S

Save Picture dialog box, 122-123
saving
    error stacks, 396-397
    files, 79
    table properties, 112-113
    tables, 586-587
    video in graphic format, 523
SCAN command, 333
scan loops (tables), 333
scope
    libraries, 253
    methods and procedures, 249-250
    variables, 247-249
scoping, 730
screen display
    Flicker-Free Draw, 181
    Outlined Move, 181
screen display types, 589
scripts, 12
Scroll Bar properties (forms), 182
scroll bars (dialog boxes), 375
SDK (Microsoft), 475
Search and Replace dialog box, 104-105
search( ) method, 232
searches
    example elements, 203-205
    multiple forms, 635
    secondary indexes, 125-126
    tables, 573, 595
second normal form, 37-38

secondary indexes, 125-126, 568-569, 730
    comparison to primary, 567-568
    created with ObjectPAL, 570
    multi-field, 569-570
    names, 576
    storing, 574-576
    tables, accessing, 580
Select All command (Edit menu), 482
Select Date Format dialog box, 169
Select Fields dialog box, 155
Select File dialog box, 199
Select Number Format dialog box, 168-169
SelectAction grouping, 259
selecting
    events, 77
    multiple objects in forms, 159
    printers, 424-425
self indicator, 404
Self object variable, 314, 315
self referential integrity, 149-150
semaphore locks, 562-563
separating menu items/popup menus, 344
Serial Number Update Program dialog box, 609
Serial Number Utility program, 608-609
serial numbers, networks, 608-609
servers
    DDE, 469-470, 728
        capabilities, 473-474
        Database Desktop, 516
        limitations, 471
    OLE, 487
    parameters, 473
    remote, accessing with DLLs, 463-466
    see also file servers
Session methods, 675-676
Session object type, 656-657
Session procedures, 676
Session type lock ( ) procedure, 557-558
sessions, 730
set comparison operators, 215-216
Set queries, 214-218
set-oriented database applications, 517-518
setAltKeyDown( ) method, 286
setChar( ) method, 286

771

setControlKeyDown( ) method, 286
setErrorCode( ) method, 270, 395
setExclusive( ) method, 563
SetFilter command (ObjectPAL), 572
setFilter( ) method, 326-327
setFocus( ) method, 291
setId( ) method, 260
setItem( ) method, 474
setMenuChoiceAttribute( ) procedure, 355
setMenuChoiceAttributeById( ) procedure, 355
setQueryRestartOptions( ) method, 564
setReadOnly( ) method, 563
setReason( ) method, 395
setReasonCode method, 270
setRetryPeriod( ) method, 564
SetShiftKeyDown( ) method, 286
setStatusValue( ) method, 553
setting
   menu attributes
      popup menus, 348-350
      pull-down menus, 355-356
   properties, 112
   tabs, 171
   variable scope, 247, 249
setTitle( ) method, 538
SetVChar( ) method, 286
setVCharCode( ) method, 286
setX( ) method, 635
setY( ) method, 635
sharing data
   troubleshooting, 508-513
   with other applications, 503
Short field types, memory usage, 129
short-circuit evaluation, 226
short-cut keys, menus, 541
Show Bands property, 187
Show Grid command (Properties menu), 180
show( ) method, 344, 539
showSpeedBar( ) procedure, 356
showSpeedBar( ) statement, 410
Shrinkable property (bands), 188
shrinking objects in forms, 190-192
significand, 229
sin( ) method, 229

single-valued relationships (tables), 138
Size field (STRUCT table), 133
Size To Fit property (forms), 182
size( ) method, 232
sizing windows, 48
   maximzing, 533
   minimizing, 533
   restoring, 533
skip( ) method, 325, 333
sliders, 50
SmallInt methods, 676-677
SmallInt object type, 657
SmallInt procedures, 677
SMARDRV.EXE file, 578
SMARTDRV, 592
software (video)
   Media Player, 525
   Video for Windows, 525
Sort Answer dialog box, 202
sorting tables
   sortTo( ) method, 337-338
   with indexes, 570-573
sortTo method( ) method, 337-338
sound, 526-527
   clips, 497
   files
      OLE fields, 526
      WAV files, 526
Sound Recorder, 526
source code
   compiling, 727
   controlling versions, 633-635
special fields, 161-162
speed (video), 525
SpeedBar, 64-67, 531, 731
   custom, 362-363
   debugger, 99
   disabling, 356
   Field View icon, 170
   forms, 587, 590
   intercepting events, 362
   main form, 414
   MDI menus, 541
   Multi-Record tool, 174
   ObjectPAL procedures, 65

program editor, 78-81
  breakpoints, 80
  check syntax, 79
  object tree, 80-81
  run, 79
  save, 79
  Quick Form icon, 151
  Quick Report option, 195
  reports, 587
  UIObjects, 156
spin boxes, 50-51
Spreadsheet Import dialog box, 507
spreadsheets
  databases, 479-485
  exporting, 506-507
  importing, 506-507
SQL (Structured Query Language), 21, 517
sqrt( ) method, 229
Stack backtrace command (Debugger menu), 95
Stacker, 592
stacks (error stack), 388, 396-397
STAFF tables, password encryption, 419
starting
  applications
    command lines, 416
    file name extensions, 414
    icons, 414
    Program Manager, 414
  Paradox for Windows configuration files, 602
statements
  debug( ), 410
  if, 622
  showSpeedBar( ), 410
  switch, 622
  while, 622
static arrays, 232-233
static linking, 459
status bar, 731
  contents (MDI), 541
  desktop, 65
  messages
    color, 594
    troubleshooting, 277-278

status( ) method, 281, 370, 553
StatusEvent methods, 677
StatusEvent object type, 657
StatusReasons constants, 716
statusValue( ) method, 553
Step Into command (Debugger menu), 98
Step Over command (Debugger menu), 98
still video images, 521-523, 527-528
  cameras, file storage, 523
  file transfer, 523
  memory, 523
  VGA cards, 527
storing indexes, 574-576
Strict Referential Integrity, 148-149
string data types (ObjectPAL), 231-232
string methods, 232, 677
String object type, 657
strings
  command, 473
  procedures, 677-678
  query, 432-433
STRUCT table, 132-134
STRUCT.DB, 132
STRUCT.DB table, 731
Structure Information dialog box, 132-133
Subject object variable, 315
substr( ) method, 232
summary calculations, 192
summary fields, 163-164
summary operators, 163
superclasses, polymorphism, 10
surrogate keys, 28, 731
swap files, 578-579
switch control structure (ObjectPAL), 224-225
switch statement, 622
SwitchIndex command (ObjectPAL), 572
switchIndex( ) method, 326-327, 589
SwitchMenu construct, 346
symmetrical outer joins, 210-211
system requirements, Paradox for Windows, 599-600
System execute( ) method, 512

773

system messages
   MsgAbortRetryIgnore, 365
   MsgInfo, 365, 367
   MsgQuestion, 365, 367
   MsgRetryCancel, 365
   MsgStop, 366-367
   MsgYesNoCancel, 366
System object type, 657
System procedures, 678-680
system setting options, 71
system-level objects, 16

T

table buffers (RAM), 604
Table Export dialog box, 504
Table Frames, 295-302
   key properties, 299-300
   properties, 297-299
   property buttons, 300
      GridStyle, 300-301
      NRows, 301
      Position, 301
      Size, 302
      TableName, 302
   ReadOnly property, 299
   structure, 295
   TableName property, 299
   Touched property, 299
   usefullness, 297
Table Frames, 175-176
Table language, 127-132
table level function restriction, 417
Table Lookup dialog box, 124-125
Table lookup field (STRUCT table), 134
table lookups, 26, 124-125
Table menu commands
   Field View, 489
   Order/Range, 570
Table methods, 683-684
Table object type, 658
Table objects, 470
table operations with TCursors, 337
Table procedures, 684-685

table properties
   duplicate records, 24
   fields, 24
      atomic, 24-25
      unordered lists, 25
   records, unordered lists, 25
Table Properties dialog box, 201-202
Table Type dialog box, 117-118
Table variable in lock( ) procedure, 558
table view, 731
table-level password protection, 417-419
TableFrame object, 731
Table Frames
   DeleteWhenEmpty property, 189
   Detach Header property, 189
   report design, 188-190
   Show All Records property, 189
Table Framestyles constants, 716
TableName property, 299
tables, 7, 12, 23, 731
   accessing
      with secondary indexes, 580
      with TCursors, 580
   action events, 258-260
   anomalies, 37
   BCNF, 40
   blocks, sizes, 131-132
   building, 117-118
   cardinality, 23
   Cascading Update capability, 208-210
   changing in reports, 194
   character support, 142
   child, 141
   comparing, 215
   controlling, 16
   converting
      delimited text files, 509-510
      Paradox to dBASE, 593
   creating with TCursors, 331
   crosstabs, 178-179, 586
   data models, 586, 594
   data normalization, avoiding problems, 43-44
   degree, 24

EXPORT.DB, 506
exporting, 504
family objects, 587
fields, 590, 595
    deleting, 128
    rearranging, 176
    reordering, 119
    sizes, 129-130
    types, 118-119
fifth normal form, 42-43
files associated with, 134-136
first normal form, 34-37
foreign keys, 28-29
forms, 134-135
fourth normal form, 41, 42
graph types, 177
graphic images, 523
graphs from table data, 176-178
importing, 504
importing files, 510-512
index files, 135
index options, 126
joining, 210-213
keyed tables, 28
linking
    to word processors, 476-478
    with indexes, 573
locking
    comparison of Paradox for DOS and Windows, 551-553
    data models, 563
    nonexistent, 562-563
    records, 553-554
    with ObjectPAL, 557-560
    with Paradox for Windows, 546-551
LOCKS.DB, 559
MB files, 135
Memo field size considerations, 130
Microsoft Access, 588
multi-valued relationships, 138
ObjectPAL, 615
opening
    exclusive/read-only, 563
    with TCursor, 330-331
parent, 141

Password Security, 126-127
placing text files, 508
printing, 590
properties, 24-25, 119-120
querying, 580
    multi-step, 582
    with indexes, 573
read-only, 141
records
    as UIObjects, 303-304
    calculated fields, 162-163
    extended fields, 170
    field display types, 165-167
    field formats, 167-170
    field properties, 164
    locking with ObjectPAL, 560-562
    manipulating with TCursors, 334
    memo fields, 170-171
    sizes, 130
    special fields, 161-162
    summary fields, 163-164
    unbound fields, 161
    word wrap, 165
referential integrity, 125, 145
    defining on preexistent tables, 146
    deleting/inserting records, 146-148
    self referential integrity, 149-150
    Strict, 148-149
relationships, 138-142
renaming, 70
reports, 134-135
restructuring, 128
saving, 586-587
scanning, 333
searching, 573, 595
second normal form, 37-38
secondary indexes, 125-126
securing with master passwords, 418
self referential integrity, 149-150
Set queries, 214-218
single-valued relationships, 138
sorting
    sortTo( ) method, 337-338
    with indexes, 570-573
STAFF (password encryption), 419
Strict Referential Integrity, 148-149

STRUCT table, 132-134
STRUCT.DB, 731
structure, 71, 128
surrogate keys, 28
Table language, 127-132
TCursors, 329
    accessing fields, 336
    assignment checks, 332-333
    closing, 332-333
    column calculations, 336
    creating, 331
    declaring, 329
    field values, 338
    moving to specific records, 334
    navigating with, 333
    opening tables, 330-331
    record manipulation, 334
    table operations, 337
third normal form, 38-40
TV files, 136
unlinked, placing in forms, 586
VAL files, 136
validity checks, 120-123
    while restructuring tables, 123-124
video, capturing full-motion, 525
viewing with indexes, 570-573
virtual, 430
see also databases; relations
TableView methods, 685
TableView object type, 658
tabs, 170-171
tabular graphs, 177
tabular layout (forms), 156
tan( ) method, 229
target indicator, 404
TCursor class
    lock( ) procedure, 558
TCursor methods, 680-683, 731
TCursor object type, 658
TCursor variables, 236
TCursors, 329, 553
    accessing fields, 336
    accessing tables, 580
    assignment checks, 332-333

    closing, 332-333
    column calculations, 336
    creating tables, 331
    declaring, 329
    field values, 338
    link relationships, 331
    moving to specific records, 334
    navigating tables, 333
    opening tables, 330-331
        attachment method, 330-331
        open method, 330
        table variable method, 330
    record manipulation, 334
    table operations, 337
    unposted records, 562
temporary files, 547-548
terminating events, 271-275
testing DDE links, 478
text
    aligning, 170
    underscoring in menus, 344
    word wrap in fields, 165
text boxes, 50
text files
    ASCII, reading, 452-455
    delimited, 505
        converting to tables, 509-510
    fixed-length
        exporting, 506
        importing, 506
    placing in tables, 508
text objects, 103, 171-172
Text Options dialog box, 505
TextAlignment constants, 716
TextDesignSizing constants, 716
TextSpacing constants, 716
TextStream methods, 685-686
TextStream object type, 453-455, 508-512, 659
TGA (Targa) files, 524
third normal form, 38-40
third-party batch tools, 512
third-party libraries, 463-466
third-party utilities, 507-508
TIF (tagged image files), 524

Index

tilde variables, 430, 431
tiling windows, 47, 535-536
Time methods, 686
Time object type, 659
Time procedures, 686
timer events, 292-293, 588
timer( ) method, 292-293
TimerEvent methods, 686
TimerEvent object type, 659
titles, application window, 538-541
title bars (dialog boxes), 375
Title text box, 66
today( ) method, 231
topic parameter, 473
touch record events, 304
Touched property, 299, 304
Trace BuiltIns dialog box, 96, 409
Trace BuiltIns command (Debugger menu), 96-97
Trace Execution command (Debugger menu), 96-97
Trace window
    code listing, 404-409
    debugging applications, 401-403
    passive application observation, 401-403
tracerClear( ) procedure, 403
tracerHide( ) procedure, 403
tracerOff( ) procedure, 402
tracerOn( ) procedure, 96, 402
tracerSave( ) procedure, 403
tracerShow( ) procedure, 403
tracerToTop( ) procedure, 403
tracerWrite( ) procedure, 403
transferring information between forms, 379-382
trapping
    action events, 258
    errors, 388-390, 397-399
    events
        at form level, 270-271
        isPreFilter( ) method, 271
        precautions, 260
    keystrokes, 285-288, 354
    menu events, 358-360
    SpeedBar events, 362

trees (object), 622-623, 730
troubleshooting
    Paradox for Windows, 647-648
    sharing data, 508-513
try-onFail control structure (ObjectPAL), 224, 226
try..endTry blocks, nesting, 399
tuples, 23, 731
    see also records
TV files, 136
twips, 346, 731
two-dimensional crosstabs, 179
type 1 errors, 386
type 2 errors, 386
type 3 errors, 386
    forcing, 391
    severity, 386
Type variables
    DDE, 473
    OLE, 497
Type window, 90
Types dialog box, 85
types of classes, 630

U

UIObject (user interface object), 731
UIObject class, 10
UIObject methods, 686-689
UIObject object type, 659
UIObject procedures, 689
UIObjects, 171, 295
    button objects, 172-173
    Contain Objects property, 159
    crosstabs, 178-179
    fields, 304-311
        assigning values, 310-311
        button objects, 305-306
        calculated fields, 309-310
        containership hierarchy, 305
        display types, 305
        Editing property, 309
        list objects, 306-309
    forms, 156-167, 316-317
        aligning, 160
        calculated fields, 162-163

containership, 158-159
duplicating, 160-161
field display types, 165-167
field properties, 164
grouping, 159
multiple object selection, 159
noise names, 157-158
overlapping, 159-160
pinning, 160
special fields, 161-162
summary fields, 163-164
unbound fields, 161
word wrap, 165
graphics objects, 172
graphs, 176-178, 311-314
methods and procedures, 317-327
MROs, 173-175, 302-303
object variables, 314-315
OLE Objects, 179-180
records, 303-304
spectrum, 296, 297
Table Frames, 175-176, 295-302
key properties, 299-300
properties, 297-299
structure, 295
usefullness, 297
text objects, 171-172
trivia, 316
unposted records, 562
see also objects
UIObjectTypes constants, 716-717
unbound fields, 161
undefined fields, 290
underscoring menu text, 344
ungrouping objects, 159
unique numeric keys, 338-339
unlabeled fields, 165
unlocking, *see* locking
unlockRecord( ) method, 325, 561-562
unordered lists of fields/records, 25
unpinning menus, 106
upper( ) method, 232
user-ready applications guidelines, 413
USER.EXE file, 371
UserMenu constant, 352

Uses method, 463
Uses window, 90, 416-417
Uses( ) method, 460-462
utilities
    compression, 513
    File Manager (Windows), 414
    Windows Control Panel, 424
Utilities Menu, 69
    Info Structure command, 195
utility forms, 636-637

V

VAL files, 136
validity checks, 731
    alphanumeric fields, 120
    default, 120
    domains, 26-27
    picture values, 120-123
    required fields, 120
    tables, 120-124
Value property (OLE UIObjects), 492
ValueEvent methods, 689
ValueEvent object type, 660
ValueReasons constants, 717
values (data types), 462
variable types, 731
variables, 731
    AnyType, 238
    cstat variable, 349
    data types, 227-238
    date and time
        creating, 230
        math operations, 230
    environment (DOS PATH), 473
    Form, 236
    global variables, 253
    in reports, 197
    object variables, 314-315
        Active, 315
        Self, 314-315
        Subject, 315
    ObjectPAL (OLE objects), 492
    OLE, declaring, 492
    Query, code listing, 430
    Query String libraries, 434

scope
    ObjectPAL, 247-250
    setting, 247, 249
Table, lock( ) procedure, 558
TCursor, 236, 329
    assignment checks, 332-333
    closing, 332-333
    column calculations, 336
    declaring, 329
    navigating tables, 333
    opening tables, 330-331
    table operations, 337
    tilde, 430-431
    versus constants, 238
    viewing, 94-95
vChar( ) method, 286
vCharCode( ) method, 286
vector file formats, 524-525
verb parameters, 493
verbs (OLE objects), 488
vertical bars (popup menus), 344
vertical mouse pointer, 49
Vertical Scroll Bar, 373
Vertical Scroll Bar property (OLE fields), 490
VGA cards (still video images), 527
video, 521-525
    applications, 521-522
    AVI (audio interleave), 525
    cameras, 521
    capture speed, 525
    capturing in tables, 525
    frame buffer, 527
    freezing, 522
    full motion, 525
    full-motion images, 521
    graphic file formats, 523-525
    hardware, 522
    image quality, 523
    Media Player, 525
    saving in graphic format, 523
    software, 525
    still images, 521-523, 527-528
        file transfer, 523
        memory, 523
        VGA cards, 527

video capture cards, 522
video clips
    action( ) method, 497
    Video for Windows, 497
Video for Windows video clips, 497
Video for Windows (Microsoft), 525
View mode, lock availablility, 551
View Source command (Debugger menu), 98
View( ) dialog box, 368
View( ) method, 233, 367-369
viewing
    declared variables, 94-95
    table structures, 132-134
    tables with indexes, 570-573
views
    QBE, 33
    relational databases, 33
    table, 731
virtual tables, 430
visibility of objects, 246

W

Wait command (Query menu), 482
Wait( ) method, 378-379
warning errors, *see* type 2 errors
WAV files (sound), 526
while control structure (ObjectPAL), 224, 226
while statement, 622
wild cards, 595
    operators, 323
    searches, 573
WIN.INI file, 602, 610
Window menu, 535-537
    Cascade option, 535-536
    program editor, 86-87
    Tile option, 535
window style constants, 376-377, 447-448
Windows
    ... (ellipsis), 57
    building menu items, 358
    built-in dialog boxes, 371-372
    Control Panel utility default printers, 424

conventions, 56-57
designing programs in ObjectPAL, 615-616
interface, 47-50
International dialog box, 167
keyboard shortcuts, 55
keycodes, 286-288
menu access keys, 57
message box, 371
mouse pointer shapes, 49
programs, executing, 592
Properties menu, 373
selecting multiple objects, 159
terminology, 56

windows
application window, 61, 531-532, 538-539, 727
cascading, 47, 535-536
child windows, 61-62, 533, 729
closing, 537
dialog boxes, 62
document window, 61, 533-537, 728
keyboard shortcuts, 537
maximized, 533-535
minimized, 533-534
Editor Window, 77
manipulating, 54-55
maximizing, 729
minimizing, 729
parent windows, 533, 729
restoring, 533
sizing controls, 48
tiling, 47, 535-536

Trace
coe listing, 404-409
passive application observation, 401-403
Type window, 90
Uses window, 90, 416-417
Windows 3.1 Object Packager, 488
Windows File Manager, 414
Windows Macro Recorder, 513
Windows Program Manager, 600-602
Windows Write, 498
WindowStyles constants, 717
Word for Windows documents, 478-479
word processing documents, 478-479
word processors
integrating with databases, 476-479
linking to tables, 476-478
word-wrap, 165, 170
WORK: aliases, 72
working directories, 731
Working Directory dialog box, 73
write table lock, 550, 552
writeProfileString( ) procedure, 455
writeQBE( ) method, 429
writeToClipboard( ) method, 494
WYSIWYG
Paradox font substitution, 153

Y-Z

year( ) method, 231
YesNoCancel dialog box, 366

If your computer uses 5 1/4-inch disks...

Paradox for Windows Power Programming comes with one 3 1/2-inch, high-density, 1.44M floppy disk. If your computer uses 5 1/4-inch disks, you may return this form to Que to obtain a 5 1/4-inch disk to use with this book. Simply fill out the remainder of this form and mail to:

Disk Exchange

Que Corporation
11711 N. College Ave., Suite 140
Carmel, IN 46032

We then will send you, free of charge, the 5 1/4-inch double-density version of the book software.

Book Title _____

Name _____ Phone _____

Company _____ Title _____

Address _____

_____

City _____

State _____

ZIP _____

By opening this package, you are agreeing to be bound by the following agreement.

This software product is copyrighted, and all rights are reserved by the publisher and author. You are licensed to use this software on a single computer. You may copy and/or modify the software as needed to facilitate your use of it on a single computer. Making copies of the software for any other purpose is a violation of United States copyright laws.

This software is sold without warranty of any kind, either expressed or implied, including but not limited to the implied warranties of merchantability and fitness for a particular purpose. Neither the publisher nor its dealers or distributors assumes any liability for any alleged or actual damages arising from the use of this program. (Some states do not allow for the exclusion of implied warranties, so the exclusion may not apply to you.)